And say: “My Lord, increase me in knowledge!”

(Koran 20:114)

Ibn al-'Arabi's Metaphysics of Imagination

THE SUFI PATH OF KNOWLEDGE

William C. Chittick

STATE UNIVERSITY OF NEW YORK PRESS

Cover photo courtesy of The Freer Gallery of Art,
Smithsonian Institute, Washington, D.C.

Published by
State University of New York Press, Albany

Printed in the United States of America.
Design by Sushila Blackman.

For information, address State University of New York Press,
State University Plaza, Albany, N.Y., 12246

Library of Congress Cataloging-in-Publication Data

Chittick, William C.
The Sufi path of knowledge : Ibn al-'Arabi's metaphysics of imagination / William C. Chittick.
p. cm.
Includes index.
ISBN 0-88706-884-7. ISBN 0-88706-885-5 (pbk.)
1. Ibn al-'Arabī, 1165-1240. 2. Sufism. 3. Imagination—Religious aspects—Islam. 4. Creative ability—Religious aspects—Islam. I. Title.
BP80.I2C48 1989
297'.4'0924—dc19 88-7040
CIP

10 9 8 7 6 5 4 3 2 1

CONTENTS

Introduction

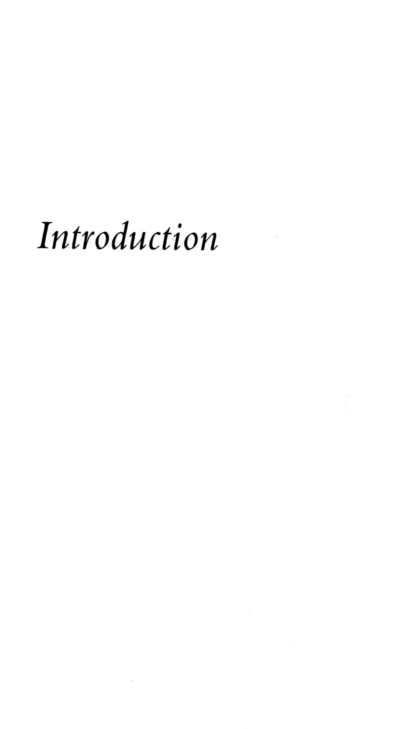

INTRODUCTION

Somewhere along the line, the Western intellectual tradition took a wrong turn. Arguments arise over when and why this happened. Many important thinkers have concluded that the West never should have abandoned certain teachings about reality which it shared with the East. They have turned to the Oriental traditions in the hope of finding resources which may help revive what has been lost and correct the deep psychic and spiritual imbalances of our civilization.

One result of this ongoing search for a lost intellectual and spiritual heritage has been the rediscovery of the importance of imagination. In putting complete faith in reason, the West forgot that imagination opens up the soul to certain possibilities of perceiving and understanding not available to the rational mind. One of the important contemporary thinkers who have pointed in this direction is the late Henry Corbin, who has bequeathed to us the word "imaginal." As Corbin has explained in his works, the "imaginal world" or *mundus imaginalis* possesses an independent ontological status and must be clearly differentiated from the "imaginary" world, which is no more than our individual fantasies. Once we lose sight of the imaginal nature of certain realities, the true import of a great body of mythic and religious teachings slips from our grasp.

All religious traditions accord a central role to imagination, though not necessarily by this name. The *mundus imaginalis* is the realm where invisible realities become visible and corporeal things are spiritualized. Though more real and "subtle" than the physical world, the World of Imagination is less real and "denser" than the spiritual world, which remains forever invisible as such. In Islam, the later intellectual tradition never tires of discussing the imaginal realm as the locus wherein spiritual realities are seen in visionary experience and all the eschatological events described in the Koran and Hadith take place exactly as described. If on the Day of Resurrection, as reported by the Prophet, "death is brought in the form of a salt-colored ram and slaughtered," this is because imaginal existence allows abstract meanings to take on concrete form. And if all the works we performed during our lives are placed in the Scales, the good deeds in the right pan and the bad deeds in the left, this is because imagination brings about the subtilization of corporeal activities.

By granting an independent ontological status to imagination and seeing the visionary realm as the self-revelation of God, Islamic philosophy has gone against the mainstream of Western thought. It offers precious assistance to those in the West who "refuse to relegate imagination to a subordinate role in an epistemological framework."[1] But in spite of Corbin's prodigious efforts, the resources of the Islamic tradition have hardly been touched. Even the teachings of Ibn al-ʿArabī, to whom Corbin dedicated his masterly study, *Creative Imagination in the Ṣūfism of Ibn ʿArabī,*[2] remain for the most part unexplored and unexplained.

Corbin performed the great service of introducing the Western world to many uniquely Islamic ways of expressing philosophical positions, but it is beyond the capacity of a single individual to bring out everything worthy of consideration. Moreover, in his zeal to revive the honor due to the imaginal realm, Corbin tended to de-emphasize the cornerstone of Islamic teachings, *tawḥīd*, the "declaration of God's Unity." It is as if Corbin was so entranced by the recovery of the imaginal that he had difficulty seeing beyond it.

From the point of view of the Islamic intellectual tradition, the tendency to become transfixed by the multiple apparitions of the One represents a danger inherent in the current revival of interest in imagination. It is clear, for example, that certain varieties of Jungianism divinize the imaginal world, giving to the soul an autonomous status never granted to it by the great traditions. Man's own domain of microcosmic imagination is posited as the Real, since "God" is merely the soul's projection. But this—in the Islamic view—is to fall into the error of associating other gods with God (*shirk*), the opposite of *tawḥīd*. We are left with polytheistic multiplicity, and the "gods" are reinstated as real entities possessing insuperable differences.

Corbin never fell into such a position, which would have betrayed the central teaching of the texts with which he was concerned. Nevertheless, if his approach to Islamic thought is to be understood as reflecting the concerns of his sources, it needs to be tempered by more attention to the ultimate Unity lying behind the theophanic facade of created existence. At the same time, certain studies of Ibn al-ʿArabī which have been concerned almost exclusively with his metaphysical and philosophical teachings have gone to the other extreme, failing to emphasize the essential role which Ibn al-ʿArabī accords to imagination. In fact, his metaphysics cannot be understood without grasping imagination's importance, and his view of imagination cannot be understood outside the realm of metaphysics. The present study is an attempt to bring these two sides of Ibn al-ʿArabī's teachings back into balance. It is hoped that just as Ibn al-ʿArabī has played an important role in reviving imagination as a topic of religious and philosophical concern in the West, so also he may provide a pointer toward the One in the midst of imaginal multiplicity.

The Life and Works of Ibn al-ʿArabī

Few Muslim spiritual authorities are so famous in the West as Muḥyī al-Dīn Muḥammad ibn ʿAlī ibn al-ʿArabī (A.H. 560–638/A.D. 1165–1240). In the Islamic world itself, probably no one has exercised deeper and more pervasive influence over the intellectual life of the community during the past seven hundred years. He was soon called by his disciples and followers al-Shaykh al-Akbar, the "Greatest Master," and few who have taken the trouble to study his works would dispute this title, though some would argue over the direction in which his greatness lies.[3]

The Shaykh was born in Mursiya in al-Andalus (Murcia in present-day Spain). His father seems to have been a government employee in the service of Muḥammad ibn Saʿīd Mardanīsh, the ruler of Murcia. The family must have held a high social position, since his maternal uncle was ruler of Tlemcen in Algeria and he himself was on familiar terms with several local kings in his later life. When the Almohad dynasty conquered Murcia in 567/1172, the family moved to Seville, where his father was again most likely involved with government service. Ibn al-ʿArabī himself was employed in the early part of his career as a secretary to the governor.

In 590/1193, at the age of thirty, Ibn al-ʿArabī left Spain for the first time, traveling to Tunis. Seven years later, a vision instructed him to go to the East. He made the pilgrimage to Mecca in 599/1202, and from there traveled extensively in the central Islamic lands, staying for various lengths of time in Egypt, Iraq, Syria, and Rūm (present-day Turkey), though he never went to Iran. In 620/1223 he settled in Damascus, where he and a circle of disciples remained until his death in 638/1240. He spent his life in study, writing, and teaching. At the same time, he was involved in the social and political life of the community. He was on good terms with at least three local kings, one of whom became well-versed in his writings. In a document dated 632/1234, he gives permission to the Ayyubid Muẓaffar al-Dīn Mūsā, who ruled in Damascus between 627/1229–30 and 635/1238, to teach all his works, of which he lists 290. In the same document, he mentions by name ninety masters of the religious sciences with whom he himself had studied.

Ibn al-ʿArabī provides many details of his personal life in his works, and we can be grateful that the major scholarly task of bringing these together and analyzing them has finally been accomplished, in a forthcoming book by Claude Chodkiewicz-Addas.[4] The best account in English is provided by the autobiographical descriptions of Ibn al-ʿArabī's meetings with some of his contemporaries, *Sufis of Andalusia*, along with the translator's introduction.[5] The reader of that work will soon realize that Ibn al-ʿArabī lived in a universe foreign to our own, where the extraordinary and miraculous were everyday occurrences.

One of the most obvious of the miraculous sides to the career of the Greatest Master was his literary production. Osman Yahia, in his two-volume history and classification of Ibn al-ʿArabī's works, estimates that Ibn al-ʿArabī wrote 700 books, treatises, and collections of poetry, of which 400 are extant. The *Futūḥāt al-makkiyya* alone will fill a projected 17,000 pages in Yahia's critical edition. One of the most daunting prospects faced by a scholar is to read the whole *Futūḥāt*, not to mention the other works available in printed editions or manuscripts. The problem is not simply the sheer volume of his production. His whole corpus stands at an extremely high level of sophistication and demands familiarity with all the Islamic sciences. This helps explain why the Shaykh al-Akbar, in spite of the intrinsic interest of his works and his wide-spread influence, has been relatively neglected by modern scholars.

The *Futūḥāt al-makkiyya* is a vast encyclopedia of the Islamic sciences within the context of *tawḥīd*, the profession of God's Unity that forms the core of Islam. The book includes 560 chapters, several of which would be major books if published separately. Ibn al-ʿArabī discusses in copious detail the Koran, the Hadith, events in the life of the Prophet, the detailed rulings of the Shariʿa, the principles of jurisprudence, the divine names and attributes, the relationship between God and the world, the structure of the cosmos, the make-up of the human being, the various human types, the path by which human perfection may be attained, the stages of the ascent to God, the ranks and kinds of the angels, the nature of the jinn, the characteristics of time and space, the role of political institutions, the symbolism of letters, the nature of the interworld between death and Resurrection, the ontological status of heaven and hell, and so on. The list could be extended for pages.

Though the *Futūḥāt* is but one of Ibn al-ʿArabī's works, most of the topics about which he has written are discussed in some detail within it. However, he frequently points out that what he knows and could put down in writing if it were opportune or necessary to do so bears no relationship with what he has written. As he remarks matter-of-factly—and, one suspects, without exaggeration—, "What we deposit in every chapter, in relation to what we have, is but a drop in the ocean" (II 578.19).[6] In one ninety-chapter section of the *Futūḥāt*, he provides in each chapter a list of the related topics which he could have discussed, and these lists alone will fill more than 400 pages of the *Futūḥāt* in its new edition.[7]

The Meccan Openings

What is the significance of Ibn al-ʿArabī's life and writings for Islamic intellectual history? More specifically, since this question can be answered from many points of view, how did he and his followers perceive the significance of his work? One way to gain a certain insight into this question is to meditate upon the title of his magnum opus, *al-Futūḥāt al-makkiyya*, "The Meccan Openings."

In Ibn al-ʿArabī's technical vocabulary, "opening" (*futūḥ*) is a near synonym for several other terms, such as unveiling, tasting, witnessing, divine effusion, divine self-disclosure, and insight. Each of these words designates a mode of gaining direct knowledge of God and of the unseen worlds without the intermediary of study, teacher, or rational faculty. God "opens up" the heart to the infusion of knowledge. The word "opening" suggests that this type of knowledge comes to the aspirant suddenly after he had been waiting patiently at the door. It involves neither "self-exertion, raising up the gaze, nor seeking" (II 505.17), that is, seeking after that particular knowledge, since man must always seek after God Himself. Opening is the type of knowledge given to the prophets (though it is not equivalent to scripture): They receive it directly from God without rational inquiry or reflective consideration.

> The prophets and the friends among the Folk of Allah have no knowledge of God derived from reflection. God has purified them from that. Rather, they possess the "opening of unveiling" through the Real. (III 116.23)

If a person wants to achieve opening, he must discipline himself according to the norms of the Shariʿa and the Ṭarīqa (the spiritual path) under the direction of a spiritual master or "shaykh" who has himself traversed the path. In several verses the Koran tells us that God may bestow knowledge upon His servant if He wills. Most commonly, Ibn al-ʿArabī quotes the verse, "Be godfearing and God will teach you" (2:282). This "godfearingness" which prepares the disciple for God's teaching entails his complete absorption in putting the revealed Law into practice and invoking (*dhikr*) the name of God under a shaykh's guidance. Until the disciple reaches opening, he will have to seclude himself from people through spiritual retreats (*khalwa*), though after full opening, retreat and presence in society (*jalwa*) are the same. As Ibn al-ʿArabī remarks, if a person wants to gain knowledge of things as they are in themselves, "He should follow the path of the great masters and dedicate himself to retreat and invocation. Then God will give direct awareness of that to his heart" (I 120.12). "Unveiling comes to them in their retreats when the divine lights dawn within them, bringing sciences purified of corroding stains" (II 600.3).

The knowledge which is opened up to the seeker is the knowledge of the Koran, the Divine Speech. "Nothing is opened up to any friend of God (*walī*) except the understanding of the Mighty Book" (III 56.2).

> The perfect inheritor (*wārith*) of the Prophet among the friends of God is he who dedicates himself exclusively to God through His Shariʿa. Eventually God will open up in his heart the understanding of what He has sent down upon His messenger and prophet, Muḥammad, through disclosing Himself to him in his inward dimension (*bāṭin*). (I 251.3)

Opening is not a goal that every disciple will reach. The least of the necessary qualifications is the "godfearingness" referred to earlier, an attribute which Muslims have always perceived as the epitome of human perfection. As the Koran says, "The most noble among you in God's eyes is the most godfearing" (49:13). Innumerable factors combine to make up an individual's preparedness for opening. One disciple may practice sincerely and assiduously throughout his life and never have his heart opened up to the unseen world. Another may practice for a relatively short period of time and reach the goal. The nature of the opening itself depends largely upon the individual human nature. Ibn al-ʿArabī never tires of reminding us of the saying of Junayd, "The water takes on the color of the cup."

It should be noted that "opening" in the technical sense cannot be applied to any and every sort of "inrush" (*wārid*) from a world normally closed to the psyche. Ibn al-ʿArabī, like other Sufis, provides many criteria for distinguishing among different types of paranormal perceptions. Like others, he divides the "incoming thoughts" (*khawāṭir*) which reach the heart into four categories: divine (*ilāhī*), spiritual (*rūḥānī*), ego-centric (*nafsānī*), and satanic (*shayṭānī*).[8] One of the tasks of the spiritual master is to discern the source of the incoming thought and give instructions to the disciple so that he can maintain his psychic and spiritual balance. Confusion among the different kinds of inspiration poses tremendous dangers for the soul in this world and the next. From the Sufi perspective, one of the most obvious signs of the deviation of most contemporary "spirituality"—especially of the "New Age" variety—is its inability to discern the source of inrushes.[9]

Ibn al-ʿArabī's extraordinary spiritual career was marked by many signs, not the least of which being the fact that he reached opening at a young age in the space of an hour or two. His disciple Shams al-Dīn Ismāʿīl ibn Sawdakīn al-Nūrī (d. 646/1248) quotes him as follows:

> I began my retreat at the first light (*fajr*) and I had reached opening before sunrise. After that I entered the "shining of the full moon"[10] and other stations, one after another. I stayed in my place for fourteen months. Through that I gained all the mysteries which I put down in writing after opening. My opening was a single attraction in that moment.[11]

Ibn al-ʿArabī experienced this opening while still a youth. His famous encounter with the chief judge of Seville, the great jurist and philosopher Ibn Rushd (known to the Latin West as Averroes, d. 595/1198), took place after the completion of this retreat. He tells us that his father, a good friend of Ibn Rushd, had told the judge something of his son's experiences.

> Ibn Rushd was eager to meet me, because of what he had heard and what had reached him concerning what God had opened up for me in my retreat. . . . I was still a youth (*ṣabī*). My face had not yet put forth a beard, and my mustache had not yet grown.[12] When I entered in upon him, he stood up in his place out of love and respect. He embraced me and said, "Yes." I said, "Yes." His joy increased because I had understood him. Then I realized why he had rejoiced at that, so I said, "No." His joy disappeared and his color changed, and he doubted what he possessed in himself.
>
> He said, "How did you find the situation in unveiling and divine effusion? Is it what rational consideration gives to us?"
>
> I replied, "Yes and no. Between the yes and the no spirits fly from their matter and heads from their bodies." His color turned pale and he began to tremble. He sat reciting, "There is no power and no

> strength but in God," since he had understood my allusion. . . .
>
> After that, he sought from my father to meet me in order to present to me what he himself had understood: He wanted to know if it conformed with or was different from what I had. He was one of the great masters of reflection and rational consideration. He thanked God that in his own time he had seen someone who had entered into the retreat ignorant and had come out like this—without study, discussion, investigation, or reading. He said, "This is a state that we had confirmed rationally, but we had never seen anyone who possessed it. Praise belongs to God, that I should live in the time of one of its possessors, those who have opened the locks upon its doors. Praise belongs to God, who singled me out to see him!" (I 153.34)[13]

Ibn al-ʿArabī confirms, though rather allusively, Ibn Sawdakīn's report that he gained all his knowledge through his initial opening and that his writings consisted of the gradual expression of that knowledge in verbal form. The Shaykh al-Akbar does not mention the term "opening" itself in this account, but he alludes to it through mention of "knocking on the door." He is commenting on these verses found towards the beginning of the *Futūḥāt*:

> When I kept knocking on God's door
> I waited mindfully, not distracted,
> Until there appeared to the eye the glory of His Face
> and a call to me, nothing else.
> I encompassed Being in knowledge—
> nothing is in my heart but God.
> (I 10.26)

> Everything we have mentioned after that [vision of the glory of God's Face] in all our speech (*kalām*) is only the differentiation of the all-inclusive reality which was contained in that look at the One Reality. (II 548.14)

Though all Ibn al-ʿArabī's knowledge may have been included in undifferentiated form in the initial opening, this does not imply that the door stayed closed to him after that. Quite the contrary, his soul was constantly being unveiled by the inrushes of divine wisdom. He frequently met with the Prophet Muḥammad and other prophets in the unseen world, and many of the great contemporary or past Sufis would appear to him in the imaginal realm. In the case of Ibn al-ʿArabī at least, once the door to the invisible world was opened, it stayed open.

This brings us to the second element in the title of the *Futūḥāt*, the adjective "Meccan." Ibn al-ʿArabī explains that the particular openings which make up the contents of this work began during his pilgrimage to Mecca in the year 598/1202. We know that he began writing the *Futūḥāt* in the next year, and he was not to finish the first redaction until after settling in Damascus twenty-one years later. In dedicating the *Futūḥāt* to one of his disciples, he alludes to the role of Mecca by mentioning God's "house" and "sanctuary."

> God set up in my thoughts that I make known to my dear friend—God preserve him—some of the gnostic sciences which I had acquired in my absence and, likewise, that I bestow upon him—God ennoble him—some of the pearls of knowledge which I had gained in my exile. Hence I wrote for him this unique treatise, which God has brought into existence as an amulet against the impediments to knowledge for every pure companion, every verifying Sufi, and for my dear friend, blameless brother, and approved son, ʿAbdallāh Badr al-Ḥabashī al-Yamanī, the freedman of Abū Ghanā'im ibn Abi'l-Futūḥ al-Ḥarrānī.[14] I named it "The Treatise of the Meccan Openings concerning the True Knowledge of the Mysteries of the Master and the Kingdom." Most of what I have deposited in this treatise was opened up for me by God when I was circumambulating His noble House or while I was sitting in a state of waiting mindfully for Him in His noble and exalted Sanctuary. (I 10.16)

The *Futūḥāt*, then, is essentially a compendium of some of the sciences which were given to Ibn al-ʿArabī during his experiences of opening. He frequently stresses this point in explaining the manner in which he wrote the work. His words are not the result of any reflective or rational process, but bestowed by the Divine Presence.

> We are not one to quote the words of the philosophers, nor the words of anyone else, since in this book and in all our books we only write that which is given by unveiling and dictated by God. (II 432.8)
>
> This book is not a place for that which is given by the proofs of the reflective powers, only for that which is given by divine unveiling. (II 389.6)
>
> The aim of our book is not to speak about considerative and reflective relationships. Its subject is only the sciences of unveiling given by God. (II 655.5)
>
> The books we have composed—this and others—do not follow the route of ordinary compositions, nor do we follow the route of ordinary authors. . . . My heart clings to the door of the Divine Presence, waiting mindfully for what comes when the door is opened. My heart is poor and needy, empty of every knowledge. . . . When something appears to the heart from behind that curtain, the heart hurries to obey and sets it down in keeping with the commanded bounds. (I 59.12)[15]

Koranic Hermeneutics

Islamic civilization is clearly logocentric. Ibn al-ʿArabī places himself squarely in the mainstream of Islam by basing all his teachings upon the Koran and the Hadith. In this respect he parts company with the philosophers and proponents of Kalām, who were far more likely to derive their sciences from other sources. Ibn al-ʿArabī confirms his own logocentrism by claiming repeatedly that the knowledge gained through opening pertains to the meaning of the Koran. This is a point of fundamental importance, too often forgotten in studies of the Shaykh. The "Meccan Openings," like the Shaykh al-Akbar's other works, are nothing if not commentary upon the Holy Book.

In order to enter into the universe of Ibn al-ʿArabī's Koranic hermeneutics, one must first cast away all preconceived notions of how a text should be read. In the Shaykh's view, the Koran is the concrete, linguistic embodiment of Real Being, God Himself. At the same time, the revealed Speech is dominated by the attributes of mercy and guidance — perfectly in keeping with Being Itself, since, according to the famous hadith, "God's mercy precedes His wrath." The Divine Speech guides through its "signs" (*āyāt*) or verses, just as the cosmos —which is also the Speech of God, articulated within the "Breath of the All-merciful"—gives news of God through its signs, which are the phenomena of nature. The revealed, written Speech can be more readily understood than the revealed, cosmic Speech. It provides the key through which "opening" can take place—the opening of the door to comprehension of the signs within the macrocosm and the microcosm, the universe around us and within us. Ibn al-ʿArabī frequently quotes the Koranic verse, "We shall show them Our signs upon the horizons and in themselves, until it is clear to them that He is the Real" (41:53).

The revealed Book is the actual, true, authentic embodiment of God's Speech. Its every letter is full of significance, since the book manifests the divine realities in both its form and meaning. It is true that the same thing can be said about the cosmos, but the written Book has the advantage of having been given a linguistic form that necessarily corresponds with Absolute Truth, which is God. This linguistic mode of existence appeals directly to the distinguishing feature of human beings, the *nuṭq* or "rational speech" which makes them "rational animals" (*ḥayawān nāṭiq*). The Book is the *barzakh* or isthmus between man's intelligence and God's knowledge of things as they are in themselves. It provides the God-given and providential means whereby man can come to know things in themselves, without the distortions of egocentrism.

If all of Ibn al-ʿArabī's works are essentially Koranic hermeneutics, this is because ultimate truth can only be perceived with the help of divine guidance, and divine guidance has taken certain specific forms. "Enter houses by their doors," the Koran commands (2:189). One cannot take God's house by storm. One enters by the door, when invited. Any attempt to climb through the windows would display blatant discourtesy (*sū' al-adab*), an attribute which automatically disqualifies the would-be hermeneut.

Because the Book in its actual, revealed form is the embodiment of the divine mercy and guidance, Ibn al-ʿArabī displays tremendous reverence for the literal text. The linguistic form of the text takes precedence over all else. Certain Western scholars have portrayed Ibn al-ʿArabī as a great practitioner of esoteric commentary (*ta'wīl*), whereby the literal meaning of the text becomes a window through which one looks into the invisible realm. One can agree with this statement, so long as it is understood that no Muslim commentator has been as concerned as the Shaykh to preserve the Book's literal sense. Ibn al-ʿArabī never denies the literal and apparent meaning. But he frequently adds to the literal sense an interpretation based upon an opening which transcends the cognitive limitations of most mortals. He often tells us that God may unveil meanings of the text to the gnostic which others have never perceived, and these unveilings can be trusted as long as they do not gainsay or contradict the literal meaning. They are additional interpretations which can add to our understanding of the manner in which the Divine Reality discloses Itself. At the same time, no matter how true they may be, they can never have the slightest effect upon the commands and prohibitions of the revealed Law.

Ibn al-ʿArabī's basic principle of Koranic interpretation is a simple one, perfectly logical once one accepts that "There is no god but God and Muḥammad is His Messenger": God intends every meaning which a speaker of the language can understand from the literal sense of the text. It is God who created the speakers of the language, brought the language into existence, and revealed the Book. God's purpose in revelation was clarification, not obfuscation. "God sent no messenger save with the tongue of his people, that [the messenger] might make clear to them" (Koran 14:4). But God had to provide a scripture in the language of the recipients which could guide a whole tradition over history, not simply a few tribesmen of one generation. God spoke in a language which would meet the spiritual needs of all those who encounter the Book. Hence, Ibn al-ʿArabī is constantly analyzing the meaning of words as they have been understood by the speakers of the Arabic language to whom the Koran is addressed, though not necessarily as the specialists in various sciences have defined them.

The Shaykh treats each word of the Koran and the Hadith with the utmost reverence. No word is accidental. God and His Messenger never speak without saying exactly what they mean. We cannot replace one word with another and say that this is what was really meant. Nor can we interpret the meaning, by "taking the word back" (*ta'wīl*) to its archetype in the world of divine realities, if that means denying or denigrating the literal sense. It is vitally important to understand the meaning of each individual word and to realize that each expresses in a concrete mode a certain dimension of the Divine Reality not denoted by any other.

The Study of Ibn al-ʿArabī in the West

A great deal can be learned about Ibn al-ʿArabī by showing the sources of his teachings in earlier writings. Michel

Chodkiewicz's excellent study of "sanctity" (*walāya*) and related concepts, *Le sceau des saints*, provides a sound outline of the type of work that needs to be done for dozens if not hundreds of technical terms.[16] But it is not the purpose of the present work to contribute anything to the task of pinpointing the sources of Ibn al-ʿArabī's teachings. In spite of the importance of this task, a second task appears even more essential to the present writer, and that is to answer such questions as the following: What was Ibn al-ʿArabī actually talking about? What are his basic teachings? How did he himself perceive the goal of his writings? Implicit in these questions is another: What does Ibn al-ʿArabī have to contribute to the intellectual and spiritual needs of the present age?

Questions such as these underlie the two most comprehensive works we possess on Ibn al-ʿArabī's teachings, the aforementioned study by Corbin and Toshihiko Izutsu's *Sufism and Taoism—A Comparative Study of Key Philosophical Concepts.*[17] Both works combine great erudition with a sympathetic understanding of their subject. Izutsu's study is unique for the clarity of the exposition and the careful attention paid to the linguistic nuances of Ibn al-ʿArabī's work. It is limited by a number of factors, and I mention these not to criticize Izutsu's invaluable study, but to situate it within a wider context. First, Izutsu deals almost exclusively with a single work of Ibn al-ʿArabī, the *Fuṣūṣ al-ḥikam*. To understand the significance of this point, we need to take a brief look at the *Fuṣūṣ*.

The *Fuṣūṣ* played a special role among Ibn al-ʿArabī's writings from the beginning. The Shaykh himself tells us in its preface that it was handed to him by the Prophet in a "heralding vision" (*mubashshira*). The second generation *Fuṣūṣ* commentator Mu'ayyid al-Dīn al-Jandī (d. 690/1291) informs us that Ibn al-ʿArabī forbade his disciples from having the *Fuṣūṣ* bound along with any other book.[18] But the *Fuṣūṣ* is a short work (180 pages in the printed edition) and undertakes a relatively specific task. In general, it aims to clarify the Koranic picture of the major prophets, thereby showing how the earthly career of each prophet manifests a specific divine reality or archetype. As a result, the *Fuṣūṣ* says a great deal about the divine names, prophetology, ontology, and several other important topics of Ibn al-ʿArabī's immediate concern. But it emphasizes certain doctrines while leaving out anything but allusions to several major dimensions of Ibn al-ʿArabī's overall teachings. Moreover, Ibn al-ʿArabī makes no attempt to explain what he does discuss with any detail or clarity. Hence the text has always been read in the Islamic world with a commentary or a teacher or both.

It is important to grasp the central role which the *Fuṣūṣ* has played in the Islamic intellectual tradition. No other book of Ibn al-ʿArabī has been as widely read or commented upon. But the tradition, providentially no doubt, took the interpretation of the *Fuṣūṣ* in a specific direction, and that direction happens to be one which often appeals to modern intellectuals cut off from spiritual practice. Beginning with the first important commentator on the *Fuṣūṣ*, Ibn al-ʿArabī's step-son Ṣadr al-Dīn al-Qūnawī (d. 673/1274), practically all *Fuṣūṣ* commentators have discussed the text largely within the context of Islamic philosophy.[19] This, of course, is *Islamic* philosophy, so it does not contradict the commands and prohibitions of Islamic Law. All those commentators about whom anything is known were devout practitioners of Islam and Sufism. They observed the Shariʿa with care, and they had no need to be reminded of its importance, since it was an integral part of their everyday lives. Hence, their special attention to the philosophical dimensions of the text did not run contrary to other, more spiritual and practical dimensions of the text, but it did tend to obscure them.

Qūnawī, a Persian, had a profoundly different intellectual make-up from his master. For one thing, Qūnawī's works are crystal clear and eminently systematic, while no one would say the same about the works of the Shaykh al-Akbar.

Qūnawī was the spiritual inheritor of Ibn al-ʿArabī and the guide of a large number of disciples.[20] At the same time he was known as a great master of the religious sciences, Hadith in particular, and people came to Konya from all over the Islamic world to study with him. Not all of them, and perhaps not many of them, would have been his disciples on the Sufi path.

Qūnawī was better versed in Peripatetic philosophy than Ibn al-ʿArabī and made active attempts to harmonize it with the intellectual expression of Sufism. This attempt at harmonization appears in the manner in which he brings the discussion of *wujūd* (Being, existence) to the forefront. Philosophy was generally defined as the study of *wujūd* qua *wujūd*. Ibn al-ʿArabī frequently discusses *wujūd*, but there is no special internal reason why his followers would have extracted this particular term from his writings and placed it at the center of their concerns. This was done as a result of various external factors personified by Qūnawī himself. He and his disciples set the stage for the later understanding of Ibn al-ʿArabī's works throughout the Islamic world, since the tradition of *Fuṣūṣ* commentary goes straight back to Qūnawī. The first full commentary on the *Fuṣūṣ* was written by Jandī, who was Qūnawī's spiritual disciple and who undertook the work at the instruction of his master. Then Jandī's student ʿAbd al-Razzāq Kāshānī (d. 730/1330) and Kāshānī's student Dāwūd Qayṣarī (d. 751/1350) wrote what are probably the two most influential commentaries of the tradition. Qūnawī's influence is clear in all these works. In the case of Qayṣarī, even the Arabic style reflects Qūnawī's works. In all these commentaries, discussion of *wujūd* stands at the forefront. Qayṣarī's long introduction to his commentary is a masterly summa of philosophical Sufism in an eminently systematic style.[21]

Though Qūnawī's influence helped determine the direction in which the *Fuṣūṣ* was to be interpreted, he was in fact the instrument whereby an inevitable process occurred. The study of Ibn al-ʿArabī could not have been reserved for those who had the requisite spiritual aspiration and "godfearingness." Since Ibn al-ʿArabī dealt with questions of interest to all sorts of scholars, his works were soon being read by many of the learned, not only Sufis. The Shaykh himself consciously employed the terminology of Kalām and philosophy—not to speak of jurisprudence—and he often criticizes the approach of the contemporary authorities of these sciences. The learned masters could not be blamed for reading him or attempting to answer his criticisms.

In short, Ibn al-ʿArabī helped bring the teachings of Sufism into the mainstream of Islamic intellectuality, which in any case was moving more toward philosophy than Kalām. In addition, from the 7th/13th century onward, Islamic intellectuality tends toward synthesis. Many authors contributed to the harmonization of divergent intellectual perspectives, such as Suhrawardī al-Maqtūl (d. 587/1191), the founder of the "Illuminationist" school of philosophy, and Naṣīr al-Dīn Ṭūsī (d. 672/1274), the first systematic Shiʿite theologian and the great revivifier of the teachings of Avicenna. It was only logical that Sufism should play a major role in this harmonization of different intellectual streams. Al-Ghazālī (d. 505/1111) had begun this task long before Ibn al-ʿArabī, and Ibn al-ʿArabī himself contributed to it by employing the terminology of all the intellectual perspectives. But Ṣadr al-Dīn Qūnawī played an especially important role by systematizing Ibn al-ʿArabī's teachings and placing emphasis upon those dimensions of his thought which could easily be reconciled with the philosophical approach. Especially significant in this respect is the correspondence which Qūnawī initiated with Ṭūsī, the great Peripatetic. In his Persian letter accompanying the first of the two Arabic treatises which he sent to Ṭūsī, Qūnawī tells him that his purpose in posing various questions concerning the Peripatetic position was to combine the conclusions derived from logical proofs with those gained by unveiling, opening, and face to face vision of the unseen world.[22]

To return to Izutsu's outstanding study of Ibn al-ʿArabī's teachings: Izutsu limits himself to an analysis of the mainly philosophical and metaphysical discussions of the *Fuṣūṣ*. Moreover, he quotes copiously from the writings of Kāshānī to explain Ibn al-ʿArabī's meaning, and, as was pointed out, Kāshānī is a third-generation commentator on the *Fuṣūṣ*, firmly entrenched in the line of Qūnawī and the movement to bring Ibn al-ʿArabī's teachings into harmony with philosophy. Hence Izutsu's study is especially valuable for showing how the *Fuṣūṣ* was read by the later commentators and how the Shaykh's teachings were being integrated into the philosophical tradition, but it does not necessarily reflect the central concerns of the *Fuṣūṣ* itself, nor, with greater reason, those of Ibn al-ʿArabī.

Moreover, Izutsu's personal interests lie mainly in the abstract discussions of philosophy, not in the *mundus imaginalis*, nor in the practical sides of Islamic spirituality. He is one of the few non-Muslim scholars who have grasped the tremendous philosophical and linguistic riches waiting to be mined in later Islamic thought, and he has made unique contributions to the study of this tradition.[23] But his personal predilections deeply color his perception of Ibn al-ʿArabī. The latter is presented not so much as he is in himself, but as one source for data to be employed in Izutsu's philosophical project, to which he seems to be alluding in the expression, "Toward a Metaphilosophy of Oriental Philosophies."[24]

The second vitally important study of Ibn al-ʿArabī is Corbin's *Creative Imagination in the Ṣūfism of Ibn ʿArabī*. Corbin has been able to present Ibn al-ʿArabī as a thinker worthy of our most serious consideration because of the contributions he can make to the philosophical and hermeneutical concerns of the continental tradition. Corbin's rhetorical flourishes and passion for his subject put his work into a unique category. Few would doubt the relevance of Ibn al-ʿArabī to modern thought after reading Corbin. But Corbin, like Izutsu, has certain limitations. More than Izutsu, Corbin is concerned with his own philosophical project, as elaborated in dozens of books, several of which have now been translated into English. Any reader of *Creative Imagination* soon begins to wonder where Ibn al-ʿArabī ends and Corbin begins. The lines are not clear, especially if one does not have access to the Arabic texts. Certainly we come to realize that Ibn al-ʿArabī is a precious larder from which all sorts of delicious vittles can be extracted. But most people familiar with the original texts would agree that Corbin has highly individual tastes. Moreover, like Izutsu, though not to the same extent, Corbin deals mainly with the *Fuṣūṣ*, making few references to relevant passages in Ibn al-ʿArabī's other works.

While Izutsu places stress on Ibn al-ʿArabī's abstract metaphysical teachings, Corbin emphasizes the Shaykh's depiction of a visionary pleroma where God reveals Himself uniquely to each spiritual aspirant, leading him into the *mundus imaginalis* and beyond. Izutsu stresses the God who can be understood through reason, while Corbin depicts the God of theophany who can be grasped by imagination. Where both authors come together is in failing to bring out the practical sides to Ibn al-ʿArabī's teachings and his insistence on weighing all knowledge in the "Scale of the Law," the norms revealed through the Koran and the Sunna of the Prophet.

The only other study of Ibn al-ʿArabī which is as firmly grounded in the texts and as seminal as these two is Chodkiewicz's *Le sceau des saints*, though it is more limited in scope, making no attempt to provide a broad overview. By placing the concept of "sanctity" within its historical perspective and showing how Ibn al-ʿArabī understands it, Chodkiewicz has contributed important insights into both the theoretical and practical sides of Ibn al-ʿArabī's teachings. His stress on the importance of practice and the observance of the Shariʿa provides a highly beneficial antidote to some of the filtered and refined potions fed to us by Izutsu and Corbin. But the self-imposed limitations of the study leaves us craving for more. Chodkiewicz's forthcoming anthology of the *Futūḥāt*, with selections in both French and English, promises to be a major step forward in our understanding of the full range of Ibn al-ʿArabī's teachings.[25]

The Present Work

The present study is an attempt to lead the reader into Ibn al-ʿArabī's own universe in a language accessible to nonspecialists. In writing the book, I tried to avoid any preconceptions as to what Ibn al-ʿArabī should be saying or what he has to offer. Instead, my goal was to translate or "carry over" his teachings as they are actually found, mainly in the *Futūḥāt*, into a language which does justice to his concerns, not our concerns. I have tried to open the door to Ibn al-ʿArabī's larder and allow the reader to look in, if not actually step inside. Naturally, certain dainties have attracted my attention more than others, and it is these which I tend to pick out.

The form of the book reflects several specific goals, foremost among them the wish to preserve the overall context of Ibn al-ʿArabī's teachings as he himself presents them. This meant that I have tried not to extract the essence of what he is saying, in contrast to most other studies. Rather, I have allowed him to express himself in his own words and within the context of the particular Koranic verses or hadiths which he is explicating at the moment. One cannot separate out the "interesting teachings" without doing harm to the whole. I have also avoided making connections between Ibn al-ʿArabī's ideas and those of other Sufis, other Muslim intellectual authorities, other religious traditions, and the contemporary world, since these are fields of investigation which know no limits. Perhaps others will be inspired to follow up the obvious leads.

Some people might object that I should have translated a single work instead of picking and choosing. But there are many drawbacks to that approach, especially at the present state of our ability to understand the Shaykh's writings on the one hand and then to express them within the confines of an alien universe of discourse on the other. Ibn al-ʿArabī's *Fuṣūṣ al-ḥikam* has been translated into English several times, in each case with mixed results. The best of these translations, that by R.W.J. Austin, still leaves a great deal to be desired, even on the level of conveying accurately the sense of the text.[26] In the original Arabic, much of the text is unintelligible without detailed commentary, which none of the translators have provided. A commentary sufficient to situate the work within Ibn al-ʿArabī's world view and to explain his meaning in every case would be far longer than the *Fuṣūṣ* itself. As with most of Ibn al-ʿArabī's major writings, the *Fuṣūṣ* contains everything, but in such an allusive and undifferentiated form that it is impossible to grasp the meaning without detailed explanation.

One of the advantages of working with the *Futūḥāt* is that Ibn al-ʿArabī is not afraid to go into detail. If he does not explain a topic fully in one passage, he is likely to throw a good deal of light on it elsewhere. The translator can choose the clearest and most complete exposition of various points and leave out the allusions to other teachings not completely relevant to the point he is trying to clarify. Perhaps even more importantly, the text of the *Futūḥāt* is available to us in an excellent edition. Though originally published in Cairo in 1911, it surpasses the standards of most modern critical editions published in the East. Moreover,

Osman Yahia's new edition, with incredibly detailed apparatus, is a great boon to the scholar, though unfortunately, only ten volumes have appeared (of a projected thirty-seven).

It will be a long time before anyone will be able to translate a major work of Ibn al-ʿArabī into comprehensible English without extensive notes and commentary, or even with extensive notes and commentary. His writings pose many difficulties. They are full of allusions to all sorts of esoteric wisdom, and frequently even the prose takes on a symbolic and visionary aura that is practically impossible to fathom. One of the major difficulties presented even by those passages in his writings which are relatively clear is the interrelationship of all discussions with everything else. In order to understand one point, one has to understand all points. This is why, in traditional circles, it was not uncommon for a master to spend several hours commenting on each line of the *Fuṣūṣ*, and a single reading of the text could take many years.

The interrelatedness of Ibn al-ʿArabī's teachings helps explain the repetitions which are characteristic of his style and which have been preserved in the translations and my own commentary. But most repetitions add new nuances and fresh interrelationships not discussed in other contexts. Any attempt to avoid repetition would mean tearing the ideas out of context and imposing upon them a systematic exposition foreign to the original texts.

Ibn al-ʿArabī never tires of stressing the unique characteristics of the knowledge he and other "Folk of Allah"—as he refers to his peers—are trying to impart. Because their science derives from divine opening and not discursive thought, it is intimately interrelated on all levels, though reason often fails to see the connections.

> In its root, the existence of the cosmos is tied to the Being who is Necessary through Himself. Hence each part of the cosmos is tied to every other part, and each is an interconnecting link on a chain. When man begins to consider the science of the cosmos, he is taken from one thing to another because of the interrelationships. But in fact, this only happens in the science of the Folk of Allah. Their science does not follow the canon of those of the learned who know only the outward appearances of phenomena. The canon of the Folk of Allah ties together all parts of the cosmos, so they are taken from one thing to another, even if the scholar of outward appearances sees no relationship. This is knowledge of God. . . .
>
> He who knows the Koran and realizes it will know the science of the Folk of Allah. He will know that their science does not enter into limited chapters, nor does it follow the canon of logic, nor can it be weighed by any scale. It is the scale of all scales. (III 200.26)
>
> Most people work contrary to this direct tasting [of the divine things]. That is why their speech is not tied together. He who considers their speech looks for a root to which all their words go back, but he does not find it. But each part of our speech is interrelated with the other parts, since it is one entity, while these things I say are its differentiation. A person will know what I am saying if he knows the interconnection of the verses of the Koran. (II 548.15)

I began this book with the idea of providing a more or less comprehensive overview of Ibn al-ʿArabī's teachings in the style of my study of Rūmī, *The Sufi Path of Love*. Several months of writing made it clear to me that I could not possibly provide a reasonable survey of Ibn al-ʿArabī's teachings under one cover, so I divided the topics into several major headings, with the idea of publishing a second volume at a later date. As the book originally developed, I wrote ten chapters on cosmology, anthropology, and the cosmic role of perfect man (*al-insān al-kāmil*) after Chapter 8, but it soon became obvious that I could not do justice to these topics along with the other topics which needed to be discussed. I put those chapters aside with the hope of coming back to them on another occasion. In the notes I refer to them as *Cosmology*.[27]

I am painfully aware of the inadequacies of my own explanations of the Shaykh's teachings. I cannot claim to understand everything he is talking about, and in any case I have usually been forced to oversimplify my own comments, since one cannot keep on qualifying oneself in every paragraph. The reader should keep in mind that all my own explanation is tentative, and much of what Ibn al-ʿArabī himself says is modified by what he says in other contexts. In any case, summaries and simplifications of his teachings are unavoidable as soon as we want to gain an overview of his ideas. Definitions have to be provided for terminology, however tentative these may be.

In each chapter I have been torn between the wish to do justice to the topic by presenting it in its full context, and the knowledge that the book will have to have certain limits to be published and read. More than anyone else, I know that compromises have been made and that the book represents nothing close to a final statement of Ibn al-ʿArabī's positions. I too have been forced to offer but a few table scraps from the Shaykh's inexhaustible kitchen.

❉

Though but a preliminary and incomplete survey of Ibn al-ʿArabī's teachings, the present book brings to fruition some twenty years of study. I began reading Ibn al-ʿArabī's works in the original language at Tehran University, where I edited a commentary on one of his treatises as a Ph.D. dissertation under the guidance of Seyyed Hossein Nasr, a project which was completed in 1973 and published in 1977. During those years, Toshihiko Izutsu spent three months of the year in Tehran, and in 1972 he graciously accepted to teach the *Fuṣūṣ* to myself and two others. We finally completed the text in 1978, when Izutsu was teaching full time at the Imperial Iranian Academy of Philosophy, which had recently been founded under the directorship of Nasr. The late Henry Corbin also taught at the Academy, and his intellectual presence was always palpable. I also had the opportunity to study some of the works of Ibn al-ʿArabī's followers with the sage of Mashhad, Sayyid Jalāl al-Dīn Āshtiyānī. To all these teachers I owe a tremendous debt of gratitude, and to all of them I submit my apologies for the inadequacies which remain in the present work.

I first conceived of this book in 1983, soon after publishing *The Sufi Path of Love*. At that time I began reading the *Futūḥāt* systematically. As I moved forward in the text, I read more and more slowly. As my understanding increased, I took detailed notes on passages that at first I would have skimmed. Soon I was finding unexpected ramifications on every page. It began to appear that it would take many, many years to finish the text. In the meantime I had applied to the National Endowment for the Humanities for a Fellowship for Independent Study and Research to write a book on Ibn al-ʿArabī, and this was granted for 1986–87. I gratefully accepted this generous gift and began writing the book without having finished the *Futūḥāt*, not to mention many other works of the Shaykh which I could have consulted. Since I am completely convinced of the truth of Ibn al-ʿArabī's claim that everything he writes is intimately interrelated, I have reason to hope that the texts presented here will not portray his teachings in an unbalanced manner.

1

Overview

1. THE DIVINE PRESENCE

Finding God

How can I find God?

Ibn al-ʿArabī maintains that all human beings must seek to answer this question. Having answered it, they must then set out to verify the truth of their answer by finding God in fact, not in theory. He refers to those who have successfully verified the truth of their answer as the People of Unveiling and Finding (*ahl al-kashf wa'l-wujūd*). They have passed beyond the veils that stand between them and their Lord and stand in His Presence. The path they have traversed is open to everyone. It is the path brought by the prophets and followed by the friends of God (*al-awliyā'*), and it is the path set down in incredible detail in Ibn al-ʿArabī's works. To understand how he conceives of the problem, the path, and the goal is the major task of the present study. We begin by examining the question: "How can I find God?"

"Finding" renders the Arabic *wujūd*, which, in another context, may be translated as "existence" or "being." The famous expression "Oneness of Being" or "Unity of Existence" (*waḥdat al-wujūd*), which is often said to represent Ibn al-ʿArabī's doctrinal position, might also be translated as the "Oneness" or "Unity of Finding." Despite the hundreds of volumes on ontology that have been inspired by Ibn al-ʿArabī's works, his main concern is not with the mental concept of being but with the experience of God's Being, the tasting (*dhawq*) of Being, that "finding" which is at one and the same time to perceive and to be that which truly is. No doubt Ibn al-ʿArabī possessed one of the greatest philosophical minds the world has ever known, but philosophy was not his concern. He wanted only to bask in the constant and ever-renewed finding of the Divine Being and Consciousness. He, for one, had passed beyond the veils, though he was always ready to admit that the veils are infinite and that every instant in life, in this world and for all eternity, represents a continual lifting of the veils.

To find God is to fall into bewilderment (*ḥayra*), not the bewilderment of being lost and unable to find one's way, but the bewilderment of finding and knowing God and of not-finding and not-knowing Him at the same time. Every existent thing other than God dwells in a never-never land of affirmation and negation, finding and losing, knowing and not-knowing. The difference between the Finders and the rest of us is that they are fully aware of their own ambiguous situation. They know the significance of the saying of the first caliph Abū Bakr: "Incapacity to attain comprehension is itself comprehension." They know that the answer to every significant question concerning God and the world is "Yes and no," or, as the Shaykh expresses it, "He/not He" (*huwa lā huwa*).

Chodkiewicz points out that it would not be far from the mark to say that Ibn al-ʿArabī never writes about anything except sanctity, its paths, and its goals.[1] The saints, a term which will be translated here in one of its literal meanings as "friends (of God)," have found God in this life and dwell in His Presence. Ibn al-ʿArabī often refers to them as the "gnostics" (*ʿārifūn*). They see and recognize God wherever they look. The Koranic verse, "Whithersoever you turn, there is the Face of God" (2:115) has become the description of their spiritual state. Others are prevented from seeing Him by veils, but God's friends know that He is the veils and the others. Not that the friends are muddle-headed. They do not say "All is He"[2] and leave it at that. They say, "All is He, all is not He," and then proceed to clarify the various points of view in terms of which the situation can be perceived. If they happen to be among those friends whom Ibn al-ʿArabī considers of the highest rank—the "Verifiers" (*al-muḥaqqiqūn*)—they will have verified the truth of their vision of God on every level of existence and finding, not least on the level of intelligence and speech, the specific marks of being human. Hence they and Ibn al-ʿArabī in particular will provide sophisticated expositions of the exact nature of the ontological and epistemological ambiguity that fills the Void and is commonly referred to as the "world." The bewilderment of the Verifiers in respect to God as He is in Himself never prevents them from finding Him as Light and Wisdom and from employing the fruits of those divine attributes to illuminate the nature of things and put each thing in its proper place.

"How can I find God?" This question means: How can I remove the veils that prevent me from seeing God? We dwell now in the situation of seeing the Not He in all things. How can we also perceive the universe as He?

We ourselves are included among the "things" of the universe. So "How can I find God?" also means: How can I remove those veils that prevent me from *being* God in that respect where the "He" must be affirmed. "Finding," it needs to repeated, is never just epistemological. It is fundamentally ontological. Being precedes knowledge in God as in the world; nothing knows until it first exists. And as the oft-quoted Sufi saying maintains, "None knows God but God." Both knowledge and being are finding.

Worlds and Presences

The mystery of He/not He begins in the Divine Self and extends down through every level of existence. In clarifying the manner in which God is found —in affirming the "He" in all things— Ibn al-ʿArabī also affirms the Not He and explains the nature of everything that fits into that category, i.e., "everything other than God" (*mā siwā Allāh*), which is how Muslim thinkers define "the world" (*al-ʿālam*). He also speaks in detail about "worlds" in the plural. These might best be conceived of as subsystems of the Not He considered as a single whole. Two such worlds are the "greater" and the "lesser" worlds, i.e., the macrocosm (the universe "out there") and the microcosm (the human individual). Three more are the spiritual, imaginal, and corporeal worlds, referred to in concrete imagery as the worlds of light, fire, and clay, from which were created respectively the angels, the jinn, and the body of Adam. In order to distinguish between these two senses of the term world, in what follows *ʿālam* in the sense of the world as a whole will be translated as "cosmos" or "universe," while in the sense of one world in relation to other worlds, it will be translated as "world." When reference is made to "cosmology," what is meant is the study of the cosmos in the sense defined here, that is, the study of "everything other than God." In contrast, modern cosmology has in view not the cosmos as a whole, but a single one of the many worlds.

Considered as other than God, the sum total of everything that exists is the cosmos or all the worlds. But considered as not other than God and as somehow identical with the He (*al-huwa*), the existing things are more likely to be referred to in terms of the "presences" (*ḥaḍra*). The term "presence" is used to refer to most of the "worlds," though not to "the cosmos" as such. Thus the spiritual, imaginal, and corporeal "worlds" are also referred to as "presences." The sense of the term is that, for example, the "Presence of Imagination" (*ḥaḍrat al-khayāl*) is a domain in which everything that exists is woven out of images. As a result, all things in this domain are "present" with imagination. In the same way, all things that reside in the Presence of Sense Perception (*ḥaḍrat al-ḥiss*) can be perceived by the senses. Ibn al-ʿArabī's followers, beginning with Qūnawī, wrote in detail about the "Five Divine Presences," by which they meant the five domains in which God is to be "found" or in which His Presence is to be perceived, i.e., (1) God Himself, the (2) spiritual, (3) imaginal, and (4) corporeal worlds, and (5) perfect man (*al-insān al-kāmil*).[3]

In the last analysis, there is but a single presence known as the Divine Presence (*al-ḥaḍrat al-ilāhiyya*), which comprehends everything that exists. Ibn al-ʿArabī defines it as the Essence, Attributes, and Acts of Allah (II 114.14). Allah is known as the "all-comprehensive" (*jāmiʿ*) name of God, since it alone designates God as He is in Himself in the widest possible sense, leaving out nothing whatsoever of His Reality. Other names, such as Creator, Forgiving, and Vengeful, designate Him under certain specific aspects of His Reality.

The Divine Presence is that "location" where Allah is to be found, or where we can affirm that what we find is He. It includes the Essence (*dhāt*) of Allah, which is God in Himself without regard to His creatures; the attributes (*ṣifāt*) of Allah, also called His names (*asmāʾ*), which are the relationships that can be discerned between the Essence and everything other than He; and the acts (*afʿāl*), which are all the creatures in the cosmos along with everything that appears from them. Hence the term "Divine Presence" designates God on the one hand and the cosmos, inasmuch as it can be said to be the locus of His activity, on the other.

Ibn al-ʿArabī most often uses the term presence to refer to the sphere of influence of one of the divine names. For example, God is Powerful, so the "Presence of Power" is everything in existence that comes under the sway of His power, including the whole of creation. But the Presence of Power is more constricted, for example, than the Presence of Knowledge. No matter how powerful God may be, He cannot make Himself ignorant of what He knows. This way of thinking, which infuses Ibn al-ʿArabī's writings, has far-reaching implications for theological speculation.

"Where can I find God?" One obvious answer: Wherever He is present. But how is God present in things? God is certainly present through the properties of His Essence, which is He Himself, His very Being. Allah, God as described by the all-comprehensive name, has an influence upon everything in the cosmos. Everything that exists, by the fact of existing, manifests something of the Divine Presence, which by definition embraces all that exists. But every name of God has its own presence, which means that God makes Himself present to His creatures in various modalities. In each case it is God who reveals Himself, who is present in the created thing, but God as the Abaser (*al-mudhill*) is not the same as God as the Exalter (*al-muʿizz*). "Thou exaltest whom Thou wilt and Thou abasest whom Thou wilt" (Koran 3:26). God as the Life-Giver (*al-muḥyī*) is not the same as God as the Slayer (*al-mumīt*). God encompasses all things, but some are exalted and some abased, some alive and some dead.

"Where can I find God?" Wherever He is present, which is everywhere, since all things are His acts. But no act is identical with God, who encompasses all things and all acts, all worlds and all presences. Though He can be found everywhere, He is also nowhere to be found. He/not He.

Being and Nonexistence

From the first, Islam's primary teaching has been that God is one. It did not take long before theologians and philosophers were struggling with the perennial intellectual task of explaining how multiplicity could have arisen from a reality that is one in every respect. Ibn al-ʿArabī sees one explanation in the doctrine of the divine names, which provides the infrastructure for most of his teachings. But even more fundamental is the question of the nature of existence itself. Before talking about God and His attributes, we can search for Oneness and uncover the root of multiplicity in the nature of existing things.

We return to the word *wujūd*, "finding," "being," or "existence." Ibn al-ʿArabī employs the term in a wide variety of ways. Without getting embroiled at this point in philosophical niceties, we can discern two fundamental meanings that will demand two different translations for a single term. On the one hand we "find" things wherever we look, both in the outside world and inside the mind. All these things "exist" in some mode or another; existence can be said to be their attribute. The house exists and the galaxy exists in the outside world, the green-eyed monster exists in the hallucinations of a madman, on the film screen, and on the written page. The modes are different, but in each case we can say that something possesses the attribute of being there. When Ibn al-ʿArabī speaks about any specific thing or idea that can be discussed, he uses the term existence in this general sense to refer to the fact that something is there, something is to be found. In this sense we can also say that God exists, meaning, "There is a God."

In a second sense Ibn al-ʿArabī employs the word *wujūd* when speaking about the substance or stuff or nature of God Himself. In one word, what is God? He is *wujūd*. In this sense "finding" might better convey the sense of the term, as long as we do not imagine that God has lost something only to have found it again. What He is finding now He has always found and will ever find. Past, present, and future are in any case meaningless in relation to God in Himself, since they are attributes assumed by various existent things in relation to us, not in relation to Him. But "finding" is perhaps not the best term to bring this discussion into the theological and philosophical arena where Ibn al-ʿArabī wants it to be considered. We are better off choosing the standard philosophical term "Being," which has normally been chosen (along with "existence") by Western scholars when they have wanted to discuss the term *wujūd* in English. However, one needs to keep in mind the fact that "Being" is in no way divorced from consciousness, from a fully aware finding, perception, and knowledge of the ontological situation. Since this point tends to be forgotten when the term is discussed, I will have occasion to come back to it, hoping for the reader's indulgence.

In what follows, "Being" in upper case will refer to God as He is in Himself. For Ibn al-ʿArabī, Being is in no sense ambiguous or questionable, though our understanding of Being is something else again. Being is that which truly is, while everything else dwells in fog and haziness. Hence, when we say that something—anything other that God—"exists," we have to hesitate a little in saying so. The statement is ambiguous, for just as a thing pertains to existence, so also it lies in the grasp of existence's opposite, nonexistence (*ʿadam*). Every existent thing is at one and the same time He (Being) and Not He (not-being, absolute nothingness). Only God is Being without qualification, without hesitation, without doubt.

God is sheer Being, utter Plenitude, pure Consciousness. Any given entity in the cosmos is at best a dim reflection of some of these qualities. Ibn al-ʿArabī commonly employs the term "existent" (*mawjūd*) to refer to the existing things, a term which, through its derivative grammatical form, suggests the derivative nature of the existence that is ascribed to the things. As will become clear when we discuss the "immutable entities" (*al-aʿyān al-thābita*), this ascription of existence to the things is in any case a mode of speaking more than a strict description of the actual situation. In fact, existence is but the reflected brilliance of Being, and there is only a single Being, God Himself.

God is Light, as the Koran affirms (24:35). Like so many other Muslim thinkers, at least from the time of al-Ghazālī, Ibn al-ʿArabī identifies Light with Being and employs the symbolism of visible light to explain the relationship between Being and nonexistence. God is Light and nothing but Light, while the things are so many rays reflected from Light's substance. In one respect they are Light, since nothing else can be found; in another respect they are darkness, since they are not identical with Light itself. But darkness has no positive reality of its own, since its defining characteristic is the absence of Light. In the same way the defining characteristic of each existent thing is its absence of Being. Though it reflects Being in one respect, it is nonexistent in another. He/not He.

Being or Light is that which by its very nature finds itself, though it cannot be perceived—i.e., embraced, encompassed, and understood—by "others." First, because there is nothing other than Light that might do the perceiving. There is only Light, which perceives itself. Second, because if we accept that certain things "exist," or that there are rays of light shining in an area which we can call the Void, these things or rays can only perceive themselves or their likes, not something infinitely greater than themselves of which they are but dim reflections. The shadow cannot perceive the sunlight, and the sunlight cannot embrace the sun. Only the sun knows the sun. "None knows God but God."

How does manyness arise from Oneness? Being is Oneness, while nothingness as such does not exist in any respect. But we already know about Being that It is Light, so It radiates and gives of Itself. Hence we have three "things": Light, radiance, and darkness; or Being, existence, nonexistence. The second category—radiance or existence—is our particular concern, since it defines our "location" for all practical purposes. Its most obvious characteristic is its ambiguous situation, half-way between Being and nonexistence, Light and darkness, He and Not He. Ibn al-ʿArabī sometimes calls it existence, and sometimes nonexistence, since each attribute applies to it. "Nonexistence" can thus be seen to be of two basic kinds: Absolute nonexistence (*al-ʿadam al-muṭlaq*), which is nothingness pure and simple, and relative nonexistence (*al-ʿadam al-iḍāfī*), which is the state of the things considered as Not He.

Our classification of the kinds of reality has gradually become more complex. We began with Being and existence, then looked at Being and nonexistence, then at Being, existence, and nonexistence, and now we turn to a fourth picture of the basic structure of reality: Being, relative nonexistence, and absolute nonexistence, the last of which we can call "nothingness." Only Being truly is, while nothingness has no existence except of a purely speculative and mental kind. So "everything other than God"—the cosmos—is relative nonexistence. But anything which is relatively nonexistence is also relatively existent.

Plurality and manyness arise from the very nature of existence (we could also say, from the very nature of nonexistence, but then the discussion would take a different turn; that perspective will come up in due time). It is plain to everyone that "brightness" is not all of a single intensity. Some brightness is stronger, some weaker; some is closer to light, some farther away. We can also say that some existents are more intense than others, but here the point is not so obvious. To make the point clear, it is best to talk not about Being itself but about the attributes of Being, i.e., those qualities that are denoted by the divine names, and examine how they are reflected in existence.

Take "finding," for example, which is identical with consciousness and self-awareness, or with "knowledge" as a divine attribute (and also as a human attribute in the context of Sufi texts). It should be obvious that some people are more aware than others, some more knowledgeable than others. This is Ibn al-ʿArabī's doctrine of *tafāḍul*, "ranking in degrees of excellence," or "some being preferred over others," or "some surpassing others." The term is derived from such Koranic verses as, "God has caused some of you to surpass others in provision" (16:71). Knowledge is among the greatest bounties which He has provided for His creatures, but He has not given it to everyone equally. The Koran says, "We [God] raise in degrees whomsoever We will, and above each one who possesses knowledge is someone who knows [more]" (12:76).[4] And it asks, "Are they equal—those who know and those who know not?" (39:9).

Existence or the cosmos is a vast panorama of ranking in degrees in every conceivable quality and attribute. No two things are exactly the same. Two things must differ in at least one attribute, or else they would be the same thing. The attributes depend upon Being, though they gain specific coloring from nothingness. Without first existing, a thing cannot be large or small, intelligent or ignorant, living or dead. Without light, there can be no red or green or blue. Everywhere we look we see hierarchies of attributes. If someone knows, someone else knows more, and someone else less. No two existents know exactly the same thing or the same amount. If we shared in God's infinite knowledge, we would be able to discern a hierarchy of the knowing things in creation for all eternity from the least knowledgeable to the most knowledgeable. Each individual thing at any point in the trajectory of its existence would fit into a specific niche in the hierarchy. And the same thing can be said about every attribute that pertains to Being as well as about that global unity of Being's manifest attributes known as "existence." There is a gradation in the intensity of existence—or light—to be perceived in all things. No two things are exactly the same in the degree or mode of their existence.

The Divine Attributes

"Allah," the all-comprehensive name, refers to all attributes of Being at once. It also alludes to Being's relationship with the whole hierarchy of existence that reflects Its attributes in varying intensities, a hierarchy that is called, in the language of the theologians, the "acts of God." Other divine names refer to relatively specific attributes of Being, such as Life, Knowledge, Desire, Power, Speech, Generosity, and Justice. According to a saying of the Prophet, there are ninety-nine of these "most beautiful" divine names, though other names are expressed or implied in the Koran and various prophetic sayings. Each name enunciates an attribute of God, Sheer Being. The effect (*athar*) or property (*ḥukm*) of each name can be traced within existence, if, that is, we are given the insight and wisdom to do so. This in fact is the task that Ibn al-ʿArabī undertakes in the *Futūḥāt*, though he is fully aware that every book in the universe would be insufficient to record all the properties of the divine names, all the "words" of God. As the Koran puts it, "Though all the trees in the earth were pens, and the sea—seven seas after it to replenish it—[were ink,] yet would the words of God not be spent" (31:27).

As was pointed out earlier, the name Allah refers to God's Essence, attributes, and acts. The Essence is God in Himself without reference to anything else. As such God is unknowable to any but Himself. He is, as Ibn al-ʿArabī quotes constantly, "Independent of the worlds" (Koran 3:97), and this includes the knowledge possessed by the worlds. God as the Essence is contrasted with God inasmuch as He assumes relationships with the cosmos, relationships denoted by various divine names, such as Creator, Maker, Shaper, Generous, Just, Exalter, Abaser, Life-Giver, Slayer, Forgiver, Pardoner, Avenger, Grateful, and Patient.

Inasmuch as God's Essence is Independent of the worlds, the cosmos is Not He, but inasmuch as God freely assumes relationships with the worlds through attributes such as creativity and generosity, the cosmos manifests the He. If we examine anything in the universe, God is Independent of that thing and infinitely exalted beyond it. He is, to employ the theological term that plays a major role in Ibn al-ʿArabī's vocabulary, "incomparable" (*tanzīh*) with each thing and all things. But at the same time, each thing displays one or more of God's attributes, and in this respect the thing must be said to be "similar" (*tashbīh*) in some way to God. The very least we can say is that it exists and God exists, even though the modalities of existence may be largely incomparable. Many scholars have employed the terms "transcendence" and "immanence" (or "anthropomorphism") in referring to these two ways of conceptualizing God's relationship with the cosmos, but I will refrain from using these words in an attempt to avoid preconceptions and capture the nuances of the Arabic terminology.

When Ibn al-ʿArabī speaks about the Essence as such, he has in view God's incomparability. In this respect there is little one can say about God, except to negate (*salb*) the attributes of created things from Him. Nevertheless, the Essence is God as He is in Himself, and God must exist in Himself before He reveals Himself to others. Both logically and ontologically, incomparability precedes similarity. It is the ultimate reference point for everything we say about God. A great deal can indeed be said about Him—that, after all, is what religion and revelation are all about—but once said, it must also be negated. Our doctrines, dogmas, theologies, and philosophies exist like other things, which is to say that they also are He/not He. Discerning the modalities and relationships, distinguishing the true from the false and the more true from the less true, is the essence of wisdom.

When Ibn al-ʿArabī speaks about God's attributes and acts, he has in view the divine similarity. In this respect many things can be attributed to God, although it is best to observe courtesy (*adab*) by attributing to Him only that which He has attributed to Himself in revelation. What He has attributed to Himself is epitomized by His names and attributes, the discussion of which delineates Ibn al-ʿArabī's fundamental approach to the exposition of the nature of things. The attributes are reflected in the acts, i.e., all things found in the cosmos. God's "power" is reflected passively in everything He has made and actively in suns, volcanoes, seas, bees, human beings, and other creatures. His Hearing is found in every animal and perhaps in plants as well. His Speech is certainly reflected in the cries, calls, and chirps of animals, but only in the same way that a glowing ember may be said to manifest the light of the sun. Only in the human being, the crown of that creation with which we are familiar, can speech reach a station where it expresses intelligence and truth and, in prayer, becomes discourse between man and God. "Call upon Me," says God in the Koran—to man, not to monkeys or parrots—"and I will answer you" (40:60).

For Ibn al-ʿArabī the divine names are the primary reference points in respect to which we can gain knowledge of the cosmos. In the *Futūḥāt* he constantly discusses words and technical terms that were employed by theologians, philosophers, and Sufis before him. For example, he has chapters devoted to many of the states (*aḥwāl*) and stations (*maqāmāt*) that are discussed in detail in Sufi works. These represent the psychological, moral, and spiritual attributes and perspectives that mark degrees of spiritual growth which travelers on the path to God must experience, assimilate, and in most cases pass beyond. Examples include attributes that are paired and usually must be actualized together, such as hope and fear, expansion and contraction, intoxication and sobriety, annihilation and subsistence; and other attributes which are viewed as marking a kind of ascending hierarchy, such as awakening, repentance, self-examination, meditation, ascetic discipline, abstinence, renunciation, desire, refinement, sincerity, confidence, satisfaction, gratitude, humility, joy, certainty, courtesy, remembrance, good-doing, wisdom, inspiration, love, jealousy, ecstasy, tasting, immersion, realization, and unity.[5] Ibn al-ʿArabī devotes about 200 chapters of the *Futūḥāt* to such terminology. The point to be made here is that his characteristic mode of approach is to discuss briefly what previous masters have said about these qualities and then to bring out what he calls the "divine root" (*al-aṣl al-ilāhī*) or the "divine support" (*al-mustanad al-ilāhī*) of the quality in question. What is it about God—Allah, the all-comprehensive Reality—that allows such a quality to be manifested in existence in the first place and then to be assumed by a human being? In a few cases the answer is immediately clear. "Love" is attributed to God in many places in the Koran, so the love that the spiritual traveler acquires must be a reflection of that divine love. But in most cases the divine root can only be brought out by a subtle analysis of Koranic verses and hadiths. Invariably, these analyses circle around the names and attributes that are ascribed to God in the revealed texts.

It must be concluded—from the above and a great deal more evidence that will present itself naturally in the course of the present book—that the divine names are the single most important concept to be found in Ibn al-ʿArabī's works. Everything, divine or cosmic, is related back to them. Neither the Divine Essence nor the most insignificant creature in the cosmos can be understood without reference to them. It is true that the Essence is unknown in Itself, but it is precisely the Essence that is named by the names.[6] There are not two realities, Essence and name, but a single reality—the Essence—which is called by a specific name in a given context and from a particular point of view. A single person may be father, son, brother, husband, and so on without becoming many people. By knowing the person as "father" we know him, but that does not mean we know him as brother. Likewise, by knowing any name of God we know God, but not necessarily in respect of another name, nor in respect to His very Self or Essence.

In the same way, God's creatures must be known in terms of the divine names for any true knowledge to accrue. Every attribute possessed by a creature can be traced back to its ontological root, God Himself. The existence of the creature derives from God's Being, its strength from God's power, its awareness from God's knowledge, and so on.

Obviously there are many more attributes in creation than those delineated by the ninety-nine Most Beautiful Names. So the task of explaining the divine root of a thing through language is not at all straightforward.[7] If it were, the *Futūḥāt* would fill 100 pages instead of 17,000. However this may be, it is sufficient for present purposes to realize that the Essence manifests Itself in the divine names, and the names in turn are revealed through the divine acts.

The Divine Acts

The term "acts" has many synonyms that Ibn al-ʿArabī is more likely to employ, though each synonym has its own connotations and nuances that can only become clear when it is explained in detail and employed in context. Acts are found in the intermediate domain known as existence, so their state remains forever ambiguous. To what extent they reflect the light of Being is always at issue. The word acts itself implies their existence, since the acts pertain to the Divine Presence, and by definition God is Sheer Being. In a similar way the synonymous term "creatures" (*khalq, makhlūqāt*) demands that the acts be the result of the activity of the divine name "Creator" (*khāliq*), whose business is to bring things out from nonexistence into existence. Here also, the term emphasizes the light of Being reflected in the things of the cosmos. Another common term applied to anything in the cosmos is "form" (*ṣūra*). As Ibn al-ʿArabī says, "There is nothing in the cosmos but forms" (II 682.20). But the term "form" normally calls to mind a second reality which the form manifests. X is the form of y. This second reality is often called the "meaning" (*maʿnā*) of the form.

At first sight the term "existents" (*mawjūdāt*) clearly affirms the reality of the created things, but a more careful analysis makes it ambiguous, since existence itself stands in an intermediary situation. Nevertheless, we can contrast "existents" with "nonexistents" (*maʿdūmāt*), in which case a clear distinction must be drawn. Here the point is that there are degrees of participation in the light of Being.

Those things that are "existent" can be "found" in the outside world through our senses. But those things that are "nonexistents" cannot be found. However, they are not pure nothingness, since "nonexistence" is an ambiguous category, not too much different from existence. The nonexistence of the things is clearly a relative (*iḍāfī*) matter. For example, a person may claim that galaxies are nonexistent, and in relationship to his understanding, this may be a true statement. On another level, your fantasies are nonexistent for me, existent for you. On the cosmic level, any creature which can be found in the outside world is existent as long as it continues to be found there. But when it is destroyed or dies or decays, it ceases to be found in its original form, so it is nonexistent.

Any creature that God has not yet brought into existence is also nonexistent, though it certainly exists in some mode, since it is an object of God's knowledge. It is "found" with God. He knows that He will bring it into the cosmos at a certain time and place, so it exists with Him, but is nonexistent in the cosmos.

Ibn al-ʿArabī employs the term "objects of [God's] knowledge" (*maʿlūmāt*) synonymously with the term "nonexistent things." Both terms denote things or creatures as found with God "before" or "after" they have existed in the cosmos. However, it needs to be kept in mind that these things never "leave" God's knowledge, so everything existent in the cosmos at this moment is also a "nonexistent object of knowledge." Here again its situation is ambiguous.

One of the more common and probably best known terms that Ibn al-ʿArabī employs for the nonexistent objects of God's knowledge is "immutable entity"

(*ʿayn thābita*). Entity here is synonymous with "thing" (*shay'*), and "thing," as should be apparent from the way I have been employing the term all along, is "one of the most indefinite of the indefinites" (*min ankar al-nakirāt*), since it can be applied to anything whatsoever, existent or nonexistent (though it is not normally applied to God as Being). The "existent things" are the creatures of the cosmos (though never ceasing to be nonexistent objects of God's knowledge). The "nonexistent things" are objects of knowledge, also called the "immutable entities." These things or entities are immutable because they never change, just as God's knowledge never changes. He knows them for all eternity. Here of course we enter onto the very slippery ground of free will and predestination, one of Ibn al-ʿArabī's favorite topics.

When discussing *wujūd*, the central concern of the Muslim Peripatetics such as Avicenna, Ibn al-ʿArabī often borrows the Peripatetic term *wājib al-wujūd*, Necessary Being, that which by its very nature *is* and cannot not be; this is what we have been referring to as "Being." In this context the entities are called the "possible things" (*mumkināt*), since they may or may not exist in the cosmos. In respect to their own possibility, which is their defining characteristic, their relationship to existence and nonexistence is the same. An "immutable entity" is a nonexistent possible thing. If God "gives preponderance" (*tarjīḥ*) to the side of existence over nonexistence, it becomes an existent entity, an existent possible thing. Like "entity" and "thing" and unlike "existent," the ontological status of a possible thing has to be specified.

These few words that are employed in various contexts as synonyms for the term "acts" all share a certain ambiguity in terms of their referents. To repeat, this is because they are used to describe the domain of existent things, which is ambiguous by nature. Only Being—the Necessary Being—is absolutely unquestionable and unambiguous. But since It is utterly free of every limitation that can be applied to anything else, we can only know It by negating from It all the ambiguities of "that which is other than Being." Things, immutable entities, existent entities, acts, creatures, existents, nonexistents, possible things, and anything else we can name are in themselves "Not He." This is what might be called God's radical transcendence, His utter and absolute incomparability. From this point of view, true knowledge of God can only come through negation. This is the classical position of much of Islamic theology, but, however essential and true, it must be complemented—in Ibn al-ʿArabī's view—with the acknowledgment that the acts do possess a certain derivative actuality and existence, all the more so since we are situated in their midst and cannot ignore them. Everything other than God is Not He, which means that everything other than God is not Reality, not Being, not Finding, not Knowledge, not Power, etc. Nevertheless, we do "find" the effects of these attributes in the existent things, and this lets us know that He is present. "We are nearer to [man] than the jugular vein" (Koran 50:16). "Whithersoever you turn, *there* is the Face of God" (2:115).

The Macrocosm

The existent things are not scattered randomly, in spite of their ambiguous status. God is the Wise, and wisdom (*ḥikma*) discerns the proper place of things and puts them where they belong. God is also "Uplifter of degrees" (*rafīʿ al-darajāt*), so He arranges all things according to the requirements of their own attributes and qualities. This is the source of the "ranking in degrees" (*tafāḍul*) already mentioned. These names provide important theological roots for the various cosmological teachings found in the works of Muslim authors. Like many other Muslim cosmologists, Ibn al-ʿArabī bases his scheme largely on the data of the Koran and the Hadith. In the present work I can only provide a brief outline of the cosmos as he pictures it.

The Koran and Hadith are full of terms, many of them presented as complementary pairs, that suggest the dimensions of the cosmos: Light and darkness, the heavens and the earth, this world and the next world, the origin and the return, spirit and body, life and death, sun and moon, day and night. All these Koranic pairs find an appropriate place in Ibn al-ʿArabī's cosmology. To them must be added various sets of terms such as stars, planets, and mansions of the moon; earth, air, water, and fire; animals, plants, and inanimate objects; and so on throughout the natural universe. It is well known that few if any sacred texts pay as much attention as the Koran to natural phenomena, which the Koran calls the "signs" (*āyāt*) of God. Add to these texts the indigenous knowledge of the Arabs and the Greek and Persian legacies that were very early taken over by the Muslims, and one begins to have an idea of the rich sources of Islamic cosmology.

To gain an overview of Ibn al-ʿArabī's system, it may be best to suggest some of the implications of one of the most basic and suggestive of all pairings, that of "light" (*nūr*) and "darkness" (*ẓulma*). We have already seen that God is the Light of the heavens and the earth, and that Light is synonymous with Being. The "darkness" which stands opposite this uncreated Light of God is "nothingness," absolute nonexistence. But there is also a created light that pertains to the cosmos. *Nūr*, like *wujūd*, is applied to both God and the creatures. The angels (*malāʾika*), for example, are—according to the Prophet—created from light, which is to say that their very substance is woven from light. This is not the Light which is God, for God in Himself is infinitely incomparable, even with the greatest of the angels, all of whom are His creatures. So the light out of which the angels have been shaped and formed is the immediate radiance of Light or Being. Then there are other creatures who are dark in relation to the angels, since they have been made out of clay. These things cannot be pure and utter darkness, since they exist. Their light or existence is obscured by their distance from the Absolute Light which is the source of cosmic light, but it is real light. These creatures created out of relative darkness—that is, extremely dim light—inhabit the earth, which itself is basically "clay" (earth and water), though the more luminous elements, air and fire, also play important roles (the four elements are known as the "pillars" [*arkān*] of terrestrial existence).

The slightest meditation on the relationship between light and darkness shows that they are relative things. In a dark room, a candle is a bright light, but in the desert at noon it is virtually nonexistent. Fireflies fill the nights of June with radiance, but no one finds them in the daytime. The moon is a marvelous lamp, but it quickly flees the scene when the sun appears. Much of the terminology that Ibn al-ʿArabī employs in referring to existent things possesses this same relativity, and indeed one can say that every attribute that is applied to every existing thing in the universe has to be understood in relative terms. This type of relativity fits into the category of "ranking in degrees" or *tafāḍul*. If an angel is made out of light, it is nevertheless dark in relation to God. If a stone is dark, it is nevertheless light in relation to nothingness. If one person is intelligent, someone can always be found who is more intelligent. The only absolutes are the Divine Essence on the one hand and "nothingness" on the other. These are the two poles between which the cosmos takes shape.

All the basic terms that Ibn al-ʿArabī employs to describe the structure of the cosmos must be viewed in relative terms. When we say that there are "two" basic kinds of existent, those made of light and those made of clay, this means that pure created light and pure clay are, relatively speaking, two cosmic poles. Between them all the existent things in the cosmos are arranged according to any attribute that one wants to take into account. When Ibn al-ʿArabī speaks about the "hierarchy of the cosmos" (*tartīb al-ʿālam*), as he does in great detail in many passages of the *Futūḥāt*, he has in view the various degrees of existence or finding, the "ontological levels" (*marātib al-wujūd*) of the universe, or in other words, the various degrees in which the creatures participate in the Divine Presence. But when he has in view the various positive divine attributes such as knowledge, power, or generosity, then he uses the term *tafāḍul* or ranking in degrees to describe how each creature reflects or participates in these attributes to a different extent.

Some of the most important pairs of terms that are used to relate the existent things to the two poles of the cosmos are luminous (*nūrānī*) and dark (*ẓulmānī*), subtle (*laṭīf*) and dense (*kathīf*), spiritual (*rūḥānī*) and corporeal (*jismānī*), unseen (*ghayb*) and visible (*shahāda*), high (*ʿulwī*) and low (*suflī*). Each term designates a relative situation. What is subtle in relation to one thing is dense in relation to another. When it is said that the angels are luminous, subtle, spiritual, unseen, and high, a relationship is envisaged with all those things that are dark, dense, corporeal, visible, and low. It is not forgotten that the angels are in fact dark and dense in relationship to the infinite Light of God.

Viewed in the context of relative contrast and conflict, each attribute is taken to be incompatible with its opposite. This means that the angels have no direct relationship with the things of the corporeal world. Light does not perceive the darkness, nor does darkness comprehend the light. The angels are pure unitive awareness, while the corporeal things, as such, are conglomerations of unconscious parts and conflicting bits. Each part, which may be viewed as a relatively independent corporeal thing, has come into existence through a temporary marriage of the four elements in a specific balance that gives it its elemental characteristics (e.g., the ascending or fiery element may dominate over the descending or earthy element). But viewed as a continuous hierarchy, the existent things are ranged between the most intense created light and the most intense darkness (= the least intense light), and this tells us that there must be innumerable degrees of intermediate creatures between "pure" light and "pure" darkness. In this context, it needs to be remembered, "pure" means the most intense in existence; it does not signify absolute, since Absolute Light is God, while absolute darkness is sheer nothingness.[8] These intermediate degrees are known as *barzakh*s (literally "isthmuses").

A *barzakh* is something that stands between and separates two other things, yet combines the attributes of both. Strictly speaking, every existent thing is a *barzakh*, since everything has its own niche between two other niches within the ontological hierarchy known as the cosmos. "There is nothing in existence but *barzakh*s, since a *barzakh* is the arrangement of one thing between two other things . . . , and existence has no edges (*ṭaraf*)" (III 156.27). Existence itself is a *barzakh* between Being and nothingness. In the hierarchy of worlds which makes up the cosmos, the term *barzakh* refers to an intermediate world standing between the luminous or spiritual world and the dark or corporeal world. The term is relative, like other cosmological terms, but it helps us to situate existent things in the cosmos with a bit more precision. Instead of saying that things are either spiritual or corporeal, we can now say that they may also be *barzakhī*, that is to say, neither spiritual nor corporeal but somewhere in between.

The term *barzakh* is often used to refer to the whole intermediate realm between the spiritual and the corporeal. In this sense the term is synonymous with the World of Imagination (*khayāl*) or Images (*mithāl*). From this perspective, there are basically three kinds of existent things: spiritual, imaginal or *barzakhī*, and corporeal. The imaginal world is more real than the corporeal world, since it is situated closer to the World of Light, though it is less real than the spiritual and luminous realm of the angels. "Imaginary" things possess a certain kinship with imaginal things, but only as a sort of weak reverberation. Nevertheless, we can gain help in understanding the nature of the World of Imagination by reflecting upon our own mental experience of imagination.

The most specific characteristic of the things found within the domain of imagination, on whatever level it is considered, is their intermediary and ambiguous status. When we understand the pairs of terms mentioned above as extreme "poles" or as relatively absolute ontological situations, then we can see that nothing found on the imaginal level corresponds to one or the other of the two poles. Imaginal existents are neither luminous nor dark, neither spiritual nor corporeal, neither subtle nor dense, neither high nor low. In every case they are somewhere in between, which is to say that they are "both/and." When we consider the pairs of terms which denote the extremes as relative terms, then all of them apply to imagination, depending on the perspective. Imaginal things are subtle in relation to the corporeal world, but dense in relation to the spiritual world. They are luminous in relation to visible things, but dark in relation to unseen things. Ibn al-ʿArabī often employs expressions like "corporealization of the spirits" (*tajassud al-arwāḥ*) and "spiritualization of the corporeal bodies" (*tarawḥun al-ajsām*) to explain what sorts of events take place in the imaginal realm. It is here, he says, that the friends of God have visions of past prophets or that, after death, all the works of a person will be given back to him in a form appropriate to the intention and reality behind the work, not in the form of the work itself.

Those Muslim thinkers who deal with the imaginal world—and there are many, as Corbin's researches have helped to show[9]—love to point to dreams as our most direct and common experience of its ontological status. In the dream world, the things we perceive share in the luminosity of our own consciousness, yet they are presented to us as corporeal and dense things, not as disembodied spirits. Since the World of Spirits manifests directly the unity of the divine, angels have no "parts," while the world of corporeal things appears to us as indefinite multiplicity. But the world of dreams combines unity and multiplicity. A single dreaming subject perceives a multiplicity of forms and things that in fact are nothing but his own single self. Their manyness is but the mode that the one consciousness assumes in displaying various facets of itself.

It was just said that the most specific characteristic of imaginal things is their intermediary and ambiguous situation. From everything we have said about existent things in general, it should be clear that all existent things share in a similar ambiguity, since they are neither Being nor nothingness, but somewhere in between. Existence as a whole, as was said above, is a *barzakh*, an intermediary realm between Being and nothingness. Hence existence as a whole can be called "imagination." When Ibn al-ʿArabī uses the term imagination, he most often has in mind the intermediary realm between the spiritual and corporeal worlds. But sometimes he means existence per se. In a few passages he clarifies the distinction between the two kinds of imagination by calling the cosmos "nondelimited imagination" (*al-khayāl al-muṭlaq*) and the imaginal world "delimited imagination" (*al-khayāl al-muqayyad*). The accompanying diagram shows the overall structure of Ibn al-ʿArabī's most elementary cosmological scheme. Note that there are two intermediary domains, existence as such (= nondelimited imagination), which stands between Being and nothingness, and the imaginal world (= delimited imagination), which stands between the spiritual and the corporeal worlds.

It needs to be kept in mind that the cosmos is "imagination" only in the specific sense of the term as defined above. In no sense does this imply that things "out there" are imaginary, any more

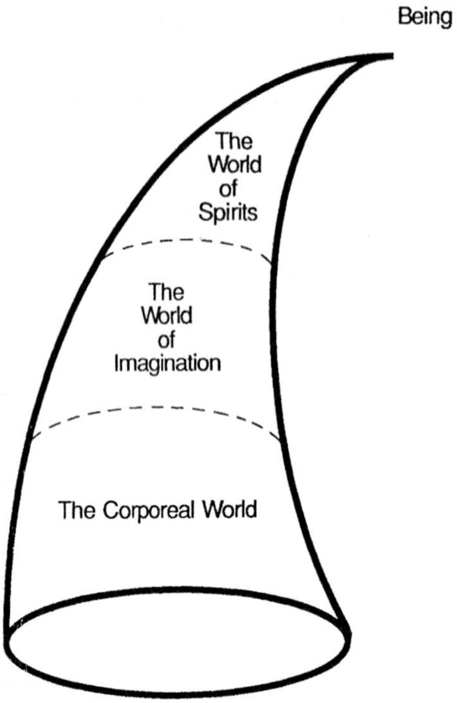

Nondelimited Imagination. (Ibn al-ʿArabī describes nondelimited imagination as a "horn made out of light" [I 306, translated in Chapter 7])

than we ourselves are imaginary. We ourselves are part of the cosmos and partake of its ontological status, and it provides our only path to true knowledge of ourselves and of God. Moreover, the cosmos is God's imagination, not our imagination. He imagines everything other than Himself, but by so doing, He gives all things a certain mode of real and seemingly independent existence. This nondelimited imagination of God is also God's self-manifestation (*ẓuhūr*) or self-disclosure (*tajallī*), terms that will be discussed in detail as we go along. For now, it is sufficient to look at one implication of the term "self-manifestation."

According to the Koran (57:3), God is the Outward or Manifest (*ẓāhir*) and the Inward or Nonmanifest (*bāṭin*). It can be said that God is Nonmanifest in the sense that His Essence in Itself remains forever unknown to the creatures, while He is Manifest inasmuch as the cosmos reveals something of His names and attributes. The question arises as to which divine attributes are revealed by the divine acts. The answer is that, generally speaking, every name of God has loci of manifestation (*maẓāhir*; sing.: *maẓhar*) in the cosmos, some obvious and some hidden. The universe as a whole manifests all the names of God. Within the existent things is found every attribute of Being in some mode or another. Even such attributes as incomparability and unknowability that apply in a strict sense only to the Essence can be found in a relative sense among the possible things. Or again, one could say that every divine attribute is found in an absolute sense in God alone, but in a relative sense in the creatures. The cosmos considered as a single whole is the locus of manifestation for all the divine names, or what comes down to the same thing, for the name Allah, which is the name that brings together all the other names. Hence, says Ibn al-ʿArabī, God created the cosmos in His own image, or, to use a better translation of the Arabic term *ṣūra*, in His own "form." So also, as the Prophet reported, "God created Adam upon His own form." Hence the universe is a great man (*insān kabīr*),[10] while man is a "small universe" (*ʿālam ṣaghīr*).

The Microcosm

So far we have been leaving human beings out of the picture. The reason should be obvious: They do not fit neatly into any of the categories discussed so far. Are they corporeal things? Yes, but they also have a spiritual dimension. Are they dense, dark, low? Yes, but also—in their inward dimensions, at least potentially—subtle, luminous, and high. In other words, human beings can be described by most if not all of the attributes that are attributed to the cosmos. Speaking about the general human situation without reference to specific individuals, it can be said that human beings embrace a hierarchy of all things within existence, from the most luminous to the darkest. They were created from God's Spirit breathed into the clay of this world (Koran 15:28–29, 32:7–9, 38:71–72), so they combine the most intense light of existence and awareness with the dullest and most inanimate dust of the universe.

The microcosm reflects the macrocosm in two ways which are of particular significance for Ibn al-ʿArabī's teachings: as a hierarchy of existence and as a divine form, a theomorphic entity. The three basic worlds of the macrocosm—the spiritual, imaginal, and corporeal—are represented in man by the spirit (*rūḥ*), soul (*nafs*), and body (*jism*). That the spirit should be spiritual and the body corporeal presents no difficulties. But what does it mean to say that the soul pertains to the imaginal world?

The human spirit is also God's spirit. The Koran attributes the spirit breathed into Adam to God with the pronouns "His" (32:9) and "My" (15:29, 38:72). Hence this spirit is called the "attributed spirit" (*al-rūḥ al-iḍāfī*), i.e., attributed to God, a term which suggests its ambiguous status, both divine and human at once. The spirit possesses all the spiritual or angelic attributes, such as luminosity, subtlety, awareness, and oneness. Clay stands at the opposite pole of the existent cosmos: dark, dense, multiple, dispersed. No connection can be established between the one and the many, the luminous and the dark, without an intermediary, which in man's case is the soul, the locus of our individual awareness. The spirit is aware of God, though not of anything less than God. But we—at least before we have refined our own souls—have no awareness of the spirit. Clay is unaware of anything at all. The soul, which develops gradually as a human being grows and matures, becomes aware of the world with which it is put in touch in a never-ending process of self-discovery and self-finding. Ultimately it may attain to complete harmony with the spirit.

The soul is luminous and dark, subtle and dense, one and many. In some human beings its luminous or ascending tendency dominates, in others its dark or descending tendency. Here the Koranic revelation uses the language of guidance and misguidance, prophets and satans. Without discussing this question, it is easy to see that there must be a vast hierarchy of souls, ranging from the most spirit-like luminosity to the most clay-like darkness. The soul—that is to say our own self-awareness—represents an unlimited possibility for development, whether upward, downward, or sideways.

Just as the soul can be spoken about in terms of the single divine and cosmic attribute of light, so also it can be discussed in terms of every name of God. "God created Adam upon His own form" means that He placed within man every one of His own attributes, just as He placed all of His attributes within the cosmos. But in the cosmos they are scattered and dispersed, while in man they are gathered and concentrated. In the cosmos the divine names are relatively differentiated (*mufaṣṣal*), while in man they are relatively undifferentiated (*mujmal*). The growth of the human soul, the process whereby it moves from darkness to light, is also a growth from death to life (*ḥayāt*), ignorance to knowledge (*ʿilm*), listlessness to desire (*irāda*), weakness to power (*qudra*), dumbness to speech (*kalām*), meanness to generosity (*jūd*), and wrongdoing to justice (*qisṭ*). In each case the goal is the actualization of a divine attribute in the form of which man was created, but which remains a relative potentiality as long as man does not achieve it fully. All the "states" and "stations" mentioned earlier can be seen as stages in the process of actualizing one or more of the divine names.

Cosmic Dynamics

In most of the previous discussion, the macrocosm and microcosm have been envisaged as relatively static entities. But a little meditation upon the human state has been sufficient to remind us that the microcosm hardly stands still. Humans may be made of three worlds, but the relationship among the worlds does not remain the same throughout a person's life. People may have been created in the divine form, but there is an immeasurable difference between someone who has brought out the divine knowledge and power which had previously been latent within himself and someone else who has remained ignorant and weak. And just as the microcosm represents a gradual manifestation of the divine names, so also does the macrocosm.

The outstanding feature of the cosmos is its ambiguous status, the fact that it is He/not He. In other terms, the cosmos is imagination, and imagination is that which stands in an intermediary situation between affirmation and denial. About it one says "both this and that," or, "neither this nor that." The universe is neither Being nor nothingness, or both Being and nothingness. It is "existence" in the way this term has been defined. This description of the cosmos is basically static and nontemporal. What happens when we take time into consideration? Another dimension of ambiguity is added. In other words, if we take an existent thing at any moment in time without reference to past or future and try to define its situation, we will come up with a hazy sort of definition, a not very successful attempt to pinpoint its situation between Being and nothingness and in relation to the divine names. But if we look at that thing in the next moment in time, ambiguity has increased, since the situation has changed, relationships have altered, and we need a new definition in order to take the changes into account. Just as no two things in the cosmos considered synchronistically are exactly the same—since each fits into its own particular niche on each of the cosmic hierarchies that are defined by luminosity, knowledge, power, and the other divine attributes—so also no single thing considered temporally is exactly the same in two successive moments. This is Ibn al-ʿArabī's well-known doctrine of the "renewal of creation at each instant" (*tajdīd al-khalq fi'l-ānāt*), a term derived from such Koranic verses as, "No indeed, but they are in confusion as to a new creation (*khalq jadīd*)" (50:15).

All things change constantly because none of them is the Essence of God, which alone is absolutely changeless and eternal. Certain angelic or other creatures may survive for countless aeons and from our point of view appear to be "eternal," but in the end, "Everything is annihilated except His Face" (Koran 28: 88). Compared to Eternity, the longest duration imaginable is but the blink of an eye. Moreover, no angel remains fixed in its place. Angels have wings—two, three, and four according to the Koran (35:1)—so they flap them. Every flap takes them to a new situation. Galaxies may last from one "big bang" to the next, or the universe may exist "steadily" and "forever." But one glance allows us to understand that physical reality is constantly changing, slowly or quickly. If we need the tools of modern physics, we can employ them to convince ourselves that "solidity" and permanence are but illusions. When the veil is lifted, says the Koran, "You will see the mountains, that you supposed to be fixed, passing by like clouds" (27:88).

All things change constantly because "Each day He is upon some task" (Koran 55:29). God's tasks (*shu'ūn*), says Ibn al-ʿArabī, are the creatures, and His "day" (*yawm*) is the indivisible moment (*ān*). Each instant God's relationship to every existent thing in the cosmos changes, since each instant He undertakes a new task. To employ another of Ibn al-ʿArabī's favorite expressions, "Self-disclosure never repeats itself" (*lā takrār fi'l-tajallī*). In the traditional Islamic world, brides were kept veiled from their husbands until the wedding night. Then came *jilwa*, "the removal of the bride's veil." From the same root we have the word *tajallī*, "self-disclosure" or "God's unveiling Himself to the creatures." The cosmos, made upon God's form, is His unveiling, and He never repeats the manner in which He shows His Face, for He is infinite and unconstricted. The Divine Vastness (*al-tawassuʿ al-ilāhī*) forbids repetition.

The evanescent and changing nature of existence, or the cosmos as ever-renewed creation and never-repeated divine self-disclosure, is evoked by one of Ibn al-ʿArabī's best-known names for the substance of the universe, the "Breath of the All-merciful" (*nafas al-raḥmān*). God breathes out, and while breathing, He speaks. But only His Speech is eternal, not His spoken words as words. Every word appears for an instant only to disappear from the created cosmos forever (though it remains immutably present in His knowledge). Every part of every existent thing is a "letter" (*ḥarf*) of God. The creatures are words (*kalima*) spelled out by the letters, the trajectory of a creature's existence is a sentence (*jumla*), and each world a book (*kitāb*). All the words and all the books are uttered by the All-merciful, for God "embraces all things in mercy and knowledge" (Koran 40:7). Through knowledge He knows all things, both in their nonexistent state as immutable entities and in their existent state as things in the cosmos. Through mercy He has pity on the nonexistent things by answering their prayers to be given existence. For possibility (*imkān*) is a prayer, a call to the Necessary Being, who at every instant recreates the cosmos in a new form as the sun throws out fresh light. His infinite Mercy—identified by Ibn al-ʿArabī's followers explicitly with Being Itself—answers every prayer for existence.

When considering the transformations and transmutations undergone by the cosmos at each instant, it is well to remember that from a certain point of view the direction of the movement is away from the Center, just as light shines out only to dissipate itself in indefinite distance, and words are uttered only to dissolve into space. It is true that everything returns to God. This is a Koranic leitmotif and a principle of Islamic belief. But the mode of return is different from the mode of appearance. As Ibn al-ʿArabī points out, the corporeal universe continues moving down and away from its spiritual root.[11] Nevertheless, things disappear only to be taken back to God. The Return takes place in a "dimension" of reality different from that of the Origination. Ibn al-ʿArabī declares that everything which disappears from manifestation goes back to nonmanifestation from whence it arose. Every death is a birth into another world, every disappearance an appearance elsewhere. But the overall movement never reverses itself, since the cosmic roads know only one-way traffic. To return to "there" from "here," we have to take a different route than the one by which we came.

The Return to God

All things return to God, but most of them go back in roughly the same form in which they came. Speaking for the angels, Gabriel is quoted as saying, "None of us there is but has a known station" (Koran 37:164). Ibn al-ʿArabī remarks that his words apply in fact to every kind of creature except two: human beings and jinn.[12] A pear tree enters this world as a pear tree and never leaves as a pumpkin. A rhinoceros does not become a monkey or a mouse. Only human beings (leaving jinn out of the picture) come into the universe as a tremendous potentiality for growth and maturation, but also for deviation, degradation, and deformation. Outwardly they remain human as long as they stay in this world, but inwardly they may become almost anything at all. They come in as men, but they may leave as pumpkins or monkeys or pigs.

On the one hand, human beings return to God by the same invisible route followed by other creatures. They are born, they live, they die, and they are gone, no one knows where. The same thing happens to a bee or an oak tree. This is what Ibn al-ʿArabī and others call the "compulsory return" (*rujūʿ iḍṭirārī*) to God. Whether we like it or not, we will travel that route. "O man, you are laboring toward your Lord laboriously, and you shall encounter Him!" (Koran 84:6). On the other hand human beings possess certain gifts which allow them to choose their own route of return (this is the "voluntary return," *rujūʿ ikhtiyārī*). Man can follow the path laid down by this prophet or that, or he can follow his own "caprice" (*hawā*) and whims. Each way takes him back to God, but God has many faces, not all of them pleasant to meet. "Whithersoever you turn, there is the Face of God" (2:115), whether in this world or the next. If we want to know what these faces are like, we can get a rough idea by meditating upon the "divine roots" of all things, God's names. He is full of Mercy (*raḥma*), but He is not above showing His Wrath (*ghaḍab*). He is the Forgiver (*al-ghafūr*) and the Blessing-giver (*al-munʿim*), but He is also the Avenger (*al-muntaqim*) and the Terrible in Punishment (*shadīd al-ʿiqāb*). Each of these names represents a "face" of God, and no one can think that the properties (*aḥkām*) of each name are the same. Paradise, says Ibn al-ʿArabī, is the locus of manifestation for God's mercy, while hell is the locus of manifestation for His wrath.

What will decide the divine face to which a person returns? This is one of the most complex of all issues, not least because it immediately moves us into the realm of free will and predestination, one of the most puzzling of all questions that arise when the divine things (*al-ilāhiyyāt*) are discussed. The brief answer to the question, "Are we free?" (or, "Are we predestined?") is "Yes and no," and it remains to sort out the different perspectives from which our ambiguous situation can be understood. For the present, we will look only at the freedom that sets human beings apart from other creatures and allows them to "choose" their route of return to the Divine Reality. Later Ibn al-ʿArabī will be quoted on the subtleties of various divine relationships which counterbalance the appearance of freedom. But we need to begin with the fact that human beings experience themselves as free agents and that their freedom is sufficiently real in the divine scheme of things for God to have sent thousands of messengers warning human beings to make proper use of it.

The divine root of human freedom and of the fact that we choose the route by which we return to God is the fact that God created man upon His own form. In its primordial nature (*fiṭra*) every human microcosm is the outward form (*ṣūra*) of an inward meaning (*maʿnā*) that is named "Allah." Allah, the all-comprehensive name, denotes not only the Essence of God but also the sum total of every attribute that the Essence assumes in relationship to the creatures. However, human beings do not enter the world as full-fledged divine forms. They start out as a sort of infinite potentiality for actualizing the all-comprehensive name. At the beginning they are only empty shells, the dimmest of apparitions dancing on the farthest of walls. Between the apparition and Absolute Light stands a yawning chasm, an endless void. True, the apparition in relation to absolute darkness is light, but in effect it is shadow. To connect the apparition to the Light which it manifests is the human task. This involves a process through which light is intensified and darkness overcome. The dim apparition remains on the wall for all to see—the body remains a fixed reality until death—but the human consciousness travels in the direction of the Light.

Different people make different choices. Some prefer to play with apparitions, some seek out various degrees of light, some turn their gaze to the Absolute Light and can be satisfied with nothing less. The degrees of light's intensity are practically limitless. Every degree can become a person's waystation (*manzil*), but a "waystation" exists only for the traveler to move on to the next. The journey goes on forever. How can the finite encompass the Infinite?

All paths do not lead in the direction of Absolute Light. A person may continue to wander in apparitions in this world and the next, or become transfixed by one of the innumerable *barzakh*s or interworlds that fill the chasm. Here we meet the imponderables of human destiny. Few are the human beings who have witnessed the interworlds with the clarity and perspicacity of Ibn al-ʿArabī and returned to map them out.

When human beings return to God, whether by compulsion or their own free choice, they go by way of the intermediate worlds. The general characteristics of these worlds have to be sought out in the divine names which they manifest. The Koran tells us to pray, "Guide us on the straight path" (1:5). Just as this straight path of return can be imagined as an ascent through an ever increasing intensity of light that opens up into the Infinite Light of God, so also it can be envisaged in terms of many other divine attributes. To increase in light is to increase in life, knowledge, desire, power, speech, generosity, justice, and so on. This is the process of actualizing all the divine names that are latent within the primordial human nature by virtue of the divine form.

Assuming the Traits of God

One of the most common terms that Ibn al-ʿArabī employs to describe the process whereby man comes to manifest the divine attributes is *takhalluq*, "assuming the traits." The term must be understood in relation to one of its root meanings as found in the word *khuluq*, which may be translated as "character" in a general sense or "character trait" in a specific sense. Its full connotations cannot be understood without reference to a few of its antecedents in the tradition.

In the most important scriptural use of the term, the Koran addresses the Prophet, telling him that he has a "*khuluq ʿaẓīm*" (68:4). English translators have rendered the expression as "mighty morality" (Arberry), "sublime nature" (Dawood), "tremendous nature" (Pickthall), "sublime morals" (Muhammad Ali), "sublime morality" (Habib), "tremendous character" (Irving), etc. These translations show an attempt to bring out the term's moral and ethical connotations on the one hand and its ontological roots on the other, for it is separated only by pronunciation (not in the way it is written) from the term *khalq*, "creation." For an Ibn al-ʿArabī, the "tremendous character" of the Prophet has to do not only with the way he dealt with people, but also with the degree to which he had realized the potentialities of his own primordial nature, created upon the form of God. Qualities such as generosity, justice, kindness, benevolence, piety, patience, gratitude, and every other moral virtue are nothing extraneous or superadded to the human condition. On the contrary, they define the human condition in an ontological sense. Only by actualizing such qualities does one participate in the fullness of existence and show forth the qualities of Being.

Just as a person's character is referred to by the term *khuluq*, so also each of his moral traits, whether good or bad, is called by the same term. The word's plural, *akhlāq*, may be translated as "moral traits," though in a philosophical context it is usually rendered as "ethics." A few of the hadiths in which this term is employed can suggest some of the connotations it carries in the tradition. The Prophet was asked, "Which part of faith is most excellent?" He replied, "A beautiful character." "The most perfect of the faithful in faith is the most beautiful of them in character." "The best thing in the Scale on the Day of Judgment will be a beautiful character." "Every religion has its moral character, and the moral character of Islam is modesty (*al-ḥayā'*)." "The Prophet used to command people to observe noble character traits (*makārim al-akhlāq*)." "I was sent [as a prophet] to complete the beautiful character traits (*ḥusn al-akhlāq*)." "Among the best of you is the most beautiful in character traits."[13]

It is not difficult to see the connection between good character traits and the divine names. Note first of all that the adjective "beautiful" employed in many of these hadiths is the same as that which is applied to the "Most Beautiful Names." Many moral traits are also divine attributes, such as repentance (corresponding to the name *al-tawwāb*), faith (*al-mu'min*), generosity (*al-karīm*), justice (*al-ʿadl, al-muqsiṭ*), forgiveness (*al-ghaffār, al-ghafūr*), pardon (*al-ʿafū*), patience (*al-ṣabūr*), gratitude (*al-shakūr*), forbearance (*al-ḥalīm*), wisdom (*al-ḥakīm*), love (*al-wadūd*), dutifulness (*al-barr*), and clemency (*al-ra'ūf*). Moreover, if the question is asked, "What are God's 'character traits'?," one can answer only by listing His names. For Ibn al-ʿArabī, the expressions "assuming the character traits of God" (*al-takhalluq bi akhlāq Allāh*) and "assuming the traits of God's names" (*al-takhalluq bi asmā' Allāh*) are synonymous, and they are identical with the spiritual path of the Sufis.

Theomorphic Ethics

In Ibn al-ʿArabī's way of looking at things, human beings assume many of the traits of God, to a certain degree and more than any other terrestrial creatures, as a matter of course by the fact of living a life in the divine/human form. A normal child cannot grow up without manifesting life, knowledge, desire, power, speech, hearing, sight, and other divine attributes. Especially significant here is the degree to which humans display the attributes of knowledge (or intelligence[14]) and speech, since these are fundamental in setting them apart from other creatures. The presence of the qualities just mentioned (leaving aside for a moment the question of the intensity of their manifestation) is the mark of theomorphism and the sign of being human. But a person who aspires to become more than a human animal will have to actualize other divine qualities which are likely to remain latent in the "natural" human state, that is, those traits which have a specifically moral connotation, such as generosity, justice, forbearance, and gratitude.

It must always be kept in mind that Sufi ethics, Ibn al-ʿArabī's in particular, is grounded in ontology. In other words, noble character traits are not extraneous qualities that we might acquire if we aspire to become good human beings but which have no real bearing upon our mode of existence. On the contrary, they define our mode of existence, since they determine the extent to which we participate in the fullness of the Light of Being. It is easy to conceive of existence as light and to understand that a more intense light is a more intense existence, and that absolute Light is Sheer Being. But one must also understand every divine attribute and moral trait as a mode—or color, if you like—of light. Absolute Being is sheer generosity. To gain proximity to Being by increasing the intensity of one's existence is to become more generous by the very nature of things. Greed, impatience, injustice, cowardice, arrogance, and avarice are not only moral faults but also ontological lacks. They mark the weakness of the reflected Light of Being in the human individual.[15]

Everyone who has studied traditional ethics knows that one cannot become virtuous and ethical through wishy-washy do-goodism. A work like Naṣīr al-Dīn Ṭūsī's *Nasirean Ethics* makes abundantly clear that a key ingredient in the virtuous human soul is equilibrium among the moral traits, and this depends on an intelligent and wise discernment of relationships and aspects.[16] Too much justice without generosity will end up in tyranny, and too much forgiveness without justice will lead to chaos. In ethics and morality, balance is everything. So also is the case, Ibn al-ʿArabī would add, in assuming the traits of the divine names, which is what ethics and morality are all about. It is especially difficult to assume the traits of the names because all the names do not stand on the same level. Hence, some must be displayed before others, and some must even be avoided until God bestows them on man in accordance with His wisdom.

It is clear that a certain hierarchy exists among the names. For example, God does not do something (power) without wanting to (desire). He cannot desire to do something without discerning its situation (knowledge). And He cannot have knowledge without existing in the first place (life). Human attainment to generosity and justice presupposes a certain degree of intelligence and speech. But where this question takes on special importance is in divine names such as Magnificent (*al-mutakabbir*), Overbearing (*al-jabbār*), Overwhelming (*al-qahhār*), Inaccessible (*al-ʿazīz*), Tremendous (*al-ʿaẓīm*), and All-high (*al-ʿalī*). In Ibn al-ʿArabī's view, the person who actualized these qualities most patently was the Pharoah of the Koran, who said, "I am your lord the most high" (79:24). But we do not have to search that far, since most any office has its own would-be pharoah. Obviously these divine qualities cannot be displayed in isolation from other qualities, or moral disaster ensues.

The general principle that determines which names should be acquired and which should be avoided derives from the relative ontological status of the names. It can be stated succinctly in terms of the well-known prophetic saying, "God's Mercy precedes His Wrath." This means that Mercy always takes priority over Wrath within the divine acts. The whole of the cosmos is nothing but the Breath of the All-merciful. Wrath, then, is an offshoot of mercy in relation to certain creatures. However, it may take aeons before those creatures realize that the wrath they had been tasting in the concrete form of infernal punishment was in fact mercy. From the human perspective, there is a real and fundamental difference between mercy and wrath, even if, in the divine overview, wrath derives from and leads back to mercy. In short, mercy pertains to the very nature of Being Itself, so it encompasses "all things" (as the Koran insists [7:156, 40:7]), but wrath is a subsidiary attribute of Being assumed in relation to specific existents for precise and determined reasons.

A similar analysis could be made of many corresponding pairs of divine attributes, such as forgiveness and vengeance. Several sets of contrary divine names describe the faces of Being turned toward the creatures. These attributes can be divided into two broad categories, the names of beauty (*jamāl*) and the names of majesty (*jalāl*), or the names of gentleness (*luṭf*) and the names of severity (*qahr*). The created properties of these two sets of attributes provide a significant parallel with the two fundamental perspectives on the Divine Being discussed earlier: incomparability and similarity.

Inasmuch as God is incomparable with all created things, He can only be understood in terms of the attributes denoting His distance, transcendence, and difference. In this respect, human beings sense the majesty and tremendousness of God and perceive Him as Magnificent, Overbearing, Overwhelming, Inaccessible, All-high, Great, Slayer, King. These attributes demand that all created things be infinitely far from Him. The things are totally Not He; He is Being and they are nonexistence. To the extent any relationship can be envisaged between the Creator and His creature, He is the stern and distant father (though Islam avoids this particular analogy because of its Christian connections). The human situation in this respect is total slavehood or servanthood (*ʿubūdiyya*). God is self-sufficient and independent (*al-ghanī*), while man is utterly poor (*al-faqīr*) toward Him. Man cannot aspire to assume the divine traits of majesty or even to gain proximity to them, since they mark the difference between God and creation, between Being and nonexistence. To claim such attributes for oneself is, in effect, to claim divinity, an unforgivable sin.

When God's similarity with the creatures is affirmed, the situation appears in a different light. In respect of His similarity, God is seen as immanent and near. He appears in the guise of gentleness, mercy, beauty, generosity, love, forgiveness, pardon, bestowal, and beneficence. Because He possesses these attributes, the existence of every individual creature is a matter of His immediate concern. In this respect one might say that "She" is a compassionate mother who never fails to look out for the welfare of Her children.[17] The human response to this relationship is love, devotion, and the desire to move nearer to the Source of light. It is in this respect that human beings are created upon God's form and can actualize the fullness of their theomorphic nature. If in the first respect man is God's slave, in the second respect he may become His "vicegerent" (*khalīfa*) and "friend" (*walī*)—two important technical terms.

Incomparability and the names of majesty are demanded by the fact of God's Being and our nonexistence. But our nonexistence is somehow woven with existence. The dimmest light is nevertheless light. And the dimmest light is more real than total darkness. Mercy—which is Being and Light—pervades everything that exists. In contrast, Wrath is like the repercussion of nothingness. It is God's answer to a nonexistent thing which has been given existence through generosity and compassion, and yet claims a right to exist. Incomparability affirms the reality of Being in the face of everything that is not-being, but similarity affirms the ultimate identity of all existence with Being. Incomparability says Not He, similarity says He. And He is more real than Not He. The attributes of similarity and beauty overcome those of incomparability and majesty in the same way that light erases darkness, mercy overcomes wrath, and nearness negates distance.

But man cannot claim light and nearness for himself. His first task is to be God's servant, to acknowledge His majesty and wrath, and to avoid any attempt to assume as his own those attributes which pertain to incomparability. He must seek out mercy and avoid wrath. It is true that man is a theomorphic entity, made upon the form of all the divine names, but there is a right way and a wrong way to assume the divine traits. Once a human being has been infused with the divine mercy and filled with its light, the attributes of majesty appear within him as a matter of course. But they always present dangers. The sin of Iblis (Satan) was to perceive that the light within himself was more intense than in Adam and to say as a result, "I am better than he—Thou created me of fire and him of clay" (Koran 7:12, 38:76). As a result he claimed a greatness which did not in fact belong to him. Or, as Ibn al-ʿArabī might say, he came to manifest the divine name Magnificent outside of its proper limits within the created world. He claimed incomparability for himself and as a result came face to face with the divine Wrath. The only thing a person can ever claim for himself is nonexistence, which, in religious terms, is to be God's servant. Indeed, Ibn al-ʿArabī places servanthood at the highest level of human realization. After all, it was through his servanthood that Muḥammad was worthy to be God's Messenger (*ʿabduhu wa rasūluhu*). Total obliteration before the divine incomparability results in a full manifestation of the divine similarity. Not He is simultaneously He.

The priority of mercy over wrath can also be explained in terms of the precedence of unity over multiplicity. God in Himself is One Being, while existence appears as an indefinite multiplicity of things. The divine names stand as a kind of *barzakh* between Oneness and manyness. There is but a single Being, yet the names represent a multiplicity of faces that Being assumes in relation to the created things. The Essence Itself, or Being considered without the names, is what Ibn al-ʿArabī sometimes calls the Unity of the One (*aḥadiyyat al-aḥad*) in contrast to Being considered as possessor of the names, which is the Unity of Manyness (*aḥadiyyat al-kathra*). God as such, taking both perspectives into account, is then the "One/Many" (*al-wāḥid al-kathīr*). Here Oneness precedes manyness, since, without Being the many things cannot exist. In the same way, light precedes the colors, and mercy precedes wrath.

From the perspective of Unity and multiplicity, the Divine Presence appears as a circle whose center is the Essence and whose full deployment is the acts in their multiple degrees and kinds. The concentric circles surrounding the Center represent the ontological levels, each successive circle being dimmer and weaker than the preceding circle. Here the divine names are the relationships that the Center assumes in respect to any place on the circle. Each "place" can be assigned coordinates in terms of its distance from the Center (i.e., its degree on the ontological hierarchy) and its relationship with other points situated on the same concentric circle (i.e., its relationship with things in its own world). But the situation is made incredibly complex because of the nature of the Center, which can be viewed in respect of any ontological attribute—any name of God. The Center is not only Being, it is also Absolute Life, Knowledge, Desire, Power and so on. The Center is One, yet it assumes a relationship with each location on the circle in terms of each attribute. Desire has one effect upon each specific point, while Power has another effect. By the same token, each point is both passive (in relation to the activity of the attribute) and, to the extent that it is colored by the attribute and displays it as its own, active toward other points on the circle. When light shines upon the moon, the moon illuminates the night sky. When any attribute of Being displays its properties within a given existent, those properties are reflected in the direction of other existent things in an indefinite concatenation of relationships.

This cosmos of interrelating "points," each reflecting the Center in its own unique fashion, is by no means static. All sorts of movements can be discerned on any given concentric circle or between the various circles, the ultimate significance of which can only be judged in terms of the changing relationship with the Center. But this much is relatively clear: The "precedent attributes" of God display their properties ever more clearly as one moves toward the Center, while the secondary and subsidiary attributes become stronger as one moves toward the periphery. Where is mercy? With Being, Light, Knowledge, Unity. Where is wrath? With nonexistence, darkness, ignorance, multiplicity, dispersion.

The dispersive movement toward the periphery is a positive creative force. Without it, Light would not shine and the cosmos would not come into existence. The divine attributes manifest themselves in an undifferentiated mode (*mujmal*) at the level of the intense light of the angels and in a boundlessly differentiated mode (*tafṣīl*) at the level of the sensory cosmos in its full spatial and temporal extension. But once this full outward manifestation is achieved, it is time for the unitive movement to take over, and an active and conscious participation in this movement is the exclusive prerogative of human beings.

Man enters into the corporeal world where the differentiated attributes of Being begin their reintegration into an all-comprehensive unity, since he is created upon the divine form even as an infant. The attribute which rules over the return to the center is "Guidance" (*hidāya*), while the dispersive movement within the human sphere that prevents and precludes the return toward the Center is called "Misguidance" (*iḍlāl*). The unitive movement finds its fullest human expression in the prophets and the friends of God, who are the loci of self-disclosure for the divine name the "Guide" (*al-hādī*). The dispersive movement finds its greatest representatives in Satan and his friends (*awliyāʾ al-shayṭān*), who manifest the divine name "Misguider" (*al-muḍill*). Misguidance is closely allied to Wrath and therefore must be considered a branch of mercy and guidance, but the positive effects of the attribute in the long run—taking perhaps innumerable aeons—cannot obviate the negative effects in the relatively short run, effects which the Koran refers to as punishment, chastisement, and the pain of the Burning.

The prophets present guidance to mankind in the form of the divine messages, which frequently appear as scriptures. In order to achieve full humanity, people must move toward the mercy, light, and unity which stand at the center of the circle of existence. Guidance is the only door which leads in that direction. If human beings ignore the message of the prophets, they will fall into one of the innumerable paths laid down by the satans, all of whom manifest misguidance. Hence they will remain in dispersion and come under the sway of the divine wrath. Though mercy precedes wrath and manifests itself even in the midst of wrath, there is a more specific kind of mercy which leads to happiness and felicity immediately after death and at the Resurrection and which can only be actualized through putting oneself into harmony with guidance. Hence Ibn al-ʿArabī distinguishes between the "mercy of free gift" and the "mercy of obligation." God gives the first to all creatures without distinction, while He has obliged Himself to confer the second only on the "godfearing." Both mercies are referred to in the Koranic verse, "My mercy [of free gift] embraces all things, but I shall prescribe it [in specific instances] for those who are godfearing and pay the alms, and those who indeed have faith in Our signs, those who follow the Messenger" (7:156). The first mercy manifests itself even in chastisement and infernal wretchedness, while the second displays itself only as felicity.

The Scale of the Law

By way of the voluntary return man strives to assume God's character traits, or to manifest the divine names in whose form he was created. But what are the divine names? What is "manifestation"? How can it be achieved? How can an apparition on an infinitely distant wall get up and walk back to the sun? How can darkness, which has no real taste or understanding of light, become light? How do we, blind and ignorant shadows of existence, discern the difference between Being and nothingness? Can ignorance become knowledge, listlessness desire, weakness power, dumbness speech, greed generosity, wrongdoing justice? How can a bare specter woven of ambiguities be transformed into clarity, discernment, wisdom, certainty? How can we distinguish the properties of mercy from the properties of wrath within the created universe, where all things appear confused? Once having seen how God's mercy and love manifest themselves, how do we ourselves become mercy and love? Ibn al-ʿArabī answers these and similar questions the same way other Muslims answer them: Stick to guidance and avoid misguidance, follow the prophets and flee the satans.

Like all Muslims Ibn al-ʿArabī considers prophecy and revelation facts of human existence, phenomena that have been observed wherever there have been people, from the time of Adam—the first prophet—down to Muḥammad, the last of the prophets. All human beings have access to and are required by their very humanity to follow the revealed guidance. The Shaykh discusses the nature and function of prophecy (which has now come to an end) and the process of becoming a "friend of God" (which will continue until the end of time) in voluminous detail. For the full significance of the whole range of his teachings to be understood, they must always be tied back to the reality of prophecy and friendship, as Chodkiewicz has illustrated so well in *Le sceau des saints*.

One of the most common terms that Ibn al-ʿArabī employs in referring to revelation in both a general sense and the specific sense of the Koran and the Sunna is *sharʿ*, which will be translated as "Law" and from which the well-known term Shariʿa, the revealed law of Islam, is derived. The original sense of the term is "to enter into the water to drink of it," said of animals. Secondarily it means a clear and open track or path. It came to be applied metaphorically to the clear and obvious path which leads to God, or in other words, the Law which God revealed as guidance to mankind. Ibn al-ʿArabī often speaks of revealed Law in general terms, showing plainly that he means revelation in a universal sense, given to all peoples throughout history, down to Muḥammad. But when he turns to specific applications and interpretations of principles, he always remains within the Islamic universe. He discusses Jesus, Moses, Abraham and other prophets in detail, sometimes even telling of his own encounters with them in the invisible world. But these are Muslim prophets through and through, their qualities and characteristics defined largely by the picture of them drawn in the Koran, the Hadith, and the Islamic tradition in general. No Christian or Jew, if given the chapter on Jesus or Moses from the *Fuṣūṣ al-ḥikam* without being told the author, would imagine that it had been written by an authority of his own tradition.

According to Ibn al-ʿArabī, the Law is the scale (*al-mīzān*) in which must be weighed everything having to do with God, knowledge, love, spiritual realization, and the human state in general. Without the Scale of the Law, we will remain forever swimming in a shoreless ocean of ambiguity. Only the Scale can provide a point of reference in terms of which knowledge and all human endeavors may be judged. The Law makes it possible to move toward the Center and avoid wallowing in indefinite dispersion, overcome by ignorance, multiplicity, and misguidance.

One might say that the function of the Law is to sort out relationships and put things in their proper perspective, thus providing a divine norm for human knowledge and action. Faced with He/not He wherever they look, human beings cannot possibly search out the He and cling to light without a discernment deriving from Light Itself. No doubt everyone has an inner light known as intelligence, but that also needs correct guidance to grow in intensity and begin functioning on its own. Only the friends of God have reached the station where they can follow the inner light without reference to the outer Law. But this, as Ibn al-ʿArabī would say, is a station of great danger (*khaṭar*). Iblis and countless "spiritual teachers" have been led astray by it. The law remains the only concrete anchor.

It was said earlier that in "ethics" or assuming the character traits of God—which, precisely, is the Sufi path—equilibrium is everything. The divine names must be actualized in the proper relationships, the names of beauty preceding those of wrath, generosity dominating over justice, humility taking precedence over magnificence, and so on. The perfect equilibrium of the names is actualized by the perfect assumption of every trait in the form of which human beings were created. In a word, perfect equilibrium is to be the outward form of the name "Allah," the Divine Presence. The person who achieves such a realization is known as perfect man (*al-insān al-kāmil*), one of the most famous of Ibn al-ʿArabī's technical terms.

There are many different types of perfect men. Briefly stated, all of them represent full actualizations of the name Allah, which is the "meaning" (*ma'nā*) or innermost reality of every human form. But each human being is different, which is to say that "the divine self-disclosure never repeats itself." The Divine Presence manifests itself in different modes to each individual. Some of these modes are designated by names close to Unity, others by names that relate to dispersion, and most to names that are outside the scope of the ninety-nine Most Beautiful Names. The prophets and great friends of God, as human beings, manifest the name Allah in its relative fullness. Then, in their specific functions, they display one or more of the Most Beautiful Names. They are exemplars who disclose the possibilities of the human theomorphic state. Each is a model of perfection.

The connection between the divine names and the prophets can be seen clearly in the structure of the *Fuṣūṣ al-ḥikam*, where each of the twenty-seven chapters is dedicated to a single prophet and a corresponding divine attribute.[18] The first chapter is dedicated to "the wisdom of the Divine Presence as embodied in Adam," by whom, Ibn al-'Arabī makes clear, he means the human being as such. Then the succeeding chapters are dedicated to various prophets and their attributes, it being understood that each of the prophets, as a human being, also manifests the name Allah. By dealing with the prophets as human individuals, Ibn al-'Arabī is able to investigate the properties of the divine attributes when manifested in the cosmos in specific cases. Each prophet himself becomes a kind of divine name, manifesting the Divine Presence through his earthly career. This is one reason that Ibn al-'Arabī makes extensive reference in the *Futūḥāt* to the "presences" of the prophets in exactly the same sense that he talks about the "presences" of the names. If the Presence of Power embraces everything in existence wherein the name Powerful exercises its effects and displays its properties, so also the "Presence of Moses" (*al-ḥaḍrat al-mūsawiyya*) embraces everything on the path of achieving human theomorphism that manifests the qualities of Moses. Dozens of chapters in the *Futūḥāt* dealing with the visions of the lights of Being and interpretations of the nature of the realities that fill the cosmos are labelled by the expressions "From the Presence of Muḥammad," "From the Presence of Moses," and "From the Presence of Jesus" to indicate the particular cognitive and revelational perspective that is being taken into account.

Seeing Things as They Are

Perfect man alone is able to see all things in their proper places. He is the divine sage who has so thoroughly assimilated the Scale of the Law that he witnesses through his very nature the correct relationships among things. This discernment of relationships is the most difficult of all human tasks, because of the intrinsic ambiguity of existence. There is no absolute point of reference to which man can cling, since "None knows God but God." Instead there are numerous "relatively absolute" standpoints in respect of which knowledge can be acquired. But some of these may lead to felicity, and some may not. Ibn al-'Arabī's deconstruction of all doctrinal absolutes must be grasped from the outset, or one will constantly be tempted to provide a definitive statement of "what Ibn al-'Arabī believes" without defining his standpoint on the question at issue.

The Shaykh accepts no absolutes other than the Essence of the Real—Being in Itself—on the one hand and pure and simple nothingness on the other. None knows the Essence of the Real but the Real, which is to say that there is no point of view within the contingent universe which allows us to speak for the Essence Itself. In other words, there are no absolutes in the cosmos or in the universe of discourse. Every formulation which attempts to describe the real must assume a delimited, defined, and relative standpoint. What is accepted from one point of view may have to be denied from a second point of view. The Essence alone is absolutely Real, but the Essence is forever beyond our grasp and understanding. Each standpoint in respect of which God and the cosmos are perceived becomes a "relative absolute" or a "presence" (*ḥaḍra*) from which certain conclusions can be drawn, conclusions which will be valid for that point of view. But Ibn al-ʿArabī is constantly changing his points of view, as is clearly indicated by the structure of many of his works, the *Fuṣūṣ* in particular. Each of the divine wisdoms incarnated in each of twenty-seven prophets speaks in a unique language, thus throwing new light on the self-revelation of the Unknown. Each revelation provides a unique way of looking upon God and the cosmos. So also, the spiritual "stations" (*maqāmāt*) themselves, like the "waystations" and similar concepts, all go back, in Ibn al-ʿArabī's way of seeing things, to unique perceptions of reality, delimited and defined by certain relationships and constraints. But none of these is absolute, so each can be contradicted by other points of view. The human response to these constant shifts in perspective may well be "bewilderment," which, Ibn al-ʿArabī tells us, is the station of the great friends of God. The Absolute allows for no absolutizing of anything other than Itself, which is to say that everything other than God is imagination.

This having been said, it is still fair to maintain that perfect man's vision combines the two basic points of view of incomparability and similarity, while he vacillates between them in expressing his perception of reality. The first represents the point of view of the rational faculty, which declares God's Unity (*tawḥīd*) and is perfectly able to grasp that the cosmos is ruled by a God who must be One. The second represents the point of view of imagination, which perceives God's theophany or self-disclosure in all that exists.

The rational faculty cannot perceive how God can disclose Himself in the cosmos, since, if He were similar to His acts, He would have to assume attributes which can only be applied to created things. But a healthy and sound rational faculty will grasp its own limitations and accept the truth of revelation. It will realize that God knows perfectly well what He is talking about, even if it cannot fathom what He means. Hence it will accept the literal significance of the revealed texts. It will say: "Yes, God has hands, eyes, and feet, just as the Koran and the Hadith have reported. He laughs, rejoices, forgets, and sits down. The revealed texts have said this and God speaks in accordance with the tongue of the people, so God no doubt means what He says. If He did not mean this, He could have said something else. I accept it as true, but I do not ask 'how' (*kayf*) it is true." This is the limit of the knowledge reason can attain—and only with the help of revelation.

Imagination understands in modes foreign to reason. As an intermediate reality standing between spirit and body, it perceives abstract ideas and spiritual beings in embodied form. Since in itself it is neither the one nor the other, it is intrinsically ambiguous and multivalent, and it can grasp the self-disclosure of God, which is He/not He. Reason demands to know the exact relationships in the context of either/or. But imagination perceives that self-disclosure can never be known with precision, since it manifests the Unknown Essence.

In the case of perfect man, spiritual realization has opened up the imagination to the actual vision of the embodiment of God when He discloses Himself in theophany. He does not know "how" God discloses Himself, but he sees Him doing so. He understands the truth of God's similarity with all things through a God-given vision, seeing clearly that all things are neither/nor, both/and, but never either/or.

Perfect man has submitted to the literal sense and the legal injunctions of the Divine Book. He has taken God's command, "Be godfearing and God will teach you" (2:282), literally, and he has been taught the meaning of the text, the meaning of the cosmos, and the meaning of his own soul. Hermeneutics is not a rational process, but an encounter with the divine self-disclosure, an opening of the heart toward infinite wisdom.

Human Perfection

Nondelimited Being is one in Its Essence and many through Its self-disclosures. It is both incomparable with all existent things and similar to every creature. It finds its fullest outward expression in perfect man, who manifests God's names in their total deployment. Just as God is perfect in His Essence and perfect through His names, so also perfect man displays human perfection through his essential reality, as the form of the name Allah, and through his accidental manifestations, as the outward display of all the individual divine names in the appropriate circumstances. The perfect men are fixed in their essences, which are not other than the Being of God. But they undergo constant transformations and transmutations by participating in God's ceaseless and never-repeating self-disclosure.

God created the universe to manifest the fullness of His generosity and mercy. Through the cosmos, Being displays the infinite possibilities latent within Itself. But It only manifests Itself in Its fullness through perfect man, since he alone actualizes every divine character trait, or every quality of Being. He is the human individual who has attained to the total actualization of his theomorphism, such that the name Allah shines forth in him in infinite splendor.

On the level of the outward, corporeal world, perfect man may not appear different from other human beings, certainly not in the eyes of the deniers and misbelievers. The Koran reports the words of some of Muḥammad's contemporaries as, "What ails this Messenger that he eats food and goes into the markets?" (25:7). But the corporeal world is but the distant Sun reflected in dust. The real fullness of perfect man's existence must be sought in the inward domains, the innumerable intermediate worlds that lie between his sensory shell and his divine kernel. He is in fact the "Barzakh of barzakhs" (*barzakh al-barāzikh*), the interworld who encompasses all interworlds, the intermediary who fills the gap between Absolute Being and absolute nothingness. His cosmic function is everything, because he is in effect identical with the cosmos. In perfect man the microcosm and the macrocosm have become one through an inner unity. In other terms, the macrocosm is the body, perfect man the heart. In him all things are brought together, whether divine or cosmic. Just as Allah is the "all-comprehensive name" (*al-ism al-jāmiʿ*), so perfect man is the "all-comprehensive engendered thing" (*al-kawn al-jāmiʿ*) in which the divine names receive their full manifestation on every level of the cosmos.

In perfect man can be seen the unity of the dynamic and static dimensions of Ibn al-ʿArabī's cosmology. As an existent thing who lives at once on every level of the cosmos, perfect man embraces in himself every hierarchy. But as a human individual who has come into existence and then returned to his Creator, he has tied together the Origin and the Return. He lives fully and consciously on all the levels of the descent through which light becomes separate from Light and on all the levels of the ascent through which light retraces its steps and human intelligence rejoins divine knowledge. He is the part and the Whole, the many and the One, the small and the Great, everything and All. Just as he turns round about God, so the cosmos turns round about him.

2

Theology

2. THE NAMES OF GOD

The connecting thread of the Koran is not the stories of the prophets, the legal injunctions, the threats of punishment and promises of reward, or the descriptions of nature and the cosmos, but the Most Beautiful Names, which are mentioned singly, often in pairs, and sometimes in groups throughout the text. Most of Islamic theological thinking revolves around the names revealed in the Koran. The proponents of Kalām or dogmatic theology (the Muʿtazilites and Ashʿarites) commonly used the term "attribute" instead of "name," but the upshot was the same. The names—or attributes—summarize what can be understood about God. Even the Peripatetic philosophers, who tended to avoid Koranic references in their strictly philosophical works, often spoke about God in Koranic terms. How can one discuss reality without referring to knowledge, desire, power, life, priority, and many other attributes attributed to God in the Koran?

When Ibn al-ʿArabī places the divine names at the center of the stage, he is merely bringing out what is implicit in Islamic thought. Several scholars who have studied his works have pointed out the importance of the theme to everything he writes.[1] But this theme is far too fundamental for us merely to point to its importance and refer to it in passing as we go along. As the basis of the Shaykh's dialectic, it needs thorough exposition at the outset. In order to understand the role of the divine names, however, we have to become familiar with the many technical terms which are employed synonymously, such as attributes, relationships, realities, roots, and supports. In the same way, since names establish a bridge between the phenomenal and the Nonphenomenal, it is necessary to look at some of the words used to describe the realities of the phenomenal world in terms of the names, such as properties, effects, veils, and secondary causes. And ultimately, we need to understand how the phenomena themselves are names of God.

Names, Attributes, and Relationships

The Divine Presence comprises the Essence, the Divine Attributes, and the Divine Acts, thus embracing all that is. The Essence is God in Himself without reference to the relationships that can be envisaged between Him and the existent or nonexistent things. The acts are the created things. The attributes or names are the *barzakh* or isthmus between the Essence and the cosmos. The names are "called 'names' by the Law (*shar'*), 'relationships' by sound rational faculties, and 'attributes' by imperfect rational faculties [that is, by the proponents of Kalām]" (III 289.4).[2] The names provide the only means to gain knowledge of God and the cosmos.

What are God's names? Several points need clarifying: (1) The names are different from the words which we employ in referring to them. (2) The names are relationships, not entities or existing things. (3) Each name denotes both the Essence and a specific meaning peculiar to itself. (4) The specific meaning of a name can be called its "reality" or "root." (5) The reality of the name determines the "effects" or "properties" of the name within the cosmos.

(1) The Names of the Names

The words which we call divine names are not, strictly speaking, the names themselves, but the "names of the names" (*asmā' al-asmā'*) which have been revealed by God to His servants through the Koran and other scriptures.

> You should know that the divine names which we have are the names of the divine names. God named Himself by them in respect to the fact that He is the Speaker (*al-mutakallim*) [who reveals by means of His Speech]. (II 56.33).

Revelation, through which we learn the names of the names, makes known the nature of things; without it, true knowledge of existence is impossible. Revelation is an outward form (*ṣūra*), while God's own knowledge of Himself and the cosmos is the inner meaning (*ma'nā*), the spirit and life behind the form. In a parallel manner, the outward forms of the cosmos reflect the name "All-merciful" (*al-raḥmān*), whose Breath (*nafas*) is the underlying stuff of the universe. God as the All-merciful breathes out while speaking, and the words that take form in His Breath are the existent things of the cosmos and the scriptures through which true knowledge of the nature of things is imparted to human beings. The names of the names thus possess a dual ontological reality: On the one hand they are creatures, or the manifestations of the divine names within the Breath of the All-merciful, and on the other they are the words naming God and revealed in the scriptures.

> God says, "Call upon Allah or call upon the All-merciful; whichever you call upon, to Him belong the most beautiful names" (Koran 17:110). Here God makes the Most Beautiful Names belong equally to both Allah and the All-merciful. But notice this subtle point: Every name has a meaning (*ma'nā*) and a form (*ṣūra*). "Allah" is called by the name's meaning, while the "All-merciful" is called by the name's form. This is because the Breath is ascribed to the All-merciful, and through the Breath the divine words become manifest within the various levels of the Void, which is where the cosmos becomes manifest.[3] So we only call upon God by means of the form of the name.
>
> Every name has two forms. One form is with us in our breaths and in the letters we combine. These are the names by which we call upon Him. They are the "names of the divine names" and are like robes upon the names. Through the forms of these names in our breaths we express the divine names. Then the divine names have another kind of form within the Breath of the All-merciful in respect of the fact that God is the Speaker (*al-qā'il*) and is described by Speech (*al-kalām*). Behind these forms are meanings which are like the spirits of these forms. The forms of the divine names through which God mentions Himself in His Speech are their existence within the All-merciful. Therefore "To Him [the All-merciful] belong the most beautiful names." But the spirits of those forms, which belong to the name "Allah," are

outside of the control of the Breath, not being described by any quality. So these "spirits," in relation to the forms of the names within the Breath of the All-merciful, are like meanings in relation to words. (II 396.30)

The names of the names, revealed in the scriptures, are as worthy of reverence and respect (*ḥurma*) as the names which they denote.

In respect of the fact that the Real (*al-ḥaqq*) is the Speaker, He mentions Himself by names. . . . These names themselves have names with us in the language of every speaker. In the Arabic language the name by which He named Himself in respect of being the Speaker is "Allah," in Persian "Khudāy," in Ethiopian "Wāq," in the tongue of the Franks "Creator" (*krayṭūr*), and so on in every language.[4] These are the names of those names. They are many because of the plurality of relationships. Every group venerates these names in respect of what they denote. That is why we [Muslims] are forbidden to travel to the lands of the enemy with a Koran, even though it is but a script in our hands, pages written by the hands of temporally originated creatures with ink compounded of gall nuts and vitriol. If not for the denotation, the book would neither be venerated nor despised. . . . So we have nothing in our hands but the names of the names. (II 683.29)

(2) Relationships

In the previous passage, the Shaykh alludes to the plurality of the names. Why, one might ask, does One God have many names? Does not the plurality of names demand some sort of plurality in the Divinity? Ibn al-ʿArabī answers this question in many ways. For example, he points out that the names are not existent entities (*aʿyān*). They are not like the creatures of the universe, which can be placed next to God as separate things. Rather, they are relationships, attributions, ascriptions, or correlations (*nisab, iḍāfāt*) that are envisaged between God and the cosmos.

As soon as we juxtapose God and the cosmos, we perceive a relationship between the two. The relationship may be expressed by saying that God created the cosmos, so He is its Creator (*al-khāliq*) and Author (*al-bāri'*). He also "made" and "originated" the cosmos, so He is its Maker (*al-ṣāniʿ*) and Originator (*al-mubdi'*). By bringing the creatures into existence He shows mercy to all of them, so He is the All-merciful. By guiding some on the straight path of religion, He is the Guide (*al-hādī*) and the Benefactor (*al-munʿim*). By the fact that He stands infinitely beyond the grasp of the creatures, He is the Transcendent (*al-mutaʿālī*), the Glorified (*al-subbūḥ*), and the All-holy (*al-quddūs*). In every case where a name of God is mentioned by the Koran, a relationship can be envisaged with the creatures.

Once God has created the cosmos, we see that it possesses diverse levels (*marātib*) and realities (*ḥaqā'iq*).[5] Each of these demands a specific relationship with the Real. When He sent His messengers, one of the things He sent with them because of those relationships were the names by which He is named for the sake of His creatures. These names allow us to understand that they denote (*dalāla*) both His Essence and an intelligible quality (*amr maʿqūl*) which has no entity in existence. But the property of the effect (*athar*) and reality manifest within the cosmos belongs to the quality. Examples of these intelligible qualities include creation, provision, gain, loss, bringing into existence, specification, strengthening, domination, severity, gentleness, descent, attraction, love, hate, nearness, distance, reverence, and contempt. Every attribute (*ṣifa*) manifest within the cosmos has a name known to us through the Law (*al-sharʿ*). (III 441.31)

The divine names allow us to understand many realities of obvious diversity (*ikhtilāf*). The names are attributed only to God, for He is the object named by them, but He does not become multiple (*takaththur*) through them. If they were

> ontological qualities (*umūr wujūdiyya*) subsisting within Him, they would make Him multiple.
>
> God knows the names in respect of the fact that He knows every object of knowledge, while we know the names through the diversity of their effects within us. We name Him such and such through the effect of what we find within ourselves. So the effects are multiple within us; hence the names are multiple, while God is named by them. So they are attributed to Him, but He does not become multiple in Himself through them. (III 397.8)

As relationships the names and attributes are contrasted with existent "entities" (*aʿyān;* sing. *ʿayn*), that is, the things which actually exist, whether within the cosmos (the created things, everything other than God), or outside the cosmos (God Himself, the Essence or "Entity" named by the names).

> Relationships are neither entities nor things. In respect to the realities of the relationships, they are nonexistent qualities (*umūr ʿadamiyya*). (II 516.34)
>
> Relationships are not ontological entities, nor do they become qualified by absolute nonexistence, since they are intelligible. (II 684.13)
>
> Relationships are non-entities within entities (*lā ʿayn fī ʿayn*), since they have no entities, but their properties rule over existence. . . . They have no existence except through their properties. (III 362.5)
>
> One of the characteristics of an "attribute" is that it cannot be conceived as having any existence except in that to which it is ascribed (*al-mawṣūf*), since it does not subsist in itself. . . . It has no existence in its own entity, since it denotes that to which it is ascribed. (II 300.35)

(3) The Two Denotations of the Names

Every divine name signifies or denotes (*dalāla*) two realities: the Divine Essence and a quality specific to itself that separates or "distinguishes" (*tamayyuz*) it from other divine names. Who is the All-merciful, the Creator, the Knowing, the Alive, the Desirer, the Powerful? In all cases the answer is God Himself, that is, the Essence, or He who is named by the names (*al-musammā*). But to say that God is Alive is clearly not the same as to say that He is Powerful, since the two names denote specific qualities that differ in important respects. This becomes especially clear when we contrast divine names that oppose each other. God is both Forgiving (*al-ghafūr*) and Vengeful (*al-muntaqim*), Life-giver (*al-muḥyī*) and Slayer (*al-mumīt*), Exalter (*al-muʿizz*) and Abaser (*al-mudhill*). In all cases the names refer to the Divine Essence and to diverse qualities, but there are never two entities involved. The Slayer is the Essence and so is the Life-giver.

> The names of the names are diverse only because of the diversity of their meanings (*maʿnā*). Were it not for that, we would not be able to distinguish among them. They are one in God's eyes, but many in our eyes. (IV 419.7)
>
> Were it not for the distinction, each divine name would be explained exactly as the next divine name in every respect. But the "Exalter" is not explained the same as the "Abaser," and so on, though the two are identical in respect of Unity (*al-aḥadiyya*). Thus, it is said that each name denotes both the Essence and its own reality in respect of itself. The Named is one, so the Exalter is the Abaser in respect of what is named. But the Exalter is not the Abaser in respect of itself and its own reality. (*Fuṣūṣ* 93)

In the last analysis, every name denotes all the names, since each name is identical with the Essence. In the *Fuṣūṣ al-ḥikam* Ibn al-ʿArabī provides a succinct summary of these points while explaining a saying of the Sufi Abu'l-Qāsim ibn Qasī:[6]

> Abu'l-Qāsim alluded to this point in his *Khalʿ al-naʿlayn* when he said, "Each divine name is named and described by all the divine names." This is because each name denotes both the Essence and the

meaning which it conveys and demands. In respect of its denotation of the Essence it possesses all the names, but in respect of its denotation of the meaning which belongs to it alone, it becomes distinguished from other names, as in the case of Lord (*al-rabb*), Creator (*al-khāliq*), Form-giver (*al-muṣawwir*), etc. Hence the name is the Named in respect of the Essence, but it is different from the Named in respect of the specific meaning which it conveys. (*Fuṣūṣ* 79–80)[7]

In the *Futūḥāt* the Shaykh makes the same point in reference to a saying of the famous Sufi Abū Yazīd Basṭāmī (d. ca. 261/874).

Abū Yazīd heard a Koran reciter reciting the verse, "On the day when We shall muster the godfearing to the All-merciful in droves" (19:85). He wept until his tears drummed upon the pulpit. It is also said that blood flowed from his eyes until it struck the pulpit. He cried out, saying, "How strange! Where will he who is sitting with Him be mustered?"[8]

When it came around to our time, I was asked about that. I replied: There is nothing strange except the words of Abū Yazīd. You should know that the reason for this is that the "godfearing servant" (*al-muttaqī*) is sitting with the Overbearing (*al-jabbār*), so he fears His chastisement (*saṭwa*). But the name All-merciful has no chastisement in respect of its being the All-merciful, since the All-merciful bestows mildness, gentleness, pardon, and forgiveness. Therefore the godfearing servant is mustered to it from the name Overbearing, which bestows chastisement and awe (*hayba*) and which sits with the godfearing servant in this world in respect to the fact that he has fear of Him.

You should take every divine name in this manner whenever you aim to understand its reality and its distinction (*tamayyuz*) from other names, since this is how you will find the names wherever they have been mentioned in the tongues of the prophecies. Each name has two denotations: a denotation of the Named and a denotation of its own reality through which it is distinguished from every other name. So understand! (I 210.7).

(4) Realities, Roots, and Supports

Ibn al-ʿArabī and others employ the word "reality" (*ḥaqīqa*) in a number of senses, some of which will be met in coming chapters. In the present context the Shaykh often employs it more or less synonymously with name. A reality is the Divine Essence considered in respect of a particular relationship which It assumes with the creatures. This relationship may be specified by a revealed name, in which case the name denotes the reality. Strictly speaking, the reality is then the name itself, while the revealed name is the "name of the name." The relationship may also be specified by a Koranic verse or hadith describing God but not mentioning a specific name. In this second case, the term reality is broader than name, since it can be applied to all revealed references to God.

There is no existent possible thing in everything other than God that is not connected to the divine relationships and lordly realities (*al-ḥaqāʾiq al-rabbāniyya*) known as the Most Beautiful Names. Therefore every possible thing is in the grasp (*qabḍa*) of a divine reality. (II 115.27)

Every divine reality has a property within the cosmos that does not belong to any other. These realities are relationships. The Knowing has a relationship to the reality of knowledge different from its relationship to the reality of power. The property of knowledge possessed by the Knowing has no interrelationship with the object of power (*al-maqdūr*); the Knowing is related only to the object of knowledge (*al-maʿlūm*). Moreover the object's situation in respect of being an object of power differs from its situation in respect of being an object of knowledge. (II 665.23)

Everything in the cosmos can be traced back to the divine realities or names. Hence Ibn al-ʿArabī often refers to a reality as a "root" (*aṣl*) or "support" (*mustanad*) and speaks of the phenomena of this world as being "supported" (*istinād*) by the names. Reality, root, and support may sometimes be employed synonymously with the divine names, but more often they have a broader sense, since, strictly speaking, there are a limited number of revealed names that can be attributed to God (a point explained in more detail below), while everything and every event in the cosmos can be traced back to a "reality" prefigured by the Divine Essence. Using terms such as reality, root, and support, the Shaykh does not have to worry about specifying one of the revealed names but can refer to various Koranic verses or hadiths.

> There is no property in the cosmos without a divine support and a lordly attribute. (IV 231.21)
>
> The root of the existence [of dispute among the angels] in the cosmos is the property of those divine names which have contrary properties, nothing else. This is its divine support. (III 137.23)
>
> God has made each of the four elements both producer of effects and receptive toward effects. The root of this in the divine knowledge is His words, "When My servants question thee concerning Me—surely I am near. I respond to the call of the caller when he calls to Me" (Koran 2:186). (II 453.16)
>
> The support of the "present moment" (*waqt*) in the divine things is the fact that He describes Himself with the words, "Each day He is upon some task" (55:29). (II 539.2)
>
> [One of the sciences which the traveler gains in this spiritual station] is the science of the differentiations among affairs and that to which these go back. Do they go back to a root, i.e., the divine names, or to the receptacles, i.e., the entities of the possible things, or to both? (III 126.33)

Realities, roots, and supports are all reducible to the things and situations known by God, that is, the objects of the divine knowledge (*maʿlūmāt*). In one passage Ibn al-ʿArabī explains this point while discussing the power of certain of God's friends to enter into the World of Imagination and appear to different people or even to the angels in various guises. The "root" of this, he says, is the power of "transmutation" (*taḥawwul*), which is attributed to God in a hadith found in Muslim about the Day of Resurrection: God appears to people in different guises, but they keep on denying Him until He presents Himself to them according to a mark by which they recognize Him. Then "He transmutes Himself into the form in which they saw Him the first time."[9]

> Were it not for this divine root [i.e., transmutation] and the fact that God possesses it and owns it in Himself, the reality [of transmutation] could not become engendered in the cosmos, since it is impossible for there to be something in the cosmos whose very form is not supported by a divine reality. If there were such a thing, there would be something in existence outside of God's knowledge. But He knows the things only through His knowledge of Himself, and His Self (*nafs*) is His knowledge. In His knowledge we are like forms in a dust cloud (*habāʾ*). (III 44.24)

Since God's knowledge is identical with His Essence (or else knowledge would be an independent entity), and His Essence does not change, realities and roots also do not change. They represent the way things are in truth, that is, as they are known by God Himself.

> How can a human being cease being a human being or an angel stop being an angel? If this could happen, the realities would be overthrown (*inqilāb*), God would cease being a god, the Real would become the creatures and the creatures the Real, no one could depend upon knowledge, the necessary would become possible, the impossible would become necessary, and Order (*al-niẓām*) would be corrupted. So there is no way in which the realities can be overthrown. (III 53.22)
>
> It is impossible for the realities to change, so the servant is a servant and the Lord a Lord; the Real is the Real and the creature a creature. (II 371.5)

(5) Properties and Effects

If the names, realities, roots, and supports denote the Essence in terms of relationships, they also point to things and phenomena within the cosmos, relating them back to God. The names are an intermediate stage between God and the universe. Though they have no existence separate from God and cannot be understood correctly except as relationships, they provide our only means of grasping the connection between man and God. In Ibn al-ʿArabī's terms, they are a *barzakh* or isthmus between God and the cosmos.

> The divine names are the *barzakh* between us and the Named. They look upon Him since they name Him, and they look upon us since they bestow upon us effects attributed to the Named. So they make the Named known and they make us known. (II 203.3)

Ibn al-ʿArabī employs two terms almost synonymously to refer to the manner in which the divine names are reflected within the cosmos: "effect" (*athar*, pl. *āthār*) and "property" (*ḥukm*, pl. *aḥkām*). The literal sense of *athar* is remainder, trace, mark, sign, vestige. The word is employed in such Koranic verses as "Behold the effects of God's mercy: How He brings the earth to life after it was dead" (30:50). The word *ḥukm* is frequently employed in the Koran in the sense of judgment or decision. It soon came to have significance for several of the sciences, such as jurisprudence (*fiqh*), where it means ruling, statute, prescription. The Shaykh employs the term in these meanings, but in the present context he uses it to refer to what might be called the ruling power or the governing control of the divine names in the cosmos. Here the term will be translated as "property," though on occasion it will be necessary to add a modifier to get the sense across, such as "ruling property" or "determining property." The Shaykh understands the term *ḥukm* in this sense from several Koranic verses, especially 28:88, as explained in the fifth passage quoted below.

The "effects" or "properties" of the divine names are the phenomena of the cosmos. In other words, they are the creatures—the things, the entities, the forms—considered inasmuch as they make the divine names manifest. In the Shaykh al-Akbar's vocabulary the word "creature" immediately calls to mind "Creator," "existent entity" conjures up "immutable entity," and "form" implies "meaning." In the same way, "properties" and "effects" bring to mind the names, realities, and roots. Or rather, to see the properties and effects is to see the names and realities exercising their influence and determining the nature of the cosmos. And to see the names and realities is to see the manifestation of the Essence Itself.

> No property becomes manifest within existence without a root in the Divine Side (*al-janāb al-ilāhī*) by which it is supported. (II 508.5).
>
> The "divine support" is the fact that the divine names are the support for the loci (*maḥāll*) wherein their own effects exist, so that the levels of the names may become designated (*taʿyīn*). (II 654.16).
>
> If not for the possible things, no effect of the divine names would become manifest. And the name is identical with the Named, especially when what is meant is the divine names. (III 317.12)
>
> That which turns its attention toward bringing "everything other than God" (*mā siwā Allāh*) into existence is the Divinity (*al-ulūha*) through its properties,[10] relations, and attributions; it is these which call for effects. It is impossible that there might be one that overpowers (*qāhir*) without something overpowered (*maqhūr*), or a powerful (*qādir*) without an object of power (*maqdūr*). (I 41.34)
>
> God says, "Everything is annihilated except His Face." He continues the verse with His words, "To Him belongs the property," which is what becomes manifest within the things themselves. Then He says, "And to Him you shall be returned" (28:88). In other words: You will return, after having been "others," to Me.

The property of the "other" will go, since there is nothing in existence but Me.

We can explain this with, for example, the name "human being" (*al-insān*), with all its differentiations and its different properties, such as life, sensation, faculties, organs with diverse motions, and everything that belongs to this thing named "human being." The entities within which these properties become manifest are nothing other than the human being. Hence "To the human being these properties shall be returned."

In the case of the Real, the "properties" are nothing other than the forms of the entire cosmos—that part of the cosmos which has become manifest and will become manifest. The properties derive from Him. Hence He says, "To Him belongs the property" (28:88). Then all of them return to being identical with Him. (III 419.25)

Were it not for the names, we would not fear, hope, give, worship, listen, obey, or be addressed, nor would we address the Named. Were it not for the properties which they possess—that is, the effects—you would not know the names. . . . The properties of the names beautify the names and dress them in splendor (*bahā'*), while the names beautify the Named and dress Him in splendor. Through us the names become designated, so we dress Him in the form of splendor. Within Him the names become manifest, so splendor subsists in Him, for He is the Named. (IV 419.3)

The divine name is the spirit of its effect, while its effect is its form. Sight cannot see the name, only its effect, which is its form. Thus, when a person sees the corporeal form of Zayd, he can say correctly that he saw Zayd, without any interpretation (*ta'wīl*). His words are true, even though Zayd has an unseen governing spirit (*rūḥ mudabbir*), while that spirit has a form which is his corporeality. So the effects of the divine names are the forms of the names. He who witnesses the forms says truly that he has witnessed the names. (II 499.13)

No possible thing is brought into existence without there being found within it the effects of those divine names that are connected (*muta'allaq*) to the engendered things (*al-akwān*). However, within that specific possible thing, one of the names will have a stronger effect and greater property than the others, and therefore that thing will be attributed (*nisba*) to it. In the same way [in astrology] Sunday is attributed to the planet of the seventh sphere, Monday to that of the fourth sphere, and so on for each day. Nevertheless, each planet has a property and an effect in each day. But the specific planet to which the day is attributed has a greater and stronger property than the other planets. (II 468.3)

In one passage Ibn al-ʿArabī sets out to explain that even attributes like "poverty" (*iftiqār*), which cannot be attributed to God, have their roots in the divine names. For the reality of poverty is need, and it can be said that God—in respect of certain names—has need of the cosmos. In the process of explaining this, the Shaykh brings together much of what has been said about the names to this point.

Someone may object: You have stated that there is no reality and no relationship in the cosmos that does not emerge from a divine relationship. But among the relationships is poverty. And Abū Yazīd—who, moreover, is one of the People of Unveiling and Finding—said that God said to him in one of his visions: "Approach Me through that which I do not possess—lowliness (*dhilla*) and poverty."[11]

[My answer is as follows:] You should know, O seeker of truth, that the Real possesses mercy, pardon, generosity, forgiveness and other things of this sort which have been mentioned as His Most Beautiful Names. He possesses these in reality. He also possesses vengeance (*al-intiqām*) and terrible assault (*al-baṭsh al-shadīd*). So He is Compassionate, Pardoner, Generous, Forgiver, and Possessor of Vengeance. It is impossible that the effects of these names be found within Him or that He be a locus (*maḥall*) for their effects. So toward whom is He compassionate? Whom does He pardon? To whom is He generous? Whom does He forgive? From whom does He exact vengeance? Hence one has to say that God the Creator demands created things (*makhlūq*) and the created things demand the Creator. . . . Therefore there must be a cosmos, since the divine realities demand it.[12]

We have already explained that God as an essence cannot be understood in the same way as God as a god. Therefore there are two different levels (*martaba*), though there is nothing in entified existence (*al-wujūd al-ʿaynī*) save the One Entity. In respect of Himself, He is "Independent of the worlds,"[13] but, in respect of the Most Beautiful Names which demand the cosmos because of its possibility (*imkān*)[14] in order for their effects to become manifest within it, He demands the existence of the cosmos. If the cosmos already existed, He would not have sought its existence. So the names are like a family dependent upon Him, and the master strives for the sake of his dependents. The creatures are His extended family, while the names are the immediate household. The cosmos asks from Him because of its possibility, while the names ask from Him in order for their effects to become manifest. . . .

This is what is given by the realities in themselves, and they do not change. If the realities changed, Order would be destroyed and there would be no knowledge whatsoever, no Real, and no creation. (III 316.27)

Ibn al-ʿArabī provides a definition of the divine names employing much of the above terminology in a context which reminds us that, although he expresses his ideas philosophically, he did not think them out in the philosophical manner, since they are the fruit of unveiling and opening.

While writing the present section, I fell asleep and saw a heralding vision (*mubashshira*),[15] in which it was recited to me, "He has laid down for you as Law what He charged Noah with, and what We have revealed to thee [O Muḥammad], and what We charged Abraham with, and Moses, and Jesus: 'Perform the religion, and scatter not regarding it.' Very hateful is that for the idolaters—that to which thou art calling them" (Koran 42:13), that is, the Oneness to which thou art calling them, since God is many in His properties. He possesses the Most Beautiful Names, and each name is a mark (*ʿalāma*) upon an intelligible reality which is different from other realities. When the cosmos comes from nonexistence into existence, its faces are many, and these seek the names—I mean the objects named—, even though the Entity is One. In the same way, the cosmos, in respect of being a cosmos, is one, but it is many through its properties and individuals. (III 368.27)

The Names of Engendered Existence

The engendered things (*al-kāʾināt, al-akwān, al-mukawwanāt*) are the existents or the acts, the creatures which have been brought into existence by the Divine Command "Be!" (*kun*) and which will pass out of existence when their stay in this world is over. Many names are attributed to them. Every noun that denotes something existing in the cosmos in every language in the world is a name of an engendered thing. How many of these names can also be attributed to God?

The first answer to this question is that only those names can be attributed to God which have been attributed to Him by Himself in His revelations. This is the theological principle of "conditionality" (*tawqīf*), which is based among other things on the courtesy (*adab*) that must be observed toward God.

In terms of their ascription (*iṭlāq*) to Him, His names are conditional upon having come from Him. So He is not named except as He has named Himself, even if it be known that a name designates Him, since conditionality in ascribing the names is to be preferred. God decreed all of this only so that the creatures would learn courtesy toward Him. (II 232.28)

But the Shaykh also points out that in the last analysis all names must be ascribed to God, since the acts of God denote Him inasmuch as they are the properties and effects of His names.

> Every name by which something is named and which expresses a meaning is God's name. However, it should not be ascribed to Him—and this either because of the Law, or because of courtesy toward God. (III 373.1)
>
> The names become intelligible through that which is demanded by engendered existence. But engendered existence (*al-kawn*) never ceases coming to be, so there is no end to the names. (II 69.32)
>
> "God has ninety-nine names." . . . These are "mothers,"[16] like the [360] degrees of the celestial sphere. Then every possible entity has a specific divine name which gazes upon it. The name gives the entity its specific face, through which it becomes distinguished from every other entity. The possible things are infinite, so the names are infinite, since relationships come into temporal existence along with the temporal origination of the possible things. (IV 288.1)
>
> The names of God are infinite, since they become known from that which is engendered from them, and that is infinite, even though the names are reducible to finite roots which are the "Mothers of the Names" or the "Presences of the Names." In reality one single Reality accepts all these relationships and attributions which are alluded to as the divine names. Moreover, this Reality demands that every name that becomes manifest, ad infinitum, possess a reality that distinguishes it from every other name. This reality by which the name becomes distinguished is the name itself; that which is shared [with the other names] is not the name. (*Fuṣūṣ* 65)

On the one hand the principle of conditionality demands that a name must have been revealed by God in order for us to employ it. On the other hand the nature of things allows us to understand that every name refers to the divine acts; and the acts are embraced by the Divine Presence. So God is present in all things and named by them. Nevertheless, courtesy demands that we refrain from calling Him by certain names, even many names that are implied by the text of the Koran. For example, the Koran says, "They deceived God and God deceived" (3:54), "God mocks them" (2:15), and so on. Can we call God the Deceiver and the Mocker? No, says the Shaykh:

> Among the names are those which can appropriately be designated and those which cannot. For example, the Splitter [of the Dawn] (*al-fāliq*) and the Appointer (*al-jāʿil*) have been designated, but the "Mocker" and the "Derider" have not been revealed. Nevertheless, it is He who mocks whomsoever He will of His servants. He deceives and derides whomsoever of them He will, since He has mentioned this [in the Koran]. Yet He is not named by anything of this sort. (IV 319.5)

In the text of the *Futūḥāt* Ibn al-ʿArabī sometimes denies that the names of the engendered things (*asmāʾ al-kawn* or *al-asmāʾ al-kawniyya*) can be attributed to God. When he does so, he is observing courtesy and the principle of conditionality. More commonly he maintains that the names of all things must, in the last analysis, be attributed to the One Reality which is their root, support, and source.

> There are names that are ascribed to the servant but not to the Divine Side, even though their meaning includes that. For example, the "miser" (*al-bakhīl*) is ascribed to the servant but not to the Real. But miserliness is a kind of holding back, and one of His names is "He who holds back" (*al-mānīʿ*). A person who is miserly has held back. This is true, but we ask for another way to approach the question, so we say: Every miserliness is a holding back, but not every holding back is a miserliness. He who holds back the rightful due (*ḥaqq*) of him to whom it belongs has been miserly; but the Real has recorded the words of Moses that God "gave each thing its creation" (Koran 20:50). He who has given you your creation and accomplished your rightful due has not been miserly toward you. So to hold back that of which the creatures are not worthy is not

the holding back of miserliness. To this extent we will make a distinction here between the two meanings.

In the same way the name "liar" (*al-kādhib*) pertains specifically to the servant and cannot properly be ascribed to the Real, since He tells the truth in every respect. . . .

Likewise the name "ignorant" (*al-jāhil*) is one of the names of engendered existence and it is not appropriate for the Divine Side. . . . (II 242.20, 28)

One of the ways [of looking at the nature of things is to speak of] the creatures becoming manifest in those attributes of the Real that are generally distinguished as attributes of the Real by the common people,[17] like the Most Beautiful Names and such things. This is the extent of the knowledge of the common people. But for us and for the elect, all attributes belong to God at root (*bi'l-aṣāla*). Those attributes which are attributed to the creatures—and which, according to the common people, descend (*nuzūl*) from God toward us—we call "attributes of the Real." The servant's station with God rises until he becomes adorned (*taḥallī*) by them.[18] For the common people they are names of imperfection (*naqṣ*), but for us they are names of perfection (*kamāl*), since none is named at root but God.

When He made the creatures manifest, He bestowed upon them those names which He willed to bestow and actualized the creatures through them. Creation stands in the station of imperfection because of its possibility (*imkān*) and its poverty (*iftiqār*) toward someone to give preponderance [to its existence over its nonexistence] (*al-murajjiḥ*).[19] Hence people imagined that imperfection is their root and their right (*ḥaqq*), and they judged themselves accordingly. They judged that these creaturely names (*al-asmā' al-khalqiyya*) are imperfect. When they heard that the Real had named Himself by them, they made this a "descent" from the Real to them through their attributes. They did not know that these are names of the Real at root.

According to our position (*madhhab*) concerning the creatures' becoming manifest in the attributes of the Real, the names include all creatures. Every name the creatures possess belongs truly (*ḥaqq*) to the Real and metaphorically (*musta'ār*) to the creatures. The position of the majority (*al-jamā'a*) is that this is only true for specific names, that is, the Most Beautiful Names. (III 147.16)

Ibn al-'Arabī clarifies his own position on the names of engendered existence in the context of explaining how the lover of God travels to God through His names. In the process he refers to the fact that the friends of God assume His character traits (*takhalluq*) by gaining nearness to Him.

God discloses Himself (*tajallī*) to the lover in the names of engendered existence and in His Most Beautiful Names. The lover imagines that His self-disclosure through the names of engendered existence is a descent by the Real for his sake. But from His horizon, this is not so.

When the lover assumes the traits of His Most Beautiful Names, he is overcome by the same assumption of traits that takes place in the path of the Folk of Allah.[20] The lover imagines that the names of engendered existence were created for him and not for God and that the station of the Real in them is like the station of the servant in His Most Beautiful Names.[21] The lover says: "I will enter in upon Him (*dukhūl 'alayh*) only through my own names. Then when I come out again to the creatures, I will come out to them having assumed the traits of His Most Beautiful Names." Then, when he enters in upon God through what he supposes to be his own names—i.e., those things he calls the "names of engendered existence"—he sees the signs (*āyāt*) which the prophets saw in their spiritual journeys (*isrā'*) and ascensions (*mi'rāj*) "upon the horizons and in themselves" (Koran 41:53). Hence he sees that all are His names and that the servant has no name of his own. Even the name "servant" does not belong to him. On the contrary, he has assumed it as a trait, like all the Most Beautiful Names. He comes to know that traveling to Him, entering in upon Him, and being present (*ḥuḍūr*) with Him take place only through His names and that the names of engendered existence are His names. So he corrects his error after missing what he had missed.

> This witnessing (*shuhūd*) makes up for everything that had slipped away from the lover when he differentiated between the worshiper (*al-ʿābid*) and the worshiped (*al-maʿbūd*). . . . I have not seen that this station has been tasted (*dhawq*) by any of God's friends, only the prophets and messengers. In respect of this locus of divine disclosure they described Him by what exoteric knowledge (*ʿilm al-rusūm*)[22] calls the "attributes of similarity" (*ṣifāt al-tashbīh*). People imagined that the Real described Himself with the attributes of the creatures, so they interpreted that away (*ta'wīl*). But this locus of witnessing (*mashhad*) shows that the root of every name possessed by engendered existence belongs in reality to the Real. Applied to the creatures, the name is a word without meaning, though the creatures assume its traits. (II 350.23)

Secondary Causes

In order to prove that God is named by all things, Ibn al-ʿArabī often analyzes the poverty and need (*faqr, iftiqār*) of all creatures. Every engendered existent has need of God both for its existence and its attributes, which are nothing but the properties and effects of the names. This, according to the Shaykh, is the meaning of the Koranic verse, "O people, you are the poor [or, the needy] toward God, and God—He is the Independent [or, the Wealthy], the Praiseworthy" (35:15). In one passage, the Shaykh tells us that none of the lists of the ninety-nine names which have reached us is reliable, and he quotes approvingly the opinion that only eighty-three of the ninety-nine can be known with certainty. After listing these, he writes:

> But he who truly wants to become aware of the names of God should meditate upon His words, "O people, you are the poor toward God!" In reality there is nothing in existence but His names. (II 303.13)

He explains what he means in many passages of the *Futūḥāt*, most often in the context of describing the "secondary causes" (*asbāb*) that fill the cosmos. The word *sabab*, singular of *asbāb*, means literally "rope" or "cord," and by extension is applied to connecting things or factors. Hence it also refers to a way or means of access, or to any "means" for accomplishing an end. In the Islamic sciences the term came to mean "cause," usually in the incomplete or incidental sense that might best be translated "occasion" or "mediate cause." Often a distinction was drawn between the apparent or secondary cause of a thing and the real cause, known as the Causer of Secondary Causes (*musabbib al-asbāb*), i.e., God. In the sense of "secondary causes," especially in the plural, the term becomes a common expression in Sufi writings to refer to the causes that seem to be at work in the cosmos. Since each thing in the universe is the cause of, or occasion for, other things, *asbāb* was soon a term used to refer to the existent things in general, to all the phenomena, which, in the general Islamic view, could only be the outward forms of unseen realities or "noumena." Many Sufis held that it was blameworthy to take the *asbāb* or "secondary causes" seriously, since this would mean turning one's gaze away from the Causer of Secondary Causes. But Ibn al-ʿArabī reinstates the secondary causes as fundamental constituent elements of the cosmos. God Himself established (*waḍʿ*) the secondary causes, so they play an important role in His plan. "God did not establish the secondary causes aimlessly" (II 208.16).

The secondary causes are important because they are names of God through which we come to know Him. Without them we would have no access to Him. Here one has to understand that "secondary causes" is merely another name for existent things, creatures, or divine acts. However, the term implies that something is hidden from sight, since secondary causes conceal the First Cause. Hence the term is used more or less synonymously with "forms" (*ṣuwar*)—a word which always implies that there are "meanings" behind the forms—and with "veils" (*ḥujub*), that is, the things inasmuch as they prevent us from seeing God, though they alert us to the fact that God is hidden behind them.

God established the secondary causes and made them like veils. Hence, the secondary causes take everyone who knows that they are veils back to Him. But they block everyone who takes them as lords (*arbāb*). (III 416.19)

Through the secondary causes that He has set up, He made us blind to His attentiveness (*tawajjuh*) toward bringing the things into existence. He sent down the rain, so it fell. People tilled the earth and sowed the grain, and the sun spread its rays. The grain sprouted and was harvested, milled, made into dough, chewed with teeth, swallowed, and digested by the stomach. Then the liver took over and made it into blood. Then it was sent through the veins and divided among the parts of the body. Then a vapor (*bukhār*) rose up from it, and it became the life of the body for the sake of the soul. These are the "mothers" of the secondary causes, along with the movement of the spheres, the traveling of the planets, the shining of rays. . . . All of these are established veils (*ḥujub mawḍūʿa*), the mothers of the minute secondary causes below them. A person's ears must rend all these veils to hear the word "Be!"[23] Therefore He creates in the believer the power of faith (*al-īmān*). It pervades his hearing, so he perceives the word "Be!", and it pervades his sight, so he witnesses the Engenderer of Secondary Causes (*mukawwin al-asbāb*). (II 414.1)

If secondary causes had no effect in that which is caused, God would not have brought them into existence. If their property were not intrinsic (*dhātī*) to the caused things (*al-musabbabāt*), they would not be causes and it would not be true to call them causes. This situation is known, for example, when something can only accept existence in a locus, while there is no locus, though the Giver of Existence (*al-mūjid*) desires to bring the thing into existence. Hence He must bring a locus into existence for the existence of that thing whose existence He desires. Hence the existence of the locus is a secondary cause for the existence of the desired thing to which God's desire has become connected. . . . Hence it is known that secondary causes have properties within the things that are caused. They are like the tools of an artisan (*ṣāniʿ*). The art (*ṣanʿa*) and the artifact (*maṣnūʿ*) are attributed to the artisan, not to the tools. (III 134.25)

All secondary causes brought into existence by God are forms and veils, or effects and properties of His names. In the last analysis the secondary causes denote only the Causer. They must be considered His names. This is the point Ibn al-ʿArabī wants to explain in the context of the "poverty and need" (*iftiqār*) of all things toward God. His reasoning goes something like this: God has said in the Koran that all people are poor toward Him, so this is a reality that cannot be denied. Because of His testimony, we know that poverty toward Him is an intrinsic dimension of human nature which cannot be left behind in any situation. However, when we look at people, we see that they are poor and needy toward all sorts of things, such as food, water, shelter, and other secondary causes. But at best this poverty is an extrinsic and accidental need, since we are intrinsically and essentially poor only toward God. Therefore, in fact, when we have need of the secondary causes, we have need of God. The forms and phenomena are merely veils hiding God's Reality, or rather, various names that He assumes in disclosing Himself to His creatures. Poverty toward secondary causes is in truth poverty toward the First Cause.

Though this argument might sound like sophistry to some people, it is strongly grounded in the Shaykh's ontology, a point that will become clear as we move along. It is intimately connected with the "inherent worship" (*al-ʿibādat al-dhātiyya*) that is a property of all things, as opposed to the "accidental worship" (*al-ʿibādat al-ʿaraḍiyya*) that human beings perform when they follow a religion.[24]

God says, "O people, you are the poor toward God" (35:15). Through addressing people in this way, God names Himself by every name possessed by something toward which there is poverty. This is a kind of Divine Jealousy (*al-ghayrat al-ilāhiyya*) so that no one should be poor toward any but Him.[25] (II 601.11)

To Him who is named by the name "Allah" belongs—in respect of the fact that "To Him all affairs shall be returned" (Koran 11:123)—the name of every named thing toward which there is poverty, whether mineral, plant, animal, man, celestial sphere, angel, or any such thing, whatever name is applied to it. . . . Hence He is named by every name which is possessed by every named thing in the cosmos and which has an effect within engendered existence—and everything has an effect in engendered existence. (IV 196.31)

The possible things are poor in their very essences. Poverty never ceases to accompany them perpetually, since their essences are perpetual. So God established the secondary causes through which the possible things can acquire that toward which they are poor. Hence the possible things are poor toward the secondary causes. Then God made the secondary causes themselves names for Himself. Hence the names of the secondary causes are among His names, and as a result there is no poverty except toward Him. . . . The People of Unveiling see no difference, in respect of being names of God, between those names that in common usage (*al-ʿurf*) and the Law are said to be the names of God and the names of the secondary causes. For God says, "You are the poor toward God." But in fact we observe poverty toward the secondary causes. So the names of the possible things must be the names of God, and we call upon Him by means of them. However, this call is made by our state (*duʿā' al-ḥāl*), not our words. When hunger touches us, we hurry to the food which takes away the pain of hunger. So we are poor toward it, while it is independent of us. But we are not poor toward any but God. Hence, one of His names is this very thing, that is, the form of that food, which takes the place of the spoken or written form of the divine name. (III 208.7)

To be poor toward all things is hardly something to be despised. In fact, Ibn al-ʿArabī calls it the station of perfect man (*al-insān al-kāmil*).

Know that all the levels are divine at root, though their properties become manifest within engendered existence. The highest divine level becomes manifest within perfect man, and the highest level is that of independence *from* all things. But that level is only appropriate for God in respect of His Essence. The highest cosmic level is independence *through* all things; or if you want, call it "poverty toward all things." This is the level of perfect man, for everything was created for him and for his sake and was subjected (*taskhīr*) to him,[26] since God knew of his need toward all things. So he has no independence from anything.

But one can only have need for him in whose hand is the accomplishment of the need, and that is only God, "in whose hand is the dominion of all things" (Koran 36:83). Hence God had to disclose Himself to this perfect man in the form of each thing. Thereby God delivers to him, through the form of the thing, that toward which he has need and which can only subsist through God.

Since God qualified Himself by jealousy before His servants, He made manifest the property of jealousy.[27] Hence He made clear to them that it is He who discloses Himself in the form of everything, so that there should be no poverty except toward Him specifically. For He said, "O people, you are the poor toward God." So you should understand and verify the reliance of people upon the forms of the secondary causes and their poverty toward them, while God has affirmed that people are poor toward Him, not toward anything else. Thus He makes clear to them that it is He who discloses Himself in the forms of the secondary causes, and that the secondary causes—which are the forms—are a veil over Him. (II 469.2)

3. THE DIVINE ROOTS OF HIERARCHY AND CONFLICT

Several times in the previous chapter the term "level" (*martaba*) was employed without explanation. In the last quotation we learned that the "highest divine level becomes manifest within perfect man" and that it consists of "independence from all things." For present purposes, a single point needs to be clarified in some detail: the nature of the "divine levels," of which independence is the "highest" (independence itself will be discussed in the next chapter).

The divine levels go back to the fact that the divine names denote the Essence on the one hand and a specific reality on the other, a reality which allows us to differentiate between one name and another. The highest level pertains to the name which designates the widest and greatest of these specific realities. In other words, the highest level belongs to the name Allah, which denotes the "Divinity." Levels lower than the Divinity pertain to other names, each of which refers to a reality more limited and specific than Allah, such as Knowing, Powerful, Forgiving, Vengeful, and so on. The names can be ranked in degrees in terms of the scope of the realities which they designate, and this ranking is the "root" of every hierarchy that can be perceived in the cosmos.

Many of the names exercise properties that are mutually incompatible, such as Forgiving and Vengeful, and these names also display their effects within the cosmos. These effects are the root of diversity and conflict. But in spite of the fact that the names yield multiplicity and contradictory properties in the universe, each of them denotes the One Essence, which remains incomparable with all created things. Many of the names, in fact, denote various aspects of this incomparability, and in classifying the names into different categories, it is useful to distinguish between the names of incomparability, which pertain exclusively to God, and the names of similarity, which God shares with the creatures.

Hierarchy in the Names

The word *martaba* or "level" derives from the root *r.t.b.*, the basic meaning of which is to be constant, firm, and motionless. A *martaba* or *rutba* (from the same root) is a locus wherein something is fixed, hence a "degree, grade, level, rank, standing, station, class." The most common verbal noun from the root is *tartīb*, which means to arrange or to place in degrees, grades, levels, etc., and which will usually be translated as "hierarchy," as in *tartīb al-ʿālam*, the "hierarchy of the cosmos."

A level becomes established in relation to other things or other levels, so it is a relationship. As we saw above, relationships pertain to nonexistence (*umūr ʿadamiyya*), since they are not entities. They can be perceived only in respect to different things or between the things and God. For example there is a relationship between a father and his son based on the fact that the son has come into existence through the father. The "level" here is fatherhood on the one hand and sonhood on the other. Both fatherhood and sonhood are relationships, not existent entities. Examples could be multiplied indefinitely. It is only necessary to look at two things and then rank them in respect to relationship: higher and lower, larger and smaller, brighter and darker, more intense and less intense, and so on.

> Relationships pertain only to nonexistence. This is self-evident in the prop-

erties of levels, as for example the level of a sovereign and the level of a subject among human beings. The sovereign rules over the subject according to what is demanded by the level of sovereignty. But sovereignty has no entified existence (*wujūd ʿaynī*). So the ruling property (*ḥukm*) belongs to the levels. (III 452.12)

Things are only witnessed in respect of their levels, not in their entities. For example, there is no difference between the king and his subjects in humanity. Hence the [parts of the] cosmos only become distinct through the levels. Only in respect to the levels are some parts more excellent than others.

He who knows that excellence (*sharaf*) pertains to the levels—not to his own entity—will never deceive himself into thinking that he is more excellent than anyone else, though he may say that one level is more excellent than another level. This is the station of the intelligent, the gnostics. The Messenger of God said a great deal in respect to this station concerning himself in order to teach us. [For example, God says to him in the Koran, "Say,] 'I am but a mortal like you'." Hence, he did not see himself superior to us. Then he mentioned the level, for he said, "To me it has been revealed. . ." (41:6). (III 225.32)

Ibn al-ʿArabī finds a clear reference to the divine root of the cosmic levels in the name "Uplifter of Degrees" (*rafīʿ al-darajāt*, Koran 40:15). In discussing its properties, he says that its attentiveness (*tawajjuh*)—that is, the manner in which it exercises its properties and displays its effects—is limited to

the designation (*taʿyīn*) of the levels, not bringing them into existence. For the levels are relationships; they do not become qualified by existence, since they have no entities. . . .

Moreover, you should know that every divine name has a level not possessed by any other. And every form in the cosmos has a level not possessed by any other. So the levels are infinite, and they are the "degrees." Some degrees have been uplifted, and some have been uplifted even more, whether they are divine or engendered, for the engendered levels are [in fact] divine. So there is no level that is not uplifted, and ranking in degrees (*tafāḍul*) is found in the uplifting (*rifʿa*). . . .

You should also know that, were there no forms, no entity would become distinguished from any other. And were there no levels, the measures (*maqādīr*) of things could not be known and no form could take up residence in its waystation (*manzila*). ʿĀ'isha [the wife of the Prophet] alluded to that waystation with her words, "God has placed the people in their waystations." The levels make known that which is ranked higher (*al-fāḍil*) and that over which it is ranked (*al-mafḍūl*). The levels distinguish (*tamyīz*) between God and the cosmos and they manifest the realities of the divine names in terms of their more inclusive and less inclusive connections [with the creatures]. (II 468.35, 469.11, 17)

The term "connection" (*taʿalluq*) signifies the relationship between an attribute and its object, or a name and its effect. Thus theologians speak of the "connection" of knowledge to the known, desire to the object desired, power to the object over which it is exercised, and so on. It is one of several terms the Shaykh employs to refer to the relationship between a divine name and the effects it exercises in the cosmos. He often points out that the "connections" of the names vary in scope (*ḥīṭa*) or inclusiveness (*ʿumūm*). The "connection" of the name Knowing to the things is more inclusive than that of Powerful, since the Knowing knows all things, existent or nonexistent, while the Powerful becomes connected only to those things which enter into existence. Hence the scope of some names is greater or more inclusive, that of others narrower and less inclusive.

The divine names that are attributed to the Real have various levels in attribution. Some of them depend (*tawaqquf*) upon others, some of them supervise (*muhayminiyya*) others, and some have a more inclusive connection to the cosmos and more effects within it than others. The whole cosmos is the loci of manifestation (*maẓāhir*) for these divine names. (II 34.1).

When Ibn al-ʿArabī ranks the names in degrees, most commonly he has in view the difference in scope among the names. In the following passage he is discussing the divine root of the fact that God is "Uplifter of degrees."

> We know that some names—whichever they might be—are uplifted above others in degrees, so that some may make use (*ittikhādh*) of others. We know that the degree of the Alive (*al-ḥayy*) is the most tremendous degree among the names, since it is the precondition (*al-sharṭ*) for the existence of the names.[1] We also know that the knowledge of the Knowing (*al-ʿālim*) is more inclusive in connection and more tremendous in compass (*iḥāṭa*) than the Powerful (*al-qādir*) and the Desiring (*al-murīd*), since names like these have less inclusive connections than the Knowing. They are like gatekeepers (*sadana*) for the Knowing. . . .
>
> There is a similar situation to be seen in the fact that the degrees of the Hearing (*al-samīʿ*), the Seeing (*al-baṣīr*), the Thankful (*al-shakūr*), and the rest of the names—including the Clement (*al-raʾūf*), the Compassionate (*al-raḥīm*), and the other names —are less inclusive in connection. All of them stand lower than the Knowing (*al-ʿalīm*) in degree. (IV 228.12, 18)

Though Ibn al-ʿArabī states in the passage quoted at the end of the last chapter that the highest level is "independence," elsewhere he speaks of "divinity" (*al-ulūha* or *al-ulūhiyya*) as the highest, since the two levels are in fact practically synonymous. The Divinity is the highest level and the Essence stands "beyond" the Divinity, which is to say that the Essence is not a level. Or rather, Divinity is the Level of the Essence. This is a key theme in the Shaykh's metaphysics and deserves a good deal of attention.

"Divinity," it should be noted at the outset, is the verbal noun connected both to the proper name Allah and to the generic term *ilāh*, "god." Ibn al-ʿArabī frequently uses the latter term in discussing what it means to be a god. It will usually be translated as "god" with lowercase g, or with capital letter when accompanied by the definite article, i.e., "the God." The name Allah often has a specific technical significance, in which case it will be retained in translation. In other cases it is merely the vaguest and most general name that can be applied to the ultimate Reality, synonymous with *al-ḥaqq*, "the Real." The latter name is sometimes employed to contrast with the term *al-khalq* ("creation" or "the creatures"), and sometimes it is used as the most general of divine names to avoid mentioning a specific relationship. Thus, Ibn al-ʿArabī commonly employs *al-ḥaqq* in a sentence like, "The Real can be viewed in respect of the Essence or in respect of the name Allah."

As stated earlier, the terms Essence and Divinity are applied to the same Reality, but from different points of view. In respect of the Essence, nothing positive can be said about God; attributes must be negated from Him. But in respect of the Divinity, all names can be ascribed to Him. In other words, God cannot be understood in a positive, affirmative way in respect of His Essence, but He can be understood so in respect of His names. In the same way, levels—which, like the names, are relationships—can only be discerned in respect of the Divinity, not in respect of the Essence. So the Essence itself is not a level, and the first level that can be discerned in all that exists is God as Divinity. Hence Ibn al-ʿArabī often talks about the "Essence" and the "Level" as contrasting points of view in respect to the Real.

> In respect of His Essence, "Allah is Independent of the worlds" (Koran 3:97), so we speak about Him only inasmuch as He is a god. Hence we speak about the Level, not about the Entity. In the same way we speak about the sovereign in respect of the fact that he is a sovereign, not the fact that he is a human being. There is no

profit in speaking except about the realities of the levels, since it is through them that ranking in degrees is understood among the entities. (I 441.15)

The divine names—that is, the level which is called a "god"—possess free disposal (*al-taṣrīf*) and exhibit properties within those things described by them [that is, those creatures which display the effects of the names in the cosmos]. (III 317.15)

The names do not become intelligible unless relationships become intelligible, and relationships do not become intelligible unless the loci of manifestation (*al-maẓāhir*) known as the "cosmos" become intelligible. Hence the relationships are temporally originated (*ḥudūth*) through the temporal origination of the loci of manifestation. . . . So the relationships are temporally originated, and the names are subordinate (*tābiʿ*) to them. But the names have no existence, though their properties are intelligible. . . . That which is denoted by the name Allah demands the cosmos and everything within it. So this name is like the name "king" or "sovereign." Hence it is a name of the Level, not the Essence.[2] (II 57.1, 10)

There are two fundamental levels: God and the cosmos, independence and poverty, or Lordship (*rubūbiyya*) and servanthood (*al-ʿubūdiyya*). All the other levels have to do with the various modalities that tie these two basic levels together.

Know that the wisdom (*al-ḥikma*) in all things and in every single affair belongs to the levels, not the entities. The most tremendous (*aʿẓam*) of the levels is the Divinity, while the lowest (*anzal*) of the levels is servanthood. Hence there are only two levels, since there are only a Lord and a servant. However, the Divinity possesses properties, every one of which requires (*iqtiḍā'*) a level.

The property may subsist through the God. Then He exerts the property upon Himself; this is the property of the level exerted upon the meaning (*al-maʿnā*). None exerts this property except the Owner of the Level (*ṣāḥib al-martaba* [i.e., the Essence]), since the level itself is not the existence of an entity; it is only an intelligible quality and a known relationship through which properties are exercised and which possesses properties. This is one of the most marvelous of things: that the nonexistent (*al-maʿdūm*) displays effects![3]

The property may also subsist through something that exists other than God, either as an ontological quality or as a relationship. So nothing exercises effects except the levels.

In the same way servitude (*ʿubūda*) has properties, each of which has a level. The property may subsist through the servant's self, so that nothing exercises properties upon him except himself. Then he is like the deputy of the level, which has made this property incumbent upon him. Or he exercises the property upon his like (*mithl*) or upon some other (*ghayr*). For the servant, there is nothing but the like or the other.

In the case of God, there is nothing but the other, not the like, since He has no like.[4] As for the properties that return to Him because of the properties of the Level, these are: the Necessity of His Being through His Essence, the judgment that He is Independent of the cosmos, His obligating (*ījāb*) Himself to help the faithful through mercy, and all the attributes of majesty (*nuʿūt al-jalāl*) required by the profession of incomparability and the negation of likeness (*nafy al-mumāthala*).

As for the properties which are required in their essences by His demanding the other (*ṭalab al-ghayr*), these are things like all the attributes of creatures. They include attributes of generosity (*karam*), bountifulness (*ifḍāl*), munificence (*jūd*), and bestowing existence (*ījād*).

There must be [concrete answers to the questions] "Toward whom?" and "Upon whom?," so there must be the other, and only the servant is other. There is no effect demanded by the servant unless it has a necessary root in God, so it is made necessary by the Level. There is no escape from this. God also possesses exclusive properties from this Level that are not sought by the creatures, as was explained.

Because the servant is a servant, his level demands certain properties that only subsist through the servant by his being specifically a servant. They pervade every servant by his very essence. . . .

As for the fact that the level of the servant exercises effects upon his master, this is because the master attends to the best interests (*maṣāliḥ*) of his servant so that the property of masterhood will remain with him. A person who does not attend to the best interests of his servant has been dismissed from the level, for the levels possess the property of appointing (*tawliya*) and dismissing (*'azl*) in their essence, not extraneously, no matter who may possess them. . . .

Do you not see that the level of Him who has no place (*makān*) required Him to create a heaven to make into a Throne (*'arsh*)? Then He mentioned that He "sat upon it" (Koran 20:5) so that people could supplicate Him and seek their needs from Him. Otherwise the servant would remain bewildered, not knowing where to turn, since God created the servant possessing directions (*jiha*). So the Real attributed to Himself aboveness (*fawqiyya*) in terms of heaven and the Throne and the fact that He encompasses all directions. He did this through His words, "Whithersoever you turn, there is the Face of God" (Koran 2:115), and His words, "Our Lord descends to the heaven of this world every night and says, 'Is there any repenter? Is there any supplicator? Is there anyone asking for forgiveness?'"[5] And His Prophet said about Him, "God is in the kibla of him who performs the prayer."[6]

All of these are properties of the levels, if you have intelligence. If the levels were to disappear from the cosmos, the entities would have no existence whatsoever. So understand! (III 408.11,28,32)

Ranking in Degrees

As already remarked, the Shaykh al-Akbar often refers to hierarchy, whether in the divine names or in the cosmos, by the term *tafāḍul*. The word derives from the root *f.ḍ.l.*, the basic meaning of which is "to exceed," and by extension, to excel and surpass. The Shaykh's use of the term is based upon several Koranic verses in which God is said to have made certain things surpass other things or be more excellent than other things. God's ranking of the things in degrees, by making some of them more excellent than others, establishes a hierarchical order throughout the cosmos. This ranking, and therefore all order in the universe, goes back to the names, as does all knowledge, which is basically the discernment of order and relationships among things.

God sent down the cosmos in keeping with the levels so that they might be fully inhabited (*ta'mīr*). If there were no ranking in degrees in the cosmos, some of the levels would remain inoperative (*mu'aṭṭal*) and uninhabited. But there is nothing in existence inoperative; on the contrary, all of it is fully inhabited. Every level must have inhabitants whose properties will be in keeping with the level.[7] Hence He made some parts of the cosmos more excellent than others.

The root of this in the divine things (*al-ilāhiyyāt*) is the divine names. How can the compass (*iḥāṭa*) of Knowing compare with that of Desiring and Powerful? For Knowing is distinguished from Desiring, and Desiring from Powerful, by the level of that to which connection is established. Knowing has the most inclusive compass, so it is greater and more excellent than Desiring and Powerful, through something which neither of them possesses in respect of being Desiring and Powerful. For He knows Himself, but He is not described as having power over Himself, nor as desiring His own existence. Part of the reality of desire is that it only becomes connected to that which is nonexistent,[8] but God exists. And one of the characteristics of power is that it only becomes connected to the possible thing, or that which is "necessary through the Other" (*al-wājib bi'l-ghayr*),[9] but He is the Necessary Being through Himself. So from here ranking in degrees becomes manifest in the cosmos according to the ranking in degrees of the levels. Therefore there must be ranking in degrees among those who inhabit the levels. Hence there must be ranking in degrees in the cosmos. (II 527.11)

The realities of the relationships are arranged in a real hierarchy (*tartīb ḥaqīqī*), not one established by convention (*waḍ'ī*).

Take, for example, the priority of Alive (*al-ḥayy*) over Knowing, the inclusion of Desiring within the compass of Knowing, and the inclusion of the Powerful within the compass of Desiring. Desiring does not undertake that which pertains to Powerful, Knowing does not undertake that which pertains to Desiring, Alive does not undertake that which pertains to Knowing, Knowing does not undertake that which pertains to Alive, Desiring does not undertake that which pertains to Knowing, Powerful does not undertake that which pertains to Desiring. And the entity (*ʿayn*)[10] of Knowing is the entity of Alive, Desiring, and Powerful; the entity of life is the entity of knowledge, desire, and power; the entity of life is the entity of Alive, Knowing, Desiring, and Powerful. And so on with the rest. So the relationships are diverse, but the Entity is One. (II 608.26).

The Names Personified

The divine names are relationships and attributions, not real entities that can be distinguished from God or the creatures. Ibn al-ʿArabī stresses this point constantly, for to deny it would be to introduce multiplicity into the One God. To counter certain criticisms which might arise from a misunderstanding of what follows, we quote him once again on this matter:

Those things which we affirm are the relationships themselves. The Law refers to them as names. Each name possesses a meaning not possessed by any other name, and that meaning is attributed to the Essence of the Real. The considerative thinkers (*nuẓẓār*) who follow Kalām call that meaning an "attribute" (*ṣifa*), while the Verifiers[11] call it a "relationship" (*nisba*). . . .

The relationships are distinct from one another. You can not equate desire with power, speech, life, or knowledge. The name Knowing bestows what is not bestowed by Powerful, and Wise bestows what is not bestowed by any other name. So make them all "relationships" or "names" or "attributes." It is best to make them names, no doubt, since the Divine Law has not mentioned attributes or relationships in respect to the Real, only names. God said, "To God belong the Most Beautiful Names" (Koran 7:180), and they are nothing other than these relationships.

Do the names have ontological entities or not? Here there is a dispute among the considerative thinkers (*ahl al-naẓar*). As for us, there is no dispute: They are relationships and names which designate intelligible, non-ontological realities. Therefore the Essence does not become multiple through them, since a thing can only become multiple through ontological entities, not through properties, attributions, and relationships. (IV 294.11)

Ibn al-ʿArabī directs all of his teachings at *tawḥīd*, affirming the Unity of God and the consequent unity of all things that exist. No one with any sense of what he is trying to do would think of accusing him, for example, of making the divine names into lesser gods.[12] That is why he can safely speak of the names as God's close family members—as we saw in the last chapter—in an analogy which would not have won too much favor among the proponents of Kalām.

How can the existence of the cosmos be explained? As we have seen above, the cosmos is demanded or sought (*ṭalab*) by the names. Once we have a universe, we see that the existent things stand in certain relationships with the Divine Reality. Those relationships demand that God be named by certain names. Hence God possesses those names, and He has possessed them for all eternity, since they designate His Reality, and realities do not change. As a result, we see that those names demand creation, since without it, they would remain virtualities. It is only through the creatures that the properties and effects of the names come to be understood and seen. If there were no universe, the names would never become manifest. In a section on the divine name

All-provider (*al-razzāq*), the Shaykh explains that God not only gives all creatures their daily provisions, He also provides the names with their provision and happiness by creating the universe.

> The first provision to become manifest from All-provider is the provision through which the names are nourished, that is, the manifestation of their effects within the cosmos. In that manifestation is their subsistence, bliss, joy, and happiness. . . . So the fact that the names exercise their effects upon the engendered things is their provision, through which they are nourished and subsist. (II 462.19).
>
> Though the names find delight in their own essence and perfection, they find even greater delight through the manifestation of their effects within the entities of the loci of manifestation, since thereby their authority (*sulṭān*) becomes manifest. This is what the poet alludes to by acting as their spokesman in the following verse. He refers to them indirectly with the pronoun "we." . . .
>
> Though we sit in the seat of joy,
> none but you can complete our joy.
>
> The "seat of joy" which belongs to the names is the Presence of the Essence, while the "completion of their joy" is that which their realities demand in the loci of manifestation, which are alluded to as "you." (II 61.27)

Ibn al-ʿArabī goes much further in personifying the names than merely attributing joy and delight to them. In several passages he describes how the names gathered together and discussed their situation "before" their properties and effects became manifest. The Shaykh calls this imaginative depiction, which is more reminiscent of a polytheistic myth than a Muslim theological discussion, "The Conference, Discussion, and Concurrence of the Divine Names in the Arena of Debate."[13] Note, however, that at the beginning of his longest description of this "Conference," quoted below, he is once again careful to point out that the names are only relationships and attributions, and that it would be a serious mistake to ascribe any sort of ontological independence to them.

> You should know that "divine names" is an expression for a state that is bestowed by the realities. So pay attention to what you will hear, and do not imagine manyness or ontological combination (*al-ijtimāʿ al-wujūdī*). What we want to explain in this section is only the hierarchy of the intelligible realities, which are many in respect of relationships, but not in respect of real existence, for the Essence of the Real is One in respect of being the Essence. However, we know in respect of our existence, our poverty, and our possibility that there must be a Preponderator (*murajjiḥ*) by whom we are supported. We also know that our existence must demand from that Support diverse relationships. Hence the Lawgiver (*al-shāriʿ*)[14] alluded to these relationships as the "Most Beautiful Names." In respect of being the Speaker (*al-mutakallim*), He named Himself by the names at the level of the Necessity of His Divine Being, which cannot be shared by anyone, for He is One God, and there is no other God.
>
> After this introduction concerning the origin of this matter and the production of effects and the giving of preponderance to the possible cosmos, I say:
>
> The names gathered together in the presence of the Named. They gazed upon their own realities and meanings and sought the manifestation of their own properties in order that their entities might become distinct through their effects.[15] For Creator—who is Ordainer[16]—, Knowing, Governor, Deployer, Author, Form-giver, Provider, Life-giver, Slayer, Inheritor, Grateful, and all the rest of the divine names gazed upon their own essences. But they found nothing created, governed, deployed, or nourished. So they said, "What can be done so that these entities—within which our own properties can become manifest—may become manifest, that thereby our authority may become manifest?"
>
> So the divine names—which are demanded by some of the realities of the cosmos after the manifestation of the en-

tity of the cosmos—had recourse to the name Author. They said to it, "Perhaps you can give existence to these entities so that our properties may become manifest and our authority established, for the presence within which we now dwell is not able to display our effects." Author said, "That goes back to the name Powerful, since I am under its scope."

The root of all this is as follows: In the state of their nonexistence the possible things asked the divine names—an asking through their state of abasement and poverty—as follows: "Nonexistence has blinded us, so we are not able to perceive one another or to know what God requires you to do with us. If you were to make manifest our entities and clothe them in the robe of existence, you would be doing us a favor and we would undertake the appropriate veneration and reverence. Moreover, your sovereignty becomes genuine through our becoming manifest in actuality. Today you possess sovereignty over us only potentially and virtually. What we seek from you is what you should be seeking to an even greater degree from us." The names replied, "What the possible things have said is correct." So they fell to seeking the same thing.

When the names had recourse to the name Powerful, it said, "I am under the scope of the name Desiring, so I cannot bring any of you into entified existence without its specification (*ikhtiṣāṣ*). The possible thing itself does not give me the ability to do that. First the command of Commander must come from its Lord. When it commands the thing to enter into engendered existence, saying to it 'Be!', then it gives me the ability from itself, and I undertake to bring it into existence and immediately give it engendered existence. So have recourse to the name Desiring. Perhaps it will give preponderance to and specify the side of existence over the side of nonexistence. Then I, Commander, and Speaker will join together and give you existence."

So the names had recourse to the name Desiring. They said to it, "We asked the name Powerful to bring our entities into existence, but it deferred the command to you. What do you decree?" Desiring said, "Powerful spoke the truth. But I have no news about the property of the name Knowing in respect to you. Does it or does it not have precedent knowledge that you will be given existence, so that we can specify it for you? I am under the scope of the name Knowing. Go to it and mention your situation to it."

So they went to the name Knowing and mentioned what the name Desiring had said. Knowing said, "Desiring spoke the truth. And I have precedent knowledge that you will be given existence. But courtesy must be observed. For we have a presence which watches over us, and that is the name Allah. We must all be present with it, since it is the Presence of All-comprehensiveness (*ḥaḍrat al-jamʿ*)."

Hence all the names gathered together in the Presence of Allah. It said, "What is on your mind?" They told it the story. It said, "I am the name that comprehends your realities and I denote the Named, who is an All-holy Essence described by perfection and incomparability. Stay here while I enter in upon the Object of my denotation." So it entered in upon the Object of its denotation and told it what the possible things had said and what the names were discussing. The Essence said, "Go out, and tell each one of the names to become connected to what its reality requires among the possible things. For I am One in Myself in respect of Myself. The possible things demand only My Level, and My Level demands them. All the divine names belong to the Level, not to Me, except only the name One (*al-wāḥid*).[17] It is a name that pertains exclusively to Me. No one shares with Me in its reality in any respect, none of the names, none of the levels, and none of the possible things."

So the name Allah went out, next to it the name Speaker, acting as its spokesman to the possible things and the names. It mentioned to them what the Named had said. Knowing, Desiring, Speaking, and Powerful established their connections, and the first possible thing became outwardly manifest through the specification of Desiring and the property of Knowing. (I 322.33)

The Divine Conflict

The multiplicity of relationships that can be discerned in God results in a multiplicity of relationships in the cosmos. All things in the universe manifest the effects and properties of the divine names. Even the conflict, quarrel, strife, and war that are found in created things have their roots in God. The cosmos is a great collection of things, and things go their own ways, not necessarily in harmony with other things on the level where they are being considered. The names relate to each other in many different modes, some harmonious, and some sufficiently disharmonious that Ibn al-ʿArabī can even talk about "conflict" (*tanāzuʿ*) among the names.

> The properties of the divine names, in respect of being names, are diverse. What do Avenger, Terrible in Punishment, and Overpowering have in common with Compassionate, Forgiving, and Gentle? For Avenger demands the occurrence of vengeance in its object, while Compassionate demands the removal of vengeance from the same object. . . . So he who looks at the divine names will maintain that there is a Divine Conflict. That is why God said to His Prophet, "Dispute (*jidāl*) with them in the most beautiful way (*aḥsan*)" (Koran 16:125). God commanded him to dispute in the manner demanded by the divine names, that is, in the way that is "most beautiful."[18] (II 93.19)

The "Divine Conflict" has never-ending repercussions in this world and the next, since all change and transformation can be traced back to it. In one passage the Shaykh discusses the divine root of "calling" (*nidāʾ*), as, for example, when God calls out in the Koran, "O you who have faith. . . !" He explains that diversity and conflict in the cosmos stem from the fact that different names call the creatures in different directions.

> You should know that the divine call includes believer and unbeliever, obedient and disobedient. . . . This call derives only from the divine names. One divine name calls to someone who is governed by the property of a second divine name when it knows that the term of the second name's property within the person has come to an end. Then this name which calls to him takes over. So it continues in this world and the next. Hence everything other than God is called by a divine name to come to an engendered state (*ḥāl kawnī*) to which that name seeks to attach it. If the object of the call responds, he is named "obedient" and becomes "felicitous" (*saʿīd*). If he does not respond, he is named "disobedient" and becomes "wretched" (*shaqī*).
>
> You may object and say: "How can a divine name call and the engendered thing refuse to respond, given that it is weak and must accept the divine power?" We will answer: It does not refuse to respond in respect of itself and its own reality, since it is constantly overpowered. But since it is under the overpowering sway of a divine name, that name does not let it respond to the name which calls to it. Hence there is conflict among the divine names. However, the names are equals, so the ruling property belongs to the actual possessor, which is the name in whose hand the thing is when the second name calls to it. The possessor is stronger through the situation.
>
> You may object: "Then why is a person taken to task for his refusal?" We answer: Because he claims the refusal for himself and does not ascribe it to the divine name which controls him.
>
> You may object: "The situation stays the same, since he refuses only because of the overpowering sway of a divine name. The person who is called refused because of the name." We answer: That is true, but he is ignorant of that, so he is taken to task for his ignorance (*jahl*), for the ignorance belongs to himself.
>
> You may object: "But his ignorance derives from a divine name whose property governs him." We answer: Ignorance is a quality pertaining to nonexistence (*amr ʿadamī*); it is not ontological. But the divine names bestow only existence; they do not bestow nonexistence. So the ignorance belongs to the very self of him who is called. (II 592.32)

In another context Ibn al-ʿArabī explains that the "wages" (*ajr*) mentioned in the Koran are paid to those who perform supererogatory works (*al-nawāfil*). Since human beings are God's slaves (*ʿabd mamlūk*), they are not paid wages for the acts which the religion makes obligatory for them (*farā'iḍ*), though of course the Master rewards His slaves in other ways. The root of this matter has to do with two kinds of servanthood (*ʿubūdiyya*), one toward the Essence and the other toward the divine names. The first is compulsory (*iḍṭirārī*) while the second is voluntary (*ikhtiyārī*).[19]

The prophets are God's sincere servants, not being owned by their own caprice (*hawā*) or that of any of God's creatures. But they say, "My wage falls only on Allah" (Koran 10:72, 11:29, 34:47). This goes back to their entrance under the properties of the divine names, from whence wages are paid. Through compulsion and in reality they are the servants and the possession of the Essence. But the divine names seek them to make their effects manifest through them. So they have free choice (*ikhtiyār*) in entering under whichever name they desire. The divine names know this, so the divine names designate wages for them. Each divine name wants this slave of the Essence to choose to serve (*khidma*) it rather than the other divine names. It says to him, "Enter under my command, for I will give you such and such." Then he remains in the service of that name until he is called by the Lord in respect of his servanthood to the Essence. At that point he abandons every divine name and undertakes the call of his Lord. Once he has done what He commands him to do, he returns to whichever name he pleases. That is why every person performs supererogatory works and worships as he desires until he hears the call to begin the obligatory prayer (*iqāmat al-ṣalāt*). At that point every supererogatory work is forbidden to him and he must endeavor to perform the obligatory act for his Lord and Master. Then when he finishes, he enters into any supererogatory work that he desires.

In this situation man is similar to the slave of a master with many sons. He is a compulsory servant of his master. When his master commands him, he does not occupy himself with anything but his command. But when he finishes with that, the sons of the master seek to make him their subject. Hence they have to designate for him something that will make him want to serve them. Each son would love to take him into his own service in the time that he is free from the business of his master. Hence they compete in giving him wages in order to have him devote himself exclusively to them. But he is free to choose which son to serve at that time. So man is the slave, the master is Allah, and the sons are the other divine names.

When He sees the servant troubled and helps him, then it is known that the servant is subjected to the name "Helper." Hence he will receive from Helper the wage that it has designated for him. When He sees him weak in himself and He acts with gentleness toward him, then he is subjected to the name "Gentle." And so it goes with all the names. So verify, my friend, how you serve your Lord and Master! Possess correct knowledge concerning yourself and your Master! Then you will be one of the men of knowledge who are "deeply rooted in knowledge" (*al-rāsikhūn fi'l-ʿilm* [Koran 3:7]), the divine sages (*al-ḥukamā' al-ilāhiyyūn*), and you will attain to the furthest degree and the highest place along with the messengers and the prophets! (III 64.7)

The Unity of the Essence

When we read what Ibn al-ʿArabī has to say about the multiplicity and conflict demanded by the divine names or when we meet his personifications of the names, we may forget for a moment that the names are multiple only in properties, not in existence, since each is identical in existence with the Essence. In respect of the Divine Self, the One Entity, there can be no multiplicity. But in respect of the relationships which are established with creation because of the fact that the Self is a God, numerous names and attributes can be envisaged. Each relationship we take into account—each divine name—has special effects and properties among the creatures which distinguish it from other relationships.

On the basis of these properties, we can say that one name is ranked above another. In other words, one relationship is different from another. Since there is no multiplicity in God, there is no hierarchy in God Himself. This is why the Shaykh can deny ranking in degrees in the "divine things" (*al-ilāhiyyāt*), just as he affirms that it derives from them. On the one hand he has in view the relationships inasmuch as they designate specific qualities demanding a variety of effects and properties, and on the other he has in view the identity of the names with the Divine Essence.

> There can be no ranking in degrees in the divine things, since a thing cannot be considered superior to itself. The divine realities and relationships cannot be ranked one over another, except insofar as they are attributed to something [in the cosmos], since they have no ranking in their Essence. (II 226.2)
>
> There can be no ranking in degrees among the divine names, for two reasons: First, the relationship of the names to the Essence is one relationship, so there is no ranking of degrees in this relationship. If the levels were ranked one over the other in respect of the divine realities by which they are supported, there would be superiority among the names of God. Hence some of God's names would be more excellent than others. But no one says this on the basis of Law or reason. The greater inclusiveness of a name does not prove its greater excellence. There can only be greater excellence in that which has the characteristic of accepting something, but which does not go to the effort of accepting it; or in that which may be described by something, but is not so described.
>
> Second, the divine names go back to His Essence, and the Essence is One. But ranking in degrees demands manyness. And a thing cannot be considered superior to itself. (II 61.10)

A distinction can be drawn between how God relates to the universe as the Knowing and how He relates to it as the Powerful. This is especially clear in mutually contradictory names such as the Forgiver and the Avenger. But the Essence as Essence is related to all things in an identical manner. Hence the name Allah—the name that denotes the Essence as such—is related to everything in the cosmos in the same way.

> The divine relationship between Allah and all creatures is one relationship within which there is no ranking in degrees, since ranking in degrees demands manyness. (II 580.19)
>
> The relationship of Allah to all things is one relationship with no ranking in degrees. You will not see this relationship predominating in any of the creatures, whether of the higher or lower plenum.[20] It does not establish ranking or preponderation in the cosmos. . . . But inasmuch as the cosmos is the cosmos, some parts of the cosmos preponderate over other parts and disparity becomes manifest within it. (III 157.34)

Multiplicity is not an intrinsic attribute of the names, only of that in which they display their properties. In themselves the names remain one, since God is One.

> The names of the Real do not become plural and multiple except within the loci of their manifestation. But in respect to Him, the property of number does not rule over them. (II 122.19)
>
> What "separates" (*faṣl*)[21] a thing is that which distinguishes it from association with something else. As for the divine names, separation takes place through what they designate in respect of being plural in number. Since they accept manyness, they need separation. First, they are separate from the Essence of the Named, lest their [specific] meanings be attributed to It. Second, they are separate in respect to that within which their effects become manifest. Manyness in the names is occasioned by that in which the effects are displayed, not by the name as agent, which is that which produces the effects. So the effects are the multiplicity of relationships with the One Entity. This separation is in the effects, not in the names, nor in the Named, nor in that within which the effects appear. (II 480.33)

Names of Incomparability and Names of Acts

Muslim theologians often classify the divine names into categories. Ibn al-ʿArabī is no exception, and he provides several different ways of classifying the names in his works. For the practical purpose of gaining an insight into his basic teachings, it is sufficient to grasp a single basic distinction, one which will come up in many different contexts: that between the names which negate (*salb*) various descriptions from God and other names which affirm (*ithbāt*) that He possesses attributes. These two kinds of names are most commonly called the "Names of Incomparability" and the "Names of the Acts." "Acts," it will be remembered, is a theological designation for the creatures.

As was seen in the first chapter, the Divine Presence includes the Essence, the attributes, and the acts. The attributes or names are the *barzakh* between the Essence and the acts. But these names can be divided into two categories, depending on the type of relationship which they designate between the Essence and the cosmos. In the first case, they negate various qualities from the Essence. In the second, they affirm that the Essence inasmuch as It is a god possesses various qualities.

Incomparability (*tanzīh*) signifies that the Essence cannot be judged, gauged, or known by any of the creatures. It is normally contrasted with similarity (*tashbīh*), which signifies that God as the possessor of the names establishes certain relationships with the things and that these can be known and judged to a certain degree. The names of acts thus demand the "similarity" of the created things with God.

The "Divine Presence" is a name for an Essence, attributes, and acts; or, if you prefer, you can say "for attributes of acts and attributes of incomparability." (IV 196.11; cf. II 579.14)

The names that demand incomparability are the names which the Essence demands in Itself, while the names which demand similarity are the names which the Essence demands inasmuch as It is a god. The names of incomparability are those such as Independent (*al-ghanī*) and One (*al-aḥad*) and all those which can only be possessed by Him, while the names of similarity are those such as Compassionate, Forgiving, and everything by which the servant may truly be qualified in respect of being a locus of manifestation, not in respect of his own entity. (II 57.30)

There are two kinds of divine attributes: divine attributes which require the declaration of incomparability, like All-great (*al-kabīr*) and All-high (*al-ʿalī*), and divine attributes which require the declaration of similarity, such as the Magnificent (*al-mutakabbir*), the Self-exalted (*al-mutaʿālī*), and everything by which the Real described Himself and by which the servant is also qualified. (I 691.1)

The names are of two kinds: One kind is all lights (*anwār*); these are the names that denote ontological qualities. Another kind is all darknesses (*ẓulam*); these are the names that denote incomparability. (II 110.30)

We have no knowledge of God except through attributes of incomparability or attributes of acts. He who supposes that he has knowledge of positive attributes of the Self (*ṣifa nafsiyya thubūtiyya*) has supposed wrongly. For such an attribute would define (*ḥadd*) Him, but His Essence has no definition. This is a door locked to engendered existence (*al-kawn*), a door that cannot be opened. It belongs only to the Real. (II 619.15)

4. THE ESSENCE AND THE DIVINITY

The Divine Essence is God in Himself, without reference to the relationships which may be established between God and the creatures. In contrast, the Divinity is the Essence considered in relation to created things. Only negative attributes can be ascribed to the Essence; we can say what It is not, but not what It is. Ibn al-ʿArabī sometimes says that no name whatsoever can be applied to the Essence, since It is absolutely unknowable. But considered as the Divinity, God accepts all names and attributes, both positive and negative.

As a level, the Divinity has to be considered in relationship to other levels, such as creature, servant, vassal and "divine thrall." In this respect the name Allah is strictly analogous to divine names such as Knowing and Powerful, both of which have to be understood in terms of their objects. But the Essence transcends levels and relationships, and hence cannot be known, since it is impossible to "get a bearing" on It. The Shaykh frequently criticizes the theologians for claiming to provide positive knowledge of God Himself, whereas God's "independence" from the worlds demands that He stand beyond rational understanding. But in spite of God's absolute independence of all created things, He tells us of His generosity and mercy, and such attributes demand creation, though they do not impose constraints upon Him as Essence.

Both Essence and Divinity are denoted by the name Allah, which brings together all the divine names and hence is the "coincidence of opposites" (*jamʿ al-aḍdād*). The opposition and contrariety found among the names explain the strife and turmoil of the cosmos, which is the locus in which the properties of the contrary names are displayed. The names encompassed by the name Allah are mutually opposed not only in a horizontal sense, but also in a vertical sense; here we come back to the distinction between the names of incomparability and the names of acts or similarity. True knowledge of God demands knowing Him through both kinds of names.

The Divinity

The word "Divinity" (*al-ulūha, al-ulūhiyya*), derives from the root *'.l.h.*, from which we have the name "Allah" as well as the word *ilāh* or god. As was pointed out in the previous chapter, the "Level" to which the name Allah refers is the Divinity, while the "Entity" to which it refers is the Essence. Level and Entity are the same reality, of course, since we are dealing here with a single Being. But to speak of Divinity is to envisage relationships with creatures, while to speak of the Essence is to envisage the Reality Itself, without any relationships. About God as Divinity we can say that certain relationships are established with Him. Then we can talk about these relationships, which are known as the "divine names," but we cannot talk about God in Himself, the Essence, in terms of any relationships.

> Interrelationship (*munāsaba*) between the Real and creation is neither intelligible (*maʿqūl*) nor existent. Nothing comes from Him in respect of His Essence. Everything denoted by the Law or taken by the rational faculty (*al-ʿaql*) as a denotation is connected to the Divinity, not the Essence. God in respect of being a god is that by which the possible thing is supported in its possibility. (II 579.9)
>
> It is not correct for the Real and creation to come together (*ijtimāʿ*) in any mode whatsoever in respect of the Essence, only in respect of the fact that the Essence is described by Divinity. Divinity is one of the properties which rational faculties are able to perceive on their own. In our view, anything that the rational fac-

ulty is able to perceive on its own can be known prior to being witnessed (*shuhūd*). But the Essence of the Real is outside this judgment, for It is witnessed before It is known. Or rather, It is witnessed, but not known, just as the Divinity is known, but not witnessed.[1]

How many a rational man among the considerative thinkers, claiming a firm rational faculty, has maintained that he has acquired knowledge of the Essence in respect of his reflective consideration (*al-naẓar al-fikrī*)! But he is mistaken, since he wavers (*mutaraddid*) in his reflection between negation (*salb*) and affirmation (*ithbāt*). The affirmation returns to himself, since he only affirms that which he considers in respect of the fact that the Real is Knowing, Powerful, Desiring, and so on with all the names. The negation returns to nonexistence and negativity (*al-nafy*), and negativity cannot be an attribute of the Essence, since the attributes of the essences of existent things are only positive (*thubūtī*).[2] So this reflective thinker, wavering between affirmation and negation, has gained nothing of knowledge of God. (I 41.9)

The loci of manifestation (*maẓāhir*) belong to the Level, not to the Essence. Hence He is not worshiped except inasmuch as He is a god; nor does anyone assume the traits (*takhalluq*) of His names except in inasmuch as He is a god. Nothing is understood from His loci of manifestation within His loci of manifestation except that He is a god. Were the Essence to make the loci of manifestation manifest, It would be known. Were It known, It would be encompassed (*iḥāṭa*). Were It encompassed, It would be limited (*ḥadd*). Were It limited, It would be confined (*inḥiṣār*). Were It confined, It would be owned (*mulk*). But the Essence of the Real is high exalted above all this. (II 597.17)

Since the Essence is unknowable, no one can conceive of Its opposite; no relationship at all can be envisaged. But the Divinity demands relationships. From this principle arises Ibn al-ʿArabī's well-known doctrine of the *ma'lūh* or "divine thrall." The word is a past participle derived from the same root as *ilāh*, "god." Literally it means that which is "godded over," or the object in respect of which a god is a god. It is nearly synonymous with *marbūb*, "vassal," the past participle from the same root as *rabb*, "lord."

The Divine Essence cannot be understood by the rational faculty, since there is nothing "other" (*siwā*) than It. But the Divinity and the Lordship (*al-rubūbiyya*) can be understood by this faculty, since the "others" in relation to them are the divine thrall and the vassal. (II 257.28)

We have already seen the Shaykh employing past participles derived from various divine attributes in a number of passages. For example, he has asked how there can be someone powerful without an object of power (*maqdūr*), or a knower without an object of knowledge (*maʿlūm*). In respect of God, he says, the same principle is involved. When we speak of the names, they are relationships, or better, "correlations" (*iḍāfa*); each name demands two correlative terms (*mutaḍā'if*), the name itself and the object to which it is connected (*taʿalluq*). The name Allah is not outside of this principle, only the Essence, since It is not a correlative term, but the Entity Itself. As soon as we say that It is related to something, we are talking about the "level" of the Essence, not the Essence in Itself.

In the first passage below, Ibn al-ʿArabī is discussing the spiritual state of "freedom" (*ḥurriyya*) achieved by the friends of God. In the last analysis, he says, the creature can never be free.

In reality there is no existing entity that possesses freedom, since the correlations prevent that. The reality of freedom is found only in the fact that the Essence is "Independent of the worlds" (Koran 3:97), even though the cosmos becomes manifest from It and through It, not through anything else. Since the Essence is "Independent of the worlds," It is free, while the cosmos is poor and needy toward It. The creatures of the cosmos have no freedom whatsoever. They are demanded by the Divinity through the properties It has prescribed for them, properties without which the Divinity would have no manifestation; hence correlations become manifest. Therefore the situation is dependent (*mawqūf*) from two sides, each side depending upon the other. So it is impossible for freedom to subsist in either of the correlatives. (II 502.33)

The relationship between Lord and vassal exists. Through it the Lord is the vassal's Lord. But there is no relationship between the vassal and the Essence of the Lord. Hence nothing comes out of the Essence . . . , since the Essence does not turn Its attentiveness toward bringing the things into existence in respect of being the Essence. It only does so inasmuch as Power is attributed to It and there is nothing to prevent it. This is what is known as the Divinity. (II 609.2)

God as the Lover (*al-muḥibb*) has no name that can denote His Essence. The divine thrall, who is God's beloved, looks at His effects within himself, then names Him by those effects. The Real in turn accepts the way the thrall names Him. The divine thrall says, "O Allah!" Allah says, "Here I am." The vassal says, "O Lord!" The Lord says, "Here I am." The created one says, "O Creator!" The Creator says, "Here I am." The one provided for says, "O All-provider!" The All-provider says, "Here I am." The weak one says, "O Strong!" The Strong says, "I respond to thee." (II 360.6)

Since the cosmos has no subsistence except through God, and since the attribute of Divinity has no subsistence except through the cosmos, each of the two is the provision (*rizq*) of the other; each takes nourishment (*taghadhdhī*) from the other so that its existence may subsist. The very property of each demands that this be so.

We are His provision,
  since He feeds upon our existence,
just as He is the provision
  of engendered things, without doubt.
He preserves us in engendered existence
  and we preserve the fact that He
is a god. In these words
  there is no lie,
nor any heedlessness;
  for in every state engendered existence
admits bondage to and possession by
  the Owner of the Kingdom (*malik al-mulk*).

Temporally originated existence (*al-wujūd al-ḥādith*) and Eternal Being (*al-wujūd al-qadīm*) are tied to each other through correlation and property, not through the existence of the entity (*wujūd al-ʿayn*). For example, a human being exists in entity in respect of the fact that he is a human being. In the state of his existence, he has no fatherhood (*ubuwwa*) as long as he does not have a son who gives that attribute to him, or as long as it is not supposed that he has a son. In the same way, he is not called an "owner" (*mālik*) as long as he does not have possessions through which it is said that he is an owner. In the same way, the possessions, though they exist in entity, are not called possessions until someone owns them.

Hence God, in respect of His Essence and Being, is Independent of the worlds. But in respect of the fact that He is a lord, He demands vassals, without doubt. So in respect of Entity, He makes no demands; but in respect of Lordship (*al-rubūbiyya*), He demands vassals either in existence or supposition (*taqdīr*).

We have mentioned that every attribute in the cosmos must be supported by a divine attribute, but not by the Attribute of the Essence, which God merits in His Essence and through which He is Independent. Nor is the essential attribute which is merited by the cosmos [based upon a divine attribute]; through it the cosmos is poor, or rather a servant, for the cosmos is more worthy of this latter than of the attribute of poverty. (III 363.32)

The Divinity . . . confronts the creatures through Its own [specific] essence [as Divinity] and It confronts the Essence through Its own essence. That is why It discloses Itself (*tajallī*) in many forms, transmuting (*taḥawwul*) Itself and undergoing continual change (*tabaddul*) within them. It has a face toward creation through which It discloses Itself in the forms of creation; It has a face toward the Essence through which It becomes manifest to the Essence. So the created things do not know the Essence except from behind this *barzakh*, which is the Divinity. Nor does the Essence exercise properties within the created things except through this *barzakh*, which is the Divinity. We have verified It, and we have found it no different from the Most Beautiful Names by which we call upon It. So the Essence compels (*jabr*) the cosmos only through the divine names, and the cosmos knows nothing of the Real but these Most Beautiful Divine Names. (IV 208.33)

The Unknowability of the Essence

God is known through the relations, attributions, and correlations that become established between Him and the cosmos. But the Essence is unknown, since nothing is related to It. In proof of this assertion, the Shaykh often cites the Koranic verse, "God warns you about His Self" (3:28,30), which he frequently explains in terms of the prophetic saying, "Reflect (*tafakkur*) upon all things, but reflect not upon God's Essence."[3]

In respect of Itself the Essence has no name, since It is not the locus of effects, nor is It known by anyone. There is no name to denote It without relationship, nor with any assurance (*tamkīn*). For names act to make known and to distinguish, but this door [to knowledge of the Essence] is forbidden to anyone other than God, since "None knows God but God." So the names exist through us and for us. They revolve around us and become manifest within us. Their properties are with us, their goals are toward us, their expressions are of us, and their beginnings are from us.

If not for them,
  we would not be.
If not for us,
  they would not be. (II 69.34)

Reflection (*fikr*) has no governing property or domain in the Essence of the Real, neither rationally nor according to the Law. For the Law has forbidden reflection upon the Essence of God, a point to which is alluded by His words, "God warns you about His Self" (3:28). This is because there is no interrelationship (*munāsaba*) between the Essence of the Real and the essence of the creatures. (II 230.15)

Engendered existence has no connection whatsoever to knowledge of the Essence. The only thing connected to it is knowledge of the Level, i.e., that which is named Allah. This [knowledge of the Level] is a firmly established proof (*dalīl*). It goes straight to the mark in knowing the God (*al-ilāh*). Likewise it recognizes both the names of the acts and the descriptions of majesty appropriate to Him[4] and perceives the reality in accordance with which engendered existence emerges from the Essence. The Essence is described by this Level, but It is unknown in entity or quality (*kayf*).

In our view there is no disputing the fact that the Essence is unknown. To It are ascribed descriptions that make It incomparable with the attributes of temporal things (*al-ḥadath*). It possesses eternity (*al-qidam*), and to Its Being is ascribed beginninglessness (*al-azal*). But all these names designate negations, such as the negation of beginning and everything appropriate to temporal origination.

A group of Ashʿarite theologians oppose us on this. They imagine that they have known the Real through a positive attribute of Self (*ṣifa nafsiyya thubūtiyya*). How far from the mark! How could they know that? A group of the theologians whom we have seen, including Abū ʿAbdallāh al-Kattānī, Abu'l-ʿAbbās al-Ashqar, and al-Ḍarīr al-Silāwī, author of *al-Urjūza fī ʿilm al-kalām*, have even criticized Abū Saʿīd al-Kharrāz,[5] Abū Ḥāmid [al-Ghazālī] and their likes for their statement, "None knows God but God"! (I 160.4).

God says, "In that there are signs for a people who reflect" (13:3). But reflection upon the Essence of God is impossible, so there remains only reflection upon engendered existence. That to which reflection becomes connected is the Most Beautiful Names or the features (*simāt*) of the temporally originated things. The names, all of them, are the root of engendered existence. (II 557.11)

In citing the injunction of the Shariʿa not to meditate upon the Essence of God, Ibn al-ʿArabī is not implying that it is wrong to say anything about God's

Essence. If that were his position, he would be contradicting himself constantly. What he has in mind is the peculiar mental process denoted by the words *fikr* and *tafakkur*, a process which is the domain of the proponents of Kalām and the philosophers. His own position and that of the great Sufis are not based on reflection, but on the Koran and unveiling (*kashf*), that is, knowledge given to them by God without the interference of that rational (*ʿaqlī*) or considerative (*naẓarī*) faculty known as reflection. This point will be discussed in detail beginning in Chapter 12. For now, the following passage can serve as an example of the types of criticisms the Shaykh levels at thinkers who cannot transcend the rational faculty (*ʿaql*).

> The Law has forbidden reflection upon His Essence. He has said, "God warns you about His Self" (3:28). In other words: Do not embark upon reflection about God's Self. The rational thinkers added disobedience toward the Law to their meddling (*fuḍūl*) by plunging into what has been forbidden to them. One of them said that He is a body, another that He is not a body. One said that He is a substance, another that He is not a substance. One said that He is in a direction, another that He is not in a direction. But God did not command a single one of His creatures to plunge into this sort of thing to any extent, neither him who negates, nor him who affirms.
>
> If these people were asked to verify their knowledge of a single essence in the cosmos, they would not know how to do so. If it were said to this plunger: "How does your soul govern your body? Is it inside or outside it, or neither inside nor outside? Consider that with your rational faculty! And this extraneous thing through which the animate body moves, sees, hears, imagines, and reflects—to what does it go back? To a single thing, or to many things? Does it go back to a substance, an accident, or a body?" If you were to seek from him rational proofs—not proofs derived from the Law—he would not find any rational proofs whatsoever. He would not know through the rational faculty that spirits have a subsistence and an existence after death. . . .
>
> God is One God and there is no other god. He is named by those names from the meaning of which it is understood that none are worthy of them except Him. In other words, He possesses this Level. Do not embark, my friend, upon plunging into "What?", "How much?", and "How?" That would prevent you from plunging into what has been prescribed for you [by the Law] (*taklīf*). Cling to the path of faith and works in accordance with what God has made obligatory (*farḍ*) upon you. "And remember your Lord . . . in the morning and evening" (7:205) with the remembrance (*dhikr*) which He has set down for you in the Law. . . .
>
> If this knowledge which is bestowed by reflecting upon God were a light, as is supposed, the darkness of obfuscation[6] and skepticism (*tashkīk*) would never enter the heart, yet it does enter. It is not one of the characteristics of darkness to dispel light, nor does darkness possess any authority over light. Authority belongs only to the light which dispels darkness. This shows that all those things known by the proponents of Kalām and the plungers concerning the Essence of God are not lights, even though they imagine—before any obfuscation enters in upon them—that through it they dwell in light and upon a clear sign from their Lord.[7] They do not know their deficiency until the obfuscation enters in upon them. Who knows? Perhaps the opinion which they suppose is only an obfuscation is the truth and right knowledge.
>
> You are well aware that in the Muʿtazilite's view, the proof with which the Ashʿarite affirms a question whose truth is denied by the Muʿtazilite is an obfuscation. In the same way, the Ashʿarite holds that the Muʿtazilite's proof in negating what the Ashʿarite has affirmed is an obfuscation. Moreover, there is no school of thought (*madhhab*) that does not have leaders, all of whom disagree; it does not matter if they are all described, for example, as being Ashʿarites. Abu'l-Maʿālī's position is different from the Qāḍī's position, the Qāḍī maintains a position that disagrees with the Ustādh, and the Ustādh maintains a position in which he opposes the Shaykh.[8] But all of them

claim to be Ashʿarites. And the Muʿtazilites are the same, as are the philosophers in their doctrines about God. (III 81.30)

The Independence of the Essence

As Ibn al-ʿArabī constantly quotes from the Koran, God is "Independent of the worlds" in respect of the Essence. The term *ghinā* signifies independence, wealth, and having need for nothing. God has all wealth—Being and all Its attributes—in Himself, so He is independent of the cosmos and needs nothing whatsoever from it. The opposite of *ghinā* is *faqr*, "poverty" or "need," which, as we have seen on several occasions, is the essential and inherent attribute of all created or "temporally originated" (*ḥādith*) things. Everything other than God is constantly in need of God, not only for its existence but also for every positive attribute it displays, since these attributes are nothing but the properties and effects of the divine names.

> God reported about Himself that He possesses two relationships: a relationship with the cosmos through the divine names which affirm the entities of the cosmos, and the relationship of His independence from the cosmos. In respect of His relationship of independence, He knows Himself and we know Him not. (II 533.4)
>
> In actuality the Divine Perfection is found in the penetration of power into the objects of power, desire into the objects of desire, and in the manifestation of the properties of the divine names. The Essential Perfection possessed by the Essence is absolute independence from all this. (II 588.30)
>
> God says, "O people, you are the poor toward Allah, and Allah—He is the Independent, the Praiseworthy" (Koran 35:15). In other words, He is Independent through His names, just as we are poor toward His names. That is why He mentioned [in this verse] the name Allah, which brings together all the divine names. (II 263.13)
>
> Independence from creation belongs to God from eternity without beginning (*azal*), while poverty toward God in respect of His independence belongs to the possible thing in the state of its nonexistence from eternity without beginning. (II 100.35)
>
> Freedom is a station of the Essence, not of the Divinity. It can never be fully delivered over to the servant, since he is God's servant through a servanthood that does not accept emancipation. But we have considered freedom impossible for the Real in respect of the fact that He is a god, because He is tied to the divine thrall, just as a master is tied to the existence of the slave, an owner to possessions, and a king to the kingdom. . . . The reality of correlation demands, both rationally and ontologically, the concept of two correlative terms. So there can be no freedom along with correlation. And Lordship and Divinity are correlations. But since there is no interrelationship or correlation between the Real and creation—on the contrary, He is Independent of the worlds, and this belongs to no existent essence save the Essence of the Real—no engendered thing is tied to the Essence, no eye perceives It, no limit encompasses It, and no demonstration (*burhān*) gives knowledge of It. (II 226.22)

According to the Shaykh, God in respect of being the Divinity must create the cosmos, even though, in respect of the Essence, He is Independent of the cosmos. God as Essence has nothing to do with the universe, but as Creator He demands creation, as Powerful He demands objects of power, as Lord He demands vassals, as God He demands divine thralls. Once we view the universe as already created, we see that God is Creator of the things and Revealer of the scriptures. In both respects, that which He has shown to us—the universe and the revealed texts—"speaks" of Him as Generous, Gracious, Kind, Beneficent, Bestower, Giver, and so on. All these names denote the Divinity as It is in fact, so they all demand that the cosmos have some sort of existence. One may be allowed to argue at this point that God as

Divinity could have created something else—though the Shaykh rejects this position in other contexts—but not that He could not have created. The created cosmos and the statements of the revealed books both prove that God is a Creator, and "realities do not change." This type of approach is basic to Ibn al-ʿArabī's way of thinking, and we will meet many more examples of it. For the present it is sufficient to quote a few passages which show that God as Essence is in no way constrained or compelled to create the cosmos. It is only God as the Divinity who, by the very reality of Divinity, will never refrain from creativity and generosity. As soon as we have said "Divinity," we have also said "cosmos."

> Abū Yazīd used to say, "I have no attributes."[9] So it is much more appropriate to negate any delimitation by attributes from the Real, since He is Independent of the cosmos. For attributes demand engendered things. If there were in the Real that which demands the cosmos, it would not be correct for Him to be Independent of that which He demands. (IV 319.31)
>
> Though God in His Essence is Independent of the worlds, it is known that He is described by generosity (*al-karam*), munificence (*al-jūd*), and mercy (*al-raḥma*). Hence there must be objects of mercy and objects of generosity. That is why God says, "When My servants question thee about Me—surely I am near. I respond to the call of the caller when he calls to Me" (Koran 2:186). God answers the caller through munificence and generosity.
>
> Asking through one's states (*al-aḥwāl*) is without doubt more complete than asking through one's words. Response is quicker to him who asks through his state, since he is asking through his very essence. Moreover, munificence toward someone who is distressed and needy is in actual fact a greater munificence than munificence shown toward someone who is not distressed. The possible thing in the state of its nonexistence has a more intense poverty toward God than in the state of its existence. That is why the possible thing makes no claims (*daʿwā*) in the state of its nonexistence, unlike the state of its existence. Hence effusing (*ifāḍa*) existence upon the possible thing in its state of nonexistence is a greater act of munificence and generosity [than giving it something once it exists].
>
> Though God is Independent of the worlds, this means that He is incomparable in the sense that any poverty might subsist in Him or any denotation other than His own Self might denote Him. Hence He brought the cosmos into existence out of His munificence and generosity. No intelligent person or man of faith doubts this, or the fact that munificence is an attribute of Self. For He is the Munificent, the Generous in Himself. So the cosmos must exist. If knowledge has judged that something must exist, it is impossible for it not to exist. So there must be "relationships," or "attributes" according to the position of the Attributists,[10] or "names" according to the position of others. So there must be manyness (*kathra*) in the One Entity. (III 289.23)
>
> "Chivalry" (*futuwwa*) is a divine attribute by way of meaning, but there is no word derived from it by which God is named. Both the Law and rational proofs show that He possesses independence from the cosmos absolutely. . . . One who has such independence and then brings the cosmos into existence does not bring it into existence because of His poverty toward it. He only brings the cosmos into existence for the sake of the cosmos, as an act of charity (*īthār*) toward it in spite of the fact that He alone possesses Being. This is chivalry itself.
>
> There are three reports of the divine chivalry, one Koranic and two prophetic. In the Koran God says, "I created jinn and mankind only to worship Me" (51:56). The form of chivalry here is that He created them to give them the blessing (*inʿām*) of existence, to bring them out from the evil of nonexistence, to make it possible for them to assume the traits (*takhalluq*) of the divine names, and to make them successors (*khalf*).[11] All of this is charity toward them, given that He alone possesses everything in which He has made them successors. Then He knew that making people feel obliged (*imtinān*) detracts from a blessing,[12] so He concealed (*sitr*) the blessing from them with His words, "I only created jinn and mankind to worship Me." He made it appear

that He had created them for His sake rather than for their sake.

In a prophetic report that comes from Moses, it is said that God created things for us and He created us for Him.[13] Then He concealed this with His words, "There is nothing that does not glorify Him in praise" (17:44), so that all might know through His giving knowledge that they are glorifying Him in praise. Thus we smell no whiff of feeling obliged. In this Mosaic report the property of chivalry is that He created things for us as an act of charity for us. . . .

The second prophetic report is that which has been related through the Messenger of God from God. God said, "I was a Treasure but was not known. So I loved to be known, and I created the creatures and made Myself known to them. Then they came to know Me."[14] . . . (II 231.33, 232.1)

The Name "Allah"

God may be considered in respect of Himself, in which case He is referred to as the Essence, or in respect of His Level, in which case He is referred to as the Divinity. In both cases He is called "Allah." Like most authorities, Ibn al-ʿArabī normally considers the name "Allah" a proper name (*ism ʿalam*), refusing to derive it (*ishtiqāq*) from the root *ʾ.l.h.*, from which are derived *ilāh*, "god," and *ulūha*, "divinity." This does not reflect linguistic obtuseness on his part, but rather courtesy toward God in respect of His most important revealed name.[15]

Allah is called the "all-comprehensive name," which means that it designates every name and attribute of God. Hence, as we have seen, the "Divine Presence"—that level of reality which pertains to the name Allah—includes the Essence, the attributes, and the acts. In other words, the Divine Presence embraces Being, existence, and nonexistence, or everything that can in any sense be said to be real. Every other name is included within the scope of the name Allah, a point which was explained in the "Conference of the Names." In practice this means that no one can call upon Allah in respect of the name's all-comprehensiveness; rather, everyone who calls upon Him in fact has one name or another in view. This principle is fundamental to the Shaykh's ontology and spiritual psychology. Its corollary is that things know God only through their own specific realities and worship Him only in terms of their own individual beliefs; a great deal will be said about this in later chapters.

Since every name other than the name Allah, while denoting the Essence of the Real, also denotes—because of its linguistic derivation—a meaning of negation or affirmation, no other name is as strong as this name in the unity of its denotation of the Essence. (IV 197.1)

You say "Allah." This name brings together the realities of all the divine names, so it is impossible for it to be said in a nondelimited sense (*ʿala'l-iṭlāq*). Hence states (*al-aḥwāl*) must delimit it. If words delimit it, that follows from the states. Whenever something is attributed to Allah, look to see which name is worthy of that attribution. What is sought from Allah in that situation is only the name which that attribution specifies. (III 317.28)

In respect of what the name Allah denotes, it cannot be described, since it brings together contradictory things (*al-naqīḍayn*). Though this name becomes manifest in speech, what is meant by it is only the specific name that is sought by the context of the person's state in keeping with the reality of that which is mentioned after it and in respect of which this divine name was employed. When the person who is seeking and in need of provision says, "O Allah, provide for me!"—while Allah in addition [to being All-provider] is also Withholder (*al-mānīʿ*)—then through his state this person is seeking only the name All-provider. The meaning of what he has said is nothing but, "O All-provider, provide for me!"

In consequence, he who wants a response from Allah in affairs should ask from Him only in terms of the name specific to that thing. He should not ask Him through a name that contains what he wants as well as something else. He should not ask by a name in respect of its denotation of the Essence of the Named, but only in respect of the meaning which the name carries, in respect to which it was revealed and is distinguished from the other names—a distinction through meaning, not only verbal. (II 462.7)

According to the Verifiers, it is impossible to have [the spiritual state of] intimacy (*uns*) with Allah. One can only have intimacy with a specific and designated divine name, not with the name Allah. In the same way, nothing that comes from Allah to His servants can come through the property of the name Allah alone, since Allah is the name that brings together the realities of all the divine names. Hence, nothing happens to a designated individual in engendered existence except through a designated name. Or rather, no entity[16] becomes manifest in all engendered existence—I mean in everything other than Allah—except from a designated, specific name that cannot be the name Allah.

The reason for this is that one of the properties of the name Allah is independence from the worlds, just as one of its properties is the manifestation of the cosmos and His love for that manifestation.[17] He who is Independent of the worlds does not rejoice (*faraḥ*) because of the cosmos, but Allah rejoices through the repentance of His servant.[18] So the Level of the name Allah is known, but it is impossible for its property to become manifest within the cosmos, because of the contrariety (*taqābul*) it contains. (II 541.5)

The Disputes of the Angels

The name Allah is the "totality of the contrary names" (*majmūʿ al-asmāʾ al-mutaqābila*, II 157.21), since it brings together the Forgiver and the Avenger, the Abaser and the Exalter, the Life-giver and the Slayer, and so on. Ibn al-ʿArabī often quotes the words of Abū Saʿīd al-Kharrāz, who was asked, "Through what do you know Allah?" He answered, "Through the fact that He brings opposites together (*jamʿuhu al-ḍiddayn*)"; then he recited the Koranic verse, "He is the First and the Last, the Manifest and the Nonmanifest" (57:3).[19] This is the root of the "Divine Conflict" which was discussed above, not to mention all strife and struggle that become manifest in the cosmos.

> The root of all things is difference (*tafriqa*), which first becomes manifest in the divine names. The properties of the names are different because their meanings are different. (II 518.12)
>
> The [friend of God who is the] owner of divine courtesy (*al-adab al-ilāhī*)[20] never conflicts with anyone. He only translates (*tarjumān*) for the conflicters. Those from whom he translates are the divine names, from which conflict (*nizāʿ*) arises in the cosmos. Because of them the Scale of the Law (*al-mīzān al-sharʿī*) was established in this world and the Fundamental Scale in the next world.[21] For Exalter and Abaser are disputants (*khaṣm*), as are Harmer and Benefiter, Life-giver and Slayer, and Bestower and Withholder. Facing every name stands one of the other names which is its contrary in property. The Scale established among the names is the name Arbitrator (*al-ḥakam*); this Scale decrees justly. Arbitrator looks upon the preparedness of the locus (*istiʿdād al-maḥall*) and judges it according to its preparedness by placing it in the party of one of the two contrary and conflicting names. (III 98.19)

In tracing conflict and dispute in the cosmos back to its roots in God, Ibn al-ʿArabī frequently comments on the Koranic verse, "Say: '. . . I had no knowledge of the higher plenum when they disputed'" (38:69). The higher plenum (*al-malaʾ al-aʿlā*) are the angels, the spiritual beings which populate the higher world. The Shaykh occasionally contrasts them with the "lower plenum" (*al-malaʾ al-adnā* or *al-asfal*), the creatures of the corporeal world.[22] At first sight it is not obvious why angels should dispute (*ikhtiṣām*, cf. Koran 3:44), especially since, in the words of the Koran, the angels "disobey God not in what He commands them" (66:6). They should have no reason to quarrel unless God in His infinite wisdom wants them to do so. The Koran passes over the reason for the angelic dispute without explanation. The hadith literature makes a number of references to it, and the most famous of these sayings makes it clear that the reason for their disputing is not at all obvious. The Prophet said,

> My Lord—Inaccessible and Majestic is He—came to me at night in the most beautiful form. He said: "O Muḥammad!" I said, "Here I am, my Lord, at Thy service." He said, "What is the higher plenum disputing about?" I said, "I know not, my Lord." He said that two or three times. Then He placed His palm between my shoulders. I felt its coolness between my breasts, and everything in the heavens and the earth was disclosed to me. . . . Then He said, "O Muḥammad! What is the higher plenum disputing about?" I said, "About expiations (*kaffārāt*)." He said, "And what are expiations?" I said: "Going on foot to congregations (*jamāʿāt*), sitting in the mosque after the prayers, and performing the ablutions fully in difficult circumstances. He who does that lives in good and dies in good. His offenses are like the day his mother bore him." . . .[23]

In discussing the angels' dispute, the Shaykh points out that its only root can be the diversity of the divine names.

> We know that the members of the higher plenum dispute. Hence they enter into His words, "They never cease in their oppositions, except those upon whom thy Lord has mercy" (Koran 11:118). The higher plenum oppose those objects of mercy who are their opponents. And that is why He created them, that is, for opposition (*khilāf*), since the divine names are ranked in degrees. From here opposition originates. What does Harmer have in common with Benefiter, Exalter with Abaser, Contractor with Expander? What does heat have in common with cold and wetness with dryness?[24] What does light have in common with darkness and existence with nonexistence? What does fire have in common with water, yellow bile with phlegm, movement with rest, servanthood with Lordship? Are not all of these contraries? So "they never cease in their oppositions." (II 335.12)
>
> That which is the product (*muwallad*) of mutually averse opposites (*aḍdād mutanāfira*) cannot avoid conflict (*munāzaʿa*) within itself, especially that which is the product of the four elements. For such a thing is the product of a product of a product: elements [are produced] from the spheres, [the spheres] from the constellations, [the constellations] from Nature,[25] [Nature] from the [Universal] Soul.[26] The root is the contrary divine names, from which contrariety permeates the cosmos.
>
> But we are in the last degrees. Hence there is less opposition (*khilāf*) in everything lying above [our level, which is] the level of things produced from the elements, even though opposition never ceases. Do you not see how the higher plenum were disputing? And the Messenger of God had no knowledge of them when they were disputing until God taught him that. The reason for their dispute is that the root of their configuration (*nash'a*) gives it to them. In respect of the reality upon which they were created they said [when God told them He was going to place Adam in the earth], "What, wilt Thou place therein one who will do corruption therein, and shed blood?" (Koran 2:30). This is a hidden conflict with the Lordship from behind the veil of jealousy and reverence. The root of conflict and mutual aversion is the divine names we mentioned: Life-giver and Slayer, Exalter and Abaser, Harmer and Benefiter. (II 251.29)

Incomparability and Similarity

The discussion of the divine names has been moving back and forth between the Essence and the cosmos, since the names are the *barzakh* between the two. In one respect no name can truly denote the Essence, since in Himself God is infinitely beyond all things. "None knows God but God." In another respect every divine name—and even every name of an engendered thing—denotes God, since He is the only true Reality, the Source of all existence and attributes.

The Shaykh al-Akbar constantly alternates between these two points of view. He maintains that true knowledge of God and creation can only come through combining the two perspectives. He commonly refers to them as (the declaration of God's) incomparability (*tanzīh*) and (the declaration of His) similarity (*tashbīh*). *Tanzīh* derives from the root *n.z.h.*, which means to be far away from, to be untouched by, to be free from. Hence *tanzīh* means to declare or to affirm that something is far away or free from something else. In other words, *tanzīh* is to declare that God transcends any attribute or quality possessed by His creatures. *Tashbīh* derives from the root *sh.b.h.*, which means to be similar or comparable. It signifies declaring or affirming that something is similar to something else; to compare, to liken. Hence *tashbīh* is to maintain that a certain similarity can be found between God and creation.

Ibn al-ʿArabī borrowed the two terms from Kalām, where there was a long history of dispute concerning them; as Wolfson has pointed out, the two perspectives must even be considered a basic pre-Kalām problem.[27] For the most part the dominant theologians criticized similarity as a heretical position, often citing as their opponents various obscure thinkers who claimed, for example, that God had a corporeal body. The theologians were well aware that the Koran and Hadith are full of references to God's hands, eyes, feet, laughter, and so on, but they held that these terms have to be understood as in no way similar to what is designated by the same terms when applied to human beings. Debates raged back and forth, and in the end the adopted formula held that everything the Koran said about God is true, but a person should not ask "how" (*kayf*) it is true, since that is known only to God.

For the Shaykh, incomparability and similarity derive necessarily from the Essence on the one hand and the Level of Divinity on the other. Since the Essence is unknowable and incomprehensible, nothing is comparable to It. But since the Essence in respect of being a god assumes all sorts of relationships with the creatures, those relationships—known as names and attributes—can only be grasped through our knowledge of creation. By knowing these relationships we gain real knowledge of God; this knowledge is incomplete and partial, but it is efficacious on its own level for the purposes in which it must be employed (e.g., worship). The names themselves are inconceivable without the creatures and are shared by the creatures in some manner, even if, as the Shaykh sometimes says, that manner is only a matter of a single word shared by two different things essentially different in attribute. But when he does say this, as in the following passage addressed to those schooled in the intricacies of Kalām-type argumentation, he is speaking about the distinction between the name in itself, identical to the Essence, and the specific characteristic of the name which gains a real connection to the created things.

> It is impossible for the Essence of the Real to come together (*ijtimāʿ*) with the possible thing in any attribute, since the existence of every attribute by which the possible thing is qualified disappears with the disappearance of that to which it is attributed, or the attribute disappears while the possible thing subsists . . . But the Necessary Being through Itself cannot accept that which may possibly be or not be. Since It cannot be qualified by that thing in respect of the reality of the description, there only remains a sharing of terminology (*ishtirāk fiʾl-lafẓ*). Since sharing of definition (*ḥadd*) and reality has been rejected, no single definition whatsoever combines the attribute of the Real and the attribute of the servant. . . .
>
> Hence, when we say "God is Know-

> ing" we do not mean it according to the definition and reality of the knowledge that we attribute to the temporally originated possible thing. For the attribution of knowledge to God differs from its attribution to the creature. If eternal knowledge were identical with temporally originated knowledge, a single, essential definition would bring together the two definitions. Then what was impossible for one would be impossible for the other. But we have found the situation different from this. (I 271.20)

In respect of His names, God has a certain similarity with creatures, but in respect of His Essence, He cannot be compared with them. That is why it was said earlier that God has two basic kinds of names: those which declare Him incomparable and those which declare Him similar, or names of incomparability and names of acts.[28] The first type of names negate from His Essence any similarity with the things of the cosmos. The second affirm that every reality in the cosmos has its roots in the Divine Level.

The theme of incomparability and similarity runs throughout Ibn al-ʿArabī's works. God is the coincidence of all contrary attributes. In knowing God, we must be able to put opposites together. As the Shaykh sees it, most schools of thought had failed to make this combination. More specifically, the rational thinkers, by whom he means both the proponents of Kalām—Ashʿarites and Muʿtazilites—and the philosophers (*falāsifa*) such as Avicenna, overemphasized incomparability. By ignoring imagination, which alone is able to perceive the true meaning of the Koranic depictions of similarity, they fell into a lopsided view of reality.

The rational faculty or reason (*ʿaql*), which is the specific tool by which Kalām and philosophy seek to know the nature of things, wants to negate anything from God which does not appear appropriate to its own definition of Divinity, e.g., hands, feet, and eyes. Hence, the rational thinkers "interpret" or "explain away" (*ta'wīl*) these terms wherever they find them in the revealed texts. But by explaining away such terms, these thinkers usually miss the point. In the Shaykh's view, reason places so much emphasis upon incomparability that it excludes similarity, while the Koran and Hadith have presented us with both incomparability and similarity. It is impossible to understand the full message of the scriptures by accepting only one-half of it. The rational faculty can grasp God's Unity and transcendence, while imagination is needed to perceive the multiplicity of His self-disclosures and His immanence.

To accept the full message of scripture does not imply that one believes simple-mindedly that God has hands and feet in exactly the same way that human beings have hands and feet. So difficult in fact is it to combine the points of view of reason and imagination that this task can only be achieved through God's own inspiration. "Be godfearing," the Shaykh continually reminds us, "and God will teach you" (Koran 2:282). Through "godfearingness" (*taqwā*), an important technical term in the Shaykh's vocabulary, the servant can attain to the station of direct "tasting" (*dhawq*) or the "unveiling" (*kashf*) of the realities of things. This is the true knowledge that will allow him to combine similarity and incomparability, or imagination and reason, without falling into the dangerous pitfalls of overemphasizing either side. This whole problem is central to Ibn al-ʿArabī's approach and will come more to the forefront as we move forward. For the present a few representative passages concerning incomparability and similarity need to be quoted. Detailed discussions of the relationships that exist among revelation, reason, imagination, and unveiling must be left for later chapters.

Incomparability

> *Tanzīh* is to describe the Real as having no connection with the attributes of temporally originated things. (II 672.19)

He who knows God through his considerative faculty (*naẓar*) looks upon Him as far removed (*munʿazil*) from himself through a distance that demands the declaration of incomparability. So he places himself on one side and the Real on the other, calling to Him from a "far place."[29] (III 410.18)

Some rational faculties are meddlesome (*fuḍūl*) because of the faculties which are their tools [e.g., reflection and consideration]. . . . This meddlesome nature leads them to rational consideration of the Essence of God, though the Law has prohibited reflection upon God's Essence. Such a rational faculty slips into considering the Essence, thereby transgressing and wronging itself. It sets up what it supposes are proofs . . . that the Essence of God cannot be such and such, nor can It be in such a manner. Reason negates from the Essence everything that is attributed to temporally originated things so that It will be distinct from them. Thereby it constricts the Essence and considers It delimited.[30] (II 389.1)

Ibn al-ʿArabī identifies the declaration of incomparability with the Koranic concept of *tasbīḥ* or "glorification," since the formula "Glory be to God" as employed in the Koran involves a negation of some posited or limited attribute from God. For example, the Koran says, "Glory be to God above what they describe!" (23:91, 37:159); or, "They say, 'He has taken a son,' Glory be to Him! He is the Independent" (10:68). Moreover, the Koran repeats in several verses (57:1, 59:1, 62:1, etc.) that everything in the heavens and the earth glorifies God, which is to say—in the Shaykh's interpretation—that everything declares that He is incomparable with itself.

Glorification is to declare the incomparability of the "Lord of inaccessibility above what they describe" (Koran 37:180). "Inaccessibility"[31] requires that true knowledge of Him cannot be attained. (II 580.14)

Glorification is a declaration of incomparability. It is not a laudation (*thanā'*) through a positive quality (*amr thubūtī*). He cannot be lauded except through what is worthy of Him. But that which belongs to Him is not shared in common (*mushāraka*) with anything. He can only be lauded through His names, but every one of His names known to us is assumed by the servant as his own trait (*takhalluq*), and by it he becomes qualified to the measure that is appropriate for him. [Hence there is no name worthy of God's unique Essence.]

Since it is not possible for Him to be lauded within the cosmos as is worthy, He made the glorification of Him by all things into His laudation. That is why He attributes "praise" (*ḥamd*) to the glorification, saying, "glorifies by praising Him" (Koran 13:13, 17:44), i.e., by the laudation of which He is worthy, and that is only glorification. For God says, "Glory be to thy Lord, the Lord of inaccessibility, above what they describe" (37:180). (III 148.19)

God preserves the cosmos in order that laudation of Him will continue upon the tongue of the temporally originated things through their declaring Him incomparable with the poverty that belongs to them. He does not preserve the cosmos out of concern (*al-ihtimām*) for it, nor out of solicitude (*al-ʿināya*), only so that it will be His locus of self-disclosure (*majlā*), within which the properties of His names may become manifest. (III 120.19)

When someone declares God's incomparability, his declaration is measured according to his own level, since he does not declare His Creator's incomparability except in respect of himself, since he knows only himself.[32] (III 92.3)

Declaring incomparability is diverse according to the diversity of the worlds and the fact that every knower declares the Real incomparable in the measure of his knowledge of himself. He declares Him incomparable with everything that belongs to himself, since everything that belongs to himself is temporally originated. Hence he declares the Real incomparable . . . in respect to those temporally originated qualities pertaining to himself. That is why declaring the Real's incomparability is diverse in accordance with the diversity of the declarers. For example, an accident (*ʿaraḍ*) says, "Glory be to Him who is not poor in His Being toward a locus in which to become manifest!" A substance (*jawhar*) says, "Glory be to Him who is not poor in His Being toward a bestower of existence!" A corporeal body (*jism*) says, "Glory be to Him who is not poor in His Being toward instruments (*adāh*)!" Thus, declaring incomparability has been classified according to its major categories (*ummahāt*), since there is nothing that is not either substance, body, or accident. Then each kind of creature pertains specifically to certain things that other kinds do not possess, so it glorifies God in respect of those attributes in its own station. But perfect man glorifies God through all the glorifications in the cosmos. (III 77.19)

Similarity

The sincere lover is he who passes into the attributes of the beloved, not he who brings the beloved down to his own attributes. Do you not see that the Real, when He loved us, descended to us in His hidden gentlenesses by means of that which corresponds (*munāsaba*) to us and above which His eminence and greatness are high exalted? He descended to (1) receiving us joyfully when we come to His house in order to confide in Him; (2) rejoicing at our repentance and our return to Him after our turning away from Him; (3) wonder at the young man who lacks sensual desire while he should be controlled by it, even though he has that through God's giving him success; (4) being our deputies in our hunger, thirst, and illness, and placing Himself in our way-stations. When one of His servants is hungry, He says to the others, "I was hungry, but you did not feed Me." He says to another of His servants, "I was ill but you did not visit Me." When the servants ask Him about this, He replies to them, "Verily so-and-so was ill; if you had visited him, you would have found Me with him. So-and-so was hungry; if you had fed him, you would have found Me with him. . . . " This is one of the fruits of love, when He descends to us.[33] (II 596.6)

Nowadays our companions[34] suffer extreme pain at not being able to speak without restraint about God as is appropriate and as the prophets spoke without restraint. . . . What prevents them from ascribing to God that which is ascribed to Him by the revealed books and the messengers is the lack of justice on the part of the jurists (*fuqahā'*) and the possessors of [worldly] authority (*ulu'l-amr*) who listen to them. Such people hurry to declare anyone who says about God the like of what the prophets said an "unbeliever." They have abandoned God's words, "You have a good example in the Messenger of God" (Koran 33:21). God also said to the Prophet when He mentioned the prophets and messengers, "Those are they whom God has guided, so follow their guidance" (6:90).

But the jurists have locked this door because of claimers who lie in their claims. And they have done well! The truthful servants suffer no harm because of this, since speaking and expressing such things is not indispensable. In those things of this sort which have come from the Messenger of God there is sufficiency for them, so they mention them and are happy with them, that is, such things as wonder, rejoicing, laughter, receiving joyfully, descent, withness, love, and yearning.[35] But were a friend of God to express these and similar matters on his own, he would be declared an unbeliever, and perhaps killed.

Most of the exoteric scholars (*'ulamā' al-rusūm*) lack the knowledge of this through tasting and drinking.[36] So they deny such things in the gnostics, out of envy on their part. If it were impossible to ascribe such things to God, He would not have ascribed them to Himself, nor would His messengers have ascribed them. But the envy of these people prevents them from seeing that they are rejecting the Book of God and forbidding God's mercy from reaching some of His servants. Most of the common people (*al-'āmma*) follow the jurists in this denial, in imitation of them. No! On the contrary —praise belongs to God!—the lesser part of the common people.

As for kings, for the most part they have not reached the witnessing of these realities because of their occupation with what has been turned over to them. So they support the exoteric scholars in their position, except for a few of them who have suspected the exoteric scholars in that, since these kings have seen that these authorities are dedicated to the chaff of this world—though they have no need for it—and to the love of position and leadership and to accommodating the desires of kings in that which is not permitted [by the Law].[37] So the knowers of God remain in the lowliness of incapacity and constraint, like a messenger to whom his people cry lies and in whom not one of them believes. (I 272.17)

I am amazed at . . . the Ashʿarites, in their mistakes concerning shared terminology (*lafẓ mushtarak*). How can they call this a declaration of similarity, since declaring similarity between two things only takes place through the word "like" (*mithl, ka*) in language? But this is hard to find in any Koranic verse or hadith which they have made into a declaration of similarity.

The Ashʿarites imagined that by interpreting (*ta'wīl*) they would be able to leave aside the declaration of similarity, but they did not depart from it. They only passed from declaring similarity with corporeal things (*ajsām*) to declaring similarity with temporally originated meanings (*al-maʿānī al-muḥdatha*), which are different from the eternal attributes both in reality and definition. Hence they never passed beyond declaring God similar with temporally originated things.

For example, if we were to maintain their position, we would not swerve from the "sitting upon" (*istiwā'*), which means "to take up residence" (*istiqrār*), to the "sitting upon" which means "to make oneself master of" (*istīlā'*),[38] as they swerved [in their interpretation of the Koranic verse, "The All-merciful sat upon the Throne" (20:5)]. This is especially so since "Throne" is mentioned in relation to sitting. The meaning of "making oneself master of" is nullified by the reference to the seat, and it is impossible to turn it into another meaning different from taking up residence.

I would say, for example: Declaration of similarity takes place through "sitting," and sitting is a meaning, but not through that upon which one sits, which is a corporeal body. Sitting is an intelligible, supra-sensory (*maʿnawī*) reality which can be attributed to every essence in accordance with what the reality of that essence provides. There is no need to burden oneself (*takalluf*) by turning "sitting" away from its apparent meaning. (I 43.32)

God is the Light about which is said, "Nothing is like Him" (Koran 42:11). Hence He does not accept similarity, for He has no attributes (*ṣifa*). Everyone who has attributes accepts similarity, since attributes undergo variation (*tanawwuʿ*) in their receptacles in accordance with what is given by the reality of that which is described by them. For example, the Real is qualified by knowledge, hearing, sight, power, desire, speech, and other attributes, while the creature is also qualified by them. But it is obvious that their attribution to the creature is not commensurate with their attribution to the Creator. What is more, their attribution to a human being differs from their attribution to an angel, yet both of these are created things. (II 499.7)

There are attributes by which the Real described Himself and which the exoteric scholars suppose are called hadiths of similarity or Koranic verses of similarity; [they also suppose that they are] a divine descent out of mercy to the servants, a divine gentleness. In our view these are true descriptions which, in the case of the servant, are metaphorical (*mustaʿār*), just like the other names which the servant assumes as his traits (*takhalluq*). For He is the Best of the Deceivers (*khayr al-mākirīn*, Koran 3:54, 8:30) and God mocks the mockers among His servants (Koran 2:15) with a mocking and a deception that belong to Him from whence they know not, while He does not describe Himself by temporally originated things. So this shows that these descriptions belong at root to God; they do not become manifest in the divine servant except inasmuch as he is created in God's form in all respects.[39]

The gnostics knew all of this. They also saw His words, "To Him all affairs shall be returned" (11:123). They understood that these descriptions which are manifest in the engendered things and which the exoteric scholars believe belong truly to the servant are among the affairs that are returned to God. Hence they abandoned them all to God. (II 224.3)

Combining Incomparability and Similarity

As we shall see repeatedly, the Shaykh often quotes the verse, "Nothing is like

Him, and He is the Seeing, the Hearing" (42:11), as a Koranic proof that God combines attributes of incomparability and similarity.

The rational faculty has come with one-half the knowledge of God, that is, the declaration of incomparability and the negation of multiple properties from Him. But the Lawgiver brought news of God by affirming what the rational faculty's proofs (*dalāla*) have negated from Him and establishing what the rational faculty has stripped from Him. The Lawgiver brought both things because of the perfection appropriate to God, while rational faculties remained bewildered. This is the Perfection of Divinity. . . .

The sensory and imaginative faculties demand by their essences to see Him who brought them into existence, while rational faculties demand by their essences and their proofs—such as negation, affirmation, necessity, permissibility, and impossibility—to know Him who brought them into existence.

Hence God addressed the senses and imagination with the disengagement (*tajrīd*) established by the proofs provided by rational faculties. The senses listen to God's address, and they and imagination become bewildered. They say, "We have nothing of that in our hands."

Then God addressed the rational faculties with the declaration of similarity established by the senses and imagination. The rational faculties listen and become bewildered. They say, "We have nothing of that in our hands." So God is high above the perception of rational faculties, the senses, and imagination. (II 307.19)

Sound rational faculties which recognize God's majesty are bewildered. But the people of interpretation (*ahl al-ta'wīl*) are not bewildered, nor do they hit their target, that is, by plunging into interpretation. Even if they should conform to the doctrine (*al-ʿilm*), they have committed a forbidden act about which they will be questioned on the Day of Resurrection—they and everyone who speaks about His Essence, declares Him incomparable with what He has attributed to Himself, and prefers his own rational faculty to his faith and the judgment of his own consideration to the doctrine concerning his Lord. (II 407.3)

God knew that He had deposited within the rational faculty acceptance toward that which is given both by the Real (*al-ḥaqq*) and by the reflective faculty (*al-quwwat al-mufakkira*). He well knew that He had placed in the reflective faculty free disposal within and domination over the existent things. . . . He knew that the reflective faculty had to dominate over the rational faculty by reflection upon the Essence of Him who gave it existence, i.e., God. Therefore He had pity on the rational faculty in this respect, since He knew that it would fall short of achieving what it was trying to do. Hence He addressed it through the Koran: "God warns you about His Self, and God is Clement to the servants" (3:30). He says: We have only cautioned you against rationally considering the Essence of God out of mercy and pity toward you; We know that the reflective faculty tells the rational faculty to negate the attributes We have affirmed through the tongues of Our messengers. So people reject these attributes with their proofs, are deprived of faith, and suffer everlasting wretchedness (*shaqāwa*).

Then God commanded the Messenger of God to prohibit us from reflecting upon God's Essence, as was done by some of God's servants. But the People of Consideration began to speak (*mutakallim*) about God's Essence, and their doctrines became diverse. Each of them spoke about what his own consideration required. One of them would deny exactly what the other affirmed. They did not agree on a single thing concerning God in respect of their consideration of His Essence, and they disobeyed God and His Messenger by speaking about it, since God had prohibited them from doing that out of mercy toward them. They shrank from God's mercy, "So their striving goes astray in the present life, while they think they are working good deeds" (Koran 18:104).

Some of them said, "He is a cause." Others said, "He is not a cause." Others said, "The Essence of the Real cannot be a substance, an accident, or a corporeal body; on the contrary, His Being (*inniyya*) is identical with His quiddity (*māhiyya*) and does not fit into any of the ten categories." They went on and on in this manner and became like the proverb says: "I hear the grinding, but I don't see any flour."

When the Law came, it contradicted everything proven by rational faculties. It mentioned [God's] coming, descent, sitting, rejoicing, laughter, hand, foot, and every attribute of temporally originated things that has been transmitted in the sound traditions. Then it brought "There is nothing like Him" (42:11), even though these attributes have been affirmed. If they were impossible, as the rational faculty indicates, He would not have ascribed them to Himself and the true report would be a lie. But God "sent no messenger save with the tongue of his people, that he might make clear to them" (Koran 14:4) what He sent down to them and that they might understand. The Prophet made clear, delivered the message, and called God to witness before his community that he had delivered the message.[40]

So through "Nothing is like Him" we are ignorant of the exact nature of the attribution. We understand what is intelligible from the revealed words and that what is intelligible is single, in respect of that for which the words have been coined. But the attributions are diverse in accordance with the diversity of the objects to which attribution is made, though their realities are not diverse, since realities do not change. Hence he who stops at these words and their meanings and maintains that he does not have the knowledge of the attribution to the Real is a man of knowledge and faith (*ʿālim mu'min*). But he who attributes them in a specific sense of application outside of corporealization (*tajsīm*) is neither a man of faith nor a man of knowledge.[41]

If this person who rationally considers the Essence of God were just, he would not consider God's Essence and would have faith in what has come from God, since proofs have shown him that the report-giver—the Messenger—has spoken the truth. This is what has held me back in this chapter from speaking about God's Essence in accordance with what the proofs of the rational faculty offer. Instead we turned for knowledge of these things to what has come from the transmitted sources. At the same time, we negate likeness in the attribution and [refuse to claim] correct knowledge of the reality of the revealed attribute by which the Unknown Essence has been described.

Thus have I counselled you. Understand what I have said! Remain steady in what the Shariʿa has brought for you and you will be safe. For He knows Himself best and He is most truthful in words. He has only taught us in keeping with how He is. "There is no god but He, the Inaccessible, the Wise" (Koran 3:6). "Glory be to thy Lord, the Lord of inaccessibility, above what they describe. Peace be upon the envoys, and praise belongs to God, Lord of the worlds" (37:180). (II 319.15)

The Real described Himself by things with which rational proofs declare Him incomparable. Hence these things can only be accepted by way of faith and submission, or, for him who adds it, by interpretation (*ta'wīl*) in the mode appropriate for rational consideration. The People of Unveiling, who possess the divine faculty that is beyond the stage of reason (*ṭawr al-ʿaql*), recognize this, just as the common people understand. They know why God accepts this description, even though He is incomparable through "Nothing is like Him." But this lies outside of what can be perceived by the rational faculty through its own reflections. So the common people stand in the station of declaring similarity, the People of Unveiling declare both similarity and incomparability, and the rational thinkers declare incomparability alone. Hence, God combined the two sides in His elect. (II 116.4)

The philosophers speak of becoming similar (*tashabbuh*) to God to the extent effort allows.[42] But when you verify this statement, you will see that it displays ignorance on the part of him who said it, since in fact there cannot be any "becoming similar." If an attribute subsists in someone, then it belongs to him and he has the preparedness (*istiʿdād*) for it to subsist in him. Hence the preparedness of his own essence required it. So no one is similar to anyone; rather, the attribute is found in both, just as it is found in others. What has veiled people here is priority and posteriority and the fact that the form is one. When they saw the attribute in the earlier thing, then they saw it in the later thing, they said that the later thing is similar to the earlier thing in this form. They did not know that its reality in the later thing is its reality in the earlier thing. If it were as they say, servanthood would jostle against Lordship and the realities would be nullified. Hence the servant only becomes adorned with what he himself possesses. And the Real only becomes manifest in what He possesses, whether attributes of incomparability or attributes of similarity. All of this belongs to Him. Were this not so, everything He has described Himself as possessing would be a lie. But God is high exalted [above lying]! Rather, He is as He described Himself, in terms of inaccessibility, greatness, invincibility, tremendousness, and the negation of likeness; just as He described Himself by forgetting, deception, trickery, guile, rejoicing, withness, and so on.[43] All are attributes of God's perfection. He is described by them as His Essence requires, and you are described by them as your essence requires.

The entity is one,
  the properties diverse:
The servant serves,
  the All-merciful is served. (II 483.27)

God brought the cosmos into existence only so that the cosmos might come to know Him.[44] But the cosmos is temporally originated, so nothing subsists within it that is not temporally originated. Knowledge of God subsists within the cosmos either through God's giving knowledge (*taʿrīf*), or through the faculty [i.e., reflection] which He created within it through which knowledge of God is reached, though only in a certain respect. He who declares God incomparable by means of this faculty has come to know Him and calls him who declares Him similar an unbeliever. He who declares Him similar by means of this faculty has come to know Him and is ignorant of him who declares Him incomparable, or rather, calls him an unbeliever. But he who comes to know Him through the divine knowledge-giving has combined incomparability and similarity. He declares Him incomparable in the place of incomparability, and He declares Him similar in the place of similarity. Each of these three groups possesses a knowledge of God, since not one of God's creatures is ignorant of Him, for He created them only to know Him. If He did not make Himself known to them through this faculty by which knowledge is reached—that is, reflection—or through revelatory giving of knowledge, they would not know Him and there would not occur in the cosmos that for which God created the cosmos. (III 132.9)

3

Ontology

5. EXISTENCE AND NONEXISTENCE

Ibn al-ʿArabī is known as the founder of the school of the Oneness of Being (*waḥdat al-wujūd*). Though he does not employ the term, the idea permeates his works. Simply stated, there is only one Being, and all existence is nothing but the manifestation or outward radiance of that One Being. Hence "everything other than the One Being"—that is, the whole cosmos in all its spatial and temporal extension—is nonexistent in itself, though it may be considered to exist through Being.

Stated in these terms, the "Oneness of Being" may appear to some people as another brand of "pantheism." But in fact, this simplified expression of what the Shaykh is talking about cannot begin to do him justice, especially since terms like "pantheism" are almost invariably employed with a dismissive and critical intent. When the Shaykh himself explains what he means by the statement that Being is one, he provides one of the most sophisticated and nuanced expressions of the "profession of God's Unity" (*tawḥīd*) to be found in Islamic thought.[1] His teachings did not dominate the second half of Islamic intellectual history because people were simple-minded and therefore ready to accept "pantheism" in place of *tawḥīd*—quite the contrary. What Ibn al-ʿArabī provides is an inexhaustible ocean of meditations upon the Unity of God and its relationship with the manyness of all things, a synthesis of the various currents of Islamic intellectuality that yielded endless insights into the nature of existence.

God in Himself is Being, and nonexistence has no relationship to Him. That which sets "everything other than God" apart from God is the admixture of nonexistence. Things, entities, possible things, loci of manifestation, forms, attributes—these are all names applied to that which is other than Being, to nonexistence. But "nonexistence" does not mean absolute nothingness, since the things—whether as objects of God's knowledge "before" they are found in the cosmos or as existent entities within the cosmos itself—possess certain modes of relative existence, that is, existence through the Other, who is God, the Necessary Being. In God's knowledge the things exist neither in the cosmos nor in themselves. But they do exist in God in a manner analogous to the way our thoughts exist in our minds. In the cosmos the things have no existence of their own, but they leave their marks and effects upon the Manifest, who is Being. What we actually observe in the universe is either Being colored by the properties of the nonexistent things, or the things made manifest by Being. But we never see the things themselves, since that which is nonexistent is not there to be seen; nor do we see God Himself, since God in Himself is beyond all perception and understanding. The cosmos is He/ not He. In the last analysis we see only the properties of the divine names, which are the qualities and attributes intrinsic to Being.

Being/Existence and the Existent: Wujūd *and* Mawjūd

The discussion of the Oneness of Being centers around a single word, *wujūd*, which has been translated thus far as Being, existence, and finding. In the present context, two of these translations will be employed, though sometimes it will be necessary to resort to the expression "Being/existence" to emphasize the fact that both meanings need to be understood from a given passage.

By "Being" is meant *wujūd* inasmuch as it designates God's own Reality and Essence. By "existence" is meant *wujūd* inasmuch as it designates the fact that certain things are found in the cosmos. When "existence" is discussed, it is contrasted with a thing or entity that exists. Hence one speaks of the existence of the cosmos or of a tree. But the term "Being" refers strictly to God in Himself and cannot be juxtaposed with any entity other than Being, since God's "thingness" or entity is Being Itself.

Muslim philosophers, like many thinkers in the Western tradition, distinguish between the thing itself—or its "essence" or "quiddity" (*māhiyya*)—and the existence of the thing. We can ask about anything in the universe, whether or not the thing is here to be discussed and whether or not it exists. Dragons and phoenixes are things to be discussed, even though none of us has seen one. According to this view, the existence of anything we discuss may be discerned and separated—at least by the mind—from the quiddity of the thing, except in the case of God. Or if you prefer, you can say that God's "existence" is identical to His quiddity, which is to say that He is Being. We can distinguish between a man and his existence; but we cannot distinguish between God and His Being, since He is Being as such.

The word "quiddity" derives from a literal Latin translation of the Arabic word *māhiyya*, which was coined from the sentence *mā hiya*, i.e., "What is it?" If this question is asked about any *thing*, the answer will be, it is a horse, a house, a galaxy, and so on. We can then discuss that thing without regard to whether or not it exists. But when we ask, "What is it?" about God, the only answer sufficiently broad to include God's whole reality is to say "*wujūd*" (which, for the Shaykh, is a philosophical term equivalent to the name "Allah"). God's quiddity is Being itself, and we cannot discuss His quiddity without regard to Being, since then we would be discussing something else.

Ibn al-ʿArabī took over most of the vocabulary connected to the discussion of *wujūd* from the Muslim philosophers. The term *wujūd* is not mentioned in the Koran, and the identification between it and God or the Necessary Being (*wājib al-wujūd*) seems to have been made originally in philosophical texts, not in the sources of the tradition or by the theologians and Sufis. Hence an understanding of the philosophical background of this terminology can help toward the perception of Ibn al-ʿArabī's role in synthesizing the schools of Islamic thought. But in the present work this allusion to the importance of the input from philosophy will have to suffice. The Shaykh, it should be remarked in passing, rarely employs the term *māhiyya*, preferring its synonyms such as entity and reality (cf. I

193.31), but he does use it in instructive contexts, such as the following:

> The Unity of the Essence in Itself has no known quiddity. Hence we cannot ascribe properties to It, since It is not similar to anything in the cosmos, nor is anything in the cosmos similar to It. Therefore no intelligent person undertakes to speak about His Essence, unless on the basis of a report received from Him. And even when we bring the report, we are ignorant of the relationship of that property to Him, since we are ignorant of Him. Hence we have faith in it just as He has uttered it and knows it, since, according to both the Law and reason, proofs can be offered only to negate similarity. (II 289.25)
>
> Since the Being of the Real permeates the cosmos, no one denies Him. Mistakes arise from seeking to know His quiddity, and this leads to the disagreements concerning Him which have become manifest in the cosmos. (III 164.31)

Both the philosophers and Ibn al-ʿArabī attempted to explain the relationship between the many and the One, the creatures and the Creator, the existent things and Being, the possible existents and the Necessary Being. In the context of the philosophical terminology, the basic issue can be phrased in the simple question: "If God is *wujūd*, are the things also *wujūd*?" The Shaykh answers that God alone is Being, and the "existence" of the things is identical to that Being, though the quiddities of the things as quiddities are not Being; in themselves the things are nonexistent. In other words, he replies to the question, "Are the things the same as God?," by saying, "Yes and no." They are "He/not He." The creatures dwell in an ambiguous middle ground or *barzakh* whose actual situation is exceedingly difficult to express in words. In trying to explain their situation, the Shaykh employs most of the terminology used by the philosophical and theological schools, while making full use of the possibilities provided by the Koran, the Hadith, and the writings and sayings of the Sufis.

Ibn al-ʿArabī employs a number of sets of terms to refer to the creatures. Some of these are commonly used in Islamic philosophy, others by the proponents of Kalām, and still others derive from the Koran and Hadith. The Shaykh makes no attempt to keep these sets of terms separate. Having adopted various technical terms as his own, he employs them as he sees fit without regard to the contexts from which they have been taken. To understand his broad and sweeping explanations of the nature of Being and existence, it is necessary to be familiar with all these ways of expressing the basic ideas. Hence, as the first step in understanding the richness of nuances involved in the concept of the Oneness of Being, it is necessary to define the most important relevant technical terms and to illustrate how they are employed.

The first term that needs to be understood in relation to *wujūd* is the past participle from the same root, *mawjūd*, which will be translated as existent or existent thing. An existent thing is an entity which exists on any level or in any world which is envisaged; occasionally the term is also employed to refer to God Himself as He who possesses true existence or Being, in which case it will normally be translated as the Existent Being. The objects that we find in the world around us are all existents in the corporeal world, while our ideas are existents within our minds. A given idea may correspond to something that exists "out there" or it may not. A thing known by God but not found in the created world is called "nonexistent" (*maʿdūm*), not in an absolute sense, since it possesses a certain mode of existence within God's knowledge, but in the sense that it has not been brought into spiritual, imaginal, or corporeal existence.

Possible Things

The philosophers referred to the Divine Reality as the Necessary Being (*wā-*

jib al-wujūd) in order to differentiate it from "possible things" (*mumkin*) and "impossible things" (*mumtaniʿ* or *muḥāl*). The Necessary Being is that reality which cannot not be. The impossible thing cannot come into existence within the cosmos (though it can exist in a certain fashion in the mind of man or God). The possible thing is that reality whose relationship to existence and nonexistence is equal.

> If the possible thing were an existent which could not be qualified by nonexistence, then it would be the Real. If it were a nonexistence which could not be qualified by existence, then it would be impossible. (III 275.5)

The possible thing may or may not exist, depending on circumstances. These "circumstances" go back to the desire of the Necessary Being, who must "give preponderance" (*tarjīḥ*) to the existence of the possible thing over its nonexistence for it to come into existence as a thing in the world. Hence the Necessary Being, having given existence to something, is known as the "Preponderator" (*murajjiḥ*).

> God gave preponderance to the existence of the possible things over their nonexistence because they sought this preponderance by their very essences. Hence, this was a kind of submission (*inqiyād*) of the Real to this seeking on the part of possibility, and also a gratuitous kindness (*imtinān*). For God is Independent of the worlds. But He described Himself by saying that He loved to be known by the possible things, since He was not known,[2] and one of the characteristics of the lover is to submit himself to his beloved. But in reality, He only submitted to Himself. The possible thing is a veil over this divine seeking. (III 217.7)

Among the terms Necessary Being, possible thing, and impossible thing, Ibn al-ʿArabī devotes by far the most attention to "possible thing," since his major philosophical task is to explain the nature of the existence that is attributed to the possible thing once the Preponderator has brought it into the cosmos. At the same time, he sees the fact of "possibility" (*imkān*) as one of the greatest rational arguments that can be offered to prove that "there is a God." In this sort of context the Shaykh ascribes the term *wujūd* to God not to designate His Reality, but to point out that He can in fact be "found." He does exist. Hence the term *wujūd* can be translated here as the "existence" of God rather than His "Being." In a section on the meaning of "travel" (*safar*), Ibn al-ʿArabī points out that the spiritual teachers have described many kinds of traveling. The first of these has to do with the mind's journey to find the signs (*āyāt*) of God and to understand that He exists.

> The "traveler" is he who travels with his reflection in search of the signs and proofs of the existence of his Maker (*ṣāniʿ*). In his traveling he finds no proof for that other than his own possibility. The meaning of his possibility is that existence is brought into relationship with him and the whole cosmos, and they receive it; or nonexistence is brought into relationship with them, and they receive it. The two things are equal for him, so in respect of his own essence the relationship of existence to him cannot be preferred over the relationship of nonexistence. So he is poor toward the existence of a Preponderator who will give preponderance to one of the two descriptions over the other.
>
> When the traveler reaches this waystation, passes by this watering place, and uncovers the existence of his Preponderator, he begins a second journey into the knowledge of that which should be known about this Maker who has brought him into existence. He uncovers the proof that He alone possesses attributes of incomparability, that is, that He is incomparable with the poverty that belongs to the possible thing. He understands that this Preponderator is the Necessary Being through Itself[3] for whom is permitted nothing that is permissible for the possible thing.
>
> Then he passes in his journey to another waystation, and he uncovers the

> fact that this Necessary Being through Itself cannot possibly become nonexistent. . . . (II 382.27)

The sum total of the possible things, whether or not they exist, is called the cosmos. If we accept that at a given moment some of the possible things have been given existence by the Preponderator while others have not, this has no ultimate effect upon their status as possible things. The possible things include "everything other than God" at all times, not just at the present moment.

> The "cosmos" consists of everything other than God. It is none other than the possible things, whether or not they exist. . . . Possibility is their necessary property in the state of their nonexistence as well as their existence. It is intrinsic (*dhātī*) to them, since preponderation (*tarjīḥ*) is necessary for them. Hence [through the possible things] the Preponderator is known, and that is why the cosmos is named "cosmos" (*ʿālam*)—from "mark" (*ʿalāma*)—since it is a proof of the Preponderator. (III 443.5)

Entities

For students of Ibn al-ʿArabī who have read about him only in English, the most familiar of terms employed for things in contrast to Being is *ʿayn*. The expression *ʿayn thābita* has been translated by scholars in a wide variety of manners (e.g., "permanent archetype"), most of which obscure the broad significance of the single term *ʿayn* in Ibn al-ʿArabī's vocabulary. In the present work *ʿayn* in this technical sense is translated as "entity." In this meaning it has no Koranic basis. The Shaykh acknowledges his debt to the Muʿtazilite theologians for the term *ʿayn thābita*, though he also states that they did not reach a full and true understanding of its significance.[4]

The Arabic word *ʿayn* has a wide variety of nontechnical meanings, some of which—such as "eye" or "identical with"—are often used in Ibn al-ʿArabī's writings. In its technical sense as "entity," the term refers to specificity, particularization, and designation. What sets one thing apart from another thing? The *ʿayn*s of the two things. In the writings of Ibn al-ʿArabī's followers, especially the chief expositor of his philosophical teachings, Ṣadr al-Dīn al-Qūnawī, this meaning is emphasized by the important role given to the term *taʿayyun*, the fifth verbal form from the same root. This term signifies "to be or to become an entity" or "the state of being specified and particularized." *Taʿayyun*'s grammatical connection with the term entity is well preserved by the translation "entification."[5] Though Ibn al-ʿArabī sometimes employs the term *taʿayyun*, it assumes no special importance in his works.

As was indicated in the discussion of "relationships" in Chapter 2, the Shaykh frequently employs the term "entities" to distinguish existent things from relationships. In this sense he speaks of the Entity of the Real (*ʿayn al-ḥaqq*), meaning God's Being or Essence. He also employs the expression "among the entities" (*fi'l-aʿyān*) to refer to the existent things of the cosmos. This meaning of the term gives rise to the expression "entified existence" (*al-wujūd al-ʿaynī*), which refers to anything that exists in itself, whether God on the one hand or the existent possible things on the other. Entified existence is contrasted with "mental existence" (*al-wujūd al-dhihnī*), i.e., the existence of a thing as a concept in the mind, whether or not it is found in the cosmos.[6]

When the Shaykh uses the term "Entity of God," he normally means the Essence of God. When he speaks of the "One Entity" (*al-ʿayn al-wāḥida*) he usually has in view Being inasmuch as all existence is but Its radiance and the things are Its properties and effects.

> God says, "God makes you grow up from the earth as growing things" (Koran 71:17). The earth is one, but how can the

form of grass be compared to that of trees, given the diversity of their kinds, or with the form of man, or with the forms of the animals? Yet all of this derives from an elemental reality (*ḥaqīqa ʿunṣuriyya*).[7] The elementality never disappears through the diversity of what becomes manifest within it. Thus the diversity of the cosmos in its entirety does not take it away from the fact that it is one entity in existence. In the same way Zayd is not ʿAmr, but the two are man (*al-insān*). So they are identical with man, nothing else. From here you will recognize who the cosmos is and the form of the actual situation (*al-amr*) within it, if you possess sound consideration (*naẓar ṣaḥīḥ*).

"And in your souls—what, do you not see?" (Koran 51:21). There is nothing but a rational soul, but it is intelligent, reflecting, imagining, remembering, form-giving, nutritive, growth-producing, attractive, expulsive, digestive, retentive, hearing, seeing, tasting, smelling, and feeling.[8] Moreover, the soul perceives all these affairs, the diversity of these faculties, and the diversity of these names. Yet it is nothing extraneous to any of them; on the contrary, it is identical with the form of each. So also will you find the situation in the forms of inanimate things, plants, animals, spheres, and angels [—all are identical with the One Entity]. So Glory be to Him who made the things manifest, while He is their entity!

My eyes have never gazed
  on other than His Face,
My ears have never heard
  other than His words! (II 459.21)

"Entities" are, on the one hand, the possible things as they exist in the cosmos, and on the other hand, the possible things nonexistent in the cosmos but existent in God's knowledge. If many translators have rendered *ʿayn* as "archetype," this is because God creates the cosmos in accordance with His eternal knowledge of it. Thereby He gives each thing known by Him—each entity "immutably fixed" (*thābit*) within His knowledge—existence in the universe. However, the term "archetype" may suggest that what is being discussed becomes the model for many individuals in the manner of a Platonic idea. In fact, what corresponds to the Platonic ideas in Ibn al-ʿArabī's teachings is the divine names, while the immutable entities are the things themselves "before" they are given existence in the world.[9] There is no difference between the entity known in God's knowledge and the entity in the cosmos except that in the first case it is "nonexistent" while in the second it is "existent." The immutable entity (*ʿayn thābita*) and the existent entity (*ʿayn mawjūda*) are the same reality, but one exists in the cosmos and the other does not. The difference between the two corresponds exactly to the difference between the possible thing before it is given existence and the same possible thing after it comes into existence. However, the attribute *thābita*, "immutable," helps remind us that the possible thing never leaves its state of possibility in the divine knowledge. Though the entity may "exist" in the cosmos, it is still immutably fixed and "nonexistent" in God's knowledge.

> The Real's knowledge of Himself is identical (*ʿayn*) with His knowledge of the cosmos, since the cosmos never ceases being witnessed by Him, even though it is qualified by nonexistence. But the cosmos is not witnessed by itself [in that state], since it does not have existence. This is an ocean in which the considerative thinkers (*al-nāẓirūn*) perish, those who have not been given unveiling. His Self never ceases to exist, so His knowledge never ceases to exist; and His knowledge of Himself is His knowledge of the cosmos; so His knowledge of the cosmos never ceases to exist. Hence He knows the cosmos in the state of its nonexistence. He gives it existence according to its form in His knowledge. (I 90.23)

Ibn al-ʿArabī takes a middle position between those philosophers who maintain that the cosmos is eternal (*qadīm*) and the theologians who maintain that it is temporally originated (*ḥādith*). As will be seen later on in this chapter, he holds that the cosmos is created from nonexistence, but that here "nonexistence" cannot mean absolute nothingness. In the following passage he affirms the existence of the cosmos in God's knowledge before it enters into creation and points out that the argument over whether the cosmos is eternal or temporally originated is based upon a difference in perspective.

> The cosmos is perceived (*mudrak*) by God in the state of its nonexistence. So it is nonexistent in entity, perceived by God. He sees it, then brings it into existence through the influence exercised upon it by the divine power. Hence the effusion (*fayḍ*) of entified existence falls only upon the objects of God's sight (*ru'ya*) in the state of their nonexistence. Some thinkers consider the fact that sight is connected to the cosmos in the state of its nonexistence, that it is a true sight in which there is no doubt, that [the object of sight] is what is called the cosmos, and that the Real is never qualified by first not seeing the cosmos, then seeing it; on the contrary, He never ceases seeing it. He who holds that the cosmos is eternal does so from this perspective. But he who considers the existence of the cosmos in relation to its own entity and the fact that it did not possess this state when the Real saw it maintains that the cosmos is temporally originated. (II 666.34)

None of this implies that anything ever "leaves" God's knowledge in order to come into the cosmos. What God knows, He knows eternally and immutably. But at a certain point, in keeping with what He knows, He gives preponderance to the existence of the entity over its nonexistence, and the entity is then found in the cosmos, without ever coming out of His knowledge. In one passage Ibn al-ʿArabī makes this last point in discussing the difference between the finitude of that which enters into existence and the infinity of that which remains immutable in God's knowledge. The passage makes clear that "immutability" (*thubūt*) is a mode of existence with God possessed by the entities over and above any existence they may have in the cosmos. Ibn al-ʿArabī is commenting on a *ḥadīth qudsī* which reads, "O My servants, if the first of you and the last of you and the mankind of you and the jinn of you were to stand in one place, then to ask of Me, and I were to give to each of you everything he asked, that would not diminish My kingdom by anything, any more than a needle dipped into the sea would diminish the sea."[10]

> This is because the giver and the receiver of the gift are nothing other than His kingdom, since there is nothing outside of His kingdom. However, in His kingdom there is that which is described by existence and that which is described by immutability. That which is both immutable and existent must be finite, but the immutable is infinite. That which is infinite cannot be qualified by diminishment, since that of it which gains actuality in existence is not diminished from immutability. The reason for this is that the thing in its immutability is identical to the thing in the state of its existence, except that God has clothed it in the robe of existence through Himself. So the existence belongs to God, the Real, while the thing remains in its immutability, neither diminishing nor increasing. That of it which becomes clothed in the robe of existence undergoes, as it were, entification (*taʿayyun*) and specification (*takhaṣṣuṣ*). Its limits in relation to the infinite are the limits of the needle which you dip into the sea. Look at how much [of the sea] becomes connected to it!
>
> We know that this analogy (*mithāl*) is correct. For we know that there are immutable entities which become qualified by existence, just as we know that some of the sea will become connected to the needle when you dip it in. The relationship of the sea's water to the needle is not the same in degree as the robe of existence put on by the immutable entities, since the ocean is limited and its existence is measurable and finite, but the immutable entities are infinite. That which is infinite cannot be encompassed by limits or enumerated, even though the analogy is correct, no doubt. (IV 320.14)

God is "Independent of the worlds," which means that He has no need for the existence of the cosmos. But without God's bestowal of existence (*ījād*), the immutable entities can gain no "taste" or existential knowledge of their own realities. In the same way the names have need of the things to manifest their own effects and properties.

> The fact that "God is independent of the worlds" means that He is Independent of the existence of the cosmos, not of its immutability. For through the state of its immutability the cosmos provides God sufficiency and independence from its existence, since it fulfills the right (*ḥaqq*) of the Divinity [to have a divine thrall] through its possibility [and need for a Preponderator]. . . . But the possible things . . . desire to taste (*dhawq*) the state of existence, just as they tasted the state of nonexistence. They ask the Necessary Being with the tongue of their immutability to bring their entities into existence, so that their knowledge may become tasting. Hence He brings them into existence for themselves, not for Himself. (III 306.19)

It needs to be kept in mind that the existent entities are identical with the "effects" or "properties" of the divine names. Hence the divine names rejoice when the entities enter into existence. Ibn al-ʿArabī makes this point while discussing the "divine marriage," which is one of the three basic kinds of "marriage" or "sexual union" (*al-nikāḥ*) found in the cosmos. It occurs when Being comes together with the nonexistent possible thing to produce the existent possible thing.[11]

> That which is desired from marriage may be reproduction (*tanāsul*)—I mean the birth of offspring—or it may simply be enjoyment (*iltidhādh*). The Divine Marriage is the attentiveness (*tawajjuh*) of the Real toward the possible thing in the presence of possibility through the desire of love (*al-irādat al-ḥubbiyya*), so that there may be bliss (*ibtihāj*) along with desire. When the Real turns His attentiveness toward the possible thing as mentioned, He makes manifest the coming to be (*takwīn*) of this possible thing. Hence, that which is born from this coming together is the existence of the possible thing.
>
> The entity of the possible thing is named "wife," the attentiveness through desire and love is called "marriage," and the production of the offspring is called a "bestowal of existence" upon the entity of that possible thing, or, if you prefer, an "existence." The "wedding feasts" (*aʿrās*) are the rejoicing of the Most Beautiful Names. For the marriage results in a bestowal of manifested existence upon the entities of the possible things, in order that the effects of the names may become manifest. This is because the names can have no effects within themselves, nor within the Named. Their effect and authority can only become manifest within the entity of the possible thing, because of its poverty and need for what is in the hands of the names. Hence their authority becomes manifest within the possible thing. That is why we attribute rejoicing, happiness, and wedding feasts to them.
>
> This marriage is constant and continuous in existence. There can be no cessation or divorce in this marital contract. (III 516.3)

The nonexistence of the immutable entities is a relative nonexistence. They are nonexistent in relation to the cosmos, but not in relation to God's knowledge. When the entities become manifest in the cosmos, they are said to enter into existence (even though they never leave the state of immutability). One can say that they move from relative nonexistence to existence, or from one form of existence to another form. Hence a distinction has to be drawn between the nonexistence which belongs to the possible thing and that which belongs to the impossible thing. The impossible thing can never enter into entified existence within the cosmos, even if we can think and write about it. But the possible thing may move from nonexistence into existence. The Shaykh clarifies the difference between the two kinds of nonexistence in a passage where he is commenting on the divine roots of the

Koranic verses, "If you help God, He will help you" (47:7) and "Be helpers of God!" (61:14).

The Real possesses the attribute of Being and the attribute of Necessary Being through Himself. His contrary is called absolute nonexistence (*al-ʿadam al-muṭlaq*), and it possesses an attribute through which it is called "impossible" (*muḥāl*). Because of this attribute, it never receives existence. So it has no share in existence, just as the Necessary Being through Himself has no share in nonexistence. Since the situation is like this, we [creatures] are at the level of the middle (*wasaṭ*). We receive existence in our essences and we receive nonexistence in our essences. When we turn toward either of the two, it exercises its properties within us in accordance with what its reality bestows, and we become its kingdom, so it manifests its authority within us. Hence the impossible nonexistence seeks to make us its kingdom, and the Real, the Necessary Being through Himself, seeks to make us His kingdom and to manifest His authority within us.

We have a reality that receives both descriptions, but our relationship to nonexistence is nearer than our relationship to existence, since we are nonexistent things (*maʿdūmūn*). However, we are not described by impossibility; on the contrary, we are described in that nonexistence by possibility. This means that we do not possess the power to repel from ourselves existence or nonexistence. Rather, we possess immutable and distinct entities which are addressed by the two sides. Nonexistence says to us: "Be as you are in nonexistence, for you have no right to come to be in my level." But the Real says to the entity of each possible thing "Be!" (Koran 16:40). Hence He commands each one to exist.

The posssible thing says, "We are in nonexistence. We have come to know and taste it. Now the Necessary Being has commanded us to exist. But we do not know existence, nor do we have any foot in it. So come, let us help Him against this nonexistent impossible in order that we come to know through tasting what this existence is." Hence they come into engendered existence through His word, "Be!" And once they are actualized in His grasp, they never return to nonexistence, because of the sweet pleasure of existence. They praise their own view and see the blessing of their helping God against the impossible nonexistence. So the cosmos in respect of its substantiality (*jawhariyya*) is a helper of God; as a result, it is helped [by God] forever. (II 248.24)

The Shaykh finds a Koranic reference to the transferal of the possible things from relative nonexistence to cosmic existence in the verse, "There is no thing whose treasuries are not with Us" (15:21).

It is obvious that God creates the things and brings them out of nonexistence into existence. The attribution [of the things to God's treasuries found in the verse] demands that He bring them out from the treasuries which are with Him, that is, from an existence which we do not perceive to an existence which we do perceive. So the things are never in sheer nonexistence. On the contrary, the apparent situation is that their nonexistence is a relative (*iḍāfī*) nonexistence. For in the state of their nonexistence, the things are witnessed by God. He distinguishes them through their entities, differentiating (*tafṣīl*) some of them from others. He does not see them as undifferentiated (*ijmāl*).

Hence the "treasuries" of the things, which are the "containers" (*awʿiya*) within which they are stored, are only the possibilities (*imkān*) of the things, nothing else, since the things have no existence in their entities. On the contrary, they possess immutability. That which they acquire from the Real is entified existence. Hence they become differentiated for the viewers and for themselves through the existence of their entities, while they never cease to be differentiated for God through an immutable differentiation. (III 193.3)

The engendered things (*al-kawn*) emerge from an existence, i.e., that which is comprised by these treasuries, to another existence. In other words, they become manifest from these treasuries and to themselves through the light by which their selves are unveiled. In the darkness of the treasuries they had been veiled from the vision of themselves, since they were in the state of their own nonexistence.

God also says [in the continuation of the verse], "We do not send it down except in a known measure." So that which becomes distinguished for Him is only that which exists for Him. "Measure" takes place only in the distinguishing of one entity from another. But this is not the attribute of what is nonexistent in every respect. So all of this shows that the existence of the entities belongs to God in the state of their being qualified by nonexistence in themselves. This is the fundamental, relative existence (*al-wujūd al-aṣlī al-iḍāfī*) and relative nonexistence (*al-ʿadam al-iḍāfī*). (II 587.32)

Things

The Shaykh employs the Koranic term "thing" (*shay'*) as the equivalent of the philosophical term "possible thing" and the theological term "entity." Linguistically, he points out, the word thing is "one of the most indefinite of the indefinites" (*min ankar al-nakirāt*),[12] since it can be applied to anything at all, except only God Himself.

> As for ourselves, we do not affirm that the word "thingness" can be ascribed to the Essence of the Real, since [such ascription] has not come down to us, nor have we been addressed by it, and courtesy (*adab*) is to be preferred . . . . [In the verse "Everything is annihilated" (Koran 28:88)], every *thing* is annihilated. That is why we negate from the Real the ascription of the word "thing" to Him. (II 99.20,27)

Ibn al-ʿArabī often refers to the situation of the entities—as opposed to Being Itself—as their "thingness" (*shay'iyya*). He distinguishes between their relative nonexistence in God's knowledge, called their "thingness of immutability," and their entified existence in the cosmos, called their "thingness of existence." He finds reference to the immutable state of the things in many Koranic verses, especially those which mention God's addressing the things before creating them, as, for example, "Our only speech to a thing, when We desire it, is to say to it 'Be!', and it is" (16:40).

> The Prophet said, "God is (*kān*), and no thing is with Him."[13] The meaning is as follows: He is not accompanied by thingness, nor do we ascribe it to Him. Such is He, and there is no thing with Him. The negation of thingness from Him is one of His essential attributes, just as is the negation of "withness" (*maʿiyya*) from things. He is with the things, but the things are not with Him, since "withness" follows from knowledge: He knows us, so He is with us. We do not know Him, so we are not with Him.
>
> The word *kān* denotes a temporal limitation [since it is a past tense form—and is usually translated as "was"]. But in this saying that limitation is not meant. What is meant by the word is the "being" (*kawn*) which is existence (*wujūd*) . . . . In the same sense we have in the Koran, "God is (*kān*) All-pardoning, All-forgiving" (4:99), and other instances where the word *kān* is employed. . . . For [the grammarian] Sībawayh, *kān* is a word denoting existence (*ḥarf wujūdī*). (II 56.3)

One more quotation in which Ibn al-ʿArabī is discussing God's "kingdom" (*mulk*), referred to above, can suffice to illustrate his use of the term "thing."

> God's kingdom is nothing other than the possible things, which are our own entities. So we are His kingdom, and through us He is a king (*malik*). He says, "To Him belongs the kingdom of the heavens and the earth" (Koran 2:107), while God's Messenger said in praise of God, "He is the Lord and King of everything."[14] He brought the word "thing," which is applied to both the immutable and the existent entities. (IV 319.34)

In several of the above passages we met the word *kān* and its derivatives, all of which are important terms referring to existence. When God wants to bring a thing into existence or to "engender" it, He says to it, "Be!" (*kun*), so the type of existence which a thing accquires when it "comes to be" (*takawwun*) is frequently called "engendered existence" (*kawn*). The term *kawn* is sometimes employed to refer to the whole cosmos, and sometimes to a single engendered thing. Its plural (*akwān*) is used synonymously with other terms from the same root to refer to engendered things (*ka'ināt, kawā'in, mukawwanāt*).

Loci of Manifestation

Few teachings are as basic to Sufism —or to Islam, for that matter—as the idea that something more real stands beyond the realm of appearances. In Koranic terms, all creatures are "signs" (*āyāt*) of God. Most Sufis take the position that the outward form (*ṣūra*) is a deceptive veil, even though it reveals the Divine Reality in some manner. Ibn al-ʿArabī says nothing basically different, but he radically affirms the revelatory nature of phenomena. That which appears is in fact Being, the Divine Reality Itself. The phenomena are fundamentally nonexistent, and even if one can refer to their "coming into existence," this is in fact a metaphor. What appears to us is the One Being, but colored by the properties of the nonexistent possible things.

One of the terms which the Shaykh most often employs in explaining these ideas is *maẓhar*, which is grammatically a "noun of place" derived from *ẓuhūr*, which means "manifestation, outwardness, appearance." Here the word *maẓhar* is translated as "locus of manifestation." Ibn al-ʿArabī claims to have been the first to employ the term to explain the nature of existence (II 520.21).

The Koranic basis for speaking of God in terms of "manifestations" is the oft-quoted verse, "He is the First and the Last, the Manifest (*al-ẓāhir*) and the Nonmanifest (*al-bāṭin*)" (or, "the Outward and the Inward") (57:3). For Ibn al-ʿArabī this verse must be understood literally, with no attempts to explain it away. God is Outwardly Manifest before our eyes, just as He is Inwardly Nonmanifest. On the one hand "Withersoever you turn, there is the Face of God" (Koran 2:115). This is the profession of His similarity. On the other, "Sight perceives Him not" (Koran 6:103). This is the profession of His incomparability. True knowledge of the Divine Being can only be achieved through the proper combination of these two complementary perspectives.

> God is the Manifest who is witnessed by the eyes and the Nonmanifest who is witnessed by intellects. Just as there is no object of knowledge whatsoever which is unseen by Him—on the contrary, everything is witnessed by Him—so also He is not unseen by His creatures, whether in their state of nonexistence or in their state of existence. On the contrary, He is witnessed by them in the attributes of manifestation and nonmanifestation by their insight (*baṣīra*) and their sight (*baṣar*). However, witnessing Him does not necessitate knowing that He is the object. (III 484.35)
>
> One of the mysteries of knowledge of God lies in the interrelationship between the God and the divine thrall, or the Lord and the vassal. If God did not undertake to preserve the thrall and the vassal constantly, they would immediately be annihilated, since nothing would preserve them and keep them in subsistence. Were He to become veiled from the cosmos in the Unseen, the cosmos would become naught. Hence the name "Manifest" exercises its properties forever in existence, while the name "Nonmanifest" exercises its properties in knowledge and gnosis. Through the name Manifest He makes the cosmos subsist, and through the name Nonmanifest we come to know Him. (III 65.22)
>
> God is identical with the existence of the things, but He is not identical with the things. The entities of the existent things are a "hyle" (*hayūlā*) for the things, or they are their "spirits." Existence is the

> manifest dimension of those spirits and the forms of those hylic entities. Hence, all existence is the Real Manifest, while His Nonmanifest is the things. (II 21.35)

The entities are never manifest, since God is the Manifest; the entities never exist, since God is Being. We are left with a "locus of manifestation," commonly called an existent thing, an existent possible thing, or an existent entity. Every attribute and quality found in the locus belongs to the Manifest within it. In the following passage, Ibn al-ʿArabī explains that when something "comes to be" (*takawwun*) as the result of the divine command "Be!", the situation is not as most people imagine.

> God says to the thing, "Be!" He does not address or command any but that which hears, yet it has no existence. . . .It receives coming to be. But our view of its reception of coming to be is not like your view. Its reception of coming to be is only the fact that it becomes a locus of manifestation for the Real. This is the meaning of His words, "[Be!] And it is." This does not mean that the thing "acquires existence" (*istifādat al-wujūd*). It only acquires the property of being a locus of manifestation. . . . Hence He is identical to all things in manifestation, but He is not identical to them in their essences. On the contrary, He is He, and the things are the things. (II 484.23)

God can never be identical to the things in their essences, because their essences are inherently nonexistent and exist only through Him, while He is the Necessary Being who exists through Himself and cannot not exist. In the following passage, a continuation of the above-quoted commentary on the hadith, "God is, and no thing is with Him," Ibn al-ʿArabī explains some of these points.

> The meaning of this saying is: God has Being, and no thing is with Him. In other words, there is no one whose Being is Necessary through Itself except the Real. The existence of the possible thing is necessary through Him, since it is His locus of manifestation, and He is manifest within it. The possible entity is concealed (*mastūr*) by the Manifest within it. So manifestation and the Manifest become qualified by possibility. The entity of the locus of manifestation, which is the possible thing, exercises this property upon the Manifest. Hence the possible thing is enwrapped (*indirāj*) in the Necessary Being as an entity, while the Necessary Being is enwrapped in the possible thing as a property. (II 56.16)

Being is One, and Being is the Manifest, so the Manifest is One. It follows that multiplicity is not the attribute of the Manifest, but of the loci within which It becomes manifest. Ibn al-ʿArabī discusses this in a passage in which he is explaining what the Real requires from those who profess His Unity (*tawḥīd*).

> He requires that there be no competition (*muzāḥama*). What I mean is as follows: Since God is named the Manifest and the Nonmanifest, He negated competition, since the Manifest does not compete with the Nonmanifest, nor does the Nonmanifest compete with the Manifest. Competition would take place if there were two manifests, or two nonmanifests. So He is Manifest in respect of the loci of manifestation, while He is Nonmanifest in respect of His He-ness (*huwiyya*).[15] Hence the loci of manifestation are plural (*mutaʿaddid*) in respect of their entities, but not in respect of the Manifest within them. Therefore Unity (*al-aḥadiyya*) lies in their manifestation, while plurality lies in their entities. The Real requires from those who are described by the attribute of professing His Unity that they profess His Unity in respect of His He-ness. Though the loci of manifestation are plural, the Manifest is not plural. They should not see anything unless He is the seen and the seer. They should not seek anything unless He is the seeker, the seeking, and the sought. They should not hear anything unless He is the hearer, the hearing, and the heard. Hence there is no competition, so there is no dispute. (II 93.33)

Being is One and Manifest. Hence multiplicity and distinction arise from the properties of the nonexistent things, which are many and nonmanifest. Ibn al-ʿArabī explains this while discussing a definition given by an early Sufi to the term *farq* or "dispersion": "It is the witnessing of 'others' (*al-aghyār*) as belonging to God."

> Hence the person witnesses in the very Being of the Real the properties of the immutable entities. [He sees] that Being becomes manifest only in accordance with their properties. Then limits (*ḥudūd*) become manifest and the levels of the entities become distinguished in the Being of the Real. It is said, "angels, spheres, elements, productions, genera, species, individuals." But the Entity of Being is One, while the properties are diverse in accordance with the diversity of the immutable entities, which are the "others" without doubt, though in immutability, not in existence. (II 519.10)

Self-Disclosure and Receptivity

God is the Manifest and the Nonmanifest. Through the name Manifest He discloses Himself in a manner that is primarily "ontological" by creating the universe; through the name Nonmanifest He discloses Himself in a manner that is primarily "epistemological" to the understandings and insights of His creatures. Ibn al-ʿArabī often employs the word "[self-]manifestation" (*ẓuhūr*) for the first type of divine display. He uses the term *tajallī* or "self-disclosure" synonymously, while he also employs it for God's nonmanifest display. Hence the term *tajallī* may be employed in the context of ontology, epistemology, or—as more commonly happens—without any distinction being implied between the two domains. In the Shaykh's view, existence and knowledge are two names for the same reality; it is impossible to discuss one without the other. By the same token ignorance is identical with nonexistence: "Ignorance (*jahl*) is nonexistence, while knowledge is verified existence (*wujūd muḥaqqaq*)" (III 56.5). We will return to this point later. For now it is necessary to illustrate his usage of the term self-disclosure in a sense that is primarily ontological.

Closely connected with the idea of self-disclosure is that of receptivity (*qabūl*) and preparedness (*istiʿdād*). When God discloses Himself, the extent to which a thing "receives" the self-disclosure is determined by its "preparedness" to receive it, and this in turn is determined by the thing's own reality. Receptivity is a matter of common experience, though we are more likely to think of it in terms of cognition than existence. Every teacher knows that a classroom full of students represents as many different receptivities for understanding the subject matter as there are individuals, whatever may be the reasons for the discrepancies in aptitude—e.g., environment, heredity, individual predilections, and so on. In Ibn al-ʿArabī's view receptivity must be taken into account not only on the cognitive level, but also on the existential level. Being is One, and It discloses Itself to all things in Its Oneness. But each thing represents a unique combination of attributes and properties. Each receives Being's self-disclosure to the measure of its own capacity. The receptivities of things are given broad outlines by their situation in the ontological hierarchy. Inanimate objects demonstrate one level of capacity, plants a higher level, animals a still higher level, and human beings the highest level among all created things. Perfect man alone has the receptivity to display Being in Its fullness. In the following passage Ibn al-ʿArabī explains the important role played by preparedness in the context of addressing the practical problem of why prayers are often not answered.

> God says, "The giving of thy Lord can never be walled up" (Koran 17:20). In other words, it can never be withheld. God is saying that He gives constantly, while the loci receive in the measure of the realities of their preparednesses. In the same way we say that the sun spreads its

rays over the existent things. It is not miserly with its light toward anything. The loci receive the light in the measure of their preparednesses.

Each locus attributes the effect [of light] to the sun and forgets its own preparedness. The person with a cold temperament enjoys the sun's heat, while the person with a hot temperament suffers from its heat. In respect of its essence the light is one, while each of the two people suffers from what the other enjoys. If this belonged only to the light, it would result in a single reality. Therefore the sun gives according to its own strength, while the receiver exercises a property over that giving, and necessarily so, since no result is produced without two premises.[16]

The sun blackens the face of the washerman, while it whitens the clothing. The sun whitens the clothing because of the clothing's preparedness, while it blackens the face of the washerman. In the same way, with a single blowing of air a person extinguishes a lamp and ignites a fire in tinder; but the air in itself is one. A single verse from God's Book reaches the listener as one entity. One listener understands one thing from it, another listener does not understand that thing but understands something else, while a third understands many things. Therefore each of those who consider this verse cite it in accordance with the diversity of the preparedness of their understandings.

The same thing takes place in divine self-disclosures. The Self-discloser, in respect of what He is in Himself, is One in Entity, while the self-disclosures—I mean their forms—are diverse in accordance with the diversity of the preparednesses of the loci of self-disclosure. The property of the divine gifts is the same.

Once you understand this, you will know that the gift of God is not withheld. But you want Him to give you something that your preparedness cannot receive. Then you attribute the withholding to Him in that which you seek from Him, and you do not turn your attention toward the preparedness. It is possible that a person has the preparedness to ask, but he does not have the preparedness to receive what he asks for—if it were given to him in place of being withheld. You answer, "God is powerful over everything" (Koran 2:20 etc.), and you speak the truth in that. But you forget the hierarchy of divine wisdom in the cosmos and what is demanded by the realities of the things. (I 287.10)

Once the concept of receptivity is clearly understood, it becomes a simple means for explaining the relationship between Being and the existent things. Each entity is a "receptacle" (*qābil*) for Being. To the extent it is able to receive and manifest Being, it is said to "exist," though in fact existence belongs only to God.

> The existence attributed to each created thing is the Being of the Real, since the possible thing has no existence. However, the entities of the possible things are receptacles for the manifestation of this Being. (II 69.3)

Though some of Ibn al-ʿArabī's followers drew distinctions between receptivity and preparedness,[17] for practical purposes the two terms can be used interchangeably to designate those specific characteristics of a thing which determine the manner in which Being manifests Itself through the thing. The following passages describe the nature of the preparedness:

> The entity of the servant possesses a specific preparedness that displays its effects in the Manifest and gives rise to the diversity of forms within the Manifest, which is the Entity of the Real. (II 517.23)
>
> [God says, "We shall show them Our signs upon the horizons and in themselves,] until it is clear to them that He is the Real" (Koran 41:53), nothing else. Hence the "signs" (*āyāt*) are the denotations (*dalālāt*) showing that He is the Real, Manifest in the loci of manifestation, that is, the entities of the cosmos. . . . He completed the instruction by saying, "Is it not enough that thy Lord is witness" through self-disclosure and self-manifestation "over every thing" (41:53), that is, over every entity of the cosmos? The cosmos cannot repel from itself this Manifest within itself, nor can it refuse to be a lo-

cus of manifestation. This is what is called its "possibility." If the reality of the cosmos was not possibility, it would not receive Light, that is, the manifestation of the Real within it which becomes clear to it through the signs.

Then He completed the verse by saying, "Surely He encompasses everything" (41:54) in the cosmos. "Encompassing" (*iḥāṭa*) a thing conceals that thing. Hence the Manifest is the Encompasser (*al-muḥīt*). That thing is not manifest, since the encompassing prevents its manifestation. Hence within the Encompasser that thing—that is, the cosmos—is like the spirit within the body, and the Encompasser is like the body in relation to the spirit. One of the two is visible (*shahāda*), that is, the Manifest Encompasser, while the other is unseen (*ghayb*), that is, that which is concealed by this encompassing—the entity of the cosmos. The property, which belongs to that which is described as being unseen, is found in the Manifest, which is the Visible. In accordance with their preparednesses in themselves, the entities of the thingnesses of the cosmos display properties within that which is Manifest within themselves as is given by their own realities. Hence their forms become manifest within the Encompasser, who is the Real. Hence it is said, "a Throne," "a Footstool," "celestial spheres," "angels," "elements," "productions," "accidental states." But there is nothing other than God. (II 151.3)

In discussing various stages of "annihilation" or "passing away from self" (*fanā'*) that are experienced by the travelers on the path to God, Ibn al-ʿArabī identifies the seventh and highest stage with the vision of God as the Manifest within the cosmos. As a result, the traveler can no longer claim that names and attributes belong to God:

The traveler sees the engendered thing as the Real, manifest within the entity of the locus of manifestation, but in the form of the preparedness possessed by the locus in itself. He does not see the Real as possessing any effect in engendered existence, and he has no proof through which to affirm relationships, attributes, or descriptions. Hence this witnessing annihilates him from God's names, attributes, and descriptions. Rather, if he verifies it, he will see that engendered existence is the locus of displaying effects, since the preparedness of the immutable entities—that is, the entities of the possible things—displays effects within it. Among the things which verifies this [witnessing] is the fact that He describes Himself in His Book and upon the tongues of His messengers with that by which temporally originated created things are described. (II 514.32)

Self-disclosure is illumination: The nonexistent possible thing is illuminated by the light of existence, and the ignorant thing is illuminated by the light of knowledge. Self-disclosure is never-ending, since God is Light, and the reality of light demands that it disclose itself. It may be that the darkness fails to comprehend the shining sun, but the sun never ceases to shine.

The divine self-disclosure is everlasting (*dā'im*). No veil is upon it. However, it is not known that it is it. The reason for this is that when God created the cosmos, He made it hear His speech in the state of its nonexistence. That is His word, "Be!" The cosmos was witnessed by Him, but He was not witnessed by it. Upon the eyes of the possible things was the veil of nonexistence, no other. They did not perceive the Existent Being while they were nonexistent. In the same way light dispels darkness, for darkness cannot subsist along with the existence of light. Such was the situation of nonexistence and Being.

When He commanded the possible things to come into engendered existence because of their possibility and their preparedness for reception, they rushed to see what there was, since they had the capacity (*quwwa*) to see, just as they had the capacity to hear—in respect of their immutability, not in respect of existence. When the possible thing came into existence, it became colored (*inṣibāgh*) by light, and nonexistence disappeared. The thing opened its eyes and saw that Being was Sheer Good (*al-khayr al-maḥḍ*), but it did not know what It was, nor did it know that It had commanded it to come into engendered existence. Then self-disclosure gave it a knowledge of what it saw, but not a knowledge of the fact that Being had given it its existence.

When it became colored by light, the possible thing turned its attention to the left. It saw nonexistence. So it investigated it and saw that it arose from itself like a shadow (*ẓill*) that arises from a person who faces the light. It said, "What is that?" Light said to it from the right hand side, "That is you. If you were light, shadow could have no entity. I am Light and I take away shadow. The light which you have derives from that in your essence which is turned toward Me. Thereby you come to know that you are not I. For I am Light without shadow, while you are mixed light, as a result of your possibility. If you relate yourself to Me, I receive you; and if you relate yourself to nonexistence, it receives you, for you are between Being and nonexistence, and you are between Good and evil.

"If you turn away from your own shadow, you will have turned away from your possibility. Once you have turned away from your possibility, you will have become ignorant of Me and will not know Me. For you have no proof that I am your God, Lord, and Existence-bestower except your own possibility, which is your witnessing of your shadow. But if you turn away from your light totally so that you never cease witnessing your shadow, you will not come to know that it is the shadow of your possibility. You will imagine that it is the shadow of the impossible. And the impossible and the Necessary are contraries in every respect. So if I call you, you will not respond to Me or hear Me, since that object of witnessing will make you deaf to My call.

"So look not upon Me with a gaze that will annihilate (*ifnā'*) you from your shadow. Then you would claim that you are I and fall into ignorance. And look not upon your shadow with a gaze that will annihilate you from Me. That would leave you deaf, and you would remain ignorant of why I created you. So be sometimes this and sometimes that.

"God created two eyes for you only so that you could witness Me with one and your shadow with the other. I have said to you in the manner of showing you My favors, 'Have We not appointed for him two eyes, and a tongue, and two lips, and guided him on the two highways?' (Koran 90:8-10). In other words, We made clear for him the two paths, that of light and that of shadow. '[Surely We have guided him on the way], whether he be thankful or unthankful' (Koran 76:3), for the impossible nonexistence is darkness, while the possible nonexistence is shadow, not darkness. That is why the ease of existence is found in shadow." (II 303.28)

Oneness of Being and Effects of the Names

In discussing Being and the various terms that are used to refer to the nonexistent and existent things, we have largely neglectd the divine names to which Part 2 was devoted. At this point we need to remind the reader that each thing other than God is a name of God. And since God is Being, every *thing*, every entity, every possible thing, is a name of Being.[18]

It is impossible for the things other than God to come out of the grasp of the Real, for He brings them into existence, or rather, He is their existence and from Him they acquire (*istifāda*) existence. And existence/Being is nothing other than the Real, nor is it something outside of Him from which He gives to them. That is impossible. On the contrary He is Being, and through Him the entities become manifest. (I 406.14)

He who loses sight of the Face of the Real in the things is able to make claims (*da'wā*), and making claims is identical with illness (*maraḍ*). For the Verifiers it has been established that there is nothing in Being/existence but God. As for us [creatures], though we exist, our existence is through Him. He whose existence is through other than himself is in effect nonexistent. (I 279.5)

Concerning the existents in all their differentiations, we maintain that they are the manifestation of God in the loci of manifestation, that is, the entities of the possible things in accordance with the preparednesses possessed by the possible things. Hence the attributes of the Manifest are diverse, since the entities within which It becomes manifest are diverse. Hence the existent things become distinct and plural through the plurality of the entities and their distinction in themselves. Hence there is nothing in Being/existence except God and the properties of the entities, while there is nothing in nonexistence except the entities of the possible things prepared to be qualified for existence. So in existence "they are/they are not": The Manifest is their properties, so "they are." But they have no entity in existence, so "they are not." In the same way, "He is and is not": He is the Manifest, so "He is." But the distinction among the existents is intelligible and perceived by the senses because of the diversity of the properties of the entities, so "He is not." (II 160.1)

Just as God gave the cosmos the name *wujūd*, which belongs to Him in reality, so also He gave it the Most Beautiful Names through its preparedness and the fact that it is a locus of manifestation for Him. (II 167.32)

Every name in the cosmos is His name, not the name of other than He. For it is the name of the Manifest in the locus of manifestation. (II 122.14)

Everything is the properties of the entities of the possible things within the Ontological Entity which becomes manifest in the forms as a result of the effects of the Most Beautiful Divine Names and in respect of the fact that the possible things are qualified by them. In the case of the Real, these are names, but in the case of the possible thing, they are descriptions and attributes, while the possible thing remains in the state of nonexistence. (IV 11.9)

If you are given opening[19] concerning the knowledge of the relationships of the divine names, which become manifest through the manifestation of the divine loci of manifestation within the entities of the possible things, thus becoming arranged in species, genera, and individuals . . . [then you will know that] the cause (*sabab*) for the manifestation of every property in its entity is its divine name. (II 39.27)

The entity of the servant has no rightful claim (*istiḥqāq*) in itself, since it is not the Real in any sense. The Real alone has a rightful claim on that upon which He has a rightful claim. So all the names in the cosmos which are imagined to be the rightful due (*ḥaqq*) of the servant are the rightful due of God. . . . The Real alone has a rightful claim upon all names occurring within engendered existence and manifest in property. The servant assumes their traits (*takhalluq*) and possesses nothing of his own except his entity. . . . When one of the names occurs for or is applied to any of the entities, this is only so in the respect that the entities are loci of manifestation. Hence every name is applied to nothing but the Being of the Real within the entities, while the entities remain in their root without any rightful claims. . . . Being belongs to God, and whenever Being is described by an attribute, that which the attribute names is the same as that which is named "Allah." So understand that there is no ontological named thing (*musammā wujūdī*) except God. He is named by every name, described by every attribute, qualified by every description. As for His words, "Glory be to thy Lord, the Lord of inaccessibility, above what they describe" (Koran 37:180), [the meaning is that He is above] having any partner (*sharīk*) in any of the names. So all are names of God: names of His acts, or of His attributes, or of His Essence. There is nothing in Being/existence but God, while the entities are nonexistent, in the midst of that which becomes manifest from them. . . . Hence existence belongs to Him and nonexistence belongs to you. He is an Existent Being forever, and you are nonexistent forever. (II 54.6)

The Real is the First in the Entity in which He is the Last, in the Entity in which He is the Manifest, in the Entity in which He is the Nonmanifest, and so on, through all the divine names. . . . Though the divine names and the engendered entities are plural through relationships, they are One Entity in Being. (I 462.6)

God says, "We created not the heavens and the earth, and what between them is, save through the Real"[20] (Koran 15:85), which is Sheer Being. Hence there came to be ascribed to It everything given by the realities of the entities. Limitations arose, measurements became manifest, property and decree exercised their influence. The high, the low, and the middle, diverse and parallel things, the kinds of existents—their genera, their species, their individuals, their states, and their properties—all became manifest within One Entity. Shapes became distinct within It and the names of the Real became manifest, possessing effects in that which became manifest within existence, out of God's Jealousy, lest those effects be attributed to the entities of the possible things within the Manifest within them. Since the effects belong to the divine names, and the name is the Named, there is nothing in Being/existence except God. (II 216.7)

6. *THE NEW CREATION*

Discussion of the Oneness of Being leaves us with a relatively static picture of everything that exists. Yet few concepts are as central to Ibn al-ʿArabī's teachings as change. "Everything other than God" dwells by definition in continual flux. Being alone remains unchanged, while all existence displays Being's infinite properties in kaleidoscopic variety. In Itself Being's Oneness allows for no multiplicity, yet only multiplicity can give rise to diversity of forms, whether spatially or temporally. Just as the entities display their properties within the Manifest in indefinite variety at any given moment, so at each successive moment each thing undergoes fluctuation, transformation, and transmutation.

Ibn al-ʿArabī discerns the divine roots of change in many Koranic verses, especially, "No indeed, but they are in confusion as to a new creation (*khalq jadīd*)" (50:15) and "Each day He is upon some task (*sha'n*)" (55:29). Two closely connected concepts are the lack of "repetition" (*takrār*) in the divine self-disclosure (*al-tajallī*), which means that God never displays Himself twice in exactly the same form; and the divine "vastness" (*ittisāʿ* or *tawassuʿ*), which demands the infinity of the possible things.

Infinite Possibility

The possible things in their state of nonexistence are infinite in number (*mā lā yatanāhā* or *lā nihāya lah* or *ghayr mutanāhī*). Possibility is an inexhaustible Treasury (*khizāna*) from which God continues to create forever. Ibn al-ʿArabī finds references to it in such Koranic verses as the above-quoted, "There is no thing whose treasuries are not with Us, and We send it not down but in a known measure" (15:21). For Ibn al-ʿArabī this means Being can manifest Itself through the form of any possible thing, just as water, upon which the Throne of God is placed (Koran 11:7), can take the shape of any receptacle. However, since one form excludes another form, "existence" defined as the manifest cosmos cannot be infinite. It is the nonexistent possibilities that are infinite.

> Within the Treasuries are found the individuals (*ashkhāṣ*) of the genera (*ajnās*). These individuals are infinite, and that which is infinite does not enter into existence, since everything confined (*inḥiṣār*) by existence is finite. (III 361.13)
>
> That which is with God (*ʿind Allāh*) is infinite, but it is impossible for the infinite to enter into existence. So everything that enters into existence is finite. When the finite is compared with the Infinite, it appears as little or as nothing, even if it is a great deal. (II 353.29)
>
> The possible things are infinite, and there cannot be more than the infinite. But the infinite does not enter into existence all at once (*dafʿa*); rather it enters little by little, with no end. (II 482.26)

The infinity of the possible things underlies the discussion of the continual recreation of all things. Behind the fragile appearance of the existent things which make up the cosmos stands the Infinite Ocean, forever replenishing the waves on Its surface. And just as the number of possible things is infinite, so also are the changes undergone by each possible thing. Or rather, in the last analysis, each new state, each changed situation, is a newly created possible thing, similar (*mithl*) to the first to be sure, but not identical.

> It may be that the situation of a specific species, such as man, is finite, since the individuals of this species are finite—though the individuals of the cosmos are not finite. However, there is another sense in which the creation of individual human beings is in fact infinite, though not everyone is aware of it. It is referred to in His words, "No indeed, but they are in confusion as to a new creation" (50:15). The entity of each individual is renewed (*tajaddud*) at each instant, and necessarily so, for the Real never ceases being the Agent (*fāʿil*) of existence in the possible things. This is shown by the diversity of properties of the entities in every state. The entity which has *this* specific state cannot be the same as the entity which had *that* state, the passing and disappearance of which was witnessed. (IV 320.3)

Perpetual Renewal

Ibn al-ʿArabī traces the theoretical exposition of the idea of a perpetually renewed creation back to the Ashʿarite theologians, though he criticizes their view as being incomplete. They maintained that the cosmos is composed of substances (*jawāhir*) and accidents (*aʿrāḍ*) and that the substances remain constant while "The accident does not remain for two moments (*lā tabqā zamānayn*)." The basic difference between the Ashʿarite view and that of the Shaykh al-Akbar is that he holds that substances are no different from accidents in being perpetually re-created. In the *Fuṣūṣ al-ḥikam* he goes to some lengths to describe the errors of the Ashʿarites, concluding that "They did not understand that the whole cosmos is a collection of accidents; hence it undergoes continual change (*tabaddul*) at every moment, since 'The accident does not remain for two moments'" (*Fuṣūṣ* 125).[1]

In Ibn al-ʿArabī's way of looking at things, the various kinds of substance discussed by theologians and philosophers are themselves accidents in respect to a still deeper "substance," which is Being, or the Breath of the All-merciful. All things, both "substances" and "accidents" are in fact accidents, the effects of the immutable entities found in Manifest Being. The substance of the cosmos is the One Entity.

> At root the substance of the cosmos is one. It never changes from its reality. Every form that becomes manifest within it is an accident which in actual fact (*fī nafs al-amr*) undergoes transmutation (*istiḥāla*) at each indivisible instant (*zamān fard*). The Real brings similars (*amthāl*) into existence perpetually (*ʿala'l-dawām*), since He is the Creator perpetually, while the possible things in the state of their nonexistence possess the preparedness to receive existence. (III 452.24)
>
> No nonexistence ever overcomes the cosmos in respect of its substance, nor does any form ever remain for two instants. Creation never ceases, while the entities are receivers which take off and put on [existence]. So in every instant (*nafas*) the cosmos in respect of its form undergoes a new creation in which there is no repetition. (II 677.30)

The Koranic expression *ajal* or "term" designates the moment of death foreordained by God, or the moment at which something comes to an end, or the length of something's existence. In one passage Ibn al-ʿArabī declares that God has established a "term" for every form in the cosmos, except for the entities which receive the forms.

> God says, "Every one runs to a stated term" (13:2, 31:29). And He says, "He

decreed a term, a term stated with Him" (6:2). He brought the word "every," which demands all-encompassingness and all-inclusiveness. But we have said that the entities that receive the forms have no term. So how can they escape from the property of the "every"? We say: They have not escaped. Rather, the "term" that belongs to the entity is its relationship (*irtibāṭ*) to one of the forms which it receives. Its receiving it reaches a stated term, which is the expiration of the moment of that form. When the term known to God reaches this relationship, the form ceases to exist and the entity receives another form. Hence the entities "run to a stated term" by receiving a form, just as the form "runs to a stated term" by being affirmed for that entity, which is the locus of its manifestation. Hence the "every" embraces the stated term.

God has decreed for each thing a term in a given affair which it reaches. Then the thing passes to another state in which it also runs to a stated term. And God creates perpetually at each instant (*maʿa'l-anfās*). So among the things, some remain for the length of the moment of their existence and reach their term in the second moment of the time of their existence. This is the smallest duration (*mudda*) in the cosmos. God does this so that the entities will be poor and needy toward God at each instant. For if they were to remain [in existence] for two moments or more, they would be qualified by independence (*ghinā*) from God in that duration.

This is a position which no one maintains except the Folk of Verified Unveiling among us and the Ashʿarites among the theologians. (II 639.6)

The Shaykh often returns to the affirmation of the "poverty" of the things as the reason for and proof of the constant renewal of creation. The possible things can never escape from perpetual need for a Preponderator in order to stay in existence. To maintain otherwise would be to claim that they are independent from God; but as we have seen, Independence is strictly a divine attribute, while poverty is inherent to all created things.

The cosmos is never fixed in a single state for a moment, since God is Ever-creating constantly. Were the cosmos to remain in a single state for two moments, it would be described by independence from God. But people are "in confusion as to a new creation." (III 199.9)

Divine Tasks

Ibn al-ʿArabī quotes no Koranic passage in support of the new creation more often than the verse, "Each day He is upon some task" (55:29). Frequently he explains the meaning of this "day" while discussing the various kinds of days mentioned in the Koran and the Hadith, such as the 1,000 or 50,000-year days of Koran 32:5 and 70:4.[2] Here the "day" is the shortest of all days, corresponding to the present instant or the "indivisible moment" (*al-zaman al-fard*).[3] As for the divine "tasks," they are all the things, states, and situations found in engendered existence.

He is "each day upon some task." The "day" is the indivisible moment, while the "task" is that which God causes to occur within it. (II 431.28)

"Days" are many; some are long and some are short. The smallest of them is the indivisible moment, in respect of which came the verse, "Each day He is upon some task." God named the indivisible moment a "day" because a "task" is made to occur within it. So it is the shortest and most minute of days. (I 292.15)

Though the days are diverse in their measures and in their correspondence with solar days, God's command within them is like the "twinkling of an eye" (Koran 54:50). . . . The day may even be smaller than [the twinkling of an eye] . . . ; its measure may be the supposed (*mutawahham*) "indivisible moment," which is the "day of the task." In regard to the Real, the task is one, but in regard to the receivers in the cosmos, all the receivers are tasks. Were it not for the fact that existence confines them, we would say that they are infinite. (II 82.4)

The factor that separates two similars among things is difficult to perceive through witnessing, except for him who witnesses the Real or who verifies his witnessing of a chameleon, since there is no animal that shows more clearly that the Real possesses the property of "Each day He is upon some task" than the chameleon.[4] So no attribute and no state in the cosmos remains for two moments, nor does any form become manifest twice. (II 500.6)

God says, "Each day He is upon some task." The smallest of the days is the indivisible moment. In it He is upon His tasks to the number of the indivisible parts of the cosmos which are in existence. . . . Hence He is upon some task with every part of the cosmos, in that He creates within it that which lets it remain. . . . These tasks are the states (*aḥwāl*) of the creatures, who are the loci for the existence of the tasks within them, since it is within them that He creates those states perpetually. Hence no state can remain for two moments, since, were it to remain for two moments, the Real would not be the creator of that thing in which the state remained. It would not be poor toward God and would be qualified by independence from Him. But this is impossible. (II 384.31)

Breaking Habits

Ibn al-ʿArabī sometimes employs the concept of the new creation in unexpected contexts. In one passage he brings it up while discussing the phenomenon of "charismatic acts" (*karāmāt*), the miracles performed by the friends of God. The word for "miracle" is "breaking the habit" (*kharq al-ʿāda*). Etymologically a "habit" (*ʿāda*) is "that which returns." In fact, says Ibn al-ʿArabī, there is nothing habitual, since everything is constantly renewed and nothing ever returns.

The possessor of this deputation (*niyāba* [which is the subject of the present chapter]) constantly has the power to exercise free disposal (*taṣarruf*). The common people name this "charismatic acts," "signs" (*āyāt*), and "the breaking of habits." For the Verifiers, these acts are not the "breaking of habit," but rather the bringing into existence of engendered things (*kawāʾin*). The reason is that in reality, there are no habits, since there is no repetition. So nothing returns. This is referred to in God's words concerning the people of habits, "No indeed, but they are in confusion as to a new creation" (50:15). He says: They do not know that in every instant they are in a new creation, so what they see in the first instant is not identical to what they see in the second instant. They are in confusion about this.

Hence there is no return, so there is no breaking. This is how the situation is perceived by the Verifiers from among the Folk of Allah. And the situation is nothing but this, just as we have mentioned. For it is through this that the creatures are perpetually and forever poor and the Real is the Creator and Preserver of this existence. The creature's existence is perpetual because of the new creation which He brings into existence within it in order for it to remain. (III 288.14)

In reality, the situation is new forever, so there is nothing that returns, so there is no breaking of habit. . . . The Divinity is vaster than that It should cause anything to return, but the similar things are veils upon the eyes of the blind, those "who know an outward significance of the present life, but of the next they are heedless" (Koran 30:7). That "next" is the existence of the entity of the second similar.[5] They are "heedless," so "They are in confusion as to a new creation" (50:15). But the possible things are infinite, God's power exercises its influence, and the Real is Ever-creating. So how should there be repetition? For one cannot conceive of repetition except through return. (II 372.20)

Transmutation and Transformation

One of the most explicit scriptural supports for Ibn al-ʿArabī's contention that

God can assume an indefinite number of "tasks" in keeping with each creature is found in an already mentioned hadith from Muslim's *Ṣaḥīḥ*. The text describes the scene on the Day of Resurrection, when God appears to each group of people in a variety of forms. But they deny Him in every form in which He appears. Finally, "He transmutes (*taḥawwul*) Himself into the form in which they saw Him the first time and He says, 'I am your Lord.' They answer, 'Indeed, Thou art our Lord'."[6] The term *taḥawwul*, derived from the same root as the term "state" (*ḥāl*), signifies that something undergoes a change from one state or situation or form to another, hence a transmutation. It is employed repeatedly in discussions of the nature of imagination. In the following passage, Ibn al-ʿArabī has been explaining the nature of imagination but extends the discussion to include the corporeal world as well.

> Change may take place from a form to a similar form (*mithl*) or to a dissimilar form (*khilāf*) in imagination, in the sensory domain (*al-ḥiss*), or anyplace in the cosmos, since the whole cosmos never ceases to change for all eternity, ad infinitum, because of the change of the root which replenishes it. The root of this change is the divine self-transmutation in forms mentioned in the *Ṣaḥīḥ*. From here He becomes manifest in meanings (*maʿānī*) and forms.
>
> From meaning to meaning,
> from forms to forms.
>
> Hence His words, "Each day He is upon some task," the task being the changes which He causes to occur in the engendered things (*akwān*). (III 198.28)
>
> Such is the situation of the Real with the cosmos: God has effects manifest within the cosmos; they are the states within which the cosmos undergoes constant fluctuation (*taqallub*). This is a property of His name "Time" (*dahr*).[7] . . .
>
> The Real described Himself for us by the descriptions of those things which in our view are temporally originated. In reality these are His descriptions which have become manifest within us; then [we thought that] they did not return to Him, so we described Him by descriptions worthy of His majesty. But they are His descriptions in reality.
>
> Had He not brought us into existence in the form of what He is in Himself, it would not be correct and established that we have received attributes by which He has described us and which belong rightfully (*ḥaqq*) to Him; nor would He receive attributes by which He has described Himself and which belong rightfully to us.[8] All are rightfully His. So He is the Root, and we are the branch of that Root. The [divine] names are the boughs of this tree—I mean the tree of existence (*shajarat al-wujūd*)—and we are identical with its fruit, or rather, He is identical with its fruit. . . .
>
> He has given us news on the tongue of His Messenger concerning His self-transmutation (*taḥawwul*) in forms within the places of self-disclosure. That is the root of our transmutation in states—both inwardly and outwardly—all of which takes place in Him. (III 315.11, 16)

The word *taḥawwul* or "transmutation" is practically synonymous with *istiḥāla*, the tenth verbal form from the same root. However, the latter term was often employed in discussions of the nature of the changes that take place within the corporeal world. More specifically, it was said that one of the four elements could become "transmuted" into another element in the appropriate circumstances. Hence water could be transmuted into earth or air, air into water or fire, and so forth. Though this discussion plays a certain role in Ibn al-ʿArabī's cosmological scheme, in the present context he merely perceives the transmutation of the elements as one instance of the general transmutation that takes place in all things.

> The whole cosmos is confined to three mysteries (*asrār*): its substance, its forms, and transmutation (*istiḥāla*). There is no fourth affair (*amr*). If you ask us: From whence in the divine realities does transmutation become manifest in the cosmos? We will reply:

The Real described Himself by saying, "Each day He is upon some task" (55:29). The "tasks" are diverse. He described Himself as rejoicing at the repentance of His servant; and He rejoiced at it before it came to be (*kawn*). In the same way the Prophet said, "God does not become bored that you should become bored."[9] The gnostics—who are the messengers (upon them be peace!)—have mentioned concerning God that He will become wrathful on the Day of Resurrection "with a wrath with the like of which He has not become wrathful before this and with the like of which He will not become wrathful after this," as is worthy of His majesty.[10] Hence they have described Him as having a state before this wrath in which He was not described by this wrath. The *Ṣaḥīḥ* has mentioned His self-transmutation in forms on the Day of Resurrection when He discloses Himself to His servants. And self-transmutation (*taḥawwul*) is identical with transmutation (*istiḥāla*); there is no difference between the two in manifestation.

Were this not so, it would not be correct for the cosmos to have a beginning; rather, it would be coextensive (*musāwiq*) with God in existence. But this is not so in actual fact. Just as God accepted to manifest Himself to His servants in diverse forms, so also at first He did not create, then He created.

In eternity without beginning (*al-azal*) He was described as Knowing and Powerful. In other words, He had the ability to bring the possible thing into existence, but it was up to Him whether or not to become manifest in the form of bringing it into existence. He became manifest by bringing the form of the possible thing into existence whenever He willed. And there is no difference among the possible things in their relationship to Him. For example, we know that God did not bring Zayd into existence until yesterday, or until today. So Zayd's existence has been delayed, even though the Real is Powerful. It is necessary to make the same judgment concerning the first existent of the cosmos. God is qualified by power over bringing the thing into existence, even if He does not do so. In the same way you are powerful over moving in the time of being still, even if you do not move; this does not necessitate any absurdity. For there is no difference between the presently existent possible thing which has been delayed until after other possible things, and the first possible thing, since the Real is not qualified as having brought Zayd into existence when Zayd is nonexistent.

So the form is one, if you have understood. However, the word "transmutation (*istiḥāla*)" is not ascribed to God, even though He has ascribed "self-transmutation" to Himself. . . .

The attribute of self (*waṣf nafsī*) cannot be eliminated from that which is described by it. Otherwise, the object of description would itself be eliminated, since the attribute is identical to the object. The priority (*taqaddum*) of nonexistence is an attribute of self for the possible thing, since it was impossible for the possible thing to exist in eternity without beginning. Hence it must have been nonexistent in eternity without beginning. Hence the priority of nonexistence is its attribute of self.

The possible things are distinguished in their realities and forms by their very essences, since the realities bestow that. So when God desired to clothe them in the state of existence—and there was none but God, who is identical with Being, the Existent—He manifested Himself to the possible things according to the preparednesses and realities of the possible things. They saw themselves through themselves in the Being of Him who gave them existence, while they remained in their state of nonexistence. For they have perceptions in the state of their nonexistence, just as they perceive that which perceives them in the state of their nonexistence. That is why it has been mentioned in the Law that God commanded the possible thing to come into engendered existence, and it did so.

If the possible thing did not possess the reality of hearing and perceiving the command of the Real when He turned His attentiveness (*tawajjuh*) toward it, it would not have come to be, nor would God have described it as coming to be, nor would He have described Himself as speaking to that thing described by nonexistence. In this way the possible thing possesses all the faculties by which it perceives the objects pertaining to these perceptions. When He commanded the possible things to come to be, they found no existence by which they might be qualified, since there was nothing except the Being of the Real. Hence they became manifest as forms within the Being of the Real. That is why the divine and engendered (*kawnī*) attributes interpenetrate (*tadākhul*). The creatures are described by the attributes of the Real, and the Real is described by the attributes of the creatures.

Hence he who says, "I have seen nothing but God" speaks the truth. He who says, "I have seen nothing but the cosmos," speaks the truth. He who says, "I have seen no thing," speaks the truth, because of the speed of the transmutation and the lack of stability (*thabāt*); so he says, "I have not seen anything."

As for him who says, "I have never seen anything without seeing God before it"[11]—well, that is what we say: The possible thing possesses a perception in the state of its nonexistence. So when the command arrives to come to be, it finds nothing but the Being of the Real. It becomes manifest within Being to itself, seeing God before it sees itself. When the Being of the Real clothes it, it sees itself at that time. Then it says, "I have never seen anything without seeing God before it," that is, before it comes to be within Him. So the Real receives the form of that thing. He who does not understand the situation in this manner does not understand the Real, creation, or these relationships.

So "Every thing is annihilated" in form through transformation "except its face" (Koran 28:88). The pronoun "its" refers to "thing." The thing is annihilated in respect of its form, but not in respect of its face and reality, which is nothing but the Being of the Real through which it has become manifest to itself. "To it belongs the property" (28:88); in other words, that thing exercises a property in the Face, so the properties are diverse in accordance with the diversity of the forms. "And to it you shall be returned" (28:88) in that property. In other words, to that thing will be returned the property through which the thing exercised a property upon the Face. . . . So there is nothing but annihilation and bringing into existence within a Single Entity. There is no changing (*tabdīl*) except God's. "God's creation possesses no changing" (30:30). "God's words possess no changing" (10:64). On the contrary, the changing belongs to Him, just as He possesses the affair from before and after. This is demanded by His reporting about Himself that He is "the First and the Last" (57:3). (III 254.23, 255.8)

One of Ibn al-ʿArabī's arguments to prove the new creation is that there can be no stillness (*sukūn*), that is, lack of motion (*ḥaraka*), in existence. A few of the reasons for this have already been mentioned, while others need to be discussed in the context of cosmology.

Motion has a tremendous authority which is witnessed in the corporeal bodies and their concomitants (*lawāzim*) and which is intelligible within meanings and everything whose limits are unknown. Motion permeates the existent things in the most complete manner. The first property it possesses in everything other than God is that the entities leave and pass from the state of nonexistence to the state of existence. There can be no rest (*istiqrār*) whatsoever in any existent thing, since rest is stillness, and stillness is lack of motion. (II 629.28)

The cause of the speed and lastingness of continual change is that the Root is such. Hence He gives to engendered existence in accordance with the fact that He is Ever-creating perpetually because of the reality of His Level, while engendered existence is poor and needy perpetually. Hence all existence is perpetually in motion, in this world and the hereafter, since bringing to be does not take place from stillness. On God's part there are perpetual turnings of attentiveness and inexhaustible words. That is His saying, "[What is with you comes to an end,] but what is with God remains" (16:96). With God there is turning of the attentiveness; that is His saying, "[Our only speech to a thing] when We desire it [is to say to it 'Be!', and it is]" (16:40). [By inexhaustible words we mean] the Word of the Presence (*kalimat al-ḥaḍra*), that is, His word "Be!" to every thing He desires, in the meaning that is appropriate for His majesty. "Be" is a word denoting existence, so nothing comes from it except existence. No nonexistence comes from it, since nonexistence cannot "be," since being (*kawn*) is existence. These turnings of the attentiveness and words are kept in the Treasuries of Generosity for every thing that receives existence.

God says, "There is no thing whose treasuries are not with Us" (Koran 15:21). That is what we just said. God also says, "We send it not down but in a known measure" (15:21) in respect of His name the Wise. For the authority of wisdom pertains to this divine sending down, which is to bring these things out from the Treasuries to the existence of their entities.

This is what we meant in the first sentence of this book by our words, "Praise belongs to God who brought the things into existence from a nonexistence and from its nonexistence."[12] ["Its nonexistence" means] the "nonexistence of nonexistence," which is an existence. This is the relationship defined by the fact that the things are preserved in these Treasuries, existent for God, immutable in their entities, not existent for themselves. In regard to their own entities, they come into existence from a nonexistence; but in regard to the fact that they are with God in these Treasuries, they come into existence from the nonexistence of nonexistence, which is Being.

If you want, you can give preponderance to the fact that they are in the Treasuries. Then we say: He brought the things into existence from their existence in the Treasuries to their existence in their entities. . . . And if you want, you can say: He brought the things into existence from a nonexistence, after you understand the meaning which I have mentioned to you. Say whatever you want. In any case, He brings them into existence in the place where they become manifest to their entities.

As for God's words, "What is with you comes to an end" (16:96), that is correct in the doctrine, for here the entity of the substance is addressed. Those existent things which are "with" the substance are the attributes, accidents, and phenomena which God has brought into existence in the locus (*maḥall*) [i.e., the substance]. In the second moment, or the second state—say whichever you like—after the moment or state of its existence, it ceases to exist with us. This is what He means by, "What is with you comes to an end." He renews for the substance the similars or opposites (*aḍdād*) perpetually from these Treasuries. This is the meaning of the words of the theologians, "The accident does not remain for two moments." (II 280.31)

Never-Repeating Self-Disclosures

Ibn al-ʿArabī quotes Abū Ṭālib al-Makkī (d. 386/996), author of the famous Sufi manual *Qūt al-qulūb*, as saying, "God never discloses Himself in a single form to two individuals, nor in a single form twice."[13] Abū Ṭālib's saying may have been the source for the more succinct expression of the same idea which later gains the quality of a Sufi axiom: *Lā takrār fi'l-tajallī*—"There is no repetition in self-disclosure," or, "Self-disclosure never repeats itself." The reason for this is the Divine Vastness and the infinity of the possible things. The immutable entities represent every possible form and modality that existence can assume, and these are infinite; hence, in disclosing Itself in each, Being never repeats Itself.

> The Prophet said in a hadith which unveiling has shown to be sound, "When God discloses Himself to a thing, it humbles itself to Him."[14] God discloses Himself perpetually, since changes (*taghayyurāt*) are witnessed perpetually in the manifest things and the nonmanifest things, the unseen and the visible, the sensory and the intelligible. His task is self-disclosure, and the task of the existent things is change and passage from one state to another state. Among us there are those who recognize this and those who do not recognize it. Those who recognize it worship Him in every state. Those who do not recognize it deny Him in every state. It is established in the sound tradition that the Prophet said, "Praise belongs to God for every state."[15] So he lauded Him for every state, since through His self-disclosure He bestows every state. . . .

"Each day He is upon some task" (55: 29). [The "tasks"] are divine states within engendered entities through names that are relationships specified by the changes within engendered existence. He discloses Himself as the One Entity within diverse entities in engendered existence. The entities see their forms within the One Entity; parts of the cosmos witness other parts within It. Some of them are affinitive (*munāsib*), that is, compatible (*muwāfiq*), while others are not affinitive, that is, incompatible (*mukhālif*). Hence compatibility and incompatibility become manifest in the entities of the cosmos in both this world and the hereafter, for the entities of the cosmos never cease seeing each other in that Self-disclosing Entity. That Entity's lights are reflected upon them, because of what they have acquired from It. Hence there occurs in the cosmos what occurs, in this world and the hereafter, as an effect of the reality of that Entity when the sight of the cosmos becomes connected to It. This is like a mirror facing the sun. The sun's radiance is reflected upon a piece of cotton facing the reflected light, and hence a fire breaks out. This is exactly what becomes manifest in the cosmos when parts of it leave effects upon other parts as a result of witnessing that Entity. (II 304.33)

He who knows the Divine Vastness knows that nothing is repeated in existence; rather, it is imagined that the existence of things similar in form is identical to that which is past. But these are their similars, not their exact entities; what is similar to a thing is not identical with it. (II 432.12)

The appearance of multiplicity in the cosmos does not negate the oneness of the Self-discloser (*al-mutajallī*), any more than the multiplicity of a person's thoughts and situations negates the oneness of his self.

Though self-disclosure never repeats itself, the Self-discloser is known to be One. For example, man knows that he himself fluctuates in states, thoughts, acts, and awareness. All of this takes place in diverse forms. In spite of this fluctuation and transmutation, he knows his own entity and self and that his he-ness remains the same without ceasing, in spite of his fluctuation. So also is the form of self-disclosure: Though it is many and never repeats itself, yet people do not remain ignorant of the knowledge of Him who discloses Himself in these forms while One in Entity; the qualities He assumes do not veil Him. (III 282.21)

In the following passage, Ibn al-ʿArabī is discussing the station (*maqām*) of "satisfaction" (*riḍā*), which he, like other Muslims, recognizes as an important character trait that must be developed in the path of spiritual growth. But he points out that satisfaction is not always desirable, especially in the matter of knowledge.

For the exoterics abandoning satisfaction
  is a stain.
For the Folk of finding God it
  is a sign
of their having realized
  the Entity of their Creator,
in respect of the fact that in Him
  they are obliterated and affirmed. . . .

God is much vaster than that a person should be satisfied with a little of what comes from Him. Rather, one should be satisfied with Him, but not with what comes from Him, since satisfaction with what comes from Him cuts off the Men[16] from their aspirations (*himma*). God commands His Prophet with His words, "Say: 'My Lord, increase me in knowledge!'" (20:114), even though he had actualized the knowledge of "the ancients and the later folk" and had been given "the all-comprehensive words."[17] So there is nothing too great to be sought from God, since that which is sought from Him is infinite and hence has no end where we should come to a halt. So make your seeking of increase vast, if you are among those who know God! And since the vastness of the possible things accepts no finitude, what do you suppose about the Divine Vastness? (II 213.23)

That which is past never returns, since were it to return, something in existence would repeat itself, but there is no repetition, because of the Divine Vastness. (II 185.27)

The fact that all existent entities are different means that each is able to receive the divine self-disclosure only to the extent of its own preparedness. This means, as will be seen in detail later on, that each belief (*iʿtiqād*) about God is unique to the believer who holds it. In fact, the object of our belief is only ourselves, since God stands far beyond our capacity to conceptualize or understand. By the same token, even if we should attain to the state of "presence" (*ḥuḍūr*) with God, the God with whom we are present is determined by our ability to encompass Him; we can never encompass God, so we are only present with ourselves. Ibn al-ʿArabī makes this point while discussing man's return (*rujūʿ*) to God, through which he moves "away from" this world and by which God "returns" to man.

> The realities demand that you will not be present except with yourself. The actual situation is that when you are present through "presence" with Him who is present, you cannot be present with Him except in keeping with the limits given by your level; hence you have become present with yourself, not with Him. For He does not disclose Himself to you except to the measure that your level allows. So understand this! You will profit from it. Do not let it be hidden from you while you are returning to Him away from that from which you are returning, lest you imagine that you are returning to that which is higher than you. For you will not be returning except from yourself to yourself.
>
> The Real does not return to you except through you, not through Himself. For it is not in the capacity of the creature to endure Him. That is why His returnings undergo variation (*tanawwuʿ*), His self-disclosures are diverse, and His loci of manifestation are multiple without repetition. But in Himself He is Incomparable with multiplicity and change. "Nothing is like Him" (42:11) in that which is attributed to His Essence. (II 589.28)

Boredom

God's perpetual self-disclosures to the creatures mean that creation is renewed at each instant. Hence, no one with any understanding of the nature of the things can suffer boredom (*malal*), whether in this world or the next.

> The men of knowledge (*al-ʿulamāʾ*) are forever joyful, but others remain in the shadows of bewilderment, wandering astray in this world and the next. Were it not for the renewal of creation at each instant, boredom would overcome the entities, since Nature requires boredom. This requirement decrees that the entities must be renewed. That is why the Messenger of God said about God, "God does not become bored that you should become bored." So the boredom of the cosmos is identical with the boredom of the Real. But no one in the cosmos becomes bored except him who has no unveiling and does not witness the renewal of creation constantly at each instant and does not witness God as Ever-creating perpetually. Boredom takes place only as the result of unceasing companionship (*istiṣḥāb*). (III 506.17)

In the following passage Ibn al-ʿArabī is discussing the nature of "curtaining" (*sitr*), which is the opposite of disclosure. God does not really place anything behind a curtain, but our ignorance prevents us from seeing the realities as they are in themselves. "He placed no veil upon you but yourself" (III 215.3). "You are identical with the curtain over yourself" (III 229.12). "The greatest of veils are two, one supra-sensory (*maʿnawī*), that is, ignorance, and the other sensory: you yourself" (III 214.26). It is only ignorance which leads us to think that God is curtained and not self-disclosing.

> Some people do not know that at every instant God has a self-disclosure which does not take the form of the previous self-disclosure. When such a person lacks this perception, he may become the un-

> ceasing companion of a single self-disclosure, and its witnessing may become drawn out for him. . . . Hence boredom will overcome him, but boredom in this station is lack of reverence (*iḥtirām*) toward the Divine Side, since "They are in confusion as to a new creation" (50:15) at every instant. They imagine that the situation is not changing, and so a curtain is let down over them because of the boredom which leads to irreverence, after God has deprived them of knowledge of themselves and Him. So they imagine that they are they in each instant; and they *are* they in respect of their substantiality, but not in respect of their attributes. (II 554.16)

Between lover and beloved the pleasure (*ladhdha*) of encounter (*liqā'*) is greater than the pleasure of unceasing companionship. That is why God keeps Himself separate from His lover. It also explains the bliss of paradise: Everyone in the Garden is constantly parted from the bliss he enjoys and thereby experiences the ever-renewed encounters with the divine display.

> The Beloved keeps Himself absent (*ghayba*) from the lover for the sake of imparting knowledge and teaching courtesy in love. For if the lover is truthful in his claim, while God tests him by the absence of his Beloved, then there will appear from the lover a movement of yearning to witness Him. Through this yearning he shows the truth of his claim; thereby his station is increased, and his reward through bliss in his Beloved is multiplied. For the pleasure which he finds at encounter is greater than the pleasure of unceasing companionship. This is similar to the frightened person who finds the sweetness of reaching security: The sweetness of unceasing security is not nearly as intense. So the bliss (*na'īm*) of the frightened person is multiplied. That is why the folk of the Garden dwell in a bliss that is renewed at each succeeding instant in all their senses, their meanings, and the divine self-disclosures; they are constantly in delight (*ṭarab*). Hence their bliss is the greatest of blisses—because of expecting separation and imagining there will not be companionship. Since man is ignorant of this level, he seeks unceasing companionship. But the man of knowledge seeks the unceasing companionship of the *renewal* of bliss and of the discernment between the two blisses, so that he may enjoy a new bliss.
>
> In fact, it is like this in actual fact, even though not everyone recognizes it, nor does every eye and rational faculty witness it. For in actual fact [existence] is renewed at each instant. But a person who is ignorant does not witness the renewal of bliss, so he becomes bored. Were this ignorance to be lifted from him, so also would boredom be lifted. Boredom is the greatest proof that man has remained ignorant of God's preserving his existence and renewing his blessings at each instant. May God verify us through the most complete unveiling and the most inclusive locus of witnessing! (II 653.25)

The Heart

One of the words employed above as a synonym for transformation was *taqallub* or "fluctuation." From the same root we have the word *qalb* or "heart." As a verbal noun, *qalb* is more or less synonymous with *taqallub*. The dictionaries define *qalb* as "reversal, overturn, transformation, change" and *taqallub* as "alteration, transformation, change, fluctuation, variableness, inconstancy." Thus the Shaykh sees the heart as a place of constant change and fluctuation. He finds the divine root of the heart's fluctuating nature mentioned in various hadiths. For example, the Prophet said, "The hearts of all the children of Adam are like a single heart between two of the fingers of the All-merciful. He turns (*taṣrīf*) it wherever He desires. O God, O Turner of Hearts, turn our hearts toward obeying Thee!"[18] In many hadiths God is called the "Turner of hearts" (*muṣarrif al-qulūb*) or "He who makes hearts fluctuate" (*muqallib al-qulūb*).[19]

In Islamic texts in general and Ibn al-'Arabī in particular, the heart is a locus for knowledge rather than for sentiments or feelings. The Koran employs the term about 130 times and often attributes understanding and intelligence to the healthy heart. Ibn al-ʿArabī compares the heart to the Kaʿba, making it the "noblest house in the man of faith" (III 250.24). He also declares that it is the Throne of God (*al-ʿarsh*) in the microcosm, alluding here to the oft-quoted *ḥadīth qudsī*, "My earth and My heaven embrace Me not, but the heart of My believing servant does embrace Me."[20] This "embracing" (*saʿa*) takes place through "knowledge of God (*al-ʿilm bi Allāh*)" (III 250.26). The heart possesses such a tremendous capacity (*wusʿ*) because of its connection to the All-merciful, between whose two fingers it dwells. Moreover, according to the Koran, it is the All-merciful who "sat upon the Throne" (20:5); and God's mercy "embraces all things" (7:156). The only other divine attribute which possesses such an all-embracing nature is knowledge; in the words of the angels who bear the Throne, "Our Lord, Thou embracest all things in mercy and knowledge" (Koran 40:7).

> The heart is His Throne and not delimited by any specific attribute. On the contrary, it brings together all the divine names and attributes, just as the All-merciful possesses all the Most Beautiful Names (Koran 17:110). (III 129.17)

The infinite capacity of the heart places it beyond delimitation (*taqyīd*) by anything whatsoever. Like Being it is Nondelimited (*muṭlaq*), free and absolved from all limitations and constraints. To the extent a person verifies the nature of things by means of his heart, he can understand God and the cosmos. But to the extent that he follows the way of his reason or rational faculty (*ʿaql*), he will remain in constant constriction and binding. Here the Shaykh points to the root meaning of the term *ʿaql*, closely connected to the "fetter" (*ʿiqāl*) used to hobble a camel. Reason strives to define and delimit God, but that is impossible. The heart frees God of all constraints and absolves Him of all limitations. The heart alone is able to perceive God's self-disclosures through the faculty of imagination.

> "Surely in that," that is, in the constant change in the cosmos, "there is a reminder" of the constant change of the Root, "for him who has a heart" (Koran 50:37), since the heart possesses fluctuation (*taqlīb*) from one state to another. That is why it is called "heart" (*qalb*). He who explains "heart" as meaning "reason" has no knowledge of the realities, for "reason" is a "delimitation" (*taqyīd*), the word *ʿaql* being derived from "fetter." But if he means by "reason," which is delimitation, what we mean by it, that is, that which is delimited by fluctuation so that it never ceases undergoing transformation, then he is correct. . . .
>
> We know that one of the attributes of Time (*al-dahr*) is transmutation (*taḥawwul*) and fluctuation (*qalb*) and that "God is Time."[21] It has been established that He undergoes transmutation in forms and that "Each day He is upon some task" (55:29). . . . If man examines (*murāqaba*) his heart, he will see that it does not remain in a single state. So he should know that if the Root were not like this, this fluctuation would have no support. But the heart is between two of the fingers of its Creator, who is the All-merciful. . . . So "He who knows himself knows his Lord."[22] And in the hadith of the fingers there are divine glad tidings, since he attributed the fingers to the All-merciful. Hence He does not cause the heart to fluctuate except from one mercy to another mercy, even though there is affliction (*balāʾ*) in the various kinds of fluctuation. But there lies in affliction's midst a mercy hidden from man and known to the Real, for the two fingers belong to the All-merciful. (III 198.33)

In discussing the spiritual station of "longing" (*raghba*), Ibn al-ʿArabī points out that in Sufi terminology there are three kinds of longing, all of which take place in the heart. One of these is "longing for the reality (*al-ḥaqīqa*)." In explaining the meaning of this expression, he refers to two other spiritual stations, "stability" (*tamkīn*) and its opposite, "variegation" (*talwīn*). According to most authorities, stability is a higher station than variegation, but Ibn al-ʿArabī holds that variegation is in fact higher, since it corresponds to the nature of things, the divine self-transmutation in forms. Hence, he says, the Verifiers attain to the station of "stability in variegation" (*al-tamkīn fiʾl-talwīn*), just as they actualize the heart "which is delimited by fluctuation so that it never ceases undergoing transformation," as said above.

> In existence the "reality" is variegation. He who is stable in variegation is the Owner of Stability. The heart longs to witness this reality. God made the heart the locus of this longing to bring the actualization (*taḥṣīl*) of this reality near to man, since there is fluctuation in the heart. God did not place this longing in the rational faculty, since reason possesses delimitation. If this longing were in the rational faculty, the person might see that he is fixed in a single state. But since it lies in the heart, fluctuation comes upon him quickly. For the heart is between the fingers of the All-merciful, so it does not remain in a single state in the reality of the situation. Hence it is fixed in its fluctuation within its state in accordance with its witnessing of the way the fingers cause it to fluctuate. (II 532.30)

Since the heart is connected to the two fingers of the All-merciful, mercy is the heart's fundamental reality. It cannot but return to the divine mercy in the end (*biʾl-maʾāl*). This has important eschatological consequences, as Ibn al-ʿArabī often reminds us.

> Do you not see that the heart lies between the two fingers of the All-merciful? That which causes it to fluctuate is only the All-merciful; no other divine name enters in upon it along with the All-merciful. This name gives to it only what it possesses in its own reality, and His Mercy "embraces all things" (7:156). Hence you will not see anything in the heart's fluctuation which leads to distress (*ʿanāʾ*), chastisement (*ʿadhāb*), and wretchedness (*shaqāʾ*), unless there is also a hidden mercy along with it, since the heart lies between the fingers of the All-merciful, who causes it to fluctuate. If He wills, He keeps it straight (*iqāma*), and if He wills, He causes it to swerve (*izāgha*) from that straightness, so this is a relative inclination [from straightness].
>
> Hence the heart ends up (*maʾāl*) at mercy by the property of the authority of this name. He whose heart swerves is like him whose heart goes straight. This is a glad tidings from God to His servants. "O My servants who have been immoderate toward yourselves!"—here He does not mention one kind of immoderation (*saraf*) rather than another, so in this immoderation He includes all the states of those who are immoderate—"Despair not of God's mercy," since that which has made you swerve is the fingers of the All-merciful; "surely God forgives all sins" (Koran 39:53).
>
> This is a report which accepts no abrogation (*naskh*). This verse should be combined with His words, "God does not forgive that any should be associated with Him" (Koran 4:48).[23] We conclude that a person is punished for his associating others with God as God wills, then the fingers of the All-merciful display their properties within him. So he ends up with the All-merciful. Those kinds of swerving less than associating others with God which are forgiven are forgiven after punishment. These are the people of major sins (*kabāʾir*) who will be taken out of the Fire through intercession after they have become coals as long as they have not associated others with Him.[24] Faith in this is mandatory. There are also those who are forgiven without punishment. So there is no escape from ending up in mercy. (II 171.24)

The heart is the place of love for God, since only the heart can know God in order to love Him. The perfect lover of God accepts Him and loves Him in every form He assumes through His self-transmutation. Ibn al-ʿArabī explains these points in answering one of al-

Tirmidhī's questions:[25] " What is the goblet of love (*ka's al-ḥubb*)?"

> The goblet of love is the lover's heart, not his reason or his sense perception. For the heart fluctuates from state to state, just as God—who is the Beloved—is "Each day upon some task" (55:29). So the lover undergoes constant variation in the object of his love in keeping with the constant variation of the Beloved in His acts. The lover is like the clear and pure glass goblet which undergoes constant variation according to the variation of the liquid within it. The color of the lover is the color of the Beloved. This belongs only to the heart, since reason comes from the world of delimitation; that is why it is called "reason," a word derived from "fetter." As for sense perception, it obviously and necessarily belongs to the world of delimitation, in contrast to the heart.
>
> This can be explained by the fact that love has many diverse and mutually opposed properties. Hence nothing receives these properties except that which has the capacity (*quwwa*) to fluctuate along with love in those properties. This belongs only to the heart. In order to ascribe something like this to God, look at His words, "I respond to the call of the caller when he calls to Me" (2:186); "God does not become bored that you should be bored"; "When someone remembers (*dhikr*) Me in himself, I remember him in Myself."[26] All the revealed Law (*al-sharʿ*), or most of it, is of this type.
>
> The wine is precisely what becomes actualized in the cup. And we have explained[27] that the cup is identical with the locus of manifestation, the wine is identical with the Manifest within it, and the drinking (*shurb*) is that which is actualized from the Self-discloser in His locus of self-disclosure. (II 113.33)

Nondelimitation

God in Himself is free of any constraints, "Independent of the worlds," "nondelimited" (*muṭlaq*) by any attribute whatsoever. As a result, the Divine Essence can only be discussed in terms of negative (*salbī*) qualities. But God is not only Nondelimited, He is also free of delimitation (*taqyīd*) by nondelimitation (*iṭlāq*). In other words, since He is free from all limitations, He is also free from the limitation of being free; as a result He can delimit Himself through all constraints and limitations, without thereby becoming delimited by them. In His self-delimitation—which becomes manifest through His self-disclosure and self-transmutation—He remains eternally free from limits and bounds.

> God possesses Nondelimited Being, but no delimitation prevents Him from delimitation. On the contrary, He possesses all delimitations. Hence He is Nondelimited Delimitation; no single delimitation rather than another exercises its property over Him. (III 162.23)

Just as God is not delimited by nondelimitation, so also He is not incomparable with similarity. This is a restatement of Ibn al-ʿArabī's basic objection to those who limit themselves to a rational understanding of the Divine Reality. The rational thinkers imagine that God's incomparability means that He cannot in any way be similar. On the contrary, says Ibn al-ʿArabī, His very incomparability proves that He cannot be limited by any limitations whatsoever, including that limitation which is to declare Him incomparable and only incomparable. Hence He is also similar.

> God delimits Himself by self-transmutation only to open up the servant to the knowledge that the actual situation is infinite, and that which is infinite does not enter under delimitation. That which accepts transmutation from one form to another accepts transmutation within forms ad infinitum. . . . So the servant comes out of the limits of delimitation through [witnessing God's] delimitation, in order to know that the Object of his witnessing is Nondelimited Being. Hence his witnessing is also nondelimited in keeping with the nondelimitation of its Object.

Hence the transmutation from form to form gives him a knowledge he did not have. . . .

The greatest ascetic discipline (*riyāḍa*) of the knowledgeable servant is to refrain from denying Him in any form and from delimiting Him by incomparability, for He is absolutely incomparable with any declaration of incomparability which delimits. (II 483.7)

The fact that God can choose to delimit Himself because of His nondelimitation explains why He has created the cosmos, even though He is "Independent of the worlds."

When a thing's reality is such that it is delimited, it cannot be nondelimited in any respect as long as its entity remains, for delimitation is its attribute of self (*ṣifa nafsiyya*). If a thing's reality is to be nondelimited, it can receive no delimitation whatsoever, for its attribute of self is to be nondelimited.

However, it is not in the capacity of the delimited thing to receive nondelimitation, since its attribute is incapacity (*ʿajz*). Even if the divine preservation accompanies the thing in order that its entity should remain in existence, poverty is inseparable from it. But the Nondelimited delimits Itself if It wills and does not delimit Itself if It wills. For that is one of Its attributes through being Nondelimited: Its will (*mashīʾa*) is nondelimited. From here the Real has obligated (*ījāb*) Himself and entered into the covenant (*al-ʿahd*) with His servant. He said concerning obligation, "Your Lord has written," that is, obligated, "for Himself mercy" (Koran 6:54). Hence He has obligated Himself. No "other" has obligated that upon Him, so He is not delimited by other than Himself. Hence He delimited Himself toward His servants as a mercy toward them and a hidden gentleness.

God said concerning the covenant, "Fulfill My covenant, and I shall fulfill your covenant" (2:40). Hence He prescribed (*taklīf*) for them and He prescribed for Himself. They have proofs that He speaks the truth in His words, so He mentioned that to put them at ease.

Now all of this—I mean His entering under delimitation for His servants—is in respect of the fact that He is a god, not in respect of the fact that He is an essence. For the Essence is Independent of the worlds, but the king is not independent of the kingdom, since, if there were no kingdom, he could not be called "king." Hence the Level [of Divinity] bestows delimitation, not the Essence of the Real. (III 72.20)

The "gnostics through Him" (*al-ʿārifūn bihi*) know God through God, not through any human faculties; they combine the declaration of God's incomparability (*tanzīh*) with the affirmation of His similarity (*tashbīh*). They recognize that through His very nondelimitation He assumes every constraint and boundary.

When the gnostics know Him through Him, they become distinguished from those who know Him through their own rational consideration (*naẓar*), for they possess nondelimitation, while others have delimitation. The gnostics through Him witness Him in each thing or in the entity of each thing, but those who know Him through rational consideration are removed far from Him by a distance which is required by their declaration of His incomparability. Hence they place themselves on one side and the Real on the other. Then they call to Him "from a far place" (Koran 41:44). (III 410.17)

The nondelimitation of the gnostics, who are also called the "Folk of Allah," means that they are able to discern God in all things. Since God—Being—in His nondelimitation assumes every delimitation, the gnostics gaze upon Him through an all-inclusive witnessing. It is only they who recognize God in every form into which He transmutes Himself on the Day of Resurrection.

The science of the sects (*niḥal*) and the creeds (*milal*) is a science which the person of faith need not study or consider. But it is incumbent upon the Folk of Allah to know the doctrine of every sect and creed concerning God, in order to witness Him in every form and in order not to stand in the place of denial. For He permeates existence, so no one denies Him except those who are limited. But the Folk of Allah follow Him whose folk they are, so His property flows over them. And His property is the lack of delimitation. Hence He possesses all-pervading Being (*wujūd*), while they possess all-pervading witnessing (*shuhūd*). That person who delimits His Being delimits the witnessing of Him; he is not one of the Folk of Allah. . . .

God describes Himself as "sitting [upon the Throne]" (20:5), "descending to the heaven [of this world],"[28] and exercising free disposal "in every direction" of engendered existence, "toward which He turns" (2:148). So "Whithersoever you turn, there is the Face of God" (2:115). But "Turn your face towards the Holy Mosque" (2:144), since this does not eliminate the property of God's Face being wherever you turn. However, God has chosen for you that you should turn your face toward something that will give you felicity (*saʿāda*), but [this turning occurs] in a specific state, which is the daily prayer. God did not place this delimitation upon other spatially located things (*ayniyyāt*). Hence for you He combined delimitation and nondelimitation, just as for Himself He combined incomparability and similarity. He said, "Nothing is like Him, and He is the Hearing, the Seeing" (42:11). (III 161.13)

We began this chapter with the "new creation." We conclude with two passages which connect the new creation to the divine nondelimitation and tie it in with the heart, the rational faculty, and the combination of incomparability and similarity.

In the view of the Verifiers, the Real is too exalted "to disclose Himself in a single form twice or to two individuals." The Real never repeats anything, because of His nondelimitation and the Divine Vastness, since repetition amounts to constraint (*ḍīq*) and delimitation. (II 657.13)

After those who had faith in God came to know Him through considerative proofs, their rational faculties saw that God still asks them to know Him. So they came to know that there is another knowledge of God which is not reached by way of reflection. Hence they employed ascetic discipline, retreats (*khalwa*), spiritual struggle (*mujāhada*), cutting off of attachments (*qaṭʿ al-ʿalāʾiq*), isolation (*infirād*), and sitting with God with the aim of freeing the locus (*tafrīgh al-maḥall*) and sanctifying the heart (*taqdīs al-qalb*) from the stains of reflective thoughts (*afkār*), for these thoughts take engendered things as their object. They heard that the Real descends to His servants and seeks to win them over. So they knew that the path to Him in respect of Him is nearer to Him than the path of their reflection—especially for those who have faith. They may have heard His words, "When someone comes to Me running, I come to him rushing,"[29] or that the heart of the person of faith embraces God's majesty and tremendousness.[30]

So the servant turned his face totally toward Him and cut himself off from every faculty that takes him away from Him. When the servant turned his face, God effused from His light a divine knowledge, teaching him by way of witnessing and self-disclosure that God is not received or rejected by any engendered thing. That is why He said, "Surely in that is a reminder for him who has a heart" (50:37). He mentions only the heart because the heart is known through constant fluctuation in states, since it does not remain in a single state. So also are the divine self-disclosures. Hence he who does not witness the self-disclosures in his heart denies them. For the rational faculty delimits, like all other faculties except the heart. The heart does not delimit, but quickly fluctuates in every state. That is why the Lawgiver said, "The heart is between two of the fingers of the All-merciful; He makes it fluctuate as He desires." The heart fluctuates with the fluctuation of self-disclosures, but the rational faculty is not like that.

The heart is the faculty (*quwwa*) which is beyond the stage of reason. If in this verse God had meant by "heart" the rational faculty, he would not have said, "for him who has a heart," since every human being has a rational faculty, but not every human being has been given the faculty which is beyond the stage of reason and which is named "heart" in this verse.

That is why He said, "for him who has a heart."

Fluctuation in the heart is equivalent to the divine self-transmutation in forms. Hence knowledge of the Real from the Real comes only through the heart, not reason. Then the rational faculty receives knowledge from the heart, just as it receives from reflection. So the heart does not "embrace" Him except by overturning (*qalb*) what is with you. The meaning of "overturning what is with you" is as follows: You attach your knowledge to Him and apprehend (*ḍabṭ*) some specific thing in your knowledge. But the highest thing you apprehend about Him in your knowledge of Him is that He cannot be apprehended and is nondelimited, and that He does not resemble anything, nor does anything resemble Him. Hence He is not apprehended, but He is apprehended by His being distinguished from that which is apprehended. So that which cannot be apprehended has been apprehended. This is like your words, "Incapacity to attain comprehension is itself comprehension."[31]

The Real can only be embraced by the heart. The meaning of this is that the Real cannot be judged to receive (*qabūl*), nor not to receive. For the Essence and Ipseity (*inniyya*) of the Real are unknown to engendered existence, especially since He has given reports of Himself in the Book and the Sunna through contradictory things (*naqīḍayn*). He declares Himself similar in one place and incomparable in another. He declares Himself incomparable through His words, "Nothing is like Him," and similar through His words, "And He is the Hearing, the Seeing" (42:11). Hence thoughts of similarity were dispersed, and thoughts of incomparability were scattered.

In reality, he who professes incomparability has delimited Him and confined Him in his declaration of incomparability and emptied Him of similarity, while he who professes similarity has also delimited and confined Him in his declaration of similarity and emptied Him of incomparability. But the truth is found in combining the statements of the two groups. He is not declared incomparable in any manner that will remove Him from similarity, nor is He declared similar in any manner that will remove Him from incomparability. So do not declare Him nondelimited and thus delimited by being distinguished from delimitation! For if He is distinguished, then He is delimited by His nondelimitation. And if He is delimited by His nondelimitation, then He is not He. So He is the Delimited by the attributes of majesty by which He has delimited Himself, and He is the Nondelimited by the names of perfection which He has named Himself. And He is the One, the Real, the Disclosed (*al-jalī*), the Hidden (*al-khafī*). There is no god but He, the All-high, the Tremendous. (I 289.20)

7. *COSMIC IMAGINATION*

No one will find true knowledge of the nature of things by seeking explanations in "either/or." The real situation will have to be sought in "both/and" or "neither/nor." Ambiguity does not grow up simply from our ignorance: it is an ontological fact, inherent in the nature of the cosmos. Nothing is certain but Being Itself, yet It is the "coincidence of opposites" (*jamʿ al-aḍdād*), bringing all opposites together in a single reality.

The deeper we delve into the nature of existence, the more clearly we are faced with its fundamental ambiguity. Everything that exists in the cosmos takes its existence and attributes from the Divine Reality. By affirming the reality of the thing, we affirm the Reality of God, but at the same time we deny that the "thing" is God. The thing is only God in its existence and attributes, not in its specific existential thingness, where it is precisely the thing. The more one discusses this situation, the more language becomes convoluted and the observers and listeners confused and bewildered. This is as it must be, since the universe is He/not He.

The clearest access shared by all human beings to the nature of existence, which is "everything other than God," is our own imagination, especially dreams. The more deeply we delve into our own imagination, the more clearly we see that its characteristics coincide with those of existence itself. Just as our imagination is the *barzakh* between our spirits and bodies, so also existence is the *barzakh* between Being and nothingness. Everything that we observe in imagination on a microcosmic scale takes place on a macrocosmic scale in the Nondelimited World of Imagination, which is existence. Just as the world we observe in dreams is spiritual and corporeal, intelligible and sensory, meaning and form, so also the world that God observes in His "dream" is built of Being and nothingness. When we wake up and want to understand our dreams, we try to interpret them or go to an interpreter to do this for us. So also, when we die and thereby "wake up" to the cosmic dream of God, we will find the interpretation of our dream (even though that "waking up" is itself another stage in the cosmic dream).

Without knowledge of imagination and its functioning, on whatever level it is envisaged, many fundamental religious teachings cannot be understood. It is because of their ignorance of imagination that the Peripatetic philosophers and the theologians insisted upon "interpreting"—that is, "explaining away"—all the revelational data that does not accord with the laws of logic and reason. Others simply gave up trying to understand such things and said, "God says so, so it must be true." But this is not to give intelligence its full credit, since there are modes of gaining knowledge of the true situation through the power of imagination, which can perceive the divine self-disclosures for what they are.

Ibn al-ʿArabī's dialectic of negation (*nafy*) and affirmation (*ithbāt*) is hardly new in Islamic thought. The Koran often negates the very things it affirms, a fact that has led to a great deal of theological squabbling. We have seen a few examples of the Koranic mode of combining affirmation and negation in the opposing and contrary divine names, or in some of Ibn al-ʿArabī's favorite verses, such as "Nothing is like Him, and He is the Hearing, the Seeing" (42:11). The most concise traditional expression of the form of this dialectic is found in the Muslim declaration of faith, the "witnessing" (*shahāda*), "[There is] no god but God," which is made up of both negation and affirmation and is considered the definition of *tawḥīd*, the "declaration of God's Unity" that is the heart of Islam.

He/Not He

The Koranic verse that Ibn al-ʿArabī cites more often than any other to show the radical ambiguity of existence was revealed after the battle of Badr, which turned in favor of the Muslims when the Prophet picked up a handful of sand and threw it in the direction of the enemy. Concerning the Prophet's throwing of this sand, the Koran says, "You did not throw when you threw, but God threw" (8:17). The verse affirms the individual reality of the Prophet, then negates it by saying that God in fact was the reality behind the appearance. In a passage about the One Entity—Sheer Being—and the effects of the names which become manifest as the entities of the possible things, the Shaykh concludes, "There is none in Being/existence but God." He continues,

> But the clear formulation of this question is terribly difficult. Verbal expression (*ʿibāra*) falls short of it and conceptualization (*taṣawwur*) cannot define it, because it quickly escapes and its properties are contradictory. It is like His words, "You did not throw," so He negated, "when

you threw," so He affirmed, "but God threw," so He negated the engendered existence (*kawn*) of Muḥammad and affirmed Himself as identical (*ʿayn*) with Muḥammad, since He appointed for him the name "God." (II 216.12)

In discussing the "lover" (*muḥibb*), a name which applies both to the servant and to God, Ibn al-ʿArabī declares that the lover is "obliteration in affirmation" (*maḥw fī ithbāt*), and cites a number of Koranic verses that allude to this point.

> The "affirmation" of the [servant as] lover becomes manifest in the fact that religious prescriptions (*taklīf*) are made for him. . . . His "obliteration" in the midst of this affirmation appears in God's words, "God created you and what you do" (37:96); "Nothing of the command belongs to thee" (3:128); "Surely the command belongs to God entirely" (3:154); "You did not throw when you threw, but God threw" (8:17); "[Expend of] that in which He has made you vicegerents" (57:7). This is all an extremely clear explanation of "obliteration in affirmation" in God's Book. The lover has no free disposal (*taṣarruf*) except in that for which God disposes Him. His love has put him at a loss to desire anything other than what is desired for him. In actual fact the reality refuses anything but that. Everything that appears from the lover is God's creation, and the lover is the object of the act (*mafʿūl*), not the agent (*fāʿil*). Hence he is the locus within which affairs take place, so he is obliterated in affirmation.
>
> As for the "obliteration in affirmation" of God considered as the Lover, that is as follows: The eye falls only upon the act of the servant, so this is the "obliteration" of the Real. But rational proofs and unveiling allow only for the Being of the Real, not the existence of the servant and the engendered things. This is the affirmation of the Real. Hence He is obliterated in the World of the Visible (*ʿālam al-shahāda*), affirmed in the World of Witnessing (*ʿālam al-shuhūd*). (II 355.33)

The root of the cosmos or "everything other than God" is God, while the cosmos is nothing but the Being of God within which appear the properties of the nonexistent entities, properties which themselves are the effects of the divine names. So what we see are the names, and the cosmos is the outward form of all the names in differentiated mode (*tafṣīl*), just as the human being is the outward form of all the names in undifferentiated mode (*ijmāl*).

> Hence the cosmos became manifest as "alive, hearing, seeing, knowing, desiring, powerful, and speaking."[1] It works in His manner, as He said, "Say: Each works according to His manner" (Koran 17:84). The cosmos is His work, so it became manifest in the attributes of the Real. If you say concerning it, "It is God," you have spoken the truth, for God says, "but God threw." If you say concerning it, "It is creation," you have spoken the truth, for He says, "when you threw." So He clothed and bared, affirmed and negated: He/not He, unknown/known. "To God belong the most beautiful names" (7:180), and to the cosmos belongs becoming manifest through them by assuming their traits (*takhalluq*). (II 438.20)

Ibn al-ʿArabī likes to quote a hadith about Adam from the collection of Tirmidhī, part of which reads as follows:

> While His two hands were closed, God said to Adam, "Choose whichever you like." Adam replied, "I choose the right hand of the Lord, though both hands of my Lord are right and blessed." Then God opened it, and within it were Adam and His seed. He said, "My Lord, what are these?" God replied, "These are your seed."[2]

One of the passages in which Ibn al-ʿArabī comments on this hadith reads as follows:

> Adam was in that hand while he was also outside of it. Such also is the case in this question: When you consider, you will see that the cosmos is with the Real in this manner. This is a place of bewilderment (*ḥayra*): He/not He. "You did not throw when you threw, but God

threw." . . . Would that I knew who is the middle, the one who stands between the negation—His words "You did not throw"—and the affirmation—His words "But He threw." He is saying, "You are not you when you are you, but God is you." This is the meaning of our words concerning the Manifest and the loci of manifestation and the fact that He is identical with them, even though the forms of the loci of manifestation are diverse. In the same way we say concerning Zayd that he is one, despite the diversity of his bodily parts. His foot is not his hand, but it is Zayd when we say "Zayd." It is the same with all his bodily parts. His nonmanifest and his manifest, his unseen and his visible, are diverse in form, but each is identical with Zayd and not different from him. (II 444.13)

The "other" (*al-ghayr*) is in reality affirmed/not affirmed, He/not He. (II 501.4)

Imagination

According to Ibn al-ʿArabī, the reality of "He/not He" finds its clearest expression in the cosmos through imagination (*khayāl*). In dreaming, for example, which is a function of imagination, a person sees corporeal things which are not corporeal things. The objects he sees possess corporeal forms, yet they dwell not in the world of corporeal bodies, but in that imaginal world which is the soul. Imagination can take a "meaning" (*maʿnā*)—that is, a reality of the world of intelligible things without any outward form—and give to it a sensory form (*ṣūra maḥsūsa*), as we will see in detail below. This occurs in spite of the fact that in normal circumstances "meanings" and "sensory forms" are mutually exclusive, since meanings belong to the World of Intelligence and are free of any sort of matter or substratum (*mādda*), while sensory forms belong to the external world of corporeal bodies. The following description of the three kinds of possible things may help to clarify the distinction between meanings and sensory forms:

Among the possible things there are three levels of known things (*maʿlūmāt*): (1.) A level that belongs to meanings disengaged (*mujarrad*) from substrata; the characteristic of meanings is that rational faculties perceive them through proofs or a priori (*bi ṭarīq al-badāya*). (2.) A level whose characteristic is to be perceived by the senses; these are the sensory things. (3.) A level whose characteristic is to be perceived either by the rational faculty or by the senses. These are imaginal things. They are the meanings that assume shape (*tashakkul*) in sensory forms; they are given form by the form-giving faculty (*al-quwwat al-muṣawwira*), which serves the rational faculty. (II 66.14)

In spite of the fact that meanings and sensory forms are mutually contradictory, imagination possesses the strength to combine the two; hence, says Ibn al-ʿArabī, it manifests the divine name the "Strong" (*al-qawī*).

God possesses strength because of the inaccessibility (*ʿizza*) of some—or all—of the possible things, that is, the fact that they do not accept opposites. One of the effects of strength is the creation of the World of Imagination in order to make manifest within it the fact that it brings together all opposites (*al-jamʿ bayn al-aḍdād*). It is impossible for sense perception or the rational faculty to bring together opposites, but it is not impossible for imagination.

Hence the authority and strength of the Strong only became manifest in the creation of the imaginal faculty (*al-quwwat al-mutakhayyila*) and the World of Imagination, which is the closest thing to a denotation (*dalāla*) of the Real. For the Real is "the First and the Last, the Manifest and the Nonmanifest" (Koran 57:3). Abū Saʿīd al-Kharrāz was asked, "Through what have you known God?" He answered, "Through the fact that He brings opposites together." Then he recited this Koranic verse.

Were all this not in a Single Entity, there would be no profit, since no one denies the relationships. One person may have a multiplicity of relationships, so he is father, son, paternal uncle, maternal uncle, and so on, yet he is he, no one else.

> Hence nothing has truly gained possession of the [Divine] Form except imagination. And this is something that no one can deny, since he finds imagination in himself and he sees it in his dreams. Hence he sees the impossible existence as existent. (IV 325.2)

The visions of God's friends often involve the "embodiment" (*tajassud*) of angels or prophets or even God, though these objects of vision do not in fact possess bodies. In a similar way the cosmos itself consists of nonexistent meanings displayed or "embodied" in Manifest Being, so the cosmos as a whole is nothing but "imagination."

> The Prophet said, "I saw my Lord in the form of a youth."[3] This is like the meanings that a sleeper sees in his dreams within sensory forms. The reason for this is that the reality of imagination is to embody that which is not properly a body (*jasad*); it does this because its presence (*ḥaḍra*) gives this to it.
>
> None of the strata (*ṭabaqāt*) of the cosmos makes known the situation as it really is except this imaginal presence, for it makes contraries come together, and within it the realities become manifest as they are in themselves. The truth of affairs is that you should say concerning everything that you see or perceive, through whatever faculty perception takes place, "He/not He," just as God said, "You did not throw when you threw."
>
> You do not doubt in the state of dreaming that the form you see is identical with what it is said to be; and you do not doubt in the interpretation (*taʿbīr*) when you wake up that it was not it. You will not doubt in sound rational consideration that the situation is "He/not He."
>
> It was said to Abū Saʿīd al-Kharrāz, "Through what have you known God?" He replied, "Through the fact that He brings opposites together." So every entity qualified by existence is it/not it. The whole cosmos is He/not He. The Real manifest through form is He/not He. He is the limited who is not limited, the seen who is not seen.
>
> This situation becomes manifest in the imaginal presence when a person is asleep or absent (*ghaybūba*) from outward sensory things in whatever manner. Imagination in sleep is the most complete and general in existence, since it belongs to both the gnostics and the common people. As for the [spiritual] states of absence (*ghayba*), annihilation (*fanāʾ*), obliteration (*maḥw*), and the like, the common people do not experience them in respect of the divine things (*al-ilāhiyyāt*).
>
> God has brought no engendered thing into existence as it is in itself except in this presence. . . . Hence God brought this imaginal presence into existence in order to make manifest the situation which is the Root as It is in Itself. So know that the Manifest in the loci of manifestation—which are the entities—is the Real Being (*al-wujūd al-ḥaqq*), and that It is not It, because of the shapes and attributes which are those of the possible entities through which It became manifest. (II 379.3)

The root *kh.y.l.*, from which *khayāl* is derived, is employed a single time in a relevant meaning in the Koran. In telling the story of Moses and the sorcerers, the Koran says that the sorcerers threw down their staffs, which promptly turned into serpents. As a result, Moses "was *made to imagine*, by their sorcery, that their ropes and staffs were sliding" (20:16). The term is used in a similar sense in a small number of hadiths. These few instances were sufficient to allow al-Ghazālī to provide detailed discussions of imagination as an Islamic concept, just as al-Fārābī and Avicenna had employed the term largely on the basis of Greek sources.

For Ibn al-ʿArabī the term "imagination" (*khayāl*) designates a reality or "presence" that becomes manifest in three different loci: In the cosmos as such, where existence is identical to imagination; in the macrocosm, where the intermediate world between the spiritual and corporeal worlds is imaginal; and in the microcosm, where the human soul considered as a reality distinct from spirit and body pertains to imagination. He also uses the term in a still narrower sense, to designate the "faculty of imagination" considered as one of the several faculties of the soul, along with reason, reflection, and memory. Ibn al-ʿArabī sometimes distinguishes clearly among these meanings, but he is more likely to discuss imagination in general terms or in one or more of these meanings without making specific reference to the distinction among them.

Ibn al-ʿArabī names imagination in its widest sense "Nondelimited Imagination" (*al-khayāl al-muṭlaq*), since it designates the situation of all existence. He calls the intermediate world of imagination "discontiguous imagination" (*al-khayāl al-munfaṣil*), since it exists independently of the viewer. And he names the soul along with the faculty of imagination "contiguous imagination" (*al-khayāl al-muttaṣil*), since these are connected to the viewing subject. In the present context, our primary concern is to understand how all existence can be considered identical with imagination.

> God created another creature. If you say concerning it that it is existent, you will have spoken the truth, and if you say it is nonexistent, you will have spoken the truth. If you say that it is neither existent nor nonexistent, you will have spoken the truth. It is imagination, and it has two states: a state of contiguity, which it possesses through man and certain animals, and a state of discontiguity. To the latter outward perception becomes connected while remaining separate from it in actual fact, as in the case of Gabriel's appearance in the form of Diḥya,[4] or a jinn or an angel which becomes manifest from the world of curtaining. (III 442.3)
>
> The difference between contiguous imagination and discontiguous imagination is that the contiguous kind disappears with the disappearance of the imaginer, while the discontiguous kind is an autonomous presence, constantly receptive toward meanings and spirits. It embodies them in accordance with its own characteristics, nothing else. Contiguous imagination derives from the discontiguous kind. (II 311.19)

Ibn al-ʿArabī often employs the term *mithāl*, "image," as a synonym for imagination. The basic difference between the manner in which he uses the terms is that *khayāl* refers both to the mental faculty known as imagination and the objective world "out there" known as imagination, whereas *mithāl* is never used for the faculty. The root meaning of *mithāl* is to resemble, to look like, to imitate, to appear in the likeness of. This root is employed much more commonly in the Koran and Hadith than *kh.y.l.* For example, the Koran repeatedly speaks about "similitudes" (*mathal*) and God's "striking of similitudes," that is, His explanation of various points by means of imagery and symbolism rather than explicit formulation. But the most significant use of the root for the present context is probably the single occurrence of the word *tamaththul*, which means "to appear in the image of" or "to become imaginalized." Concerning Gabriel's appearance to Mary at the annunciation the Koran says, "He became imaginalized to her as a man without fault" (19:17). In the Hadith the Prophet often employs this term *tamaththul* and its near synonym, *tamthīl*. For example, in a famous hadith that became an important principle in the science of interpreting dreams, he says, "Satan cannot become imaginalized (*tamaththul*) in my image (*mithl*)" or "in my form."[5]

What is imagination in general, without reference to the various loci in which it may become manifest? According to the Shaykh, imagination is fundamentally an intermediate reality; as such, it is intrinsically ambiguous and can best be defined by saying that it is neither this nor that, or both this and that. Hence it is a *barzakh*, or the *barzakh* par excellence.

> A *barzakh* is something that separates (*fāṣil*) two other things while never going to one side (*mutaṭarrif*), as, for example, the line that separates shadow from sunlight. God says, "He let forth the two seas that meet together, between them a *barzakh* they do not overpass" (Koran 55:19); in other words, the one sea does not mix

with the other. Though sense perception might be incapable of separating the two things, the rational faculty judges that there is a barrier (*ḥājiz*) between them which separates them. The intelligible barrier is the *barzakh*. If it is perceived by the senses, it is one of the two things, not the *barzakh*. Any two adjacent things are in need of a *barzakh* which is neither the one nor the other but which possesses the power (*quwwa*) of both.

The *barzakh* is something that separates a known from an unknown, an existent from a nonexistent, a negated from an affirmed, an intelligible from a non-intelligible. It is called *barzakh* as a technical term (*iṣṭilāḥ*), and in itself it is intelligible, but it is only imagination. For, when you perceive it and are intelligent, you will know that you have perceived an ontological thing (*shay' wujūdī*) upon which your eyes have fallen. But you will know for certain by proofs that there is nothing there in origin and root. So what is this thing for which you have affirmed an ontological thingness and from which you have negated that thingness in the state of your affirming it?

Imagination is neither existent nor nonexistent, neither known nor unknown, neither negated nor affirmed. For example, a person perceives his form in a mirror. He knows for certain that he has perceived his form in one respect and he knows for certain that he has not perceived his form in another respect. . . . He cannot deny that he has seen his form, and he knows that his form is not in the mirror, nor is it between himself and the mirror. . . . Hence he is neither a truth-teller nor a liar in his words, "I saw my form, I did not see my form." (I 304.16)

The cosmos is Nondelimited Imagination since everything other than God displays the properties of imagination. The continual creation and constant transformation of the cosmos are nothing if not the appearance of the reality of He/not He.

The reality of imagination is continual change in every state and manifestation in every form. There is no true existence that does not accept change except God, and there is nothing in verified Being (*al-wujūd al-muḥaqqaq*) except God. As for everything other than He, that dwells in imaginal existence (*al-wujūd al-khayālī*). But when the Real becomes manifest within this imaginal existence, He only becomes manifest in keeping with its reality, not in His Essence, which is True Being (*al-wujūd al-ḥaqīqī*). That is why it is mentioned in the sound hadith that He undergoes transmutation in His self-disclosure to His servants. This is also the meaning of His words. "Everything is annihilated," since no state, whether engendered (*kawnī*) or divine (*ilāhī*), remains in the cosmos, "except its face" (28:88), meaning its essence, since the face of a thing is its essence. So you will not be annihilated. But how can the form *into* which He transmutes Himself be compared with the form *from* which He transmutes Himself? The form from which He transmutes Himself shares in annihilation.

Everything other than the Essence of the Real is in the station of transmutation, speedy and slow. Everything other than the Essence of the Real is intervening imagination and vanishing shadow. No engendered thing remains in this world, the hereafter, and what is between the two, neither spirit, nor soul, nor anything other than God—I mean the Essence of God—upon a single state; rather, it undergoes continual change from form to form constantly and forever. And imagination is nothing but this. . . . So the cosmos only became manifest within imagination. It is imagined in itself. So it is it, and it is not it.

Among the things that confirm what we have mentioned is the verse, "You did not throw when you threw" (8:17). Hence He negated the same thing that He affirmed. In other words: You imagined that you threw, but there is no doubt that He threw. That is why He said "when you threw." Then He said: The throwing is correct, "but God threw," that is: You became manifest, O Muḥammad, in a form of God. Hence your throwing hit the mark in a manner in which the throwing of no mortal man hits the mark. (II 313.12)

Dreams

Like other authorities before him who spoke of imagination, Ibn al-ʿArabī often cites dreams as the most common human experience of the nature of imaginal things. In dreams we see things that are not things. We can say to someone, "I saw you in a dream last night," knowing full well that the statement is not completely true nor completely false. What we saw was both the person and not the person; it was our own self and not our own self. It was both this and that, or neither this nor that. Dreams are in fact a God-given key to unlock the mystery of cosmic ambiguity and the constant transmutation of existence. The new creation is never more clearly witnessed than in the world of dreams.

> The only reason God placed sleep in the animate world (*al-ʿālam al-ḥayawānī*) was so that everyone might witness the Presence of Imagination and know that there is another world similar to the sensory world. Through the speed of the transmutation of the imaginal form He calls the attention of intelligent dreamers to the fact that in the sensory world of fixed engendered existence there are transmutations at every instant, even though the eyes and the senses do not perceive them, except in speech and movement. In other than these two kinds, people do not perceive the form of the transmutations and changes except through insight (*baṣīra*), that is, unveiling, or through sound reflection upon some of these forms, since reflection falls short of [perceiving] them all. (III 198.23)

People know that dreams need interpretation (*taʿbīr*). The word *taʿbīr* derives from the root *ʿ.b.r.*, which signifies "crossing over," hence, to traverse, to ford, to pass. The interpreter (*muʿabbir*) is he who passes from the sensory form of the dream to the meaning which has put on the clothing of form. From the same root we have "*ʿibāra*" or "[verbal] expression," which is a passage from understanding to exposition.

The Muslims have always considered dream interpretation an important science. It is mentioned as a prophetic science in the Koran, and the Prophet himself used to practice it, so several Hadith collections have chapters dedicated to "interpretation" and "dream-visions" (*ru'yā*). In one hadith that Ibn al-ʿArabī frequently quotes, the Prophet said, "In a dream I was given a cup of milk, so I drank it until I saw that even my fingertips were quenched. Then I gave the rest to ʿUmar." When asked to interpret the dream, he replied, "Knowledge."[6]

> Through the science of interpretation a person comes to know what is meant by the forms of images when they are displayed to him and when sense perception causes them to rise in his imagination during sleep, wakefulness, absence, or annihilation. (II 152.5)
>
> Reporting (*ikhbār*) about things is called "expression" (*ʿibāra*) and interpreting dreams is called "interpretation" (*taʿbīr*). This is because the expresser/interpreter "crosses over" (*ʿubūr*) by means of what he says. In other words, by means of his words he passes (*jawāz*) from the presence (*ḥaḍra*) of his own self to the self of the listener. Hence he transfers his words from imagination to imagination, since the listener imagines to the extent of his understanding. Imagination may or may not coincide (*taṭābuq*) with imagination, that is, the imagination of the speaker with that of the listener. If it coincides, this is called his "understanding" (*fahm*); if it does not coincide, he has not understood. . . . We only make this allusion to call attention to the tremendousness of imagination's level, for it is the Absolute Ruler (*al-ḥākim al-muṭlaq*) over known things. (III 454.1)

When the nature of the cosmos is truly "verified" (*taḥqīq*), the knower sees it to be a form of imagination, in need of interpretation like a dream. Among the traditional texts that Ibn al-ʿArabī cites to support this point is the well known saying, usually attributed to the Prophet, "People are asleep, and when they die, they awake."[7] This of course is a gloss on the Koranic verse, "[On the Day of Resurrection] every soul will come, along with it a driver and a witness: 'You were heedless of this, so We have now unveiled from you your covering and your sight today is piercing'" (50:22).

Ibn al-ʿArabī refers to some of these points in a short discussion of sleep in Chapter 188 of the *Futūḥāt* on the station of "dreams" (*ru'yā*).

Dreams have a place, a locus, and a state. Their state is sleep (*nawm*), which is an absence from manifest sensory things that produces ease (*rāḥa*) because of the weariness (*taʿb*) which overcomes the soul in this plane in the state of wakefulness because of motion, even if the motion is in pursuit of its own inclination. God says, "We appointed your sleep for a rest" (Koran 78:9); in other words, We appointed sleep for you as an ease in which souls can relax.

Sleep is of two kinds. One is a transferal (*intiqāl*) within which there is a certain amount of rest, or the reaching of individual desire, or an increase of weariness. The second kind is only rest. It is the pure and correct sleep concerning which God said that He appointed it as a rest for the weariness which reaches the bodily instruments, organs, and parts in the state of wakefulness. God made night its time, even if it takes place in the daytime, just as He appointed the daytime for livelihood, even if it is acquired at night.[8] But the property belongs to that which dominates.

As for the sleep which is transferal, that is the kind within which there are dreams. The instruments [of the soul] are transferred from the manifest side (*ẓāhir*) of sense perception to its nonmanifest side (*bāṭin*) in order to see what has become established in the Treasury of Imagination (*khizānat al-khayāl*)—to which the senses have lifted up what they have acquired from sensory objects—and what has been formed by the form-giving faculty, which is one of the assistants of this Treasury. Thus the rational soul, to which God has given ownership of this city [of the human being], looks upon what has been placed in its Treasury, as is the habit of kings, who enter into their treasuries when they are alone to gain knowledge of what is in them.

To the extent that the instruments (*ālāt*), which are the organs (*jawāriḥ*), and the assistants, which are the sensory faculties, have been perfected, there will be storing away. Hence there are perfect treasuries, because of the perfection of life, and imperfect treasuries, as in the case of a man born blind, since the forms of colors are not transferred into the treasury of imagination; or the case of a man born deaf, since the form of sounds and verbal letters are not transferred into his imagination's treasury. . . .

Moreover, God discloses Himself within this Treasury in the forms and attributes of Nature, as in the Prophet's words, "I saw my Lord in the form of a youth."[9] . . .

I call this state a "transferal" because meanings are transferred from their disengagement (*tajrīd*) from substrata into a state of being clothed in substrata, like the manifestation of the Real in the forms of corporeal bodies, or of knowledge in the form of milk, or similar things. . . .

Dreams are interpreted, but that which is perceived by sense perception is not interpreted. However, when man ascends in the degrees of gnosis, he will come to know through both faith and unveiling that he is a dreamer in the state of ordinary wakefulness and that the situation in which he dwells is a dream. That is why God mentions various things which happen in manifest sense perception. Then He says, "So take heed [literally, "pass beyond"]!" (Koran 59:2); and He says, "Surely in that there is a 'lesson' [literally, "passage"]" (3:13). He says: Cross over and pass beyond that of it which has become manifest to you and go to the knowledge of its nonmanifest side and of the place from which it has come. The Prophet said, "People are asleep, and when they die they awake." But they are not aware. Hence we said "faith." . . .

All of existence is sleep and its wakefulness is sleep. So all of existence is ease, and ease is mercy, for mercy "embraces all things" (7:156), and all things end up (*ma'āl*) in mercy. . . . Though there may be weariness along the way, it is a weariness in ease. . . .

Verification shows that the forms of the cosmos—which belong to the Real in respect to the name the "Nonmanifest"—are the forms of a dream to the Dreamer. The interpretation of the dream is that those forms are His states, nothing else. In the same way, the forms of a dream are the states of the dreamer, nothing else. Hence He sees only Himself.

This is [indicated by] His words, He "did not create the heavens, the earth, and what is between them except through the Real" (30:8), and the Real is Himself. Hence he says concerning the gnostics, "They know that God, He is the Evident Real" (24:25), that is, the Manifest Real, for He is the One/Many (*al-wāḥid al-kathīr*).

He who takes heed of and passes beyond (*iʿtibār*) dreams will see a formidable thing. What he cannot perceive in any other respect will become clear for him. That is why the Prophet, when he saw his companions in the morning, used to say to them, "Has any of you seen a dream?"[10] For the dream is a kind of prophecy (*nubuwwa*).[11] . . .

As for the locus of dreaming, that is this elemental plane; it has no other locus. Angels do not dream, since dreaming belongs specifically to the animate elemental plane. Dreaming's locus in the divine knowledge is the transmutations in the forms of self-disclosure. So everything within which we are the dream of the Real dwells in the ease of the disappearance of fatigue and weariness, nothing else.

As for the place, that is within the sphere of the moon specifically; in the next world, it is in that which is within the sphere of the fixed stars. . . . (II 378.24, 379.24, 380.4)

The Manifestation of the Impossible

Understanding imagination is the key to various kinds of knowledge that are normally hidden from our rational minds, since imagination is able to combine opposites and contradictions. For example, only imagination provides the means to grasp the meaning of the revealed reports concerning life after death, reports which are full of logically impossible occurrences.

After knowledge of the divine names and of self-disclosure and its all-embracingness, there is no knowledge more complete [than knowledge of imagination] . . . , for it is the center-piece of the necklace; to it the senses climb up, and to it meanings descend, while it never leaves its place. (II 309.17)

[Through imagination one perceives] what is perceived in the Garden: "Its fruits are . . . neither cut off, nor forbidden" (Koran 56:33), even though people eat them, nor are they prohibited from that. So people eat them without their being cut off . . . , while the entity of the fruit remains on the tree. . . . Everything of this sort that has come in the Book and the Sunna is accepted by the faithful and confirmed by the Folk of Unveiling. But the considerative thinkers (*aṣḥāb al-naẓar*) deny it; or, if they accept it, they accept it through a farfetched interpretation (*ta'wīl baʿīd*), or by submitting themselves to Him who said it, since the speaker is God or His messenger. But if something of this sort should become manifest to you as an individual, they are ignorant of it and deny it, attributing it to the corruption (*fasād*) of your imagination. Hence they admit what they deny, for they affirm imagination and its corruption. But its corruption does not point to its nonexistence. Its "corruption" is the fact that it does not coincide with what is truly sound in their view.

But in our view, it is indifferent whether you call it "sound" or "corrupt." Its entity and the fact that the form dwells in imagination have been established. So let it be sound or corrupt—I do not care. Our goal is only to establish the existence of imagination. We are not trying to show the soundness or corruption of what becomes manifest within it.

Hence it has been established that imagination possesses a governing property (*ḥukm*) in every mode and over every state, the sensory and the intelligible, senses and rational faculties, forms and meanings, the temporally originated and the eternal, the impossible, the possible, and the Necessary.

He who does not know the level of imagination has no true knowledge whatsoever. If this pillar of true knowledge has not been actualized by the knowers, they have not a whiff of true knowledge. (II 312.23, 31)

Ibn al-ʿArabī devotes many passages to demonstrating the all-comprehensive nature of imagination, the fact that it rules over all things. In one of the more interesting of these passages, he is explaining the nature of the Trumpet—mentioned in ten Koranic verses—which will be blown by the angel Seraphiel on two different occasions. On the first occasion it will cause everyone in the heavens and the earth to swoon, and on the second it will awaken them and gather them all together for the accounting with God. In a complicated analysis of the imagery, Ibn al-ʿArabī identifies the Trumpet itself with the World of Imagination. Here only a few relevant sections from his discussion can be quoted. It will be helpful to know that the word for "Trumpet" is *ṣūr*, which may also be read *ṣuwar*, in which case it is the plural of the word "form" (*ṣūra*).

> The Prophet was asked about the Trumpet. He replied, "It is a horn of light that Seraphiel has put to his mouth."[12] Hence he gave news that it has the shape of a horn, so he described it by wideness (*saʿa*) and narrowness (*ḍīq*), since a horn is wide and narrow. . . .
>
> You should know that the wideness of this horn is exceedingly wide. There is nothing among the engendered things that is wider. That is because it exercises its properties through its reality over every thing and non-thing. It gives form to absolute nonexistence, the impossible (*muḥāl*), the Necessary, and possibility. It makes existence nonexistent and nonexistence existent. Concerning it, or rather in respect to this presence, the Prophet said, "Worship God as if you see Him" and "God is in the kibla of him who performs the prayer."[13] In other words: Imagine that He is in your kibla and that you are facing Him, so that you will attend to Him, have shame before Him, and observe courtesy in your prayer. For if you do not do these things, you will not have observed courtesy.
>
> Had the Lawgiver not known that you have a reality known as "imagination" which possesses this property, he would not have said to you "*as if* you see Him" with your eyes. For rational demonstration prevents the "as if," since it declares through its proofs that similarity is impossible. As for sight, it perceives nothing but a wall. Hence we come to understand that the Lawgiver has addressed you in order that you will imagine that you are facing God in your kibla, which according to the Law you must face in your prayers. At the same time God says, "Withersoever you turn, there is the face of God" (2:115). The "face" of a thing is its reality and entity. Hence imagination has given form to that which, according to rational demonstration, cannot possibly have form or assume forms (*taṣawwur*). Hence imagination is wide.
>
> As for its narrowness, that is because imagination does not have the capacity to accept any affair, whether sensory, suprasensory (*maʿnawī*), relations, attributions, the majesty of God, or His Essence, except through form. If imagination tried to perceive something in other than a form, its reality would not allow that, since it is nothing but fantasy (*wahm*). That is why it has the greatest narrowness, for it can never disengage meanings from substrata. Hence sense perception is the nearest thing to imagination, since imagination takes forms from sense perception, then it discloses meanings through those sensory forms. This derives from its narrowness. It is narrow in order that nothing may be described by lack of delimitation, by non-delimitation in existence, and by "He performs whatsoever He desires" (11:107) except God alone, about whom it is said, "Nothing is like Him" (42:11).
>
> Imagination is the widest known thing. Yet in spite of this tremendous wideness by which it exercises its properties over all things, it is incapable of receiving meanings disengaged from substrata as they are in themselves. That is why it sees knowledge in the form of milk, honey, wine, and pearls. It sees Islam in the form of a dome and a pillar. It sees the Koran in the form of butter and honey. It sees religion in the form of a cord. It sees the Real in the form of a human being or a light.[14] Hence it is the wide/narrow, while God is the "Wide" absolutely, the Knower of that in which He creates His creatures. . . .
>
> As for the fact that the "horn" is of "light," that is because light is the cause of unveiling and manifestation. Without light, eyesight would perceive nothing. Hence God made imagination a light

through which the assumption of forms by all things—whatever it might be, as we said—may be perceived. Its light penetrates into sheer nonexistence and gives it the form of an existence. Hence imagination is more worthy to be called "light" than all other creatures described by luminosity. Its light does not resemble other lights, and through it self-disclosures are perceived. This is the light of the eye of imagination, not the light of the eye of sense perception. So understand! For this will benefit you by giving you the knowledge of the fact that imagination is a light, and you will know that imagination hits the mark [and thus you will be distinguished] from him who does not know.

He who does not know is the one who says, "This is corrupt imagination." That is because this person lacks the knowledge to perceive the imaginal light which God has given to him. In the same way, this person accuses sense perception of missing the mark in some of its perceptions, but its perception is correct, since the judgment belongs to something else [i.e., the rational faculty], not to it. That which judges misses the mark, not sense perception. Imagination is the same way: It perceives through its light what it perceives, but it has no judgment. The judgment belongs to something else, that is, the rational faculty. Hence missing the mark cannot be attributed to imagination, for there is no corrupt imagination whatsoever; on the contrary, all of it is sound.

As for our companions, they have been mistaken concerning this horn. Most of the rational thinkers have made its narrowest part the center, while its highest [and widest] part they have made the Supreme Sphere, above which there is no sphere. They have held that the forms which it contains are the forms of the cosmos. Hence they have made the widest part of the horn the highest part of the cosmos, and the narrowest part the lowest part of the cosmos. But the situation is not as they have supposed. On the contrary, since imagination—as we have said—gives form to the Real and to everything in the cosmos below Him, even nonexistence, its highest part is narrow, while its lowest part is wide. This is how God created it, for the first thing He created from it was narrow, and the last thing He created was wide, the part which is fixed to the animal's head.

There is no doubt that the Presence of Acts and engendered things is wide. That is why the knower has no wideness in his knowledge except to the extent of what he knows of the cosmos. Then, when he wants to pass on to knowledge of the Unity of God, he never ceases ascending from wideness toward narrowness, little by little. The higher he ascends in knowledge of the Essence of the Real through unveiling, the fewer his sciences become. Finally there remains no object of knowledge but the Real alone. This is the narrowest of what there is in the horn. So in reality, the horn's narrow part is the highest, and within it there is complete excellence. This is the first thing that appears of the horn when God causes it to grow up from the head of the animal. It never ceases to go up in the form of its narrowness, while its bottom becomes wider. Hence the tip never changes in its state; it is the first creation. (I 306.3)

The *barzakh* is the widest of presences and the Meeting Place of the Two Seas (Koran 18:60)—the Sea of Meanings and the Sea of Sensory Things. The sensory thing cannot be a meaning, nor can the meaning be a sensory thing. But the Presence of Imagination—which we have called the Meeting Place of the Two Seas—embodies meanings and subtilizes the sensory thing. It transforms the entity of every object of knowledge in the viewer's eye. So it is the self-ruling ruler (*al-ḥākim al-mutaḥakkim*), that which rules and is not ruled over, even though it is a creation. (III 361.5)

According to the principles of Peripatetic philosophy, the "impossible" (*muḥāl*) cannot come into existence, in contrast to the "possible," which may or may not come into existence, and the Necessary, which cannot not exist. But "imagination" is a domain in which contraries meet and impossible things take place. The rational faculty holds to the principles of its philosophy, but imagination observes contradictory and mutually exclusive things actually occurring.

In reality imagination is one of the presences of sense perception, since it joins meanings to sensory forms. Hence the impossible is imagined as a sensory thing and it comes into existence in the hereafter, or wherever God desires, as a sensory thing. That is why this takes place in the "here-after" (*al-ākhira*) not the "here-before" (*al-ūlā*), for imagination stands in a degree which is posterior to sense perception, since it takes the forms with which it clothes the impossible and other things from sense perception. Hence, wherever it is found, it is only found in the "here-after." So pay heed!

Which faculty is more tremendous than that which makes the thing which cannot possibly exist into an existent sensory thing which can be seen? For example, a corporeal body exists simultaneously in two places. Just as this is imagined here, so it happens likewise in sense perception in the hereafter. . . .

The levels have interpenetrated, and the impossible thing has been made into the possible thing, that is, joined to its level, while the possible thing has become joined to the level of the impossible thing. The reason for this is the penetration of the Real into creation and creation into the Real through self-disclosure in the divine and engendered names. So the situation is the Real in one respect, creation in another respect, in each and every engendered thing. The Divine Presence comprehends the property of the Real in creation and creation in the Real. (IV 282.18)

How wide is the Presence of Imagination! Within it becomes manifest the existence of the impossible thing. Or rather, nothing becomes manifest within it in verification except the existence of the impossible thing. For the Necessary Being—who is God—does not receive forms, yet He becomes manifest in forms in this presence. Thereby impossible existence has received existence in this presence. Within it corporeal bodies are seen in two places, as Adam saw himself outside the hand of the Real. Yet, when the Real opened His hand, Adam and his seed were within it. So he was in the hand, and he himself was outside the hand. In such a way this presence receives only the existence of impossible things.

In the same way a person is sleeping in his home and he sees himself in his ordinary form in another city and another situation contrary to his own situation. Yet, for him who recognizes the situation of existence as it is, that is he, nothing else. Were it not for the trace of imagination, rational thinkers would not be able to "suppose the impossible" (*farḍ al-muḥāl*) when seeking a proof for something. For if the impossible did not receive existence in some presence, it could not be supposed or presumed. (II 312.4)

Sleep is a state in which the servant passes from the witnessing of the world of sense perception to the world of the *barzakh*, which is the most perfect world. There is no world more perfect, since it is the root of the origin of the cosmos; it possesses true existence and controlling rule (*taḥakkum*) in all affairs. It embodies meanings and changes that which does not subsist (*qā'im*) in itself into that which does subsist in itself. It gives form to that which has no form. It turns the impossible into the possible. It exercises free disposal in affairs as it wills.

Since imagination possesses such nondelimitation, though it is a creature created by God, what do you think about the Creator who created it and gave it this capacity? How can you wish to judge that God is delimited and say that God is not capable of doing the impossible? Yet you witness in yourself imagination's power over the impossible, though imagination is one of God's creatures. You do not doubt what you see when imagination embodies meanings for you, showing them to you as self-subsistent individuals. In the same way God will bring the works of the children of Adam [on the Day of Resurrection], even though they are accidents (*aʿrāḍ*), as self-subsistent forms placed in the Scale to establish justice.[15] He will bring death, even though it is a relationship—farther than the accident from embodiment—"in the form of a salt-colored ram."[16] Here He means that it is extremely clear, so He described it as "salt-colored," that is, white. Then all the people will recognize it. So this is an impossible thing decreed. So where is the judgment of the rational faculty about God and the corruption of its interpretation (*ta'wīl*)? (II 183.8)

8. THE SUPREME BARZAKH

Being is one and changeless, while the existent things never remain still for an instant. The source of this constant agitation must be sought in the relationship between God and nothingness, a relationship which is made possible by the *barzakh* which stands between the two. To differentiate this "Supreme Barzakh" (*al-barzakh al-aʿlā*) or "Barzakh of Barzakhs" (III 46.31) from the *barzakh* which lies between the world of the spirits and the world of corporeal bodies and which corresponds to the soul in the microcosm, we will refer to it simply as the Barzakh.

The Barzakh is known by many names, one of which—"Nondelimited Imagination"—has already been discussed in some detail. Others include the Cloud, the Breath of the All-merciful, the Real Through Whom Creation Takes Place, the Universal Reality, Nature, and the Reality of the Perfect Man. These are not exact synonyms, since each is employed within a specific context and does not necessarily overlap with the others in all cases.

The Cloud

The Prophet was asked, "Where (*ayn*) did our Lord come to be (*kān*) before He created the creatures (*khalq*)?" He replied, "He came to be in a cloud, neither above which nor below which was any air (*hawā*ʾ)."[1] Ibn al-ʿArabī explains that the word *ʿamā*ʾ means a thin cloud surrounded by air. By describing the Cloud in this fashion, the Prophet informed his listeners that it is different from any cloud they have seen or heard described. "He negated the air so that they would know that it is not similar [to ordinary clouds] in every respect" (II 310.5). Normally clouds are pushed this way and that by the air that surrounds them, but by negating the air the Prophet showed that nothing controls the Cloud other than God, "since it is the nearest of existent things to God" (II 310.24). The "before" mentioned in the hadith has nothing to do with time, but is employed to get a point across (*tawṣīl*). "It denotes a relationship (*nisba*) through which the listener will be able to understand" (I 148.18).

This hadith is normally translated, "He *was* in a cloud," but Ibn al-ʿArabī makes clear that "He came to be"—a meaning equally allowable by the Arabic—is how he understands it. He tells us that there are five instances in which God "comes to be" (*kaynūna*) according to the Koran and the Hadith.

> (1) Coming to be in the Cloud, which is what we just mentioned; (2) coming to be in the Throne, as indicated by His words, "The All-merciful sat upon the Throne" (Koran 20:5); (3) coming to be in the heaven, as indicated by the words, "Our Lord descends each night to the heaven of this world";[2] (4) coming to be in the earth, as in His words, "He is God in the heavens and the earth" (6:3); and (5) an all-inclusive coming to be, since He is with the existent things in all their levels wherever they might come to be, as He explained in relation to us with His words, "He is with you wherever you come to be" (57:4). All of these are relationships in keeping with His majesty, without asking "how" (*takyīf*), without declaring Him similar (*tashbīh*), and without conceptualization (*taṣawwur*). (II 310.6)

Within the Cloud the cosmos in its entirety takes shape. The Cloud is Nondelimited Imagination, since it gives form (*taṣwīr*) to all engendered things (*kā*ʾ*ināt*). Every existent thing becomes manifest within it, so it is called God's "Manifest" in the words, "He is the First and the Last, the Manifest and the Nonmanifest" (Koran 57:3, II 310.12–15).

Though Ibn al-ʿArabī usually maintains that the the Cloud is identical with the Breath of the All-merciful, sometimes, as in the following passage, he distinguishes between the two and says that the Cloud comes into existence through the Breath.

> Contiguous imagination derives from one of the faces of Nondelimited Imagination, which is the All-comprehensive Presence and the All-inclusive Level. This Cloud becomes configured within the Breath of the All-merciful, inasmuch as the All-merciful is a god, not inasmuch as He is only All-merciful. All existent things become manifest within the Cloud through "Be!", or one hand, or two hands.[3] In contrast, the Cloud itself becomes manifest only through the Breath. Were it not for the fact that the word "Breath" has come in the Law, we would not have applied the term, though we knew the reality.
>
> The root of the Breath is the property of love. Love has a movement (*ḥaraka*) within the lover, while "breath" is a movement of yearning (*shawq*) toward the object of love, and through that breathing enjoyment is experienced. And God has said, as has been reported, "I was a Treasure but was not known, so I loved to be known." Through this love, breathing takes place, so the Breath becomes manifest, and the Cloud comes into being. (II 310.17).

As the Barzakh, the Cloud stands between God and nothingness and shares in the attributes of both. Through the intermediary of the Barzakh, God takes on the attributes of the creatures, and they become clothed in His qualities. God in His Essence remains incomparable, but He discloses Himself by means of the Barzakh, thus being called similar. Hence the rational faculty is unable to grasp the nature of the Barzakh without outside help, since on its own it can only perceive incomparability. To understand the nature of the Barzakh, we have to fall back on imagination. Through the Barzakh, the immutable entities in God's knowledge are able to find existence in the cosmos, just as through imagination, meanings without form come to be seen in the clothing of forms.

> The Cloud is the Barzakh standing between meanings—which have no entities in existence—and luminous corporeal bodies and Nature.[4] Take, for example, [the meanings] "knowledge" and "movement," the first within souls and the second within corporeal bodies. The meanings become corporealized in the Presence of Imagination, like knowledge in the form of milk. In the same way, relationships become entified, even though they have no entities, whether in the soul or in corporeal bodies. Thus a thing's "constancy" is a relationship in terms of that which is constant within the thing, but this constancy becomes manifest in the form of a sensory cord within the presence of contiguous imagination.[5] In the same way spirits become manifest in the forms of bodies having shapes, such as Gabriel in the form of Diḥya, or those angels which became manifest as dust on the Day of Badr.[6] All this takes place in discontiguous imagination. (II 311.12)

In short, the Cloud is identical with Nondelimited Imagination considered as the very substance within which all things in the cosmos take shape. In making this point, Ibn al-ʿArabī refers to the hadith of God's self-transmutation on the Day of Resurrection, when people continue to deny Him until He manifests Himself to them in a form which they recognize.

> The Real is denied in one form and accepted in another; the Entity is one, but the forms are diverse. This is exactly what we mean by the diversity of forms, that is, the forms of the cosmos, within the Cloud. In respect of being forms, the forms are imaginalized things (*mutakhayyalāt*), while the Cloud within which they become manifest is Imagination. . . . So also is His self-disclosure to hearts and within the entities of the possible things. He is the Manifest, and He is also the forms in accordance with what is bestowed upon Him by the entities of the possible things through their preparednesses, such that He becomes manifest

within them. The possible things are the Cloud, while the Manifest within the Cloud is the Real. Hence the Cloud is the Real Through Whom Creation Takes Place. The diversity of the entities of the possible things derives from their own immutability; they exercise properties over Him who manifests Himself within them. (II 311.33)

The cosmos is a collection of "imaginalized" forms that take shape within the Cloud. The Cloud—like all clouds—undergoes constant transformation in its outward form, though its substance remains the same. Hence the term "Cloud," like the term "imagination," is employed to call attention to the evanescence of all created existence.

In the state of its existence the cosmos is nothing but the forms which the Cloud receives and which become manifest within it. So the cosmos—if you look upon its reality—is nothing but a vanishing accident, that is, its ruling property is its evanescence (*zawāl*). This is shown by His words, "Everything is annihilated except its face" (28:88). The Prophet said, "The truest verse sung by the Arabs is the line of Labīd, 'Is not everything other than God unreal (*bāṭil*)?'"[7] In other words, other than God has no reality of its own through which it is fixed, since it exists through other than itself . . .

So the immutable substance (*al-jawhar al-thābit*) is the Cloud, which is nothing other than the Breath of the All-merciful. The cosmos is all the forms which become manifest within it; so they are accidents which may be made to vanish. These forms are the possible things. Their relationship to the Cloud is the relationship of the forms which the viewer sees in a mirror to the mirror. The Real is the sight (*baṣar*) of the cosmos, so He is the viewer. (III 443.8)

The Breath of the All-merciful

Ibn al-ʿArabī quotes two hadiths as the source for the expression "Breath of the All-merciful" (*nafas al-raḥmān*): "Do not curse the wind, for it derives from the Breath of the All-merciful!" "I find the Breath of the All-merciful coming to me from the direction of Yemen."[8] He explains that in both cases the word *nafas* alludes to a kind of *tanfīs* (a word from the same root), which means to air, to cheer up, to comfort, to relieve, to remove sorrow.[9] In the first hadith the Prophet is referring to the fact that wind is one of the means whereby God gives comfort and relief to His servants and in the second to the comfort certain of his Companions gave to him in face of the opposition of his own family to his prophetic mission.

The Shaykh compares the Breath of the All-merciful to the human breath in order to provide an analogy for the creative process. Each characteristic of breath becomes the starting point for the explanation of a dimension of the relationship between God and creation. Thus breath is a vapor, relieves constriction in the breast, and is the vehicle for words; in the same way the Breath of the All-merciful is a Cloud, relieves the constriction of the immutable entities (or the divine names)—which desire to see the outward manifestation of their properties—and is the vehicle for God's words, which are the creatures. These ideas are all intertwined, but the third is most central to the concept of God's Breath and is closely connected to the imagery of Book, verses, words, and letters provided by the Koran.

Each creature is a word (*kalima*) of God. As Koranic proof for this point, Ibn al-ʿArabī often quotes the verse "The Messiah, Jesus son of Mary . . . was His word that He cast into Mary" (4:171) to show that a created thing may be called a "word." In many other verses he finds allusions to the idea that all things are God's words, especially the verse already quoted, "Though all the trees in the earth were pens, and the sea—seven seas after it to replenish it—[were ink,] yet would the words of God not be spent" (31:27; cf. 18:109). As Ibn al-ʿArabī understands this verse, "The existent things are the words of God which are not spent" (II 390.24), since the possible things are infinite.

In one passage the Shaykh explains the mutual love that exists between God and the creatures in terms of vision (*ru'ya*) and audition (*samā'*). God's love for the creatures stems from His vision of them within Himself as identical with Himself. Seeing them as the "Hidden Treasure," "He loved to be known." The creature's love for God derives from hearing the word "Be!", which brings them into existence. They are, in effect, identical with this word; each is the word "Be!" in a specific form.

> One of the characteristics of the Lover, should He possess form, is to breathe, since in that breathing is found the enjoyment of what is sought. The Breath emerges from a root, which is Love for the creatures, to whom He desired to make Himself known, so that they might know Him. Hence the Cloud comes to be; it is called the Real Through Whom Creation Takes Place. The Cloud is the substance of the cosmos, so it receives all the forms, spirits, and natures of the cosmos; it is a receptacle ad infinitum. This is the origin of His love for us.
>
> As for our love for Him, its origin is audition, not vision. It is His words to us—while we were in the substance of the Cloud—"Be!" Hence the Cloud derives from His breathing, while the forms which are called the cosmos derive from the word "Be!" So we are "His words which are not spent." . . . When we heard His speech, while we were immutable in the substance of the Cloud, we were not able to keep back from existence. We became forms within the substance of the Cloud. Through our manifestation within the Cloud He gave us an existence belonging to the Cloud. A thing whose existence had been intelligible gained entified existence. This is the cause of the origin of our love for Him. (II 331.23)

The existent things or words come into existence within the Breath as the result of God's speech (*qawl*). The Koran describes this speech as the single word "Be!", yet this word is addressed to each "thing" in the state of its nonexistence.

> God says, "Our only speech to a thing, when We desire it"—here "Our speech" refers to the fact that He is a speaker (*mutakallim*)—"is to say to it 'Be!'" (16:40). "Be!" is exactly what He speaks. Through it that to which He says "Be!" becomes manifest. . . . Thereby the entities become manifest within the Breath of the All-merciful, just as letters become manifest within the human breath. The thing that comes to be is a specific form, like a form painted upon wood. (II 401.29)

The analogy between the letters that take shape in the human breath and the All-merciful Breath provides the basis for one of the Shaykh's major modes of describing the cosmos. Just as the Arabic alphabet has twenty-eight letters through which the names of all things may be pronounced, so also the cosmos has twenty-eight basic "letters" which combine to produce all created things. Each letter of the alphabet issues from a particular point, known as the "place of articulation" (*makhraj*), within the vocal apparatus. Depending on how the breath passes through the throat and mouth, that is, which "place of articulation" is employed, letters are produced which may be guttural, velar, palatal, dental, labial, and so on. In the same way each letter/reality of the cosmos manifests Being in a specific mode different from other modes. Each, therefore, is connected to a specific divine name. Here we cannot go into detail concerning this cosmology; it will be sufficient for our purposes to be aware of the fundamental correspondence between the human and divine breaths.

> From the Breath of the All-merciful become manifest the letters of engendered existence and the words of the cosmos in accordance with the different levels of the places of articulation within the breath of the human breather, for the human being is the most perfect of all configurations

(*nash'a*) in the cosmos. These places of articulation are twenty-eight letters. Each letter has a name which is determined by its own place of vocalization (*maqṭaʿ*). The first of these letters is *hā'* and the last is *wāw*. (II 394.21)

The Shaykh analyzes the letters of the Arabic alphabet phonetically in some detail, showing in the process how each letter arises at a different point of vocalization and can thus be ranked in degree, beginning with *hā'* at the deepest level of the breath and *wāw* at the very end. Between these two letters, which correspond to the First Intellect and the level or utmost limit (*ghāya*) of each existent thing, all letters are articulated and all things in the cosmos come into existence.[10] He summarizes his conclusions in the following terms:

The Real is the root of the One, Unique Being, which does not accept number. Though He is One in Entity, He is named Alive, Self-subsistent, Inaccessible, Magnificent, Overbearing—ninety-nine names for One Entity and many properties. What is understood from "Alive" is not what is understood from the name Desiring, nor Powerful, nor Potent. So also it is with each letter of the alphabet.

The letters emerge from the breath of the human breather, who is the most perfect of configurations. Through him and his breath become manifest all the letters, for he is upon the Divine Form through the Breath of the All-merciful and the manifestation of the letters of engendered existence; so also is the domain of words. All these words are the human breath—twenty-eight letters precisely, because the entities of the divine words issue forth from the All-merciful Breath as twenty-eight words, each having many faces. They issue from the Breath of the All-merciful, which is the Cloud within which our Lord came to be before He created the creatures.

So the Cloud is like the human breath. The manifestation of the cosmos when the Cloud extends into the Void in accordance with the levels of the engendered things is similar to the human breath extending from the heart to the mouth. The manifestation of the letters in the path of the breath and in words is similar to the manifestation of the cosmos from the Cloud, which is the Real's All-merciful Breath, within the ordained levels along the supposed extension—not within a body—which is the Void filled by the cosmos.

Just as the first letter—the first of the entities of the cosmos—which became manifest from this Breath came to be when it sought to go out to the utmost limit, which is the end of the Void, so also the utmost extension of the breath is at the lips.

The *hā'* becomes manifest first and the *wāw* last. There is no intelligible letter beyond the *wāw*. Hence the genera of the cosmos are limited, but its individuals (*ashkhāṣ*) are infinite in existence, for they come into temporal being as long as the secondary cause exists, and this cause never comes to an end. Hence the bringing into existence of the individuals of the species never comes to an end. (II 395.1)

The places of articulation which determine and specify words correspond to the preparednesses of the immutable entities. In the process of becoming manifest, Being is colored by the properties of the entities. In the act of speaking, the human breath is defined by the various points of articulation. In bringing the cosmos into existence, the Breath of the All-merciful assumes the contours defined by the immutable entities. The "Breath" defines the dynamic interrelationship between God as the Nonmanifest (*al-bāṭin*) and God as the Manifest (*al-ẓāhir*).

God described Himself as having a Breath. This is His emergence from the Unseen and the manifestation of the letters as the Visible. The letters are containers (*ẓarf*) for meanings, while the meanings are the spirits of the letters. (III 95.19)

The breath of the breather is none other than the nonmanifest of the breather. Then the breath becomes manifest as the entities of letters and words. It does not become manifest through anything super-

> added to the nonmanifest, so it is identical with the nonmanifest. The preparedness of the places of articulation to designate the letters within the breath is the same as the preparedness of the immutable entities of the cosmos within the Breath of the All-merciful. What becomes manifest is the property determined by the preparedness of the cosmos, which is manifest within the Breath. That is why God said to His Prophet, "You did not throw when you threw, but God threw" (8:17). . . . For the letters are not other than the Breath, nor are they the same as the Breath; the word is not other than the letters, nor is it the same as the letters. (II 396.13, 27)

Relief Through Mercy

Mercy (*raḥma*) can be divided into two basic kinds, referred to in the formula, "In the name of God, the All-merciful (*al-raḥmān*), the All-compassionate (*al-raḥīm*)." The terms All-merciful and All-compassionate both derive from the word *raḥma*. The first kind of mercy, known as essential (*dhātiyya*) mercy or the mercy of free gift (*al-imtinān, al-minna*) is all-inclusive (*ʿāmma*), since no existent thing is excluded from it. God bestows it upon all creatures without distinction. "Existence itself is a mercy for every existent thing" (II 281.27). The second kind, known as the mercy of obligation (*wujūb*) is specific (*khāṣṣa*), since its bestowal becomes obligatory for God only in the case of certain servants who come to deserve it. Both kinds of mercy are referred to in the Koranic verse, "My mercy [in the all-inclusive sense] embraces all things, but I shall prescribe it [in the specific sense] for those who are godfearing and pay the alms, and those who indeed have faith in Our signs, those who follow the Messenger" (7: 156).[11]

> God says, "My mercy embraces all things." It is either a gratuitous gift or obligatory. There are servants whom it embraces as a property of obligation, and there are others whom it embraces as a property of gratuitous gift. But the root is the divine gratuitous gift, bounty (*al-faḍl*), and bestowal of blessing (*al-inʿām*), since at first there was no engendered existence to deserve it. Hence, the very manifestation of engendered existence derives from gratuitous gift. (III 93.25)

The Divine Breath is ascribed to the All-merciful because God embraces all things in respect of this name. Through the Breath He brings all things into existence. This all-inclusive mercy which becomes manifest through the Breath "precedes God's wrath," with important eschatological consequences that have already been mentioned: Since all things originate in this mercy, all return to it in the end (*bi'l- ma'āl*).

> God attributed a Breath to Himself, ascribing it to the name "All-merciful," only to tell us—once our entities have become manifest and the messengers of this affair have come to us—that mercy comprises and includes all things and that all people and creatures end up with mercy. Nothing becomes manifest from the All-merciful but objects of mercy (*marḥūm*). (III 420.2)

Mercy is rest, repose, and ease (*rāḥa*). By bringing the cosmos into existence, God shows mercy toward all things. The things in themselves are nonexistent, immutable entities, unable to display their properties because of their nonexistence. Just as the names desire the outward manifestation of their effects, so also the entities desire to display themselves. In fact, says the Shaykh, "Through the Breath of the All-merciful God gave relief (*tanfīs*) to the divine names" (II 487.34).

> The cosmos issues from the Breath of the All-merciful because He relieved His names of the lack of displaying effects which they were finding in themselves. (II 123.26)

As long as the names—or the entities—do not find the outward manifestation of their properties, they dwell in distress (*karb*). The Breath of the All-merciful removes their distress.

> Were it not for straitness (*ḥaraj*) and constriction (*ḍīq*), the All-merciful Breath would have no property. "Giving relief" is to eliminate straitness and constriction, and nonexistence is identical with straitness and constriction, since the nonexistent thing possesses the possibility of coming into existence. Hence, when the possible thing knows its possibility while in the state of nonexistence, it is distressed, since it yearns for the existence allowed by its reality in order to take its share of good (*khayr*). The All-merciful relieves this straitness through His Breath, since He brings the possible thing into existence. Hence His "giving relief" is His elimination of the property of nonexistence within the possible thing. Every existent except God is a possible thing and therefore possesses this property.
>
> The Breath of the All-merciful bestows existence upon the forms of the possible things, just as the human breath bestows existence upon letters. Hence the cosmos is the words of God in respect to this Breath, as He said, "His word that He cast into Mary" (Koran 4:171), a word which is the very entity of Jesus. God reported that His words will not be spent, so His creatures will never cease coming into existence and He will never cease being a Creator. (II 459.1)
>
> Through the All-merciful Breath God relieves every distress in His creatures. The constriction which overtakes or is found by the cosmos stems from the fact that the creatures' root lies in contraction (*qabḍa*). Everything contracted is constrained (*maḥṣūr*), and everything constrained is confined (*maḥjūr*). But since man comes into existence upon the Divine Form, he finds confinement intolerable. So God relieves that in him through this All-merciful Breath, inasmuch as His breathing is a property of the Love by which He described Himself in the saying, "I loved to be known."[12] God makes man manifest through the All-merciful Breath. Hence this Divine Breathing is identical with the existence of the cosmos, and the cosmos comes to know Him as He desired. So the cosmos is identical with mercy, nothing else. (II 437.20)

Ibn al-ʿArabī discusses the Breath of the All-merciful to demonstrate the motive behind the creation of the cosmos and the energizing power that makes the cosmos undergo constant transformation. The analogy of God's Breath with the human breath provides a far-reaching illustration of his whole metaphysics and cosmology. The following passages tie much of the preceding chapter into the present context.

> According to a hadith, which is sound on the basis of unveiling but not established by way of transmission (*naql*),[13] God said something like this: "I was a Treasure but was not known. So I loved to be known, and I created the creatures and made Myself known to them. Then they came to know Me." . . . We have explained elsewhere that love attaches itself only to something that is nonexistent. The thing may come into existence, but it is nonexistent at the moment.[14] The cosmos is a temporally originated thing, while "God is, and nothing is with Him." He knew the cosmos through His knowledge of Himself. Hence He made manifest in engendered existence nothing other than what the engendered thing was in itself. It was as if the engendered thing were nonmanifest and became manifest through the cosmos. The Breath of the All-merciful made the cosmos manifest in order to release the property of love and relieve what the Lover found in Himself. So He knew Himself through witnessing in the Manifest, and He mentioned Himself on the basis of knowledge in terms of that which He made manifest: This is His mention of the Cloud which is attributed to the Lord before He created the creatures. This is a mention of that which is all-inclusive (*ʿāmm*) and undifferentiated (*mujmal*). All the "words" of the cosmos are undifferentiated within this All-merciful Breath, while their differentiations (*tafāṣīl*) are infinite. (II 399.28)
>
> God is described by Being, while "nothing is with Him": No possible thing is described by existence. Rather, I say

that the Real is Being/existence itself. This is the meaning of the saying of the Messenger of God, "God is, and nothing is with Him." He says: God is an Existent Being, but nothing of the cosmos is existent.

God Himself mentioned the origin of this affair—I mean the manifestation of the cosmos in its [existent] entity. He said that He loved to be known in order to show munificence (*jūd*) to the cosmos by its knowing Him. But He knew that He could not be known in respect of His Heness, nor in the respect that He knows Himself. The only knowledge of Him which the cosmos could actualize was that it know that He cannot be known. This much is called "knowledge," as was said by Abū Bakr: "Incapacity to attain comprehension is itself comprehension." For he knew that there is something in existence that is not known—that is, God—and especially not by the existent things in respect of the fact that they possess nonexistent immutable entities coextensive (*musāwiq*) with the Necessary Being in eternity without beginning. In the same way they have an auditory connection in the state of immutability—not in existence—to the address of the Real when He addresses them, and they have the power to obey it. Likewise they have all the faculties, such as knowledge and sight. They possess each of these as an immutable thing and a verified but not existential property. . . .

God is qualified by love for us, and love is a property that demands that he who is described by it be merciful toward himself. Hence the breather finds ease in his breathing, for the breather's exhalation of breath is the same as mercy toward himself. So nothing emerges from Him except the mercy "which embraces all things" (7:156). It extends to the whole cosmos, that which is and that which has not yet come to be, ad infinitum. The first form assumed by the Breath of the All-merciful was the Cloud. So it is an All-merciful Vapor within which there is mercy; or rather, it is mercy itself. . . .

Through and in the Cloud the cosmos becomes manifest, for the cosmos cannot possibly become manifest as a property of the Nonmanifest. Hence the Real must possess a manifestation through which the forms of the cosmos may become manifest, and this is none other than the Cloud, which is the name the Manifest, the All-merciful. (III 429.4)

The Real Through Whom Creation Takes Place

The word *ḥaqq* is a noun and adjective signifying truth, correctness, rightness, appropriateness, real, sound, valid, and so on. The term is employed in a wide variety of contexts in the Koran, the Hadith, and the religious literature. In the present discussion, we will limit ourselves to its underlying ontological sense, which can be rendered as "real" or "truly real."

As pointed out earlier, Ibn al-ʿArabī and many other Muslim authorities consider the terms Allah and *al-ḥaqq* basically synonymous and employ them interchangeably. Often Ibn al-ʿArabī will use the term Allah rather than *al-ḥaqq* to call attention to the specific properties of the name Allah itself, rather than the Reality which is being named. Thus, for example, by mentioning the name Allah he may be stressing that it denotes God inasmuch as He possesses all names, or inasmuch as He must be conceived vis-a-vis the divine thrall (*ma'lūh*) or the servant (*ʿabd*). In both these instances the Divinity rather than the Essence is taken into view, and in such discussions, *al-ḥaqq* may serve better to denote God as such, as embracing both Essence and Divinity. But the term *al-ḥaqq* itself often calls to mind its own contraries, *al-khalq*, "creation" or "creatures," and *al-bāṭil*, "falsehood" or "unreal." When *al-ḥaqq* is being used in such a context, then the term Allah may better serve to designate God as such. In addition, the term *ḥaqq* can be used as an equivalent to *wujūd* in the ambivalent sense of Being/existence, whereas the name Allah is almost always reserved for Being.

In order to clarify some of the usages of the name *al-ḥaqq*, a few typical passages can be quoted. In the first, the word is used in contradistinction to creation in exactly the same sense that Allah is used in contradistinction to servant. Ibn al-ʿArabī is discussing Independence and poverty, which, as we have seen, correspond to the philosophical terms Necessity and possibility.

> Independence and poverty can never be brought together. Hence poverty has no station with God in His Being, nor does Independence have any station with the servant in his existence. . . . Poverty is an attribute of creation, and Independence is an attribute of the Real. . . . Nothing brings together the Real and creation. (II 654.24)

In the second passage, *al-ḥaqq* is employed synonymously with Being (and as we have seen repeatedly, "Being is Allah"), while a distinction is made between *wujūd* as Being and *wujūd* as existence, or uncreated and created *wujūd*. In this context, Ibn al-ʿArabī would not use the term Allah, since one cannot speak of Allah as "created."

> Concerning the entities of the cosmos, it is said that they are neither identical with the Real, nor other than the Real. On the contrary, *wujūd* is all Real. However, some of what is Real is described as created, and some is described as not created, while all of it is existent. (III 419.34)

In the third passage, Ibn al-ʿArabī is discussing the properties of the "unreal" (*al-bāṭil*), which is used as the opposite of *al-ḥaqq* in several Koranic verses, in particular 17:81: "The Real has come and the unreal has vanished away; surely the unreal is ever certain to vanish." As Ibn al-ʿArabī points out elsewhere, "*Al-Bāṭil* is the same as nonexistence, and its opposite is *al-ḥaqq*" (II 129.23).

> There is nothing in existence save God, His names, and His acts. He is the First in respect to the name Manifest, and He is the Last in respect to the name Nonmanifest. So existence is all Real. There is nothing of the unreal within it, since what is understood from applying the word unreal is nonexistence. (III 68.12)

In the fourth passage, Ibn al-ʿArabī points to the paradoxical situation of all existent things—"everything other than God"—in terms of the unreal and the Real. Since the unreal is nonexistent, it cannot exist, yet the world is full of the unreal, or that which is not God. In other words, the cosmos is He/not He, Real/unreal. But inasmuch as it exists, it can only be Real, since the unreal does not exist.

> The unreal becomes manifest in the form of the Real. But the unreal is nonexistence. It has no existence, while the form is existent, so it is Real. So where is the entity of the unreal which became manifest, when the form is only Real? (III 97.13)

With some idea of the complexity of the idea of "*al-ḥaqq*," we can turn to Ibn al-ʿArabī's use of the term, the Real Through Whom Creation Takes Place (*al-ḥaqq al-makhlūq bihi*). He tells us that he has taken the term from the writings of ʿAbd al-Salām ibn Barrajān of Seville (d. 536/1141).[15] Ibn Barrajān in turn derived it from such Koranic verses as "We created not the heavens and the earth and all that between them is, in play; We created them not save through the Real, but most of them know it not" (44:38–39); "We created not the heavens and the earth, and what between them is, save through the Real" (15:85).[16] In most passages where Ibn al-ʿArabī mentions this term, he merely provides it as a synonym for the Cloud or the Breath of the All-merciful. In a few passages he provides brief definitions which are worth noting.

> When the Real brought the cosmos into existence, He opened up His Form within the Cloud, which is the Breath of the All-merciful, i.e., the Real through whom

takes place the creation of the levels and entities of the cosmos. (II 391.33)

The Cloud is identical with the Breath of the All-merciful. It is a breathing (*nafkh*) in the Being of the Real, so through it creation takes shape (*tashakkul*) within the Real. Hence it is the Real through whom takes place the creation of the forms of the cosmos which become manifest within it and the diversification of the divine self-disclosure which appears within it. (II 313.24)

The Cloud is the Real through whom takes place the creation of everything. It is called the "Real" since it is identical with the Breath, and the Breath is hidden within the Breather—for this is what one understands from "breath." Hence the Breath has the property of the Nonmanifest, but when it becomes manifest it has the property of the Manifest. So it is the First in the Nonmanifest and the Last in the Manifest, "and it has knowledge of everything" (Koran 57:3),[17] for within it becomes manifest every named thing. This includes both the nonexistent thing, the existence of whose entity is possible, and the nonexistent thing whose entity has been given existence. (II 310.25)

In the next passage, Ibn al-ʿArabī is again explaining that the Barzakh is an intermediate reality where the "impossible" takes place, since meanings, which have no forms, assume forms within it.

The Cloud is the seat of the name "Lord" [who was "in it" before He created the creatures], just as the Throne is the seat of the All-merciful (Koran 20:5).[18] The Cloud is the first thing [in the ontological hierarchy] concerning which the question "Where?" can be posed. From it become manifest place-occupying receptacles and levels. . . . From it become manifest loci which receive corporeal meanings in sensory and imaginal form. It is a noble existent, whose meaning is the Real. It is the Real through whom takes place the creation of every existent other than the Real. It is the meaning within which are immutably established and fixed the entities of the possible things. It receives the reality of "where," the containership of place (*ẓarfiyyat al-makān*), the level of rank (*rutbat al-makāna*), and the name of locus (*maḥall*). There are none of the names ot God between the world of the earth and the Cloud except the names of acts. (II 283.9)

In the following passage, Ibn al-ʿArabī summarizes the manifestation of the cosmos "through the Real" in a commentary on the particular type of *tawḥīd* or declaration of God's Unity that is expressed in a Koranic verse where the divine name Real is mentioned: "Then high exalted be God, the King, the Real! There is no god but He, the Lord of the noble Throne" (23:116).

This is the *tawḥīd* of the Real, which is the *tawḥīd* of the He-ness. God says, "We created not the heavens and the earth and all that between them is, in play" (21:116, 44:38). This is the same in meaning as His words, "What, do you think that We created you only for sport?" (23:115). Hence, "There is no god but He" [in the above Koranic passage] is a description of the Real.

That within which the existence of the cosmos has become manifest is the Real; it becomes manifest only within the Breath of the All-merciful, which is the Cloud. So it is the Real, the Lord of the Throne, who gave the Throne its all-encompassing shape, since it encompasses all things. Hence the root within which the forms of the cosmos became manifest encompasses everything in the world of corporeal bodies. This is nothing other than the Real Through Whom Creation Takes Place. Through this receptivity, It is like a container within which comes out into the open (*burūz*) the existence of everything it includes, layer upon layer, entity after entity, in a wise hierarchy (*al-tartīb al-ḥikamī*). So It brings out into the open that which had been unseen within It in order to witness it. (II 415.18)

The Universal Reality

The term "reality" (*ḥaqīqa*) is often used as a synonym for entity. The "reality of a thing" is then the immutable entity of an existent thing, or the thing as it is known by God. The properties of the existent thing are determined by its own reality or immutable entity. We have seen that the divine names are referred to as "realities" and that they are the archetypes of all created things. The "reality" of human knowledge is the divine name Knower, the reality of cosmic life is the divine name Alive, and so on. If we consider the ninety-nine names of God as the universal realities of the cosmos, then each immutable entity can be called a particular reality.

One way of defining "reality" is to call it the nonmanifest dimension of something that is manifest. The reality of an existent thing is not what we see of it, but its immutable entity which is seen only by God and certain of His friends. And in considering the term reality (*ḥaqīqa*), one must always keep in mind that it is sometimes employed synonymously with "real," a word from the same root.

> The Real is named the Manifest and the Nonmanifest. . . . "Reality" is the manifestation of the attribute of the Real from behind a veil, which is the attribute of the servant. Once the veil of ignorance is lifted from the eye of insight, people see that the attribute of the servant is identical to the attribute of the Real. But in our view, the attribute of the servant is the Real Itself, not the attribute of the Real, since the Manifest is a creature and the Nonmanifest is Real, and the Nonmanifest is the source (*mansha'*) of the Manifest. [In the same way] the limbs [of a person] follow and obey what the soul wants from them. The soul is nonmanifest in entity but manifest in property, while the limb is manifest in property but has no nonmanifest [dimension of its own], since it has no property [of its own]. (II 563.19)

If the realities of the existent things of the cosmos are the immutable entities and the divine names, what is the reality of the divine names? In one sense, we can answer that their reality is the Divine Essence Itself (*al-dhāt*), which is *dhāt al-asmā'*, "possessor of the names." But strictly speaking, the Essence is beyond knowledge or conceptualization, so this answer, though it may be true, does not provide us with any new way of looking at things. In fact, says Ibn al-ʿArabī, the "Reality of Realities" (*ḥaqīqat al-ḥaqā'iq*)—also known as the "Universal Reality" (*al-ḥaqīqat al-kulliyya*)—can be discussed and conceptualized. This doctrine Ibn al-ʿArabī claims as belonging exclusively to the Sufis, though he does recognize that the Muʿtazilites had understood something similar.[19]

Another question: Where are the realities of things? We have seen that the first thing about which "whereness" can be posited is the Cloud, which was named in answer to the question, "Where was our Lord before He created the creatures?" And the name "Lord" demands the term "vassal." It can be employed as a description of any divine name that calls for the existence of an entity. Thus the Knower is the Lord, and the known thing is its vassal, the Creator is the Lord and the created thing is its vassal, the Powerful is the Lord and the object of power is its vassal. A "reality" by definition is a nonmanifest root which has a manifest branch, just as the Creator is a nonmanifest root and the created thing is a manifest branch. Hence in this sense of the term, a reality is a Lord, while the thing that manifests the reality in the cosmos is the vassal. According to this perspective, the question asked from the Prophet can be rephrased as follows: "Where were the realities before the vassals were brought into existence?" The answer is known: in the Cloud. Hence the Cloud is the Reality of Realities, whereas the Divine Essence or He-ness Itself, which cannot be conceived as the Lord of anything, is beyond the Cloud.

> Lordship is the relationship (*nisba*) of the He-ness to an entity, but the He-ness in Itself does not require any relationship;

> rather the immutability of the entities demands relationships with the He-ness. (II 94.15)

It is characteristic of a *barzakh* to stand between two stools. Is the Cloud God, or is it creation? Is it existent or is it nonexistent? To these sorts of questions, one has to answer equivocally, since here we have the whole mystery of Nondelimited Imagination: He/not He. Inasmuch as the Barzakh may be said to embrace both the attributes of God and the attributes of creation, it is called the Universal Reality, since it brings together all realities without exception.

The Reality of Realities defines the sphere of intelligibility of all things. Through it the relationships are established without which nothing could be known. It is not a separately existing thing—unlike God on the one hand or the cosmos on the other. Ibn al-ʿArabī describes it as *maʿqūl*, "intelligible" or "conceived of by reason (*ʿaql*)." This means that we are able to conceive of it even though it has no existence as such. It exists only through the relationships that are established between God and creation. After all, it possesses the attributes of those things that it embraces, which are the divine names and the immutable entities. As we have seen on more than one occasion, neither names nor entities are existent as such; they represent relationships that are established between the Nonmanifest and the Manifest. When we conceive of the totality of these relationships, we call it the "Universal Reality."

> The Reality of Realities is neither existent nor nonexistent, neither temporally originated nor eternal, but eternal in the eternal and temporally originated in the temporally originated. It is conceived of by the rational faculty, but it does not exist in its own essence. The same is the case, for example, with the attribute of knowing, speaking, and so on. (*Azal* 9)
>
> The Universal Reality becomes manifest in the Eternal as eternal and in temporally originated things as temporally originated. It is the manifestation of the divine realities and the lordly forms (*al-ṣuwar al-rabbāniyya* [= the divine names]) within the immutable entities, which are described by possibility and which are the loci of manifestation for the Real. But none knows the relationship of this manifestation to this locus of manifestation except God. (II 103.28)

In one passage Ibn al-ʿArabī speaks of "the four objects of knowledge," the four basic concepts which embrace all that can be known. These are: (1) God as Essence, though we cannot know the Essence as such; (2) the cosmos as a whole, that is, everything other than God, the macrocosm; (3) the human being, in which all God's attributes are brought together in undifferentiated mode, i.e., the microcosm; (4) the Universal Reality, which brings together all three of these realities. The Shaykh then describes the Universal Reality:

> The Universal Reality belongs to both the Real and the cosmos. It is described neither by existence nor by nonexistence, neither by temporal origination nor by eternity. If the Eternal is described by it, it is eternal; if the temporally originated thing is described by it, it is temporally originated. No object of knowledge, whether eternal or temporally originated, is known until this reality is known. But this reality does not come into existence until those things described by it come into existence. If something exists without a precedent nonexistence, like the Real and His attributes, one says that this reality is an eternal existent, since the Real is described by it. If something exists after nonexistence, like the existence of everything other than God, then this reality is temporally originated and existent through something other than itself; then one says concerning it that it is temporally originated. In each existent thing it accords with its own reality, since it does not accept division, since within it there is no "whole" or "part." One cannot attain to knowledge of it disengaged from form through a logical demonstration or a proof. By this Reality the cosmos came into existence through the Real. But this

Reality is not existent, that the Real should have brought us into existence from an eternally existent thing and we should be called eternal.

In the same order of things, you should know that this Reality is not described as prior to the cosmos, nor is the cosmos described as posterior to it. But it is the root of all existent things. It is the root of substance, the Sphere of Life (*falak al-ḥayāt*), the Real Through Whom Creation Takes Place, and so forth. It is the all-encompassing intelligible sphere. If you say that it is the cosmos, you are correct; that it is not the cosmos, you are correct; that it is the Real or not the Real, you are correct. It accepts all of that. At the same time it becomes plural through the plurality of the individual things of the cosmos, and it is declared incomparable through God's incomparability. (I 119.3)

The Reality of Realities possesses temporal origination in the temporally originated thing and eternity in the Eternal. This becomes manifest in the sharing (*ishtirāk*) of names. He has named you with what He has named Himself. But He has not named *you*, rather [He has named] the Universal Reality which brings together the Real and creation. So [for example] you are the knower, and He is the Knower. However, you are temporally originated, so the attribution of knowledge to you is temporally originated, while He is Eternal, so the attribution of knowledge to Him is eternal. But knowledge in itself is a single thing which has come to be qualified by the attribute of him who is described by it. (IV 311.26)

In the following passage Ibn al-ʿArabī is discussing the symbolism of the Cloud, which he shows to be identical with the Universal Reality, though he does not mention the latter by name. The word for "air" (*hawā'*) employed in the hadith of the Cloud is closely connected in origin and meaning to the word "caprice" (*hawā*), which is a Koranic term signifying the self-centered and ignorant willfulness of those who follow their own desires as another god, thus becoming guilty of the only unforgivable sin, *shirk*, or "associating another reality with God." "Have you seen him who has taken his caprice to be his god?" (25:43). "Who is further astray than he who follows his caprice without guidance from God?" (28:50). Caprice is an airiness and lightheadedness that turns a person away from right guidance. In what follows Ibn al-ʿArabī employs the term *ahwā'*, which is the plural of both "air" and "caprice," to bring out one of the implications of the air mentioned in the hadith of the Cloud. I translate the term as "airs," hoping to call to mind that a person who "puts on airs" is acting merely for the sake of appearance and outward show, not because the reality of things would demand it. That God should "put on airs" is diametrically opposed to the idea that He creates "through the Real."

The Prophet said that our Lord is in a Cloud, neither above which nor below which is any air. Thereby he declared God incomparable with the idea that He turns things about because of airs. He alluded to that Being with a word which denotes a cloud, which is the place where airs turn things about. Then he denied that there should be any air above or below that Cloud. Hence it possesses everlasting immutability. It is neither on air nor in air. . . .

God described Himself among His creatures with the words, "He governs the affair, He differentiates the signs" (Koran 13:2). In the same way He said, "We turn about the signs" (6:105). He who has no understanding imagines that God's states undergo change. But He is high exalted and far too holy for change. Rather, the states change, but He does not change with them. For He rules over properties. Nothing rules over Him. Hence the Lawgiver mentioned [in this hadith] the attribute of immutability which does not accept change, for the hand of airs does not turn about His signs, since the Cloud does not accept airs.

This Cloud is that which we have mentioned as eternal in the eternal and temporally originated in the temporally originated. This is like your words, or identical with your words, concerning Being/existence. When you attribute it to the Real, you say it is Eternal, but when you attribute it to creation, you say that it is temporally originated. So the Cloud inasmuch as it is a description of the Real is a divine description (*waṣf ilāhī*), but inasmuch as it is a description of the cosmos it is an engendered description (*waṣf kiyānī*). Its descriptions are diverse according to the diversity of the entities which are described.

God says concerning His beginningless and eternal Speech, "There comes not to them a remembrance from their Lord temporally originated (*muḥdath*), [but they listen to it yet playing, diverted their hearts]" (21:2). Hence He described His Speech as temporally originated, since it came down upon a temporally originated person, in respect to whom there originated in time something which he did not know. So it is temporally originated for him, without doubt.

As for this temporally originated thing: Is it temporally originated in itself or not? If we say that it is the attribute of the Real of which His majesty is worthy, we will say that it is eternal, without doubt. For He is far too exalted for temporally originated attributes to subsist within Him. So the Speech of the Real is Eternal in itself and eternal in relationship to God, but also temporally originated, just as He said to him to whom He sent it down. In the same way, one of the faces of its eternity, in respect to him to whom it is sent down, is its relationship to temporal origination. This also demands that it possess the attribute of eternity, since, were temporal origination to be removed from the created things, there could be no relationship of eternity, nor could eternity be conceived. The reason for this is that relationships which have opposites can only be conceived through opposites. (II 63.2)

Ibn al-ʿArabī finds an allusion to the Universal Reality in the hadith, "All *ḥaqq*s have a [single] reality."[20] Here by *ḥaqq* he seems to understand "real thing." If *al-ḥaqq* with the definite article is the Real, then *ḥaqq* without the article refers to any manifestation of the Real. But the Real Itself is the Essence, beyond the specification of any name. Once the Real is specified by a name, that is, a relationship which is established between it and creation, that name becomes the reality of the creature to which it is related. The one reality to which every real thing relates can only be the Universal Reality, which embraces all names and all entities.

The Universal Reality is the spirit of every *ḥaqq*. Should a *ḥaqq* be empty of it, it ceases to be a *ḥaqq*. That is why the Prophet said, "All *ḥaqq*s have a reality." In this saying he employs a word which, when free of delimiting contexts, demands all-inclusiveness (*iḥāṭa*), that is, the word "all." In the same way the concept of knowledge, or life, or desire [includes all knowledge, all life, all desire].

In reality, the Universal Reality is a single intelligible thing (*maʿqūl*). When a specific quality (*amr*) is attributed to it, it then possesses a name which comes into temporal being (*ḥudūth*). Then when that specific quality is attributed to an essence which is known to have existence, even though its reality is not known, that specific quality is attributed to that determinate essence in accordance with what it requires. If that essence is described by eternity, then this specific quality is described by eternity. If it is described by temporal origination, then the quality is described by the same. But the quality in itself is not described by existence, since it has no entity, nor by nonexistence, since it is an intelligible thing, nor by temporal origination, since the Eternal cannot be described by that; it cannot be a locus for temporally originated things. Nor is the quality described by eternity, since the temporally originated thing accepts description by the quality, and the temporal thing is not described by the eternal, nor can the eternal dwell (*ḥāll*) in the temporal. Hence it is neither eternal nor temporally originated. If the temporally originated thing is described by it, it is named temporally originated, and if the eternal is described by it, it is named eternal. It is truly eternal in the eternal, and it is truly temporally originated in the temporally originated, since it stands opposite everything that becomes described by it in its own essence.

For example, both the Real and the creature are described by knowledge. It is said concerning God's knowledge that it is eternal, since He who is described by it is eternal. Hence His knowledge of the things is eternal, without any beginning. It is said concerning the knowledge of the creature that it is temporally originated, for he who is described by it at first was not, and then he came to be. Hence his attributes are like himself: Their property did not become manifest within him until after the existence of his entity. Hence his knowledge is temporally originated like himself. But knowledge in itself does not change from its own reality in relation to itself. In every essence it accords with its own reality and entity. But it has no existential entity except the entity of that which it describes. So it remains in its root: an intelligible thing, not an existent thing.

The example of this in the sensory realm is whiteness in every white thing and blackness in every black thing. This is in the case of colors. The same holds true in shapes: rectangularity in every rectangular thing, roundness in every round thing, octagonality in every octagon. The shape keeps its own essence in every thing that has shape; it accords with the intelligibility of its own reality. That which the senses perceive is only the thing which has shape, not the shape, while the shape is an intelligible concept. Were the thing which has shape identical with the shape, shape could not become manifest in a similarly shaped thing. But it is obvious that the one thing possessing shape is not the same as the other.

These are similitudes struck for the universal realities by which the Real and the creature are qualified. In the case of the Real they are "names," and in the case of the creature they are "engendered things" (*akwān*). (II 432.16)

When Ibn al-ʿArabī discusses the Supreme Barzakh as Universal Reality or Reality of Realities, he also refers to it as the Third Thing (*al-shay' al-thālith*). He divides things into three kinds: that which exists in itself (i.e., the Necessary Being), that which exists through the other (i.e., everything other than God), and the Third Thing, which is neither existent nor nonexistent.[21]

Nature

Ibn al-ʿArabī calls the Supreme Barzakh by several other names, such as the Reality of the Perfect Man and the Muhammadan Reality; these and other names call to mind related concepts which would take us far from the concerns of the present work. However, it will be fitting to conclude this section with a brief analysis of one more synonym for the Supreme Barzakh, i.e., Nature. This term is fundamental to all philosophical cosmology. By identifying the Barzakh and Nature, Ibn al-ʿArabī relates his cosmological teachings, which grow up from the various names which can be applied to the Barzakh, directly to the philosophical tradition. By discussing Nature here, we open a door to cosmology as such, especially since Ibn al-ʿArabī gives the term two basic meanings, the second of which refers to a reality which is itself a *barzakh* between Nature as the Supreme Barzakh and the things of the cosmos. But to develop the concept in any detail would take us in the direction of analyzing Ibn al-ʿArabī's visionary cosmos in detail, and this is the task for another book.

The root *ṭ.b.ʿ.*, from which the words *ṭabīʿa* and *ṭabʿ* are derived, means to provide with an imprint, to impress, to mark with a seal or a special characteristic. Hence "nature" signifies the sum total of the peculiarities which are stamped into something, that is, the thing's characteristics, character, temperament, or constitution. The word *ṭabīʿa* alludes to the feminine side of a male/female, active/receptive, or yang/yin relationship. To speak of *ṭabīʿa* is to mention an "impression" and at the same time to point to a reality which has made the impression, a fact which is brought home in the Koranic usage of the word *ṭabʿ*, which refers to God's "sealing" the hearts of the unbelievers. Hence, the word calls to mind receptivity toward an activity coming from above. In this respect, the sense of *ṭabīʿa* is not much different from "sign" (*āya*); to say that everything in existence displays the "signs" of God is to say that all "Nature" is receptive toward God's creative command.

Though Nature is viewed primarily as receptivity, both activity (*fāʿiliyya*) and receptivity (*qābiliyya*)—or the quality of being acted upon (*infiʿāliyya*)—are manifest through it, since the higher principle that acts upon Nature possesses both active and receptive dimensions. In other words, though Nature is receptive to that which instills form into it, the forms that are instilled may be active or receptive, male or female, yang or yin. Moreover, Ibn al-ʿArabī sometimes shifts the point of view from which he considers Nature and sees it as an active instead of a receptive principle.[22]

From one point of view Nature is darkness, since that which acts upon it is either God—through His command (*amr*) or Word (*kalima*)—or the spirit, and these are light. Yet, the Shaykh insists that Nature at root is also a kind of light, or else it could not begin to display its properties in the spiritual world between the Universal Soul and the Dust (Hyle or Prime Matter; II 647.34). He says that true darkness is the Unseen, since it is neither perceived, nor does perception take place through it. But in common experience we perceive darkness around us, which shows that "darkness is a kind of light" (II 648.4); if it were not light, it could not be perceived. Hence Nature also, though it may be called darkness in relation to the Spirit which infuses it with life, is light in relation to absolute nothingness.

When Nature is envisaged as that which is receptive toward the effects of the divine names, it is synonymous with the Cloud. Just as the Breath of the All-merciful becomes manifest through the letters and words which take shape within it, so Nature appears only through its effects on various levels of the cosmos. In itself it remains forever unseen. Nature is the "highest and greatest mother" (*al-umm al-ʿāliyat al-kubrā*; IV 150.15), who gives birth to all things, though she herself is never seen. She is the receptivity that allows the existent things to become manifest.

When Nature is envisaged as that which is receptive to the First Intellect working within the cosmos, then she is the "second mother," the "daughter of the Greatest Nature" (*al-ṭabīʿat al-ʿuẓmā*, III 420.34), and she makes her presence felt between the Universal Soul and the Dust. Her children are all the forms which become manifest from the Dust to the lowest level of existence.

> Nature is absent in entity from existence, since it has no entity within existence, and from immutability, since it has no entity there. Hence it is the Verified World of the Unseen (*ʿālam al-ghayb al-muḥaqqaq*). But Nature is known, just as the impossible (*al-muḥāl*) is known, except that, though Nature is like the impossible in having neither existence nor immutability, it has an effect and brings about the manifestation of forms. But the impossible is not like that. (III 397.5)
>
> There is nothing in existence but the One/Many (*al-wāḥid al-kathīr*). Within it become manifest the enraptured angels, the Intellect, the Soul, and Nature.[23] Nature is more worthy to be attributed to the Real than anything else, since everything else becomes manifest only in that which becomes manifest from Nature, that is, the Breath, which permeates the cosmos. . . . So look at the all-inclusiveness of Nature's property! And look at the inadequacy of the property of the [First] Intellect, for in reality it is one of the forms of Nature. Or rather, it is one of the forms of the Cloud, and the Cloud is one of the forms of Nature.
>
> As for those who have placed Nature in a level below the Soul and above the Hyle, this is because they have no witnessing. If a person is a possessor of witnessing and holds this view, he wants to refer to the Nature which becomes manifest through its property in the translucent corporeal bodies, that is, in the Throne and what it surrounds. This second Nature is to the first as the daughter is to the woman who is the mother; like her mother, she gives birth, even if she is a daughter born from her. (III 420.15)

Nature in relation to the Real is like the female in relation to the male, since within it becomes manifest engendering, i.e., the engendering of everything other than God. It is an intelligible reality.

When some people saw the power of Nature's authority and did not know that this power lies only in its reception to that which the Real engenders within it, they attributed and ascribed the engendering to Nature itself. "They forgot" God through Nature, "so He made them forget themselves" (Koran 59:19), since He turned them away from the signs (*āyāt*) of their own souls. This is what is meant by God's words, "I shall turn away from My signs those who wax proud in the earth without the Real" (7:146). . . .

The Real possesses entified and intelligible existence, while Nature possesses intelligible existence but not entified existence. Thereby creation's property may stand between existence and nothingness. Creation accepts nonexistence in respect of Nature and accepts existence from the side of the Real. Hence everything other than God is described by the reception of both nonexistence and existence. . . . Were this not so, it would be impossible for an existent created thing to accept nonexistence or a nonexistent thing to accept existence. In this manner you must understand the realities; and there is no way to do so except by not turning away from the signs. . . .

Nature possesses reception and the Real possesses bestowal (*wahb*) and the exercise of effects (*ta'thīr*). Nature is the highest, greatest mother of the cosmos, of whom the cosmos never sees the entity, only the effects, just as it never sees anything of the Real but His effects, never His Entity. (IV 150.1,9)

A woman in relation to a man is like Nature in relation to the Divine Command (*al-amr al-ilāhī*), since the woman is the locus of the existence of the entities of the children, just as Nature in relation to the Divine Command is the locus of the manifestation of the entities of the corporeal bodies. Through it they are engendered and from it they become manifest. So there can be no Command without Nature and no Nature without Command. Hence engendered existence depends upon both. . . . He who knows the level of Nature knows the level of the woman, and he who knows the Divine Command knows the level of the man and the fact that the existence of all existent things other than God depends upon these two realities. (III 90.18,28)

The most specific properties of Nature are the "four natures" (*al-ṭabā'i' al-arba'a*), that is, heat, cold, wetness, and dryness. Two of them are active and two receptive. Heat is active and its effects appear as dryness, while cold is active and displays its activity as wetness (II 439.10). Heat is the secondary cause or root of the existence of dryness, and coldness the root of wetness (I 122.25; Y 2,239.10). But all four natures are receptive in relation to the Divine Command or the First Intellect; like Nature itself they are all mothers. "All of the natures are acted upon (*infi'āl*) in relation to that from which they have emerged" (I 293.17).

Heat and cold as well as wetness and dryness display opposition (*taḍādd*) and mutual aversion (*tanāfur*). As a result, everything that displays the properties of Nature—that is, everything other than God—reflects this opposition and conflict. The "Dispute of the Angels" is but an early result of the innate characteristics of Nature.

Know that subtlety (*luṭf*) cannot possibly turn into density (*kathāfa*), since realities do not change. But that which is subtle can become dense, like a hot thing which becomes cool, or a cold thing which becomes hot.

The spirits possess subtlety. When they become embodied (*tajassud*) and are manifested in the form of corporeal bodies, they become dense in the eye of him who looks upon them, for corporeal bodies, whether or not they are translucent (*shaffāf*),[24] are dense. . . .

The reason for the density of the spirits, even though they belong to the World of Subtlety, is that they were created from Nature. Though their bodies are made of light, this is the light of Nature, like the light of a lamp. That is why they accept density and become manifest within the forms of dense bodies.

In the same way, the property of Nature leaves the effect of conflict within them, since within Nature there is contrariety and opposition, and opposites and contraries conflict with those who stand opposite them. Such are the words of the Messenger of God as related from him by God, "I had no knowledge of the higher plenum when they disputed" (Koran 38:69). Hence God describes them as disputing. Through the reality which allows them to dispute they become embodied within the forms of dense corporeal bodies. (II 472.10)

The spirits are all fathers, while Nature is the Mother, since it is the locus of transmutations. (I 138.29)

From a certain point of view, the lower Nature may be seen as the source of evil, since it is basically darkness in contradistinction to the light of the spirit. In the following passage Ibn al-ʿArabī refers to the angelic or spiritual world as the "World of Command" as opposed to the "World of Creation," that is, the Visible World. The name "World of Command" derives from many Koranic allusions, one of the most relevant being, "They [the angels] are honored servants who precede Him not in speech and act according to His Command" (21:27).

The world of creation and composition (*tarkīb*) requires evil (*sharr*) in its very essence, but the World of Command is a good (*khayr*) in which there is no evil. That world saw man's creation and composition from the mutually averse natures. It knew that mutual aversion is conflict (*tanāzuʿ*) and that conflict leads to corruption (*fasād*). Hence it said [after God had created Adam and was about to place him in the earth], "What, wilt Thou place therein one who will do corruption therein, and shed blood?" (Koran 2:30). . . . Then there occurred what the angels had said. They saw that God said, "God loves not those who do corruption" (5: 64), and "God loves not corruption" (2: 205), so they disliked what God disliked and loved what God loved, but God's decree in creation followed the course determined by the Inaccessible, the All-knowing.

The evils which became manifest within the world of composition derive from its Nature, which was mentioned by the angels. The good which becomes manifest within it derives from its Divine Spirit, which is light. Hence the angels spoke the truth. Therefore God said, "Whatever evil visits you is from yourself" (Koran 4:79). Since the World of Creation is like this, it is incumbent upon every rational person to seek protection in this light. . . . All evils are ascribed to the World of Creation, and all good is ascribed to the World of Command. (II 575.25)

Though everything other than God belongs to the domain of Nature, there are many degrees of existents, which means that Nature's luminosity is greatest at the highest levels and decreases as we move down from the "subtle" toward the "dense" levels of existence.

The angel is more excellent than man in worship, since it never flags, as is demanded by the reality of its plane. Its calling God holy is inherent, since its glorification derives from a presence with Him who is glorified. The angel glorifies only Him who brought it into existence. In its very essence it is purified of all heedlessness. Its natural, luminous plane does not distract it from constant glorification of its Creator, even though the angels, in respect to their plane, dispute. . . .

Man is not given the power of the angel in this, since the mixture (*mizāj*) of Nature is diverse in individuals. This is self-evident in the World of the Elements, and even more so in the case of him who has a closer relationship to Nature than the elements. To the extent that Nature's various productions stand as intermediaries between disengaged Nature and these things which are produced from it, the veil becomes more dense and the darknesses pile up. For example, how can the last human being existent from his Lord in respect to the time when He created Adam's body with His two hands be compared to Adam? For Adam says, "My Lord created me with His two hands." His son Seth says, "Between me and my Lord is my father." Such are the natural existents in relation to Nature, whether they be angel, celestial sphere, element, mineral, plant, animal, man, or the angel

> created from man's soul, which is the last natural existent.[25] (II 109.6)

Here we cut short our discussion of cosmology. If certain dimensions of the previous passages remain unclear, perhaps this can be remedied on another occasion. But the exact status of the First Nature, the Supreme Barzakh as such, can never be completely clarified. And this follows from its reality. Discussing the Barzakh has led to a certain amount of perplexity and bewilderment, since its fundamental nature is imagination—intrinsic ambiguity. The more it is analyzed, the more confused the accounts become. Part of the problem stems from our tendency to think in terms of logical concepts rather than analogies and images. Since existence is an imaginal reality, reason can understand it only with the help of analogies and comparisons which appeal to the imagination. But imaginal realities cannot be pinned down. If you say the cosmos is He, I have to reply that it is not He. And if you try to hold me to that, I will say yes and no. This is the whole mystery of existence.

> Engendered being is only imagination,
> yet in truth it is the Real.
> He who has understood this point
> has grasped the mysteries of the Path.
> (*Fuṣūṣ* 159)

What is the Barzakh? It is the cosmos as revelation, the face of God manifested as existence. It is the reality of "Whithersoever you turn, there is the Face of God" (2:115). Is it God? Yes and no. He/not He. The more we analyze it, the more puzzled we become. The desire for a clear, logical, and totally coherent picture of the universe merely reflects the ignorance of the seeker. Ultimate Reality in Itself cannot be known, and It "never repeats Itself" in Its self-disclosures. So how can we constrict and define Its self-disclosures? Our highest and clearest perception of It, as Ibn al-ʿArabī frequently reminds us, is "the incapacity to comprehend It," whether in Itself, or as It reveals Itself. How can we know the reality of anything at all, given the fact that both the existence and attributes of each thing go back to the One, who is unknowable?

But this does not mean that man should give up searching for knowledge, since the explicit divine command is to pray, "My Lord, increase me in knowledge!" (20:114). The dead end we reach in trying to analyze things through the rational faculty should serve rather to alert us to the fact that there are other modes of knowing God and self. If "imagination" seems a shaky ground upon which to stand, this is because we have forgotten what must guide the imagination: God's revelations. True and valid knowledge of all things is in fact available, within limits, and these limits are set down by the revealed Laws. If Ibn al-ʿArabī constantly reminds us that reason is incapable of finding true knowledge on its own, this is because he wants to point to the firm handle provided by the Koran and the Hadith. Hence we turn from Ibn al-ʿArabī's description of Reality to a concern far more basic to his writings: How do we gain personal knowledge of the Real? How do we find God?

4

Epistemology

9. *KNOWLEDGE AND THE KNOWER*

Few concerns are as central to Islam as the search for knowledge (*ʿilm*). In the Koran God commands the Prophet, by universal Muslim consent the most knowledgeable of all human beings, to pray, "My Lord, increase me in knowledge!" (20:114). Muslims must imitate him in this quest. "Are they equal," asks the Koran, "those who know and those who know not?" (39:9). The answer is self-evident. Hence, as the Prophet said, "The search for knowledge is incumbent upon every Muslim."[1]

Both the form and content of Islamic knowledge are epitomized by the Shahāda, the "witnessing" that defines *tawḥīd*, "There is no god but God." Knowledge concerns itself first with God. "Other than God" comes into the picture only to the extent that one must know the other in order to gain knowledge of God. In fact, of course, no knowledge of God can be gained without intermediary, so "other than God" is as important for knowledge, if not more important, than God Himself. But the other must be known with a view toward God. All things must be taken back to the One, which is precisely the sense of the word *tawḥīd*.

Knowledge and Knowledge

In contrast to many Sufis who emphasize love more than knowledge (albeit within the cognitive context of Islam), Ibn al-ʿArabī approaches God primarily through knowing Him. In this respect he follows the path of most Muslim authorities. However, when the jurists, for example, speak of the "search for knowledge," they have in mind the learning of the details of God's Law. And when the proponents of Kalām (the Mutakallimūn) or the Peripatetic philosophers search for knowledge, they employ reason (*ʿaql*) as their primary tool, even if the former emphasize the understanding of the Koranic revelation and the latter emphasize the ability of reason to function independently of revelation. For Ibn al-ʿArabī, these kinds of knowledge are all useful and good, but they can become obstructions to gaining the most real and useful of knowledges, which is taught by God Himself.

In any case, knowledge is one of the greatest goods and should always be sought.

> God never commanded His Prophet to seek increase of anything except knowledge, since all good (*khayr*) lies therein. It is the greatest charismatic gift (*karāma*). Idleness with knowledge is better than ignorance with good works. . . . By knowledge I mean only knowledge of God, of the next world, and of that which is appropriate for this world, in relationship to that for which this world was created and established. Then man's affairs will be "upon insight"[2] wherever he is, and he will be ignorant of nothing in himself and his activities.
>
> Knowledge is a divine attribute of all-encompassingness, so it is the most excellent bounty of God. Hence God said, "[Then they found one of Our servants, whom We had given mercy from Us], and whom We had taught knowledge from Us" (18:65), that is, as a mercy from Us. So knowledge derives from the mine of mercy. (II 370.4)

Knowledge is the most all-encompassing of the divine attributes, which is to say that "God is Knower of all things" (Koran 4:176, 8:75, etc.). "Not a leaf falls, but He knows it" (6:59). Nothing escapes His knowledge of Himself or the other. "Our Lord embraces all things in knowledge" (Koran 7:89). The only attribute said to have the same all-encompassing nature is mercy, which is practically identical with existence.[3] "Our Lord," say the angels in the Koran, "Thou embracest all things in mercy and knowledge" (40:7).

Knowledge cannot be defined in the sense of delineating its essential nature and determining its bounds (*ḥadd*), since it embraces all bounds. Nothing is more luminous than knowledge to throw light upon it. The seat of knowledge, for Ibn al-ʿArabī as for other Muslim authorities, is the heart.

> Know—God confirm you—that knowledge is for the heart to acquire (*taḥṣīl*) something (*amr*) as that thing is in itself, whether the thing is nonexistent or existent. Knowledge is the attribute gained by the heart through this acquisition. The knower is the heart, and the object of knowledge is that acquired thing. Conceiving of the reality of knowledge is extremely difficult. (I 91.19)

Like other authors, Ibn al-ʿArabī employs two words for knowledge, *ʿilm* and *maʿrifa*. Sometimes he distinguishes between them, but for the most part he does not. The Koran ascribes only *ʿilm* to God, never *maʿrifa*, so in the case of God, the latter term is rarely employed. When discussing knowledge as a human attribute, many Sufis placed *maʿrifa* at a higher stage than *ʿilm*, and in this context it would be fair to translate the first as gnosis and the second as knowledge. Then *maʿrifa* is equivalent to the direct knowledge called unveiling, witnessing, and tasting, about which a good deal will be said in later chapters.

Ibn al-ʿArabī often speaks of the "gnostics" as the greatest friends of God, employing the term *ʿārifūn* (plural of *ʿārif*, from the same root as *maʿrifa*); sometimes he accords an equal rank to the "knowers" *ʿulamāʾ* (plural of *ʿālim*, from *ʿilm*), though he is more likely to employ the latter term for the exoteric scholars (*ʿulamāʾ al-rusūm*). It would be possible to translate the two words consistently as "knowledge" (*ʿilm*) and "gnosis" (*maʿrifa*), but this would make a distinction between them that is unwarranted in many contexts. When appropriate, the distinction will be drawn in translation, but otherwise "knowledge" will be used for both terms; when the context is particularly significant, the Arabic term will be mentioned in brackets. On occasion *maʿrifa* will be translated as "true knowledge" to indicate the specification which the term conveys. Often, particularly in verbal form, it can be rendered accurately as "to recognize."

As in English, the word "knowledge" can mean either the act of knowing or that which is known. This is especially the case when the plural is employed. On these occasions it will often be more natural to translate *ʿilm* as "science" and *maʿrifa* as "gnostic science." Sometimes

ʿilm is employed to refer to the well-known teachings of Islam or Sufism, in which case it may be translated as "doctrine."

Ibn al-ʿArabī was perfectly aware that various Sufis—not to speak of theologians and philosophers—disagreed concerning the relationship between *ʿilm* and *maʿrifa*. Though he tells us his own position in certain passages, he does not always hold to it. In the following he talks about the divergence of his "companions" (*aṣḥāb*), that is, the great Sufis of Islamic history.[4]

> Our companions have disagreed concerning the station of *maʿrifa* and the *ʿārif* and the station of *ʿilm* and the *ʿālim*. A group maintain that the station of *maʿrifa* is lordly (*rabbānī*) and the station of *ʿilm* divine (*ilāhī*), including myself and the Verifiers (*al-muḥaqqiqūn*), like Sahl al-Tustarī, Abū Yazīd, Ibn al-ʿArīf, and Abū Madyan.[5] Another group maintain that the station of *maʿrifa* is divine and the station of *ʿilm* below it; I maintain that also, since they mean by *ʿilm* what we mean by *maʿrifa*, and they mean by *maʿrifa* what we mean by *ʿilm*. Hence the disagreement is verbal. . . . We have spoken in great detail about the difference between *maʿrifa* and *ʿilm* in *Mawāqiʿ al-nujūm*. There I explained that when I asked the person who maintains the superiority of the station of *maʿrifa*, he replied with that which the opponent replies concerning the station of *ʿilm*. So the disagreement lies in the names, not in the meaning.[6] (II 318.30)

At the beginning of the long chapter on *maʿrifa* in the *Futūḥāt*, Ibn al-ʿArabī tells us that the Sufis who affirm *maʿrifa*'s superiority to *ʿilm* mean to say that it is a form of knowledge which can be achieved only through spiritual practice, not by book learning or study with a teacher. It is the knowledge to which the Koran refers when it says, "Be god-fearing, and God will teach you" (2:282):

> For the Tribe, *maʿrifa* is a path (*maḥajja*). Hence any knowledge which can be actualized only through practice (*ʿamal*), godfearingness (*taqwā*), and wayfaring (*sulūk*) is *maʿrifa*, since it derives from a verified unveiling which is not seized by obfuscation. This contrasts with the knowledge which is actualized through reflective consideration (*al-naẓar al-fikrī*), which is never safe from obfuscation and bewilderment, nor from rejection of that which leads to it. (II 297.33)
>
> Our companions among the Folk of Allah apply the name "gnostics" to the knowers (*al-ʿulamāʾ*) of God, and they call the knowledge of God by way of tasting "gnosis." They define this station by its results and concomitants, which become manifest through this attribute in its possessor.
>
> When Junayd was asked about gnosis and the gnostic, he replied, "The water takes on the color of its cup." In other words, the gnostic assumes the character traits of God, to the point where it seems as if he is He. He is not He, yet he is He. (II 316.9)

The importance of practice in actualizing certain "gnostic sciences" (*maʿārif*) helps explain why knowledge without practice is not true knowledge. Ibn al-ʿArabī provides a metaphysical explanation for this point by saying that knowledge by itself pertains only to the domain of God as the Nonmanifest, while knowledge along with practice embraces the domains of both the Nonmanifest and the Manifest. Hence it is broader in scope and more perfect.

> The rulings (*aḥkām*) revealed by the Law comprise certain gnostic sciences which are not unveiled unless the rulings are put into practice. This is because the Manifest has a stronger—that is to say, more inclusive (*aʿamm*)—property than the Nonmanifest, since the Manifest possesses the station of both creation and the Real, while the Nonmanifest possesses the station of the Real without creation. But in relation to Himself He is not Nonmanifest, only Manifest. (II 533.2)

The Usefulness of Knowledge

The Prophet used to pray, "I seek refuge in God from a knowledge which has no use (*lā yanfaʿ*)."[7] Useless knowledge is that which is disconnected from its source and origin, i.e., from the Divine Reality. Any knowledge outside of *tawḥīd* leads away from God, not toward Him. But knowledge within the context of *tawḥīd* allows its possessor to grasp the interconnectedness of all things through a vast web whose Center is the Divine. All existent things come from God and go back to Him. Likewise all true and useful knowledge comes from God and takes the knower back to Him. It is true that in the last analysis, all knowledge without exception comes from God, but if we do not recognize this and understand the manner in which it leads back to Him, that knowledge will be of no use to us, if not positively harmful.

> The root of every knowledge derives from knowledge of the divine things,[8] since "everything other than God" derives from God. (I 170.8)
>
> Everything in engendered existence must be supported by divine realities and comprised within knowledge of the divine things, from which all knowledges branch out. (I 293.5)

Again, true and useful knowledge is knowledge of God, or knowledge of the cosmos inasmuch as it displays the signs of God and points to Him. In a hadith already quoted, in which the Prophet tells us that God taught him the knowledge of why the Higher Plenum disputes, God placed His palm between the Prophet's shoulders. In explaining one of the meanings of this hadith, the Shaykh refers to the Koranic verse, "I created the jinn and mankind only to worship Me" (51:56). He alludes to the fact, well known to his readers, that many of the Koran commentators, beginning with the Prophet's companion Ibn ʿAbbās, interpreted the words "to worship Me" as meaning "to know Me."[9]

> The Prophet said, "When God struck His palm between my shoulders, I came to know the knowledge of the ancients and the later folk"[10] through that placing of the palm. So through that striking God gave him the knowledge he mentioned. By this knowledge he means knowledge of God. Knowledge of other than God is a waste of time (*taḍyīʿ al-waqt*), since God created the cosmos only for knowledge of Him. More specifically, this is the case with what is called "mankind and jinn," since He stated clearly that He created them to worship Him. (IV 221.20)

Useful knowledge takes a person back to God, that is, God as the Merciful, the Forgiving, and the Beneficent, not God as the Wrathful and the Vengeful. For all knowledge is ultimately from God and leads back to Him, but not all of it leads to the same face of God. We have already quoted Ibn al-ʿArabī on this point:

> What do the Avenger, the Terrible in Punishment, and the Overpowering have in common with the Compassionate, the Forgiving, and the Gentle? For the Avenger demands the occurrence of vengeance in its object, while the Compassionate demands the removal of vengeance from the same object. (II 93.19)

Simply put, useful knowledge leads to deliverance (*najāt*), which is none other than happiness or "felicity" (*saʿāda*) and the avoidance of "wretchedness" (*shaqāʾ*) in the stages of existence after death. "For any creature who has individual desires (*aghrāḍ*), felicity is to attain, in his actual situation, to all the individual desires created within him" (II 673.18). It is to enter the Garden by becoming a locus of manifestation for the divine names of gentleness and beauty. In contrast, wretchedness is to burn in the Fire through being overcome by the properties of the names of severity and majesty.

> Because the next world is an abode of recompense (*jazāʾ*) . . . wretchedness and felicity become manifest there. Wretchedness belongs to the divine wrath (*ghaḍab*), while felicity belongs to the divine approval (*riḍā*). Felicity is the infinite expanse of mercy. Wrath will be cut off, according to the prophetic report, so its

> property will come to an end, but the property of approval will never come to an end. (III 382.34)

Felicity is achieved through nearness or proximity (*qurb*) to God. In the words of the Koran, "The Outstrippers, the Outstrippers! They are those brought near [to God], in the Gardens of Delight . . ." (56:11), and this nearness is achieved on the foundation of knowledge. "All felicity lies in knowledge of God" (IV 319.10). But in order to achieve felicity, man must seek nearness to God in respect of His merciful names, not His wrathful names. Ibn al-ʿArabī makes this point while discussing the station of nearness, which, as a Sufi term, had usually been defined as "undertaking acts of obedience."

> The nearness which the Sufis define as "undertaking acts of obedience" is a nearness to the servant's felicity through his being safe from wretchedness. The "felicity" of the servant lies in his attaining to all his individual desires without exception, and this takes place only in the Garden. As for this world, he must necessarily abandon those of his individual desires which detract from his felicity. The "nearness" of the common people and of people in general is nearness to felicity. The person obeys in order to gain felicity. . . .
>
> Were it not for the divine names and their properties among the engendered things, the property of nearness and distance (*buʿd*) would never become manifest within the cosmos. In each moment (*waqt*) every servant must be the possessor of nearness to one divine name and the possessor of distance from another name which, at that moment, has no ruling property over him. If the property of the name which rules over him at the moment and which is qualified by nearness to him gives him safety from wretchedness and possession of felicity, this is the nearness desired by the Tribe. It is everything that bestows felicity upon the servant; if it does not bestow felicity, the Tribe does not refer to it as "nearness." (II 558.34)

Any knowledge which does not lead back to God by a road of felicity does not deserve to be called "knowledge." Ibn al-ʿArabī often refers to it instead as "surmise" (*ẓann*), a Koranic term, frequently discussed in the religious sciences, which may also be translated as opinion, conjecture, or supposition.

> If anyone sets up in himself an object of worship which he worships by surmise, not in certitude (*qaṭʿ*), that will avail him nothing against God. God says, "[They have no knowledge thereof; they follow only surmise,] and surmise avails naught against the Real" (53:28). Concerning their worship, He says, "They follow only surmise and the caprice of their souls" (53:23). God attributes to them worshiping other than God only by way of surmise, not by way of knowledge, for in actual fact, that cannot be knowledge.
>
> Hence you come to know that knowledge is the cause of deliverance. If a person should become wretched on the way, in the end (*maʾāl*) he will reach deliverance. So how noble is the rank of knowledge! That is why God did not command His Prophet to seek increase in anything except knowledge, for He said to him, "Say: 'My Lord, increase me in knowledge!'" (20:114). He who understands our allusions will know the distinction between the people of felicity and the people of wretchedness. (II 612.6)

The knowledge which leads to God and felicity is not, of course, a theoretical knowledge. It is a knowledge conjoined with practice or good works (*ʿamal*). Knowledge and practice are so closely connected in the Islamic consciousness that Ibn al-ʿArabī rarely bothers to remind his readers of the relationship.

> In our view, knowledge requires practice, and necessarily so, or else it is not knowledge, even if it appears in the form of knowledge. (III 333.17)
>
> In our own view, God's deceiving (*makr*) the servant is that He should provide him knowledge which demands practice, and then deprive him of the practice. (II 529.34)

Ibn al-ʿArabī provides a wide definition of the term "practice," including within it both inward (*bāṭin*) and outward (*ẓāhir*) activities.

> There is an outward practice, which is everything connected to the bodily parts, and an inward practice, which is everything connected to the soul (*nafs*). The most inclusive inward practice is faith in God and what has come from Him in accordance with the words of the Messenger, not in accordance with knowledge of it. Faith embraces all acts which are to be performed or avoided. (II 559.20)

One of al-Ḥakīm al-Tirmidhī's questions which Ibn al-ʿArabī answers in the *Futūḥāt* is "What is prostration (*sujūd*)?" Literally, the word signifies being lowly and bending the head to the ground. As a technical term in the Islamic sciences, it signifies the placing of the forehead on the ground during the canonical prayer (*ṣalāt*); it is the servant's supreme act of humility before his Lord. In answering al-Tirmidhī, Ibn al-ʿArabī goes to the heart of this richly symbolic act:

> Everything which prostrates itself bears witness to its own root from which it is absent by being a branch. When a thing is diverted from being a root by being a branch, it is said to it, "Seek that which is absent from you, your root from which you have emerged." So the thing prostrates itself to the soil which is its root. The spirit prostrates itself to the Universal Spirit (*al-rūḥ al-kull*) from which it has emerged. The inmost consciousness (*sirr*) prostrates itself to its Lord by means of whom it has achieved its level.
>
> All roots are unseen (*ghayb*). Do you not see how they become manifest in trees? The roots of trees are unseen, for the act of bringing to be (*takwīn*) is unseen. No one witnesses the embryo coming to be in the womb of its mother, so it is unseen. Some animals come to be inside an egg; when the animal is perfected, the egg breaks. The root of the existence of the things is the Real, and He is unseen by them.
>
> Kings are saluted because subjects stand below them. The king possesses highness and tremendousness. Hence, when a person below him enters in upon him, he prostrates himself before him, as if to say, "My station in relation to you is the station of the low in relation to the high." People consider a king in respect of his rank and level, not in respect of his [human] configuration, since they are equal to him in that configuration.
>
> The angels prostrate themselves to the level of knowledge. Their prostration is their words, "We have no knowledge" (2:32), so they are ignorant.[11]
>
> Shadows prostrate themselves because of witnessing those who are outside of themselves, the objects [which throw the shadows].[12] The shadow of the object becomes hidden from the light by the root from which it arose, lest the light annihilate it. Hence the shadow has no subsistence in existence except through the existence of the root. Hence the cosmos has no subsistence except through God. . . .
>
> When the heart prostrates itself, it never rises up, since its prostration is to the divine names—not to the Essence—for the names have made it a "heart" (*qalb*); the names make it fluctuate from state to state in this world and the next. That is why it is called a "heart."[13] When the Real discloses Himself to the heart as the Cause of Fluctuation (*muqallib*), it sees itself in the grasp of Him who makes it fluctuate. And He is the divine names, from which no created thing is separate. The names rule over the creatures. The heart of him who witnesses them prostrates itself, but the heart of him who does not witness them does not prostrate itself; he is the one who makes claims (*muddaʿī*) by saying "I." On the Day of Resurrection the reckoning and the questioning will be directed toward the person who has such an attribute, as also the punishment, if he is punished. He whose heart has prostrated itself has no claims (*daʿwā*), so he will have no reckoning, questioning, or punishment.
>
> Hence there is no state more noble than

the state of prostration, since it is the state of attainment to the knowledge of the roots. And there is no attribute more noble than knowledge, since it yields felicity in the two worlds and ease in the two stations. (II 101.29)

Limits to Knowledge

All knowledge is knowledge of God, while God in Himself, in His very Essence, cannot be known. Nothing can be known of God except what He discloses of Himself. He discloses His names and the entities—the creatures—which are precisely the properties and effects of His names and attributes. But He never discloses Himself as Essence. "None knows God but God."

The objects of God's knowledge are infinite, though only a finite number exist at any given time and only a finite number can be known by a finite thing. God Himself is infinite in the direction of the Essence, which is to say that He also cannot be known. For man, the seeker of knowledge, the acquisition of knowledge is endless, since the objects of knowledge are endless. This is the secret of man's felicity. Knowledge, the greatest good, is also the greatest joy and the greatest pleasure. The never-ending trajectory of man's life in the next world has to be explained in terms of his constant growth in knowledge. For the felicitous, this knowledge is totally congruent and harmonious with their own souls, which have been shaped in this world through faith and practice, and hence every increase in knowledge is an increase in felicity. For the wretched, knowledge of things as they actually are is a searing torture, since it contradicts their beliefs and practices in this world. Every new knowledge—every new self-disclosure, recognized now for what it is—is a new misery. It is only the precedence of God's mercy over His wrath which eventually alleviates the pain of knowing.

The infinity of knowledge is one of Ibn al-ʿArabī's frequent themes. In the following he explains one of the terms of the Sufi vocabulary, "quenching" (*rī*), the third in a hierarchy of terms which begins with "tasting" (*dhawq*) and "drinking" (*shurb*). The Sufis had often discussed whether the gnostic's thirst is ever quenched. Ibn al-ʿArabī takes a firm negative stand:

God commanded His Prophet to say, "My Lord, increase me in knowledge" (20:114). The thirst of him who seeks increase is never quenched. God did not command him to seek for a determined time or within limited bounds. On the contrary, the command was absolute. Hence he seeks increase and bestowal in this world and the next.

Concerning the situation at the Day of Resurrection, the Prophet said, "I will praise Him," that is, when he intercedes with Him, "with words of praise which God will teach me and which I do not know now."[14]

God never ceases creating within us ad infinitum, so the knowledges extend ad infinitum. By "knowledge" the Tribe means only that which is connected to God through unveiling (*kashf*) or denotation (*dalāla*). "The words of God are never exhausted;"[15] these "words" are the entities of His existent things. Hence the thirst of the seeker of knowledge never ceases. He never experiences "quenching," because his preparedness (*istiʿdād*) seeks to gain a knowledge. Once this knowledge has been gained, it gives to him the preparedness for a new knowledge, whether engendered or divine. What he gains lets him know that there is something demanded by the new preparedness—which has been occasioned by the knowledge acquired through the first preparedness—, so he becomes thirsty to gain this [new] knowledge. Hence the seeker of knowledge is like him who drinks the water of the sea. The more he drinks, the thirstier he becomes. Bringing to be (*al-takwīn*) is never cut off, so objects of knowledge are never cut off, so knowledges are never cut off. How can there be quenching? No one believes in quenching except him who is ignorant of what is created within himself constantly and continuously. And he who has no knowledge of himself has no knowledge of his Lord.[16]

One of the gnostics said, "The soul is an ocean without shore," alluding to infinity. But everything which enters into existence or is qualified by existence is finite. That which does not enter into existence is infinite, and that is only the possible things (*al-mumkināt*). Hence only the temporally originated thing (*muḥdath*) can be known, since first the object of knowledge was not, then it was, then there was another. If the object of knowledge were to be qualified by existence, it would be finite and one could be satisfied with it. . . .

He who has no knowledge imagines that he knows God, but that is not correct, since a thing cannot be known except through positive attributes of its own self, but our knowledge of this is impossible, so our knowledge of God is impossible. So Glory be to Him who is known only by the fact that He is not known! The knower of God does not transgress his own level. He knows that he knows that he is one of those who do not know. (II 552.12)

The potential infinity of the objects of human knowledge goes back to the fact that the creatures have already been "taught" this knowledge, for it is latent in the cosmos through God's nearness or self-disclosure to all things. Since we already know everything, coming to know is in fact a remembrance or recollection (*tadhakkur*). In the process of explaining this, Ibn al-ʿArabī refers to the "taking (of Adam's seed) at the Covenant" (*akhdh al-mīthāq*), when the children of Adam bore witness to God's Lordship over them before their entrance into the sensory world. The Koran says, "When thy Lord took from the children of Adam, from their loins, their seed, and made them testify touching themselves: 'Am I not your Lord?' They said, 'Yes, we testify'" (7:172).

This waystation includes the fact that God deposited within man knowledge of all things, then prevented him from perceiving what He had deposited within him. Man is not alone in this. On the contrary, the whole cosmos is the same. This is one of the divine mysteries which reason denies and considers totally impossible. The nearness of this mystery to those ignorant of it is like God's nearness to His servant, as mentioned in His words, "We are nearer to him than you, but you do not see" (56:85) and His words, "We are nearer to him than the jugular vein" (50:16). In spite of this nearness, the person does not perceive and does not know, except inasmuch as he follows the authority [of the Koran]. Were it not for God's report, no rational faculty would point to this fact.

In the same way, all the infinite objects of knowledge that God knows are within man and within the cosmos through this type of nearness. No one knows what is within himself until it is unveiled to him instant by instant. It cannot be unveiled all at once, since that would require restriction (*ḥaṣr*), and we have said that it is infinite. Hence man only knows one thing after another, ad infinitum.

This is one of the most marvelous of divine mysteries: that the infinite should enter into the existence of the servant, just as infinite objects of knowledge enter into the Real's knowledge, while His knowledge is identical with His Essence. The Real's knowing the infinite is different from His depositing it in the servant's heart, since the Real knows what is within Himself and what is within the soul of His servant through designation (*taʿyīn*) and differentiation (*tafṣīl*), while the servant knows it only in an undifferentiated mode (*ijmāl*). But there is no undifferentiation in the Real's knowledge of the things, though He possesses knowledge of undifferentiation in respect to the fact that it is known to the servant in himself and in others. In short, everything known by man and by every existent thing, without cease, is in reality a recollection and a renewal (*tajdīd*) of what he had forgotten.

This waystation demands that the Real may sometimes place the servant within a station where his knowledge takes the infinite as its object. This is not impossible in our view; what is impossible is that the infinite should enter into existence, not that it be known.

Then God made the servants forget this, just as He made them forget the fact that they bore witness against themselves at the taking of the covenant, even though it happened and we have come to know about it through the divine report. So man's knowledge is always recollection. Some of us, when reminded, remember that we once knew that knowledge. Such was Dhu'l-Nūn al-Miṣrī.[17] Others of us do not remember that, though we have faith that we witnessed it. (II 686.4)

Since knowledge of the Essence as Essence is impossible, in respect to the Essence we must declare God's incomparability, even if we declare His similarity in respect to His self-disclosure.

Do not let manyness veil you from the *tawḥīd* of Allah! I have explained to you the object of your *tawḥīd*, without addressing myself to the Essence in Itself, since reflection upon it is forbidden according to the Law. The Messenger of God said, "Reflect not upon God's Essence," and God says, "God warns you about His Self" (3:28), that is, that you must not reflect upon It and judge by some matter that It is such and such.

But God did not forbid talking about the Divinity, though It is not grasped by reflection, and the Folk of Allah declare witnessing It to be impossible. However, the Divinity has loci of manifestation within which It becomes manifest, and the vision of the servants becomes connected to these loci, while the religions have mentioned this sort of thing.

We have nothing of knowledge other than attributes of declaring incomparability and attributes of acts. He who supposes that he possesses knowledge of a positive attribute of Self has supposed wrongly, for such attributes would limit (*ḥadd*) Him, while His Essence has no limits. This is a door which is locked toward engendered existence and cannot be opened. The Real alone has knowledge of it.

The Messenger of God gave news of the knowledge of the Real which God taught him. He said, "O God, I ask Thee by every name by which Thou hast named Thyself or taught to any one of Thy creatures or kept to Thyself in the knowledge of Thy Unseen."[18] Hence He has names known only to Himself and going back to Him. Through "keeping them to Himself" He has withheld them from the knowledge of His creatures. His names are not proper names (*ʿalam*), nor are they substantives (*jāmid*). They are only His names by way of praise, encomium, and laudation. Hence they are "beautiful" because of what is understood from their meanings. They contrast with proper names, which simply denote the entities named by them, neither in praise nor in blame. . . .

In this waystation one gains knowledge of the curbing and checking experienced by him who says that he has known the Essence of the Real. This person will not have his ignorance uncovered for him until the hereafter. Then he will know that the situation of his knowledge is different from what he had believed it to be and that he does not know either in this world or the next. God says, "There will appear to them from God what they had never reckoned" (39:47), making this a general statement. Hence there will appear to every group which believed something which does not correspond to the actual situation the negation of the belief. The verse does not say how this will be negated, whether by incapacity [to know the reality] or by knowledge of the contrary, but both of these situations will exist in the next world. . . .

If knowledge were in actual fact the knowledge of certainty, then it would not change, but it is only a reckoning and a surmise which has veiled its possessor through the form of knowledge. He says that he knows, and the Real says to him that he surmises and reckons. What does the one station have in common with the other? For not every affair is known, and not every affair is unknown.

The most knowledgeable of the knowers is he who knows that he knows what he knows and that he does not know what he does not know. The Prophet said, "I count not Thy praises before Thee,"[19] since he knew that there is something that cannot be encompassed. Abū Bakr said, "Incapacity to attain comprehension is itself comprehension." In other words, he comprehended that there is something which he is incapable of comprehending. So that is knowledge/not knowledge.

Man will come to know on the Day of Resurrection that his reflection is incapable of comprehending what he had reckoned he had comprehended. He will be chastised by his reflection, through the fire of its being uprooted, since the argument of the Law stands against it, for the Law had explained and clarified that upon which it is proper to reflect. . . .

There is no blessing greater than the blessing of knowledge, even though God's blessings cannot be counted in respect of the causes which bring them about. (II 619.11,27, 620.9)

God has no tongue by which He explicates for us except what the messengers have brought from Him. God's explication (*bayān*) is true explication, not that which reason supposes it explicates through its demonstrations. "Explication" is only that which admits no equivocality, and that occurs only through sound unveiling or plain report-giving. If a person's reason, consideration, and demonstration rule over his Law, he has not counselled his own soul. How great will be his regret in the next world when the covering is lifted and he comes to see in sensory form that which he had interpreted as a meaning! God will deprive him of the joy of knowing it in the next world. Or rather, his regret (*ḥasra*) and pain (*alam*) will be multiplied, since there he will witness the ignorance which had made him turn away from that manifest dimension to the meaning in this world and negate that which was denoted by the manifest dimension.

The regret of ignorance is the greatest of regrets: God is unveiled for him in the place where he had not been praising Him and no joy accrues to him. On the contrary, he is exactly like someone who knows that he is about to be overcome by an affliction. He suffers terrible pain from this knowledge, for not every knowledge brings about joy. (IV 313.22)

The Infinity of Knowledge

The Essence of God, as Essence, can never be known. What can be known is "everything other than God," that is, everything other than the Essence as such: the self-disclosure of the Essence through the divine names and the cosmos. The "cosmos" includes all the possible things, whether or not they exist at any given moment, and these are infinite. There are as many possible objects of knowledge as there are possible things, so human knowledge is potentially infinite. But just as all possible things cannot exist at once, so also all objects of knowledge cannot be known at once. There always remains an infinity of objects to be known. The greatest and most knowledgeable of all human beings was told to pray, "My Lord, increase me in knowledge!", and this increase continues forever, in this world and the next. There is nothing static about paradise, since it is the continuous self-disclosure of the divine Reality in forms of mercy, knowledge, and bliss.

God possesses relationships, faces, and realities without limit. Though they all go back to a single Entity, yet the relationships are not qualified by existence, so they are not touched by finitude. . . . The relationships are infinite, so the creation of the possible things is infinite. Hence creation is constant in this world and the next, and knowledge undergoes temporal origination constantly in this world and the next. That is why He commanded [His servants] to seek increase in knowledge. Do you think He is commanding them to seek increase in the knowledge of the engendered things? No, by God, He commanded them only to seek knowledge of God by considering the engendered things which are temporally created. Each engendered thing gives them knowledge of the divine relationship from which it became manifest. That is why the Prophet alerted hearts through his words in his supplication, "O God, I ask Thee by every name by which Thou hast named Thyself or taught to any one of Thy creatures or kept to Thyself in the knowledge of Thy Unseen." The names are divine relationships, and the Unseen is infinite. Hence there must be constant creation, and the knowledge of the created knower must be finite in every state and time and receptive toward a knowledge which he does not have, a temporally originated knowledge whose object is God or a created thing which provides evidence of God. (II 671.5)

God cannot be measured in differentiated mode (*tafṣīl*), since increase in knowledge of God will never be cut off in this world or the next. Here the actual situation is infinite. (III 317.31)

The human soul gains security (*amān*) through its being supported by manyness (*kathra*). "Allah" brings together all the names of good. When you verify the knowledge of the divine names, you will find that the names of taking to task (*akhdh*) are few, while the names of mercy embraced by the name Allah are many. That is why God commanded you to flee (*farār*) to Allah (Koran 51:50). So know this!

There is no divine name that does not wish to attach you to itself and delimit you, so that through you its authority may become manifest. At the same time, you know that felicity lies in increase. But you will not have increase without passing to the property of another name. Thereby you may gain a knowledge which you did not have, though that which you possess will not leave you. This establishes "flight." But you are warned that the name which is with you must not continue to determine your property. So you flee to the place of increase. Thus "flight" is a property that accompanies the servant in this world and the next. (II 156.17)

Certain Sufis extolled the benefits of "renunciation" or "asceticism" (*zuhd*). Ibn al-ʿArabī considers renunciation useful perhaps at the early stages of the path, but hardly a mark of perfection, since to renounce this world one has to renounce the secondary causes (*asbāb*), which are our only means of knowing God. In fact, the whole cosmos is constantly singing God's praises by the very fact of its existence, and thus it serves as the clearest possible denotation of its Maker. The claim to "have renounced everything other than God" may serve a rhetorical purpose and alert some people to the direction in which efforts should be directed, but such renunciation is impossible and undesirable in any case, since to renounce the cosmos is to renounce the possibility of increasing one's knowledge of God.

God never ceases gazing upon the entities of the possible things in the state of their nonexistence. The divine munificence never ceases showing kindness toward them by bringing them into existence in accordance with His precedent knowledge, such that some are brought into existence before others. Since the entity of the Universal Substance (*al-jawhar al-kull*)[20] cannot subsist without certain possible things existing within it—things which cannot subsist in themselves—the divine preservation preserves their subsistence, though in their own essences they do not accept existence except in the time of their existence. So the divine munificence never ceases bringing into existence those possible things which are necessary for the subsistence of the Universal Substance, within which God opened up the forms of the cosmos, for God never ceases creating constantly and preserving creation constantly.

In the same way, had God not caused the mystery of life to permeate the existent things, they would not possess rational speech (*nuṭq*). And were it not for the fact that they are permeated by knowledge, they would not speak in praise of God, who brought them into existence. Hence God says, "There is nothing that does not glorify Him in praise [but you do not understand their glorification]" (Koran 17:44). . . .

"Renunciation" of things can occur only through the ignorance and lack of knowledge of the one who renounces and through the veil which covers his eyes, that is, the lack of unveiling and witnessing. . . . If he only knew or witnessed the fact that the whole cosmos speaks by glorifying and lauding its Creator and that it witnesses Him, how could he renounce it, as long as it has this attribute?

Man's entity, essence, and attributes are part of the cosmos. God has let him witness and shown him His signs upon the horizons, that is, everything outside of himself, and in himself,[21] that is, everything which he himself possesses. Even if he were able to come out (*khurūj*) of the other, how could he come out of himself?

He who comes out of the cosmos and himself has come out of God, and he who comes out of God has come out of possibility and joined himself with impossibility. But he is a possible thing in his very reality, so he cannot join the impossible. Hence his claim to have come out of everything other than God is sheer ignorance. . . .

His ignorance makes him imagine that the cosmos is far removed from God and that God is far removed from the cosmos. Hence he seeks to "flee" (*farār*) to God. But this is an imaginary flight, and its cause is the lack of tasting (*dhawq*) of the things and the fact that he heard in recitation, "So flee to God!" (51:50). This verse is correct, except that the one who is fleeing did not pay attention to what is mentioned in the following verse, that is, His words, "And set not up with God another god" (51:51).

Had he known this completing verse, he would have known that God's words, "So flee to God" refer to the flight from ignorance to knowledge. The situation is one and unitary. He imagined some ontological thing, attributing divinity to it and taking it as a god, but this was a nonexistent impossible thing, neither possible nor necessary. This is what is meant by the flight which God commands. Flight is "to Him" in respect of the attribution of Divinity to Him. . . .

God did not create man a knower of all things. On the contrary, He commanded His Prophet to seek from Him an increase in knowledge, since He said to him, "Say: My Lord, increase me in knowledge!" (20:114). Hence in every state he takes from knowledge that which gives him felicity and perfection. The cosmos and man were created with innate knowledge of God's existence and of the fact that the temporally originated thing is poor toward Him and in need of Him. Since this is the situation, everyone who has this attribute must flee to God in order to witness his own poverty and the pain in the soul which poverty gives to him and in order that God may give him independence inasmuch as he cuts himself off from everything but Him. Perhaps He will take away the pain of his poverty through that which gives joy, which is independence (*ghinā*) through God.

However, this is a goal which cannot be actualized in any respect. Were anyone to gain independence through God, he would be independent of God, and being independent of God is impossible. So being independent through God is impossible. Nevertheless, God gives the seeker something during his seeking through which He makes him independent; the joy which he finds eliminates the pain of that specific poverty, not the pain of the universal poverty which cannot disappear from the possible thing—since poverty is its essential description—whether in the state of nonexistence or in the state of existence. Therefore God places within the soul of the possible thing something through which he finds within himself the joy which eliminates the pain of seeking. Then God occasions another seeking of something else or of the subsistence of that thing he has gained; and so it continues forever, in this world and the next.

Since this is a person's state, he must withdraw and flee from those affairs which divert him from this situation, so that God may unveil his insight and his sight. Then he will witness the situation as it is in itself and he will know how to seek, from whom to seek, who does the seeking, and so on. He will know the meaning of God's words, "Surely God is the Independent, the Praiseworthy" (31:26), that is, praised for His independence. . . .

Once this is established, you will know that the Messenger of God used to go alone to the cave of Ḥirā' to devote himself to God therein and flee from seeing people, since he used to find in himself straitness and constriction in seeing them. Had he gazed upon the face of God within them, he would not have fled from them, nor would he have sought to be alone with himself. He remained like this till God came to him suddenly. Then he returned to the creatures and stayed with them. . . .

Every seeker of his Lord must be alone with himself with his Lord in his inmost consciousness, since God gave man an outward dimension (*ẓāhir*) and an inward dimension (*bāṭin*) only so that he might be alone with God in his inward dimension and witness Him in his outward dimension within the secondary causes, after having gazed upon Him in his inward dimension, so that he may discern Him within the midst of the secondary causes. Otherwise, he will never recognize Him. He who enters the spiritual retreat (*khalwa*) with God does so only for this reason, since man's inward dimension is the cell of his retreat. (III 263.16,35, 265.1)

10. ACQUIRING KNOWLEDGE

Knowledge can be acquired through reflection, unveiling, or scripture. The human subtle reality (*al-laṭīfat al-insāniyya*), also called the "soul" (*nafs*), knows in a variety of modes. When it knows through reflection, the mode of its knowing is called "reason" (*ʿaql*). When it knows directly from God, the mode of knowing is called the "heart" (*qalb*), which is contrasted with reason. Whatever the means whereby the soul acquires knowledge, the knowing subject is one. There are not two different entities known as "reason" and "heart," though there is a real difference between the modalities of knowing. As we have already seen, reason knows through delimitation and binding, while the heart knows through letting go of all restrictions. *ʿAql*, as shown by its root meaning, is that which limits the free and ties down the unconstricted. *Qalb* means fluctuation, for the heart undergoes constant change and transmutation in keeping with the never-repeating self-disclosures of God.

The Rational Faculty

"Reason" or the "rational faculty" is one of the fundamental powers of the human soul. From one point of view it defines the human state, setting man apart from all other animals. Spiritual beings may also possess the faculty known as *ʿaql*, but then it might be more accurate to say that the spiritual being is itself an *ʿaql*. In such contexts, the word can be translated better as "intellect." Thus, for example, the First Intellect is the luminous pole of creation, sometimes identified with the Breath of the All-merciful. In discussing the spiritual world, Ibn al-ʿArabī will often speak of angelic beings, disengaged from loci of manifestation, known as "intellects, souls, and spirits."[1] As a human faculty *ʿaql* almost always implies restriction and confinement, though on occasion the Shaykh will employ the term in a sense which suggests that it has transcended its limitations and become identical with the heart, in which case it might be better to speak of man's "intellect." For the adjective *ʿaqlī*, the term "rational" will be employed, though in some contexts "intelligible" will render it better. As for the active participle *ʿāqil*, this often refers to the "rational thinker" or "possessor of reason," in which case it has a rather negative connotation, but it may simply mean the person who uses his reason correctly, in which case "intelligent person" translates it more exactly.

By its nature reason perceives (*idrāk*), whether through an inherent, intuitive knowledge that needs nothing from outside, or through various instruments, such as the five senses and "reflective consideration" (*naẓar fikrī*). "Reflection" (*fikr*) is the power of thought or cogitation, the ability of the soul to put together the data gathered by sense perception or acquired from imagination in order to reach rational conclusions. It belongs only to human beings. "Consideration" (*naẓar*) refers to the specific activity of reason when it employs reflection. It is the investigation of phenomena as well as the thought processes whereby reason reaches conclusions. In this meaning *naẓar* is practically synonymous with *fikr*. However, the latter term designates a specific faculty possessed by reason, while the term *naẓar* is used in a wide variety of other meanings in keeping with its literal sense of "to look." Thus it is employed to refer to the gaze of the physical eye, reason, or the heart, that is, to the sensory, the rational, and the supra-rational levels. The terms "reflective consideration," "reflection," and "consideration" all refer especially to the endeavors of the rational thinkers, such as the philosophers and the proponents of Kalām. Terms such as "possessors of consideration" (*ahl al-naẓar*) and "those who consider" (*al-nuẓẓār*) are used synonymously with "people of reflection" (*ahl al-fikr, aṣḥāb al-afkār*), the "people of rational faculties" (*ahl al-ʿuqūl*), and "the rational thinkers" (*al-ʿuqalāʾ*).

Reason, reflection, and consideration can be treated as distinct realities, each with a positive role to play. But when misused, they share certain common denominators which allow Ibn al-ʿArabī to lump their possessors into a single category.

> There are six things which perceive: hearing, sight, smell, touch, taste, and reason. Each of them—except reason—perceives things incontrovertibly (*ḍarūrī*). They are never mistaken in the things which normally become related to them. A group of the rational thinkers have erred on this point by attributing error to sensation. That is not the case; the error belongs only to that which passes judgment.
>
> Reason perceives its objects in two modes. One kind of perception is incontrovertible, as in the case of the other things which perceive. Another kind is not incontrovertible; in order to gain knowledge, it needs six instuments, including the five senses which we just mentioned and the reflective faculty (*al-quwwat al-mufakkira*). There is no object of knowledge which can be known by a created thing and cannot be perceived by one of these modes of perception. (I 213.30)

Reason has a second, closely related meaning which plays an important role in Islamic moral and spiritual teachings. It is the opposite of "passion" (*shahwa*), that is, any desire which has an object not sanctioned by the Law. Thus the Koran says, "Then there succeeded after them a later generation who have neglected prayer and followed passions" (19:59). In itself passion is positive, since it is one of the constituent faculties of the animate soul, through which all animals, including human beings, remain alive. It manifests Nature (*ṭabīʿa*), the loving and nurturing mother through whom all things are sustained.

> There are two passions. The first is accidental (*ʿaraḍī*). It is the passion which one must not follow, since it is false. Though it may have its benefits on some days, the possessor of reason should not follow it. . . . The second passion is inherent (*dhātī*), and it is incumbent upon him to follow it. For within it lies the well-being (*ṣalāḥ*) of his constitution (*mizāj*), since it is agreeable to his nature. In the well-being of his constitution lies the well-being of his religion, and in the well-being of his religion lies his felicity. However, he must follow this passion according to the Divine Scale (*al-mīzān al-ilāhī*) established by the Lawgiver, and that is the ruling of the established revealed Law. (II 191.6)

As Ibn al-ʿArabī points out, the very existence of the rational faculty, which is able to discern between right and wrong and judge accordingly, has made passion a negative human condition.

> God created the faculty named "reason," placing it within the rational soul, to stand opposite natural passion when passion exercises control over the soul by diverting it from the occupation proper to it as specified by the Lawgiver. (II 319.13)
>
> God placed reason [within the soul] to stand opposite passion. Were it not for

reason, natural passion would be praiseworthy. (II 190.8)

Shahwa is a synonym or near synonym of the term *hawā*, "caprice," which is the tendency in man which turns him away from divine guidance.[2]

God said to His prophet David, "Give rulings among men by the Real, and follow not caprice, [lest it mislead you from the path of God]" (38:26). He also said "Have you seen him who has taken his caprice to be his god?" (25:43). Caprice is nothing save the desire of the servant when it opposes (*mukhālafa*) the Scale of the Revealed Law (*al-mīzān al-mashrū*ʿ), which God has established for him in this world. (III 305.16)

Just as passion is made negative by the existence of reason, so also caprice becomes a negative force only because of the existence of the Law.

There can only be caprice when there is the ruling of the Shariʿa. This is indicated by God's words to David, "Give rulings among men by the Real, and follow not caprice" (38:26). In other words: Follow not what you love, but follow what I love, which is the ruling which I have delineated for you. Then God said, "Lest it mislead you from the path of God." In other words: Lest caprice bewilder you, ruin you, and make you blind toward the path which I have laid down as Law for you and upon which I have asked you to walk. . . . . So here "caprice" is everything man loves. The Real commands man to abandon his loves if they correspond to something other than the path of the revealed Law. (II 336.5)

In a vision I saw caprice and passion, whispering together. God has given to this caprice a penetrating power through which it dominates over most rational faculties unless they are protected by God. Caprice halted in that place and said, "I am the god worshiped by every existent thing." It turned away from reason and everything that came to it through tradition (*naql*). The satans followed it, while passion was in front of it. Finally it reached the center of the Fire, and a carpet of tar was laid down for it. But it relied upon something which it imagined would deliver it from God's chastisement. Then God came between it and that upon which it relied and depended. Then it and everyone who followed it was destroyed. (II 583.16)

There is nothing stronger than caprice except man, since he is able to root out his caprice through his rational faculty, which God has brought into existence within him. So he manifests his rational faculty through its ruling power over his caprice. (II 451.1)

Inasmuch as reason rules over passion and caprice, it leads man on the path of his felicity, which is the path of the Law. In this respect it plays a positive role.

A king said to one of his sitting companions who used to offer sound opinions and considerations when he sought counsel from him, "Whom do you think I should place in charge of the affairs of the people?"

He replied, "Place in charge of them a man of reason, for the man of reason will go to great lengths to acquit himself. If he has the knowledge, he will give rulings according to what he knows. If he does not have the knowledge of the ruling for a given occurrence, then his rational faculty will make him ask the person who knows the divine ruling revealed in the Law for that situation. Once he comes to know it, he will rule accordingly. This is the benefit of reason.

"Many of those who desire religion and exoteric knowledge (*al-ʿilm al-rasmī*) are governed by their passion. But the man of reason is not like that, since the rational faculty refuses everything except qualities of excellence (*faḍā'il*). For reason delimits its possessor, not allowing him to enter into that which is improper. That is why it is called 'reason,' from 'fetter'." (III 333.20)

According to Ibn al-ʿArabī, all created things know God through an inborn knowledge, with the exception of man and the jinn. They alone were given reflection in order to gain knowledge of God.

The angels, like inanimate things (*jamādāt*), have an innate (*mafṭūr*) knowledge of God; they have no rational faculties and no passion. Animals are born with both knowledge of God and passion. Mankind and the jinn have an innate passion and cognitions (*maʿārif*) in respect of their outward forms, but not in respect of their spirits.[3] God placed the rational faculty within them so that they can bring passion into line with the Scale of the Law; thereby He prevented them from having to contend with passion outside the locus designated by the Law. God did not bring the rational faculty into existence for them to acquire sciences. That which He gave them with which to acquire sciences was the reflective faculty. That is why their spirits were not given innate cognitions as were the spirits of the angels and everything other than mankind and the jinn. (III 99.12)

Reflection

Reflection, as we have seen, is one of the six instruments by which the rational faculty gains knowledge, the other five being the senses. If reflection is employed properly, it will aid in the acquisition of right knowledge of God and thereby lead to felicity. If it is employed improperly, it can be one of man's greatest obstacles.

Reflection is a faculty found only in human beings. It derives from their exclusive possession of the divine "form," the fact enunciated in the hadith, "God created Adam upon His own form."[4] In reading the following passage, one needs to remember that "soul" (*nafs*) is that dimension of man and other animals which stands between the disengaged spirit and the corporeal body; it is the domain of imagination, which is neither the pure light of spirit nor the darkness known as clay.

In the view of the people of unveiling, the souls of men and jinn and the souls of the animals have two faculties, one cognitive (*ʿilmī*) and one practical (*ʿamalī*). These are manifest in all those animals like bees, spiders, and birds which make nests, and in other animals. The souls of men and jinn, in contrast to other living things, possess a third faculty—the reflective faculty—which is not possessed by animals nor by the Universal Soul (*al-nafs al-kulliyya*).[5] The human being acquires certain sciences by way of reflection, while it shares with the rest of the cosmos in taking sciences through the divine effusion (*al-fayḍ al-ilāhī*) and with some of them—like the animals—in having innate knowledge (*bi'l-fiṭra*), such as an infant's accepting its mother's breast and drinking milk. Nothing other than man acquires sciences which stay with it by way of reflection.

In man reflection stands in the station of the divine reality referred to in the text, "He governs (*tadbīr*) the affair, He differentiates (*tafṣīl*) the signs" (13:2), as also in His words in the sound hadith, "I never waver (*taraddud*) in anything I do [the way I waver in taking the soul of a man of faith who hates death, while I hate to do ill to him]."[6] This reality is not possessed by the First Intellect, nor by the Universal Soul. It pertains to that which is specific to man because of the Form upon which no other thing was created. (I 260.18)

Like other tools, reflection can be used for good and evil ends. But human beings possess no higher tool, since all other tools are controlled through it. Ibn al-ʿArabī calls it an "affliction" (*balā'*), that is, a test and a trial which may very well lead to man's ruin.

God afflicted man with an affliction with which no other of His creatures was afflicted. Through it He takes him to felicity or wretchedness, depending upon how He allows him to make use of it. This affliction with which God afflicted him is that He created within him a faculty named "reflection." He made this faculty the assistant of another faculty called "reason." Moreover, He compelled reason, in spite of its being reflection's chief, to take from reflection what it gives. God gave reflection no place to roam except the faculty of imagination. God made the faculty of imagination the locus which brings together everything given by the sensory faculties. He gave to it another faculty called the "form-giver" (*al-muṣawwira*). As a result, nothing is actualized within the faculty of imagination unless it is given by the senses or the form-giving faculty. The material with which the form-giver works is the impressions of the senses (*maḥsūsāt*). Hence it composes forms which have no existence in entity, though all the parts exist in the sensory realm.

Reason is a plain creature (*khalq sādhij*). It possesses nothing of the considerative sciences. It is said to reflection: "Discern (*tamyīz*) between the real and the unreal found in the faculty of imagination." Reflection considers in accordance with what occurs to it. It may fall upon an obfuscation (*shubha*) or upon a proof (*dalīl*) without knowing which it is. However, it supposes that it knows obfuscations from proofs and that it has fallen upon knowledge. It does not consider the incapacity of the material by which it supports itself to acquire the sciences. Then the rational faculty accepts the sciences from reflection and judges accordingly. Hence the rational faculty has more ignorance than knowledge of what is not near to it.

Then God prescribed for the rational faculty that it should come to know Him, in order that it might turn to Him for knowledge of Him, not to other than Him. But reason understood the contrary of what the Real meant by His words, "Have they not reflected?" (7:184); "[Thus do We differentiate the signs] for a people who reflect" (10:24). Hence reason supports itself by reflection and makes it a leader which it follows. It remains heedless of what the Real meant by "reflection." For He addressed reason in order that it might reflect and come to understand that the only way to know God is for God to give it knowledge. (I 125.33)

The fundamental function of reflection is to lead man to the understanding that he cannot reach knowledge of God through his own resources. Through reflection, man sees that reason delimits and defines everything that it knows, while the Divine Essence is beyond delimitation and definition. Hence the only knowledge about God which reflection can hand over to reason is the knowledge of what God is not. Through reflection reason can grasp God's incomparability. But to gain any positive and affirmative knowledge of God, any statement about what God is rather than what He is not, it must have recourse to revelation.

Know that except for men and jinn, everything other than God has knowledge (*maʿrifa*) of God, receives revelation (*waḥy*) from God, and knows who it is that discloses Himself to them. That is innate to all of them, and all of them are felicitous. That is why God said, "Have you not seen how before God prostrate themselves all who are in the heavens and all who are in the earth?"; so here He makes an all-inclusive statement. Then He differentiates to clarify to mankind what has come down upon them. He says, "The sun and the moon, the stars and the mountains, the trees and the beasts, and many of mankind" (22:18). "Many of mankind" is explained by His words, "Those who have faith and do deeds of righteousness, and few they are not" (38:24), that is, they are many.[7] This is the same as His words [in the previous verse], "Many of mankind." He continues by saying, "And many merit the chastisement" (22:18).

The reason for this is that, in respect of the reflective faculty placed within his rational soul which exists between light and Nature, God charged man to acquire knowledge (*maʿrifa*) of God through reflection, taking this knowledge freely from God. God also gave man the rational faculty, as He gave it to other existent things. To the rational faculty He gave the attribute of acceptance (*qabūl*), and He enamored it of the reflective faculty in order for it to derive knowledges from it. . . .

When God gave to human beings the reflective faculty, He set up for them marks (*ʿalāʾim*) and denotations (*dalāʾil*) which denote their temporal origination (*ḥudūth*), since they subsist through their own entities. He also set up for them marks and denotations which denote eternity (*qidam*), which consists of the negation of beginning from God's existence. These latter denotations are identical with those which He set up to denote temporal origination. Their negation (*salb*) from the Eternal Essence named God is itself the denotation, nothing else.

Hence denotations have two faces, though they are one in entity. Their affirmation (*thubūt*) denotes the temporal origination of the cosmos, while their negation denotes Him who brought the cosmos into existence. When man considers with this consideration, he says, "I have come to know (*maʿrifa*) God through the denotations which He has set up for us to know ourselves and Him. They are the 'signs' (*āyāt*) set up upon the horizons and within ourselves that it may become clear to us that He is the Real, and it has become clear to us." This is what we call "self-disclosure" (*tajallī*), for self-disclosure is put there in order to be seen. It is referred to in God's words, "We shall show them Our signs upon the horizons and in themselves, until it is clear to them that He is the Real" (41:53). In other words, the self-disclosure which they come to see is a mark. It is a mark of Himself, so it becomes clear to them that He is the Real who is sought. Hence God completed this verse by saying, "Is not your Lord sufficient?", that is, sufficient as a denotation of Himself? The clearest of denotations is a thing's denoting itself by its own manifestation.

People's rational faculties gained this knowledge of declaring God's incomparability by means of that which they attributed to the essences of the cosmos. It was a single denotation which went back and forth between negating knowledge of God and affirming knowledge of the cosmos. (II 305.12)

Ibn al-ʿArabī makes clear in many passages, including the continuation of the above, that this knowledge of God's incomparability can be attained by reflection without revelation. But there is a good deal of knowledge about God and the next world that can only come through a revealed Law; and again, there is no way to actualize the felicity of the next world without following the Law.

The creatures are divided into "wretched" and "felicitous." Because Light pervades all existent things, the dense and the subtle, the dark and the not-dark, all existent things confess to the existence of their Maker, without any doubt or uncertainty. They confess that the Absolute Unseen (*al-ghayb al-muṭlaq*) belongs to Him. His Essence cannot be known through affirmation; rather, He is incomparable with anything appropriate for temporally originated things. . . .

Then the divine reports (*al-akhbār al-ilāhiyya*) come on the tongues of the angels,[8] who pass them on to the messengers, who pass them on to us. When a person has faith in these reports, leaving his reflection behind him, accepting them through the attribute of acceptance which pertains to his rational faculty, and attesting to the truthfulness of the report-giver in what he has brought, while acting as required, he is called "felicitous." . . . He will be recompensed with the promised good in the Abode of Constancy and permanent bliss. . . .

But if a person does not have faith in these reports, making his own corrupt reflection his leader and following it, and rejecting the prophetic reports either by denying the root or by a corrupt interpretation . . . , he is called "wretched." He is so because of the darkness within him, just as the felicitous person has faith because of the light within him. He will be recompensed, with the evil which was promised for denial, in the Abode of Ruin and lack of constancy through the existence of permanent chastisement. (II 648.7)

The Folk of Allah understand what God meant when He commanded human beings to seek knowledge. Hence they abandon reflection and return directly to God.

The Folk of Allah display their poverty toward God through their faith in Him, in order to reach knowledge of Him, which He has prescribed in the Law. They know that what God desires for them is their return (*rujūʿ*) to Him in that and in every state. One of them says, "Glory be to Him who has set down no path to knowledge of Him except incapacity to know Him!" Another says, "Incapacity to attain comprehension is itself comprehension." The Prophet said, "I count not Thy praises before Thee." God says, "They encompass Him not in knowledge" (20:110). Hence they return to God in knowledge of Him. They leave reflection in its own level and give it its full due (*ḥaqq*): They do not make it pass on to that about which it is improper to reflect. And reflection upon the Essence of God has been prohibited, while God has said, "God warns you about His Self" (3:28). So God gives to them whatever knowledge of Himself which He gives to them, and He allows them to witness those of His creatures and loci of manifestation which He allows them to witness. They come to know that what is impossible for reason by way of reflection is not impossible as a divine relationship. (I 126.13)

Consideration

The Arabic term *naẓar*, which is being translated here as "consideration," means to look, to gaze, to inspect, to investigate. For the proponents of Kalām, it denotes the process of investigation and reasoning whereby conclusions are drawn. Ibn al-ʿArabī uses the term technically to denote the speculative activities of rational thinkers in general, theologians and philosophers in particular. If reflection denotes the faculty of reason whereby thought takes place, consideration denotes the specific kind of sophisticated rational thinking indulged in by the learned.

Like reflection, *naẓar* is a mental activity commanded by the Koran, and in this sense Ibn al-ʿArabī sees it as totally positive. But he holds that the learned classes have forgotten the original goal of consideration, just as they have forgotten the proper use of reflection.

Reflection is a state which offers no preservation from error. Hence it is a station of danger (*khaṭar*). He who possesses it does not know if he is mistaken or correct, since reflection accepts either. If the possessor of reflection wants his reflection to be mostly correct in knowledge of God, he should study each verse which has come down in the Koran in which reflection (*tafakkur*) and taking heed (*iʿtibār*) are mentioned. . . . For in the Koran God has mentioned nothing worthy of reflection and declared nothing productive of heed or connected with reflection without there being correctness along with it. . . . But if you go beyond the verses of reflection to the verses of reason, the verses of hearing, the verses of knowing, or the verses of faith and employ reflection therein, you will never be correct. . . .

In the same way, the verses of consideration can be classified along with reflection, like His words, "What, do they not consider how the camel was created?" (88:17), or like His words, "Have they not considered the dominion of the heaven and the earth?" (7:185). (II 230.19)

Consideration has an important role to play, but it must be limited to that role. Those who depend upon consideration are misled when they deal with things which should be left, for example, to faith. The possessor of consideration (*ṣāḥib al-naẓar*) is not wrong to consider. He is wrong to depend upon consideration in all domains.

The possessor of consideration is delimited by the ruling power of his reflection, but reflection can only roam in its own specific playing field (*maydān*), which is one of many fields. Each faculty in man has a playing field in which it roams and beyond which it should not step. If it goes beyond its field, it falls into error and makes mistakes and is described as having deviated from its straight way. For example, visual unveiling may discover things where rational arguments stumble, because the arguments have left their proper domain. The rational faculties which are described as misguided have been led astray only by their own reflective processes, and their reflective processes have gone astray by moving about in that which is not their own abode. (II 281.15)

The greatest error of the possessors of consideration is to interpret the revealed

Law and to explain away those parts of it which do not accord with their own understandings of God and the cosmos. The only way to escape the errors to which reason, consideration, and reflection are prone is to adhere firmly to the Scale of the Law, which puts each thing back in its proper place. In this way the seeker opens himself up to the possibility of gaining knowledge and certainty directly from God, as man was meant to do. This is the way of unveiling, or the witnessing of God's self-disclosure in all things.

> The eye is never mistaken, neither it nor any of the senses. . . . The rational faculty perceives in two modes: through an inherent (*dhātī*) perception in which it is like the senses, never being mistaken; and by a non-inherent perception. The second is what it perceives through its instruments (*āla*), which are reflection and sense perception.
>
> Imagination follows the authority (*taqlīd*) of that which sense perception gives to it. Reflection considers imagination and finds therein individual things (*mufradāt*). Reflection would love to configure a form to be preserved by the rational faculty. Hence it attributes some of the individual things to others. In this attribution it may be mistaken concerning the actual situation, or it may be correct. Reason judges upon this basis, so it also may be mistaken or correct. Hence reason is a follower of authority, and it may make mistakes.
>
> Since the Sufis saw the mistakes of those who employ consideration, they turned to the path in which there is no confusion so that they might take things from the Eye of Certainty (*ʿayn al-yaqīn*) and become qualified by certain knowledge. (II 628.27)

Following Authority

In whatever knowledge it acquires, reason follows authority, so the wisest course is to follow the authority of God. "Following authority" (*taqlīd*) is a major topic of discussion in such schools of Islamic thought as principles of jurisprudence (*uṣūl al-fiqh*). The word is derived from the same root as *qilāda*, "necklace" or "collar." One person follows the authority of another by taking his words and deeds as a collar around his own neck. Following authority is often contrasted with *ijtihād*, individual striving to draw conclusions concerning the rulings of the Law, or mastery of the Law. It may also be contrasted with *taḥqīq*, "verification," which for Ibn al-ʿArabī delineates the station of the great gnostics, those who have verified the truth of their knowledge through unveiling and direct vision. Though Sufis often criticize following authority as the business of the common people, the Shaykh bestows upon it an elevated degree in the hierarchy of human situations, with the proviso, or course, that man follow God's authority, nothing else. In any case, says the Shaykh, following authority is inescapable. The question boils down to what or whom we choose to follow.

> Reason is full of meddling because reflection governs over it, along with all the faculties within man, since there is nothing greater than reason in following authority. Reason imagines it has God-given proofs, but it only has proofs given by reflection. Reflection's proofs let it take reason wherever it wants, while reason is like a blind man. No, it is even blinder in the path of God. The Folk of Allah do not follow the authority of their reflections, since a created thing should not follow the authority of another created thing. Hence they incline toward following God's authority. They come to know God through God, and He is as He says about Himself, not as meddlesome reason judges.
>
> How is it proper for an intelligent man to follow the authority of the reflective faculty, when he divides reflective consideration into correct and corrupt? Necessarily, he has need for a criterion (*fāriq*) with which to separate the correct from the corrupt, but he cannot possibly distinguish between correct and corrupt reflective consideration through reflective con-

sideration itself. Necessarily, he has need for God in that.

As for us, when we want to discern correct reflective consideration from the corrupt so that we may judge by it, we first have recourse to God, asking Him to bestow upon us knowledge of the object without the use of reflection. The Tribe depends upon this and acts in accordance with it. This is the knowledge of the prophets, the friends, and the possessors of knowledge among the Folk of Allah. They never transgress their places with their reflective powers. (II 290.14)

No one can have knowledge unless he knows things through his own essence. Anyone who knows something through something added to his own essence is following the authority of that added thing in what it gives to him. Nothing in existence knows things through its own essence other than the One. The knowledge of things and not-things possessed by everything other than the One is a following of authority. Since it has been established that other than God cannot have knowledge of a thing without following authority, let us follow God's authority, especially in knowledge of Him.

Why do we say that nothing can be known by other than God except through following authority? Because man knows nothing except through one of the faculties given to him by God: the senses and reason. Hence man has to follow the authority of his sense perception in that which it gives, and sense perception may be mistaken, or it may correspond to the situation as it is in itself. Or, man has to follow the authority of his rational faculty in that which it gives him, either the incontrovertible (*ḍarūra*) or consideration. But reason follows the authority of reflection, some of which is correct and some of which is corrupt, so its knowledge of affairs is by chance (*bi'l-ittifāq*). Hence there is nothing but following authority.

Since this is the situation, the intelligent man who wants to know God should follow His authority in the reports He has given about Himself in His scriptures and upon the tongues of His messengers. When a person wants to know the things, but he cannot know them through what his faculties give him, he should strive in acts of obedience (*ṭāʿāt*) until the Real is his hearing, his seeing, and all his faculties.[9] Then he will know all affairs through God and he will know God through God. In any case, there is no escape from following authority. But once you know God through God and all things through God, then you will not be visited in that by ignorance, obfuscations, doubts, or uncertainties. Thus have I alerted you to something which has never before reached your ear!

The rational thinkers from among the people of consideration imagine that they know what consideration, sense perception, and reason have bestowed upon them, but they are following the authority of these things. Every faculty is prone to a certain kind of mistake. Though they may know this fact, they seek to throw themselves into error, for they distinguish between that within which sense perception, reason, and reflection may be mistaken and that within which it is not mistaken. But how can they know? Perhaps that which they have declared to be a mistake is correct. Nothing can eliminate this incurable disease, unless all a person's knowledge is known through God, not through other than Him. God knows through His own Essence, not through anything added to It. Hence you also will come to know through that through which He knows, since you follow the authority of Him who knows, who is not ignorant, and who follows the authority of no one. Anyone who follows the authority of other than God follows the authority of him who is visited by mistakes and who is correct only by chance.

Someone may object: "How do you know this? Perhaps you may be mistaken in these classifications without being aware of it. For in this you follow the authority of that which can be mistaken: reason and reflection."

We reply: You are correct. However, since we see nothing but following authority, we have preferred to follow the authority of him who is named "Messenger" and that which is named "the Speech of God." We followed their authority in knowledge until the Real was our hearing and our sight, so we came to know things through God and gained knowledge of these classifications through God. The fact that we were right to follow this authority was by chance, since, as we have said, whenever reason or any of the faculties accords with something as it is in itself, this is by chance. We do not hold that it is mistaken in every situation. We only say that we do not know how to distinguish its being wrong from its being right. But when the Real is all a person's faculties and he knows things through God, then he knows the difference between the faculties' being right and their being mistaken. This is what we maintain, and no one can deny it, for he finds it in himself.

Since this is so, occupy yourself with following that which God has commanded you: practicing obedience to Him, examining (*murāqaba*) the thoughts that occur to your heart, shame (*ḥayā'*) before God, halting before His bounds, being alone (*infirād*) with Him, and preferring His side over yourself, until the Real is all your faculties, and you are "upon insight"[10] in your affair.

Thus have I counselled you, for we have seen the Real report about Himself that He possesses things which rational proofs and sound reflective powers reject, even though they offer proofs that the report-giver speaks the truth and people must have faith in what he says. So follow the authority of your Lord, since there is no escape from following authority! Do not follow your rational faculty in its interpretation (*ta'wīl*)! (II 298.2)

If on the one hand the Sufis follow the authority of God, on the other hand they pass beyond mere following authority by "verifying" the knowledge they have received through the revealed Law. Thus *taḥqīq* completes and perfects *taqlīd*.

This Tribe works toward acquiring something of what the divine reports have brought from the Real. They start to polish their hearts through invocations, reciting the Koran, freeing the locus [of God's self-disclosure] from taking possible things into consideration, presence (*ḥuḍūr*), and self-examination (*murāqaba*). They also keep their outward dimension pure by halting within the bounds established by the Law, for example, by averting the eyes from those things such as private parts which it is forbidden to look upon and by looking at those things which bring about heedfulness and clear seeing. So also with the hearing, tongue, hand, foot, stomach, private parts, and heart. Outwardly there are only these seven, and the heart is the eighth. Such a person eliminates reflection from himself completely, since it disperses his single-minded concern (*hamm*). He secludes himself at the gate of his Lord, occupying himself with examining his heart, in hopes that God will open the gate for him and he will come to know what he did not know, those things which the messengers and the Folk of Allah know and which rational faculties cannot possibly perceive on their own.

When God opens the gate to the possessor of this heart, he actualizes a divine self-disclosure which gives to him that which accords with its own properties. Then he attributes to God things which he would not have dared attribute to God earlier. He would not have described God that way except to the extent that it was brought by the divine reports. He used to take such things through following authority. Now he takes them through an unveiling which corresponds with and confirms for him what the revealed scriptures and the messengers have mentioned. He used to ascribe those things to God through faith and as a mere narrator, without verifying their meanings or adding to them. Now he ascribes them to Him within himself, with a verified knowledge because of that which has been disclosed to him. (I 271.27)

Unveiling

In many passages Ibn al-ʿArabī explains the difference between two basic kinds of knowledge: That which can be acquired by the rational faculty, and the "gnosis" which can only come through spiritual practice and the divine self-disclosure. In general, he refers to this second kind of knowledge as "unveiling" (*kashf*), "[direct] tasting" (*dhawq*), "opening" (*fatḥ*), "insight" (*baṣīra*), and "witnessing" (*shuhūd, mushāhada*), though he employs other terms as well, and often distinguishes among the various terms.

The way of gaining knowledge is divided between reflection (*fikr*) and bestowal (*wahb*), which is the divine effusion (*fayḍ*). The latter is the way of our companions. . . . Hence it is said that the sciences of the prophets and the friends of God are "beyond the stage of reason" (*warāý ṭawr al-ʿaql*). Reason has no entrance into them through reflection, though it can accept them, especially in the case of him whose reason is "sound" (*salīm*), that is, he who is not overcome by any obfuscation deriving from imagination and reflection, an obfuscation which would corrupt his consideration. (I 261.9)

Two ways lead to knowledge of God. There is no third way. The person who declares God's Unity in some other way follows authority in his declaration.

The first way is the way of unveiling. It is an incontrovertible knowledge which is actualized through unveiling and which man finds in himself. He receives no obfuscations along with it and is not able to repel it. He knows no proof for it by which it is supported except what he finds in himself. One of the Sufis differs on this point, for he says, "He is given the proof and what is proven by the proof in his unveiling, since, when something cannot be known except through proof, its proof must also be unveiled." This was the view of our companion Abū ʿAbdallāh [Muḥammad] ibn al-Kattānī in Fez. I heard that from him. He reported about his own state, and he spoke the truth. However, he was mistaken in holding that the situation must be like that, for others find the knowledge in themselves through tasting without having its proof unveiled. This kind of knowledge may also be actualized through a divine self-disclosure given to its possessors, who are the messengers, the prophets, and some of the friends.

The second way is the way of reflection and reasoning (*istidlāl*) through rational demonstration (*burhān ʿaqlī*). This way is lower than the first way, since he who bases his consideration upon proof can be visited by obfuscations which detract from his proof, and only with difficulty can he remove them. (I 319.27)

At the beginning of the introduction to the *Futūḥāt*, Ibn al-ʿArabī explains that the various kinds of knowledge can be ranked according to excellence:

The sciences are of three levels. [The first] is the science of reason, which is every knowledge which is actualized for you by the fact that it is self-evident or after considering proofs, on condition that the purport of that proof is discovered. . . .

The second science is the science of states (*aḥwāl*), which cannot be reached except through tasting. No man of reason can define the states, nor can any proof be adduced for knowing them, naturally enough. Take for example knowledge of the sweetness of honey, the bitterness of aloes, the pleasure of sexual intercourse, love, ecstasy, yearning, and similar knowledges. It is impossible for anyone to know any of these sciences without being qualified by them and tasting them. . . .

The third knowledge is the sciences of the mysteries (*asrār*). It is the knowledge which is "beyond the stage of reason." It is knowledge through the blowing (*nafth*) of the Holy Spirit (*rūḥ al-qudus*) into the heart (*rūʿ*),[11] and it is specific to the prophet or the friends of God. It is of two sorts:

The first sort can be perceived by reason, just like the first of the kinds above. However, the person who knows it does not acquire it through consideration; rather, the level of this knowledge grants it.

The second sort is divided into two kinds. The first kind is connected to the second kind above, but its "state" is more noble. The second kind is the sciences of reports (*akhbār*), and concerning them one can say that they are true or false, unless the truthfulness of the report-giver and his inerrancy in what he says have been established for the one who receives the report. Such is the report given by the prophets from God, like their reporting about the Garden and what is within it. Hence the words of the Prophet that there is a Garden is a science of reports. But his words that at the resurrection there is a pool sweeter than honey is a science of states, a science of tasting. And his words, "God is, and nothing is with Him," is one of the sciences of reason, perceived by consideration.

The knower of this last kind—the science of mysteries—knows and exhausts all sciences. The possessors of the other sciences are not like that. So there is no knowledge more noble than this all-encompassing knowledge, which comprises all objects of knowledge. (I 31.11)

True knowledge is unveiled by God, without the intermediary of reflection or any other faculty. According to a saying often cited in Sufi texts, "Knowledge is a light which God throws into the heart of whomsoever He will."

Sound knowledge is not given by reflection, nor by what the rational thinkers establish by means of their reflective powers. Sound knowledge is only that which God throws into the heart of the knower. It is a divine light for which God singles out any of His servants whom He will, whether angel, messenger, prophet, friend, or person of faith. He who has no unveiling has no knowledge (*man lā kashf lah lā ʿilm lah*). (I 218.19)

There is no knowledge except that taken from God, for He alone is the Knower. He is the Teacher whose student is never visited by obfuscations in what he takes from Him. We are those who follow His authority, and what He has is true. So we are more deserving in our following His authority of the name "learned masters" (*ʿulamāʾ*) than the possessors of reflective consideration, those who follow the authority of consideration in what it gives to them. Necessarily they never cease disagreeing in knowledge of God. But the prophets, in spite of their great number and the long periods of time which separate them, had no disagreement in knowledge of God, since they took it from God. So also are the Folk and Elect of Allah: The later ones affirm the truthfulness of the earlier ones, and each supports the others. (II 290.25)

11. THE SCALE OF THE LAW

Despite the complexity of Ibn al-ʿArabī's teachings, he offers a single basic solution for all questions and confusion. The Koran puts it succinctly: "Obey God, and obey the Messenger and those in authority among you; if you should quarrel on anything, refer it to God and the Messenger" (4:59). God and the Messenger have set up the Scale of the Law (*al-mīzān al-sharʿī*), the norm which applies to every human situation and puts everything in its proper place. All knowledge and practice must be weighed in the Scale

The Revealed Law

Both in Islamic texts and in English, the term "Shariʿa" is often used to refer to Islamic law as codified in the science of jurisprudence (*fiqh*). In this meaning, the term excludes Islamic intellectuality, that is to say, most of the discussions that occupy the philosophers or an Ibn al-ʿArabī, such as metaphysics, cosmology, psychology, anthropology, prophetology, eschatology, and so on. But when Ibn al-ʿArabī employs the term *sharīʿa* or the closely related term *sharʿ*, he often has in mind a more basic sense of the term, which is the "wide road" of Islam, including all the teachings on every level that can properly be called Islamic. Hence *sharʿ* or *sharīʿa* in the sense of "revealed Law" means for him not just the legal statutes that guide activity, but also the intellectual principles which determine correct knowledge and the moral principles and practical guidelines which give birth to noble character traits.

In employing the term *sharīʿa* Ibn al-

ʿArabī may also mean the whole outward dimension of Islam as opposed to the *ṭarīqa* ("[spiritual] path") and *ḥaqīqa* ("reality") which make up its inward dimension. Thus the term "learned masters of the Shariʿa" (*ʿulamāʾ al-sharīʿa*) means those scholars who have devoted themselves to jurisprudence and other rational sciences, but who are not acquainted with Islam's more inward dimensions; these are the "exoteric scholars" (*ʿulamāʾ al-rusūm*).

The term *sharʿ* does not necessarily denote the revealed Law of Islam, since every religion sent by God is a *sharʿ*, and religion in general may also be called *sharʿ*, especially when it is being contrasted with the path of reason. The term *sharīʿa* may be used in the same way, though mainly in the plural (*sharāʾiʿ*), when it can perhaps best be translated as "revealed religions."

Ibn al-ʿArabī frequently affirms the validity of religions other than Islam, and in so doing he is simply stating the clear Koranic position. His teachings on this point are far-ranging and cannot be dealt with here, though they will be touched upon in several contexts.[1] For the present, a single quotation can suffice to provide his basic view. In discussing one of the thirty-six *tawḥīd*s or "declarations of God's Unity" found in the Koran, Ibn al-ʿArabī declares that the nineteenth *tawḥīd* is expressed by the following verse: "We never sent a messenger before thee except that We revealed to him, saying, 'There is no god but I, so worship Me!'" (Koran 21:25).

> This is a *tawḥīd* of the I-ness. . . . It is like God's words, "Naught is said to thee but what was already said to the messengers before thee" (41:43).
>
> In this verse God mentions "worship" (*ʿibāda*), but no specific practices (*aʿmāl*), for He also said, "To every one [of the prophets] We have appointed a Law and a way" (5:48), that is, We have set down designated practices. The periods of applicability of the practices can come to an end, and this is called "abrogation" (*naskh*) in the words of the learned masters of the Shariʿa. There is no single practice found in each and every prophecy, only the performance of the religion, coming together in it, and the statement of *tawḥīd*. This is indicated in God's words, "He has laid down for you as Law what He charged Noah with, and what We have revealed to thee [O Muḥammad], and what We charged Abraham with, and Moses, and Jesus: 'Perform the religion, and scatter not regarding it'" (42:13). Bukhārī has written a chapter entitled, "The chapter on what has come concerning the fact that the religion of the prophets is one," and this one religion is nothing but *tawḥīd*, performing the religion, and worship.[2] On this the prophets have all come together. (II 414.13)

The benefit of the Law is that it provides knowledge which is inaccessible to reason without God's help, and this knowledge, as we have already seen, provides the only means to achieve ultimate felicity. In other words, human beings cannot reach God's saving mercy without the Law.

> The opponents of the Folk of the Real[3] hold that the servant's reason can give him knowledge of some—though not all—of the ways to gain nearness (*qurba*) to God. But there is nothing true in this statement, since no one knows the path which brings about nearness to God and bestows endless felicity upon the servant except him who knows what is in the Self of the Real. And none of God's creatures knows that except through God's giving knowledge of it, just as God has said: "They encompass nothing of His knowledge save such as He wills" (2:255). There is no subject in this book of ours nor in any other book more difficult for all groups to understand than this. (III 79.28)
>
> God loves us for our sake. This is shown by the following: He has given us knowledge of our best interests (*maṣāliḥ*) in this world and the next. He has set up for us proofs so that we might know Him and not be ignorant of Him. He has provided for us and blessed us, in spite of our negligence after coming to know Him and after the proofs which have been es-

tablished for us that every blessing in which we move about is His creation and returns to Him and that He has brought it into existence only for our sake, so that we may be blessed by it and dwell in it. He left us in charge to do as we will.

Then, after this complete beneficence, we failed to thank Him, while reason requires that a benefactor be thanked. We had already come to know that none does good but God, and that among His good doing toward us was that He sent a messenger to us to teach us knowledge and courtesy (*adab*). So we knew what He Himself wanted for us, since He laid down the path of our felicity as the Law. He clarified it and warned us against ignoble affairs and told us to avoid base and blameworthy moral traits. . . . So we came to know that if He did not love us, there would not have been any of this. (II 328.19)

The Law provides a wide variety of knowledge, which can be divided into two main sorts—rulings (*ḥukm*) and reports (*khabar*)—and a large number of subdivisions. In Ibn al-ʿArabī's view, these divisions manifest the very nature of the revelatory Divine Word (*al-kalimat al-ilāhiyya*), which descends from God in a manner which he often describes.[4] Once the single Word passes by God's Throne and reaches His Footstool (*kursī*), it becomes differentiated into rulings and reports. Hence the five general categories of actions set down in the Shariʿa—incumbent, recommended, indifferent, reprehensible, and forbidden—have a strict ontological basis. In the following passage Ibn al-ʿArabī is describing the contents of a full revelation, or that which is brought by a "messenger" (*rasūl*). The revelation given to a "prophet" (*nabī*) in the limited sense of the term does not have the same scope.[5]

The station of messengerhood is the Footstool, since, beginning at the Footstool, the Divine Word becomes divided into reports and rulings. The friends and prophets possess only reports, while the prophets of the religions and the messengers possess both reports and rulings.

Then rulings become divided into commands (*amr*) and prohibitions (*nahy*).

Then commands become divided into two kinds: that in which man is free to choose, which is called "indifferent" (*mubāḥ*), and that in which he is encouraged. This second kind of command becomes divided into two sorts: (1) If a person refrains from the first sort, he is blamed by the Law; this is the "incumbent" (*wājib*) or "obligatory" (*farḍ*). (2) If he performs the second sort, he is praised, and if he refrains from it, he is not blamed; this is the "recommended" (*mandūb*).

Prohibition is divided into two kinds: (1) Prohibition in which he who does something is blamed, which is the "forbidden" (*maḥẓūr*), and (2) prohibition in which he who refrains from a thing is praised, though he is not blamed if he does it; this is the "reprehensible" (*makrūh*).

As for reports, they also are divided into two kinds: One kind is concerned with the situation of the Real, and the other with the situation of the cosmos.

Reports concerning the Real become divided into two kinds: (1) A kind which can be known, and (2) a kind which cannot be known. That which cannot be known is His Essence. That which can be known is divided into two kinds: (a) One kind demands the negation of likeness (*mumāthala*) and interrelationship (*munāsaba*); these are the attributes of incomparability and negation, such as "Nothing is like Him" (42:11) and the name All-holy (*al-quddūs*). (b) The second kind demands likeness; these are the attributes of Acts and every divine name that demands the cosmos. (II 257.17)

The Scale

The term "Scale" (*mīzān*) derives from a root which means "to weigh" (*wazn*). As Ibn al-ʿArabī points out, the Koranic term refers both to a pair of scales—or two pans and an indicator, called a "tongue" (*lisān*)—and to a steelyard or lever scale (*qabbān*), which makes use of weights (*raṭl*).[6] The Koran uses the word in sixteen verses in several contexts, such as describing the Scale which will be set up on the Day of Judgment to weigh the works of the servants. Ibn al-ʿArabī summarizes the various meanings which have been given to the term in commenting on the beginning of sura 55 of the Koran, "The All-merciful," especially verses 7-9:

"He set up the Scale" in order to weigh the two weighty ones (*al-thaqalān* [the jinn and mankind]). "'Exceed not the Scale!'" by overdoing or underdoing for the sake of loss; "'but set up the weighing with justice'," as in the equilibrium of the human configuration, since man is the indicator of the Scale, "'and cause not loss in the Scale'!", that is, do not underdo by giving preponderance to one of the two pans, unless because of excellence. God also says, "We set up the Scales of justice" (21:47).

Know that there is no art (*ṣanʿa*), level, state, or station which does not have a scale ruling over it in both knowledge and practice. Meanings have a scale in the hand of reason known as "logic" (*manṭiq*); it includes two pans, known as "premises." Speech has a scale known as "grammar" (*naḥw*), by which words are weighed in order to verify the meanings which the words of that language denote. Every possessor of a "tongue" has a scale, which is the known quantity to which God has joined him by sending down provisions, for He says "[There is no thing whose treasuries are not with us], and We send it not down but in a known measure" (15:21); "[Had God expanded His provision to His servants, they would have been insolent in the earth]; but He sends down in measure whatsoever He will" (42:27).

God created man's body in the form of the scale. He made the two pans his right hand and his left hand, while He made the "tongue" the pillar of himself. So man belongs to whichever side to which he inclines. God joined felicity to the right hand and wretchedness to the left.[7]. . . God's words, "He gave each thing its creation" (20:50), pertain to the Divine Scale. . . .

Know that the whole situation is restricted to knowledge and practice. Practice is of two kinds, that which pertains to the sensory realm (*ḥissī*) and that which pertains to the heart (*qalbī*). Knowledge is also of two kinds: Rational (*ʿaqlī*) and Law-defined (*sharʿī*). Each kind has a known weighing (*wazn*) with God when He bestows it. He asks from the servant, when He prescribes the Law for him, to "set up the weighing with justice," so he must not exceed or cause loss in it. God also says, "Go not beyond the bounds in your religion" (4:171); this is the meaning of "Exceed not the Scale". "And say not as to God but the truth (*al-ḥaqq*)" (4:171), which is the sense of His words, "Set up the weighing with justice." Hence God seeks justice from His servants in their interaction with Him and with everything other than Him, whether their own souls or others. Hence, when God gives the servant success to set up the weighing, there remains no good that He has not given him.

For example, God has placed health and well-being in the equilibrium of the four natures[8] such that none of them preponderates over the others, while He placed illnesses, diseases, and death in the preponderance of one over the others. Hence equilibrium is the cause of subsistence, while disequilibrium (*inḥirāf*) is the cause of destruction and annihilation. (III 6.13,26)

The specific scale which concerns us here is the Law, which is "the scale established within the cosmos to establish justice (*ʿadl*)" (II 463.16). Through it God shows man the way to right knowledge of both Himself and the cosmos and defines the path which leads to His mercy and gentleness in the next world.

He who desires the path of knowledge and felicity should not let the Scale of the Law drop from his hand for a single instant. For God keeps the scale in His hand, without letting it slip; "He lowers the Just Scale (*qist*) and raises it."[9] This "Just Scale" is the state possessed by existence. Were the Real to let the Scale drop from His hand, the cosmos would immediately be annihilated through that dropping.

In the same way, no one for whom the

Law is prescribed (*al-mukallaf*), or rather, no human being, should let the Scale established by the Law drop from his hand as long as he is prescribed for by the Law,[10] for, should he let it drop from his hand for a single instant, the whole of the Law will be annihilated, just as the cosmos would be annihilated were the Real to let the Scale drop from His hand. For the Law has a ruling which applies to every movement and rest of the person for whom it is prescribed so he cannot put down the Scale as long as the Law subsists. This is the Scale which pertains to him inasmuch as he is prescribed for by the Law. (III 239.19)

Wisdom and Courtesy

Justice (*ʿadl*), which is achieved through the Scale, is closely allied to "wisdom" (*ḥikma*). Justice is to put everything in its proper place, while wisdom is to act as is proper (*kamā yanbaghī*) in every situation, it being understood that proper activity is impossible without discernment of the right relationships. Ibn al-ʿArabī follows a well-known formula in defining the "sage" or "possessor of wisdom" (*al-ḥakīm*)—whether God or man—as "He who does what is proper for what is proper as is proper" (II 163.26). Wisdom is the hallmark of the perfect friends of God, possessed in its fullness only by the "People of Blame," the highest of the perfect men.[11]

Since wisdom puts things in their proper places, it rules over *tartīb*, that is, arrangement, order, and hierarchy. "The name Wise arranges affairs within their levels and places the things within their measures" (II 435.15). It is the perfect combination of knowledge and practice. As Ibn al-ʿArabī explains, God's name the "Wise" has a compound meaning, since it shares the properties of two other names:

The name Wise has a face toward the Knowing (*al-ʿālim*) and a face toward the Governing (*al-mudabbir*), for the Wise has two properties: It determines the property of the places of affairs, and it determines the actual putting of the things into their places. How many a knower there is who does not put a thing in its place! And how many a placer of things who puts them in places on the basis of chance, not knowledge! (I 389.31)

The Prophet said, "Give to everyone [or everything] who has a right (*ḥaqq*) his [or her or its] right."[12] Here the term *ḥaqq* may also be translated as "rightful due" or simply "due." The right of a person (or a thing) is that which he deserves on the basis of his nature and in keeping with the Law. Among those people and things to which something is due, the Prophet mentioned one's Lord, other people (guest, wife, friend), and dimensions of one's self (soul, body, eye). One of the divine roots of giving each thing its due is the principle enunciated by the Koranic verse, "God gave each thing its creation, then guided" (20:50).

[The gnostics] "give each thing its due," just as God "gives each thing its creation." (III 106.18)

The distinguishing feature of the gnostics . . . is that they verify that which distinguishes the realities. This belongs only to those who know the order of God's wisdom in affairs and who "give each thing its due." (II 480.31)

The Real described Himself as "governing the affair" (10:3) only so that we might know that He does nothing except that which is required by the wisdom of existence (*ḥikmat al-wujūd*). He puts everything in its own place, for if He did not put it there, He would not be giving wisdom its full due. But He it is who "has given everything its creation." (III 163.19)

The perfection of every state lies in its existence, for God says, "He gave each thing its creation." When a person understands and verifies this verse, he has no way to plunge into meddling (*fuḍūl*) [with God's wisdom in affairs]. However, meddling is also one of God's creations, so God "has given" meddling "its creation;

then He guided," that is, He explained that he who begins to meddle is named the "one who occupies himself with what does not concern him"[13] and the one who is ignorant of that which in fact does concern him. (II 654.20)

The person who gives each thing its due is not only wise, but also "courteous" (*adīb*). Few concepts have been as important in shaping the Islamic ethos as "courtesy" or "etiquette" (*adab*), which, in the view of the religious scholars, goes back to the Prophet's Sunna. He who has courtesy has achieved perfect refinement of words and deeds by weighing himself in the Scale of the Law as embodied in the person of the Prophet. He always puts things in their proper places, says the proper thing at the proper time, and acts according to the requisites of divine wisdom. It is he alone among all human beings who "gives each thing its due."

The Prophet said, "God taught me courtesy, so how beautiful is my courtesy!"[14] There are two ways to know the stations in which the creatures—whether the friends of God or others—stand with God. The first way is unveiling. The person sees the stations of the creatures with God and deals with each group in accordance with its station with Him.

The second way is to cling to the Divine Courtesy. "Divine Courtesy" (*al-adab al-ilāhī*) is that which God has laid down as Law for His servants through His messengers and on their tongues. The revealed religions (*al-sharā'iʿ*) are God's rules of courtesy (*ādāb Allāh*) which He set up for His servants. He who gives God's Law its full due (*ḥaqq*) has gained the courtesy of the Real (*al-ḥaqq*) and come to know the friends of the Real. (IV 58.26)

Among the divine rules of courtesy is everything that has come in the Koran in the mode of "Do this" and "Avoid that." So consider this in the Koran and gain a share of the Divine Courtesy, then put it into practice. Then you will be given success, God willing. (II 655.26)

The man of courtesy (*al-adīb*) is he who brings together all noble character traits (*makārim al-akhlāq*) and knows the base character traits without being described by them. He brings together all the levels of the sciences, both those which are praiseworthy and those which are blameworthy, since, in the eyes of every intelligent person, knowledge of a thing is always better than ignorance of it. Hence courtesy brings together all good (*jimāʿ al-khayr*). (II 284.28)

The first thing which God has commanded for His servant is "bringing together" (*jamʿ*), which is courtesy. "Courtesy" (*adab*) is derived from "banquet" (*ma'daba*), which is to come together for food. Likewise courtesy is to bring together all good. The Prophet said, "God taught me courtesy." In other words: He brought together in me all good things (*khayrāt*); for he then says, "How beautiful is my courtesy!" In other words: He made me a locus for every beautiful thing (*ḥusn*).

It is said to man, "Bring together the good things," for God placed His servant in this world as a doer and a collector who collects for His sake everything He has designated for him. Hence in this world he gathers together, so God created him only for gathering together. If he gathers together what he has been commanded to gather and collect, he will be "felicitous" and the Real will give him everything he collected and will favor him. Hence his recompense is everything he gathered together plus the beautiful divine praise for carrying the Trust (*amāna*), justice, and lack of wrongdoing and treachery. (II 640.23)

The divine root of courtesy is that God creates the world in order to manifest the properties of His names, and each name requires specific situations. These situations, when viewed as a whole, may be called the "cosmos," the "existent things" and so on. Among these names are the "secondary causes" (*asbāb*), as discussed in an earlier chapter. Since God has established the secondary causes for a purpose, the men of courtesy give each cause its due. Those pseudo-spirituals who would ignore God's wisdom in creation and go "straight to Him" without the means He has established are far from Verification. Nevertheless, what they say has a certain validity for those who are still traveling within the "states" (*aḥwāl*) and have not passed to the more advanced "stations" (*maqāmāt*) of the gnostics.

> The great ones (*al-akābir*) never rely upon any of the things, only upon God. But those who have refused to accept the existence of the secondary causes have refused to accept that thing whose existence the Real has established. Therefore they are blamed by the High Tribe.[15] This refusal to accept the secondary causes is an imperfection in station but a perfection in state, praiseworthy during wayfaring (*sulūk*) but blameworthy at the end (*al-ghāya*). (II 602.22)

Ibn al-ʿArabī clarifies the relationship between wisdom and the secondary causes while explaining the term "obliteration" (*maḥw*), which, he tells us, the Sufis employ to mean "the removal of the attributes of habit and the elimination of the cause (*ʿilla*)" (II 552.32).

> God would never remove the wisdom in things. The secondary causes are veils established by God which will not be removed. The greatest of these veils is your own entity. Your entity is the cause of the existence of your knowledge of God, since such knowledge cannot exist except in your entity. So it is impossible for you to be removed, since God wants you to know Him. Hence He "obliterates" you from yourself. Then you do not halt with the existence of your own entity and the manifestation of its properties. Thus God obliterated the Messenger of God in the property of throwing, though the throwing existed from him. God said, "You did not throw," so He obliterated him, "when you threw," so He established the secondary cause, "but God threw" (8:17). However, God only threw with the hand of His Messenger. In the same way, He says in the *Ṣaḥīḥ*. "I am his hearing, his sight, and his hand."[16]
>
> The "elimination of the cause" through obliteration lies only in the property, not in the entity. Were the cause and secondary cause to vanish, the servant would vanish, but he does not vanish. So wisdom requires that the secondary causes be kept in subsistence while the servant's reliance upon them be obliterated. (II 553.5)

The "wisdom" that requires the subsistence of the secondary causes has to do with letting each reality play its proper function. Thus, for example, the wisdom in keeping the individual entity in existence and never "obliterating" it has to do with the divine attributes of mercy and jealousy.

> The poet says:
>
> You veil your heart from the mystery
> of His Unseen:
> If not for you, He would not have set a
> seal upon the heart.[17]
>
> For He made you identical with His curtain (*sitr*) over you. Were it not for this curtain, you would not seek increase in knowledge. . . . Look at your human nature (*bashariyya*). You will find it identical with the curtain of yourself from behind which He speaks to you. For He says, "It belongs not to any human being that God should speak to him, except by revelation, or from behind a veil" (42:51). Hence, He may speak to you from yourself, since you yourself are His veil and His curtain over yourself. And it is impossible for you to cease being human, for you are human in your very essence. Though you should become absent from yourself or be annihilated (*fanāʾ*) by a state that overcomes you, your human nature subsists in its entity. Hence the curtain is let down, and the eye falls upon nothing but a curtain, since it falls upon a form.
>
> All this is required by the Divinity in respect of jealousy (*ghayra*) and mercy. He is "jealous" lest the "other" (*ghayr*) perceive Him and He be encompassed by him who perceives Him.[18] But He "encompasses everything" (Koran 4:126), so He is not encompassed by him whom He encompasses. He is "merciful" because He knows that temporally originated things cannot remain along with the "glories of His face."[19] On the contrary, they would be burned away by them, so out of mercy toward them He curtains them so that their entities may subsist. (II 554.3)

The Real established the secondary causes in the cosmos since He knew that there could be no name "Creator," neither in existence nor in supposition, without the created thing, whether in existence or supposition. In the same way, each divine name demands engendered existence, such as Forgiver, Owner, Grateful, All-compassionate, and so on. On this basis He established the secondary causes, and the cosmos became manifest such that parts of it are related to other parts. Hence no grain grows without a planter, an earth, and rain. God commanded praying for water when the rain does not come in order to affirm in the hearts of His servants the existence of the secondary causes. That is why no servant is addressed by the Law to leave aside the secondary causes, for his reality does not require that. On the contrary, God designated for him one cause rather than others. He said to him: I am your cause, so depend upon Me. "Put all your trust in God, if you have faith" (Koran 5:23).

The Man (*al-rajul*) is he who affirms secondary causes, for if he were to negate them, he would not come to know God and would not know himself. The Prophet said, "He who knows himself knows his Lord." He did not say, "knows the Essence of his Lord," since the Lord's Essence possesses nondelimited Independence. How could the delimited thing know the Nondelimited? But the "Lord" demands the vassal, without doubt. So in "Lord" there is a whiff of delimitation. Through this the created thing knows its Lord. That is why God commanded him to know that "There is no god but He" in respect of His being a god, since "god" demands the divine thrall. But the Essence of the Real is Independent of attribution, so there is no delimitation.

The affirmation of secondary causes is the clearest proof that he who affirms them has knowledge of his Lord. He who abolishes them has abolished that which cannot correctly be abolished. It is only proper for him to support the First Cause, who is He who created and established these secondary causes.

He who has no knowledge of what we are alluding to has no knowledge of how to travel the path to knowledge of his Lord through the Divine Courtesy. For the person who abolishes secondary causes has shown discourtesy toward God. He who dismisses that which God has appointed has shown discourtesy and given the lie to God through dismissing the appointee. So look at the ignorance of him who misbelieves in secondary causes and maintains that they must be abandoned! He who abandons what the Real has established is a contender, not a servant, an ignoramus, not a knower. I counsel you, my friend, lest you be among the ignorant and the heedless! . . .

So the divine man of courtesy (*al-adīb al-ilāhī*) is he who affirms what God has affirmed in the place where God has affirmed it and in the manner in which He has affirmed it and who negates what God has negated in the place where God has negated it and in the manner in which He has negated it. (III 72.32)

God did not establish the secondary causes aimlessly. He wanted us to stand up for them and rely upon them with a divine reliance. The Divine Wisdom makes this known. . . . So the divine and courteous sage is he who places the secondary causes where God has placed them. (II 471.25)

No one abolishes the secondary causes except him who is ignorant that God has put them there. No one affirms the secondary causes except a great learned master, a man of courtesy in knowledge of God. (II 123.4)

The sage among God's servants is he who puts each thing in its place and does not take it beyond its level. He "gives to each that has a due its due" and does not judge anything according to his individual desire (*gharaḍ*) or his caprice (*hawā*). Incidental desires have no affect upon him. The sage considers the abode where God has settled him for a fixed term and he considers, without increase or decrease, the scope of the activity within this abode which God has laid down for him in the Law. Then he walks in the manner which has been explained to him and he never lets the Scale which has been set up for him in this abode drop from his hand. (III 35.35)

The courteous sage follows the Scale of the Law in all his activities. More than that, he follows the Scale of God's knowledge, by means of which the Law itself was established.

There is another Scale, besides the Scale of the Law, which man must not put down and which will remain in his hand in this world and the next. That is the Scale of Knowledge; the Scale of the Law is one of the properties of this Scale of Knowledge. This Scale is like the Scale in the hand of the Real. Through it man witnesses the Real's weighing. Its relationship to the Scale of the Real is the relationship of one person who has a scale in his hand to another person who has a mirror. The person with the mirror sees in it the scale, the weighing, and the weigher. He comes to know the form of the situation through witnessing his own existence. . . .

The Unseen which weighs, the weighing, and the Scale are the Presence of the Real, while the mirror is the presence of man (*ḥaḍrat al-insān*). The weighing belongs to God, while the witnessing belongs to him whose soul is a mirror. He is the truthful man of felicity.

God unveils this mystery to whom He will in order to show him in his mirror the form of the divine creation and how things emerge and become manifest in existence from Him. This situation is indicated by the words of Abū Bakr: "I have never seen anything without seeing God before it." Hence he saw from whence that thing emerged.

The possessor of this unveiling is "ever-creating" (*khallāq*), and that is what the Real desires from him through this unveiling. Or rather, he comes to know through this unveiling that he is ever-creating and has always been such, though he was not aware. His unveiling gives him knowledge of the actual situation. He does not become ever-creating through the unveiling.

God commands the person who has this unveiling to "give each thing its due" in its form, just as God "gave each thing its creation" in its form. Then no claim will be directed against him by any created thing, just as no claim is directed against the Real by any created thing. This is the benefit of this unveiling.

When the Real sets him in one of his acts which he is commanded to do or forbidden from doing, he looks upon what it has of the Real (*al-ḥaqq*) before it. Then he gives that act its full due (*ḥaqq*). If it is one of the affairs whose performance is commanded, he gives it its due in its plane, so that it stands up faultless in creation and balanced in configuration. Hence that act possesses nothing more which is due to it from its performer. So to God belongs creation (*al-khalq*) and to the servant belongs the due (*al-ḥaqq*). The Real "gave each thing its creation" and the creation "gives each thing its due." Hence the Real enters into creation, and creation enters into the Real in this situation.

If the affair should be one of those things which are forbidden, then what is due for the servant is that he not bring it into existence and not make manifest any entity for it. If he does not act in this manner, he has not given it its due, and it directs a claim against him. Hence he has not given everything its due. In the due he fails to stand in the station of the Real in creation. Hence there is an argument against him. In this manner you should know affairs and the divine commands.

The form of avoiding acts (*tark*) on God's part is that He does not bring into existence one of two possible things, since the other thing, whose existence has been given preponderance (*al-murajjaḥ*), already exists. Hence, in respect of the fact that He did not bring it into existence, God "avoided" it.

We bring this question to your notice because we know that you will not find it in any other book, since it is difficult to conceive of, but easy to reach for him toward whom God shows solicitude. You will be given courtesy with God and allowed to preserve the Sharīʿa for His servants. This is one of the mysteries stored away with God which does not become manifest except to the gnostics through God. It is not proper to conceal it from any of God's creatures. If its knower conceals it, he has misadvised God's servant, and "He who misadvises us is not one of us;"[20] in other words, misadvising is not part of the Prophet's Sunna. . . .

The courteous man is he who creates in this abode through works (*ʿamal*), not through saying "Be!" Rather, he says, "In the name of God, the All-merciful, the All-compassionate." Thereby he is safe from his practice being shared by Satan.

. . . When we name God over our works when beginning them, we perform them alone and are preserved from Satan's sharing in them, for it is the divine name which conducts the work and comes between us and him. Some of the people of unveiling witness this repulsion of Satan by the divine name when the servant begins a work. (III 239.23, 240.25)

The Scale of Reason

There is much that reason cannot come to know on its own (*bi'l-istiqlāl*), that is, without the guidance of the Law. Ibn al-ʿArabī constantly criticizes the rational thinkers for the wrong sources they employ in gaining knowledge and the fact that they do not make full use, if any at all, of the Law. Somehow they fail to notice that man is a creature utterly in need of a Creator, and that the faculty of reflection, also created by the Creator, cannot be a sufficient means to know the Creator. Because of God's utter incomprehensibility in His Essence, man must come to know God through God, or at the very least, through the revealed guidance of God. Any attempt to know God without taking the Law into account is simply a lack of wisdom and courtesy. But a rational faculty which follows the Law is well-guided and "sound" (*salīm*).

The following passage is taken from a chapter explaining the meaning of "God's wide earth" (*arḍ Allāh al-wāsiʿa*), which is mentioned in three Koranic verses, including: "O My servants who have faith, surely My earth is wide, so worship Me!" (29:56), and "But was not God's earth wide, so that you might have emigrated in it?" (4:97). The second verse quotes the words of the angels to the evildoers whose souls they have taken after death, asking them why they did not do good works.

Since God established the secondary causes, He does not abolish them for anyone. What God does is to give to some of His servants enough of the light of guidance so that they can walk in the darkness of the secondary causes. . . . The veils of secondary causes are lowered down and will never be lifted, so wish not for that! If the Real makes you pass beyond a secondary cause, He will only make you pass to another secondary cause. He will not allow you to lose secondary causes completely, for the handhold to which God commanded you to cling fast (3:103) is a secondary cause, and that is the revealed Law. It is the strongest and most truthful of secondary causes, and it holds in its grasp the light by which one can be guided in the darknesses of the land and sea of these secondary causes.[21] For he who does such and such—which is the secondary cause—will be recompensed with such and such. So wish not for that which cannot be wished for, but ask God to sprinkle that light upon your essence. . . .

You should know, dear brother, that the earth of your body is the true "wide earth" within which the Real commanded you to worship Him. This is because He only commanded you to worship Him in His earth as long as your spirit resides in the earth of your body. When it leaves your body, this prescription by the Law will drop away from you, even though your body will continue to exist in the earth, buried within it. Thus you know that this "earth" is nothing other than your body. He made it "wide" because of the faculties and meanings which are found only in this human, bodily earth.

As for His words, "So that you might have emigrated in it," this is because the body is a place of both caprice and reason. So "you might have emigrated" from the earth of the caprice that is within it to the earth of the reason that is within it, while you were in the body; for you were in the body, and you never left it. If caprice put you to work, it ruined you and you were destroyed. But if the rational faculty within whose hand is the lamp of the Law put you to work, you were saved and God saved you through it. For God took the sound rational faculty, clear of the attributes of imperfection and obfuscations, and opened the eye of its insight to perceive affairs as they are in themselves.

Therefore employ reason as it should be employed and "Give to each that has a due its due." (III 249.22)

One of the greatest proofs of reason's inability to gain sufficient knowledge for human perfection and felicity through its own independent efforts is the fact of God's having sent the prophets.

Know, my friend, that God did not send the messengers aimlessly. If reason were able to grasp the affairs of its felicity on its own, it would have no need for messengers, and the existence of the messengers would be useless (*ʿabath*).

He by whom we are supported is not similar to us, nor are we similar to Him. Were He similar to us in entity, our being supported by Him would not be preferable to His being supported by us. Hence we know with certitude, with a knowledge not visited by obfuscations in this station,[22] that He is not like us and that no single reality brings us together with Him. Hence, man is necessarily ignorant of his final end (*maʾāl*) and the place to which he will pass on. He is ignorant of that which will bring about his felicity, if he should be felicitous, or his wretchedness, if he should be wretched, with Him by whom he is supported. For he is ignorant of God's knowledge of him. He does not know what God wants from him, and why He created him. Hence he necessarily needs a divine bestowal of knowledge (*taʿrīf ilāhī*) concerning this. (III 83.7)

Another proof of reason's incapacity before the reality of God is the fact that it cannot comprehend love, though God is by definition full of love and mercy. Were reason in charge, no one would love God.

By God, were it not for the Shariʿa brought by the divine report-giving, no one would know God! If we had remained with our rational proofs—which, in the opinion of the rational thinkers, establish knowledge of God's Essence, showing that "He is not like this" and "not like that"—no created thing would ever have loved God. But the tongues of the religions gave a divine report saying that "He is like this" and "He is like that," mentioning affairs which outwardly contradict rational proofs. He made us love Him through these positive attributes. Then, having set down the relationships and established the cause and the kinship which bring about love, He said, "Nothing is like Him" (42:11).

Hence He affirmed those secondary causes which bring about love and which are denied by the rational faculty through its proofs. This is the meaning of His words, "I created the creatures and I made Myself known to them. Then they came to know Me."[23] They only came to know God through that which He reported about Himself: His love for us, His mercy toward us, His clemency, His tenderness, His loving kindness, His descent into limitation that we may conceive of Him in imaginal form (*tamthīl*) and place Him before our eyes within our hearts, our kibla, and our imagination, just as if we see Him.[24] Or rather, we do indeed see Him within ourselves, since we have come to know Him through His giving knowledge, not through our own rational consideration. (II 326.12)

Here we come back explicitly to a familiar theme of earlier chapters: The contrast between the incomparability of God that is perceived by reason and the similarity that is perceived by imagination. Rational thinkers will never gain true knowledge of God as long as they cannot grasp that God is similar through His self-disclosure just as He is incomparable in His Essence. This similarity is not a matter of poetic "imagery," but of "imaginalization" in an ontological mode. God actually manifests Himself in the forms of self-disclosure, forms which make up the contents of the cosmos and our minds. God "imaginalizes" Himself everywhere; wherever we look, we perceive His "dream." Or again: The words of God are in and around us, since we and the cosmos are the articulations of the Breath of the All-merciful. Hence, says Ibn al-ʿArabī, continuing the passage just quoted, we love God in everything that we love. The love of God that is made possible through revelation and the divine reports has a salvific function, leading to felicity. But even without revelation, love of God is a fact of existence, though it cannot lead to our felicity unless we are aware of Him whom we love. God reveals Himself in every form, thus making it necessary that we love Him in any form which we love. Just as the possible thing by definition has need of the Necessary Being to stay in existence, and just as the creature is by definition poor toward the Independent, so also all things love God by their very nature.

There are those among us who see God but are ignorant of Him. But just as no one is poor toward anyone else, so also—by God—none but God is loved in the existent things. It is He who is manifest within every beloved to the eye of every lover—and there is nothing which is not a lover. So the cosmos is all lover and beloved, and all of it goes back to Him. . . .

Though no one loves any but his own Creator, he is veiled from Him by the love for Zaynab, Suʿād, Hind, Laylā, this world, money, position, and everything loved in the world. Poets exhaust their words writing about all these existent things without knowing, but the gnostics never hear a verse, a riddle, a panegyric, or a love poem that is not about Him, hidden beyond the veils of forms. (II 326.18)

Once you have verified that to which I have alluded in this chapter, you will come to know all the divine attributes, whether eternal or temporally originated, which were brought by the Law in the Book and the Sunna and which reason rejects, since rational demonstrations are inadequate for this perception. The knowledge that the Real exists is perceived by rational faculties in respect of the fact that they reflect and furnish proofs, but existence gives to every perception in the cosmos the knowledge of the situation of the Real in Himself. There is none but a Real and he who is correct (*muṣīb*) [in his perception]. So glory be to Him who laid out the stages, placed daytime and nighttime within the reality of the day, and sent down the rulings, differentiating the Law rather than leaving it undifferentiated! (II 183.31)

Affirming Similarity

The roots of God's similarity go back to the Barzakh within which God manifests Himself in the attributes of the creatures. Ibn al-ʿArabī employs the term "Barzakh" to remind us that the realm of the divine self-disclosure is an "isthmus" between two realities, Nondelimited Being and the nonexistent things. The Barzakh is the Cloud, "within which God came to be before He created the creatures." The Cloud stands between God and the cosmos. It is neither the one nor the other, or it is both the one and the other. God in Himself is free of the attributes of the created things, while the creatures in themselves have none of God's attributes, since they do not exist. Through the Barzakh, God assumes the attributes of the creatures, and they take on His names. Without the Barzakh, God would be incomparable but in no way similar. In other words, there would be no creation. It is the Barzakh that brings the cosmos into existence and allows us to speak of His similarity to the creatures and the creatures' similarity to Him. The Barzakh is the ontological locus for *tashbīh*.

The ocean of the Cloud is a *barzakh* between the Real and creation. Within this ocean the possible thing becomes qualified by Knowing, Powerful, and all the divine names of which we are apprised, and the Real becomes qualified by wonder, receiving joyfully, laughter, rejoicing, withness (*maʿiyya*), and most of the attributes of engendered things.[25] So return what belongs to Him, and take what belongs to you! He possesses descent (*nuzūl*), and we possess ascent (*miʿrāj*). (I 41.31)

The Breath of the All-merciful is the substance of the engendered things. That is why God described Himself by attributes that belong to temporally originated things, attributes which are considered impossible by rational and considerative proofs. (II 404.9)

The substance of the cosmos is the

All-merciful Breath, within which the forms of the cosmos become manifest. . . . Hence, all the cosmos is noble (*sharīf*) in respect to its substance. There is no ranking in excellence (*tafāḍul*) within it. A maggot and the First Intellect are the same in the excellence of the substance. Ranking in excellence becomes manifest only within the forms, which are the properties of the levels. There is a noble and a more noble, a lowly and a more lowly. . . . The forms [of the cosmos] are nothing but the entities of the possible things. . . .

Do you not see that the Lawgiver, who gives reports from God, has never described the Real with any attribute within which there is differentiation without that being an attribute of a created, temporally originated thing, even though that which is described—God—is eternal? Reason, in respect of its consideration and reflection, has no entrance into this. It does not know the root of the cause of this, nor does it know that the form of the created thing lies within the substance of the cosmos. On the contrary, reason imagines that the thing is the substance itself.

If you want to be safe, worship a Lord who has described Himself as He has described Himself: Negate similarity and affirm the property! For such is the actual situation, since the substance is not identical with the form, so similarity has no property within it. That is why God says, "Nothing is like Him"—because of the lack of mutual similarity, since the realities reject that—"and He is the Hearing, the Seeing" (42:11), and thereby He affirms the forms. . . . He who does not know his Lord through His reports about Himself has gone far astray. . . .

Affairs interpenetrate and properties become united, while the entities are distinct. It is said about Zayd and ʿAmr, "In one respect he is not he." And it is said, "In another respect, he is he, since the two are human beings." That is what we say about the cosmos in respect of its substance and in respect of its form, just as God has said it: "Nothing is like Him, and He"—that is, He who has no likeness—"is the Seeing, the Hearing." But the property of hearing is not the property of sight, so He separated and joined, but He is neither separate nor joined. (III 452.30, 453.1,8)

God is the Manifest, while the loci of manifestation, though nonexistent in themselves, bestow their properties upon Him. Hence He possesses all the attributes of temporally originated things. Ibn al-ʿArabī makes this point while discussing the reality of "freedom" (*ḥurriyya*).

> In reality, one does not say that the Real is "free." One says that He is not a slave, since He can only be known through negative descriptions, not through positive descriptions of self. However, the loci of manifestation exercise a property upon Him in respect to the fact that He is the Manifest. Then all things attributed to the locus of manifestation are attributed to Him, whether these be what are commonly considered attributes of imperfection or attributes of perfection and completion.
>
> There is nothing but the Real,
> nothing more,
> so His Manifest Entity is the description
> of the slaves.
> Say not that He is they,
> but say,
> "Just as you have said,
> nothing more!"
>
> The tongues of the divine religions have spoken of this as reality (*ḥaqīqa*), not as metaphor (*majāz*), even though considerative, rational proofs negate this sort of thing from the Divine Side. But since the religions have brought it, their stalwart learned masters interpret (*ta'wīl*) the like of this because they have no unveiling, since the Real is not their sight.[26]
>
> You follow the authority of reflection
> in spite of its incapacity,
> and you have not been illumined
> for an instant by the light of God.
> Glory be to Him whose Essence
> is concealed from the eye,
> but manifest among His creatures
> through their attributes! (II 502.21)

The Barzakh or Breath of the All-merciful is one entity (*ʿayn wāḥida*), which is neither Being nor nothingness; it is imagination, which is He/not He. In this intermediary realm, every attribute necessarily goes back to God, who is the source of each reality, even the reality of "nonexistence." The nonexistent things remain immutably nonexistent, though they are qualified by their own attributes, such as obeying the divine command "Be!" when it comes to them. Then they pass from the "thingness of immutability" to the "thingness of existence," though they never really leave their state of nonexistence.

In the state of immutability, the thing obeyed the command of its Lord to come to be (*takwīn*). For a command cannot apply to something unless it is qualified by hearing (*samʿ*). The Divine Speech has no beginning and the immutable hearing has no beginning, while that which undergoes temporal origination is the existential hearing (*al-samʿ al-wujūdī*), which is a branch of the immutable hearing. Hence the state (*ḥāl*) of hearing's entity shifted (*intiqāl*), but the hearing itself did not shift, since entities do not shift from state to state. On the contrary, states clothe them in properties, so they become clothed in them. He who has no knowledge imagines that the entity has shifted.

The states (*aḥwāl*) [of the entities] demand (*ṭalab*) the divine names, but the entities themselves are not described by demand. Then the entities come to have temporally originated names and titles in keeping with the properties of the states within which they undergo fluctuation. Were it not for the states, the entities would not become distinct (*tamayyuz*). For there is only one entity,[27] which is distinct through its very essence from the Necessary Being, just as it shares with It in the necessity of immutability.

So God possesses the Necessity of Immutability and Being, while this entity possesses the necessity of immutability. The states are to this entity as the divine names are to the Real. Just as the names of the One Entity [of Being] do not pluralize or multiply the Named, so also the states do not pluralize or multiply this entity, even though manyness and number are intelligible within the names and the states. Hence it is correct to say about this entity that it is "upon the Form," that is, it corresponds to the actual situation of God.

This entity actualizes perfection through existence, which is one of the states which make it undergo fluctuation. So it is not lacking in perfection, except that it negates the property of the Necessity of Being, in order that it may be distinct from God, since that distinction is never abolished, and it can have no entrance into Necessity.

There is also another distinction, which is that the Real undergoes fluctuation in states, but states do not make Him undergo fluctuation, since it is impossible that a state should exercise a property over God. Rather, He exercises a property over it. Hence He undergoes fluctuation in them, but they do not make Him undergo fluctuation. "Each day He is upon some task" (55:29), for if they made Him undergo fluctuation, they would impose upon Him properties.

But the entity of the cosmos is not like that. States make it undergo fluctuation, so their properties and their making it undergo fluctuation become manifest within it through God's hand. The Real's undergoing fluctuation in states is obvious through descent, sitting, withness, laughter, rejoicing, approval, wrath, and every state by which the Real has described Himself. So He undergoes fluctuation in them through property. This is the difference between us and the Real; it is the clearest and most obvious difference.

Sharing (*mushāraka*) takes place in the states, as it takes place in the names, since the names are the names of the states, while that which they name is the entity. Likewise they have another relationship in which they name the Real. So He is Hearing, Seeing, Knowing, Powerful, and you are hearing, seeing, knowing, and powerful. The state of hearing, sight, knowledge, and power belongs both to us and to Him, but it has two different relationships, since He is He, and we are we. So we have instruments (*ālāt*), and we are His instruments. . . . "You did not throw when you threw, but God threw" (8:17), while the instrument was the Messenger of God. Hence the Real undergoes fluctuation in states to make manifest our entities, just as the number "one" undergoes fluctuation in the levels of the numbers to

> make manifest their entities.[28] (III 314.2)

As we saw in an earlier chapter, reason understands only one-half the knowledge of God; imagination and sense perception must supply the other half. Reason declares God incomparable, but imagination, itself manifesting the very substance of the cosmos, perceives Him as similar. The Barzakh is Nondelimited Imagination, so imagination provides the key to grasping the nature of similarity.

Ibn al-ʿArabī stresses once more the importance of imagination in Chapter 352 of the *Futūḥāt*, which is entitled, "Concerning the true knowledge of the waystation of three talismanic mysteries, which are formed and governed by the Muhammadan Presence." He explains that the meaning of the word talisman (*ṭilism*, written *ṭ.l.s.m.* in Arabic) can be understood from its palindrome, the word *musallaṭ* (written *m.s.l.ṭ.*), which means "a thing given ruling power (over something else)." A "talisman" is given the power to rule over everyone with whom it has been charged.

> Hence everything given power to rule is a talisman, as long as it keeps its ruling power. One kind of talisman has power to rule over rational faculties. It is the strongest of talismans, since it does not let the rational faculties accept from the divine reports and the prophetic sciences of unveiling anything except that which can come under their interpretation (*taʾwīl*) and the weighing of their scale. If it is not of this sort, they do not accept it. This is the most intractable ruling power in the cosmos, for the person put under its charge loses abundant knowledge of God. This talisman is reflection. God gave it power to rule over man so that he would reflect by it and come to know that he knows no affair whatsoever except through God. Then the one to whom ruling power was given inverted the affair and said, "You will not know God, O reason, except through me!"
>
> The second talisman is imagination. God gave it power to rule over meanings (*maʿānī*). It clothes them in substrata (*mawādd*) and makes them manifest through them. No meaning is able to hold itself back from imagination.
>
> The third talisman is habits (*ʿādāt*). God gave it power to rule over rational souls. . . .
>
> As for the second talisman, which is imagination: It embodies meanings and places them within the mold of sensory forms. It also acts as a talisman upon inadequate understandings, which have no knowledge of meanings disengaged from substrata. They do not witness them, witnessing instead only corporeous forms (*ṣuwar jasadiyya*).[29] Hence, he over whom the talisman of imagination exercises its ruling property is deprived of perceiving affairs as they are in themselves without their imaginalization. Such a person receives nothing of the meanings, even though he knows that meanings are not corporeous forms and only become so when he gives form to them within his imagination as distinct, spatially confined, embodied forms, thereby bringing together two contraries. He knows that they are not forms, yet he does not receive them except as forms.
>
> Even if someone desires to abolish this talisman, he can never abolish it on this plane (*nash'a*), since it has been established by God. In the same way no divine talismans—neither their entities nor their properties—can be abolished in the place where God has put their properties. However, some people remove the talismans from their proper paths, and the property of this removal can be abolished, but nothing else. Know this!
>
> The property of the possessor of this talisman will be abolished when he sees how reflection enters into the treasury of imagination, then turns away and emerges from it. He accompanies reflection to reason, in order to witness meanings disengaged from forms as they are in themselves. The first of these that he witnesses is the reality of reflection, which he had accompanied as far as reason. He sees it disengaged from the substrata which imagination had been giving to it. So he thanks God and says, "I knew it in this manner before I witnessed it," meaning thereby to show that witnessing agrees with knowledge.
>
> When he ascends to reason, he witnesses reason also as disengaged from

substrata in itself, and he becomes intimate with the world of meanings disengaged from substrata. Once he verifies this witnessing, he passes on to witnessing the Real, that is, His effect within the disengagement of the meanings. Though contingent meanings are disengaged, they are not disengaged from their contingency (*ḥudūth*) and their possibility. So the possessor of this station witnesses within them the original nonexistence which belongs to them, and he witnesses their contingency and their possibility —all of that without any material form.

When he climbs up to the Real, the first thing he witnesses is the entity of His possibility, so he is overcome by bewilderment (*taḥayyur*) in Him, since this knowledge is impossible. Then the Real takes him by the hand in that by letting him know that what he witnessed from the Real at the beginning was the possibility that goes back to the witnesser. In other words, he witnessed the reality concerning which he says, "It is possible that the Real will give me to witness Himself, and it is possible that He will not." Hence this possibility which became manifest to him from the Real at the beginning of his witnessing had given preponderance (*tarjīḥ*) to one of the two modes of possibility. At this he becomes still and his bewilderment disappears.

Then the Real discloses Himself to him without any substratum (*mādda*), since at this point he is not present in the world of substrata. He gains knowledge from God in the measure of that self-disclosure; but no one is able to designate what is disclosed to him from the Real, except the fact that He disclosed Himself without substratum, nothing else. The cause of this is that God discloses Himself to every servant in the cosmos within a reality which is not identical to His self-disclosure to any other servant, nor is it identical to what He discloses to that servant in another locus of self-disclosure. Hence, that within which He discloses Himself does not become designated, nor can it be communicated.

When this servant returns from this station to his own world, the world of substrata, the Real's self-disclosure accompanies him. Hence he does not enter a single presence which possesses a property without seeing that the Real has transmuted Himself (*taḥawwul*) in keeping with the property of that presence. But the servant has already apprehended from Him in the first place what he apprehended, so he knows that He has transformed Himself into something else. Hence after this he is never ignorant of Him or veiled from Him, since God never discloses Himself to anyone only to veil Himself after that; this is totally impossible.

When the servant descends to the world of his own imagination, having come to know affairs as they are in themselves through witnessing, while before that he had known them through knowledge and faith, he sees the Real in the Presence of Imagination as a corporeous form. Hence he never denies Him, unlike the passer-by (*ʿābir*) and the outsiders (*ajānib*).

Then he descends from the world of imagination to the world of sensation and sensory things, and the Real descends along with him through his descent, since He never leaves him. He witnesses Him as the form of all corporeal bodies and accidents which he witnesses in the cosmos, not making Him specific to one form rather than another. He sees that He is identical with himself, while he knows that He is neither identical with himself nor identical with the cosmos. But he is not bewildered in that, for he verifies that the Real accompanies him in his descent from the station appropriate to Him, beyond which there is no world. He transmutes Himself within every presence in accordance with the property of that presence.

This is a rare place of witnessing. I have seen no one who acknowledges it without having witnessed it except on the level of the world of corporeal and corporeous bodies. The cause of this is that they do not accompany the Real when He descends from the station appropriate to Him. Hence those who acknowledge this within the world of corporeal and corporeous bodies do so only as followers of authority. This is recognized by the fact that they do not stay in the company of this place of witnessing and are repeatedly overcome by heedless moments. Only when they are present with themselves do they acknowledge it. But the possessor of tasting is not heedless of this for an instant, since it is known by him.

Heedlessness occurs in relation to one thing or another thing, but not everything. The possessor of tasting witnesses the Real within everything within which the heedless person does not witness Him, such that He is not witnessed in the state of his heedlessness. He who does not possess this station through tasting is made heedless of the Real by the things, until He calls him into His presence at certain times. This is what separates the people of tasting from others, so do not deceive yourself!

I have not seen anyone who possessed this station through tasting, though my wife, Maryam bint Muḥammad ibn ʿAbdūn, told me about someone whom she had seen and she described his state to me. I understood that he possessed this witnessing, except that she mentioned various states of his which show that he was not strong in it and was weak, even though he had attained to verification of this state. (III 232.20, 234.15)

Reactions to the Revelation of Similarity

Ibn al-ʿArabī divides people into a number of groups according to their reaction to the reports of the revealed Law concerning God's attributes of similarity. He describes what happens when a messenger comes from God and is accepted by the people, but then he begins to speak about God in terms of similarity. The Shaykh maintains that this situation occurs in all religions, though as usual he employs Koranic references showing the specific Islamic examples which he has in mind.

The messenger began to describe the Real, on behalf of whom he had come, to the people, in order that they might come to know Him through a knowledge which they had not had. They had maintained that the like of this was impossible for the Real, since the people of considerative proofs had negated it from Him. These were attributes which they affirmed for the temporally originated things as proof of their temporal origination.

Once the people heard what was denied and rejected by rational, considerative proofs, they split into a number of groups.

One person turned back on his heels and had doubts about the proof which had shown him that the messenger was speaking the truth. He set up against that proof various obfuscations that detracted from it and turned him away from faith and knowledge of it. So he turned back on his heels.

One group said: "Here in our group there are some who have nothing but the light of faith. They know nothing of knowledge or its path. We do not doubt the truthfulness of this messenger or his wisdom. And one part of wisdom is to take into account the weakest. Hence, through these attributes by which the messenger described his Lord, he has addressed this weak fellow who does not possess the proofs of consideration and has nothing but the light of faith. Thereby the messenger has been merciful toward him, for his faith will not grow except through descriptions like this. And the Real can describe Himself as He likes according to the measure of the rational faculty of the recipient, even if in Himself He is different from that. The report-giver has relied upon this description, while observing the right of the weakest one. For the messenger knows that we have knowledge of God and has verified our sincerity concerning him and our dependence upon our proofs. None of this detracts anything from what we have, since we have understood what this messenger really meant." Hence this group remained firm in their faith, but in themselves they concluded that the messenger's descriptions of his Lord were impossible. They accepted it as a wisdom and a means of attracting the weakest.

Another group of those present said: "This description contradicts our proofs, but we are certain concerning the truthfulness of this report-giver. The most we can grasp in our knowledge of God is the negation of everything we ascribe to Him, since all that has a temporal origin. But the messenger has more knowledge than we concerning this relationship. So we have faith in it in order to attest to him, and we depend in that upon him and upon God, since faith in these words will not hurt us. But the attribution of this description to God is unknown to us, since His Essence is unknown by way of positive attributes or by negation, so this is not reliable. The root is ignorance of God, so ignorance of the relationship to Him of what the Real ascribes to Himself in His Book is even greater. So let us submit (*islām*) and have faith in His knowledge of what He says about Himself."

Another group of those present said: "We do not doubt concerning the proof of the truthfulness of this report-giver. But in describing God to us, he has brought various things which, if we remain with their outward significance (*ẓāhir*) and ascribe them to God just as we ascribe them to ourselves, will lead us to conclude that He is temporally originated, and He will cease being a god. However, these things have been established. So let us consider: Do these descriptions have a proper application in the tongue in which they came? For the messenger is only sent in the tongue of his people." Hence they considered various stratagems by which those descriptions could be interpreted (*ta'wīl*) and which would require incomparability and negate similarity. They applied those words in accordance with that interpretation. When it was said to them, "What called you to do that?", they replied, "Two things. First, the fact that those descriptions detract from our proofs. For we have established through rational proofs the truthfulness of the messenger's claim, but we do not accept that which detracts from rational proofs, for that would detract from the proof of his truthfulness. Second: This truthful messenger has said to us that God Himself says, 'Nothing is like Him' (42:11), and this corresponds with rational proofs. So his truthfulness in our view is strengthened through the like of this. But if we were to say what he says about God in the manner given by the outward significance of the words, and if we were to apply that description to Him just as we apply it to temporally originated things, then we would go astray. So we began interpreting in order to affirm these two points."

Another group, which is the weakest of them all, was not able to go beyond the Presence of Imagination. These people had no knowledge of the disengagement of meanings or the abstrusities of the mysteries, nor did they know the meaning of God's words, "Nothing is like Him," or His words, "They measured not God with His true measure" (6:91). In all their affairs they stopped with imagination, while the light of faith and attestation was in their hearts. They were ignorant of the language, they ascribed the affair to its outward significance, and they did not refer its knowledge back to God. They believed that the description was related to God as it was related to themselves. There is no group weaker than this group, because they have only one-half of faith, since they accept the description of similarity but have no rational understanding of the attributes of incomparability derived from "Nothing is like Him."

Those who are surely saved among the groups which have reached the truth are those who have faith in that which comes from God as God means it and knows it, while negating similarity through "Nothing is like Him."

These, my friend, are the tongues of the revealed religions in the cosmos. They have brought, for the Real Himself, [attributes such as] form, eye, hand, foot, hearing, seeing, approval, wrath, wavering, receiving joyfully, wonder, rejoicing, laughter, boredom, deception, guile, mockery, derision, running, rushing, descent, sitting, limitation through nearness, patience with injury, and other descriptions of created things of this sort.

All of this came so that we might have faith in all of it and so that we might know that the divine self-disclosure within the entities of the possible things bestows these descriptions, for there is no witnesser and nothing witnessed except God. The tongues of the religions are the proofs of the self-disclosures, and the self-disclosures are the proofs of the divine names. (II 306.9)

Those who are "surely saved" affirm God's similarity and negate it at the same time through affirming His incomparability. The divine root of the necessity for man to affirm both incomparability and similarity is the fact that he was created "upon the form" of the all-comprehensive name (*al-ism al-jāmiʿ*), Allah. Hence he contains within himself all the attributes of God. The name Allah is the "coincidence of opposites," since it includes all the contrary names. So also man, the "all-comprehensive presence" (*al-ḥaḍrat al-jāmiʿa*), combines all opposite qualities within himself.

Following authority is the root to which returns every knowledge, whether it be derived from consideration, self-evidence (*ḍarūra*), or unveiling. But in following authority, people are ranked in levels:

Some of them follow the authority of their Lord. They are the highest group, the possessors of sound knowledge.

Some of them follow the authority of their rational faculties while being possessors of self-evident knowledges, such that, were anyone to try to make them fall into doubt through some possible affair, they would not accept it. Even though they know it is possible, they would never accept it. When this is mentioned to them, they say that the affair does not detract from self-evident knowledge. There are many examples of this, but I will not mention these—for the sake of weak souls, who might accept them, and that would lead to loss and foolishness.

Some of them follow the authority of their rational faculty in respect of what their reflection gives to it.

There are only these three groups, so following authority includes all knowers.

Following authority is a delimitation, so the cosmos never leaves its reality, for the cosmos is the delimited existent and its knowledge has to be delimited like itself. . . .

Since following authority is the ruler—there being no escape and no alternative—it is best to follow the Lord in the knowledge of Him which He has revealed through the Law. Do not swerve aside from that, for He has given you reports of Himself concerning knowledge of Him. Why should you follow the authority of your rational faculty, in respect of its following the authority of its reflection, which considers Him through its evidence and gives to you the contrary of what He has given concerning knowledge of Himself?

In the cosmos, the root is ignorance (*jahl*), while knowledge is acquired (*mustafād*). Knowledge is existence, and existence belongs to God, while ignorance is nonexistence, and nonexistence belongs to the cosmos. Hence it is best to follow the authority of the Real, who possesses Being, rather than the authority of him who is created like you. Just as you have acquired existence from Him, so also acquire knowledge from Him. Halt with the reports that He has given about Himself, and pay no regard to contradiction (*tanāquḍ*) in the reports, since each report dwells within a specific level, while you are the presence (*ḥaḍra*) which comprehends all those levels.

So stand "upon a clear sign" (11:17) from your Lord, and speak not on the basis of your rational faculty, since it will turn you over to none but itself. God created you only for Him, so let not your rational faculty take you away from Him.

When He discloses Himself to that which is self-evident to your reason, you will necessarily find that you are supported by something which you cannot know through following the authority of this rational self-evidence. When He discloses Himself to you in your reason's consideration, you will find in yourself that the Support of your existence is an ontological thing which is not similar to you, since your own entity and everything by which you are described is temporally originated and in need of One to bring it into existence, just like you. Your reason will say to you in respect of its consideration that "Nothing is like" this Existent in the cosmos. And you are the whole cosmos, since every part of the cosmos shares with the whole in denotation, as we have explained.

When He discloses Himself to you in the Law, He will explain to you the disparity of the levels of the cosmos. He will disclose Himself to you in each level. So follow the authority of the Lawgiver in that until you experience unveiling. Then you will see the situation in the form of yourself.

Therefore, follow the authority of your Lord. You will see Him declared similar and declared incomparable. You will gather together and separate, declare incomparable and declare similar. And all of this is you, since it is a divine self-disclosure in the levels, and you comprehend all of them. They all belong to you and to the cosmos. They determine the properties of everyone who becomes manifest within them. So He becomes colored by them in the eye of the observer. Hence we said that they belong "to you" and "all of this is you." For "worlds" derives from "mark" (*ʿalāma*), and a "mark" denotes only that which is limited (*maḥdūd*). Hence it only denotes you, since "God is Independent of the worlds" (3:97). Hence the cosmos does not denote knowledge of His Essence, only knowledge that He exists. (III 160.13)

5

Hermeneutics

12. FAITH AND RATIONAL INTERPRETATION

Though reason cannot grasp the full significance of God's Reality on its own, it provides the indispensable support for understanding His Unity. When Ibn al-ʿArabī criticizes the rational thinkers, for the most part he has in mind people who have faith in the prophetic message, not those who have rejected it completely. Reason is the tool of the theologians and philosophers who insist on interpreting the revealed texts in keeping with their own presuppositions. The outright unbelievers are hardly worth mentioning and can be dismissed with a wave of the hand, since no one can claim human status without faith in God. What then is faith?

Faith

The word "faith" (*īmān*) is derived from the root *ʾ.m.n.*, whose basic meaning is to be or to feel secure and safe, a sense also contained in the word *īmān*. To have faith is to feel secure concerning the knowledge one has received about God and to commit oneself to putting it into practice. *Īmān* is often employed synonymously with *taṣdīq*, which means to attest, declare or acknowledge someone's truthfulness. The theologians normally define "faith" as believing (*iʿtiqād*) or attesting (*taṣdīq*) in the heart and acknowledging with the tongue, though most of them add that this belief must also be put into practice (*ʿamal*) through following the Law. The fact that "heart" is mentioned should not lead us to think that belief is emotive, since the heart is the seat of reason and unveiling. The synonym *taṣdīq* brings this out clearly, since acknowledging someone's truthfulness means that one has recognized he is speaking the truth, and truth is understood through intelligence. Hence we see Ibn al-ʿArabī defining faith as a kind of knowledge, though he also differentiates it from knowledge in many passages. In the following he shows the difference between faith and the knowledge which comes by way of evidence and proofs (*dalīl*).

> There is no need for the messenger to provide proofs to those to whom he has been sent. . . . Hence, even when the proofs exist, we do not find everyone to

whom the message is sent having faith in it, only some of them. If the proof brought about the faith, everyone would have faith. Moreover, we see faith in those who have not been provided with proofs. This shows that faith is "a light which God throws into the heart of whomsoever He will of His servants."[1] Faith does not belong to the proof itself, so we do not make proofs its precondition.

Faith is a self-evident (*ḍarūrī*) knowledge which a person finds in his heart and is not able to repel. When someone gains faith through proofs, his faith cannot be relied upon, since he will be susceptible to obfuscations detracting from his faith, because it derives from rational consideration, not from self-evidence. (II 259.1)

It may happen that a messenger brings about a miracle (*muʿjiza*), that it is known that it is a miracle, and that the observers acquire knowledge of the truthfulness of the messenger, but that they are not given faith in him. "[When Our signs came to them visibly, they said, 'This is plain sorcery';] they denied them, though their souls acknowledged them, wrongfully and out of pride" (Koran 27:14). Hence you come to know that faith is not given by the furnishing of proofs. On the contrary, it is a divine "light which God throws into the heart of whomsoever He will of His servants." It may come after proofs, and it may come after no proof whatsoever, just as God says, "[You did not know what the Book was, nor faith;] but We made it a light, whereby We guide whom We will of Our servants" (42:52). (II 374.24)

"Belief" (*iʿtiqād*) does not coincide with "faith" as defined here. Before the detailed discussion of belief in Chapter 19, it will be sufficient to say that belief is to accept something as true, while faith is not only to accept it, but also to acknowledge it verbally and put it into practice.

Faith is speech (*qawl*), practice (*ʿamal*), and belief (*iʿtiqād*). Its reality is belief, according to both the Law and lexicography; it appears in speech and practice according to the Law, but not lexicography. The person of faith (*mu'min*) is he whose speech and act (*fiʿl*) accord with what he believes. That is why God says concerning the faithful, "[Upon the day when God will not degrade the Prophet and those who have faith with him,] their light running before them and on their right hands" (66:8). Here He means by "light" the righteous works with God which they had sent ahead. "[Men and women who have submitted, men and women who have faith . . .], for them God has prepared forgiveness and a mighty wage" (33:35). The Prophet said, "The person of faith is he before whom people feel secure (*amn*) with their possessions and themselves."[2] He also said, "The person of faith is he before whose calamities his neighbor feels secure."[3] (II 26.35)

One of the differences between knowledge and faith is that faith demands that we ascribe a truth to God, whereas knowledge of the same truth does not demand its ascription to anyone.

Iblis came to Jesus in the form of an old man of outward beauty. . . . He said to Jesus, "O Jesus, say 'There is no god but God'!", being satisfied that Jesus would obey his command to this extent.

Jesus replied, "I will say it, but not on the basis of your words. 'There is no god but God'." So Iblis went away defeated.

From here you come to know the difference between knowing something and having faith in it, and you will know that felicity lies in faith. Faith is to say what you know or what you used to say from your first messenger—who is [for example] Moses—on the basis of the words of this second messenger, who is Muḥammad. You do not say it on the basis of your knowledge of your first saying of it. Then you will be seen to have faith, and felicity will come to you. But when you do not say it on the basis of his words, but you make it appear that you said it on the basis of his words, then you are a hypocrite (*munāfiq*).

God says, "O you who have faith," meaning either the People of the Book—since they were saying what they were saying on the basis of their prophets Jesus or Moses—or anyone who had faith on the basis of the previous scriptures; hence He said, "O you who have faith." Then

He says to them, "Have faith in God" (Koran 4:136). In other words: Say, "There is no god but God," on the basis of Muḥammad's words, not on the basis of your knowledge of that, nor on the basis of your faith in your first prophet. [In the second case] you will bring together two faiths, and you will have two rewards. (I 283.4)

According to a famous hadith, "Every child is born according to primordial nature (*fiṭra*); then his parents make him into a Jew, a Christian, or a Zoroastrian."[4] This primordial nature first manifested itself at the Covenant made with God before the children of Adam entered into this world. It is woven out of faith.

Original faith (*al-īmān al-aṣlī*) is the primordial nature in accordance with which God created mankind. It is their witnessing to His Oneness (*waḥdāniyya*) at the taking of the Covenant. Hence every child is born in keeping with that Covenant. However, when he falls by means of the body into the confines of Nature—the place of forgetfulness—he becomes ignorant and forgets the state which he had had with his Lord. Hence, when he reaches the state which allows rational consideration, he needs to consider proofs concerning the oneness of his Creator. If he does not reach this state, his property is the same as that of his parents. If they had faith, he will take the declaration of God's Unity from them, as a following of authority. Whatever their religion might be, he joins with them.

He whose faith is a resolute following of authority is more protected and firm in his faith than he who takes it from proofs, because of the bewilderment, unsoundness, and obfuscations to which proofs are susceptible if he should be clever, astute, and strong in understanding. Hence he has no firm foot nor any leg upon which to stand. One must fear for him.

If the faith in the declaration of God's Unity which he gains should be preceded by an associating of others with Him (*shirk*) which he inherits from his parents, from his rational consideration, or from the community of which he is a member, then his [new-found] faith will be identical with his Covenant faith, nothing else. The veil of associating comes between the servant and the Covenant faith like a cloud which comes between the eye and the sun. When the cloud passes by, the sun appears to the eye. Such is the appearance of faith to the servant when associating others with God is eliminated, if the one who associates admits the existence of God. (II 616.19)

One of the means whereby God tests the truthfulness of faith is prescription of the Law.

When God created this human configuration and ennobled him as He did through the all-comprehensiveness (*jamʿiyya*) which He placed within him, He put within him claims (*daʿwā*) in order to perfect the form of his configuration, for making claims is a divine attribute. God says, "Verily I am God, there is no god but I; so worship Me!" (Koran 20:14). Hence He claims that there is no god but He, and this is a truthful claim. No argument is directed against anyone who makes a truthful claim, and he has authority over everyone who rejects his claim. . . .

A claim is a report, and in respect of being a report both truthfulness and falsehood may equally be attributed to it and understood from it. Hence we come to know that there must be testing. The person of faith claims faith, which is attestation to the fact of God's existence and His Unity, the fact that there is no god but He, that "Everything is annihilated except His Face" (28:88), and that "To God belongs the affair, before and after" (30:4). When he claims with his tongue that this is what is enfolded within his breast and fastened in his heart, it is plausible that he may be truthful in his claim to possess this attribute, and it is plausible that he may be lying in claiming to possess it. So God tests him—to establish the argument for or against him—through the worship that He has prescribed for him in the Law. (III 248.18)

Like prescription of the Law, the sending of prophets itself is a means whereby God tests His servants. Ibn al-ʿArabī makes this point while discussing the nature of envy (*ḥasad*).

Had God willed, He would have given each person knowledge of the causes of his felicity and explained to him the proper way for him to pursue. However, He only willed to send to each community a messenger of their own kind, not of another kind. He placed the messenger before them and commanded them to follow him and to obey him, as a trial from Him, in order to set up an argument against them because of His precedent knowledge concerning them. . . .

The vicegerent of the people
  is a son of their own kind
since that is more annoying
  to their souls;
Were he not one of them,
  they would declare his truthfulness,
for they would have no envy
  toward other than their own kind.

Man knows that the beasts and all animals are below himself in level. Suppose an animal were to speak—even a black beetle—and were to say, "I am a messenger from God to you. I warn you of such and such. Do such and such!" There would be many among the common people claiming to follow it and to seek blessing from it and venerate it. Kings would obey it and they would not seek from it any sign of its truthfulness. They would make its speech the very sign of its truthfulness, even were it not so. But since other than their own kind had reached this level, they do not envy it at all. Hence, the first trial with which God tries His creatures is His sending the messengers to them from among themselves, not from other than themselves. (III 83.12)

According to the Koran, "God is the Light of the heavens and the earth" (24:35), and for Ibn al-ʿArabī as for other Sufis, His light becomes manifest not only through existence itself but also through knowledge. Thus Ibn al-ʿArabī defines *tajallī* or God's "self-disclosure," in the broadest epistemological sense of the term, as "the lights of unseen things that are unveiled to hearts" (II 485.20). Among the many forms of light or divine self-disclosure which become manifest in the cosmos is the light of knowledge, "which dispels the darkness of ignorance from the soul" (II 154.27). Likewise reason, which perceives knowledge, may also be called a light. But faith is brighter than knowledge or reason, since faith can perceive not only the knowledge of incomparability, which is accessible to the independent rational faculty, but also the knowledge of similarity perceived by imagination.

Reason possesses a light through which it perceives specific affairs, while faith possesses a light through which it perceives everything, as long as there is no obstruction. Through the light of reason, you reach the knowledge of the Divinity, what is necessary for it and impossible, and what is permitted for it and not impossible. Through the light of faith, reason perceives the knowledge of the Essence and the attributes which God ascribed to Himself. (I 44.32)

Though the created thing's knowledge has a perfect excellence whose rank is not unknown, nothing bestows felicity through nearness to God except faith. Hence the light of faith in the created thing is more excellent than the light of knowledge not accompanied by faith. But when faith is actualized along with knowledge, the light of that knowledge, born from the light of faith, is higher. Through it the person of faith who has knowledge (*al-muʾmin al-ʿālim*) surpasses the person of faith who does not have knowledge. For "God raises up . . . those" of the faithful "who have been given knowledge in degrees" (58:11) over those of the faithful who have not been given knowledge. He means here knowledge of God, for God's Messenger said to his companions, "You are more knowledgeable [than I] in the best interests of this world of yours."[5] (I 144.27)

According to the tasting of our path, it is not possible to attest to a messenger through rational proofs (*dalāla*), only through a divine self-disclosure in respect of His name "Light." When the person's inward dimension (*bāṭin*) becomes colored by that light, then he attests to the messenger. This is the light of faith. Another person does not actualize in himself anything of that light, even though in respect of rational proofs he knows that the messenger is speaking the truth. But he does not know this fact as a light thrown into the heart. Hence such people deny in spite of their knowledge. This is indicated by God's words, "They denied them, though their souls acknowledged them, wrongfully and out of pride" (27:14). Below them in this level is he about whom God says, "God has misguided him in spite of knowledge" (45:23). This knowledge is the light of knowledge of Him, not the light of faith. (II 305.35)

Ibn al-ʿArabī does not claim that a person without faith cannot enter paradise, but he does claim that only knowledge of the declaration of God's Unity (*tawḥīd*) can save without faith. The Koran declares that God can forgive any sin except *shirk* or "associating others with God," the opposite of *tawḥīd* (4:48, 4:116).

God ordained felicity for His servants through faith and knowledge of the declaration of God's Unity specifically. There is no way to felicity other than these two. Faith's objects are the reports brought by the messengers from God. Faith is an unadulterated following of authority. We accept the reports whether or not we have knowledge of them. Knowledge is that which is given by rational consideration or divine unveiling. If this knowledge is not actualized as self-evident, such that no obfuscations can detract from it for the knower, then it is not knowledge. (III 78.12)

In discussing a long hadith about intercession (*shafāʿa*) on the day of resurrection, Ibn al-ʿArabī explains that the last part of the hadith, where God Himself, the "Most Merciful of the merciful," removes from the Fire a group "who had never done any good," refers to the deliverance of those who had knowledge of *tawḥīd*, but not faith in it.[6]

Once intercession has taken place, no one who had faith in a Law will remain in the Fire, nor any person who did a work laid down by a Law in respect of its being laid down by the Law on the tongue of a prophet, even if it is the weight of a mustard seed or less than that in size. All will be taken out by the intercession of the prophets and the faithful. There will remain the people of *tawḥīd*, those who knew *tawḥīd* through rational proofs and did not associate anything with God, though they had no faith in a Law and "had never done any good whatsoever" in respect of their following one of the prophets. They have not a dust mote of faith, or they have even less. They will be brought out by the "Most Merciful of the merciful," though "they had never done any good," that is, any act laid down in a Law in respect of its being laid down in a Law. There is no good greater than faith, but that is a good which they did not do.

The following is a hadith related by ʿUthmān quoted in Muslim's *Ṣaḥīḥ*: The Messenger of God said, "He who dies, knowing"—he did not say "having faith"—"that there is no god but God will enter the Garden."[7] Nor did he say, "saying"; on the contrary, he mentioned only knowledge. God has precedent solicitude toward such as these in the Fire, since the Fire, by its very essence, cannot accept everlastingly in any respect one who declares God's Unity. The most complete mode of *tawḥīd* is faith on the basis of knowledge, such that the two are brought together.

You may object, "Iblis knows that God is One." I reply: You are right, but he was the first to set down associating others with God as a custom (*awwal man sann al-shirk*). Therefore he must bear the punishment of those who associate,[8] and their punishment is that they do not come out of the Fire. This holds if it is established that he died declaring God's Unity. But how do you know? Perhaps he died associating others with Him because of some obfuscation which came over him in his rational consideration (*naẓar*). We have already spoken of this question in earlier chapters. So Iblis will never leave the Fire. (I 314.9)

Just as reflection and consideration can act as a nearly irremovable "talisman" upon man's reason, so also they can cause "intoxication." Many Sufis employed the terms intoxication (*sukr*) and sobriety (*ṣaḥw*) to indicate two "states" which mark the two basic modes in which the travelers experience the divine self-disclosures. In discussing intoxication as a standard Sufi term of this sort, Ibn al-ʿArabī shows that it can be applied on three basic levels, the same three levels that he perceives in many other realities. These are the "natural" (*ṭabīʿī*), the rational or intelligible (*ʿaqlī*), and the divine (*ilāhī*), corresponding to sense perception (including imagination), reason and spirit, and God.[9]

God says, "Rivers of wine, a pleasure to the drinkers" (47:15). This is the science of states (*aḥwāl*), so intoxication belongs to him within whom there is delight and pleasure. The Sufis have defined it as "An absence (*ghayba*) brought about by a strong inrush (*wārid*)," but it is only an "absence" from everything that contradicts joy, delight, happiness, and the disclosure of wishes (*amānī*) as forms subsisting within the entity of the possessor of this state.

The Men of Allah are ranked in levels in intoxication, as we shall mention, God willing:

The first is "natural intoxication." It is the delight, pleasure, joy, and happiness found by souls through the inrush of wishes, when those wishes stand up before them in their imagination as forms subsisting within it which they govern and control. Their poet says,

When I become intoxicated,
  I am lord of palace and throne.

He sees the fact that he owns these things as the utmost limit of his wish. When he is intoxicated, the form of palace and throne stand up before him as his possessions which he controls within the presence of his imagining and imagination. This is given to him by the state of intoxication, since it has a strong effect upon the imaginal faculty. Those of the Folk of Allah who halt with imagination possess this natural intoxication, since they never cease examining those affairs desired by them which can be actualized through imagination. Finally that becomes firm with them and rules over them, like the Prophet's words, "Worship God as if you see Him" or like His words, "God is in the kibla of him who performs the prayer." . . . In the case of some of those who achieve this station, God causes the imaginalized form to remain with them in the state of their sobriety. He establishes it for them as a sensory object after it had been imaginal. This was the case with the garden which Iblis made to appear to Solomon at the level of discontiguous imagination (*al-khayāl al-munfaṣil*) in order to tempt him, while Solomon knew nothing of that. He prostrated himself to God in gratitude for His giving it to him, so God made it subsist for him as a garden to enjoy at the sensory level, and Iblis went away a loser. . . .

"Rational intoxication" is similar to natural intoxication in that it takes things back to that which its own reality requires, not to that which is required by the situation in itself. The divine report comes from God to the possessor of this station making attributes of temporally originated things the attributes of God. So he refuses to accept these things in this mode, since he is intoxicated by his proof and demonstration. Hence he rejects the report in accordance with what his own consideration requires, while he is ignorant of God's Essence and whether or not It accepts this description. Or rather, he imagines that It does not accept it. Hence, because of its intoxication, this rational faculty stretches out its legs on another's carpet. He falls on God because of his intoxication, and God excuses him in that, since the drunkard is not taken to task for what he says. For he disengages from God that which God has attributed to Himself.

When this man of reason, after having been intoxicated, becomes sober through faith, he no longer rejects the truthful report and the true word. He says: "God knows better about Himself and what He attributes to Himself than reason, for reason is a created thing, and the created thing cannot judge the Creator." Everything made is ignorant of its maker, for the garment is ignorant of the weaver; such also are the elements (*arkān*) in relation to the celestial spheres, and such also are the spheres in relation to the Soul, the Soul in relation to the Intellect, and the Intellect in relation to God. The most any of those who know can know is their poverty toward their maker and their being supported by him in their existence. None of them can judge anything about its maker, especially when the maker gives reports about himself in certain affairs. The thing which is made can only accept the reports. If it rejects them, that is because it is intoxicated.

The wine which reason drinks is its proof and its demonstration. It is helped in that by the descriptions which it is given by certain divine reports which agree with its demonstration and proof. Such is an intoxication of reason. Natural intoxication is the intoxication of the faithful, while rational intoxication is the intoxication of the gnostics.

There remains the intoxication of the perfect among the Men. It is intoxication with God. The Messenger of God said concerning it, "O God, increase my bewilderment in Thee!",[10] for the drunkard is bewildered. (II 544.16)

Interpretation

Faith demands unquestioning acceptance of the divine reports that have come through revelation, while reason interprets anything which it does not consider appropriate for the Divine Reality. The word Ibn al-ʿArabī uses for this type of interpretation is *ta'wīl*, a Koranic term employed in seventeen verses, though not in a blameworthy sense. The literal meaning of the term is to return, to take back, and to take back to the origin. By extension it means to discover, explain, and interpret. Many Muslim authorities held that *ta'wīl* and *tafsīr* or "commentary" are basically synonymous when applied to the Koran, but most authorities drew various distinctions between the two terms, with *ta'wīl* normally designating a more mystical and esoteric sort of interpretation. The history of these two terms and their interrelationship is one of the many monographs on Islamic thought waiting to be written. In the present context, we can only look at Ibn al-ʿArabī's own use of the term *ta'wīl*.

Those who have been introduced to Ibn al-ʿArabī through the writings of Henry Corbin have learned that *ta'wīl* is one of the cornerstones of his thought. One cannot object to Corbin for saying that Ibn al-ʿArabī interprets the verses of the Koran, but one can object to his choosing the word *ta'wīl* to designate the process, since Ibn al-ʿArabī does not use it in the positive sense in which Corbin understands it.[11] Without doubt, Corbin was led to employ the term because of *ta'wīl*'s primary importance in Shiʿite thought. As he remarks, "It is not possible to utter the word *ta'wīl* without suggesting Shīʿism."[12] Corbin means to imply that Ibn al-ʿArabī leaned toward Shiʿite beliefs, but in fact Corbin is merely expressing his own conviction that anyone as important as Ibn al-ʿArabī had to be influenced by Shiʿism.[13] This is not to claim that Ibn al-ʿArabī never employs the term *ta'wīl* in a positive sense corresponding roughly to what Corbin had in mind. But such rare passages—one is quoted below—invariably speak of *ta'wīl* in its Koranic context and do not contradict Ibn al-ʿArabī's generally critical views of *ta'wīl*.

For the most part, Ibn al-ʿArabī considers *ta'wīl* as interpretation of the Koran and the sayings of the Prophet in a way that will not compromise the principles of rational thought. Instead of having faith in the literal accuracy of the revelation and trying to understand it on God's terms (e.g., through the practice of the religion and "godfearing"), the interpreter accepts the supremacy of reason and its ability to judge all things. In effect, reason becomes the scale in which everything else must be weighed, including the Word of God. Practically all modern hermeneutics and scriptural exegesis fit neatly into the category of *ta'wīl* as Ibn al-ʿArabī understands it.

Perhaps the most famous Koranic usage of the term *ta'wīl*, frequently cited in Shiʿite sources, is the following:

> It is He who sent down upon thee the Book, wherein are verses which are the Mother of the Book, and others ambiguous. As for those in whose hearts is swerving, they follow the ambiguous part, desiring dissension, and desiring its interpretation; but none knows its interpretation, save only God and those firmly rooted in knowledge; they say, "We have faith in it; all is from our Lord" (3:7).

The above reading of the verse is followed by those who maintain that *ta'wīl* is a valid mode of knowledge, such as most Shiʿites. But many authorities read the verse with a full stop separating "God" and "those firmly rooted in knowledge": "None knows its interpretation save only God. And those firmly rooted in knowledge say, 'We have faith in it'." Ibn al-ʿArabī accepts the first reading, but without ignoring the implications of the sentence "We have faith in it." In the following passage, he explains this verse while commenting upon another Koranic verse, "Had they performed the Torah and the Gospel, and what was sent down to them from their Lord, they would have eaten both what was above them, and what was beneath their feet. Some of them are a moderate people, but many of them—evil are the things they do!" (5:66).

> Know, dear friend—God illuminate your insight and beautify your awareness—that the sciences are of two kinds: One kind is bestowed (*mawhūb*). It is referred to in God's words, "They would have eaten what was above them" (5:66). It is the result of godfearing, as God has said, "Be godfearing, and God will teach you" (2:282). He also said, "If you are godfearing, He will give you discrimination" (8:29). And He said, "The All-merciful: He taught the Koran" (55:1–2).
>
> The second kind of sciences is earned (*muktasab*). God alludes to it in His words, "what was beneath their feet," alluding to their hard work (*kadd*) and their effort (*ijtihād*). These are the people of "moderation." . . .
>
> [The ones upon whom the sciences are bestowed] are the ones who lift up the Book of God and that which has been sent down to them from their Lord. They are the ones who "vie in good works, outracing to them" (23:61). Some of them outrace to good works, and others lift up the Book from its bed, since interpretation on the part of the learned (*ʿulamā'*) has made the Book lie down after it had been standing. The person to whom God has given success comes and makes the Book stand up after it had been lying down. In other words, he declares it incomparable with his own interpretation and exerting effort through reflection. Hence he stands up in worship of his Lord and asks Him to give him success in understanding what He meant by the words included in the Book and revelation, that is, the meanings themselves, purified of substrata. Then God gives to such people untainted knowledge. God says, "None knows its interpretation, save only God and those firmly rooted in knowledge." God teaches them that to which the written, revealed word goes back (*mā ya'ūl ilayhi*), that is, the meanings He had deposited within it. They do not employ their reflection, since in itself reflection is not preserved from error for anyone. That is why God says, "And those firmly rooted in knowledge; they say, . . . 'Our Lord, make not our hearts to swerve,'" in other words, through reflecting upon what Thou hast sent down, "after Thou hast guided us" to take from Thee the knowledge which Thou hast sent down upon us. "And bestow upon us mercy from Thee; Thou art the Bestower" (3:8). Hence they asked Him in respect of bestowal, not in respect of earning. . . .
>
> The verse continues, "Some of them are a moderate people." These are the people of earning, who interpret God's Book and do not make it stand up through the practice for the sake of which it was sent down. They do not observe courtesy (*adab*) in taking it. These people are of two types:
>
> A few of them are the "moderate" in that. They are the ones who draw near to the truth, and they may achieve the truth in what they interpret, in virtue of compatibility, but not by virtue of certitude, for they do not know exactly what God meant in what He sent down, since that can only be known by way of bestowal,

which is a divine report-giving by which God addresses the heart of the servant within the mystery (*sirr*) which stands between them.

The second type are they who are not moderate but instead plunge deeply into interpretation such that no correspondence (*munāsaba*) remains between the revealed words and the meaning. Or else they establish the words by way of declaring similarity and do not refer the knowledge of it back to God. They are the ones concerning whom God says, in the same verse, "But many of them—evil are the things they do!" (II 594.28)

One of the first negative results of *ta'wīl* is that it weakens faith.

The degrees of nearness to God are made known by the knowledge of the Lawgiver, who acts as God's spokesman. God commanded us to have faith in the Koran's clear (*muḥkam*) and ambiguous (*mutashābih*) verses. Let us accept everything that the Prophet has brought, for if we interpret any of it, saying, "In fact, this is what the Speaker meant by His words," then the degree of faith will disappear from us. Our proof will rule over the report, thereby rendering the ruling property of faith ineffectual.

When this happens, the person of faith comes forward with sound knowledge. He says to the person who has this proof: "Your certitude that your consideration has allowed you to understand the aim of the Clarifier in that which He has clearly spoken is ignorance itself and the lack of sound knowledge. Even if it happens to coincide with knowledge, your faith has left you, and felicity is tied to faith and to sound knowledge based upon doctrine. 'Sound knowledge' is that along with which faith remains." (II 660.7)

The person who interprets the revealed reports has faith in his own interpretation, not in the reports. Hence he is not able to escape from his own limitations.

The messengers and the divine knowledge-giving brought that which rational faculties declare impossible. Hence the rational faculties were forced to interpret some of it in order to accept it, and to submit and admit their incapacity in other affairs which accepted no interpretation whatsoever. The upshot was that a person had to say: "This affair has an aspect known only to God and inaccessible to our rational faculties." All of this is to make souls feel comfortable—it is not knowledge—in order that they will not reject anything brought by prophecy. And this is the state of the intelligent person of faith, while he who has no faith accepts none of this.

Many reports have been revealed which rational faculties declare impossible, some concerning the Highest Side, and others concerning realities and the overturning of entities. That which concerns the Highest Side includes everything requiring faith by which God described Himself in His Book and upon the tongue of His messengers and the outward significance (*ẓāhir*) of which reason cannot accept on the basis of its proofs, only by means of interpreting it with some far-fetched interpretation. Then reason's faith is in its own interpretation, not in the report. . . .

The views of the rational and reflective thinkers concerning God diverge in accordance with the measure of their consideration. The god worshiped by reason devoid of faith is as if he were—or rather, he is—a god put there in accordance with what has been given by that rational faculty's consideration. Hence the god's reality is diverse in respect to each rational faculty, and rational faculties conflict. Each group among the people of rational faculties declares that the others are ignorant of God. Even if they should be Muslim considerative thinkers all of whom interpret, each group declares the others unbelievers.

But no disagreement has been related from the messengers, from Adam down to Muḥammad, concerning the descriptions they attribute to God. On the contrary, all of them speak with a single tongue. All the books they brought speak about God in a single tongue. No two of them disagree. Some of them attest to the truth of the others, in spite of the great lengths of time and the prophets' not having met. . . .

In the same way, those who have faith "upon insight"—the Muslims who have surrendered (*taslīm*) themselves and do not allow themselves to enter into interpretation—are either of two people. They are either a man who has faith and has surrendered and turned over the knowledge of all to God until he dies, thus being a follower of authority (*muqallid*), or a man who puts into practice the branches of the rulings (*furūʿ al-aḥkām*) which he knows and who has firm faith in that which the messengers and books have brought. Then God lifts the veil from his insight and makes him a possessor of insight in his own situation, just as He did with His Prophet and Messenger and the people toward whom He was solicitous. He gave them unveiling and insight, and they called to God "upon insight," just as God said concerning His Prophet, giving news on his behalf: "I call to God upon insight, I and whoever follows after me" (12:108). Those who "follow after him" are the knowers through God, the gnostics. Though they are neither messengers nor prophets, they "stand upon a clear sign"[14] from their Lord in their knowledge of Him and what has come from Him. (I 218.21)

Many of the learned have interpreted the Law in order to gain favor with those in power and thereby attain to high positions. Ibn al-ʿArabī frequently criticizes the worldly *ʿulamāʾ* for this shortcoming.

When the winds of caprice dominate over souls and the learned seek high degrees with kings, they leave the clear path and incline toward far-fetched interpretations. Thus they are able to walk with the personal desires of the kings in that within which their souls have a caprice, and the kings can support themselves by a Shariʿite command. It may happen that the jurist (*faqīh*) does not himself believe the interpretation, but he gives pronouncements (*fatwā*) in accordance with it. We have seen a group of the judges and jurists who were like this.

Al-Malik al-Ẓāhir Ghāzī ibn al-Malik al-Nāṣir Ṣalāḥ al-Dīn ibn Ayyūb[15] reported to me, after we had discussed such things, as follows: He called a slave and said, "Bring me the wallet." I said to him, "What is the story of the wallet?" He replied, "You are ignorant of the ugly things (*munkarāt*) and the wrongdoing (*ẓulm*) that go on in my country and kingdom. I, by God, believe as you do, that all of it is ugly. But, by God, my friend, not a single ugly thing happens without the legal pronouncement of a jurist. I have his own handwriting with me saying it is permissible. So God's curse be upon them!

"A jurist named so and so," and he specified for me the most excellent jurist of his country in religion and mortification (*taqashshuf*), "gave me a pronouncement that it is not necessary to fast during the month of Ramaḍān itself. On the contrary, what is obligatory for me is fasting during one month of the year, and I can choose it myself. So," said the sultan, "I cursed him inwardly and did not show that to him. He is so and so," and he named him for me. God have mercy on all of them!

You should know that God has given Satan power from the Presence of Imagination. He has given him an authority from it. Hence, when Satan sees a jurist inclining toward an act of caprice which will ruin him with God, he embellishes for him his evil action by means of a strange interpretation which will provide it with a good aspect in his rational consideration. (III 69.30)

The Rational Thinkers

Both Kalām and philosophy based their views of God on reflection and rational consideration. Ibn al-ʿArabī discusses their positions in all sorts of contexts and his remarks deserve detailed scholarly attention. He criticizes them mainly for their reliance upon reflection, which, in his view, undermines whatever they say. He makes this point while explaining how man should "take heed" (*iʿtibār*) as is urged by the Koran.

Among the people who take heed are possessors of tasting. They take heed on the basis of tasting, not reflection. Taking heed may also be based on reflection. The stranger to these matters is confused by the form, and concerning each he says, "This is one who takes heed." He does not know that taking heed may derive from reflection or from tasting and that taking heed in the people of tasting is the root, while in the people of reflection it is the branch. . . .

Is there anything which cannot be reached by way of unveiling and finding? We say that there is nothing, and we forbid reflection totally, since it makes its possessor heir to deceit and lack of sincerity. There is nothing whose knowledge cannot be attained through unveiling and finding. In contrast, occupying oneself with reflection is a veil. Others refuse to accept this, though not a single one of the Folk who follow Allah's path refuses it. Those who refuse belong to the people of consideration and reasoning among the exoteric scholars, those who have not tasted the states. If they had only tasted the states—like the divine Plato among the sages! But that is rare among these people. If they had only found their breath emerging from the place where the breath of the People of Unveiling and Finding emerges!

Those among the people of Islam who dislike Plato only dislike him because of his relationship to philosophy and because of their ignorance of the meaning of this word. In reality the "sages" are those who know God and all things and who also know the station of that which is known. And God, "He is the Sage, the All-knowing" (Koran 43:84). "He who has been given wisdom has been given much good" (2:269). Wisdom is the knowledge of prophecy, as God said about David: "God gave him the kingship and wisdom, and He taught him such as He willed" (2:251). The meaning of "philosopher" is lover of wisdom, since *sophia* in Greek is "wisdom," and *phil* is "love," so the word means "love of wisdom." Every man of intelligence loves wisdom.

However, the mistakes of the People of Reflection in the divine things (*ilāhiyyāt*) are more than their hitting the mark, whether they are philosophers, Muʿtazilites, Ashʿarites or any other sort of the people of consideration. Hence philosophers are not blamed only because of this name. They are blamed because they make errors in the knowledge of God by opposing the reports brought by the messengers. They did this by judging through consideration on the basis of their corrupt reflection concerning the root of prophecy and messengerhood and concerning that by which these two are supported. Hence the situation became confused for them.

If, while loving wisdom, they had sought it from God, not from reflection, they would have hit the mark in everything. As for the people of consideration among the Muslims other than the philosophers, such as the Muʿtazilites and the Ashʿarites, Islam had already reached them and exercised its property over them. Then they began to defend it in accordance with what they understood from it. So they have hit the mark at the root and are mistaken in some of the branches, since they interpret Islam in accordance with what they are given by their reflection and rational proofs. They hold that if they were to apply to God some of the words of the Lawgiver in accordance with the outward significance of the words, while the proofs of reason hold this to be impossible, they would fall into unbelief. Hence they interpret these words. They do not know that God has a faculty in some of His servants which bestows a judgment different from what the rational faculty bestows in certain affairs, while it agrees with reason in others. This is a station which is outside the stage of reason, so reason cannot perceive it on its own. No one has faith in [what reason holds to be impossible] except him who has this faculty in his person. He knows reason's incapacity and the truth of what it denies.

Faculties are ranked in degrees, and they provide [knowledge] in keeping with the realities according to which God has brought them into existence. Thus, if the property of sight were presented to the faculty of hearing, it would declare it impossible, and so on with all the faculties. Reason is one of the faculties. Or rather, it acquires from all the faculties, while it gives nothing to any of them. . . .

Everyone who makes a mistake is mistaken only in the relationship. He attributes something where it does not belong. The Folk of Allah take the relationship and put it in its proper place, joining it to its object. This is the meaning of "wisdom," since the Folk of Allah—the messengers and the friends of God—are the sages in reality, and they are the people of "much good." (II 523.2)

Certain of the Muʿtazilites came close to Ibn al-ʿArabī's position on the question of the "nonexistence" of the entities. He often supports them on this and criticizes the Ashʿarites, though he also points out that the Muʿtazilites did not perceive the whole picture.

The Prophet related that God said, "I was a Treasure but was not known. So I loved to be known, and I created the creatures and made Myself known to them. Then they came to know Me." In the words, "I was a Treasure," one finds an affirmation of the immutable entities which were upheld by the Muʿtazilites. (II 232.11)

Know that there are three objects of knowledge, without a fourth. The first is Nondelimited Being, which does not become delimited. This is the Being of God, the Necessary Being through Himself. The second object of knowledge is nondelimited nothingness, which is nonexistence in itself. It never becomes delimited. It is the impossible (*al-muḥāl*). It stands opposite Nondelimited Being. . . .

Two contradictories never stand opposite each other without a separator (*fāṣil*) through which each is distinguished from the other and which prevents the one from being described by the attribute of the other. If a scale were to judge this reality which separates Nondelimited Being from nothingness, it would find its measure equal, without increase or decrease. This is the Supreme Barzakh, or the Barzakh of Barzakhs. It possesses a face toward Being and a face toward nothingness. It stands opposite each of these two known things in its very essence. It is the third known thing. Within it are all possible things. It is infinite, just as each of the other two known things is infinite.

The possible things have immutable entities within this Barzakh in the respect in which Nondelimited Being looks upon them. In this respect the possible things are called "things." When God wants to bring a "thing" into existence, He says to it, "Be!", and it is. In the respect in which nondelimited nothingness gazes upon the Barzakh, it has no existent entities. Hence God says "Be!", which is a word denoting existence (*ḥarf wujūdī*). If the thing had already come to be (*kāʾin*), He would not have said to it "Be!" . . . The possible things exist in respect of this Barzakh. Through them God has a vision of the things before they come to be. When any human being who possesses an imagination and the power to imagine imagines something, his gaze extends into this Barzakh, though he does not know that he is looking upon that thing in this presence.

In relation to the entities which are embraced by this Barzakh, the existent possible things which God brings into existence are like shadows in relation to corporeal bodies. Or rather, they are the true shadows. It is they which God described as prostrating themselves to Him along with the prostration of their entities,[16] for those entities never cease prostrating themselves to Him before they come into existence. So when their shadows come into existence, they come into existence prostrating themselves to God, since their entities from which they come into existence have prostrated themselves to God. These shadows are heaven, earth, sun, moon, star, mountain, tree, crawling creature, and every existent thing. . . .

The Barzakh Presence is the shadow of Nondelimited Being in respect of the name "Light" (*al-nūr*), which is ascribed to God's Being. That is why we call it a shadow. The existence of the entities [in the cosmos] is the shadow of that shadow. Sensory shadows are the shadows of these existent things within the sensory world. Since the property of a shadow is to disappear, not to remain immutable, and since the possible things—even if they exist—have the property of nonexistence, they are called "shadows" to separate them from Him who has nondelimited immutability in Being, that is, the Necessary Being, and from that which has nondelimited immutability in nothingness, that is, the impossible. Thus the levels are distinguished.

When the existent entities become manifest, they are within this Barzakh, for there is no presence into which they go in order to gain the state of existence. Within the existent entities, the existence that becomes actualized (*ḥuṣūl*) is finite, but bringing into existence (*ījād*) is infinite. So there is no existent form which is not identical to its own immutable entity, while existence is like its clothing (*thawb*). . . .

If you have doubts about the situation of this Barzakh and are of the Folk of Allah, look at His words, "He let forth the two seas that meet together, between them a *barzakh* they do not overpass" (Koran 55:19). In other words, if not for that *barzakh*, the two would not be distinguished from each other and the situation would be confused, and this would lead to the overturning of the realities (*qalb al-ḥaqā'iq*).

There are never two opposite things unless there is a *barzakh* between them "which they do not overpass." In other words, the one thing is not described by those attributes of the other through which the distinction between them is made. . . .

The Barzakh is like the dividing line between existence and nonexistence. It is neither existent nor nonexistent. If you attribute it to existence, you will find a whiff of existence within it, since it is immutable. But if you attribute it to nonexistence, you will speak the truth, since it has no existence. I wonder at the Ashʿarites! How could they reject him who says that the nonexistent is a thing in the state of its nonexistence and that first it possesses an immutable entity, then existence is added to the entity? . . .

The reason that immutability is attributed to this Barzakh, which is the possible thing between Being and nothingness, is that it stands opposite the two things by its very essence. This is as follows: Nondelimited nothingness stands before Nondelimited Being like a mirror. Within the mirror, Being sees its own form. This form is the entity of the possible thing. That is why the possible thing has an immutable entity and a thingness in the state of its nonexistence, and that is why it comes out in the form of Nondelimited Being. That also is why it is qualified by infinity, and it is said concerning it that it is infinite. (III 46.27, 47.25)

Acts of God and Acts of Man

Nothing is as crucial to an understanding of the nature of our own existence as the immutable entities—or call them the possible things, the existent/nonexistent things, the creatures, the objects of God's knowledge, the loci of manifestation. We have seen that Ibn al-ʿArabī's own position on the things can be epitomized by the expression He/not He. The things pertain to "imagination," since they are neither existent nor nonexistent.

The nature of the things was constantly discussed and disputed in Kalām. Most commonly, however, the problem was posed in terms of human acts (*afʿāl*) or works (*aʿmāl*). Clearly God created man, but to what extent or in what respect does He also create his acts? If we say in every respect, then our perception of free choice is false and the sending of the prophets becomes meaningless. But if we say that man is free, what happens to God's omnipotence? In short, this problem brings up the question of free will and predestination, surely the perennial theological stumbling block. Ibn al-ʿArabī's allusions to the theologians most often occur within this context.

As is well known, the Ashʿarites upheld the view that the acts belong to God, and thus they stressed predestination. In contrast, the Muʿtazilites attributed the acts to the servant, thus upholding free choice. In attributing the acts to one side or the other, each group took an extreme position, and Ibn al-ʿArabī praises them for this, since they thereby avoided "associating" (*shirka*) God with the creatures or the creatures with God. Both upheld the declaration of unity (*tawḥīd*), though here we see Ibn al-ʿArabī employing this word in a sense not usually given to it.[17] He is in the midst of discussing the nature of the "motion" (*ḥaraka*) which is found in the sensory realm:

People disagree as to the cause of this motion. Is its cause life, the world of the breaths (*ʿālam al-anfās*),[18] or nothing other than the divine command?

Know that the real situation is the existence of the divine command in the world of the breaths. The command turns toward this engendered world and brings it into motion, while the cosmos accepts the motion through its nature. In the same way, wind turns toward the trees to bring them into motion through its blowing. The observer sees the motion of the branches because of the blowing of the wind. Knowledge sees that if the branches were not free to move in their places, they would not find the wind when it blows. So they have a governing property over the wind in one respect, and no property in another respect. The goal to be realized by the wind bringing the trees into motion is the elimination of the corrupt vapors of the trees, so that there may not be deposited within them that which causes illness and disease in the cosmos when animals feed upon the trees. . . . Hence the blowing of the winds is directed toward the best interest of the cosmos. . . . So the wind is a secondary cause which is desired and which leaves no effect upon what it causes, since here the effect belongs to Him who set up the secondary causes and made them a veil over Himself, in order that the creatures may be distinguished according to their excellence in recognizing God and in order that he who associates others with Him will be separated from him who declares His Unity.

He who associates others is absolutely ignorant, since association in this sort of affair is not correct in any respect, for the bringing of acts into existence does not take place through association. That is why the Muʿtazilites did not join up with those who associate, since they declared the unity of the acts of the servants in the servants. They did not give the servants any associates. They attributed the acts to the servants in accordance with reason, while the Law declares that they spoke the truth in that. The Ashʿarites declared the unity of the acts of all possible things in God without any classification according to reason, while the Law supports them in that, though only through certain plausible senses (*muḥtamalāt wujūh*) of its address. The arguments of the Muʿtazilites are stronger outwardly, while the position of the Ashʿarites in this is stronger in the view of the people of unveiling among the Folk of Allah. But both groups are upholders of *tawḥīd*. (II 629.33)

The Ashʿarite position is strong in the view of unveiling because in the final analysis, everything returns to God, and this is seen most clearly through visionary experience.

I was not able to free myself to ascribe the creation of works to one of the two sides [that is, God or man]. It was difficult for me to distinguish between the "performance" (*kasb*) upheld by one group [the Ashʿarites] and the "creation" upheld by another group [the Muʿtazilites]. Then God acquainted me through a visual unveiling (*kashf baṣarī*) with His creation of the first created thing, before which there was no created thing, since there was none but God. He said to me, "Is there anything here that gives rise to obscurity and bewilderment?"

I replied that there was nothing. He said, "So also is every temporally originated thing that you see. No one and no creature has any effect upon any of them. I create the things at (*ʿind*) the secondary causes, not by means of the secondary causes, so they come to be at My command. . . ."

I said to Him, "What dost Thou say if I should address Thy words,'Do!' and 'Do not do!' "

He replied, "If I should make something clear to you, observe courtesy, since the Presence does not put up with dispute (*muḥāqaqa*)."

I said, "But that is exactly what we are doing. And who is the disputer, and who the observer of courtesy? For Thou art the Creator of courtesy and dispute. If Thou shouldst create dispute, there is no escape from its property, and if Thou shouldst create courtesy, there is no escape from it."

He said, "So it is. Therefore listen when the Koran is recited and give ear to it."

I said, "That belongs to Thee. Create listening so that I may listen and create giving ear so that I may give ear. And nothing addresses Thee now save that which Thou hast created."

He said, "I create only what I know, and I know only the object of knowledge as it actually is. 'To God belongs the conclusive argument' (6:149).[19] I have already let you know this, so cling to it in witnessing, since there is nothing else.

Then your mind will be at ease. But do not be secure until the prescription of the Law is cut off, and it will not be cut off until you cross over the Narrow Bridge. Then people will worship by their own essences, not by the command or prohibition demanded by what is obligatory, recommended, forbidden, or reprehensible."[20] (II 204.8)

The Ashʿarites avoided the contradiction involved in declaring that God creates the acts and then punishes His servants for evil deeds by their doctrine of *kasb*, "acquisition," or more accurately, "performance."[21] Man performs the acts but does not create them, while God creates the acts but does not perform them. Ibn al-ʿArabī is not especially pleased with this idea and often criticizes it, as will be seen below.

The Muʿtazilite argument, like the Ashʿarite position, is based upon certain select Koranic verses which clearly support what they want to say. The Koran is full of verses which indicate God's total control over His creation, yet it frequently attributes choice and responsibility to man. In effect, each group "interpreted" the verses cited by their opponents, but read the verses supporting their own position literally.

If you attribute the act to the power (*qudra*) of the servant, a support can be found for that in the divine report-giving, and if you attribute the act to God, a support can also be found for that in the divine report. As for rational proofs, they contradict each other among the rational thinkers, though not in actual fact. However, it is extremely difficult for rational thinkers to discern a proof from an obfuscation; and it is also difficult in respect to the divine report-giving and in respect of the reality of the servant. For the servant is commanded, and a command is only given to someone who possesses power to do what he is commanded and is able to refrain from what is prohibited to him. Hence it is difficult to negate the act from the person to whom the Law is addressed, that is, the servant, since then there would be no wisdom in addressing him.

Other divine reports and rational proofs show that the act attributed to the servant belongs only to God. Hence there is a contradiction both in the revealed reports and the view of reason. This results in bewilderment and causes the disagreement which has occurred in this question between the rational thinkers in their consideration of their proofs and the people of reports in their proofs. The truth of the matter is known only to the people of unveiling among the Folk of Allah.

The fact that man was created in the Form demands that the existence of the act belong to him, and this is confirmed by his being addressed by the Law. Sensory perception bears witness to this, so it is stronger in proof. The fact that at root all of this goes back to God does not detract from it, since the going back does not contradict this explanation. Hence the arguments of those who uphold "performance" are weak, not because they uphold performance—for their opponents also uphold it, since it is a report of the Law and a rational affair which man knows in himself. No, their arguments are weak because they negate the effect of the temporally originated power. (II 604.11)

One of the several types of "annihilation" (*fanāʾ*) which the spiritual traveler may experience is the "annihilation of acts." Ibn al-ʿArabī explains as follows:

The servant is annihilated from his acts through God's standing over them. This is indicated by His words, "What, He who stands over every soul for what it performs" (13:33). Hence the servants see the act as belonging to God from behind the veil of the engendered things, which are the locus wherein the acts become manifest. This is indicated by God's words, "Surely thy Lord is wide in concealment"[22] (53:32), that is, His covering is wide. All engendered things are His covering, while He is the one who acts (*fāʿil*) from behind this covering, "but they are unaware" (7:95).

Those of the theologians who affirm that the acts of the servants are a creation of God are aware, but they do not witness, because of the veil of "performance" through which God has blinded their in-

> sight. In the same way, He has blinded the insight of him who saw that the acts belong to the creatures when He placed him with that which he witnesses with his eyes. So this one is "unaware," and he is the Muʿtazilite. The other one "does not witness," and he is the Ashʿarite. Both have blinders over their eyes. (II 513.17)

Since all acts are ultimately God's, all of them are praiseworthy in themselves. But inasmuch as the acts become attached to the servant who is addressed by the Law, some of them are blameworthy. In the next world, once a person has left the arena of the Law, he will see that all his evil acts were in fact—in relation to God though not in relation to himself—good acts. This, in Ibn al-ʿArabī's view, is one of the meanings of the Koranic statement, "God will change their evil deeds into good deeds" (25:70).

> This verse means that he will see as good exactly what he had been seeing as evil. Before this, its goodness had been hidden from him by the rulings of the Law. When he reaches the place of the abolition of the Law's rulings, that is, the hereafter, and the covering is removed, he will see the good that was in all his works. It will be unveiled to him that the one who acted was God, no one else. So the acts were God's, and His acts are all perfect in goodness, without any imperfection or ugliness. The evil and ugliness which had been attributed to the acts were because of opposition to God's rulings, not because of the entities of the acts.
>
> Anyone who has the covering removed from his insight and sight, whenever that might be, will see what we just mentioned. But the time of the removal varies. Some people see that in this world. They are the ones who say that all God's acts are good, that there is no one who acts except God, and that the servant has no act other than the performance which is attributed to him. This "performance" consists of the free choice (*ikhtiyār*) which he has in the work. As for temporally originated power, that has no effect upon anything according to their view, since it does not go beyond its own locus.
>
> The gnostics among the Folk of Allah see that there is no temporally originated power whatsoever, so in their view it has no effect upon anything. What in fact takes place is that one divine name prescribes the Law for another divine name, addressing it within the locus of an engendered servant. The servant is then called "the one for whom the Law is prescribed" (*mukallaf*) and the address is called "prescribing the Law."
>
> Then there are those who say that the acts which emerge from the creatures are the creation of the servants, like the Muʿtazilites. When the covering is removed from them, the actual situation will become clear to them, either to their benefit or to their loss. (III 403.21)

By Ibn al-ʿArabī's own admission, his position on the acts wavers. Or rather, it depends on the point of view he has in mind. That which allows him to ascribe acts to man is the fact of man's being made upon the divine form and his ability to assume the traits of all God's names and attributes (*takhalluq*). Since God's attributes are within him, he manifests God's desire and power. Inasmuch as he is the form of God and not God Himself, his decisions and acts belong to himself.

Ibn al-ʿArabī points out that the disagreement in this question goes back to an argument over the manner in which God discloses Himself. Some say He discloses Himself in the acts of the creatures, and some disagree. Those who are aware of His self-disclosure attribute the acts to God. Those who are not aware attribute them to the creatures. Hence the difference among the theologians goes back to the fact that one group says the acts are "He," the other says they are "not He."

> Then there is "self-disclosure in the acts." It is the relationship which is the manifestation of the engendered things from the Essence from which they come to be and the manifestation of the loci of manifestation from the Essence from which they become manifest. It is alluded to in God's words, "I did not let them witness the creation of the heavens and the earth" (18:51). As for this self-disclo-

sure, God has fixed its occurrence in the beliefs of one group and has not allowed another group to accept it. God has established in one group the belief that it happens, and in another group the belief that it does not happen. And He has mentioned that He discloses Himself within the forms of beliefs.[23]

Someone may recognize that his own acts and those of others are created by God. But he witnesses them deriving from his own power, even though he knows that they derive from the divine power. At the same time, he does not witness how His power or the power of another becomes connected to the object of power when the object is brought into existence and made to appear from nonexistence. Such a person will refuse to accept that God discloses Himself in acts except to the extent that it occurs here. Hence he refuses to accept the self-disclosure in acts.

Someone else recognizes that his own acts are created by himself, not by the eternal power. However, he does not recognize them through witnessing except in the state of their existence, nor does he see—if he is fair—his power becoming connected to bringing them into existence. Rather, he only witnesses the bodily limb becoming connected to the motion that takes place. Such a person will uphold the occurrence of this self-disclosure.

There is a disagreement over this among the people of this affair which will not be lifted either in this world or the next. Each one of them has been established in his belief by God. In the next abode He will preserve the one in the imaginal perception (*wahm*) that He discloses Himself to him in his acts, and He will preserve the other in his knowledge that He does not disclose Himself in his acts. (II 606.33)

My dear son, the gnostic Shams al-Dīn Ismāʿīl ibn Sawdakīn al-Nūrī,[24] called my attention to something which had been verified for me, but in a different mode. . . . I mean self-disclosure in acts, that is, whether or not it is correct. Sometimes I would negate it in one respect, and sometimes I would affirm it in the respect in which the address of the Law required and demanded it, since man is addressed by the Law for the sake of works. It is impossible that one who is Wise and All-knowing would say, "Do!" and "Act!" to him whom He knows will not do and will not act, since he has no power. But the divine command for the servant to do works has been established, like, "Perform the prayer, and pay the alms" (2:43 etc.), "Be patient, vie you in patience, and be steadfast" (3:200), "Struggle" (5:35) and so on. Hence, there has to be some connection between the servant and what he does in respect of the act, by means of which he comes to be called the one who acts and does. If this is so, then to the extent of that relationship, self-disclosure will occur within him.

In this way I was affirming self-disclosure within the acts. And this is an approved way, extremely clear, showing that temporally originated power has the relationship of connection to that work which is prescribed for it in the Law. I saw that the argument of the opponent was flimsy and extremely weak and defective. Then one day, when this son Ismāʿīl ibn Sawdakīn was conferring with me about this question, he said to me, "Which proof of the attribution and ascription of the act to the servant and of self-disclosure within him is stronger than the fact that his attribute is that God has created man upon His own form? Were the act to be disengaged from him, it would no longer be correct for him to be upon His form and he could not accept the assumption of the traits of the names. But it is established for you and for the People of the Path without any disagreement that man is created upon the form, and so also assumption of the traits of the names is established."

No one can know the joy that came to me through his calling my attention to this. Hence it is possible that the master (*ustādh*) gain something from the disciple (*tilmīdh*) which God has decreed he will attain only in this way. (II 681.24)

The proper human attitude toward the acts adds another dimension to the question. Though one group may ascribe all acts to God, in fact "courtesy" (*adab*) demands that only good and beautiful acts be ascribed to God, while evil and ugly acts must be ascribed to the servants. Man must see all good as belonging to

God and all evil as belonging to himself, thereby putting everything in its proper place and becoming qualified by justice, wisdom, and courtesy. In one passage where Ibn al-ʿArabī classifies the names of God into various categories, he provides a distinction between the "names of acts" and the "names of deputation" (*niyāba*) which helps clarify this point.

> God says, "To God belong the most beautiful names, so call Him by them" (7:180). . . . Know that some of God's names are features (*maʿārif*), such as the well-known names. These are the obvious names.
>
> Some of the names are hidden things (*muḍmarāt*), like the [pronouns] *ka* and *tā*ʾ of address, the *tā*ʾ of the first person, the third person pronoun . . . , and the first person plural pronoun, as in "Surely We sent down." . . .
>
> Some of the names are denoted by acts, though no names are built from [the acts mentioned in such verses as] "God derides them" (9:79) or "God mocks them" (2:15).
>
> Some of the names are names of deputation: They belong to God, but they act as His deputies, such as when we say, "[He has appointed for you] shirts to protect you from the heat" (16:81). Every name given to every act ascribed to every engendered thing among the possible things functions as God's deputy, since all acts belong to God. Whether blame or praise becomes connected to the act, this connection exercises no effect upon what is given by sound knowledge. Hence every act attributed to a created thing acts as God's deputy within that thing. If it occurs in a praiseworthy way, it is attributed to God in laudation, since God loves to be lauded—so has it been recorded in the *Ṣaḥīḥ* from the Messenger of God.[25] But if blame becomes connected to it, or a defect is joined to it, we do not attribute it to God.
>
> An example of the praiseworthy is the words of Abraham, "He heals me" (26:80). But concerning illness he said, "Whenever I am sick" (26:80). He did not say, "Whenever He makes me sick," even though nothing made him sick but God. God made him sick just as He healed him.
>
> Another example is [the words of Khaḍir], "I desired to damage it" (18:79). This courteous and just knower alluded to himself by desiring to damage. But he said concerning the praiseworthy act, "Thy Lord desired" (18:82) in the case of the two orphans. Then in the place of praise and blame he said, "We desired," with the plural pronoun (18:81), because of the blame involved in killing the youth without any retaliation for a soul slain, and the praise involved in God's protecting his parents by his being killed. Hence he said "*We* desired," without specifying. Such is the state of the Courteous (*al-udabā*ʾ). Then he said, "I did not act"—that is, "He did not act"—"on my bidding" (18:82); on the contrary, the whole affair belongs to God. (IV 318.26)
>
> The distinguishing marks of works which lead to felicity are that man performs the works in a state of presence (*ḥuḍūr*) with God in all his movements and rests and that he witnesses the attribution of the acts to God in respect of their coming into existence and their praiseworthy relationship. But if he should attribute their blameworthy relationship to God, he has been discourteous and displayed his ignorance of the knowledge of the prescription of the Law (*taklīf*), of the Law's object, and of whom it addresses, that is, the person to whom it is said, "Act!"
>
> If the one to whom the Law is addressed had no relation to the act whatsoever, he would not have been told to act, and the whole of the Shariʿa would be a game, but it is true in itself. Hence the servant must have a sound relationship with the act, a relationship in respect of which he is told to perform the act. This relationship is not connected to his desire (*irāda*), as held by those who uphold performance. On the contrary, it is a subtle phenomenon of power included within the divine power and known through proofs, just as the light of the stars is included within the light of the sun. Through proofs you know that the stars possess a light which spreads over the earth, but you do not perceive it with your senses because of the overwhelming power of the light of the sun. In the same way, sense perception tells us that the acts of the servants belong to them in the sensory realm and according to the Law and that the divine power is included within

them. Reason perceives the divine power, but the senses do not, like the light of the stars included in the light of the sun. But in fact the light of the stars is identical with the light of the sun, and the stars are its loci of disclosure.[26] All the light belongs to the sun, but the senses attribute the light to the stars and then say that the light of the stars has been included within the light of the sun. But in reality, there is only the light of the sun whose light is included in itself, since there is no other light. (II 659.1)

The theological problem of the ascription of the acts to God or the servant can never have a simple solution, since it is one more version of the question, "What is a thing in relation to God?" The radical ambiguity of existence does not allow a straightforward answer. Those who see with penetrating vision will always affirm that the thing is He/not He, while those who cannot gain a complete knowledge of the situation will affirm one or the other. The rational thinkers are tied and bound by their own means of knowledge, while the people of heart fluctuate with the actual situation. The people of reason will say, "The acts are God's" (Ashʿarites) or "The acts are man's" (Muʿtazilites), but the Folk of Allah will follow the Koranic path by saying, "You did not throw when you threw, but God threw" (8:17). Ibn al-ʿArabī alludes to many of these points in discussing those whom the Koran calls the "strugglers" (*mujāhidūn*), that is, those who carry out the *jihād*, the struggle against their own limitations. In the following passage, Ibn al-ʿArabī differentiates the strugglers in an absolute sense from those who struggle in a specific and delimited sense.

The "strugglers" are the people of effort, toil, and putting up with difficulties. They are four kinds: Those who struggle without being delimited by anything, as mentioned in God's words, "God has preferred the strugglers over those who sit at home" (4:95). The second kind are the strugglers delimited by the path of God, as in His words, "The strugglers in the path of God" (4:95). The third kind are those who struggle in Him, as in His words, "Those who struggle in Us, surely We shall guide them on Our paths" (29:69). . . . The fourth kind are those who struggle in God "as is His due" (22:78); thereby He distinguishes them from those who struggle in Him without this delimitation. . . .

We now come to the strugglers whom God has not delimited by any specific attribute, not "in the path of God," nor "in Him," nor "as is His due." They are the strugglers through God, who does not possess the attribute of delimitation, so struggling through Him takes place in all things. It is the all-pervasive struggle. . . .

The "strugglers" among His servants are those who do not become delimited, just as God has made them nondelimited. They waver in the acts, the entities of which emerge within themselves. Should they attribute them to God? But there are those acts which courtesy does not allow us to attribute to Him and of which God has declared Himself quit, as in His words, "A declaration of being quit on God's part" (9:1), that is, "Let them attribute it to themselves." There are also acts which courtesy demands that we attribute to Him and which have a true relationship with Him.

The strugglers saw that God said, "You did not throw when you threw," so He negated and then affirmed exactly what He negated. Then He said, "But God threw" (8:17). Hence He placed the affirmation between two negations, so the negation is stronger than the affirmation, since it surrounds what is affirmed. Then He said in the same verse, "That He might test the faithful [with a good test]." Hence we come to know that God has bewildered the faithful, which is His testing of them through what He mentioned: the negating and the affirming of the throwing. And He made it "a good test." In other words, if the servant negates the throwing from Him, he will be correct, and if he affirms it in Him, he will be correct. There only remains which of the two correct views is better for the servant, though both are good. And this is a place of bewilderment (*ḥayra*). (II 145.29, 147.26)

13. KNOWING GOD'S SELF-DISCLOSURE

God's self-disclosure appears in two modes—ontological and cognitive, or as existence and as knowledge—but Ibn al-ʿArabī usually does not distinguish between them. Sometimes he deals primarily with one mode, but more commonly he describes self-disclosure in terms which apply to both. We need to keep in mind that *wujūd* or Being/existence means also "finding." It is a subjective experience as much as an objective occurrence. God's "Being" is identical with His knowledge, that is, His self-consciousness. The expression *wājib al-wujūd* has been consistently translated in Western sources as "Necessary Being" or "necessary existence," but it can also be rendered as "necessary finding" or "necessary awareness." God finds Himself and cannot not find Himself. The possible thing may or may not find itself and God, depending upon whether or not God gives preponderance to its finding over its not-finding (*ʿadam*). The Verifiers are the People of Unveiling and Finding (*ahl al-kashf wa'l-wujūd*), since the reality of things has been disclosed to them and they have found God in both the cosmos and themselves.

Finding Light

In Sufi terminology—as opposed to philosophical terminology—*wujūd* had long been used in the context of discussions of *samāʿ*, "listening" or "audition," that is, the "spiritual concert" which the Sufis employed as a means of opening themselves up to the inrushes of knowledge and awareness. In this context, the term *wujūd* is contrasted with two other words from the same root, *wajd* and *tawājud*. Briefly, *wajd* signifies "ecstasy." As Ibn al-ʿArabī puts it, quoting a classical definition, *wajd* is "the states (*aḥwāl*) that come upon the heart unexpectedly and annihilate it from witnessing itself and those present" (II 537.1).[1] *Tawājud* signifies "inviting ecstasy, since it is self-exertion in order to experience ecstasy" (II 535.26). *Wujūd* then means "Finding (*wijdān*) the Real (*al-ḥaqq*) in ecstasy" (II 538.1).

> In the view of the Tribe *wujūd* is finding the Real in ecstasy. They say that if you are a possessor of ecstasy, but you do not witness the Real in that state—for it is witnessing Him which annihilates you from witnessing yourself and witnessing those present—then you are not a possessor of ecstasy, since you do not possess the finding of the Real in it.
>
> Know that finding (*wujūd*) the Real in ecstasy is not known, since ecstasy is an unexpected occurrence (*muṣādafa*), and that through which the unexpected occurs is unknown, for it could have come through some other situation. Since its property is not connected to the audition, the Real is found therein in an unknown mode. . . .
>
> The finding of the Real in ecstasy is diverse among the finders because of the property of the divine names and the engendered preparednesses. Each breath of engendered existence possesses a preparedness not possessed by any other breath. The "Possessor of the Breath" (*ṣāḥib al-nafas*) is the one who is described by ecstasy. His ecstasy takes place in keeping with his preparedness, while the divine names watch and guard. The engendered thing has nothing of God but ascription to His names and His solicitude (*ʿināya*). Hence the finding of the Real in ecstasy takes place in keeping with the divine name which watches over him, and the divine names go back to the Self of the Real. . . .
>
> For the gnostics, the term "ecstasy" loses its property of being a technical term. They apply it everywhere. In their

view, there is no possessor of sound ecstasy—whoever may experience it—unless God is found (*wujūd*) in that ecstasy in a mode known to those who are gnostics through God. Hence they take from every possessor of ecstasy the finding of Him that comes to him in ecstasy, even if the possessor of that ecstasy does not recognize it as the finding of the Real. But the gnostic recognizes this. Hence he takes from every possessor of ecstasy the finding of the Real which he brings. He recognizes that the Real discloses Himself in that ecstasy in the form in which this report-giver delimits Him—that is, the one who gives a report concerning the finding of what he finds in his ecstasy. (II 538.1,21)

Ibn al-ʿArabī knows full well that most people understand *wujūd* as discussed in the context of "listening" or *samāʿ* in a different sense from the *wujūd* which is discussed in the context of existence and nonexistence. Nevertheless, he sees the meanings as basically identical. In order to indicate the identity, I translate *wujūd* in the following as existence/finding.

God says, "[God is] Listening, Knowing" (Koran 9:98), and He says, "[God is] Listening, Seeing" (22:61). Hence He places listening before knowledge and sight. The first thing we knew from God and which became connected to us from Him was His speech (*qawl*) and our listening (*samāʿ*). Hence existence/finding derived from Him. In the same way, in this path we say that every *samāʿ* without an ecstasy possessing existence/finding is not truly a *samāʿ*. This is the level of *samāʿ* to which the Folk of Allah refer and to which they listen.

Thus, when the singer sings, the one worthy of *samāʿ* sees God's speech "Be!" to the thing before it comes to be. The readiness to come into existence possessed by the listener to whom it is said "Be!" corresponds (*bi manzila*) to ecstasy in *samāʿ*. Then its existence/finding in its entity by means of His speech "Be!"—as He says, "[We say to it] 'Be!' and it is" (16:40)—corresponds to the existence/finding found by the ones worthy of *samāʿ* in their hearts and given to them by the *samāʿ* in the state of ecstasy. So he who has not listened to the *samāʿ* of existence/finding has not listened. Hence the Tribe has placed existence/finding after ecstasy.

The cosmos can have no existence without Speech on God's part and listening on the part of the cosmos. Hence the existence of the paths of felicity only becomes manifest, and the differences between them and the paths of wretchedness only become known, through the Divine Speech and the engendered listening. Therefore all the messengers came with Speech, such as the Koran, the Torah, the Gospels, the Psalms, and the Scriptures.[2] There is nothing but speech and listening. There can be nothing else. Were it not for Speech, we would not know what the Desirer desires from us. Were it not for hearing (*samʿ*), we would not reach the point of gaining what is said to us. Through Speech we move about, and as a result of Speech, we move about in listening. Hence Speech and listening are interrelated. Neither can be independent from the other, since they are two terms of a relationship. Through Speech and listening, we come to know what is in the Self of the Real, since we have no knowledge of Him except through the knowledge that He gives to us, and His giving of knowledge takes place through His Speech. (II 366.27)

In short, we come to find our own existence through listening to the Divine Speech, which is "Be!" By the same token, we come to find God through listening to His Speech in the form of revelation. Finding and existence are two aspects of the same reality, which at root is God's own Finding of Himself, His Necessary Being. All goes back to Him and His names.

God's Being is Light (*nūr*), as we have seen in an earlier chapter. The impossible thing or nothingness is darkness (*ẓulma*), and the existence of the cosmos is a domain of brightness or shadow between the two.

Light is perceived, and through it perception takes place. Darkness is perceived, but through it no perception takes place. . . . God is sheer Light, while the impossible is sheer darkness. . . . Creation is the Barzakh between Light and darkness. . . .

God says, "And to whomsoever God assigns no light, no light has he" (24:40). The light "assigned" to the possible thing is nothing other than the *wujūd* of the Real. Just as He has described Himself as obligating Himself through mercy and help, in verses like, "Your Lord has written for Himself mercy" (6:54) and "It is ever a duty incumbent upon Us to help the faithful" (30:47), so also He has described Himself as "assigning" to the possible thing: Were there no light, the possible thing would find no entity for itself, and it would not be qualified by *wujūd*. That which becomes qualified by *wujūd* has become qualified by the Real, since there is nothing in *wujūd* but God. Though Being is One Entity, the entities of the possible things have made It many, so It is the One/Many (*al-wāḥid al-kathīr*). . . . Without Him, we would not be found, and without us, He would not become many through the many attributes and the names diverse in meaning which He ascribes to Himself. The whole situation depends upon us and upon Him, since through Him we are, and through us He is. But all of this pertains specifically to the fact that He is a god, since the Lord demands the vassal through an inherent demand, whether in existence or supposition. But "God is Independent of the worlds" (3:97). . . . The cosmos is not independent of Him in any sense, since it is a possible thing, and the possible thing is poor toward the Preponderator.

The dark and luminous veils through which the Real is veiled from the cosmos are the light and the darkness by which the possible thing becomes qualified in its reality because it is an intermediary (*wasat*). It only looks upon itself, so it only looks upon the veil. Were the veils to be removed from the possible thing, possibility would be removed, and the Necessary and the impossible would be removed through its removal. Hence the veils will be hung down forever, and nothing else is possible. (III 274.25, 276.9,18)

Through the Being of God, which is Light, all perception takes place.

Were it not for light, nothing whatsoever would be perceived, neither object of knowledge, nor sensory object, nor imaginal object. The names of light are diverse in keeping with the names set down for the faculties. The common people see these as names of the faculties, but the gnostics see them as names of the light through which perception takes place. When you perceive sounds, you call that light "hearing." When you perceive sights, you call that light "seeing." When you perceive objects of touch, you call that light "touch." So also is the case with objects of imagination. . . . The faculties of smell, taste, imagination, memory, reason, reflection, form-giving, and everything through which perception takes place are all light.

As for the objects of perception (*mudrakāt*), if they did not have the preparedness to accept the perception of the one who perceives them, they would not be perceived. Hence they first possess manifestation (*ẓuhūr*) to the perceiver, then they are perceived. And manifestation is light. Hence every perceived thing must have a relationship with light, through which it gains the preparedness to be perceived.

Hence every object of knowledge has a relationship to the Real, and the Real is Light. So every object of knowledge has a relationship to light. . . . So there is no object of knowledge but God. (III 276.32, 277.12)

Like *wujūd*, light is both ontological and epistemological. The word *idrāk* or "perception" in Arabic means primarily to reach, to attain, to overtake. It is sometimes translated by classical authors into Persian by *yāft*, that is, "finding," a word which is also employed to translate *wujūd*.[3] So the "perception" which takes place through light is the "finding" that takes place through *wujūd*. The "perceived things" (*mudrakāt*) are the "found" or "existent things" (*mawjūdāt*). Since light in itself is the Real, one stage of finding God has to do with the elimination of darkness from the heart, the darkness connected to engendered existence. Hence in *Iṣṭilāḥāt* Ibn al-ʿArabī offers the following definition of light: "Any divine inrush which dispels engendered existence from the heart" (14; II 130.1). Likewise revelation is light:

> The Koran is "light" because of its verses which dispel misleading doubts. . . . Every verse it brings acts as evidence (*dalāla*) because of the fact that it is light. For light dispels darknesses. (III 96.7)

Just as Being is the Manifest, so also light is manifestation, and all manifestation takes place through it.

> There is nothing stronger than light, since it possesses manifestation, and through it manifestation takes place. Everything has need of manifestation, and there is no manifestation without light. (II 466.20)

Just as light is being, finding, and manifestation, so also it is knowledge, which, as we have seen, is a "light which God throws into the heart of whomsoever He will." Ibn al-ʿArabī makes this connection clear in discussing the vision (*ru'ya*) of God promised to the faithful. He mentions in passing that real knowledge of God derives from God's unveiling the mysteries and opening the door to direct knowledge of Him, a state known technically as the "opening of unveiling" (*futūḥ al-mukāshafa*).

> There is not one of us who will not see his Lord and speak to Him face to face. All of this will be a giving of knowledge through the form in which He discloses Himself to us, which is the form in which He created us. We know for certain that the tasting of the messengers is far beyond the tasting of their followers. So do not suppose that when Moses asked to see his Lord (Koran 7:143), he was lacking the vision which was the state of Abū Bakr in his words, "I have never seen anything without seeing God before it." This is not the vision that Moses was seeking from his Lord, since he already possessed this vision through the elevation of his level. . . .
>
> Tasting and tradition (*naql*) allow no doubt as to the fact that there will be vision of God. But reason doubts this, since vision of God is one of the things which throws rational faculties into bewilderment and concerning which they come to no conclusions. . . .
>
> The prophets and the friends among the Folk of Allah have no knowledge of God derived from reflection. God has purified them from that. Rather, they possess the "opening of unveiling" through the Real. Among those who see Him is he who sees Him without delimitation. Another sees Him through Him. Another sees Him through himself. Another does not see Him with himself, though he has seen Him and does not know that he has seen Him. This last group possesses no "mark" (*ʿalāma*)[4] and does not know the form of His manifestation in existence.
>
> Among them is he who does not see Him because he knows that His Entity becomes manifest here to the cosmos only in the forms of the properties of the entities of the cosmos, while He is their locus of disclosure. Hence the seer perceives only the form of the property, not the Entity. Hence he knows that he has not seen Him. "To God belongs the highest similitude, and He is the Inaccessible," who is not seen in respect of His Heness, "and the Wise" (16:60) in His self-disclosure, lest it be said that He was seen.
>
> Look at the form manifest to the eye in a polished surface and verify your vision. You will find that the form has come between you and your perception of the polished surface, which is its locus of disclosure. So you will never see the surface. The Real is the locus of disclosure for the forms of the possible things. Hence the cosmos sees only the cosmos in the Real. . . .
>
> The object of vision (*mar'ī*), which is the Real, is light, while that through which the perceiver perceives Him is light. Hence light becomes included in light. It is as if it returns to the root from which it became manifest. So nothing sees Him but He. You, in respect of your entity, are identical with shadow, not light. Light is that through which you perceive all things, and light is one of the things. So you perceive light only inasmuch as you carry light in your shadow itself. Shadow is ease, and darkness is a veil. When the star of the Real rises and enters into the servant's heart, the heart is illuminated and irradiated. Then bewilderment and fear disappear from the possessor of the heart, and he gives news of

his Lord explicitly, through hints, and by means of various modes of report-giving. (III 116.18)

The Lights of Self-Disclosure

For the Sufi to give news of God, the light of God must first dawn in his heart. This dawning of light is called by many names, "self-disclosure" (*tajallī*) being one of the most common. As we have seen on several occasions, this term, like *wujūd* and light, has both ontological and epistemological dimensions. God discloses Himself through the cosmos and through all knowledge. The following passage is typical:

> God brought the cosmos into existence as two sides and a center. He made one side like the point of a circle and the other side like its circumference, while He configured the cosmos between the two sides within levels and circles. He named the circumference the "Throne," the central point the "earth." Everything between the two is the circles of the elements and the celestial spheres. He made them all loci for the individuals of the species and genera which He created in the cosmos.[5]
>
> Then God disclosed Himself in an all-inclusive, all-encompassing self-disclosure, and He disclosed Himself in a specific, individual self-disclosure. The all-inclusive self-disclosure is an all-merciful self-disclosure, as indicated in His words, "The All-merciful sat upon the Throne" (20:5). The specific self-disclosure is the knowledge of God that belongs to each and every individual. Through the second self-disclosure there is entrance and exit, descent and ascent, motion and stillness, joining and separation, infringement, and that which stays in its place. He distinguished parts of the cosmos from other parts through place, position, form, and accident. Hence no distinction takes place except through Him, for He is identical to what becomes distinguished and to that through which distinction takes place. He is with each existent thing wherever it is through the manifest form that is attributed to that existent thing. All of this is known by the knowers of God by way of witnessing and finding. (III 101.20)

We saw in the last chapter that one of the definitions of self-disclosure is "the lights of unseen things that are unveiled to hearts" (II 485.20). Self-disclosure is a light, so it is existence and knowledge. But the term self-disclosure places stress upon the dynamic nature of light and existence, the fact that the two are constantly moving from nonmanifestation into manifestation.

> The divine loci of self-manifestation (*al-maẓāhir al-ilāhiyya*) are called "self-disclosures." The fundamental Light is nonmanifest within them and unseen by us, while the forms in which self-disclosure takes place are the locus within which the loci of manifestation become manifest. Hence our sight falls upon the loci of manifestation. (II 575.17)

Since knowledge is intrinsic to existence/light, the self-disclosure which brings about existence also brings about knowledge. All things know God to the extent that they share in existence and light, and to the extent of their knowledge they constantly glorify God. However, those creatures who possess rational speech (*nuṭq*) do not perceive God's self-disclosure immediately.

> Life is intrinsic to all things, since it derives from the divine self-disclosure to each and every existent thing. He created the existent things to worship and know Him, and not one of His creatures would know Him unless He disclosed Himself to it. Then it comes to know Him through itself, since no created thing has the capacity to know the Creator. . . . Self-disclosure is forever constant, witnessed by and manifest to all existent things, except the angels, mankind, and the jinn, since this constant self-disclosure belongs only to that which has no rational speech, like all inanimate things and plants.
>
> As for those things which have been given rational speech and the ability to express what is in themselves—that is,

the angels, mankind, and the jinn in respect of their governing spirits and their faculties[6]—for them self-disclosure occurs from behind the veil of the unseen. Hence the angels' knowledge derives from God's giving knowledge (*taʿrīf*), while the knowledge of mankind and the jinn derives from consideration (*naẓar*) and reasoning (*istidlāl*). But the knowledge possessed by their bodies and by all created things below them derives from the divine self-disclosure. (III 67.15)

Everything perceived on any level of existence is a divine self-disclosure. Only God's Essence is never disclosed, which is to say that God does not disclose Himself as Essence, only as other than the Essence.

The self-disclosure of the Essence is unanimously declared impossible (*mamnūʿ*) by the People of the Realities. They also agree unanimously that self-disclosure in loci of manifestation, that is, self-disclosure in the form of beliefs, takes place, as does self-disclosure in rational concepts (*maʿqūlāt*). These last two are the self-disclosure through which man "takes heed" (*iʿtibār*), since these loci of manifestation—whether they be the forms of rational concepts or the forms of beliefs—are bridges over which one "crosses" (*ʿubūr*) through knowledge. In other words, man knows that behind these forms there is Something which cannot be witnessed and cannot be known and that beyond that Object of knowledge which cannot be witnessed or known there is no reality whatsoever to be known. (II 606.30)

Ibn al-ʿArabī divides self-disclosure into different kinds in a number of passages. One of these can suffice to illustrate the types of knowledge which the spiritual traveler is given when God illuminates his heart.[7]

Lights are of two kinds: a light having no rays and radiant light. If self-disclosure takes place through radiant light, it takes away sight. It was alluded to by the Messenger of God when it was said to him, "O Messenger of God, hast thou seen thy Lord?" He replied, "He is a light. How should I see Him?"[8] He means "radiant light," since the rays take away sight and prevent perception of Him from whom the rays derive. The Prophet also alluded to this with his words, "God has seventy veils of light and darkness; were they to be removed, the Glories of His Face would burn away everything perceived by the sight of His creatures."[9] Here "glories" are the lights of His Reality, since the "face" of something is its reality.

As for the light which has no rays, it is the light within which self-disclosure takes place without rays. Then its brightness does not go outside of itself and the viewer perceives it with utmost clarity and lucidity without any doubt. At the same time, the presence in which he dwells remains in utmost clarity and utmost limpidness, such that nothing of it becomes absent from him. Concerning this self-disclosure the Prophet said, "You shall see your Lord just as you see the moon on the night when it is full."[10] One of the things he meant by this declaration that vision of God is similar to seeing the moon is that the moon itself is perceived, since the moon's rays are too weak to prevent sight from perceiving it. . . .

Then the Prophet said in the same hadith, "or just as you see the sun at noon when there is no cloud before it." At this time its light is strongest, so all things become manifest through it and sight perceives everything it falls upon when this sun is unveiled to it. But when it desires to verify its vision of the sun itself in this state, it is not able to do so. This declaration of similarity shows that this self-disclosure does not prevent people from seeing one another. In other words, they will not be annihilated. That is why he declared similarity with both the vision of the full moon and the vision of the sun, and he did not restrict himself to one of the two. He emphasized that people will subsist in this locus of witnessing by his words in the rest of the hadith, "You will not be harmed and you will not be crowded."

When I entered into this waystation, the self-disclosure without rays fell upon me, so I saw it knowingly. I saw myself through it and I saw all things through myself and through the lights which things carry in their essences and which are given to them by their realities, not through any extraneous light. I saw a tremendous place of witnessing, in sensory form—not in intelligible form—, a form of the Real, not a meaning. In this self-disclosure there became manifest to me the manner in which the small expands in order for the large to enter into it, while it remains small and the large remains large, like the camel which passes through the eye of the needle.[11] That is contemplated in sensory, not imaginal, form, and the small embraces the large; you do not know how, but you do not deny what you see. So glory be to Him who is exalted high beyond a perception that satisfies rational faculties and who preferred the eyes over rational faculties! "There is no god but He, the Inaccessible, the Wise" (Koran 3:6).

Through this self-disclosure—which makes the power of the eyes manifest and prefers them over rational faculties—God makes manifest the incapacity of rational faculties. And through His self-disclosure in radiant light He makes manifest the incapacity of the eyes and the power of the rational faculties, preferring them over the eyes. Thus everything is qualified by incapacity, and God alone possesses the perfection of the Essence. (II 632.29)

Since God alone is perfect in every respect, man is forever imperfect. Even "perfect man" is imperfect in relation to God's perfection, which explains why God commanded the most perfect of all perfect men, the Prophet Muḥammad, to pray, "My Lord, increase me in knowledge" (20:114). Ibn al-ʿArabī analyzes this Koranic verse in relation to the divine self-disclosure in chapter 19 of the *Futūḥāt*, "On the cause of the decrease and increase of knowledge":

Every animal and everything described by perception receives a new knowledge at each instant in respect of that perception. However, the person who perceives may be among those who do not pay any attention to the fact that it is knowledge, even though, in fact, it is knowledge. So if a knower's knowledge should be described as decreasing, that is because perception may separate him from many things which he would perceive if not for this obstruction. He is like the person who has been struck by blindness or deafness or something similar.

Since sciences are high and low in accordance with the object of knowledge, spiritual aspirations (*himma*) attach themselves to the noble and high sciences, those which, when man comes to know them, purify his soul and magnify his level. The science with the highest level is knowledge of God, and the highest way to knowledge of God is knowledge of self-disclosures. Below that is the knowledge of rational consideration. There is no knowledge of God below consideration. Most people have only beliefs, not sciences.

These sciences are those concerning which God commanded His Prophet to seek increase. . . . He meant the sciences of self-disclosure—for self-disclosure is the noblest way to gain sciences—and these are the sciences of tastings.

Know that increase and decrease has another chapter which we shall also mention, God willing. It is as follows: God placed within each thing—and the soul of man is one of the things—a manifest dimension (*ẓāhir*) and a nonmanifest dimension (*bāṭin*). Through the manifest dimension, man perceives things which are called "entities," and through the nonmanifest dimension, he perceives things which are called "knowledge." God is the Manifest and the Nonmanifest, so through Him perception takes place. For it is not in the power of anything other than God to perceive something through itself; it can only perceive through that which God places within it.

God's self-disclosure to whomsoever He discloses Himself in whatsoever world it may be, whether unseen or visible, takes place from His name the Manifest. As for His name "Nonmanifest," the reality of this relationship demands that self-disclosure never occur within it, neither in this world nor in the next, since "self-disclosure" consists of His manifestation to the one to whom He discloses Himself in that particular locus of disclosure, so it belongs to the name "Manifest." The signification of the relationships does not change. . . .

When God discloses Himself, either out

of gratuitous kindness or in answering a request, He discloses Himself to the manifest dimension of the soul, and perception takes place through sensation in a form within the *barzakh* of imaginalization (*tamaththul*). Then if the person who perceives the self-disclosure is one of those who have knowledge of the Shariʿa, increase will take place in the sciences related to the rulings of the Law. If he is a logician, it takes place within the sciences of the scales of meanings. If he is a grammarian, it will take place in the sciences of the scale of speech. So it is in the case of anyone who is proficient in any of the sciences of the engendered things and the non-engendered things: Increase occurs within his soul in that knowledge with which he concerns himself.

The people of this path know that the increase occurs because of the divine self-disclosure to these classes of people, for they cannot deny what has been unveiled to them. But those other than the gnostics sense the increase and attribute it to their own reflective processes. Other than these two groups find the increase but do not know that they had sought increase in anything. Their likeness is as God said: "[The likeness of those who have been loaded with the Torah, then they have not carried it,] is as the likeness of an ass carrying books. Evil is the likeness of the people who have cried lies to God's signs" (62:5), the "signs" being these increases and their root. . . .

Self-disclosure also occurs through the name Manifest to the nonmanifest dimension of the soul. Then perception takes place through "insight" (*baṣīra*) in the world of realities and meanings disengaged from substrata. These are called "plain texts" (*naṣṣ*), since the "plain text" has no confusion within it, nor any sort of equivocality. This only takes place within the meanings. Hence the possessor of meanings is at rest from the toil of reflection. When self-disclosure takes place in his case, he is increased in the divine sciences, the sciences of the mysteries, the sciences of the nonmanifest, and everything connected to the next world. This pertains exclusively to the people of our path. . . .

When I say that decrease of sciences in man is a fault, I only mean the divine sciences, since the reality demands that there is no decrease whatsoever and that man constantly and forever undergoes increase in knowledge in respect of that which he is given by his senses and the fluctuations of his states in himself and his thoughts. Hence he increases in sciences, but there is no profit in them. . . .

From the time man begins to climb the ladder of ascent (*miʿrāj*), he receives divine self-disclosure in accordance with the ladder of his ascent. Each individual among the Folk of Allah has a ladder specific to him which no one else climbs. Were one person to climb another's ladder, then prophecy could be earned (*iktisāb*), since each ladder by its essence gives a specified level to each person who climbs it. The men of knowledge would then climb the ladder of the prophets, and they would attain to prophecy through their climbing. But that is not the situation. If it were, the Divine Vastness would disappear through repetition of the affair. But it has been established for us that there is no repetition in that Side.

However, all the steps of the meanings for the prophets, the friends, the faithful, and the messengers are the same. No ladder has a single step more than any other. The first step is *islām*, which is submission (*inqiyād*). The last step is annihilation (*fanāʾ*) in going up (*ʿurūj*) and subsistence (*baqāʾ*) in coming out (*khurūj*). Between the two steps are the other steps: faith, virtue (*iḥsān*), knowledge, declaring holy, declaring incomparable, independence, poverty, abasement, exaltation, variegation, and stability in variegation. Then comes annihilation if you are leaving [the ladder], or subsistence if you are entering it [from the top].

When you leave each step, the sciences of self-disclosure decrease in your nonmanifest dimension to the measure in which they increase in your manifest dimension, until you reach the last step. If you are leaving the ladder and you have attained to the last step, God becomes manifest through His Essence in your manifest dimension in keeping with your measure. Then you make Him manifest in His creation, and nothing of Him whatsoever remains in your nonmanifest dimension. The self-disclosures of the nonmanifest dimension disappear from you completely.

When He calls you to enter in upon

Him, this is the first step; He discloses Himself to you in your nonmanifest dimension to the measure that the self-disclosure decreases in your manifest dimension. When you reach the last step, He manifests Himself in His Essence to your nonmanifest dimension, and there remains no self-disclosure whatsoever in your manifest dimension. All this takes place because the servant and the Lord always remain together in the perfection of the existence of each in himself. The servant always remains servant and the Lord Lord throughout this increase and decrease. (I 166.4)

Naming the Perception of Light

As we have already seen, Ibn al-ʿArabī employs a number of terms to refer to the perception of God's self-disclosure. Probably the most often used and the most general in meaning is "unveiling" (*kashf*). If that which is perceived by the heart is looked upon primarily in relation to the source, it is usually called "self-disclosure." If it is looked upon primarily in relation to him who perceives, it is more likely to called "unveiling." For the most part unveiling takes a visionary form. The person who experiences unveiling "sees" the lights as "loci of manifestation" (*maẓhar*) within the imaginal world.

One of the several terms that is often employed as a virtual synonym for unveiling is "tasting" (*dhawq*). Just as Ibn al-ʿArabī can say that "He who has no unveiling has no knowledge" (I 218.21), he can also say that "Any knowledge not derived from tasting is not the knowledge of the Folk of Allah" (II 574.27).

When the possessor of knowledge is assailed by obfuscations, that is not knowledge. Knowledge comes only through tastings. That is what we call "knowledge." (II 473.29)

It could be imagined that when man possesses the knowledge of something, he possesses the "tasting" of it, but such is not the case. Tasting derives only from a self-disclosure. Knowledge may be gained through the transmission of a true, sound report. (II 546.5)

Often Ibn al-ʿArabī speaks of tasting as a knowledge connected more to spiritual and psychological "states" (*aḥwāl*) than to entities. In other words, unveiling alludes to an experience that may be conveyed through describing the imaginal forms in which it occurs, while tasting—like tasting an apple in the sensory realm—cannot be described but must be experienced.

The knowledge of tasting given by each existent thing cannot be given by any other existent thing. Man may find in himself a distinct taste in each bite of an apple he eats, a taste not found in any other bite. The apple is one, yet he finds a sensory distinction in each bite, even if he is not able to explain it. (II 671.29)

When Ibn al-ʿArabī defines tasting as a standard technical term of Sufism, he makes it one of the stages of unveiling, contrasting it with "drinking" (*shurb*) and "quenching" (*rī*).

"Tasting" is the first beginnings of self-disclosure, which give rise to drinking. . . . "Drinking" is the middle of self-disclosure within a station (*maqām*) that calls for quenching, though it may be in a station that does not call for quenching, and it may be that the constitution of the drinker does not accept quenching. . . . "Quenching" is the final stages of drinking in every station. (II 133.2)[12]

In the view of the Tribe tasting is "the first beginnings of self-disclosure." It is a state which comes upon the servant suddenly in his heart. If it should stay for two instants or more, it is "drinking." . . .

The saying, "the first beginnings of self-disclosure" lets us know that every self-disclosure has a beginning, that is, a tasting that belongs to the self-disclosure. This only takes place if the self-disclosure should be within (1) forms or (2) the divine or engendered names, nothing else. If the self-disclosure should take place within (3) meaning, then its beginning is itself, since it has no property after the beginning which man can gain gradually, [in contrast to the first two kinds, within which] he gains gradually the meanings of those (1) forms within which self-disclosure takes place, or the meanings of each and every (2) name. Hence he sees at the beginning what he does not see from that name afterwards.

But for the possessor of (3) meaning, the beginning of each thing is identical with its entity. He gains nothing after this all-inclusive giving of knowledge. Then he differentiates when he expresses this one reality. This is what is meant by our words at the beginning of this book:

[When I kept knocking on God's door
  I waited mindfully, not distracted,]
Until there appeared to the eye the glory of His Face
  and a call to me, nothing else.
[I encompassed Being in knowledge—
  nothing is in my heart but God.][13]

For its beginning was itself, and everything we have mentioned after that in all our speech is only the differentiation of that all-inclusive reality which was contained in that look at the One Entity. Most people work contrary to this tasting. That is why their speech is not tied together. He who considers their speech looks for a root to which all their words go back, but he does not find it. But each part of our speech is interrelated with the other parts, since it is one entity, while this is its differentiation. A person will know what I am saying if he knows the interconnection of the verses of the Koran in the way that some of them are arranged next to others. Then he will know the factor that brings together (*al-jāmiʿ*) two verses, even if there is an obvious distance between them; yet the factor is correct. There must be some interrelating factor which brings the two verses together, and that is what gives the interrelationship with the neighboring verses, for this is a divine arrangement. I have seen no one who attempted to investigate this except Rummānī, the grammarian.[14] He has a commentary on the Koran, and someone who has seen it reported to me that he walks on this road, but I have not seen it myself. (II 548.4)

In one passage Ibn al-ʿArabī distinguishes between unveiling and tasting by saying that the first is something that one sees outside oneself, while the second is one's own, inward experience. He is describing the mysteries which the traveler comes to perceive upon entering into the waystation (*manzil*) of familiarity (*ulfa*).

> When you enter into this waystation, you join with a group of the messengers and you receive sciences from their specific tasting which you did not possess. For you these will be an unveiling, just as for them these had been a tasting. You gain from them the science of proofs and marks, so nothing is hidden from you in earth or in heaven when He discloses Himself to you. On the contrary, you distinguish and recognize each thing, while others, who have not reached this station, are ignorant of it. This is a knowledge of unveiling, since you witness it through the mark (*ʿalāma*). You do not see it from yourself, since it is not your own tasting. (II 605.20)

In the following passage Ibn al-ʿArabī employs the term tasting in a broad sense to refer to all knowledge given by God to His messengers, His prophets, and His friends. At the same time, he clarifies the distinction which he commonly draws among these three highest types of human being.

> The speech of the folk of God's path derives from tasting, and no one has any tasting of the share that a messenger receives from God, since the tastings of the messengers are specific to the messengers, the tastings of the prophets are specific to the prophets, and the tastings of the friends are specific to the friends. A messenger may have all three tastings, since he is a friend, a prophet, and a messenger [all at once]. Khaḍir said to Moses, "What thou hast never encompassed in knowledge" (18:68). He says: I have a knowledge taught to me by God and unknown to you, and you have a knowledge taught to you by God and unknown to me. This is "tasting."
>
> I was in a gathering within which there was a group of gnostics. One of them

asked another, "From which station did Moses ask for vision of God?" The other said, "From the station of yearning (*shawq*)." I said, "Be not heedless of this principle of the way: 'The final stages of the friends are the first states of the prophets.' Hence the friend has no tasting of the state of the Law-bringing prophets, so he cannot taste it. One of our principles is that we only speak on the basis of tasting, but we are neither messengers nor Law-bringing prophets. So how can we know from which station Moses asked to see his Lord? True, if a friend of God had asked that, you might be able to answer, for it is within the realm of possibility that you would also have that tasting. But we have come to know by way of tasting that the tasting of the station of the messengers is impossible for any one other than a messenger." (II 51.23)

The Sufis distinguish between various "states" (*aḥwāl*) which one may experience upon the path to God and the "stations" (*maqāmāt*) which one must pass through in order to reach Him. In general the states are fleeting and may or may not come, while the stations are the necessary foundation for actualizing human perfection. More will be said about the former in Chapter 15 and the latter in Chapter 17. For the moment it is enough to recall that one of the standard ways of distinguishing between states and stations is to say that states are divine "bestowals" (*mawāhib*), while the stations are "earnings" (*makāsib*). In a similar way, knowledge acquired through tasting is a bestowal. Nevertheless, this does not mean that God may give tasting to just anyone. The servant must first have exerted himself and made himself worthy of it. The Shaykh uses the term "opening" (*fatḥ*) in the following as a near synonym for unveiling.

"Opening through tastings" is a knowledge gained by him who knows it through exerting himself to acquire it. . . . This knowledge belongs exclusively to the people of the path, that is, the Folk and Elect of Allah. It is the science of states. Though states are "bestowals," they are only bestowed upon those who have a specific attribute. If that attribute does not produce states in this world for everyone, yet it will necessarily produce them in the next world. But since there is no condition that this producing should take place in this world, it is said concerning the knowledge of the states that the states are "bestowals." This knowledge of them is to gain them through tasting. By "through tasting" is meant at the beginning of self-disclosure.

Take for example, "trust" (*tawakkul*), which is reliance upon God in what He does or promises. The tasting of trust which is added to knowledge of trust is that the person does not become agitated when he lacks that upon which the soul relies. Instead, the soul relies upon God, not upon the specific secondary cause. Hence he finds in himself a confidence in God greater than the confidence found by someone else who has the secondary cause which would lead to it. For example, someone is hungry, and he does not have the secondary cause—the food—which will eliminate his hunger. Another person is hungry, and he has the means to eliminate his hunger. The person who has the secondary cause is strong through the existence of the food which will eliminate the hunger, but the other person, who does not have it, equals him in calm and lack of agitation, since he knows that his provision—if he is to receive any more provision—must reach him. This lack of agitation in a person who has such an attribute while he does not possess the secondary causes is called "tasting."

Every competent person feels the difference between these two individuals. The person who has the knowledge but not the tasting is agitated by not having that which will eliminate his hunger, even though he knows that his provision—if any provision remains for him—must reach him. Nevertheless, he finds no calm with God in his soul. The possessor of tasting is the one who finds the calm, just as the one who possesses the appropriate secondary cause finds it. There is no difference between them in calm; or rather, the possessor of tasting may be stronger. (IV 221.2)

Unveiling takes place when God illuminates the heart, enabling it to see into the unseen world. "Opening" (*fatḥ*, *futūḥ*), as discussed in the introduction, is for God to "open the door" to the unseen world through disclosing Himself to the heart, or to "open up" the heart to direct knowledge of Him. The term also signifies the beginning of something, and hence it is often used to refer to that stage of the spiritual ascent when a person enters into the realm of unveiling. The door is opened for him, and he no longer has to follow an authority outside himself.

> If the seeker desires divine loci of witnessing and lordly sciences, he should multiply his nightly vigils and continually multiply within them his concentration (*jamʿiyya*). If scattered lights should appear to him such that between each light darkness is interspersed, and if those lights have no subsistence but disappear quickly, this is one of the first marks of acceptance and opening. Those noble lights will never cease becoming manifest to him through his acts of spiritual struggle (*mujāhada*) and his striving until a greatest light is unveiled for him. Then the obstructions which prevent people from reaching these knowledges will be removed and mysteries of which he had nothing in himself and by which he was not described will be unveiled for him in their stations. (II 626.3)

There are two basic worlds, the "unseen" and the "visible." The outward eye or "sight" (*baṣar*) perceives the visible world, while the inward eye or "insight" (*baṣīra*) perceives the unseen world.

> The cosmos is two worlds . . . , the Unseen . . . and the Visible. The second world is perceived by sight, while the world of the Unseen is perceived by insight. (III 42.5)
>
> God says, "Sight perceives Him not" (Koran 6:103), that is, the sight of any eyes, whether the eyes of faces or the eyes of hearts. For hearts perceive only through sight, and the eyes of faces perceive only through sight. Wherever there is sight, perception occurs. Sight in the rational faculty is called the "eye of insight," while sight in the outside world (*al-ẓāhir*) is called the "sight of the eye." The eye in the outside world is the locus for sight, while insight in the inside world (*al-bāṭin*) is the locus for that eye which is sight in the eye of the face. Sight's names are diverse, but it is not diverse in itself.
>
> Just as eyes do not see Him through their sight, so also insights do not see Him with their eyes. The Messenger of God said, "God is veiled from intellects just as He is veiled from sight; the Higher Plenum seeks Him just as you yourselves seek Him."[15] (IV 30.5)
>
> The World of the Unseen is perceived through the eye of insight, just as the World of the Visible is perceived through the eye of sight. Sight perceives nothing of the World of the Visible except darkness, so long as the veil of darknesses or similar impediments are not lifted. Once the impediments are lifted and lights spread out upon the sensory objects, and once the light of sight meets the light of the locus of manifestation, then the seer sees objects with sight.
>
> In the same way, the eye of insight is veiled by such things as rust (*rayn*), passion (*shahwa*), and gazing upon "others" (*aghyār*) within the dense natural world.[16] These things come between it and the vision of the World of Dominion, that is, the World of the Unseen. But when man applies himself to the mirror of his heart and polishes it with invocation and the recitation of the Koran, he thereby gains some light. And God possesses a light called the "light of existence" which is deployed over all existent things. When these two lights come together, unseen things are unveiled as they are in themselves and as they occur in existence.
>
> However, there is a subtle meaning that separates the two lights: Sense perception is veiled by impediments, excessive distance, or excessive nearness. But the eye of insight is not like that, since nothing veils it except the rust, covering,[17] and the like which we just mentioned. However, there is also a subtle veil which I shall mention:
>
> The light which becomes deployed from the Presence of Munificence upon the World of the Unseen within the ontological presences does not pervade all of them and does not become deployed from Him over all of them in respect to this person who experiences unveiling. This only takes place in the measure desired by God. It is the station of "revelation."[18]
>
> For ourselves our proof for this is that

> we taste it. For others, the proof is His words to the Prophet, "Say: . . . 'I know not what shall be done with me or with you. I only follow what is revealed to me'" (46:9), and this in spite of the extreme Muhammadan lucidity. This is also indicated by God's words "[It belongs not to any human being that God should speak to him, except by revelation,] or from behind a veil" (42:51). (II 241.1)

Unveiling takes place through light, but the light that comes from God must coincide with the light inside the heart. Sometimes a person may perceive an excess of radiance in self-disclosure so that he does not gain in knowledge. This is because his own light is not equal to the task of matching the outside light. In explaining this, Ibn al-ʿArabī reminds us of the definition of darkness: "That which is perceived but through which no perception takes place."

> When the darkness of ignorance takes up residence in the heart, it makes it blind. Then the heart is not able to perceive those realities in respect of perceiving which it is called a "knower" (*ʿālim*). God says, "Why, is he who was dead, and We gave him life, and appointed for him a light to walk by among the people as one whose likeness is in the darknesses?" (6:122). Here [by light and darkness] He means knowledge and ignorance.
>
> But it is not true that everything which is "perceived, and through which perception does not take place" is darkness, since when light is stronger than the light of sight, man perceives it, but he does not perceive through it. That is why the Messenger of God said concerning God, "His veil is light." Hence unveiling only takes place through a light which is equivalent to the light of sight. Do you not see that bats only come out in light which is equivalent to the light of their sight? (III 369.31)

Ibn al-ʿArabī employs the term *mukāshafa*, from the same root as *kashf* or unveiling, in basically the same meaning as *kashf*. In his chapter on opening (*futūḥ*), he discerns three kinds of opening: opening of expression (*ʿibāra*) in the outward dimension, opening of sweetness (*ḥalāwa*) in the inward dimension, and opening of unveiling (*mukāshafa*) through God.

> What brings all of this together is that whatever comes to you without self-exertion, or raising up your gaze, or seeking, is "opening," whether outward or inward. Opening has a mark in him who tastes it, which is that he does not take from the opening of anyone else, or from the conclusions of reflection. One of the conditions of opening is that it not be accompanied by reflection or be acquired through reflection.
>
> Our shaykh, Abū Madyan, used to say concerning opening, "Feed us with 'fresh flesh' as God said; feed us not with dried meat."[19] In other words: Do not tell us concerning opening anything but what has been opened up to you in your hearts. Do not tell us about the opening of others. By this he wanted to raise the aspiration of his disciples (*aṣḥāb*), so that they would strive to take from God. (II 505.17)
>
> When the shaykhs ask their disciples questions in order to teach them how to take from God, they do not allow them to reflect upon the answer, lest their answer be the result of reflection. They say, "Answer only with that which comes to your mind immediately when I ask you the question. Look at what is cast into your heart when the question enters it. Mention it at the outset of the idea." If the disciples do not follow this instruction, the shaykh does not accept their answers. (II 558.14)
>
> In this path, it is not proper for the shaykh to apprise the disciple (*murīd*) of what will take place when he gains a knowledge in himself through opening. . . . Otherwise, the disciple may make that form manifest, while his inward self is devoid of that which would demand that form.
>
> You may object, "But it is not proper for the shaykh to conceal that from the disciple." I will reply: On the contrary, it is proper for him to conceal it and even incumbent. He knows that when the meaning which necessitates the manifestation of that form takes up residence in the

disciple, the disciple will have to manifest that form. Then the shaykh will know that God has given the disciple the aptitude to become one of the People of the Real. But if the shaykh were to give him knowledge of the meaning which necessitates that form, while the ego (*nafs*) is disposed to treachery and untruthfulness, then he might make that form manifest without the meaning, and there could be a misunderstanding. Thus, for example, the hypocrite manifests the form of the man of faith in outward practice, while his inward dimension is devoid of that which would necessitate that practice. (III 272.32)

Ibn al-ʿArabī explains the "opening of unveiling" as follows:

> The third kind of opening is the opening of unveiling, which brings about knowledge of the Real. The Real is greater and more exalted than that He should be known in Himself, but He is known through the things. Hence unveiling is the cause of knowledge of the Real in the things. The things are like curtains over the Real. When they are raised, unveiling takes place. . . .
>
> The Real is not known in the things without the manifestation of the things and the lifting of their properties. The eyes of the common people fall only upon the properties of the things, but the eyes of those who have the opening of unveiling fall only upon the Real in the things. Among them is he who sees the Real in the things, and among them is he who sees the things while the Real is within them. Between these two there is a difference. When opening takes place, the eye of the first falls upon the Real and he sees Him in the things, but the eye of the second falls upon the things, and then he sees the Real within them because of the existence of the opening. (II 507.30)
>
> Engendered existence is darkness, while light is the Evident Real. Light and darkness never come together, just as night and day never come together. On the contrary, each of them conceals its companion and makes itself manifest. He who sees the day does not see the night, and he who sees the night does not see the day. The actual situation is manifest and nonmanifest, since He is the Manifest and the Nonmanifest. So there is a Real and a creation. If you witness creation, you will not see the Real, and if you witness the Real, you will not see creation. So you will never see both creation and the Real. On the contrary, you will witness this in that and that in this—a witnessing through knowledge—since one is a wrapper and the other enwrapped. (II 496.11)

Witnessing and Vision

Another important synonym for unveiling is "witnessing" (*shuhūd, mushāhada*). This term has a wider sense than unveiling since it is commonly used for sight as well as insight. It is employed in typical fashion as a synonym for unveiling in the first passage below, where Ibn al-ʿArabī is discussing one of the many kinds of lights which may be seen by the heart during self-disclosure. In the process, he touches upon one of his favorite eschatological themes, the fact that mercy and light will overcome in the end, so the "final end" (*ma'āl*) for everyone will be felicity. In the second passage, he tells us that witnessing, like unveiling, can be divided into several kinds.

> The first self-disclosure [being discussed here] is the lights of meanings disengaged from substrata. Such a light is any knowledge which is unconnected to a body, a corporeal thing, an imaginal thing, or a form, and which we do not know in respect of our giving form to it (*taṣawwur*). On the contrary, we come to understand it as it is in itself—though in accordance with what we are. This cannot happen until I become a light. As long as I am not a light, I will not perceive anything of this knowledge. This is indicated by the words of the Prophet in his prayer, "Make me into a light!"[20] God says, "God is the light of the heavens and the earth" (24:35), so He only gives him light from Himself. In the same way He says, "And the earth" of the Resurrection "will shine with the light of its Lord" (39:69).

In other words, there will be no sun there, and the lack of light is darkness, but there must be witnessing, so there must be light, for that is the day when God comes to judge and decree. Hence He only comes within his name Light, so "the earth will shine with the light of its Lord." Then each "soul will know" through that light "what it has sent before and left behind" (82:5), since it will see it all made present, unveiled for it by that light.

Were it not for the light that belongs to the souls, there could be no witnessing (*mushāhada*), since witnessing (*shuhūd*) only takes place when two lights come together. When a person has a share of light, how can he be wretched forever? For light does not come from the world of wretchedness. And there is no soul which does not have a light, through which its works will be unveiled to it. It will become happy through everything good, and as for the evil, "It will wish if there were only a far space between it and that day" (3:30). That is why God finishes this verse with the words, "God is Clement to the servants," for He has appointed for them lights whereby they perceive, and they have come to know that light has no share in wretchedness. Hence the final end must be the agreeable and attaining the individual desire (*gharaḍ*), and this is what is called "felicity." For in this verse He said, "[The day] every soul," not just some specific souls rather than others, "[shall find what it has done of good brought forward, and what it has done of evil]." He mentions good and evil. Existence is light, while nonexistence is darkness, so evil is nonexistence, while we are in existence, so we are in good. If we become ill, yet we will become well, since the root is the Restorer, and He is Light. (II 485.29)

God has let His servants know that He has presences (*ḥaḍarāt*) designated for specific affairs and that He has called His servants to enter into them and gain from them. Thus He has made the servants poor and needy in respect to these presences. Some people accept these presences and some reject them out of ignorance. Among these presences is the presence of witnessing (*mushāhada*), which possesses diverse waystations (*manzil*), even though a single presence embraces them all. Among the people in this presence, some witness Him in the things, some witness Him before the things, some after them, some with them, and some witness Him Himself, in accordance with the diversity of many stations (*maqām*), which are known by the folk of God's path, the possessors of tasting and drinking. (II 601.18)

The term *shuhūd* is of special interest, since certain Sufis in India—especially Shaykh Aḥmad Sirhindī (d. 1624)—undertook to criticize the idea of *waḥdat al-wujūd* or the "Oneness of Being" in the name of *waḥdat al-shuhūd* or the "Oneness of Witnessing," and the controversy between the supporters of the two positions has reverberated down to recent times. But we have already seen that Ibn al-ʿArabī never employs the term *waḥdat al-wujūd*, and that *wujūd* in his usage signifies not only Being/existence but also the "finding" of God by God Himself or by the servant; as such it is a synonym for *kashf*, and the great Sufis are the "People of *kashf* and *wujūd*." We saw above that the knowers of God recognize His self-disclosure "by way of *shuhūd* and *wujūd*" (III 101.31). These few indications are enough to show that when Ibn al-ʿArabī was designated as the great expositor of *waḥdat al-wujūd* and criticized in terms of *waḥdat al-shuhūd*, Ibn al-ʿArabī's own position was not the real issue.[21] By the seventeenth century there was a received wisdom concerning what he had said, and it was this that became the object of debate. In the present context, we can only point to the wide range of meanings covered by both *wujūd* and *shuhūd*.

When Ibn al-ʿArabī distinguishes between *wujūd* and *shuhūd*, he usually considers *wujūd* as belonging to God and *shuhūd* as belonging to the servant. God is present and finds Himself in all things, and man witnesses this presence and finding to the extent of his capacity. *Wujūd* as such belongs to the Nonmanifest, though its reverberations fill the cosmos. In contrast, *shuhūd* is the vision of self-disclosure and belongs to the manifest realm.

> Everyone in *wujūd* is the Real,
> and everyone in *shuhūd* is creature.
> (III 306.8)

> The Folk of Allah follow Him whose folk they are, so His property flows over them. And His property is the lack of delimitation. Hence He possesses the all-inclusiveness of *wujūd*, while they possess the all-inclusiveness of *shuhūd*. That person who delimits His *wujūd* has delimited his own *shuhūd*. He is not one of the Folk of Allah. (III 161.15)
>
> The cosmos has nothing of the cosmos except a *wujūd* and a *shuhūd* in this world and the next, without end and without being cut off, for the entities become manifest and are seen. (IV 324.30)
>
> The gnostics are . . . the people of *shuhūd* within *wujūd*. I only ascribe *wujūd* to them because of the temporal origination of the properties, which do not become manifest except within an existent/found thing (*mawjūd*). (II 529.22)

If *shuhūd* can be distinguished from *mushāhada*, it may be in the sense that *shuhūd* is used more generally, as a synonym for seeing and vision on any level of existence, whereas *mushāhada* is more often used as a synonym for unveiling. In his *Iṣṭilāḥāt al-ṣūfiyya* Ibn al-ʿArabī gives three meanings to *mushāhada* as a technical Sufi term. I quote from the longer version of *Iṣṭilāḥāt* with additions in brackets from chapter 209, where he provides an expanded definition in connection with unveiling (*mukāshafa*).

> "Witnessing" is [the witnessing of creation in the Real, which is] to see the things by the proofs of declaring His Unity (*tawḥīd*). It is also [the witnessing of the Real in creation, which is] to see the Real within the things. It is also [the witnessing of the Real without creation, which is] the reality of certainty (*yaqīn*) without any doubt. Witnessing follows unveiling, or it may be said that it is followed by unveiling. (II 132.4, 495.23)

Ibn al-ʿArabī often distinguishes witnessing from vision (*ru'ya*) by referring to another well-known term of the Sufi vocabulary, *shāhid* or "witness," that is, that which gives information or testimony about what has been seen. In *Iṣṭilāḥat* 7, Ibn al-ʿArabī defines "witness" as "The trace which witnessing (*mushāhada*) leaves in the heart of the witnesser (*mushāhid*). This is the witness, and in reality, it is what the heart retains from the form of the witnessed (*mashhūd*)." The longer version of *Iṣṭilāḥāt* has "vision of the witnessed" in place of "form of the witnessed" (II 132.25). In other words, the divine self-disclosure leaves a trace in the heart, which gives testimony and "witnesses to" what has been seen.

In chapter 266 of the *Futūḥāt* on the "witness," the Shaykh provides a slightly different definition: "The witness is the subsistence of the forms of the loci of witnessing (*mashāhid*) in the soul of the witnesser. So the form of the witnessed in the heart is identical to the witness, and through it the witnesser experiences bliss (*naʿīm*)" (II 567.5). Then he explains the difference between witnessing and vision:

> The witness is the actualization of the form of the witnessed in the soul during witnessing. Hence the witness gives something different from what is given by vision, since vision is not preceded by knowledge of the object of vision (*al-mar'ī*), while witnessing is preceded by knowledge of the witnessed, a knowledge which is named "belief" (*ʿaqīda*). Hence in witnessing there occurs admission and denial, but there is nothing in vision but admission, never any denial. The witness is called by that name because it gives witness to the viewer of the correctness of his belief. Hence every witnessing is a vision, but not every vision is a witnessing, "but they do not know" (Koran 2:13). (II 567.10)
>
> When the Sufis define witnessing as the "reality of certainty without doubt and hesitation," this refers to a witnessing that takes place outside the Presence of Imaginalization. An example of the [witnessing

within the Presence of Imaginalization] is the divine self-disclosure in the hereafter which will be denied. Then, when He transmutes Himself into the mark (*ʿalāma*) by which they recognize Him, they admit to Him and recognize Him.[22] He is identical to the one denied at first and to the one recognized at last. They do not admit except to the mark, not to Him. Hence they only recognize Him as limited (*maḥṣūr*), so they do not recognize the Real.

This explains why we make a distinction between vision and witnessing. We say concerning witnessing that it is the witnessing of the witness which comes into the heart from the Real. It is this witnessing which is delimited by a mark. But vision is not like that. That is why Moses said, "Give me vision that I may gaze upon Thee" (7:143). He did not say, "Let me witness," since He was witnessed by him, never unseen (*ghayb*) by him. How should He be unseen for the prophets when He is never unseen by the friends, the gnostics? (II 495.27)

Despite the distinctions Ibn al-ʿArabī sometimes draws between vision and witnessing, in practice it is often difficult to say why he has chosen one term over the other. Like the other terms employed to refer to the perception of self-disclosure, vision seems to have both a general meaning, according to which it is more or less synonymous with unveiling, tasting, and witnessing, and a specific meaning, where it signifies a special kind of unveiling in certain contexts. In the following passage, where Ibn al-ʿArabī is discussing the station of "sobriety" (*ṣaḥw*), he tells us how the gnostic "sees" (*ru'ya*), that is, has a vision of, his Lord. This vision does not differ significantly from the "witnessing" mentioned above.

Some of the sober are sober through their Lord, and others through themselves. He who is sober through his Lord never addresses any but his Lord in his sobriety, nor does he hear any but Him. His eye falls only upon his Lord in all the existent things. He will have one of two stations:

He may see the Real from "behind" the veil of the things inasmuch as He has encompassed them, as indicated in His words, "Allah is behind them, encompassing" (85:20).

Or he may see the Real as identical with the things. Here the Men of Allah are divided into two kinds. One kind sees the Real as identical with the things in the properties and the forms. Another kind sees the Real identical with the things in respect to the fact that He is the receptacle for the properties and characteristics of the forms, not in respect of the forms themselves, since the forms are some of the properties of the immutable entities.

As for the person who is sober through himself, he only sees his own likeness and similitudes. He says only "Nothing is like Him." His station and state do not allow him to complete the verse through tasting, even if he recites it. That is His words, "He is the Hearing, the Seeing" (42:11).

The possessor of the first tasting says, "He is the Hearing, the Seeing," through both tasting and recitation. Hence the possessor of the sobriety of self sees that the Real is far removed from himself, like him who places Him in his kibla when he prays. He does not see that it is He who performs the prayer. (II 547.24)

Whatever term Ibn al-ʿArabī applies to the acquisition of knowledge of God, one must always remember that the knower acquires knowledge through God's self-disclosure, not His Essence. Vision may be higher than witnessing, and witnessing higher or lower than unveiling, but these are modes of knowledge which are acquired by other than the Essence of God, and hence the Essence Itself is never known. None knows the Essence but the Essence.

In respect to His Essence and His Being, nothing stands up to the Real; He cannot be desired or sought in His Essence. The seeker seeks and the desirer desires only knowledge (*maʿrifa*) of Him, witnessing of Him, or vision of Him, and all of these are *from* Him; they are not He Himself. (II 663.9)

Perceiving the Veil

That which comes from God is always colored by the receptacle which receives it. As Junayd said, "The water takes on the color of its cup." This principle—to which Chapter 19 is devoted—is of fundamental importance in Ibn al-ʿArabī's teachings, since, from the creaturely point of view at least, it explains all diversity and all multiplicity. It explains why religions must be different, and why the beliefs of the followers of the same religion diverge. It is the principle of continual creation and of "Self-disclosure never repeats itself" viewed from the side of the receptacle. It also has important applications to the question of "states" and "stations" on the spiritual path. Why is it that practically every book written on the stations provides an original description? Is it that Sufis cannot agree whether there are seven, ten, forty, 100, or 1000 stations on the path? Not at all. There is no question of agreement, since there is no argument. It is simply that each person who has traveled the path to God speaks from his own viewpoint and recounts his own experience. And "Self-disclosure never repeats itself." Ibn al-ʿArabī applies the principle of non-repetition to a question he was asked about witnessing:

> When two gnostics come together in a single presence of witnessing (*ḥaḍra shuhūdiyya*) with God, what is their property? I was asked this question by our shaykh, Yūsuf ibn Yakhlaf al-Kūmī[23] in the year 586 [1190]. I said to him as follows:
>
> Master, this is a question which is supposed but which does not occur, unless the self-disclosure happens to take place in the Presence of Images (*ḥaḍrat al-muthul*), like the dream of the dreamer or the state of an Incident.[24] But in the Reality, no, since the Presence does not embrace two such that something else might be witnessed along with It. On the contrary, the witnesser does not even witness himself in that Presence, much less another, extraneous entity.
>
> However, one can conceive of this situation in the self-disclosure of images (*mithāl*). Once the two gnostics come together, then one of two things is true: Either (A) they have been brought together with each other in a single station, higher [than their own stations], or lower, or in between; or (B) they have not come together.
>
> (A) If they have been brought together in a single station, the station must require the declaration of (a) incomparability, or (b) similarity, or (c) both at once. In any case, the property of the self-disclosure in respect of manifestation is one, but in respect to what the recipients of self-disclosure find, it is diverse in tasting, because of their diversity in entities: The one gnostic is not the other, neither in natural or spiritual form, nor in location. Though the one is *like* the other, he is not identical with him.
>
> The most that can happen is one of the following: (1) Each of them fully realizes (*taḥaqquq*) the knowledge of himself. But the self of the one is different from the self of the other. Hence the one acquires knowledge which is not acquired by the other. Hence we know that they have come together while remaining apart.
>
> (2) One of them fully realizes the knowledge of himself, while the other is annihilated from the witnessing of himself. Then they have remained apart while coming together, or one of them gives what is given by the object of desire (*murād*) and the other gives what is given by him who desires (*murīd*). In any case, they are different in existence (*wujūd*), while coinciding (*muttafiq*) in state and witnessing (*shuhūd*).
>
> (a) If the station requires the declaration of incomparability for each of them, the utmost that each can do is to declare Him incomparable with the form that belongs to himself, so the two are different, without doubt, even if they be alike (*mithl*).
>
> (b) If the station requires the declaration of similarity, its state is like the first. So also (c) if it requires bringing together both incomparability and similarity. For bringing the two together is to combine them in a middle presence. So the one state is like the other.

Hence the two gnostics never come together in existence, even if they come together in witnessing.

(B) They may not be brought together by a single station. Rather, each of them stands in a station which is different from the station belonging to the other while he becomes manifest in the form which belongs to the other. Then, although they come together in form, each will be given a power whereby he will witness the presence of the other upon the carpet of the object of his witnessing, since the object of witnessing is a self-disclosure in an imaginal form. It is this self-disclosure and object of witnessing within which the two will come together in what is addressed to them and what they witness, if the Object so desires. But in any other presence, neither witnessing, addressing, nor vision allows for any "other."

Should this be their situation, then their property is that of two people who have been brought together by a single station in the knowledge of self, or the annihilation of one of them, or one of them stands in the station of the object of desire and the other in that of him who desires—such that he who desires gives news of severity and strength while the object of desire gives news of softness and tenderness.[25] There is no other possibility. Neither of them will give news of what was acquired by his companion. Each will be instructed (*ilqā'*) according to the affinity (*munāsib*) required by the specific constitution which brought about the diversity of the forms of their spirits at their original configuration.

When each of them returns to his companions, he will say—even if one of them is in the West and the other in the East—"In this hour I witnessed so-and-so. I saw him face to face and came to know his form. Among his qualities is such and such," and he will describe his attributes as they actually are. He among them who does not have knowledge of the realities will then say, "The Real gave to him the like of what He gave to me." But that is not the situation. Neither of them heard what the other heard, and that is because they differ in affinity, as we said. But if he is one of the people of realities and complete knowledge and he is asked what the other gained, he will reply, "I know only what is required by my own form and I am not he, for the Real does not repeat a form." (II 475.32)

The forms in which the Real shows Himself are not the Real Himself, but the veils which hide the Essence. The gnostic never sees God directly, since he never sees anything but His self-disclosure. And that is precisely His veil.

> God says, "Those are they whom God has guided," i.e., to the good and the better, "and those—they are the possessors of the kernels" (39:18). In other words, they bring out the kernel (*lubb*) of the affairs hidden by the shell (*qishr*). The eye falls only upon the veil, while that which is veiled belongs to the possessors of the kernels. This alerts us to the form of the veil within which the Real discloses Himself. Then He transmutes Himself from it into another veil. In reality, there is nothing but passage from veil to veil, since no divine self-disclosure ever repeats itself. Hence the forms must be diverse, while the Real is behind all of that. We possess nothing of Him but the name Manifest, whether in vision or veil. As for the name Nonmanifest, it remains forever nonmanifest. It is the intelligible kernel perceived by the possessors of the kernels. In other words, they know that there is a kernel and it is over Him that a veil has become manifest. . . . Hence, he who maintains that there is vision speaks the truth, and he who holds that there is no vision speaks the truth. (IV 105.3)

He who sees the Real plainly and openly
  sees Him only from behind a veil.
He does not recognize it, yet it exists through Him—
  this is indeed a marvelous affair!
No seer sees anything
  but his own bliss or chastisement.
The form of the Seer has disclosed itself to him
  while he is the Seer—no, he is the veil.

It has been mentioned in the *Ṣaḥīḥ* that the Real discloses Himself within forms and undergoes transmutation within them. This is what we mean by "veil." It has been established by reason, the Law, and unveiling—and unveiling yields exactly the same as the Law—that the Real accepts no change. As for reason, the proofs of that are well known, and this book is not their place, since this book is based upon the Law and the results of unveiling and witnessing. . . .

As for the Law, that is His words, "Nothing is like Him" (42:11). If He underwent changes in His Essence, this property would not be true. But it is true, so it is impossible for Him to undergo change in His Essence. . . .

The forms seen by sight and perceived by rational faculties, and the forms imaginalized by the faculty of imagination are all veils, behind which the Real is seen. . . . Hence the Real remains forever Unseen behind the forms which become manifest within existence. The entities of the possible things in the thingness of their immutability and with all the variations in their states witnessed by the Real also remain unseen. The entities of these forms manifest within Being, which is the Entity of the Real, are the properties of the entities of the possible things in respect of the states, variation, change, and alteration which they have in their immutability. These become manifest within the Entity of Real Being. But the Real does not change from what He is in Himself. . . .

Hence the veils are forever let down, that is, the entities of these forms. He is not seen except from behind a veil, just as He does not speak except from behind a veil. . . .

He never manifests Himself to His creatures except within a form, and His forms are diverse in each self-disclosure, since "He never discloses Himself in a single form twice or in a single form to two individuals."[26] Since He is so, the actual situation cannot be apprehended by reason or the eye. Reason cannot delimit Him by one of those forms, since He destroys that delimitation by the next self-disclosure. But in all that He is God. . . .

All of this—praise belongs to God—is in actual fact imagination, since it never has any fixity in a single state. But "People are asleep," and the sleeper may recognize everything he sees and the presence in which he sees it, "and when they die, they awake" from this dream within a dream.[27] They will never cease being sleepers, so they will never cease being dreamers. Hence they will never cease undergoing constant variation within themselves. Nor will that which they perceive with their eyes ever cease its constant variation. The situation has always been such, and it will always be such in this life and the hereafter. (IV 18.32, 19.22,34)

14. UNDERSTANDING THE KORAN

The knowledge acquired by reason through reflection is confined and constricted by the instrument of knowledge. The light thrown into the heart by God also has certain limitations, since it is a created light deposited within a created receptacle, but the fact that God has taken the initiative and "bestowed" (*wahb*) the knowledge makes it radically different from the knowledge "earned" (*iktisāb*) through personal efforts. Reason is limited by its inability to perceive God's self-disclosure in all things, so it denies His similarity and explains away the revelatory reports which refer to it. In contrast, unveiling perceives the self-revelation in the forms of the cosmos, so it knows for certain the literal truth of the Koranic statements.

According to Ibn al-ʿArabī, one can never doubt the accuracy of the revealed text in its literal form. To suggest that God's "real meaning" lies below the surface or has to be found through interpretation is to cast aspersions upon God and amounts to blatant ill manners and discourtesy (*sū' al-adab*). The literal sense of the text must always be honored. If, after that, God "opens" up one's understanding to perceive other meanings which preserve the literal sense while adding new knowledge, one accepts the new understanding and thanks God. However, one cannot interpret the text on the basis of "common sense" or "scientific fact" or any other product of reason. One does not go charging into the text without preparation. If a person has not fulfilled the requirements of the Law upon himself and has not searched for the interpretation from God through faith, practice, and godfearing (*taqwā*), he has no basis upon which to understand the text.

The preconditions for understanding preclude the possibility of a "novel" or "original" interpretation. The required piety, godfearing, strict adherence to the Shariʿa and the Sunna, deep respect for those who have gone before in the way of the Prophet, and the acknowledgment of one's own nothingness in the face of the Divine Teacher all work against any attempts at innovation. A new interpretation must first take into account those interpretations that have been made by one's spiritual forebears and not contradict them. If it adds another dimension to the tradition and harmonizes with previous interpretations, while the interpreter possesses all the requisite personal qualities, then it might be valid.

The Goal of Rational Inquiry

Ibn al-ʿArabī frequently claims that the knowledge acquired by means of unveiling is superior to that which is earned through the efforts of intellectual investigation and rational inquiry. Nevertheless, he does not denigrate rational knowledge. He merely points out its limitations. Certain subjects lie "beyond the stage of reason," so man can gain no knowledge of them without the help of revelation. In the first passage below, he has just mentioned the great divergence of views among the rational thinkers concerning God's Essence, attributes, and acts.

This book is not a place for that which is given by the proofs of the reflective powers, only for that which is given by divine unveiling. So we will not list these proofs systematically as their supporters have established them in their books.

Then these rational thinkers turned their consideration toward transmitted knowledge (*al-samʿiyyāt*), which is our knowledge. We rely upon it in the outward rulings of the Law and we take it through divine unveiling while exerting ourself through godfearing. Then God undertakes to teach us through self-disclosure. We witness that which rational faculties cannot perceive through their reflective powers, but concerning which transmitted knowledge has come. Reason has declared it impossible, the reason of the man of faith has interpreted it, and the simple man of faith has simply assented to it.

The lights of unveiling have come with the news that it is forbidden to reflect upon the Essence. We saw that the Essence is contrary to that which rational faculties prove through their reflective powers, since the possessors of unveiling witness the right hand of God, His hand, His two hands, the eye and the eyes attributed to Him, the foot, and the face. They witness such attributes as rejoicing, wonder, laughter, and self-transmutation from form to form—all of this.

Hence the God who is worshiped by the faithful and the people of witnessing among the Folk of Allah is not the same as that worshiped by the people who reflect upon God's Essence. They are deprived of knowledge of Him, since they have disobeyed God and His Messenger by reflecting upon the Essence of God. They have transgressed the level of speech (*kalām*) and rational consideration—the fact that He is one God—and gone on to that for which they have no need. Some have done that who wished for God, like Abū Ḥāmid al-Ghazālī and others, but this is a place where feet slip, even if Abū Ḥāmid made this a covering for himself, since in some places he called attention to the opposite of that. But in short, he was discourteous. (II 389.6)

The word *kalām*, translated as "speech" in the above passage, is also the name of the discipline of the theologians, and this, in fact, may be what Ibn al-ʿArabī has in mind, since he makes it synonymous with rational consideration (*naẓar*), the specific mental activity through which the theologians reach their conclusions. He is saying that the proper domain of theological reflection is the existence and Unity of God, nothing else. This point needs to be emphasized, since there is just as much danger in ignoring reason as there is in ignoring imagination. Those who fail to utilize the full possibilities of reason run the risk of falling into *shirk*, associating other gods with God, the opposite of *tawḥīd*. And *tawḥīd* alone is a knowledge sufficient for salvation. If someone ignores the proper perceptions of reason, he will perceive the manyness of God's self-disclosures, but like contemporary contextualists, he will claim that there is no supreme Reality lying behind the myriad forms of imaginal "experience." The Shaykh, a true representative of the "perennial philosophy," would agree that "The water takes on the color of the cup." But the innate resources of the healthy rational faculty—the "intellect"—pierce the veils of self-disclosure and perceive the One.

The gnostic never ceases understanding God's Oneness, even if he sees God's self-disclosures in all things. He declares God incomparable because he perceives through his rational faculty that "Nothing is like Him," and he declares Him similar because he perceives His presence in all things through imagination and the senses. Though Ibn al-ʿArabī sometimes says that unveiling can perceive all knowledge, he says that this is only partly true in the case of *tawḥīd*, and he repeatedly affirms the positive role of reason in perceiving God's Unity.

> God has commanded us to gain knowledge of the declaration of His Unity, but He has not commanded us to know His Essence. On the contrary, He forbade that with His words, "God warns you about His Self" (3:28). So also the Messenger of God forbade us to reflect on the Essence of God. "Nothing is like Him" (42:11), so how can one reach the knowledge of His Essence? But He said, commanding us to declare His Unity, "Know that there is no god but God" (47:19). Hence there is no knowledge of Him except in respect of the fact that He is a god. This is the knowledge of God's appropriate attributes, through which He becomes distinguished from that which is not a god and from the divine thrall. This is the knowledge commanded by the Law, [but one cannot know His Essence,] since "None knows God but God."
>
> In the view of both the people of consideration and the people of unveiling, unequivocal rational proofs have been established that He is One God, since there is no god but He. Then, after rational proof of His *tawḥīd* and the self-evident rational knowledge of His existence, we see that the people of the path of God—the messengers, prophets, and friends—have brought other modes of knowledge, various attributes of God which rational proofs consider impossible. (I 271.7)
>
> You say concerning the Real that He is Hearing and Seeing. He has a hand, two hands, hands, eyes, leg, and everything He has ascribed to Himself. None of these can be ascribed to Him by the rational faculty, since it knows that they can only be ascribed to temporally originated things. Were it not for what has been brought by the Law and the divine prophetic reports, we could not ascribe these things to Him rationally. However, we negate the declaration of similarity and do not discuss anything specific, since we are ignorant of His Essence. We negate similarity only because of His words, "Nothing is like Him" (42:11), not because of what has been given by rational proofs. Thereby nothing judges Him except His own Speech. This is how we want to meet Him when we meet Him and He unveils from our insight and our sight the covering of blindness. . . .
>
> But there can be no unveiling in the knowledge of *tawḥīd*. . . . *Tawḥīd* is not something ontological (*amr wujūdī*). It is merely a relationship, and relationships cannot be seen through unveiling. They can only be known by way of proofs. For unveiling is a vision. Vision only becomes

connected to its object through the qualities (*kayfiyya*) which the object possesses. But does the Divine Side have any qualities? Rational proof negates that He should have any. . . . But if God should embody these meanings in the Presence of Imaginalization—like knowledge in the form of milk—then this knowledge can be attained through unveiling. (II 291.30)

When the misbelievers were invited to the profession of the Unity of God, they replied, "'What, has he made the gods One God?' This is indeed a marvelous thing" (38:5). People understand the sentence, "This is indeed a marvelous thing," as the words of the misbelievers, since the Prophet had invited them to profess the Unity of God, but they believed that the gods were many. But in our view, this sentence represents the words of the Real or the words of the Messenger. . . .

Man knows that God does not come to be through the making of a maker, since He is a god in Himself. That is why God chides them with His words, "Do you worship what you yourself carve?" (37: 95), since it is self-evident (*ḍarūra*) to reason that "God" cannot be receptive toward effects. But here was a block of wood which they played with, or a stone which they used to throw around. Then they took it and made it a god, abasing themselves before it and displaying need for it, calling upon it in fear and craving. It is this which is marvelous, given the fact that they have rational faculties. (II 590.31)

Ibn al-ʿArabī discusses the necessity of the rational faculty for understanding *tawḥīd* while speaking of the meaning of "death," which already in the Koran is a clear synonym for ignorance, as in the verse, "Why, is he who was dead, and We gave him life, and appointed for him a light to walk by among the people as one whose likeness is in the darknesses, and he comes not forth from them?" (6: 122). Part of the discussion is based upon the Shaykh's often repeated assertion that there is no real need to prove the existence of God, since a sound rational faculty perceives it innately. "The affirmation of His existence is self-evident to reason, because of the fact that preponderance has been given to one of the two properties of the possible thing" (II 289.9).

When the spirit, through which the body experiences life in the sensory world, departs from the body, this is called "death." It occurs for spirit and body after they had been described as being joined, a joining which is the cause of life.

In the same way, "death" occurs for the soul through lack of knowledge. You may object: "Knowledge of God, which is the life of the souls, is an added factor, while ignorance is fixed within them before the existence of knowledge. So how can you describe the ignorant person as dead?"

We reply: Knowledge of God is the precedent property of the soul of every human being because of the "taking at the Covenant," when He made them testify against themselves. Then, when the souls came to inhabit the natural bodies in this world, knowledge of the profession of God's Unity left them. Then, after that, God brought some souls to life through knowledge of the profession of His Unity, and He brought them all to life through knowledge of God's existence, since knowledge of God's existence is self-evident to the rational faculty. That is why we called the ignorant person "dead."

God says, "Why, is he who was dead," that is, because God has taken away from him the spirit, which is knowledge of God, "and We gave him life and appointed for him a light to walk by among the people." In other words, God returned his knowledge to him and he came to life through it, just as He will return the spirits to their bodies in the next world on the Day of Resurrection. As for God's words in the rest of the verse, "as one whose likeness is in the darknesses" (6: 122), here He means to contrast this with the light by which man walks among the people.

But this light is not life itself. "Life" is the admission of the existence of God, while the "light which is given" is knowledge of the declaration of God's Unity.

The "darknesses" are the ignorance of the declaration of His Unity, while "death" is ignorance of His existence. That is why, in the verse of the taking at the Covenant, God mentioned only that we admitted His existence, not that we declared His Unity. He did not address Himself to *tawḥīd* in that verse. He says, "Am I not your Lord?" They answer, "Yes" (7:172), thereby admitting Lordship, that is, the fact that He is their master. But a slave may be owned by two people in a partnership. Then, when one of these two masters says to him, "Am I not your lord?", the slave must answer "yes" and attest to him. That is why we say that in this verse man admits only that God exists as his Lord, i.e., his owner and master.

This explains why, in the above verse, after saying "And We gave him life," God added something else. He was not satisfied until He said, "and We appointed for him a light to walk by among the people." He means by "light" the knowledge of the declaration of God's Unity, nothing else. For it is this knowledge which establishes eminence and felicity. Any other knowledge does not stand in the same station. . . .

In this waystation man comes to understand that when the one knows the many, the one becomes ignorant of itself, because of its witnessing manyness. This can be explained as follows:

The spirit cannot rationally understand (*ʿaql*) itself without the body, which is the locus of "how many" and manyness. It never witnesses itself alone in the respect that it is undivided in itself. It does not know its humanness without the existence of the body along with it. That is why, when it is asked about its own definition and reality, it replies, "a feeding, sensory, rational body." This is man's reality, the definition of his essence and self. Hence, when man is asked about his definition in respect of being human, he always takes into account this manyness in his definition. He does not rationally understand his unity (*aḥadiyya*) in his essence. He only perceives the unity of the genus, not the unity of his own reality. When man learns through acquired knowledge that he is one in his entity, this is the knowledge of reflective proofs, not the knowledge of tasting, witnessing, and unveiling.

In the same way, the object of man's knowledge of God is the declaration of the Unity of the Divinity (*tawḥīd al-ulūha*), that which is named "Allah," not the *tawḥīd* of the Essence, since the Essence cannot be known at all. Hence the knowledge of Allah's *tawḥīd* is a knowledge of reflective proofs, not a knowledge of unveiled witnessing, since knowledge of *tawḥīd* can never be acquired through tasting. It becomes connected to the levels. (II 618.15)

Reason versus Unveiling

Ibn al-ʿArabī usually mentions the great al-Ghazālī with praise, calling him one of "our companions." Sometimes, however, as in the first passage quoted above, he criticizes him for entering into the arena of theological and philosophical reflection.[1] In another passage, he points out that occupying oneself with such concerns is an obstruction on the path to God. He is discussing the station of "unlettered knowledge" (*al-ʿilm al-ummī*). In employing the term *ummī*, he has in mind the sobriquet of Muḥammad, the "unlettered Prophet" (Koran 7:158). Like many other authorities, Ibn al-ʿArabī understands this to mean that the Prophet's knowledge came only from God, not from reflection and consideration. To employ another term derived from the Koran, his knowledge was "from God" or "God-given" (*ladunnī*): "We had taught [Khaḍir] knowledge *from Us*" (18:65).

For us, being "unlettered" does not contradict memorizing the Koran or the prophetic hadiths. In our view, that person is "unlettered" who does not employ his reflective consideration and his rational judgment to bring out the meaning and mysteries which the Koran embraces. He does not use rational proofs to attain to the knowledge of divine things. And he does not employ the juridical proofs, analogies, and assigning of causes that occupy the legal authorities (*al-mujtahidūn*) in order to grasp the rulings of the Law.

When the heart is safe from reflective consideration, then, according to both the Law and reason, it is "unlettered" and receptive toward the divine opening in the most perfect manner and without delay. It is provided with God-given (*ladunnī*) knowledge in all things to an extent unknown except to a prophet or one of His friends whom He has given of it through tasting. Through this knowledge the degree and plane of faith are perfected. Through it the one who receives it becomes aware of the correctness and the mistakes of reflective powers and in what respect soundness and disorder are attributed to them. All of this comes from God.

The person also comes to know, while judging the unreal (*bāṭil*), that there is nothing unreal in existence, since everything that enters into existence, whether entity or property, belongs to God, not to other than Him. Hence there is nothing useless or unreal in any entity or property, since there is no act that does not belong to God, there is no agent but God, there is no property that does not belong to God, and there is no property-giver except God.

It is unlikely that he who already has knowledge of these things will gain from the divine, God-given knowledge the same thing which the unlettered one among us will gain, he who beforehand had no knowledge of what we mentioned. This is because the scales of rational thought and the outward aspects of the scales of legal investigation among the jurists reject much of what we have mentioned, since the greater part of this affair lies beyond the stage of reason and its scale, which cannot be used here, and beyond the scale of the legal authorities among the jurists, though not beyond "jurisprudence" (*fiqh*), since what we mentioned is identical with sound jurisprudence and genuine knowledge. In the story of Moses and Khaḍir there is a strong proof of what we have mentioned. So [if this is the case with Moses, a prophet, then] what is the state of the jurist? Where do the locatedness (*ayniyya*) and similar things which both the Lawgiver and unveiling attribute to God stand in relation to those things which reason and the ruling of the legal authority hold to be the scales of speculative consideration and the demonstrations of the rational faculty?

God gives His servant mercy by coming between him and his considerative knowledge and legal ruling in respect of Himself. Then He assists him in that through divine opening and a knowledge which He gives him "from Himself." Concerning His servant Khaḍir God said, "[Then they found] one of Our servants"—thereby relating him to the pronoun which denotes the plural (*jamʿ* [=bringing together, gathering])—"whom We had given mercy from Us"—employing the plural pronoun—"and whom We had taught knowledge from Us" (18:65), again with the plural pronoun. In other words: God had brought together (*jamʿ*) for him in this unveiling knowledge of the manifest and the nonmanifest, knowledge of the secret and the open, knowledge of judgment and wisdom, knowledge of reason and convention (*waḍʿ*), knowledge of proofs and obfuscations.

He who is given all-inclusive knowledge and is commanded to employ it, like the prophets and those whom God wills among His friends, is denied (*inkār*), but this individual denies the sciences given to no one. Even if he makes a ruling different from someone else, he knows the place of that person's knowledge and in what respect he makes rulings. He gives to sight and to all the other senses their due in their ruling, and he gives to reason and to all the other spiritual faculties their rulings. He gives to the divine relationships and the divine opening their rulings. Thus it is that the divine knower (*al-ʿālim al-ilāhī*) excels everyone else. This is the "insight" which the Koran mentions in His words, "Say [O Muḥammad!]: This is my way. I call to God upon insight, I and whoever follows after me" (12:108). This complements His words, "It is He who has raised up from among the unlettered people a Messenger from among them" (62:2). The "unlettered prophet" is he who calls upon insight while being unlettered, while the "unlettered people" are those who call to God upon insight along with him. They are his "followers" in the ruling, since he is the head of the group.

The legal authority and the reflective thinker will never be "upon insight" in their rulings. The legal authority may make a ruling today concerning a Shariʿite case and tomorrow something may happen that will make clear to him that he was mistaken in yesterday's ruling. . . . Were he upon insight, he would not rule mistakenly in his first consideration. . . .

The situation of the rational thinker is the same. This happens when a group of rational thinkers exercise consideration and consider the proofs exhaustively. They discover the purport of the proofs, and this gives them knowledge of what has been proven. Then another time you see that an adversary has stood up against them from another group—like a Muʿtazilite, an Ashʿarite, a Brahmin (*barhamī*), or a philosopher—offering something else which contradicts the proof about which the first person was certain. This detracts from his proof, so he considers it and sees that his first position was a mistake and that he had not treated the pillars of his proof exhaustively and had upset the scale in that without being aware. How can this be compared with insight?

Since this does not happen in that which is self-evident (*ḍarūriyyāt*) to reason, the property of insight in people of this station is like that which is self-evident to rational faculties. A person must rejoice in knowledge like this.

Some of what the "unlettered" realize has been related from Abū Ḥāmid al-Ghazālī, the spokesman for the people of this path. He said, "When I desired to join their way, to take from whence they were taking, and to ladle from the ocean from which they were ladling, I retreated into myself and withdrew from my rational consideration and my reflection. I occupied myself with invocation, and a knowledge was kindled in me which I had not had. I rejoiced in that and I said to myself, 'I have gained what the Tribe has gained.' I studied it and I found therein a juridical faculty like what I had had before. Hence I came to know that that knowledge was not pure for me. I returned to my retreat and put into practice what the Tribe practices, and I found the like of what I had found the first time, but clearer and higher. I became happy and studied it, but I found therein the juridical faculty which I had had. The knowledge had not become pure for me. I repeated all that many times, and the state stayed the same.

"Thus I was distinguished from other considerative thinkers and the possessors of reflective powers through this measure, but I did not reach the degree of the Tribe in that. I came to know that writing upon what has been erased (*maḥw*) is not the same as writing upon that which has not been erased. Do you not see the trees? In some of them, the fruit precedes the flower; that is like the level of the learned men of consideration when they enter into the path of God, such as the jurist and the theologian. In other trees, the flower is not preceded by any fruit. That is the unlettered person whose God-given knowledge is not preceded by any reflective, outward knowledge. Hence that God-given knowledge comes to him most easily."

This can be explained as follows: Since there is no agent but God, while this jurist and theologian comes to the Divine Presence with his scale to weigh God, not recognizing that God gave him those scales only to weigh with them *for* God, not to weigh God Himself, he is deprived of courtesy. And he who lacks courtesy is punished by ignorance of the God-given knowledge of opening. Hence he will not be upon insight in his affair.

If he should have an ample rational faculty, he will know from whence he is stricken. Among them are those who enter in and leave their scale at the door. Once they come back out, they take it along to weigh with it for God's sake. This is the best state of those who enter upon God with the rational faculty. However, the heart of such a person is attached to what he left behind, since in his soul he will return to it. Hence he is deprived of the sought-for Truth to the extent that his mind is attached to what he has left behind, because of the regard he pays to it.

Even better than this person is the state of him who smashes his scale. If it is made of wood, he burns it, and if it is something that melts, he melts it. Or he freezes it, so that it ceases being a scale. If its substance remains, he does not care. But this is exceedingly rare. I have not heard that anyone has done it, though we can suppose it, and it is not impossible that God should strengthen one of His

> servants until he does something like this. (II 644.17)

The ideal rational faculty is that which accepts from God the knowledge of Him that He gives to it and does not try to go beyond its own limitations by reflecting upon Him. Hence the virtue of reason is to accept or receive (*qabūl*) unveiling and revelation.

> I have opened for you a door to gnostic sciences which are not attained by reflection, though rational faculties can attain to their acceptance, either through divine solicitude, or through the polishing of the heart by invocation and recitation of the Koran. Then the rational faculty will accept what is given to it by the self-disclosure and it will know that what has come is outside its own power in respect of its reflection and that its reflection can never give that to it. It will thank God for configuring it within a configuration that accepts the like of this—the configuration of the messengers, the prophets, and the people of solicitude among the friends. That takes place so that it will know that its acceptance is nobler than its reflection. (I 305.21)

The Shaykh makes the same point while reminding us of the limitations of reason, the fact that it constricts and binds reality by its very nature. In fact, he points out, "reason" is merely a name given to the cognitive act of distinguishing between ourselves and God. True love of God will never be actualized until the spell of reason is broken and separation is overcome.

> Love for God exercises its property over the lover to the extent of his rational faculty, since his reason delimits him, so it is his shackle. God addressed only those who have rational faculties (*al-ʿuqalāʾ*). They are the ones who are delimited by their own attributes and who distinguish them from the attributes of their Creator. When dissimilarity occurs, delimitation takes place, and the rational faculty comes to be. Hence the proofs of the rational faculties distinguish between the Real and the servant and the Creator and the creature.
>
> He who stands with his reason in the state of his love will not be able to accept anything from the ruling authority of love except what is required by his considerative proof. But if a person stands with his reason's acceptance, not its consideration, accepting from God that whereby He describes Himself, then the ruling power of love will dominate over him in accordance with what his reason has accepted. Hence reason stands between consideration and acceptance, and the property of love within the considering reason is not the same as its property within the accepting reason. Understand this, for here there are mysteries!
>
> God is the Lover. The relationship between us and our rational faculty is the relationship between Him and His knowledge. Nothing comes to be except that about which He has precedent knowledge. In the same way, nothing occurs from us except what is required by our rational faculty. Hence the property of His love among His creatures does not go beyond His knowledge, and the property of our love for Him does not go beyond our reason, whether its consideration or its acceptance. So understand! (II 358.22)
>
> The people of witnessing and finding surpass others. Though the attribute may be the same, he who knows his station with God is not like him who does not know it. "Say: 'Are they equal—those who know and those who know not?' Only those who possess the kernels remember" (39:9). This verse tells us that they knew, then forgetfulness overcame some of them. Some of them continue to be ruled by the property of forgetfulness. "They forgot God, so He forgot them" (9:67). Others are reminded and remember. These are the "possessors of the kernels."
>
> The "kernel" (*lubb*) of the rational faculty is that which becomes the food of the rational thinkers. So the "possessors of the kernels" are those who employ reason as it should be employed, in contrast to the "men of rational faculties," who are the people of the shell (*qishr*). They have missed the kernel, while the possessors of kernels have seized it. The men of rational faculties have not employed what they

> should have employed, since reason must be employed as a shell upon a kernel. Reason is properly employed through its attribute of accepting everything that comes from God. But reason without a kernel does not accept that in respect of its reflection. That is why the Folk of Allah are the people of the kernels. The kernel is their food, so they employ that within which is their sustenance. (III 120.32)

The Character of Muḥammad

What is the nature of this divine book whose truths cannot be grasped through rational interpretation? As is well known, the word Koran, Arabic *qur'ān*, derives from the root *q.r.'.*, and is generally said to mean "recitation." But the primary significance of the root is "gathering" and "collecting together," and some of the early authorities maintained that this is the significance of the name. From this point of view, the two primary names of the holy book, al-Qur'ān and al-Furqān (the latter of which means "separation" or "discrimination") together mean that the Koran gathers everything together and at the same time separates everything out into clear and distinct domains. Ibn al-ʿArabī often employs the term Koran strictly in accordance with this literal meaning, which is particularly significant to him because it is synonymous with the word *jamʿ*, "bringing together," "gathering," or "all-comprehensiveness." The name Allah is the "all-comprehensive name" (*al-ism al-jāmiʿ*) of God, since it gathers together in itself all other names. Perfect man is the "all-comprehensive engendered thing" (*al-kawn al-jāmiʿ*), because he gathers within himself everything in the Divine Reality and everything in the cosmos. The Koran is "al-Qur'ān," because it gathers together all the revealed scriptures that were sent down before it and thereby all knowledge of God.

> The Koran is one book among others except that, to the exclusion of all other books, it alone possesses all-comprehensiveness (*jamʿiyya*). (III 160.34)

Ibn al-ʿArabī comments upon the all-comprehensive nature of the Koran in many contexts, most commonly in conjunction with the perfect and all-comprehensive character of the Prophet, which made him the only possible receptacle for the Koran.

> The Koran unveils all the knowledges sent down in the scriptures and contains that which is not contained by them. He who has been given the Koran has been given the perfect luminosity (*ḍiyā'*) which comprises every knowledge. . . . Because of the Koran it is true to say that Muḥammad was given the "all-comprehensive words" (*jawāmiʿ al-kalim*). So the sciences of the prophets, the angels, and every known tongue are comprised in the Koran and elucidated by it to the "Folk of the Koran." (II 107.20)

The "Folk of the Koran" are those whom we have met elsewhere as the "Folk of Allah," since, according to a hadith, "The Folk of the Koran are the Folk of Allah and His elect."[2] In Ibn al-ʿArabī's view, "The most felicitous people with God are the Folk of the Koran" (II 443.4).

Ibn al-ʿArabī provides long and frequent commentaries on various sayings of the Prophet to show his superiority over all other messengers, prophets, and friends of God. Thus the Prophet said that on the Day of Resurrection he will be singled out for the "banner of praise"[3] and the "praiseworthy station."[4] He was given "the knowledge of those of old and the later folk."[5] He said, "I will be the master of mankind on the Day of Resurrection."[6] He "was given the all-comprehensive words (*jawāmiʿ al-kalim*)"[7] and "was a prophet when Adam was between water and clay."[8] Only a few brief comments on some of these sayings can be quoted here.[9]

When God taught Adam the names (Koran 2:30), he was in the station second to the station of Muḥammad, since Muḥammad had already come to know the all-comprehensive words, and all the names are words. (II 88.15)

Muḥammad was the greatest locus of divine self-disclosure, and thereby he came to know "the knowledge of the ancients and the later folk." Among those of old was Adam, who had knowledge of the names. Muḥammad was given the all-comprehensive words, and the words of God are never exhausted.[10] (II 171.1)

The Messenger of God said, "I will be the master of mankind on the Day of Resurrection." The reason for this is his perfection. He said, "Were Moses alive, he would find it impossible not to follow me,"[11] because of the all-inclusiveness of the Prophet's messengerhood and the all-embracingness of his Law; for he was singled out for things never given to any prophet before him, and no prophet was ever singled out for anything that Muḥammad did not possess, since he was given the all-comprehensive words. He said, "I was a prophet when Adam was between clay and water," while every other prophet was only a prophet during the state of his prophethood and the time of his messengerhood. (III 141.7)

In his answers to al-Ḥakīm al-Tirmidhī, Ibn al-ʿArabī defines the "banner of praise" (*liwāʾ al-ḥamd*) which will belong to the Prophet on the Day of Resurrection and explains why the Prophet deserves that banner.

The "banner of praise" is the praise of praises, the most complete praise, the highest and most elevated praise in level. People gather around a banner, since it is the mark of the level and existence of the king. In the same way, all praises gather around the praise of praises, since it is the correct praise which has nothing equivocal about it, nor any doubt or suspicion that it is a praise, since it denotes by its very essence, since it itself is a banner.

You might say concerning a person, "He is generous," or that person might say about himself that he is generous. This laudation may be true and it may not. But when it is found that he bestows by way of disinterested kindness and beneficence, this very bestowal gives witness to the generosity of the bestower. Hence no equivocality enters into it. This is the meaning of the praise of praises called the "banner of praise." It is named a "banner" because it brings together all praises. . . .

In order to merit the banner of praise, the Prophet will praise his Lord by the Koran, which brings together all praises. That is why it is called *qurʾān*, that is, "bringing together" (*jāmiʿ*). . . . The Koran did not descend upon anyone before him and it is not proper for it to descend except upon someone who possesses this station. For He should not be praised except by the praises which He has set down in the Law, in respect of the fact that He has set them down in the Law, not in respect of the fact that His Perfection demands attributes of praise. That is the divine laudation. But if He were praised in accordance with what is demanded by His attributes, that would be the praise of common usage (*ʿurf*) and reason. But such a praise is not worthy of His majesty. (II 88.5,21)

The Koran employs the expression "mother of the Book" (*umm al-kitāb*) in three verses, and the term has been explained in various ways. One of the most common interpretations is that it refers to the Fātiḥa, the first chapter of the Koran. One of al-Tirmidhī's questions is, "What is the interpretation of 'Mother of the Book'?" Parts of Ibn al-ʿArabī's answer throw light on his understanding of the relationship between the Prophet and the Koran:

A "mother" is that which brings together (*jāmiʿ*). Hence we have "mother of the cities" [that is, Mecca, the place of coming together for the pilgrimage]. The head is the "mother of the body." It is said [in reference to the brain], "the mother of the head," since it brings together all the sensory and supra-sensory (*maʿnawī*) faculties that belong to man. The Fātiḥa is the "mother" of all revealed books, which are the Tremendous Koran, that is, the tremendous totality that has been brought together (*majmūʿ*) comprising all things.

Muḥammad was given the "all-comprehensive words." Hence his Law comprises all revealed religions (*sharā'i'*). He was a prophet when Adam had not yet been created. Hence from him branch out the Laws to all the prophets. They were sent by him to be his deputies in the earth in the absence of his body. If his body had existed, none of them would have a Law. Hence he said, "Were Moses alive, he would find it impossible not to follow me."

God says, "We sent down the Torah, wherein is light and guidance; thereby the prophets, those who are Muslims, judge for those who are Jews" (5:44). We are the Muslims, and the learned masters among us are prophets.[12] We judge the people of each Shariʿa by their Shariʿa, since the Shariʿa of our Prophet has established it. His Law is its root, and he was sent "to all people" (34:28), while this belonged to no other prophet. "People" extend from Adam to the last human being, and among them there have been Laws, so they are the Laws of Muḥammad in the hands of his deputies. For he is sent out "to all people," so all the messengers are his deputies, without doubt.

When the Prophet himself became manifest, there remained no ruling that did not belong to him and no ruling authority which did not go back to him. But his level demanded that when he became manifest in his own entity in this world, he should be singled out for something that was not given to any of his deputies. That something had to be so great that it comprised everything which was scattered among his deputies and something in addition. Hence God gave him the Mother of the Book, which comprised all the scriptures and books. It became manifest among us as an epitome, seven verses which comprise all verses. (II 134.21)

According to a famous hadith, the Prophet's wife ʿĀ'isha was asked to describe the character (*khuluq*) of God's Messenger. She replied, "Have you not read the Koran?" The questioner said that he had. She said, "Surely the character of the Prophet was the Koran."[13] The Prophet is the most perfect of the perfect men, the locus of manifestation par excellence for the divine name Allah. Hence the Prophet synthesizes everything and possesses all knowledge. "He encompasses the knowledge of all knowers who know God, whether those who had gone before or those who would come after" (III 142.27). To say that his character is the Koran means, according to the literal sense of the term, that he brings together in himself all noble character traits, just as the revealed Koran brings together all knowledge. In other words, it is the Prophet who has assumed as his character traits all the names of God, since he "brings together all things" by being the *qur'ān*, "that which brings together." "The character of the messenger of God was the Koran and the assumption of the divine names as his own traits" (III 61.2). Coming to know the Koran is to come to know the Prophet, God, and all things.

God says, "Surely thou art upon a tremendous character (*khuluq ʿaẓīm*)" (68:4). . . . When ʿĀ'isha was asked about the character of the Messenger of God, she answered, "His character was the Koran." She said that because he was unique in character, and that unique character had to bring together all noble character traits (*makārim al-akhlāq*). God described that character as being "tremendous," just as He described the Koran in His words, "the tremendous Koran" (15:87). So the Koran is his character. If a person in the community of the Messenger who has not met the Messenger of God desires to see him, let him look upon the Koran. When he looks upon it, there is no difference between looking upon it and looking upon God's Messenger. It is as if the Koran takes the configuration of a corporeal form which is named Muḥammad ibn ʿAbdallāh ibn ʿAbd al-Muṭṭalib. The Koran is God's Speech and His attribute, so Muḥammad in his entirety is the attribute of God. "So he who obeys the Messenger has obeyed God" (Koran 4:80), since "He does not speak out of caprice" (53:3), for he is the tongue of God. (IV 60.33)

The lovers of God are called the "carriers of the Koran" (*ḥamalat al-Qur'ān*). Their Beloved brings together (*jāmiʿ*) all attributes, so they are identical with the Koran. When asked about the Prophet's character, ʿĀ'isha said, "His character was the Koran." She did not answer with anything but this. (II 346.12)

The Context of the Koran

It is not uncommon for contemporary scholars to criticize Ibn al-ʿArabī or other Koran interpreters for reading the Koran out of context. But the context of a text is defined by one's own understanding of the text's limitations and horizons. Ibn al-ʿArabī had many good reasons for claiming that "Every existent thing finds in the Koran what it desires" (III 94.2). Modern scholars find historical and literary contexts, and traditional Muslims find the Speech of God, escaping all human attempts to delimit and define it.

If we accept the primacy of historical and literary considerations in the text of the Koran, then perhaps Ibn al-ʿArabī read it out of context. But Ibn al-ʿArabī himself does not accept the primacy of such considerations, since, at best, they are the products of the reflective power of reason and as such are constricted and confined within limited, created horizons. Moreover, contemporary rational faculties can certainly not be described as wholesome and "sound" (*salīm*), since they are governed by the prejudices and presuppositions of a scientistic and materialistic age. A sound rational faculty would at least have faith in the divine origin of the Koran. Once its divine origin is accepted, then there is room for discussion about what God means and what He does not mean in a text. But as long as that is not accepted, there is not much room for exchange between the modern interpreter and the traditional hermeneut.

It has already been said that *ta'wīl* is not an appropriate term to indicate Ibn al-ʿArabī's method of interpretation, since he himself almost invariably uses the term to refer to a mental process pertaining to reflective thought whereby every verse which does not coincide with a preconceived idea of God's incomparability is explained away. More generally, *ta'wīl* is to take one's understanding of God as the standard or "scale" by which to weigh the revelation. Everything which corresponds to that understanding is accepted, while everything else is interpreted to bring it into line with that understanding. Man becomes the standard for judging the revelation, and the Koran is no longer the standard for judging man. Ibn al-ʿArabī rejects this approach entirely, insisting instead that man must allow himself to be judged, shaped, and formed by the Divine Speech. Man must devote himself to worship and godfearing, to recitation of the Koran, and to all the spiritual disciplines set down by the Law and the Way. He must constantly pray to God to enlighten him as to the meaning of the Holy Book and to increase him in knowledge. When and if God unveils to him the meaning of a verse or a portion of the Book, he must weigh his unveiling in the scales of the Law and the tradition. Only if it harmonizes with these can it be taken seriously. In any case, there is no guarantee that man will be given such understanding. The Koran is much too sacred to be taken by storm. It must give of itself when and if it wants.

To come back to the question of "context," for Ibn al-ʿArabī, the Koranic context is the divine knowledge, from which nothing is hidden. Once we come to know that the text is God's own Speech, historical considerations are of no account—at least not for understanding what *God* meant by the text, since there is no denying that the Koran can throw light on any number of phenomena connected to the historical situation at the time of Muḥammad. But for the most part these phenomena are of no interest to Ibn al-ʿArabī, since they pertain to "useless knowledge," that is, knowledge which has no bearing on ultimate human felicity.

As we will see below, Ibn al-ʿArabī's basic answer to anyone who would criticize his Koran commentary is that any interpretation supported by the literal text is valid. He might say something like this: I do not object to your interpretations, though I consider them bound and constricted by your limited perspective. And you should not object to my interpretations, since they are supported by the literal text, usually much more so than yours. If you say that my interpretation is wrong, you are saying that God could not have meant that in this verse, and you reach this conclusion through your constricting rational faculty, which would tie God down to your idea of what He is. But God cannot fit into your constrictions. Or rather, though He discloses Himself within them, He also stands infinitely beyond them. I base my interpretation upon a meaning which God has unveiled to me, so it is His meaning. Your interpretation at best is based upon your own understanding of the text. Unveiling allows me to see that your interpretation is also correct in a certain limited way. It is unfortunate that you cannot make the same concession to me. Instead, you prefer to squeeze God into your own mold.

As Ibn al-ʿArabī well knows, denial is one of the characteristic traits of reason and the Law, nor does he himself refrain from denying wrong views on these levels. Both affirmation and denial have positive roles to play.

> In this waystation, a person comes to know the coming together of opposites, which is the existence of the opposite within its own opposite. This is the strongest knowledge by which one can know oneness (*waḥdāniyya*), since the witnesser witnesses a state in which it is impossible for him not to know that the entity of the opposite is itself identical with its opposite. Hence he perceives Unity in manyness, though not in the manner of the arithmeticians (*aṣḥāb al-ʿadad*), since that way is illusory, while this is a witnessed, verified knowledge.
>
> One of those who excelled in this blessed station among the early generations was Abū Saʿīd al-Kharrāz.[14] I had taken this vision on his authority until I myself entered the station, and I gained what I gained. I came to know that it is the truth, and that the people who deny (*inkār*) it are correct, since they deny it on the basis of reason. The rational faculty can do nothing else in respect of its consideration. He who gives to the extent of his own capacity in respect of what the point of view demands has fulfilled the right of the situation. This is where our feet are established and fixed. So we do not deny the claims of anyone who makes claims, except as we are commanded to deny, so we deny according to the Law. This denial is also a reality; we only witness a condition that demands denial. In the same way we deny it on the basis of reason.
>
> The Law has a power (*quwwa*) whose reality will not allow it to be overstepped, just as reason also has such a power. Tasting also has a power by which we put it into practice, just as we put into practice everything else which has a power in accordance with its power. We live with the present moment (*waqt*). With reason we deny what reason denies, since then our present moment is reason, but we do not deny it by unveiling or the Law. With the Law we deny what the Law denies, since our present moment is the Law, but we do not deny it by unveiling or by reason. As for unveiling, it denies nothing. On the contrary, it establishes each thing in its proper level. He whose present moment is unveiling will be denied, but he will deny no one. He whose present moment is reason will deny and be denied, and he whose present moment is the Law will deny and be denied. So know that! (II 605.14)

Since the Koran is God's Speech, and since God's knowledge embraces all things, God knows every possible meaning that can be understood from the text. He also *intends* every one of those meanings, though not necessarily for everyone. Other scriptures also, by being the Speech of God, share in this attribute. In the following passage, Ibn al-ʿArabī uses the verbs *taʾawwul* and *taʾwīl*, "to interpret," in a neutral sense.

Every sense (*wajh*) which is supported (*iḥtimāl*) by any verse in God's Speech (*kalām*)—whether it is the Koran, the Torah, the Psalms, the Gospel, or the Scripture—in the view of anyone who knows that language (*lisān*) is intended (*maqṣūd*) by God in the case of that interpreter (*muta'awwil*). For His knowledge encompasses all senses. . . . Hence, every interpreter correctly grasps the intention of God in that word (*kalima*). This is the Truth, "[a Mighty Book:] to which falsehood comes not from before it nor from behind it; a sending down from One Wise, Praiseworthy" (41:42) upon the heart of him whom He chooses from among His servants. Hence no man of knowledge can declare wrong an interpretation which is supported by the words (*lafẓ*). He who does so is extremely deficient in knowledge. However, it is not necessary to uphold the interpretation nor to put it into practice, except in the case of the interpreter himself and those who follow his authority. (II 119.21)

We say concerning the senses of a verse that all are intended by God. No one forces anything upon God. On the contrary, it is an affair verified by God. The reason for this is as follows: The verse of God's Speech, of whatever sort it may be—Koran, revealed book, scripture, divine report—is a sign or a mark signifying what the words (*lafẓ*) support in all senses and intended by the One who sent down His Speech in those words, which comprise, in that language, those senses. For He who sent it down knows all those senses without exception. He knows that His servants are disparate in their consideration of those words and that He has only prescribed His address as Law for them to the extent that they understand it.[15] Hence, when someone understands a sense from the verse, that sense is intended by God in this verse in the case of the person who finds it.

This situation is not found outside God's Speech. Even though the words might support a sense, it may be that it was not intended by the speaker; for we know that he is incapable of encompassing all the senses of the words. . . .

Hence, everyone who comments (*tafsīr*) the Koran and does not go outside of what the words support is a true commentator. However, "He who comments according to his own opinion (*ra'y*) becomes an unbeliever"—so it has been recorded in the *Ḥadīth* of al-Tirmidhī.[16] But the commentary will not be "according to his own opinion" until the speakers of that language do not recognize that sense in that word. (II 567.19)

The Commentary of the Folk of Allah

Ibn al-ʿArabī usually remarks on Koran commentary in the context of his own interpretations of a verse. In the following he is discussing the profession of God's Unity, *tawḥīd*. He points out the difference between the terms *aḥad* and *wāḥid*, both of which mean "one," and explains one of the senses of the word *aḥadiyya* or "unity," which derives from *aḥad*.

The word *aḥad* is applied in the Koran to other than God. God says, "Let him not associate one[17] with his Lord's worship" (18:119). In respect to the commentary on meaning practiced by the Folk of Allah, what is understood from this verse is that He is not worshiped in respect of His Unity, since Unity contradicts the existence of the worshiper. It is as if He is saying, "What is worshiped is only the 'Lord' in respect of His Lordship, since the Lord brought you into existence. So connect yourself to Him and make yourself lowly before Him, and do not associate Unity with Lordship in worship. Do not make yourself lowly before Unity as you make yourself lowly before Lordship. For Unity does not know you and will not accept you. Hence you would be worshiping Him who is not worshiped, desiring Him who cannot be desired, and practicing without object. That is the worship of the ignorant." Hence God negates the worship of the worshipers from having a connection to Unity, since Unity is established strictly and only for Allah. As for everything other than Allah, it has no Unity whatsoever. This then is what we understand from this verse in respect of our way of Koranic commentary.

The exoterics (*ahl al-rusūm*) also take

their share from this verse, commentating upon its meaning. They ascribe the mentioned "one" to the associates which people take. This also is a sound commentary. For the Koran is the shoreless ocean, since He to whom it is ascribed intends all the meanings demanded by speech—in contrast to the speech of created things.

When you know this, you will know what God meant when He said to His Prophet, "Say: 'He is God, One'" (112:1), that is, He has no associate in this attribute.

As for the term *wāḥid*: We considered the Koran. Does God ascribe it to other than Himself, as He ascribes unity? I did not find it. But here I am not certain. If He does not ascribe it, then it is more specific than unity. It is a name of the Essence, a proper name (*ʿalam*), but it is not an attribute like unity, since attributes are a place of sharing (*ishtirāk*). That explains why unity is ascribed to everything other than God in the Koran.

The speech (*kalām*) of people and their technical terminology (*iṣṭilāḥ*) are of no account. Instead, what has come in the Koran—which is the Speech of God—must be considered. If the word *wāḥid* is found [applied to other than God] in the Speech of God, then its property is that of *aḥad*, because of what it shares in common verbally. But if the word *wāḥid* is not applied to other than God in the Speech of God, then it has to be given the characteristics which pertain to the Essence. It will be like the name Allah, by which no one else is named. (II 581.4)

Ibn al-ʿArabī sees a profound difference between the *ta'wīl* of the men of reason and the *tafsīr* performed by the Folk of Allah. Since the philosophers and theologians have neither unveiling nor firm faith that God means what He says, they try to pass from the outward or "exoteric" sense (*ẓāhir*) of the verse to the inward or "esoteric" sense (*bāṭin*). The process of interpretation is a crossing over (*ʿubūr*), as we have already seen in speaking of the "interpretation" (*taʿbīr*) of dreams. Once crossing over is made, one "gives expression" (*ʿibāra*) to the inward sense through outward forms. But in making this crossover, the rational thinkers let go of the outward sense, while the Folk of Allah, who make a similar crossover, never let go of it. Thus, the rational thinkers cannot accept that a verse such as, "Everything in the heavens and the earth glorifies God" (57:1) can be taken literally, so they try to "give expression" to its meaning through various interpretations.

Know—God confirm you, O you who seek knowledge of the things as they are in themselves—that you will never gain this knowledge unless God acquaints you with it from yourself and lets you witness it in your own essence. Then you will gain what you seek through tasting, while you become acquainted with it through unveiling. But there is no way to gain this except through a beginningless solicitude which gives you a complete preparedness to accept it; [and this preparedness will show itself] by means of ascetic discipline in the soul, bodily struggles, the assumption of the traits of the divine names, the realization of pure and angelic spirits, purification by a purity designated and detailed by the Law and not by reason, nonattachment to any engendered things, and freeing the locus [of self-disclosure] from all "others" (*aghyār*). The Real has chosen out for Himself from you only your heart, since He illumined it with faith, and it encompasses the majesty of the Real.

When someone gains this description, he sees the possible things with the eye of the Real, so he witnesses them. Even if they are not found in themselves [through existence in the cosmos], he does not lose them. When the light of faith spreads over the entities of the possible things, it may unveil to his insight—or rather, to his insight and his sight—the fact that, in the state of their nonexistence, the entities both see and are seen, hear and are heard, through an immutable sight and an immutable hearing which have no existence. The Real designates whichever of those entities which He wills. He turns toward it, but not toward others like it, through His speech which in the Arabic language is expressed as "Be!" The entity hears His command, and hurries to what is commanded. It comes to be from the word (*kalima*), or rather, it itself is the word.

In the state of their beginningless nonexistence (*al-ʿadam al-azalī*) the possible things never cease knowing Him who is the Being Necessary through His Essence. They glorify and magnify Him with a beginningless glorification and an eternal and inherent magnification. They have no existent entity, while they lose not a single property. Since the state of all the possible things is to have these attributes, which are accompanied by no ignorance, what then is their state in their existence and their becoming manifest to themselves? Is there an inanimate object which does not possess rational speech (*nuṭq*), a plant which has not realized the magnification of its Creator, an animal which does not attest through its state, or a human being not connected to his Lord? That would be impossible. Hence every possible thing in existence must glorify God with a tongue that is not understood and a dialect that not everyone comprehends. But the people of unveiling hear it, and the faithful accept it in faith and worship, for God says, "There is nothing that does not glorify Him in praise, but you do not understand their glorification. Surely He is Clement, Concealing" (17:44).

In this verse He brings the name of the veil and the curtain, that is, "Concealing."[18] He also brings the name which requires a delay in calling to account until the future and prevents calling to account in the present, that is, "Clement." For He knew that among His servants are those deprived of unveiling and faith, that is, the rational thinkers (*al-ʿuqalāʾ*), the slaves of their powers of reflection, those who halt with crossing over (*iʿtibār*). They pass from the outward sense (*ẓāhir*) to the inward sense (*bāṭin*) and separate themselves from the outward sense. Hence they "give expression" (*ʿibāra*) to it, since they are people neither of unveiling nor of faith, God having veiled their eyes from witnessing the true situation of the existent things. Nor have they been provided in their hearts with a faith to be "a light, running before them" (66:8).

As for the faithful, the truthful, the possessors of steadfastness among the friends of God, they cross over, taking the outward sense along with them. They do not cross *from* the outward sense *to* the inward sense, but they take the letter itself to the meaning, without "giving expression" to it. Hence they see things with "two eyes" and, through the light of their faith, witness "the two highways."[19] They are not able to deny what they witness, nor do they reject that about which they have certainty. For God has let them hear the rational speech of the existent things, or rather, the rational speech of the possible things before they come into existence. (III 257.16)

Commentary by Allusion

Ibn al-ʿArabī devotes Chapter 54 of the *Futūḥāt* to the "True knowledge of allusions," explaining therein why the Sufis do not always express their teachings in the clearest of languages. The word translated here as "allusion" (*ishāra*) means literally to point to or to give a sign, as for example, to nod the head in agreement. It is used in a single instance in the Koran. When Mary brought the infant Jesus to her folk, they said, "Mary, thou hast surely committed a monstrous thing! . . . Then Mary 'pointed to' the child" (19:29), that is, she made an allusion which he understood, and then he spoke in her defense. In the following passage, Ibn al-ʿArabī refers to the fact that the word *āya* or "sign" in the Koran is employed both for the verses of the Book and for the outward and inward phenomena of the cosmos. In mentioning Sufi commentaries which are called "allusions" rather than commentaries, he has in mind such works as *Laṭāʾif al-ishārāt* ("Subtle Allusions") of Abu'l-Qāsim al-Qushayrī (d. 465/1072–73).[20]

When God created the creatures, He created man in various stages (*ṭawr*). Among us are the knower and the ignorant, the just and the stubborn, the overpowering and the overpowered, the ruler and the ruled, the dominating and the dominated, the leader and the follower, the commander and the commanded, the king and the subjects, and the envier and the envied. God created no one more onerous and troublesome for the Folk of Allah than the exoteric scholars (*ʿulamāʾ al-rusūm*). Yet the Folk of Allah are those who have been singled out for His service. They are the gnostics by way of divine bestowal (*wahb*), those whom He has given His mysteries among His creatures, letting them understand the meanings of His Book and the allusions of His address. In relation to the Folk of Allah the exoteric scholars are like the pharoahs in relation to God's messengers.

Since, in accordance with God's eternal knowledge, the situation in existence occurs as we have mentioned, our companions have turned to "allusions"—just as Mary turned to allusion—because of the people of lies and deviation. The speech of our companions in explaining (*sharḥ*) His Mighty Book, "to which falsehood comes not from before it nor from behind it" (41:42), is allusions, even if it is a reality and a commentary upon its beneficial meanings. They refer it all back to their own souls, even though they discourse about it in general and discuss the mode in which it has been sent down, as known by the people of the language in which the Book was revealed. Hence God combines the two modes in them, as He said, "We shall show them our signs on the horizons and themselves" (41:53), that is, We shall show them the verses which are sent down concerning both the horizons and themselves.

Every revealed verse has two senses (*wajh*): A sense which they see within themselves and a sense which they see outside of themselves. That which they see inside themselves they call an "allusion" in order that the jurist (*faqīh*)—the exoteric scholar—will be comfortable with it. They do not say that it is a "commentary." Thereby they defend themselves against the evil of the jurists and their vile accusations of unbelief. The jurists do that because they are ignorant of the modes in which the address of the Real descends. But in this they follow the road of guidance, for God had the power to state explicitly the interpretations (*taʾawwul*) of the Folk of Allah in His Book, yet He did not do that. On the contrary, He inserted into those divine words which descend in the language of the common people the sciences of the meanings of election which He allows His servants to understand when He opens up the eye of understanding which He has provided for them.

Were the exoteric scholars to be fair, they would take into account their own souls when they consider the verse with the outward eye which is acknowledged amongst them. Then they would see that they are ranked in degrees (*tafāḍul*) in that. Some of them are better than others in speaking (*kalām*) about the meaning of that verse. Then the one who fell short would admit to the superiority of the one who did not fall short. Yet all of them walk in the same path.

Then, in spite of this superiority which they witness in what they have among themselves, they denounce the Folk of Allah when they bring something which is hidden from their perception. They do this because they believe the Folk of Allah are not men of knowledge and that knowledge can only be gained through the ordinary learning (*taʿallum*) that is well known. And they are right in that, since our companions only gain that knowledge through learning, that is, through a giving of knowledge by the All-merciful Lord. God says, "Recite: In the name of thy Lord, who created, created man of a blood-clot. Recite: And thy Lord is the Most Generous, who taught by the Pen, taught man what he knew not" (96:1-5). For it is He who says, "He brought you forth from your mothers' wombs, not knowing anything" (16:78). And He says, "He created man, He taught him the explication" (55:3-4). So God is man's teacher.

We do not doubt that the Folk of Allah are the inheritors of the messengers. God says to the Messenger, "He has taught thee what thou knewest not" (4:113). He says concerning Jesus, "He will teach him the Book, the Wisdom, the Torah, and the Gospel" (3:38). He says concerning Khaḍir, Moses' companion, "Whom We had taught knowledge from Us" (18:65).

So the exoteric scholars are right in what they say—that knowledge comes only through learning. But they are wrong in their belief that God does not teach him who is not a messenger or a prophet. God says, "He gives wisdom to whomsoever He will" (2:269), and wisdom is knowledge. He says, "whomsoever," which means anyone.

But the exoteric scholars have preferred this world to the next and the side of creation to the side of the Real. They have become accustomed to taking knowledge from books and from the mouths of men of their own kind. They think they are of the Folk of Allah because of that which they know and by which they surpass the common people. All of this has veiled them from knowing that God has servants whom He has undertaken to teach, in their inmost mystery, what He has sent down in His Books and upon the tongues of His messengers. This is sound knowledge from the Knower—Him who teaches and concerning whose knowledge no man of faith has any doubt, nor any man without faith.

Those [without faith] who say, "God does not have knowledge of the particulars (*juz'iyyāt*)," did not mean to negate His knowledge of them.[21] They only intended that His knowledge of a thing does not come to Him newly. On the contrary, He knows the particular things as inserted within His knowledge of the universals. Hence they affirmed that He has knowledge, though they are not among the faithful. They intended thereby to declare His incomparability, but they were mistaken in their way of expressing that.

God undertook, because of His solicitude toward some of His servants, to teach them about Himself through inspiration and giving them understanding of Him. After saying, "By the soul and Him who proportioned it," He says, "and inspired it as to its lewdness and godfearing" (91:8). Hence He made its lewdness distinct from its godfearing, as an inspiration from God to the soul, in order that it would avoid lewdness and practice godfearing.

Just as, at root, God sent down the Book upon His prophets, so He sends down understanding upon the hearts of some of the faithful. The prophets never said anything about God which He had not said to their hearts. They did not extract what they said from their own souls, nor from their powers of reflection, nor did they exert themselves in that. On the contrary, it came to them from God. God says, "A sending down from One Wise, Praiseworthy," and He has just said, "to which falsehood comes not from before it nor from behind it" (41:42). The root which is spoken about [i.e., the Koran] comes from God, not from man's reflection and deliberation, and the exoteric scholars know that. Hence it is only proper that the Folk of Allah, those who put the Book into practice, be more deserving of explaining the Book and explicating what God has sent down in it than the exoteric scholars. Therefore its explanation will also be a sending down from God, as was the root, upon the hearts of the Folk of Allah.

ʿAlī ibn Abī Ṭālib said in this respect, "This is nothing but an understanding of the Koran which God gives to whomsoever He will of His servants." He made this a "gift" from God, and He expressed this gift as an "understanding" from God. So the Folk of Allah are more worthy of that than others.

The Folk of Allah saw that God had given the turn of fortune in the life of this world to the people who deal in outward significance, the exoteric scholars. He gave them domination over the creatures through the pronouncements they make and He joined them to those "who know an outward significance of the present life, but of the next world they are heedless" (30:7). In their denial of the Folk of Allah, "they think they are working good deeds" (18:104). Hence, the Folk of Allah let them have their states, since they knew on what basis they are speaking. Then they protected themselves from these scholars by naming the realities "allusions," since the exoteric scholars do not deny "allusions." However, when tomorrow, the Day of Resurrection comes, the situation in all things will be as the poet said:

When the dust clears
  you will see
if you sit on a mare
  or an ass.

In the same way, the Verifier from among the Folk of Allah will be distinguished from him who claims to be worthy on the Day of Resurrection. . . .

How can the exoteric scholar be compared with the state indicated by ʿAli ibn Abī Ṭālib, when he said of himself that were he to speak of the Fātiḥa of the

Koran, he would make it carry seventy loads? Does this come from any place other than the understanding which God gave to him concerning the Koran?

Hence the name *faqīh*[22] is much more appropriate for the Tribe than for the exoteric scholar, for God says about the *faqīhs*, "[Why should not a party of every section of the faithful go forth] to gain understanding (*tafaqquh*) in religion, and to warn their people when they return to them, that haply they may be aware" (9:122). Hence God places them in the station of the Messenger in the gaining of understanding of the religion and in warning. It is he who calls to God "upon insight," just as the Messenger of God calls upon insight. He does not call on the basis of the "predominance of surmise" (*ghalabat al-ẓann*),[23] as does the exoteric scholar. When a person is upon insight from God and "upon a clear sign from his Lord" (11:17) when he calls to Him, his giving pronouncements and speaking are totally different from those of the one who gives pronouncements in the religion of God by the predominance of his surmise.

One of the characteristics of the exoteric scholar in defending himself is that he is ignorant of him who says, "My Lord has given me to understand." He considers himself superior to the one who says this and to the true possessor of knowledge. But he who is of the Folk of Allah says, "God has cast into my inmost consciousness what He meant by this ruling in this verse." Or he says, "I saw the Messenger of God in an Incident, and he gave me news of the soundness of this report which has been related from him and what it signifies for him."

Concerning this station and its soundness, Abū Yazīd addressed the exoteric scholars with his words, "You take your knowledge dead from the dead, but we take our knowledge from the Alive who does not die!"[24]

The likes of ourselves say, "My heart told me of my Lord." You say, "So and so told me." Where is he? "Dead." "And he had it from so and so." Where is he? "Dead." When someone said to Shaykh Abū Madyan, "It is related from so and so, from so and so, from so and so," he used to say, "We don't want to eat dried meat. Come on, bring me 'fresh flesh'!" Thereby he would lift up the aspirations of his companions. He meant: This is the words of so and so. What do you yourself say? What God-given knowledge has God singled out for you? Speak from your Lord, and forget about, "so and so related from so and so." They ate fresh meat, and the Giver has not died. He is "nearer" to you "than the jugular vein" (50:16).

The divine effusion is perpetual, the door to heralding visions (*mubashshirāt*) has not been shut, and "these are one of the parts of prophecy."[25] The way is clear, the door is open, the practice is set down in the Law. God rushes to meet him who comes to Him running.[26] "Three men whisper not together, but He is the fourth of them" (58:7). He is with them wherever they are.[27] If He is with you through this kind of nearness, while you claim to have knowledge of that and faith in it, why do you fail to take from Him and speak with Him? Instead you take from others, and you do not take from Him. Why do you not become "newly acquainted" with your Lord? Even rain is higher in level than you, for the Messenger of God exposed himself to the rain when it fell and uncovered his head so that the rain would strike it. When asked about that, he said, "It is newly acquainted with my Lord."[28] He said that to teach and alert us.

Our companions have chosen the term "allusion" rather than other terms for their explanations of the Book of God because of a divine teaching of which the exoteric scholars have no knowledge. This is the fact that an "allusion" only takes place through the intention of the one who alludes, not in respect of that to which the allusion is made. When an exoteric scholar asks them to explain what they mean by the allusion, they compare the allusion to a good omen. For example: A person is in a situation in which his breast becomes constricted. He is reflecting upon his situation, and one man calls out to another, whose name is Faraj ["relief"], "O Faraj!" The person whose breast is constricted hears this. He takes it as good news and says, "God's relief has come, God willing." In other words, he will be relieved from this constriction and his breast will be expanded. The Messenger of God did just this when making peace with the polytheists. They had blocked him from reaching God's House. Then a man came from among the polytheists who was called Suhayl. The Messenger of God said, "The situation has become 'easy' (*sahala*)," since he took the man's name as a good omen.[29] And the situation turned out just as the Messenger had augured. Thus everything was put in order at the hand of Suhayl. But his father did not intend that when he named him Suhayl. He gave him the name as a proper name, to distinguish him from others, though he only meant to give him a beautiful name for the sake of good.

Since the Folk of Allah saw that the Prophet took "allusions" into account, they employed them in their affairs. But they clarified their meaning, their place, and their time. They do not employ allusions in their affairs and among themselves, only when someone sits with them who is not one of them, or when the situation rises up spontaneously within themselves.

The Folk of Allah set down technical terms (*iṣṭilāḥ*) unknown to others unless learned from them. They followed a path in these terms unknown to others. In the same way the Arabs employ in their speech analogies and metaphors so that some of them may understand others. Then, when they are together with their own kind, they speak about the situation clearly and explicitly, but when someone who is not one of them is present with them, they employ the words which they have established as special terms. Then the stranger who sits with them does not know what they are doing or saying.

One of the most marvelous things in this path—it is not found in any other—is the following: Every group which has a science—logicians, grammarians, geometers, arithmeticians, astronomers, theologians, philosophers—has technical terms not known to him who comes from outside unless a master or someone familiar with it acquaints him with it. The only exception is this path [of Sufism].

The sincere seeker—and by this they know his sincerity—enters in among them and has no news of their technical terms. Then God opens up the eye of his understanding and he takes from his Lord at the beginning of his tasting, even though he had no news of the terminology they were using. He did not know that there was a people among the Folk of Allah who employed special technical terminology and that they speak using those terms which only those who have taken from them know. Then this sincere seeker understands everything they are talking about, as if he himself had established the technical terms. He shares with them in the conversation and does not find that strange from himself. On the contrary, he finds it all a self-evident knowledge which he is unable to repel. He does not know how he gained it. But the one who comes from outside, in all the other groups, never finds this unless someone has first acquainted him with the terms.

This then is what is meant by "allusion" in the view of the Tribe. They only employ allusions when outsiders are present, or in their writings and compositions, but no place else. (I 279.7)

Knowledge of Hadith

Ibn al-ʿArabī quotes sayings of the Prophet nearly as often as he quotes the Koran. In most cases, these are taken from the standard sources and would be accepted as "sound" (*ṣaḥīḥ*) by the learned masters of the science of Hadith. However, he often quotes other sayings which are not found in the standard collections and which, on occasion, have been condemned as forgeries by some of the learned. Such, for example, is the case of the famous hadiths, "He who knows himself knows his Lord," or "The first thing God created was the intellect." The Shaykh's justification for employing such hadiths is summed up by a remark he makes in passing concerning the famous saying, "I was a Treasure but was not known . . .": It is "sound on the basis of unveiling, but not established (*thābit*) by way of transmission (*naql*)" (II 399.28). Unveiling provides the means whereby the authenticity of such hadiths has been tested.

Ibn al-ʿArabī sometimes refers to the great friends of God as the "prophets among the friends," thereby meaning that they also, like the prophets, receive reports (*khabar*) from God. At the same time he frequently remarks that even reports given directly by God cannot have any effect upon the rulings (*ḥukm*) of the Law, since only the prophets in the proper sense possess the function of "Law-giving" (*tashrīʿ*). In one of the passages describing the station of the "prophets among the friends," he points to the method in which God gives them knowledge of the hadiths.

> The prophets among the friends in this community are those individuals whom God places within one of His self-disclosures. Then He makes the loci of manifestation[30] of Muḥammad and Gabriel stand before him. Then the spiritual locus of manifestation [Gabriel] allows him to hear as he addresses Muḥammad's locus of manifestation with the rulings of the Law. Once the addressing is finished and the heart of the friend who possesses this locus of witnessing is delivered from fright, he perceives through his rational faculty all the rulings of the Law comprised in that address and appearing within the Muhammadan community. This friend takes those rulings just as the Muhammadan locus of manifestation took them. . . . Then the friend is returned to himself, and he has retained in his memory everything by which the Spirit has addressed the locus of manifestation of Muḥammad. He has come to know the soundness of that address through the knowledge of certainty, or rather, the eye of certainty (*ʿayn al-yaqīn*). He takes the ruling of the Prophet, and he puts it into practice "upon a clear sign from his Lord" (11:17).
>
> There is many a weak hadith which is not put into practice because of the weakness of its line of transmission—because certain forgers (*wāḍiʿ*) transmitted it—yet which is sound in fact, since in this particular case the forger told the truth and did not forge it. The scholar of Hadith (*muḥaddith*) rejects it only because he cannot rely on that person's transmission. But that is only when this forger is the only person to transmit it, or the hadith goes back only to him. But if a reliable transmitter shares in having heard the hadith, then the hadith will be accepted by way of the reliable transmitter. But this friend may have heard the Spirit casting this very hadith upon the reality of Muḥammad, just as the Companions heard along with Muḥammad in the hadith of Gabriel concerning submission, faith, and virtue, when Gabriel confirmed the truth of what the Prophet said.[31] When the friend hears it from the Spirit who casts it, he is like the Companion who heard it from the mouth of God's Messenger, since he gains a knowledge about which he does not doubt. He is different from the Follower—who accepts it only on the basis of the "predominance of surmise"—since there is no suspicion which might impair its truthfulness.
>
> There is also many a hadith which is sound by way of its transmitters and which has been learned by this possessor of unveiling who sees this locus of manifestation. Then he asks the Prophet about this sound hadith, and he denies it and says, "I did not say it or judge by it." Thereby the friend comes to know of its weakness, so he ceases putting it into practice "upon a clear sign from his Lord," even if the people of transmission put it into practice because of the soundness of its line, though in fact it is not sound. The like of this has been mentioned by Muslim at the beginning of his book, *al-Ṣaḥīḥ*.[32] This possessor of unveiling may even come to know who forged this hadith, the line of transmission of which is supposed to be sound. Either the name of the forger would have been mentioned to him, or the form of the person would have been set up before him.
>
> These are the prophets among the friends. In no way have they their own Law, nor are they addressed with a Law. They are given only knowledge (*taʿrīf*) that this is the Law of Muḥammad, or they witness the Spirit descending upon him with a ruling in the Presence of Imaginalization, which is both outside and inside their own essence. In the case of the dreamer, this is called "heralding visions." But the friend shares with the prophet in that he perceives during wakefulness what the common people perceive during sleep. The folk of our path have affirmed that this is the station of the friends—along with other things, such as

acting by Resolve, and coming to know without any created teacher, only God; this is the knowledge of Khaḍir. If God gives the friend knowledge of this Shariʿa by which he worships according to the tongue of the Messenger of God, and He does so by removing all intermediaries—I mean the jurists and the exoteric scholars—then this is God-given knowledge, but he is not one of the "prophets" of this community. Only that one among the friends is a "prophet" who is the inheritor of a prophet in this specific fashion, that is, the witnessing of the angel when he casts to the Messenger.

These then are the "prophets among the friends." All of them are equal in that they call to God "upon insight," as God commanded His prophet to do. . . . The like of these preserve the sound Law in which there is no doubt both for themselves and for those in this community who follow them. Among the people they have the greatest knowledge of the Law, although the jurists do not concede that to them. (I 150.13)[33]

When man renounces his own individual desire, shrinks from his own ego, and prefers his Lord over all else, then God sets up before him in place of the form of his own soul the form of a divine guidance, a real form from the Real, so that he may walk proudly in diaphanous capes of light. This form is the Law of his prophet and the messengerhood of his messenger. It casts to him from his Lord that within which lies his felicity.

Some people see this in the form of their prophet, while others see it in the form of their own state. When it discloses itself to a person in the form of his prophet, he should let the eye of his understanding gaze only at what that form casts to him, nothing else, since Satan will never imaginalize himself in the form of any prophet.[34] This is the reality and spirit of that prophet, or the form of an angel in his likeness, one who knows his Law from God. Whatever the form says is correct.

We had taken many Shariʿite rulings from a form such as this which we had not learned from the learned masters, nor from books. When I presented the Shariʿite rulings which that form had addressed to me to one of the learned masters of our country, one who knew both Hadith and the schools of Law (*madhāhib*), he reported to me that everything I reported to him had been related from the Prophet in the *Ṣaḥīḥ*. Not a single word was missing. . . .

If the form becomes manifest in other than the form of his messenger, then it goes back to his state, without doubt, or to the specific waystation of the Law at that time and place in which he saw the image of the vision. However, this person sees this in wakefulness, while the common people see that while asleep. He should not take any rulings of the Law from this form when it discloses itself to him in this manner. However, he is not prohibited from taking whatever sciences and mysteries it brings—anything other than declaring lawful or unlawful—whether in beliefs or anything else. For the Divine Presence accepts all beliefs other than associating others with God (*shirk*). It does not accept that, since the associate is sheer nonexistence, and Nondelimited Being does not accept nonexistence. (III 70.23)

6

Soteriology

15. WEIGHING SELF-DISCLOSURE

How can reason merely "accept" that which comes from God, without employing its power of discernment? First, this "acceptance" is the acceptance of what comes from *God*—not just anyone—as revealed in the Koran and the Hadith. It is an acceptance based upon faith in the double testimony, "There is no god but God, and Muḥammad is His Messenger." Hence it is merely the acceptance in fact of what any Muslim accepts in theory. The unveiling that the traveler experiences adds nothing to the principles and corollaries of faith. At most it fills in some of the details. Primarily, it transforms the theoretical knowledge which makes up the content of the creed into direct vision. No longer does the traveler merely have faith that, for example, "God's hand is above their hands" (Koran 48:10), since he witnesses this face to face. Unveiling is the verification of faith.

> The knowledge of the Folk of Allah which is derived from unveiling takes the exact form of faith. The unveiling of the Folk of Allah accords with everything accepted by faith, since faith is all true (*ḥaqq*), while he who gives news of it—that is, the Prophet—gives news of it upon the basis of sound unveiling. (I 218.5)

As for reflection, reason's specific power, it has an important role to play on its own level, as was pointed out. But reflection cannot gainsay God's word. If the proofs provided by rational thought contradict revelation, the proper road is not to reject the revelation, but to recognize that the proofs are limited by the powers which have brought them into existence and that these limitations cannot give the lie to Him who created reason and its powers.

> When knowledge from God comes to you, do not place it in the scale of reflection and do not appoint any route for your rational faculty to reach it, lest you immediately perish. For the Divine Knowledge does not enter into any scale, since it set up the scale. How can the scale bring Him who established it under its property? . . .
>
> Knowledge contradicts reason, since reason is a limitation (*qayd*), while knowledge (*'ilm*) is that which is gained from a mark (*'alāma*). The mark that best denotes a thing is the thing itself. As for every mark other than the thing itself, that is

> correct in respect to us only by chance. (II 291.3)

As we have already seen in earlier chapters, the proper route is to pray for understanding from God. "Be god-fearing, and God will teach you" (2:282). But another question of fundamental importance which has not been addressed inserts itself here. Given that we enter the path and follow the guidance of God, and given that we experience an "unveiling" that makes all sorts of things clear to us that we never understood before, can we be sure that the unveiling is from God? Is there no possibility of satanic intervention and our going astray? Is not a person who claims that he is following his own "tasting" in effect claiming independence from the prophets and setting up his own religion, at least for himself?

Ibn al-ʿArabī is well aware of such dangers and discusses them in many contexts. Once again, it will only be possible to provide a few brief examples of how he deals with an important question. But his fundamental answer can be given quickly: Any knowledge, tasting, insight, witnessing, self-disclosure, or whatever that contradicts the literal sense of the Koran and the Hadith must be abandoned. Unveiling, like reason, must submit itself to the Scale of the Law.

One of the major areas in which Ibn al-ʿArabī deals with this problem is in discussing the relationship between the prophets and the friends of God, a theme which cannot be dealt with here except in passing.[1] It is sufficient to say that the friend of God (*walī*) is always a "follower" (*tābiʿ*) of the Prophet, never independent of his guidance. The friend's role is summed up by the Koranic verse mentioned above and frequently quoted by Ibn al-ʿArabī: "Say [O Muḥammad]: 'I call to God upon insight, I and whoever follows after me'" (12:108). Our task here is to ask what criteria and yardsticks can be employed in measuring "insight."

Knowledge and Practice

We saw above that the knowledge provided by the Law is basically of two kinds: Reports and rulings. Reports deal with the contents of faith. Hence, according to the standard formula derived from various Koranic verses, they comprise knowledge of God, the angels, the messengers, the scriptures, the Last Day, and the measure (*qadar*) of the good and evil that appear within the cosmos. Rulings embrace the Shariʿa proper, that is, commands and prohibitions concerning all dimensions of life and practice. To understand Ibn al-ʿArabī's position on the efficacy of unveiling, one must first clearly separate these two categories. The first may be called loosely knowledge or theory or doctrine (*ʿilm*), the second practice or works (*ʿamal*). As the Shaykh constantly reiterates, unveiling can add depth of understanding, clarity of vision, certainty, and so on to the doctrine, though it cannot change any of the doctrine's principles (*uṣūl*) or corollaries (*furūʿ*). But unveiling can add nothing to practice except understanding. The rulings and statutes of the Law are inviolable and must be followed by everyone. No possessor of unveiling can claim anything to the contrary without proving that he has gone astray.

> The traveler who wants to reach the goal safely must avoid the deceptions that lie in wait for him on the path. Once he has reached the stages of unveiling and witnessing, he will be tempted by Satan and his own caprice to depend upon himself rather than follow the Prophet. He must move forward according to the scale of knowledge derived from the revealed Law. If a divine command should come to him in that which becomes manifest to him making lawful (*ḥalāl*) for him something which has in fact been declared unlawful (*ḥarām*) by the Muhammadan Law, then he has been duped (*talbīs*) in that. He must abandon that command and return to the established ruling of

the Law. For it has been established among all the people of unveiling that there is no making lawful or unlawful and nothing of the rulings of the Law for anyone after messengerhood and prophecy have been cut off from the Folk of Allah. Hence the possessor of that command does not rely upon it. He knows for certain that it is a caprice of the soul. . . .

But it is not forbidden that the Folk of Allah be given knowledge by God concerning the soundness of a ruling of the Law in something whose textual basis is not universally acknowledged (*mutawātir*). As for that whose textual basis is universally acknowledged, if a divine knowledge-giving should arrive contrary to it, the knowledge-giving cannot be relied upon. There is no disagreement in this among the Folk of Allah who are people of unveiling and finding.

Some of those who wish for God have been duped in their states without being aware. This is a hidden deception, a strong divine guile, and a being led on step by step without their being aware.[2]

Beware lest you throw the Scale of the Law from your hand in exoteric knowledge (*al-ʿilm al-rasmī*) and in accomplishing what it sets down as rulings. If you understand from it something different from what the people understand, such that your understanding comes between you and the performance of the outward significance (*ẓāhir*) of its rulings, then do not rely upon your understanding! For it is a deception of the ego (*makr nafsī*) in a divine form without your being aware.

We have come across sincere people among the Folk of Allah who have been duped by this station. They prefer their own unveiling and that which becomes manifest to them in their understanding such that it nullifies the established ruling. They depend upon this in their own case, and they let other people observe the established ruling in its outward significance. But in our view this is nothing, nor is it anything in the view of the Folk of Allah. Anyone who relies upon it is totally confused and has left his affiliation with the Folk of Allah, thereby joining the "greatest losers" in works: "Their striving goes astray in the present life, while they think they are working good deeds" (18:104).

It may happen that the possessor of such an unveiling continues to practice the outward sense of that ruling, while he does not believe in it in respect of himself. He practices it by stipulating the outward situation (*ẓāhir*), saying to himself, "To this commandment of the Law I only give the outward dimension (*ẓāhir*) of myself, for I have gained knowledge of its secret (*sirr*). Hence its property in my inmost consciousness (*sirr*) is different from its property in my outward dimension." Hence he does not believe in it in his inmost consciousness while practicing it. If someone practices it like this—"[Whoso disbelieves in the faith,] his practice has failed, and in the world to come he shall be among the losers" (Koran 5:5). "Their commerce has not profited them, and they are not right guided" (2:16). They have ceased being the Folk of Allah and joined up with "him who has taken his caprice to be his god, and God has misguided him in spite of knowledge" (45:23). He supposes he is gaining, but he is slipping away.

So preserve yourselves, my brothers, from the calamities of this station and the deception of this unveiling! I have counselled you and I have counselled this Tribe, thus fulfilling the command that is mandatory upon me. (II 233.34)

When the friends of God climb in the ascents of their aspirations (*maʿārij al-himam*), the goal of their arrival is the divine names, since the divine names seek them. When they arrive at the names in their ascents, the names effuse upon them sciences and their own lights to the measure of the preparedness which the friends bring. They receive only in the measure of their own preparednesses. In this the friends have no need for an angel or a messenger, since these are not the sciences of Law-giving (*tashrīʿ*), but rather lights which allow them to understand that which the messenger has brought in his revelation, or the scripture that has been sent down upon him, or the book, but nothing else. It makes no difference whether the friend knows the book or has heard its details.

The knowledge of this friend can never go outside of the revelation brought by the messenger from God, or the scripture, or the book. That is the case in every friend who is the sincere devotee of his messenger, except in this community, where the friends, in respect of their sincere devotion to all the messengers and prophets, have knowledge, opening, and divine effusion in accordance with everything required by the revelation, attribute, scripture, and book of every prophet. Through this they are more excellent than the friends of God in any other community.

Each friend's unveiling in the divine sciences does not go beyond that which is given by the scripture and revelation of his prophet. In this station Junayd said, "This knowledge of ours is delimited by the Book and the Sunna."[3] Another said, "Every unveiling not borne witness to by the Book and the Sunna is nothing."

What is opened up to any friend of God is only the understanding of the Mighty Book. That is why God says, "We have neglected nothing in the Book" (6:38). Concerning the Tablets of Moses He says, "We wrote for him on the Tablets concerning everything, an admonition, and a distinguishing of everything" (7:145).

Hence the knowledge of the friend never leaves the Book and the Sunna in any way. If someone should leave them, that is not knowledge, nor is it knowledge of friendship. On the contrary, when you verify it, you will find it to be ignorance, and ignorance is nonexistence, while knowledge is verified existence.

The friend is never commanded to follow a knowledge within which there is a Law-giving which abrogates his Law. However, he may be inspired to arrange a form which has not been specified in the Law in respect of its whole, though in respect of the differentiation of its parts, you will find it to be something set down by the Law. Hence, that is the composition of various affairs set down in the Law. The friend joins some of them to others, or it is joined for him by way of casting (*ilqā'*), encounter (*liqā'*), or writing (*kitāba*). Hence he makes manifest a form which had not been manifest in the Law as a whole. The friend has this measure of Law-giving, and by doing this he does not leave the Law by which he is addressed, since the Lawgiver has set down in the Law that he should legislate to this extent, so he sets down the Law only by command of the Lawgiver. . . . If you say, "Where did God appoint that for the learned friend in the tongue of the Law?" We reply: The Messenger said, "If a person sets down a good custom (*sunna*), he will receive its reward and the reward of those who put it into practice until the Day of Resurrection, while [his receiving their rewards] will decrease nothing from their rewards."[4] Hence the Prophet has set down in his Sunna that the friend may set down a custom, though it must be something which does not oppose an established Law through making lawful that which is unlawful or making unlawful that which is lawful. Such is the friend's share in prophecy. (III 55.29)

The Inviolability of the Law

Ibn al-ʿArabī's summary of the various meanings of the term "scale" (*mīzān*) was quoted in Chapter 11. In the continuation of the same passage, he explains the various kinds of scales in accordance with his division of the "whole situation" into knowledge (*ʿilm*) and practice (*ʿamal*).

The Verifier is he who upholds the Scale in every presence, whether of knowledge or of practice, in accordance with what the Scale requires. . . .

As for the scale of rational knowledge, it is of two kinds. One kind is perceived by reason through reflection. It is called "logic" in the case of meanings and "grammar" in the case of words. But this is not the way of the people of this station. . . . Though we join them in the meanings, and necessarily so, this joining in the meanings does not have to go only by way of these words . . . , for the possessor of unveiling is "upon insight" from his Lord in that to which he calls His creatures.

Just as reason possesses reflection, so also it possesses acceptance, and this acceptance has a scale in unveiling. This scale may be known and upheld in every object of knowledge which the rational faculty can perceive on its own. However, the friend does not know the scale by way of reflection or logic. The scale of rational knowledge which comes into our path has to do with knowledge which is gained as a result of godfearing, in respect to God's words, "Be godfearing, and God will teach you" (2:282) and His words, "If you are godfearing, He will give you discrimination" (8:29). When the gnostic gains such knowledge, he considers his godfearing, the affairs in which He had feared God, and his practice; and he considers the knowledge and weighs its affinity with his godfearing in the practice he had performed, for the scales of affinities (*munāsabāt*) do not make mistakes. When he sees that the affinity between the knowledge which was opened up to him and the practice is verified, and he sees that the practice demands it, then he has earned (*iktisāb*) that knowledge through his practice. When the knowledge is outside the scale and has no affinity with it . . . , then this is one of the sciences of bestowal (*wahb*), even if it has a root in earning. . . .

As for the Scale set down by the Law, that is what you employ when God gives you one of the divine sciences—not any of the other sciences, since we are not taking into account other sciences in this specific Scale. We consider the Law, if we should be knowers of it, and if not, we ask the authorities on Hadith (*al-muḥaddithūn*) from among the learned masters of the Law. We do not ask those who have opinions of their own (*ahl al-ra'y*). We say to them, "Has it been related from any of the messengers that he said about God such and such?" If he says yes, then you weigh it against what you have come to know and what has been said to you. You understand that you have inherited from that prophet in that issue. You should also look to see if the Koran denotes this knowledge.

This way is indicated by the words of Junayd: "This knowledge of ours is delimited by the Book and the Sunna." This is the Scale. But it is not necessary in this Scale that the issue be mentioned exactly in the Book and the Sunna. That which is sought after by the Tribe is that a single principle (*aṣl*) bring together the issue and the Book or Sunna, and that this principle be derived from a Book or a Sunna on the tongue of a prophet from the time of Adam down to Muḥammad. This is because many matters enter upon the friends of God during unveiling and the divine knowledge-giving, matters which are not accepted but rather rejected by rational faculties. If the messenger or prophet speaks of these, the rational faculties accept them in faith and through interpretation, but they do not accept them from anyone else, and that because of a lack of fairness. For when the friends practice what the Law has set down for them, the Divine Presence bestows upon them fragrant blasts of divine munificence,[5] which are unveiled to them from the very entities of those divine affairs which they had accepted from the prophets to the extent God wills. Then when the friend mentions them, this person disbelieves in them, though he would have faith in exactly the same thing if brought by the Messenger. How blind is this individual's insight! The least he could say is, "If it is true as you say that you have been addressed by this, or it has been unveiled to you, its interpretation (*ta'wīl*) is such and such," if he is one of those who interpret. If he is an exoteric (*ẓāhirī*), then he could say, "There has entered into the prophetic report something similar to this." For unveiling is not a mark of prophecy, nor did the Lawgiver prohibit it, either in the Book or the Sunna. . . .

Let us now explain the scale of practice: Practice is sensory (*ḥissī*) or of the heart (*qalbī*), and its scale is of its own kind. Hence the scale of practice is to look at the Law and how it has set up the forms of practices in accordance with their most perfect goals, whether the practice is of the heart, sensory, or a combination of the two, such as the ritual prayer, [which is a combination of] the intention (*al-niyya*) and the sensory movements. The Law has set up for it a spiritual form which is grasped by the rational faculty. When you begin the practice, gaze upon that ideal image (*mithāl*) which you have taken from the Law-giver. Practice what you have been commanded in setting up that form. When you have finished, compare your prayer with the spiritual form—referred to as the ideal image which you have gained from the Law-

> giver—limb by limb, joint by joint, outwardly and inwardly. If your prayer coincides exactly with the form, without decrease or increase, then you have "set up the weighing with justice" and you have not "exceeded it" nor "caused loss" therein (Koran 55:7-9). . . .
>
> Just as the Law has set up for you the form of the praiseworthy work and explained it so that you will recognize it, so also it has set up the form of the blameworthy work so that you will recognize it and distinguish it from the praiseworthy. (III 6.34, 7.22, 8.10, 9.6)

The Law is an outward dimension (*ẓāhir*) of the Reality, while the Reality (*ḥaqīqa*) is the inward dimension (*bāṭin*) of the Law. Hence Ibn al-ʿArabī, in contrast to many Sufis, denies any real distinction between *sharīʿa* and *ḥaqīqa*, the Law and the Divine Reality which it manifests. Some people suppose that the Law only pertains to the sensory realm, and that once a person attains to the Divine Presence, all multiplicity is overcome and no more distinctions can be drawn. Ibn al-ʿArabī frequently rejects this way of looking at things by affirming the real manyness established by the "relationships"—the divine names—at the level of Divinity. There is no ontological plurality, since Being is One, but the names demand a plurality of aspects and attributions, making all sorts of distinctions necessary. The contrasts and contradictions so apparent in the revealed texts of the Law merely offer a faithful mirror of Reality itself.

> The "Reality" is the actual situation of Being (*mā huwa ʿalayhiʾl-wujūd*), with all that It entails of diversity, mutual similarity, and conflict. If you do not recognize the Reality in this, you have not recognized it. The Shariʿa is identical with the Reality. . . .
>
> There is no reality that opposes a Shariʿa, since the Shariʿa is one of the realities, and the realities are likenesses and similars. The Law negates and affirms. It says, "Nothing is like Him," so it negates, and at the same time it affirms, as He has said, "and He is the Hearing, the Seeing" (42:11). This is the word of Reality itself.
>
> Hence the Shariʿa is the Reality: Though the Reality bestows the Unity of the Divinity, it also bestows relationships within the Divinity. Hence the Reality affirms only the unity of the relational manyness, not the Unity of the One, for the Unity of the One is manifest in itself, while the Unity of Manyness is difficult to attain. Not every possessor of consideration perceives the Unity of the Many. Hence the Reality, which is the Unity of Manyness, is not discovered by everyone.
>
> When the Sufis saw that both the elect and the common people practiced the Shariʿa and that only the elect knew the Reality, they distinguished between the Shariʿa and the Reality. They made the Shariʿa pertain to the properties and rulings of the Reality which were manifest, and they made the Reality pertain to its properties and rulings which are nonmanifest. (II 563.4, 13)

The spiritual traveler who is not sufficiently rooted in the doctrine may think he no longer has need for the Law. Ibn al-ʿArabī explains this sort of danger in discussing the role of the angels in unveiling. These angels are known as the "casters" (*al-mulqiyāt*), since they cast the knowledge of unseen realities into the heart.

> The friends of God witness the angels, but they do not witness the casting itself; or they witness the casting and they know that it was done by an angel, but they do not witness the angel. No one combines the vision of the angel and the angel's casting except a prophet or a messenger. For the Tribe, this is how the friend is differentiated and distinguished from the prophet, that is, the Law-bringing prophet.
>
> God has locked the door of angelic descent with rulings of the Law, but He has not locked the door of descent with knowledge of those rulings into the hearts of the friends. He has assured that the spiritual descent with knowledge would subsist for them so that they may stand "upon insight" in their calling to God, as do those who follow after the Messenger. Hence He says, "Say: 'This is my way. I

call to God upon insight, I and whoever follows after me'" (12:108). . . .

As for how the casting takes place, understanding of that depends upon tasting, which is the state (*ḥāl*). However, I can tell you that it occurs through affinity. The heart of him who receives the casting must have the preparedness for what is cast into it. Without it, there would be no reception. But preparedness is not identical with reception, since preparedness depends upon a divine designation. Indeed, certain souls may walk upon the path which takes them to the door from behind which, when opened, there takes place this specific casting and other kinds. Then, when they reach the door, they stop until they see that through which it will be opened for them. When it is opened, the command emerges one in entity, and they receive it from outside the door to the measure of their preparedness. They perform no works in this. On the contrary, God specifies each of them with a preparedness. It is here that distinctions are drawn among the various groups, between followers and those who are not followers, between the prophets and the messengers, and between the messengers and those followers who are called in common usage the "friends."

He who has no knowledge imagines that traveling to this door is the cause by which was earned that which was gained when opening took place. Were this the case, those who experience the opening would all be equal. Hence this takes place only through the preparedness, which is not earned. It is from here that those rational thinkers who claim that prophecy is earned fall into error. (II 569.10)

The prophets established the Laws through the command of God brought by the angels of revelation. With the prophecy of Muḥammad, this sort of revelation came to an end, and anyone who claims anything of the sort is by definition an impostor.

The angels of revelation descend upon the prophets, or certain "tenuities"[6] descend from the angels upon the hearts of the friends of God. No angel ever descends with revelation upon the heart of other than a prophet, nor with any divine command whatsoever. For the Sharīʿa has been established, and the obligatory, the incumbent, the recommended, the indifferent, and the reprehensible have all been clarified.[7] Hence the divine command was cut off with the cutting off of prophecy (*nubuwwa*) and messengerhood (*risāla*). That is why the Messenger of God did not content himself with the cutting off only of messengerhood, lest someone imagine that prophecy still remains in the community, for he said, "Verily prophecy and messengerhood have been cut off, so there will be no prophet after me and no messenger."[8] Hence not a single one of God's creatures remained to whom God would give a command which would be a Law whereby he would worship.

If, for example, [someone should say that] God has commanded him to perform an obligatory act which the Prophet had commanded him to perform, then the command belongs to the Prophet. Hence that command is fantasy, a claim to a prophecy which has been cut off. If he says that God has commanded him to do something [which according to the Sharīʿa is] "indifferent" (*mubāḥ*), we would say: This means that the indifferent thing becomes incumbent upon him, in which case it abrogates the Law [of Muḥammad] which he is following, since, through this "revelation" the indifferent, made so by the Messenger, has become incumbent, so to refrain from performing it is a sin. If the one who makes these claims—the possessor of this station—leaves it indifferent as it was, then what is the profit of the command brought to him by the angel?

If he says, "No angel came with it, but God commanded me without intermediary," I would reply: This is worse than the first case, since you are claiming that God speaks to you like He spoke to Moses. But no one has maintained this, neither exoteric scholar nor possessor of tasting. Even if He did speak or talk to you, He would not cast to you through His words anything but sciences and reports, not rulings or a Law. He would never command you, since, if He did command you, it would be like what we said concerning the revelation of the angel.

If what you keep on mumbling about consists of the fact that God has created knowledge of something in your heart, well, there is nothing at any instant but the creation of knowledge in every human being. No friend of God is singled out for this over anyone else. Moreover, we have explained in this book and others the actual situation. We have declared it impossible that God should command anyone with a Shariʿa by which he himself would worship or that He should send him with it to others. But we do not declare it impossible that God should teach him—in the manner which we have stipulated and the people of our path have stipulated—in accordance with the Law by which he worships on the tongue of the Messenger, without any one of the exoteric scholars teaching him that, through heralding visions, which have assured the subsistence of the traces of prophecy among us.[9] These are dream-visions (*ru'yā*) seen by a Muslim or seen for him. They are a truth and a revelation. A person does not have to be asleep to see them; they may occur during sleep or they may occur at other times. In whichever state they occur, they are a dream-vision in imagination through sense perception, but not in the sensory realm. That which is seen imaginally may lie on the inside, within the faculty, or it may come from the outside through the imaginalization of a spiritual being or through the self-disclosure well-known to the Tribe—but it is a true imagination (*khayāl ḥaqīqī*).

If there is a harmonious constitution (*mizāj mustaqīm*) prepared for the Real, then, when the angel brings a ruling or a report containing knowledge to a prophet . . . , the human spirit encounters (*liqā'*) the [imaginal] form and the two meet, the one through giving ear (*iṣghā'*) and the other through casting (*ilqā'*), which are two lights. The constitution becomes excited and inflamed. In the two lights the native heat of the constitution is strengthened and its magnitude is increased. The color of the individual's face changes because of this. This is what is called a "state" (*ḥāl*), and it is the most intense that might be. The bodily moistures ascend in vapors to the surface of the body because of the domination of heat, and this is why the possessors of these states perspire. All of this derives from the compression (*inḍighāṭ*) undergone by the natures (*al-ṭabā'iʿ*)[10] when the two spirits meet. The strength of the hot air which brings the moistures out of the body floods the pores, so cool air cannot enter in from the outside.

When the prophet or the possessor of the state regains his composure and when the angel leaves the prophet or the spiritual tenuity leaves God's friend, then the constitution becomes calm, the heat abates, the pores begin to breathe, the body accepts and is penetrated by cold air from the outside, the constitution cools and increases in coldness, and the cold overcomes the heat, which becomes less. This is the coldness experienced by the possessor of the state and explains why he begins to shiver and puts on more clothes to warm up. Then, after that, he tells what he gained through that herald of good news (*bushrā*), if he is a friend, or that revelation, if he is a prophet. All of this takes place if the descent is that of a spiritual attribute upon the heart.

If, however, the descent is an inblowing (*nafth*), then this is "inspiration" (*ilhām*) and can occur for a friend or a prophet.[11] If something is narrated to him and he hears it without a vision, then he is a "possessor of narration" (*muḥaddath*). If he is shown the angel—given that he is a prophet in the time of the existence of prophecy—or if he is shown the tenuity as an imaginal man, or the form of an animal that addresses him with what it has brought for him, then, if he is a friend of God, he places it next to the Book and the Sunna. If it conforms (*muwāfaqa*) to them, he sees it as an address (*khiṭāb*) which is true and a bestowal of honor, nothing else. It is not an addition to a ruling, nor the occasioning of a ruling. However, it may be the explanation of a ruling or a giving of the knowledge of the actual situation, whereby that which was conjectured by him becomes known. If it does not conform to the Book and the Sunna, he sees it as addressing him with the truth and a trial for him, without doubt. He knows for certain that the tenuity is not the tenuity of an angel nor the locus of divine self-disclosure, but a satanic tenuity. For the angels have no such station; they are greater than that. Most often this sort of thing occurs for the people who hear (*ahl al-samāʿ*) from God in the creatures.

So nothing remains for the friends today, because of the end of prophethood, but God's giving knowledge. The door to the divine commands and prohibitions has been shut. He who claims these doors after Muḥammad has claimed that a Shariʿa has been revealed to him, whether it conforms to our Law or opposes it. However, in other than our time, before the Messenger of God, there was no such prohibition. That is why the righteous servant Khaḍir said, "I did not act on my bidding" (18:82), for his time allowed that; he had a Shariʿa from his Lord. God gave witness of that for him to Moses and to us, and He attested to his blamelessness. As for today, Elias and Khaḍir adhere to the Shariʿa of Muḥammad, either by way of conformity, or by way of following.[12] In either case, they have that only by way of having been given the knowledge (*taʿrīf*), not by way of prophecy. In the same way, when Jesus descends, he will only judge us by our Sunna. God will give him knowledge of it by way of knowledge-giving, not by way of prophecy, even though he is a prophet.

So preserve yourselves, my brothers, from the calamities of this place, for distinguishing it is extremely difficult! Souls find it sweet, and then within it they are duped, since they become completely enamored of it. (III 38.23)

Spiritual States

The experience of unveiling opens up an infinite expanse of previously unseen realities to the heart of the spiritual traveler. One of the major tasks of the Sufi masters is to guide the disciples through the dangers and pitfalls faced by the soul when it meets the Unknown. The realm into which the adept first enters is, after all, the World of Imagination, whose byways never end. It is the domain of the satans and other deceiving forces. One might say that unveiling opens the door to direct experience of the myriad worlds of Samsara.

The traveler needs to keep a clear head during his journeys and not be misled by the swirling forces which lie just beyond the horizons of stability and balance. For the Sufis, the Law, which governs the inward realm as much as it governs the outward, provides the indispensable framework for entering into the imaginal world. Without it the traveler will be thrown about by every blast of deceiving wind.

We have just seen a vivid description of the physiological effects of the "state" which overcomes the adept when the light of his own spirit encounters a light from the unseen world. It is well known that nowadays most people interested in the spirituality of the East desire the "experience," though they may call what they are after intimate communion with God. Those familiar with the standards and norms of spiritual experience set down by disciplined paths like Sufism are usually appalled at the way Westerners seize upon any apparition from the domain outside of normal consciousness as a manifestation of the "spiritual." In fact there are innumerable realms in the unseen world, some of them far more dangerous than the worst jungles of the visible world. No person familiar with the teachings of Sufism would dare lay himself open to such forces without the guidance of a shaykh who has himself traveled the path, faced the dangers and overcome them, and been given a mandate from heaven to guide other seekers.

Before looking at the role of the shaykh, it will be useful to look at the "states," which, in a broad sense of the term, include all the experiences and delights which so many Western seekers are anxious to achieve. As we have already seen, the "states" provide the wayfarers with the sciences of tasting. In other words, by being taken up in a state of love, yearning, fear, thanksgiving, dread, or any other positive psychological and spiritual attribute, the adept gains first-hand knowledge of the unseen realities which these states manifest. But states, in Ibn al-ʿArabī's view, are a sign of immaturity and instability. Like a madman, the possessor of the state loses his reason in the overpowering experience of his state. Hence, just as a madman is not held responsible by the Shariʿa, so also the possessor of the state is not responsible for what he experiences and does, and none of it is counted for or against him (II 358.2). The true masters have passed beyond the ruling properties of the states, always keeping a "cool head," no matter what they may experience inwardly. The masters travel within the "stations" (*maqāmāt*), which are acquired permanently and have none of the instability and fleeting nature of the states.

The word *ḥāl* or state is derived from the root *ḥ.w.l.*, from which we have *taḥawwul* or self-transmutation. The basic meaning of the root is to change from one situation to another, or from state to state. In a non-technical sense, a state may signify situation, condition, case, predicament, anything that changes, the present moment, and so on. In a broad technical sense the state is the present situation of any existent thing, though the Sufis have classified the particular psychological and spiritual states that the travelers experience into many categories, commonly as pairs of opposites.

> A "state" is for you to be subsistent or annihilated, sober or drunk, concentrated or dispersed, absent or present. . . . It was concerning the states that God commanded His Prophet to say, "My Lord, increase me in knowledge" (20:114), so that through the new knowledge he might climb to a waystation with God that he did not possess. These states do not pertain exclusively to human beings, nor to this world. Rather, they are perpetual forever in this world and the next, and they belong to every created thing. (II 498.27)
>
> God says, "He is with you wherever you are" (57:4) . . . , that is, in your states. No existent thing ceases to be in a state. Or rather, there is no entity, existent or nonexistent, which does not have a state, whether ontological or non-ontological. (II 118.22)

In the most general sense, the "states" of the things are the divine "tasks," the continually transmuting self-disclosures of God, the new creation at each instant. "Within the creatures He creates the states perpetually" (II 384.34).

A state is by definition ephemeral, as is shown by its derivation from the root *ḥ.w.l.* Some Sufis, however, have read the term as *ḥāll*, deriving it from the root *ḥ.l.l.* In this case it would mean that which dwells in something else, implying a certain permanence. Ibn al-ʿArabī explains these points in his *Iṣṭilāḥāt* while defining the term in its usual sense:

> A "state" is that which enters in upon the heart without self-exertion or the attempt to attract it. One of its conditions is that it disappear and be followed by its like and so on, until it subsides, though it may also not be followed by its like. Here there is a disagreement in the Tribe concerning the permanence of states. He who sees the succession of likes and does not know that they are likes claims that the state lasts. He derives the word from "indwelling" (*ḥulūl*). He who does not see it followed by its like maintains that it does not last and derives it from the root *ḥ.w.l.* . . . It has also been said that the state is the changing of the attributes of the servant. Once they become established and fixed, this is the "station." (II 133.25; cf. II 384.21)

As pointed out earlier, the state is also distinguished from the station by the fact that the states are bestowals (*mawāhib*) while the stations are earnings (*makāsib*) (II 157.31, 384.29).

Ibn al-ʿArabī frequently uses the term "state" in another important technical sense, closely related to the first and perhaps even more relevant to the subject at hand. In this second sense, state signifies certain dimensions of spiritual realization that differentiate advanced Sufis from ordinary individuals, and more specifically, it denotes the special powers which accrue to them as a result of their station. Hence the term state is used in conjunction with several other terms of the same type denoting the extraordinary feats or miracles which the friend of God may on occasion perform. These terms include charismatic act (*karāma*), breaking of habit (*kharq al-ʿāda*), the exercise of governing control (*taḥakkum*), free disposal (*taṣarruf*), bringing things into engendered existence (*takwīn*), and acting through Resolve (*al-fiʿl biʾl-himma*), that is, producing effects (*athar*) in the outside world through concentration. The first two terms denote the fact that something extraordinary and inexplicable takes place. The others designate the inward spiritual and mental activity which brings the extraordinary events into existence. In this meaning, the "possessor of a state" (*ṣāḥib al-ḥāl*) is he who is able to exercise these extraordinary powers.

> The possessors of states engender things through their Resolves and throw the secondary causes far from themselves. (II 573.32)

But Ibn al-ʿArabī puts no stock in "miracles," since they prove nothing about a person's situation with God and they can even be worked by magicians and practitioners of certain occult sciences. The true Sufi has the power to "break the habits" of creation if he wants, but he would only do so in exceptional circumstances and as the result of an explicit divine command. His concern is rather to observe courtesy, to put each thing in its proper place, to observe the rights of all the secondary causes, and to actualize to the extent possible his own servanthood before God. Hence, here also, a "state" may be a sign of immaturity, if not of misguidance and error.

> People may apply the word "state" and mean by it the servant's becoming manifest in the attribute of God by engendering (*takwīn*) things and producing effects through his Resolve (*himma*). This is the becoming similar (*tashabbuh*) to God which is called "assuming the traits of the names" (*al-takhalluq biʾl-asmāʾ*). This is what the people nowadays mean by "state," and we also use the term in this sense. However, we do not maintain that the state produces an effect. We maintain that the servant has the power to produce it, such that, were he to desire to make it manifest, he could do so. However, courtesy prevents him, since he wants to realize his servanthood (*ʿubūdiyya*) and keep himself hidden through his worship, so that he will do nothing disapproved.
>
> When someone sees such a servant in the extremity of his weakness, he will remember (*dhikr*) God upon seeing him. This, in our eyes, is the friend of God, and he is a divine mercy within engendered existence. This is indicated by the words of the Prophet concerning the friends of God: They are the ones who "when they are seen, God is remembered."[13] Manifest adversity from God is theirs, but they do not lift their heads toward any but God in their states. When someone like this is seen, God is remembered for having singled out such as these for Himself.
>
> Those who have no knowledge of what we say think that the friend—the possessor of the state because of whose seeing God is remembered—is he who possesses engendering (*takwīn*), acting through Resolve, and the exercise in the cosmos of governing control, overpowering sway, and authority. All of these are God's attributes, so when such people are seen, God is remembered. But this is the view of those who have no knowledge of the actual situation. What the Lawgiver meant is what I said. (II 385.12)

Ibn al-ʿArabī often contrasts "state" in this second sense with "station," but here the state is not an ephemeral gift of God, but rather the power of activity which is acquired once a traveler comes to possess a station. Through establishing himself in the stations, the wayfarer assumes the traits of the divine names. Through the state he can manifest his station in the outward world in the appropriate circumstances. Hence the possessor of the station dwells in the inward world of knowledge, while the possessor of the state is the same person who has "descended" to this outer and lower world to put the knowledge into practice.

> There is a disagreement among the Sufis concerning the station of gnosis (*maʿrifa*). Does the one who is qualified by it possess all the stations or not? The correct answer is that this knowledge does not demand a governing control or that its possessor own all the stations in respect of the states and the exercise of free disposal in the cosmos which they bestow. Its only condition is that the station be known. If the one who dwells in this station desires to exercise governing control, he descends to the state—since governing control belongs to the states—for he knows that his descent will not affect his station. But he will not descend to the state except by divine command.
>
> If a verified shaykh in this way says that the possessor of this station owns all the stations, he means through knowledge, not through state. He may be given the state, but that is not a condition. If anyone says it is a condition, he is making claims and has no knowledge of the path of God, nor of the states of the prophets and the great friends of God, and this statement must be rejected. As much as the perfect individual ascends in station, he decreases in state—I mean in this world, but not in the next world. Just as witnessing delivers one from the need to see "others," so also the station takes away the states, since fixity confronts ephemerality. (II 319.4)

In whichever of the two technical senses the term state is understood, the states present dangers to the person who experiences them. Though they are divine bestowals, yet there is always the risk of taking them too seriously, thinking that one has deserved the states, becoming proud, losing one's mental equilibrium, and so on. Hence Ibn al-ʿArabī seldom speaks of the states as positive, but rather as trials that the traveler has to undergo. The sooner they are done with, the better. He mentions their disadvantages and perils in many contexts.

> When the travelers are overcome by states, they become like madmen, and as a result they are no longer answerable to the Law [while experiencing the state]. Thereby they lose much good. That is why none of the great ones (*al-akābir*) ever seek states. They only seek stations. (III 527.26)
>
> When the lover of God possesses knowledge, he is more complete in that respect than in the fact that he is the possessor of a state. In this world a state is an imperfection (*naqṣ*), while in the next world it is a perfection (*tamām*). But knowledge is a perfection in this world, while in the next world it is a perfection and more perfect. (II 358.3)

Ibn al-ʿArabī defines the term "inrush" (*wārid*) as "every praiseworthy incoming thought (*khāṭir*) which arrives at the heart without self-exertion; or, every affair which enters in upon the heart from any divine name" (II 132. 26).[14] Though the inrushes come from God, the disciple may not always be prepared for them.

> In this station, people stand in three levels: In the first case, the inrush is greater than the strength of the soul, so it rules over the soul. He is dominated by the state and follows its ruling property, so the state turns him this way and that. He has no ability to govern himself as long as he remains in the state. If the state continues to control him until the end of his life, this is called "madness" (*junūn*) in this path, as in the case of Abū ʿIqāl al-Maghribī.
>
> In the second case, the person's rational faculty is taken away, though the animal understanding remains. He eats, drinks, and goes this way and that without self-governing or diliberation. These are called the "rational madmen" (*ʿuqalāʾ al-majānīn*),[15] since they take care of their natural livelihood, like other animals. But someone like Abū ʿIqāl was mad and totally taken from himself, so he did not eat and drink, from the time he was taken until he died. This took place over a period of four years, in Mecca.[16] He was "mad" (*majnūn*), that is totally "curtained" (*mastūr*), from the world of his own sense perception.
>
> In the third case, the inrush does not last, so the state disappears. Such a person

returns to his fellows with his reason intact. He governs his own affair, and he understands what he says and what is said to him. He turns this way and that on the basis of deliberation, like any human being. Such is the prophet and those friends who are the possessors of states.

Sometimes the person's inrush and self-disclosure are equal to his own capacity. No one sees any effect of the ruling property of the inrush over him, but one becomes aware upon seeing him, through a hidden kind of awareness, that something has happened to him, since he has to listen to the inrush in order to take what it has brought him from the Real. His state is like that of the sitting companion who is conversing with you, when another person comes with a command for him from the king. He stops talking to you and listens to what that person is saying. Once he receives the message, he returns to the conversation. In such a case, even if you do not see anything with your eyes, you notice that something has distracted him from you, as if someone were speaking to him. Or he has suddenly begun to think about something, so his senses turn toward it in his imagination, and his eyes and his gaze become dull, even while you are talking to him. You look at him, but your words do not register with him, so you become aware that his inward dimension is thinking about something else, different from what you are busy with.

Sometimes the person's capacity is greater than the inrush, so when it comes to him—while he is conversing with you—you do not become aware. He takes what the inrush casts to him, and he takes from you what you say to him, or he speaks to you.

There is no fourth kind of inrush from the Real upon the hearts of the people of this Path. (I 248.27)

The travelers seek to increase their capacity to receive inrushes so that they will not be affected by them. They also avoid those states which become manifest as extraordinary powers.

The Sufis apply the term "exile" (*ghurba*) . . . to becoming an exile from states. They say concerning exile, "It is to become an exile from the influence of states." . . . The meaning is as follows: Without doubt the possessors of states exercise a penetrating power (*nufūdh*) and governing control through which they are able to perform the miraculous breaking of habit which is famous throughout the world. But once they come to understand that the state which occurs in them and manifests an act has no effect upon that which bestows unveiling, they do not remain satisfied with it and they enter into exile from it. They say, "Halting with the state is a bane upon its possessor." They see that exile from the state is the utmost felicity and that the state is the greatest veil over man. It is the place of God's deception (*makr*), and through it man is led on step by step (*istidrāj*). No intelligent person remains in places where there is a possibility of deception. On the contrary, he should only halt in a place where he is "upon insight." (II 527.27, 528.33)

According to the Koran, God is the "Best of deceivers" (3:54, 8:30), and the Sufis have always been extremely wary of His deception (*makr*), which appears in the wiles of Satan and the lower soul. In Chapter 231 of the *Futūḥāt*, "On Deception," Ibn al-ʿArabī provides a long description of the various forms that God's deception may take. At the beginning of the chapter, he provides a succinct definition, relevant perhaps even more in our days than in his.

The Folk of Allah apply the term "deception" to the continuation of favors in spite of [the servant's] opposition [to God's command], [His] making the state subsist in spite of [the servant's] discourtesy, and the [servant's] manifestation of [miraculous] signs without a [divine] command and without being punished.

In our own view, God's deceiving the servant is that He should provide him knowledge which demands practice, and then deprive him of the practice; or that He should provide him with practice, and then deprive him of sincerity (*ikhlāṣ*) in the practice. When you see this in yourself or recognize it in someone else, know that he who has such an attribute is the object of deception.

When I was in Baghdad in the year 608

> [1211-12], I saw in an Incident that the doors of heaven had been opened and the storehouses of Divine Deception were descending like an omnipresent rain. I heard an angel saying, "What deception has descended tonight!" And I awoke terrified. I considered the way to safety from that, and I could not find it except in knowledge of the Scale set up by the Law. So if anyone desires that God give him good and preserve him from the calamities of deception, let him never let the Scale of the Law drop from his hand! (II 529.33)

In the rest of the chapter, Ibn al-ʿArabī discusses various manifestations of deception, especially as it affects the generality of the spiritual seekers (*al-ʿumūm*), the elect (*al-khuṣūṣ*), and the elect of the elect (*khuṣūṣ al-khuṣūṣ*). These last can be tempted by the desire to convince others by manifesting "signs" (*āyāt*), that is, the power that God gives to His friends to "break the habits" of the visible world and sidestep the natural "laws" to which we have become habituated by constant repetition.

> God's deception of the elect is hidden within His causing their state to subsist in spite of their discourtesy. This discourtesy is to take pleasure (*taladhdhudh*) in the state and to halt within it. This gives rise to presumptuousness in him in whom the state occurs, intrusion upon God, and failure to seek transferal from the state. God said to His Prophet, "Say: 'My Lord, increase me in knowledge'" (20:114), and He let us hear that only to alert us so that we would say this and seek increase from God. Were this specific to the Prophet, He would not have let us hear it or He would have mentioned that it was specific to him. . . .
>
> The state has a pleasure and sweetness in the soul, and as a result certain souls find it difficult to seek transferal from that which gave rise to the state. On the contrary, they only seek increase in the state itself. They are ignorant of the fact that the states are bestowals.
>
> The divine deception (*makr*) which affects the elect of the elect lies in manifesting signs and the breaking of habits without a command from God or outside of the bounds which are their scale. The friends are commanded to conceal these, just as the messengers are commanded to manifest them. When a friend is given the ability to show them and the "eye of governing control" (*ʿayn al-taḥkīm*) in the cosmos is bestowed upon him, he may be deceived because he lacks a share in what others are given and because God desires that from him. God places within such a person an urge to manifest these signs in such a way that he is unaware that this is a divine deception which points to a lack of share. Hence he is inspired in his soul to manifest the signs as a kindness to attract creatures to God, to deliver drowning men from the sea of destructive sins, and to take them away from their familiar ways. For this is one of the greatest signs by which people are called to God, which is why it was a quality of the prophets and messengers. This person sees in himself that he is one of the inheritors, and that these signs are one of the inheritances from states. This prevents him from concealing these signs in the manner that God has made mandatory for the friends, even though they possess power over them. It hides from him the fact that God has made the manifestation of signs mandatory for the messengers because, from the first, they are commanded to call to God, while the friend is not like that. The friend only calls to God by recounting (*ḥikāya*) the call and tongue of the messenger. He does not call by virtue of a tongue that speaks to him as it speaks to a messenger. And all the while the Law has been established by those who know it.
>
> So the messenger is "upon insight" in calling to God through the rulings of the Law which God has conveyed to him, but the friend is "upon insight" in calling to God by virtue of following, not by virtue of Law-giving. Hence he has no need for signs or clear proofs, for, were he to say something that contradicts the rulings of the messenger, no one would follow him, nor would he be upon insight. So there is no profit in manifesting signs. His situation contrasts with that of the messenger, for the latter establishes Law-giving and abrogates some of the Law established at the hand of other messengers. Hence he must manifest signs and marks which will be a proof that he speaks the truth when he says he brings reports from God in or-

der to take away rulings established by God on the tongue of another messenger and announce the end of the period of the ruling in that question. But the friend, in spite of his particular qualities, may abandon something obligatory, and as a result he will be imperfect in his level to the extent of that which would have been given to him if he had observed and acted in accordance with that obligatory command.

There is nothing more harmful to the servant than to interpret (*taʿwīl*) things. May God place us upon insight in our affairs and not allow us to transgress that which is demanded by our station! I ask God that He provide us with the highest station with Him possessed by the highest friend, for the door of messengerhood and prophecy is locked, and it is appropriate that no one in the cosmos ask the impossible. After the divine report-giving, this door was locked, so it is not appropriate that we ask for it. To ask for it is to beat cold iron, so no man of faith would ever ask such a thing. This is known. It is sufficient for the friend that he ask God to place him upon insight in calling to God in respect of what is required by the station of friendship and following, just as He made the Messenger call to God upon insight in respect of what is required by the station of messengerhood and Law-giving. May He preserve us from His deception and not place us among the people of imperfection (*ahl al-naqṣ*)! May He provide us with increase (*mazīd*) and advance (*taraqqī*) in this world and the next! (II 531.9)

Closely connected to the states and the miraculous acts which the immature traveler may be tempted to display is the question of various occult sciences through which similar effects can be produced in the outside world. This is a topic which could take us into many more digressions. Instead I will limit myself to a few excerpts from Chapter 273 of the *Futūḥāt*, entitled, "Concerning the true-knowledge of the waystation of the destruction (*halāk*) pertaining to caprice and the ego." Most of the chapter is taken up by the long narrative of an unusual imaginal vision in which the intellect in charge of this particular waystation showed to Ibn al-ʿArabī the forms of the "levels, realities, mysteries, and sciences encompassed by the waystation."

The intellect took my hand, and as a result the waystation became manifest to me. It said, "This is the waystation of destruction and the slaughter-ground of destruction."

I saw within it five rooms. In the first room there were four treasure chests. The first chest had three locks, the second three, the third six, and the fourth three. I wanted to open them, but the intellect said to me, "Leave it until you see the treasure chests in each room. After that you may open the locks and come to know what is within the chests." Then it took my hand and we went into the second room. I entered it and saw four chests. On the first there were six locks, on the second three, on the third four, and on the fourth six. . . .

Then we went out in order to go back to the first room, open the locks, and see what was deposited in those chests. I entered the first room and went to the first chest, and I saw that a key was hanging on each lock. Some locks had two or three keys. I looked at the first lock and saw three keys embracing 400 movements. I stretched out my hand and opened the lock. Then I also saw on the third lock three keys comprising 400 movements. I opened the third and went back to the second. Upon it were two keys. It was a layered lock consisting of two locks in one and comprising four movements in two movements.

When I opened the locks and became apprised of what was in the chests, there appeared to me the forms of knowledges to the number of the movements of the keys of each chest, no more and no less. I saw destructive knowledges. No one occupied himself with them without being destroyed—knowledges pertaining to the rational faculty and belonging exclusively to the reflective thinkers, the philosophers and the theologians. Among them I saw a knowledge which takes its possessor to perpetual destruction, and another knowledge which takes him first to destruction, then he is saved, though of course there is none of the light of the

Law within it and its possessor is deprived of felicity. Among these knowledges were many of the sciences of the Brahmins, the sciences of sorcery, and others. I gained all the sciences contained therein, so that I might avoid them. These are mysteries which cannot be made manifest. They are called the "sciences of the mystery" (*ʿulūm al-sirr*).

One of the Companions who was singled out for these sciences was Ḥudhayfa ibn al-Yamān; the Messenger of God singled him out for them. That is why among the Companions he was called "The possessor of the knowledge of the mystery." Through that knowledge he used to recognize the hypocrites. Even ʿUmar ibn al-Khaṭṭāb swore an oath before him one day: "By God, is there anything of that in me?" He said, "No, and I shall not tell of this knowledge to anyone after you." ʿUmar would never call down blessings upon a coffin until he saw that Ḥudhayfa said that blessings should be called down. If Ḥudhayfa did so, so did ʿUmar; if not, neither did he.

He who comes to know these knowledges in order to avoid them will attain felicity, but he who comes to know them believing in them and practicing them will end up in wretchedness. When I gained them and encompassed them in knowledge and kept my soul aloof from them through the divine solicitude by which God preserved me from putting them into practice and becoming qualified by their effects, I thanked God.

In these stations many of the wayfarers of this path have been destroyed, since they saw sciences which the souls love and by which they become lords and shaykhs. Souls seek superiority and leadership (*riyāsa*) over their own kind. Hence these people display these sciences and seek to practice them in the corporeal world. They are misguided and they misguide others. "They misguide many, and they have been misguided from the right way" (Koran 5:77). (II 583.21)

Spiritual Mastery

The relationship between the shaykh or spiritual guide and his disciple is one of the more complex issues in the practical dimension of Sufism and can only be touched upon in the present context. All Sufis agree that entering the path without a shaykh is impossible. If someone thinks he has done so, in fact he has gone astray. The basic reason for the absolute necessity of the spiritual master is that the path is unknown before it is traversed, and a person cannot possibly prepare himself for the dangers and pitfalls that lurk on the way. The unknowability of the path goes back to the unknowability of God. That which can be known is that which He has taught us through revelation. Traveling the path is only possible through His guidance. Though the wide and easy path of the Shariʿa is incumbent upon all, the narrow and steep path of the Ṭarīqa requires special qualifications on the part of the seeker and the person who shows the way. A second important reason for the necessity of the master is the principle set down in the Koranic verse, "Enter houses by their doors" (2:189). The door to knowledge of unseen things has been set up by God and His Prophet, and only the inheritors of the Prophet, designated by the *silsila*s or "chains of transmission" of the Sufi orders, are qualified to open those doors for others. Any attempt to enter this house by other than its door represents the utmost discourtesy toward God and His Prophet.

Even in Ibn al-ʿArabī's time there were people who claimed to be Sufi masters without possessing the proper qualifications. Often these were seekers who began with good intentions, but were then "led on step by step" through the divine deception. In other words, God continued to show them favors while they did not fulfill their part of the covenant. Instead of acting in accordance with the rules of courtesy in every situation and observing all the intricacies of the Law, they gradually were emboldened to the point of considering themselves beyond these affairs, which they saw as fit only for the common people. Thus they forgot that the Prophet and all his Companions, not to mention every friend of God, followed the Scale of the Law in all affairs.

Ibn al-ʿArabī devotes Chapter 281 of the *Futūḥāt* to "The true knowledge of the stage of reverence (*iḥtirām*) for the shaykhs." He clarifies the qualifications of the shaykh who will be able to train disciples (*murīd*) properly. He also points out that there are other "shaykhs" who are possessors of states and produce miraculous phenomena, but that such shaykhs are not qualified to lead disciples on the path. The term "companionship" (*ṣuḥba*) is a general designation for the disciple's relationship to the shaykh. As Ibn al-ʿArabī points out at the end of the passage, there is a companionship in the specific sense of undergoing training at the hands of a master, and in the more general sense of visiting the master and acquiring his blessing.

> To revere the shaykh is to show reverence for none but God, so revere him out of courtesy toward God in God.
> The shaykhs are the courteous, and proximity aids them in guiding and strengthening in God.
> They are the inheritors of all the messengers, so their words come only from God.
> You see them like the prophets among their enemies, never asking from God anything but God.
> But if a state should appear in them which distracts them from the Shariʿa, leave them with God—
> Follow not after them and walk not in their tracks, for they are God's freedmen in God.
> Be not guided by him from whom the Shariʿa has gone, even if he brings news from God!
>
> When we saw that nowadays the disciples are ignorant of the levels of their shaykhs, we said concerning that:
>
> Ignored are the measures of the shaykhs, the people of witnessings and firm rooting!
> People consider their words low out of ignorance, though they stand in a lofty degree!
>
> The shaykhs are deputies of the Real in the cosmos, like the messengers in their time. Rather, the shaykhs are the inheritors, those who have inherited the knowledge of the revealed Laws from the prophets, though the shaykhs do not set down the Law. It belongs to them to preserve the Shariʿa for everyone; it is not theirs to make the Law. It belongs to them to help the elect preserve their hearts and observe the rules of courtesy.
>
> In relation to the knowers of God, the shaykhs are like the physician in relation to the knowers of the science of Nature. The physician only knows Nature inasmuch as it governs the human body, while the knower knows it without restriction, though he may not be a physician. It may also happen that the shaykh combines the two affairs.
>
> However that may be, the share of the shaykh in knowledge of God is as follows: He has knowledge of the sources and origins of people's activities. He possesses the science of incoming thoughts (*khawāṭir*), both the praiseworthy and the blameworthy, and how a person can be duped by them when the blameworthy thought becomes manifest in the form of the praiseworthy. He knows the breaths and the complexion and what they possess and comprise of the good that is pleasing to God and the evil that is displeasing to Him. He knows the illnesses and the medicines. He knows the times, the lifetimes, the places, and the foods; that which will make the constitution sound and that which will corrupt it; and the difference between unveiling which is "true" (*ḥaqīqī*) and that which is "imaginal" (*khayālī*). He knows the divine self-disclosure. He knows the method of training (*tarbiya*) and the passage of the disciple from infancy, to youth, to old age. He knows when to stop exercising control over the Nature of the disciple and begin controlling his rational faculty,[17] and when to tell the disciple that his incoming thoughts are true. He knows the properties that belong to the soul, those that belong to Satan, and what is under the power of Satan. He knows the veils which preserve man from the satans' casting into his heart and what the disciple's self conceals from him without his being aware. When the disciple experiences opening in his inward dimension,

the shaykh differentiates for him between spiritual opening and divine opening. Through smelling (*shamm*) he discerns between those people of the path who will be wholesome for the disciple and those who will not be wholesome. He knows the adornment through which the souls of the disciples—those who are God's brides—will be adorned. The shaykhs are like the hairdresser who beautifies the bride. The shaykhs are the Courteous with God, the knowers of the rules of courtesy (*ādāb*) of the Presence and the reverence which is due to It.

The description which brings together everything in the station of the shaykh is this: He combines in himself everything of which the wayfaring disciple has need in the state of his training, his wayfaring (*sulūk*), and his unveiling until he becomes worthy of becoming a shaykh. He possesses everything the disciple needs when his mind or his heart becomes ill through some obfuscation into which he falls and whose soundness or disorder he cannot discern. Such a thing happened to Sahl ibn ʿAbdallāh over the "prostration of the heart."[18] It also happened to our own shaykh when it was said to him, "You are Jesus son of Mary."[19] The shaykh treats him with the appropriate medicine. . . . So the shaykhs are the physicians of God's religion.

Whenever a person lacks anything which a shaykh needs for the training of disciples, it is not lawful for him to sit upon the couch of the shaykh, since he will corrupt and throw into affliction much more than he will set right, like the quack who makes the healthy person ill and kills the patient. But when the individual reaches the point [which we have described], then he is a shaykh in the path of God, and every disciple must show reverence to him, serve him, observe his prescripts, and not conceal from him anything which he knows that God knows about him.

The disciple should serve the shaykh as long as he has reverence for him. But if reverence for him should fall from his heart, he should not sit with him for a single hour, for he will not gain any profit from him and will suffer loss, since companionship (*ṣuḥba*) only yields profit when there is reverence. Whenever the reverence returns to him, then he should serve him and profit from him.

The shaykhs have two states:

There are shaykhs who know the Book and the Sunna, uphold them in their outward activities, realize them in their inmost consciousness, observe God's bounds, fulfill God's covenant, uphold the precepts of the Shariʿa, never interpret (*ta'awwul*) in their pious fear, take with caution, avoid the people who mix levels, sympathize with the community at large, never hate a single one of the disobedient, love God, and hate what God hates through God's hate. No blame of any blamer ever affects them concerning God. They "command the approved, forbid the disapproved" in which there is consensus "and vie with each other in good works" (Koran 3:114). They pardon the people, venerate the old, show mercy to the young, and remove harm from the path of God and the path of the people.[20] They invite to the good—first the most incumbent, then the next most incumbent. They deliver dues (*ḥuqūq*) to their owners and behave gently toward their brothers, or rather, to all people. They do not limit their munificence to those whom they know, for their munificence is nondelimited. The old person is their father, their fellow is their brother and equal, the young person is their child. All the creatures are members of their household after whose needs they ask.

If they obey [the Law], they see that the Real has given them success to obey Him. If they disobey Him, they hurry to repentance and shame before God, blaming themselves for that which emerged from them. They never flee in their acts of disobedience to "decree and destiny" (*al-qaḍā' wa'l-qadar*), for that is discourtesy toward God. They are the easy, the pliant, the possessors of tender love, "merciful to one another. You see them bowing, prostrating" (Koran 48:21). In their face is mercy toward God's servants, as if they were weeping. Worry dominates over them more than joy, because of what is given by the place of the Law's prescription (*taklīf*).

Such as these are the ones by whom one should be guided and whose reverence is incumbent. It is they who, "when they are seen, God is remembered."

The second group of shaykhs are the possessors of states. They have a certain dispersion (*tabdīd*) and do not preserve the outward (*al-ẓāhir*) in the way that the first group does. Their states are acknowledged, but one should not become their companion. If the miraculous breaking of habit that may become manifest from them should become manifest, it is not to be relied upon, because of the discourtesy toward the Law. For we have no way to God except that which He has laid down for us as the Law. He who says there is another way to God, different from what He has laid down in the Law, has spoken falsehood (*zūr*). So a shaykh who has no courtesy is not to be taken as a guide, even if he is truthful in his state. However, reverence should be shown to him.

Know that reverence to the Real lies in reverence to the shaykh. To break the compact of obedience (*ʿuqūq*) to the one is to do the same to the other. The shaykhs are the doorkeepers of the Real, those who preserve the states of the disciples' hearts. If a person becomes the companion of a shaykh who can be followed as a guide and does not show reverence to him, his punishment is that his heart will lose the finding of the Real (*wujūd al-ḥaqq*), he will be heedless (*ghafla*) of God, and he will show discourtesy toward Him. He will intrude upon Him in his speaking and annoy Him in His level. For the finding of the Real belongs only to the Courteous. The door is closed to everyone other than the Courteous. So the disciple has no greater deprivation than to be deprived of reverence for the shaykhs. . . .

Our companions have disagreed as to the duty of a disciple in respect to another shaykh, other than his own shaykh. Is his state with him in relation to the Real the same as his state with the first shaykh or not? All of them maintain that it is incumbent to show reverence to him, without doubt; here there is consensus. But in other domains, some of them have held that his state with the second is exactly the same as his state with the first. Some have separated the two and said, "The form is not identical until the disciple knows that the second shaykh is one of those who can be taken as a guide in the path. But if he does not know that, then the two are not the same." . . .

The disciple has no goal but the Real. When his goal becomes manifest, wherever it becomes manifest, he should uphold it and stick to it. For the Men come to be known through the Real; the Real is not known through them.

The root here is that, just as there cannot be a cosmos between two gods, or a person addressed by the Law between two messengers who have brought different Shariʿas, or a woman between two husbands, so also there cannot be a disciple between two shaykhs, that is, if he is a disciple who is being trained. If it is a question of companionship and not of training, then there is no worry for a person to be the companion of all the shaykhs, since he is not under their rule. This kind of companionship is known as the companionship of "blessing" (*baraka*). However, it will not produce a Man in the path of God.

In short, reverence is the root of salvation. (II 364.28)

The relationship between the master and the disciple is not one-sided. The shaykh, like the Prophet, must always pray, "My Lord, increase me in knowledge," and it may be that in certain circumstances God will choose the disciple to impart new knowledge to the master. Ibn al-ʿArabī alludes to these points while discussing the relationship between independence (*ghinā*) and need or poverty (*faqr*).

There is a kind of discourtesy in the path of God through which God leads on the gnostics step by step. This is the shaykh's exalting himself (*ʿizza*) over the disciples who follow him because of their need for his training and his surpassing excellence. For if the shaykh does not fulfill the right of his own station, the poverty of the disciple toward him will veil him from his poverty toward his Lord in his states. Through that he will witness his independence through God, and independence through God demands exalting oneself.

The Verifier who possesses this station has another state: When he sees that the disciples have need of him because of what he has from God, he thanks God for that, since God has made the disciples poor (*fuqarāʾ*) toward him such that through their poverty toward him they make firm his poverty toward God. For it might happen that if they did not manifest their attribute of poverty toward him, he would forget his poverty toward God.

This is the state of the verified shaykh. He looks upon these disciples who have need of him with the eye with which he would look upon the person who fixed him firmly on his path so that his foot would not slip. He is like the drowning man who has found someone to take his hand. How that drowning man loves him! For he has saved his life. This shaykh sees that the disciple's right (*ḥaqq*) against him is greater than his right against the disciple. Hence the disciple through his state is the shaykh's shaykh, while the shaykh through his words and training is the disciple's shaykh. (III 19.24)

16. NAMES AND STATIONS

According to the well-known hadith, "Allah created Adam upon His own form." Since Allah is the all-comprehensive name, God created man in the form of all His names. What makes a human being human is this single characteristic which opens him up to all human possibilities. But each human being is a unique reflection of God, since "Self-disclosure never repeats itself." No single human being ever manifests the divine form in exactly the same mode in two consecutive moments, since each instant is a new creation. And some loci of manifestation are more excellent than others, since they bring the divine realities into greater actualization.

A human being manifests all the divine names, yet some of these names remain latent within him. All human beings display the basic attributes of life, knowledge, desire, power, speech, hearing, and seeing, but not in the same extent or under the same relationships. In each attribute people are ranked in degree, some possessing the attribute in greater perfection and intensity than others. The Koran states that "Above each one who possesses knowledge is one who knows [more]" (12:76), and so also is the situation with each divine attribute. But to have "more" of a divine attribute is not necessarily good. God is the Overpowering Tyrant (*al-jabbār*), and a human being who manifests this name without qualities that modify and balance it will be a monster.

What is a human being? Anything at all, since the possibilities latent within the divine form are infinite, and each human being brings them into actuality according to a unique pattern possessed by no other. What should a human being be? This is a very different question, since here we have to judge him in relationship to the Divine Reality which he manifests. But in order to compare the divine form with God Himself, we have to know God, and in Himself He is unknowable. Hence, we cannot judge on our own how a human being should manifest God or how he should go about achieving this manifestation. The Divine Reality Itself has to tell people what they should do in order to manifest the Divine Form. In other words, man needs to follow the guidance of the Law. The Law tells him to "weigh with the scale," that is, to bring all human attributes into perfect equilibrium on the basis of the norms set down in the Koran and actualized by the most perfect of all human beings, the prophet Muḥammad. "If you love God," the Prophet is commanded to say in the Koran, "follow me, and then God will love you" (3:31). To actualize the fullness of his potentiality, to reflect the names of God in perfect balance and harmony, man must put the Law into practice.

A human being possesses every name of God—every ontological possibility—within himself. But in order to attain to felicity, he must bring these attributes into actuality according to the correct scale. God possesses all possibilities, as summarized by His names. He is God precisely in virtue of the relationships which the names denote. He is Lord (*rabb*) because of the vassal (*marbūb*), Creator because of the creature, Powerful because of the object of power, Knower because of the objects of knowledge, and so on. Without the creation that actualizes His names, God would not be a god, even though, in His Essence, He is "Independent of the worlds." In the same way, man is not man until he brings the divine attributes latent within himself into actuality. He will actualize many of the divine attributes—such as life, knowledge, desire, and power—to a certain degree through the course of his natural development by the fact of being human. But these will be actualized imperfectly, and many other names and attributes cannot be actualized in their fullness without recourse to the Law. God is Generous and Just, but how does a human being become generous and just in the divine mode—not in the mode which his rational faculty, itself created by God, tells him—without clear guidelines set down by Him who alone is truly Generous and Just? God is Compassionate, Forgiving, Grateful, Pardoning, and so on. As long as these attributes are not defined and delineated by Him who is their ontological source, they remain playthings of the mind, to be accepted or rejected as human beings like, to be put into practice according to our own ideas of "charity" and "humanity," whereas in fact we do not know what charity is, what humanity is, or what any of those attributes truly are, since they all go back to roots in the Incomparable God. Without guidance from the Law, man remains a toy of his own creations, wandering this way and that in error: "Shall We tell you who will be the greatest losers in their works? Those whose striving goes astray in the present life, while they think that they are working good deeds" (Koran 18:104).

To be human is to be made upon the form of God. But few people are in fact human. Most people are what Ibn al-ʿArabī calls "animal man" (*al-insān al-ḥayawān*), that is, animals in human form, since they have not actualized the divine form which would make them human. Our humanity remains but a potentiality until we have embarked on the straight path of "assuming the traits of the divine names" (*al-takhalluq bi'l-asmāʾ al-ilāhiyya*). Then the quality of being human gradually moves from potentiality to actuality. Through this process—which Ibn al-ʿArabī identifies with the path of Sufism—man gradually assumes the divine traits with greater and greater intensity and actuality. The "scale" whereby the developing human person can be weighed remains always the revealed Law, since nothing other than God's giving news of Himself can possibly guide the finite toward the Infinite and prevent him from falling into the innumerable pitfalls which dot the way. In each stage of the journey, man acquires certain divine attributes which prepare him for acquiring more. Each name whose traits he assumes bestows upon him a new preparedness which allows him to move on to higher stages. These stages are most often called the "stations" (*maqāmāt*).

The Divine Form

The divine form upon which man was created distinguishes him from all other creatures and bestows upon him his specific characteristics and excellence. The "perfection" achieved by perfect men is to bring this form from potentiality into actuality. Any human being who does not manifest the form in its fullness remains imperfect. Only through the divine form does man become worthy of the "Trust" (*amāna*) which God offered to the heavens, the earth, and the mountains, and all refused, but man accepted (Koran 33:72). The Trust is precisely to manifest the name Allah and act as His vicegerent (*khalīfa*) in creation.

It has been mentioned in the *Ṣaḥīḥ* that God created Adam upon His form. Adam is perfect man, the epitome (*mukhtaṣar*) who became manifest through the realities of temporally originated existence and eternal Being. (II 391.1)

God created Adam upon His own form. Hence He ascribed to him all His Most Beautiful Names. Through the strength of the Form he was able to carry the offered Trust. The reality of the Form did not allow him to reject the Trust in the way that the heavens and the earth refused to carry it. (II 170.6)

The most perfect configuration which became manifest among the existent things is man, as everyone agrees. For perfect man came into existence upon the Form, but not animal man. Perfection belongs to the Form, although this does not necessitate that he be the most excellent (*afḍal*) in God's view. He is the most perfect through bringing together all things (*majmūʿ*). (I 163.21)

We are the locus wherein the divine names are disclosed. Their Essence is witnessed only within us, because of the divine form in which He created us. So our kingdom (*mulk*) is all the divine names. There is no divine name of which we do not possess a portion (*naṣīb*). (III 88.12)

God says [in a *ḥadīth qudsī*], "My earth and My heaven embrace Me not, but the heart of My believing servant does embrace Me."[1] . . . It is as if He is saying, "All My names become manifest only within the human configuration." He said, "He taught Adam the names, all of them" (2:31), that is, the divine names from which all things in engendered existence come into being. (I 216.9)

"Animal man" is the opposite of perfect man. In perfect man the Divine Form is manifest, while in animal man it remains but a virtuality. To define man as a "rational (= speaking) animal" (*ḥayawān nāṭiq*) is misleading, since the whole cosmos is animate and speaking.

Rational speech (*nuṭq*) pervades the whole cosmos. It is not the specific characteristic of man as imagined by those who make his constituting differentia (*al-faṣl al-muqawwim*) the fact that he is a "rational animal." Unveiling does not allow that man possess this definition exclusively. Man is defined specifically by the Divine Form. He who does not possess this definition is not a man. Rather he is an animal whose form resembles the outward appearance of man. (III 154.18)

The expression "Divine Form" might better be translated as the "form of the name Allah," since it is this name of the Essence, the all-comprehensive name, which turned its attentiveness towards the creation of man. In the following passage, Ibn al-ʿArabī is explaining the meaning of the hadith of the Divine Form.

Whatever is given form by a form-giver is identical with the form-giver, not other than him, since it is not outside of him. Without doubt the cosmos was given form by God in accordance with the manifestation of its entity. Man, who is Adam, consists of an individual in whom the cosmos is brought together (*majmūʿ*), for he is the small man, the epitome of the "great man" [i.e., the macrocosm]. Man cannot perceive the whole cosmos, because of its greatness and tremendous size. In contrast man is small in size, and perception embraces him in respect of his form and anatomy and the spiritual faculties that he carries. God arranged within him everything outside of him other than God. So the reality of the divine name [Allah], which caused him to appear and from which he became manifest, is connected to every part of him. Hence all the divine names are related to him; not a single name eludes him. So Adam emerged upon the form of the name Allah, since it is this name which comprises all the divine names. (II 123.35)

Those human beings who attain to perfection do so on the basis of perfect knowledge of God, which necessarily combines the declaration of God's incomparability with that of His similarity. In contrast, imperfect men, should they have faith, choose one approach or the other. In the second paragraph below Ibn al-ʿArabī criticizes, rather allusively, the theologians and rational thinkers who interpret those Koranic verses which refer to similarity through forced meanings unknown to the original recipients of the revelation.

When the servants of the Real witness Him, they see Him as possessing two relationships, the relationship of incomparability, and that of descent to the imagination through a kind of similarity.

The relationship of incomparability is His self-disclosure in "Nothing is like Him" (42:11). The other relationship is His self-disclosure in the Prophet's words, "Worship God as if you see Him," and his words, "God is in the kibla of him who performs the prayer."[2] It is also mentioned in God's words, "Withersoever you turn, there is the Face of God" (2:115)—"there" being an adverb of place, while the "Face" of God is His Essence and Reality. So also it is mentioned in all the hadiths and verses which have come with words, along with their meanings, which apply to created things. If the meanings understood in conventional language are not brought along with the words, then the person addressed by the words will gain nothing. God does not explain what He means through words which are incompatible with the language in which the divine knowledge-giving has descended. He says, "We sent no messenger save with the tongue of his people, that he might make clear to them" (14:4), that is, in their language, so that they may come to know the actual situation. The Messenger who was sent with these words never explained the words with an explanation incompatible with conventional usage. Therefore we ascribe the meanings understood from the revealed words to God just as He ascribed them to Himself. In explaining them we do not force upon them meanings which are not understood by the people in whose language the words were revealed. Then we would be among these who "distort words from their meanings" (4:46) and those who "distort God's word, and that after they had comprehended it, while they knew" (2:75) their own opposition. This is the belief of all the early Muslims (*al-salaf*), without any disagreement.

Once what we have mentioned has been established for you, that is, that the Real has these two relationships set down by the Law, while you are urged to turn the attentiveness of your heart and your worship toward these two, then you should not turn away from them, if you are perfect, nor toward one rather than another, if you are below this level of perfection, that is, toward what the proponents of Kalām say concerning God in respect of their rational faculties, or toward what those who are deficient in reason say concerning the similarity of God to His creatures. These are ignorant and those are ignorant, and the truth lies in combining the two positions.

It has been reported concerning the human configuration that "God created Adam upon His own form." In the Koran God says that He created him "with His two hands," since He wanted to point out his eminence (*sharaf*). This is shown by the context (*qarīnat al-ḥāl*), since He tells Iblis about it after Iblis claims eminence over Adam through his own configuration. God says, "What prevented you from prostrating yourself to him whom I created with My two hands?" (38:75). "Hands" here cannot be taken to mean "power" (*qudra*), because of the dual. Nor can it be taken to mean that the one hand is blessing and the other hand is power, since that is true of every existent thing, so there would be no eminence for Adam according to that interpretation (*ta'wīl*), and this would contradict the fact that His words point out Adam's eminence.

So it was these two relationships—the relationship of incomparability and that of similarity—which turned their attentiveness toward the creation of man. Hence the children of Adam emerged in three levels: (1) perfect, that is, he who combines the two relationships; (2) he who stops with the proofs of his reason and the consideration of his reflection; and (3) he who declares God's similarity according to what the revealed words give to him. There is no fourth group among those who have faith. . . .

The perfect servant stands between these two relationships, standing opposite each in his own essence. He is not divided in his essence. When something is not divided, it cannot be described as standing opposite one relationship through one thing and opposite the other relationship through something else. There is nothing but his essence, like the atom between two other atoms. . . .

In respect of his reality and subtle essence (*laṭīfa*), man stands opposite God through the relationship of incomparability. And through that very face he stands opposite God in respect of the Divine Descent to those attributes which suggest similarity; this is the other relationship.

The God who is described by these two relationships is One in Himself and in His Unity (*aḥadiyya*), so these two relationships do not impose plurality and division upon His Essence. In the same way, the perfect servant who stands opposite God through these two relationships does not possess two different faces.

Perfect man stands opposite God in respect to all relationships in their manyness, since, although they are many, they go back to these two relationships. Nor are these two anything but what is described by them. So all are One Entity. And this "all" is not ontological. I only employ it in respect of the relationships, and these have no existent entities. The Entity of God is one and the entity of the servant is one. However, the entity of the servant is immutable. It never leaves its root and never emerges from its quarry. On the contrary, God drapes it with the robe of existence. So its entity is the nonmanifest dimension of its existence, while its existence is the Entity of Him who brought it into existence. Hence nothing becomes manifest but God, no one else. The entity of the servant remains in its root. However, it acquires what it did not have: knowledge of its own essence, of Him who draped it with the robe of existence, and of recognizing those who are like itself. (II 3.28, 4.3,26)

The Stations of the Path

We saw in the previous chapter that the "state" (*ḥāl*) or present spiritual situation of the individual is by definition transitory, while a "station" (*maqām*) may have the same attributes as a state except that it is a fixed quality of the soul. States are "bestowals" while stations are "earnings."

> Every station in the path of God is earned and fixed, while every state is a bestowal, neither earned nor fixed. The state is like the flashing of lightning. When it flashes, it either disappears because of its contrary, or it is followed by similars. But if it is followed by similars, its possessor will suffer loss. (II 176.10)

Many Sufis before and after Ibn al-ʿArabī devoted books to the enumeration and description of the stations, and any general manual on Sufism includes a section discussing them. But no one else has paid as much attention to explaining all their intricacies. The Shaykh deals with "stations" in one of the six major sections of the *Futūḥāt* (Chapters 462–558). He opens this section with a general chapter entitled "On the true knowledge of the Muhammadan Poles and their waystations," thus making stations and waystations equivalent from the outset. Throughout the rest of the section, in almost 100 chapters, he employs the term "waystation" consistently in the titles. Each chapter describes a specific type of friend of God with a special connection to one Koranic verse, which is, as it were, his divine root. The chapters provide detailed commentary upon the verses and an explanation of the human possibilities to which they refer.

The Shaykh also refers to many of the "interactions" (*muʿāmalāt*; Chapters 74–189) as stations. He frequently declares that various states (Chapters 190–269) are also stations. And it is difficult to draw a clear distinction between the stations and the "waystations" (*manāzil*; Chapters 270–383) or the "mutual waystations" (*munāzalāt*; Chapters 384–461), both of which are defined as types of stations. In the following Ibn al-ʿArabī differentiates the last two terms in a manner which helps to illustrate the extent to which he refines the definitions of the various stations and states.

> The difference between a waystation and a mutual waystation is as follows: A "waystation" is a station in which God descends (*nuzūl*) to you, or within which you alight (*nuzūl*) upon Him. Notice the difference between *nuzūl* "to" (*ilā*) and *nuzūl* "upon" (*ʿalā*).[3] A "mutual waystation" is that He desires to descend to you and places within your heart a seeking to alight upon Him. Your Resolve (*himma*) undergoes a subtle, spiritual movement in order to alight upon Him and you come together (*ijtimāʿ*) with Him between these two *nuzūls*: your alighting upon Him, before you reach the waystation, and His descent to you—that is, the attentiveness (*tawajjuh*) of a divine name—before He reaches the waystation. The occurrence of this coming together outside of the two waystations is called a "mutual waystation." (II 577.32)

The Sufis normally applied the term "station" to the spiritual attitudes such as awakening, repentance, recollection, sadness, hope, sincerity, constancy, patience, and so on, though many of these same attitudes might also be described as states. Ibn al-ʿArabī devotes the section of the *Futūḥāt* on "Interactions" to some of the terms well-known in the standard Sufi works. Within these chapters he refers to these as stations, not interactions.[4] At the beginning of the section, while discussing the station of repentance (*tawba*), he explains something about the classic manner of discussing the stations in contrast to his own approach.

> Concerning this station, our shaykhs have provided definitions, which I will mention as I can, explaining what they meant by them in accordance with what the path requires. I will do the same, God willing, with each station when I find that they have said something.
>
> However, when the shaykhs were asked what something was, they did not answer by providing essential definitions (*ḥadd dhātī*). On the contrary, they answered with the result (*natīja*) of the station in him who is qualified by it. Their very answer proved that they had acquired that station through tasting and state. How many there are who know its essential definition but have no whiff of it in themselves! Such a person stands far apart from it. Indeed, he may not even have faith in the first place, but he knows both its essential and its imperfect (*rasmī*) definition. So all have agreed that answering through results and state is more complete, since the stations have no profit if they do not produce effects within the individual. They are desired for that reason, not for themselves. (II 143.6)

There are many types of stations, and Ibn al-ʿArabī classifies them from various points of view. He provides an overview near the beginning of the *Futūḥāt*. Notice that even here, he does not clearly differentiate between stations and states. Thus in the first paragraph "states" are said to be determined by their conditions, while in the third paragraph this is said to be a characteristic of a certain type of station, and in both instances "gratitude" is given as an example.

> The "station" is every attribute which becomes deeply rooted (*rusūkh*) and cannot be left behind, such as repentance. "state" is every attribute which you have at one time but not another, like intoxication, obliteration, absence, and satisfaction; or its existence depends upon a condition, so it disappears when the condition ceases to exist, like patience in adversity or gratitude for blessings.
>
> These affairs are of two kinds. The perfection of one kind is found in man's outward and inward dimensions, such as abstinence (*waraʿ*) or repentance. The perfection of the other kind is found in man's inward dimension, and if the outward dimension follows, that is all right; for example, renunciation (*zuhd*) and trust (*tawakkul*). There is no station in the path of God which exists in the outward dimension but not the inward.
>
> Among the stations are those by which man is qualified both in this world and the next world, such as witnessing, majesty, beauty, intimacy, awe, and expansion. Among them are those by which the servant is qualified until the time of death,

until the Resurrection, or until the first step in the Garden, at which point they disappear; these include fear, contraction, sadness, and hope. Among them are those by which the servant is qualified until the moment of death, such as renunciation, repentance, abstinence, struggle, ascetic discipline, withdrawal (*takhallī*), and adornment (*taḥallī*) in the way of gaining nearness. Among them are those which disappear with the disappearance of their conditions and return with the return of their conditions, such as patience, gratitude, and abstinence. (I 34.3)[5]

The lack of a clear boundary between stations and states goes back to a number of factors. In discussing the station of satisfaction (*riḍā*) Ibn al-ʿArabī points out that satisfaction is a divine attribute and like all divine attributes which are also ascribed to the creatures can be viewed in different degrees or intensities.

> The Folk of Allah have disagreed concerning satisfaction. Is it a station or a state? Those who see it as a state add it to the list of bestowals while those who see it as a station make it one of the earnings.
>
> Satisfaction is a divine attribute. When any divine attribute is ascribed to God, it accepts neither bestowal nor earning. Hence in this case its meaning is different from when it is ascribed to the creatures, where it no longer has this description. So when it is ascribed to the creatures, if it becomes fixed, it is a station, and if it disappears, it is a state. In reality it accepts both descriptions, and this is correct. Hence in the case of some people it is a state and in the case of others it is a station. Every divine attribute is of the same sort. (II 212.17)

In the above passages, Ibn al-ʿArabī alludes to the fact that stations are permanent acquisitions. Though the traveler passes on to higher stations, he never leaves behind those he has already acquired. In effect, a human potentiality latent within him has become an actuality. Once a person gains the character trait of patience, for example, he never lacks it in the appropriate circumstances.

> Passing from station to station does not mean that you abandon a station. On the contrary, you acquire that which is higher than it without departing from the station within which you dwell. It is a passage *to* the second station, but not *from* the first; or rather, it is a passing *with* the latter. Such is the passage (*intiqāl*) of the Folk of Allah. And such also is passage within meanings. When someone passes from one knowledge to another knowledge, this does not imply that he becomes ignorant of the first knowledge. On the contrary, it never leaves him. (III 225.20)

In his definition of "mutual waystation" quoted above, Ibn al-ʿArabī speaks of God's descent, and then clarifies his meaning by saying that this is the "attentiveness" (*tawajjuh*) of a divine name. The word *tawajjuh* means essentially to turn the face (*wajh*) toward something, so the term calls to mind those Koranic verses in which God's face is mentioned, such as "Whithersoever you turn, there is the face of God" (2:115). As the Shaykh frequently reminds us, in Arabic the "face" of something signifies its essence or reality. Hence, to say that God turns His face or directs His attentiveness toward someone means that He manifests His reality to that person through self-disclosure. But self-disclosure is always delimited and defined by the preparedness of the receptacle. In the case of stations, this means that God discloses Himself to the seeker under the guise of the name which provides the ontological support or the divine root for the station into which the seeker is entering. To take an extremely basic case, the wayfarer's entrance into the station of patience (*ṣabr*) corresponds to God's directing His attentiveness toward him in respect of the name the Patient (*al-ṣabūr*), though again, this is a delimited and defined patience, not the absolute patience of the Divine Reality Itself. In short, whatever the servant acquires is given by the Lord. At the same time, we are dealing here with a Lord/vassal relationship, so the divine name itself benefits from the fact that the servant enters the station which it rules, since it gains a locus in which to display its properties.

In the continuation of the discussion of waystations and mutual waystations quoted above, the Shaykh clarifies the nature of some rather more complex relationships between the servant and the divine names.

> The possessor of this state has one of three situations: (1) At the meeting [between him and the name in the mutual waystation] the benefit sought for the name from the servant and for the servant from the name is actualized. Then the name departs from him and returns to the Named, while the servant returns to the station from which he had emerged.
>
> (2) The divine name ordains that the servant return whence he had come, while the name accompanies him until it takes him back to his place of emergence.
>
> (3) The servant takes the divine name along with him and ascends to its Named. . . .
>
> A "waystation" (*manzil*) is called such only because one alights (*nuzūl*) in it [for a time], but if one should take up residence in it and does not pass on, then it is called an "abode" (*mawṭin*), because one settles down there, or a "dwelling" (*maskan*), because one feels at home there and does not pass on to another waystation. Of course the servant cannot avoid passage within the substations (*daqīqa*) of the waystation itself, without leaving it. He is like someone who moves about in the rooms of the house in which he dwells. As long as the gnostic remains the companion of a single divine name, even though he moves about in diverse modes within it, then on the whole it is his abode.
>
> It is impossible for anyone to reside for two instants (*nafas*) in a single state, so passage must occur at each instant. That is why one of the Folk of Allah declared that it is impossible for the name to be an abode or a dwelling. He imagined that every instant and every state has a divine name. But he did not know that the divine name may have a single property or it may have many diverse properties. The name remains an individual's abode as long as he moves about under the control of its properties.
>
> Some of them have said, "It is impossible to remain for two instants in one property." This is correct. However, this statement may also be read, "It is impossible to remain for two instants in the property of one [name]," and this is not correct, since the divine names have many faces. Thus, the "All-concealing" (*al-ghaffār*)[6] shields him from such and such and from so-and-so in accordance with those demands which seek him in each instant and from which the name All-concealing may properly shield him. This takes place continuously and repeatedly without any interruption by the demands of another name. That is why this name is in the intensive grammatical form: It conceals a great deal. So also is the case with the "Ever-creating" (*al-khallāq*), the "All-provider" (*al-razzāq*), and all other names which have properties within the engendered universe, when what the name demands happens repeatedly for man.
>
> Hence the divine names are waystations from one point of view and dwellings and abodes from another point of view. But in the present chapter we have explained by way of allusion and without sufficient opportunity something which will benefit the possessor of tasting. What we deposit in every chapter, in relation to what we have, is but a drop in the ocean. And that is in respect to what *we* have of it. So what is the case in respect to what it is in itself? It is the ocean which has no shore. (II 578.1)

The difference between station and state has to do with the different degrees through which a divine reality manifests itself within the servant. This difference in degree or intensity also becomes apparent within the stations themselves. It is clear that though a disciple and his shaykh may both have reached the station of gratitude, as a general rule the realization of the shaykh will be more perfect and complete. Like all other attributes in existence, each station is ranked in degrees, from him who has just barely acquired it to its full realization in the greatest of the prophets. One of the more common ways to distinguish among these degrees of realization is to divide them into three broad categories on the basis of the famous hadith of Gabriel, in which the Prophet defined "submission" (*islām*), "faith" (*īmān*), and "virtue" or "beneficence" (*iḥsān*). Ibn al-ʿArabī bases the structure of his book *Mawāqiʿ al-nujūm* on this tripartite division. In short, submission pertains to the practices of Islam, faith to the domain of conceptualization and imagination, and virtue to the direct vision of the realities of the things.[7] In the following passage, Ibn al-ʿArabī refers to this way of looking at the stations while setting down a "general rule" (*ḍābiṭ*) which can be applied to analyze each station. In the process he mentions the three basic worlds of the macrocosm and microcosm: the kingdom (*al-mulk*) or corporeal world, the invincibility (*al-jabarūt*) or imaginal world, and the dominion (*al-malakūt*) or spiritual world.[8] Though Ibn al-ʿArabī propounds this general rule toward the beginning of his discussion of the stations and makes a few references to it as he goes along, for the most part he does not employ it systematically. As in so many other cases, the rule provides an "allusion" for the people of tasting, but leaves the rest of us somewhat bewildered. Nevertheless, Ibn al-ʿArabī's application of the rule to the station he is discussing, "abstinence" (*waraʿ*), provides a relatively clear example of what he has in mind.

> Each station is either divine, lordly, or all-merciful. There is nothing other than these three presences, which include all presences. Around them all existence revolves. By them the scriptures are sent down and to them the spiritual ascents climb up. That which looks after them is three divine names: Allah, Lord, and All-merciful.
>
> When the servant comes under the determining property of one of the divine names, then one of these three names will be described by that name. The property of the name will accord with the station of the servant within whom the determining property is exercised. It will display its effects within him in respect of the fact that he has submitted (*muslim*), has faith (*mu'min*), or is virtuous (*muḥsin*). Its effects will become manifest in the servant's world of the kingdom, his world of invincibility, or his world of dominion. Within it his practice will have the property of nondelimitation, this being the practice of the Essence (*al-ʿamal al-dhātī*); or delimitation, this being the practice of an attribute. If it is the practice of an attribute, it will have the property of incomparability and negation or the attribute of an act.
>
> This is the general rule of the stations and their states, whether or not the traveler knows it. For no engendered thing is empty of these properties, though not everyone knows that. . . .
>
> The station of abstinence involves delimitation by an attribute of declaring incomparability, since its reality is avoidance and keeping to one side. It is divine. Its possessor is unknown and not recognized. His state is that he possesses a mark in himself or in that in relation to which he exercises abstinence. The name Allah gazes upon him constantly.
>
> The name Allah gazes upon him in the world of his kingdom in respect to the fact that he has "submitted" and displays its effects in his acts. As long as it prevails over his limbs, he avoids everything that would detract from this station.
>
> It gazes upon him in the world of his invincibility in respect of the fact that he has "faith" and displays its effects within him; hence he never has any false dreams. He "avoids" in his imagination just as he avoids in his outward dimension, since imagination follows sense perception. . . . But abstinence avoids falsehood. . . .
>
> When the name Allah gazes upon him in the world of his dominion and displays its effects within him, he avoids interpreting (*ta'wīl*) the divine addresses and divine self-disclosure which enter in upon him. . . . He does not try to explain what he saw or to interpret that by which he was addressed, since all of it is divine, and everything divine is unknown. In the same way, the abstainers are unknown, since abstinence is an avoidance and a refraining, and a thing can only be distinguished from the outside through activity. If the abstainer speaks about what should properly be avoided and why he avoids things, then he has violated the station of abstinence. The station has to

be unknown, but he has made known that he is an abstainer, so the property of the station has disappeared from him. Or rather, he was never in the station of abstinence and his abstaining by avoidance was defective. Hence the station cannot be conceded to him.

As for the [attributes of] "lordly" and the "all-merciful" [when applied to abstinence], they follow exactly the same pattern. So take each of them and apply them. You will see wonders! But you will be hard pressed to find this in any other book, for most people—or rather, perhaps all of them—have not explained these stations and states in accordance with what is given by the differentiation of existence. Though they knew all this, they spoke about it on the understanding that when the traveler entered into the stations and was sincere in his attentiveness, things would be explained to him as they are in themselves, and he himself would come to know their state. (II 176.12)

Assuming the Character Traits of God

The stations of the path represent every positive human attribute that the travelers strive to achieve. Through achieving them the travelers come to embody the divine realities or divine roots embraced by the name Allah, upon the form of which they were created. I employ the term "reality" and "root" rather than "name," since, as was pointed out in Chapter 2, these terms embrace everything that can properly be attributed to God, whereas the term "name" as narrowly defined refers only to the "Most Beautiful Names." Even if name is taken in a wider sense, it is stretching the resources of language to say that each Koranic verse represents a "divine name," while it does not sound strange, for example, to call a verse of God's Speech a "divine reality."

Though man is made in the form of all the names of God, he does not actualize these names until they become an established and deeply rooted part of his character (*khuluq*). When envisaging the names rather than the stations, Ibn al-ʿArabī often speaks of "assuming the traits" (*al-takhalluq*) of the names, a term which has been discussed already in some detail and mentioned in passing. In this context he employs the terms "character traits" (*akhlāq*) and "names" interchangeably, since the divine names are precisely the "character traits" of God. Thus he states in one passage that the path to God is based upon "assuming the traits of the names of God" (II 42.3), while elsewhere he says, "Assuming the character traits of God—that is Sufism" (II 267.11).

In a philosophical context the word *akhlāq*, plural of *khuluq*, is normally translated as "ethics," and it may also be rendered as "morals" or "moral qualities." However, the word "moral quality" may suggest an attribute too superficial to convey what Ibn al-ʿArabī has in mind, particularly since the word *khuluq* is closely connected both in derivation and meaning with the word *khalq* or "creation." We will see shortly that Ibn al-ʿArabī views the character traits as innate to human beings, just as the divine form is man's defining characteristic.

In Sufi texts the term *takhalluq* is frequently employed in the saying, often attributed to the Prophet, "Assume the character traits of God" (*takhallaqū bi akhlāq Allāh*).[9] Ibn al-ʿArabī does not attribute this saying to the Prophet, though he does quote the following hadith: "God has three hundred character traits. He who assumes (*takhalluq*) one of them as his own character trait will enter the Garden" (II 72.9).

Ibn al-ʿArabī points out that when Sufis speak of *takhalluq* they mean the same as what the philosophers mean when they speak of *al-tashabbuh bi'l-ilāh*, or "gaining similarity to the God" (II 126.8).[10] In one passage he refers to "gaining similarity to the Root" and identifies this process with attaining to human perfection (II 272.3).

The Shaykh sometimes gives a meaning to the word *takhalluq* that goes outside the sphere of the spiritual journey altogether, though it does point to the ontological root of character traits. In a passage already quoted he writes, "To God belong the Most Beautiful Names, and to the cosmos belongs manifestation through the names by assuming their traits" (II 438.23). Here assuming the traits of the names is synonymous with manifesting their properties and effects. It is as if Ibn al-ʿArabī has said in typical fashion, "There is nothing in existence save God, His names, and His acts" (III 68.12).

If physicians have knowledge of human anatomy (*tashrīḥ*) through dissection of the body, the Sufis gain knowledge of the true human anatomy. They analyze the names comprising the divine form, which is man's defining characteristic. They gain this knowledge in relation to the manner in which man assumes the divine character traits.

> This waystation includes the science of anatomy known by the physicians among the natural philosophers and the divine anatomy pertaining to the form which is specific to the human individual, since man was created in the form of the cosmos and the form of God.
>
> In respect of the cosmos, the science of man's anatomy is to know all the realities of the engendered things that are within him: the high and the low, the pleasant and the loathesome, the light and the darkness, in differentiated detail. Among others, Abū Ḥāmid [al-Ghazālī] has discussed and explained this science. This is the science of "anatomy" in our path.
>
> As for the second science of anatomy, that is to know the divine names and lordly relationships which are found in the human form. This will be known by the person who comes to know the assumption of the traits of the names and the divine gnostic sciences which result from their assumption. This also has been discussed by the Men of Allah in explaining the names of God, such as Abū Ḥāmid al-Ghazālī, Abu'l-Ḥakam ʿAbd al-Salām ibn Barrajān of Seville, Abū Bakr ibn ʿAbdallāh al-Maghāfirī,[11] and Abu'l-Qāsim al-Qushayrī. (II 649.23)

In a chapter explaining the Shariʿite rulings related to the imam who leads the ritual prayer and those who follow him, Ibn al-ʿArabī points out that this relationship between the imam and his followers reflects the relationship between God and man.

> The prophetic reports show that we have been charged to assume the character traits of God. The Prophet said, "God would not forbid you to take usury and then take it from you Himself."[12] There is no description by which God has described Himself by which He has not charged us to become qualified (*ittiṣāf*). This is the meaning of assuming the traits, following, and taking as an example. This is exactly the imamate in prayer. For, in reality, the imam is God, while the followers are the creatures. (I 450.22)
>
> Sincerity in love makes the lover become qualified by the attributes of the beloved. The same is true in the sincere servant's love of his Lord. He assumes the traits of His names. So he becomes qualified by "independence" from anything other than God, "exaltation" through God, "giving" through the hand of God, and "preservation" by the eye of God. The learned masters know about assuming the traits of God's names and have written many books about it.[13] Since they loved God, they became qualified by His attributes to the degree appropriate for them. (II 596.14)
>
> All the learned masters maintain that assumption of the traits of the names takes place. Thus man becomes qualified by them and is called alive, knowing, desiring, hearing, seeing, speaking, powerful. All the divine names, whether names of incomparability or names of acts, come under the scope of these seven names. Not a single one escapes them. Hence we do not mention them in detail. We have mentioned a full portion of them in our book *Inshāʾ al-jadāwil wa'l-dawāʾir.*[14] (III 398.21)

In the long chapter on love in the *Futūḥāt*, the Shaykh analyzes various dimensions of human and divine love. In discussing God's love for man, he comments upon the several Koranic verses where this is mentioned. In his usual fashion, he finds hidden meanings and allusions which would not occur to most people. Of particular relevance for the present discussion is his explanation of 61:4: "God loves those who fight in His path in ranks, as though they were a solid building." While explaining the verse, the Shaykh has in mind a hadith referring to the communal prayer: "Make your ranks solid, bring them close together, and make your necks parallel. By Him in whose hand is Muḥammad's soul, I see the satans slipping through the fissures in the ranks like young goats."[15]

> By "as though they were a solid building," God means that no fissure should enter the ranks, for fissures in the ranks are the roads of the satans, but the road is one, and that is the path of God. If the line which becomes manifest from the points should be broken, such that it is no longer solid, the line would no longer exist, and what is desired is the existence of the line. This is the meaning of "being solid"—it is for the sake of the existence of the path of God. He who does not exert himself to bring the path of God into manifestation is not one of the Folk of Allah.
>
> In the same way, the ranks of those who perform the prayers are not in the "path of God" until the people are next to each other and solidly joined together. Then the path of God itself becomes manifest. But he who does not do this, rather bringing about a fissure, has attempted to cut the path of God and eliminate it from existence. . . .
>
> On the side of God, this reality appears in the fact that His names are solidly joined together. Since they are joined together, the path of the creatures becomes manifest. Next to the name Alive is All-knowing, and there is no space between the two for another name. Next to All-knowing is Desiring, next to it Speaking, next to it All-powerful, next to it Determiner, next to it Sustenance-giver, next to it Just, next to it Governor, next to it Differentiator, next to it All-provider, next to it Life-giver. In this way the divine names are ranked so that they will bring into existence the path of the creatures, which itself has the same solidity.
>
> When this path becomes manifest—not being anything other than the solid joining together of the names—the creatures become qualified by the names. . . . The solidity of the names never ceases becoming manifest among the creatures; nothing else can be conceived of. Hence the cosmos is alive, knowing, desiring, speaking, powerful, determining, sustenance-giving, just, governing, differentiating, and so on down the list of all the divine names. In the path this is called "assumption of the traits of the names." The names become manifest within the servant, just as they become manifest, because they are solidly joined together, by bringing the straight path (*al-ṭarīq al-mustaqīm*) into existence.
>
> If a fissure should enter in upon the names in engendered existence, then God's path disappears and the paths of the satans appear, which causes fissures in the ranks, as the hadith has reported. So turn your attention toward that to which I have alerted you!
>
> When the servant stands with the names of the Real in the station possessed by the names in bringing creation into existence, and when he fights with this attribute against the enemies—who are like the satans which have penetrated the ranks—he will necessarily be helped by God, since he leaves no fissure whereby the enemy could enter. Hence God loves him who has this attribute. (II 344.15)

If God loves man because he manifests His names and attributes, so also man loves God because he assumes His character traits. When a human being loves something in this world, he loves it through that in himself which corresponds to it. Hence he only loves created things with part of himself. However, he can love another human being with his whole self, since that person is also created upon God's form. Likewise he loves God with his whole self, since all of him derives from God.

> Know that love cannot absorb (*istighrāq*) the whole of the lovers unless their

> beloved is God or one of their own kind, a woman or a man. But no other love can absorb a human being totally. We say this because in his essence a human being stands exactly opposite nothing but him who is upon his own form. When he loves that person, there is nothing in himself which does not find its corresponding part in his beloved. There remains nothing left over within him which would allow him to remain sober. His outward dimension is enraptured by his beloved's outward dimension, and his inward dimension by his inward dimension. Do you not see that God is named both Manifest and Nonmanifest? Hence love of God and love of his similars absorbs man totally, but this is not the case with anything in the cosmos not of his own kind. When he loves a form within the cosmos, he turns toward it through the corresponding part in himself; the rest of his essence remains sober in its own occupation.
>
> Man becomes totally absorbed in the love of God because he is upon His form, as reported in the hadith. Hence he turns toward the Divine Presence with his whole essence. That is why all the divine names become manifest within man. He who does not possess the attribute of love is able to assume all the traits of the names, but when he possesses the attribute of love, he is absorbed totally by love. (II 325.25)

Noble and Base Character Traits

God is the root of all "noble character traits" (*makārim al-akhlāq*). He is also the root of the "base character traits" (*safsāf al-akhlāq*), though the relationship here is more subtle and will need some explanation. For the time being, it is sufficient to note that all God's own relationships with His creatures manifest noble character traits, while base character traits are attributes which the creatures assume in certain relationships with God or other creatures. God Himself is always noble and good.

> It is obvious that God never praises any one of the noble character traits unless He Himself is more worthy [than His creatures] to observe it toward His creatures, and He never blames any of the base character traits unless the Divine Side is further away from them [than are His creatures]. (I 285.8)
>
> God did not name Himself by any name without appointing for man a share (*ḥaẓẓ*) in assuming the trait of that name. Through that share man manifests that name in the cosmos according to the appropriate measure. Hence some people have interpreted the Prophet's words, "God created Adam upon His own form," in this meaning. (I 124.14)
>
> No existent thing is named by all the divine names except man, who has been charged (*nadb*) to assume the names as his own traits. That is why he was given the vicegerency (*khilāfa*) and the deputyship (*niyāba*), and the knowledge of all the names. He was the last configuration within the cosmos, bringing together all the realities of the cosmos. (II 603.4)

Having been created in the divine form, man embraces all the divine names and contains within himself all God's character traits. The task of the spiritual traveler is to bring the names and character traits from latency into actuality in perfect balance and harmony. Since this is the case, the use of the term *takhalluq* or "assumption of traits" is problematic, since the literal meaning of the term *takhalluq* is "to exert oneself in acquiring character traits" (II 72.19), whereas, strictly speaking, man already possesses the character traits.

> All character traits are divine attributes, so all of them are noble. All of them are found in man's innate disposition (*jibilla*). That is why God addresses Himself to them. One of those who has no knowledge of the realities maintains that the character traits in man are an "assumption of traits," while in God they are actual traits. But this shows the speaker's ignorance of the true situation, unless he means that as a metaphor (*majāz*) or he maintains it in respect to the priority of God's Being over the servant's existence.

For God is the Necessary Being through Himself, while man exists through his Lord, so he acquires existence and character traits from Him. If this speaker has kept this principle in view and then speaks of "assumption of traits," then the meaning is correct. But if he means by assuming traits that the servant becomes qualified by something which belongs in reality to God; that he does not possess it until he becomes qualified by it, which explains why it is called the "assumption of a trait" rather than a "character trait"; and that the servant has no "character traits" except in respect to his innate disposition at the root of his configuration; then the speaker has no knowledge of the configuration of man nor of the knowledge given by the Prophet when he said, "God created man upon His own form." Moreover, this speaker would then have to say as follows: Those attributes which belong to the servant "in reality," but by which we see that God is also qualified, are an assumption of traits on God's part; thereby He gains attributes which belong rightfully to man. But no one who has the slightest amount of knowledge would say anything like that.

The fact is that all of the divine character traits are found in man's innate disposition. Moreover, they become manifest to him who recognizes them in every human being to the same extent that they become manifest on the Divine Side. For it cannot be that each and every one of these character traits will be put into effect in interaction with all engendered things, whether on God's part or man's part.

God is generous (*karīm*) without delimitation, and so also man is generous without delimitation. Nevertheless, even though God is generous without delimitation, among His names are Withholder (*al-māni*ʿ), Harmer (*al-ḍārr*), and Abaser (*al-mudhill*). "He forgives . . . and He chastises whomsoever He will" (2:284). He gives the kingdom, He takes away the kingdom,[16] He avenges, and He shows munificence. In spite of all this delimitation in respect to some people rather than others, He is nondelimited in attributes. And so also are the attributes in the case of man.

Hence the character traits are original (*aṣlī*) with man, not an assumption of traits. Man cannot put all of these traits into effect, even though they are nondelimited in respect to him, just as God cannot put all of them into effect in all of His creatures, even though He is nondelimited while described by them.

It cannot be said that these attributes are borrowed, unless metaphorically, as we mentioned. For God possessed these attributes while we did not exist. When we came to be, we came to be possessing them. We did not acquire them or borrow them from Him, since they are God's eternal attributes, that is, they are attributes by which He was qualified when there was no cosmos. But an attribute must have an object to which it is attributed, since it is in the reality of the attribute not to subsist in itself. But once we say that they are "borrowed," we have to say that they subsist in themselves and that God did not have them and that the temporally originated thing is the locus for the existence of the eternal. But no one who has knowledge of God would say any of this.

Hence all character traits, both the noble and the base, which become manifest from man lie in his innate disposition. They belong to him in reality, not metaphorically or as a borrowing. In the same way, God possesses every name by which He has named Himself. Or rather, He possesses every attribute of the acts by which He has described Himself, including creation, giving life and slaying, withholding and bestowal, making, deception, guile, mockery, decision, decree, and everything that has come in the revealed scriptures and about which the messengers have spoken, such as laughter, rejoicing, wonder, receiving joyfully, foot, hand, two hands, hands, eyes, and forearm. All of this is sound description, since it is His Speech about Himself and the speech of His messengers about Him. He speaks the truth, and they speak the truth, as has been shown by rational proofs.

However, all this pertains to Him as He knows it and to the extent that it is accepted by His Essence and what is proper to His majesty, nothing more. We neither declare that impossible nor try to explain how it takes place (*takyīf*). Nor do we maintain that all of this is attributed to Him in the same way that we attribute it to ourselves—we seek refuge in God! For we attribute it to ourselves to the extent of our knowledge of ourselves, so we know how (*kayf*) we attribute it. But God is far too exalted for His Essence to be known, so He is far too exalted for it to be known how we should attribute to Him what He attributes to Himself. But he who rejects something which God has affirmed for Himself in His Book or upon the tongue of His Messenger has disbelieved in him who has brought it and in God. He who has faith in parts of it and rejects parts of it has truly disbelieved. And he who has faith in all of it while declaring Him Similar by attributing it to Him as it is attributed to us, or he who supposes this, or it occurs to his mind, or he conceives of it, or he considers it possible, is ignorant, though he has not disbelieved. . . .

Thus have I explained to you the station of character traits. As for the allusions of the Sufis to the "assumption of traits," they have patched together various sayings. So also is their maintaining the "assumption of the traits of the names." We also have applied these terms in the way they apply them, but we have done so on the basis of verified knowledge and a nondelimited application while preserving divine courtesy through realization (*taḥaqquq*). But in reality these are character traits, not the assumption of traits, as we have explained to you. . . .

As for the character traits about which the people of wayfaring need to know—and all of us are wayfarers, since there can be no end (*nihāya*)—these are as follows: Common usage (*al-ʿurf*) and the Law have established the noble and base character traits. They have commanded us to bring the noble and avoid the base. Then the Law has alerted us to the fact that they are of two kinds: Some are character traits within man's innate disposition. Thus, the Messenger of God said to Ashajj ʿAbd al-Qays: "In you are two qualities (*khaṣla*) which God and His Messenger love: deliberation and forbearance."[17] In another version, not found in [the *Ṣaḥīḥ* of] Muslim, the man said, "O Messenger of God, are there things to which I am innately disposed?" The Prophet replied that there were, and the man said, "Praise belongs to God who made my innate disposition these two."[18]

The second kind of character traits are earned (*muktasab*). It is this kind in respect to which one speaks of the "assumption of traits," which is to become similar (*tashabbuh*) to him who possesses these noble traits innately, at the root of his creation.

Without doubt, putting noble character traits into practice is difficult, since doing so among the engendered things involves the meeting of opposites. Thus, when two personal motives or individual desires in two different people contradict and each one of them seeks from you that you act with him with a noble character by taking care of his desire, you cannot bring the two together. If you satisfy the one, you will not satisfy the other. Since it is impossible to bring the two together, it is impossible to make everyone satisfied and to employ a noble character with both of them. Hence it is incumbent upon man to come outside of himself in that and to turn the judgment over to the Law. He takes the Law as a scale and a leader in this matter. . . .

"Noble character traits" are only those connected to interaction with others. Other traits are not known as "noble." Rather, they are attributes which are assumed as traits in order to rectify the [divine] form or the [divine] relationship. . . .

The details of how to employ character traits with the creatures are many. Were we to explain the traits and their qualities, no book could contain the explanation.

Now that I have given you a principle (*aṣl*) concerning them, rely upon it and put it into practice: In your every motion in respect to every existent thing, look at the ruling of the Law. Deal with that thing as the Lawgiver has told you. Deal with it according to what is obligatory (*wujūb*) or what is recommended (*nadb*), and do not go beyond that. Then in all of that you will have a praiseworthy disposition, you will be secure and honored with God, and you will possess a divine light. (II 241.28, 243.9, 30)

17. PITFALLS OF THE PATH

The friend of God who has assumed the divine names as his own character traits embodies God's self-disclosure and appears in every mode of existence. But God creates the good and the evil, the ugly and the beautiful, the straight and the crooked, the moral and the immoral. Does the gnostic become manifest in these attributes? The answer, of course, is "Yes and no." Between the yes and the no lie the manifold dangers that face the traveler and would-be traveler on the path to God. In the same ambiguous region arise the oft-repeated criticisms of an alleged antinomianism and hedonism among the Sufis.

Sufism in general and Ibn al-ʿArabī in particular have been accused of innumerable misdeeds against Islam, religion, and morality. In the case of Ibn al-ʿArabī, this is not surprising, since it is extremely easy to read his works out of context. Ibn Taymiyya (d. 1328) established a solid precedent for this and has been followed by a host of critics over the centuries, including a good number of orientalists. Nowadays even many of those who believe that Ibn al-ʿArabī has a message to offer to our own century have understood him largely as Ibn Taymiyya did, though they consider this his virtue. Ibn Taymiyya must be saying from his grave, "I told you so."

As long as the Sufis expressed themselves through poetical and mysterious "allusions" (*ishārāt*), no one outside their own circles took them too seriously and they were able to communicate with those who had the "taste" to recognize their message. But Ibn al-ʿArabī brought Sufism into the mainstream of serious intellectual speculation. In doing so, he was forced by the nature of things to employ all the tools of the theologians, philosophers, grammarians, and other specialists. As a result, his works could be read only by a tiny fraction of even the learned. Hence it was easy to misrepresent him, since it was merely necessary to quote an isolated sentence from the *Futūḥāt* and say that the whole of the work is the same, and few people knew any better.

Many of the issues on which Ibn al-ʿArabī was criticized have to do with good and evil, the Law, and morality. Briefly stated, his position was read as follows: Since there is only One Being which permeates all things, God is present in everything, the good and the evil alike. Therefore there is no difference between good and evil and it is unnecessary to follow the Law or observe moral strictures. Since all is God, all is good and all is permitted. This criticism of Ibn al-ʿArabī is presented in the language of contemporary scholarship by one of the foremost Muslim thinkers residing in the West:

> The position of the Sharīʿa . . . was gravely endangered. A thoroughly monistic system, no matter how pious and conscientious it may claim to be, can not, by its very nature, take seriously the objective validity of moral standards.[1]

There is no point trying to answer this view directly, since on the one hand, what has already been said concerning Ibn al-ʿArabī's view of the Law should be more than sufficient, and on the other, those who have made up their minds will hardly be swayed by argument. Nevertheless, it will be useful to turn to a few of Ibn al-ʿArabī's own formulations dealing with the nature of this sensitive domain between the affirmation of God's omnipresent Reality and the declarations of the revealed Laws concerning good and evil. We should be able to discern how God and perfect man permeate the cosmic maze without becoming defiled by the evil that is found therein. More importantly, we will see why evil is real on its own level, a fact which necessitates the setting up of the Scale of the Law. Man faces a predicament as real as himself, and he is forced by his own nature to choose between the straight path which leads to balance, harmony, and felicity and the crooked paths which lead to imbalance, disequilibrium, and wretchedness.

In spite of the reality of the straight and crooked paths and their vital importance for determining human destiny, in certain contexts the gnostic is justified in taking "God's point of view" and saying that all paths are straight, since there is no evil in creation. But that is the point of view of God as Being, who comprehends all names and all ontological possibilities. It is not the point of view of God as Guide (*al-hādī*), who desires the perfection and felicity of mankind.

Good and Evil

To clarify the status of good and evil, Ibn al-ʿArabī first takes the concepts back to their divine roots. If the "good" (*khayr*) is that which is positive, useful, profitable, beautiful, and so on, then "There is no good but God." This is one of the meanings of the Koranic statement, "To Him belong the most beautiful (*ḥusnā*) names," since the word *ḥasan*, from which *ḥusnā* is derived, means both good and beautiful. In the final analysis Good is Being, to which all positive and beautiful attributes belong. Evil (*sharr*) is the lack of good, so it is nonexistence. This is Ibn al-ʿArabī's first definition of good and evil, but not his last, since this definition ignores the human predicament along with questions of Law and morality. As soon as the particular interests of human beings are taken into account, various derivative goods and evils must also be considered.

> There is nothing in supra-sensory (*maʿnawī*), sensory, and imaginal existence but the Real, for everything comes into existence from the Real, and the Real brings nothing into existence but the Real. That is why the Prophet said in his supplication, addressing his Lord, "The good, all of it, is in Thy hands, while evil does not go back to Thee."[2]
>
> Evil is the opposite of good, and nothing emerges from good but good; evil is only the nonexistence of good. Hence, all good is existence, while evil is nonexistence, since it is the manifestation of that which has no entity in reality. (III 373.26)
>
> "Ignorance" (*jahl*) consists of the lack of knowledge, nothing else. Hence it is not an ontological quality (*amr wujūdī*). Nonexistence is evil, and in itself nonexistence is ugly, wherever it might be supposed. That is why the sound report has reached us that the Prophet said in supplicating his Lord, "The good, all of it, is in Thy hands, while evil does not go back to Thee." Hence he did not ascribe evil to Him. Were evil an ontological quality, its coming into existence would go back to God, since there is no agent but God. Hence all of existence is good, since it is identical with the Sheer Good (*al-khayr al-maḥḍ*), who is God. (III 528.6)
>
> One of the emissaries of the Real said to me during a long speech in a mutual waystation on the subject of darkness and light: "Good lies in existence, and evil lies in nonexistence." I came to know that the Real possesses Nondelimited Being without any delimitation. He is sheer good without any evil. He stands opposite nondelimited nothingness, which is sheer evil without any good. (I 47.2)

At root the creatures are immutable entities dwelling in nonexistence, which is evil. God in respect of His all-embracing mercy gives them existence in order to bring them from evil to good. Man hangs between good and evil for the same reason that he stands in the station of He/not He.

> Since God was kind toward us through the name "All-merciful," He brought us out from evil, which is nonexistence, to good, which is existence. That is why God reminds us of His kindness through the blessing of existence, for He says, "Will not man remember that We created him aforetime, when he was nothing?"

(19:67). Hence, from the beginning, we took only mercy from Him. That is why the Prophet said, "God's mercy precedes His wrath." (II 157.15)

God made the possible things come to exist as entities only to bring them out from the evil of nonexistence, for He knows that existence is Sheer Good within which is no evil, except accidentally (*ʿaraḍ*). Nonexistence gazes upon the possible thing in respect of its being a possible thing; but at that moment it dwells in Sheer Good. Whatever reaches it from nonexistence's gazing upon it because it is a possible thing—to that extent is the evil which the cosmos finds where it finds it. Hence, when the possible thing looks toward its existence and its endlessness, it becomes happy through the fact that it is existence's companion, but when it looks upon the state by which it is qualified and which has no existence, it suffers pain through witnessing it. (III 207.33)

There is no evil in the Root. By whom then are evils supported? For the cosmos is in the grasp of Sheer Good, which is complete Being. But nonexistence gazes upon the possible thing, so in that measure is attributed to it the evil which is attributed to it. In its essence the possible thing does not possess the property of the Being which is Necessary though Its own Essence, and this is why evil presents itself to the possible thing. But the possible thing does not continue or become fixed in evil, since it dwells in the grasp of Sheer Good and Being. (III 315.6)

God brought the cosmos from nonexistence, which is evil, only for the good which He desired for it, and that is nothing but existence. Hence the cosmos exists fundamentally for felicity, and it will reach its property in the end. (III 377.14)

God created the cosmos only for felicity in its essence. Wretchedness occurs for whom it occurs as an accidental property. The reason for this is that nothing emerges from Sheer Good—which is the Being of God that gave existence to the cosmos—except that which accords with it, which is specifically good. Hence good belongs to the cosmos in its essence. But the cosmos possesses the property of possibility, since it is alternately qualified by one of the two sides [existence and nonexistence], so it does not stand in the level of the Being which is Necessary through Its own Essence, and hence evil occurs to it as an accident.

"Evil" is failure to reach one's individual desire (*gharaḍ*) and what is agreeable (*mulāʾim*) to one's nature. It stems from the fact that the thing's possibility does not prevent it from becoming connected to nonexistence. To this extent evil becomes manifest within the cosmos. Hence it only becomes manifest from the direction of the possible thing, not from the direction of God. That is why the Prophet said in his supplication, "The good, all of it, is in Thy hands, while evil does not go back to Thee," but rather to creation in respect of its possibility. (III 389.21)

Though there is no evil in Being, the existent things suffer evil to the extent they fail to share in Being. Hence the way to avoid evil is to seek refuge from it in Being. Again we are brought back to the fundamental human imperative: Man is bound by the reality of his own essence to strive after God, who is Good, Light, Knowledge, Being—everything to which he must conform in order to reach his own happiness and felicity. But God is unknown and unknowable, so the only way to reach Him is to follow the Law as He makes it known to us.

The Two Commands

From the point of view of Sheer Being, there is nothing but good. But as soon as existence is taken into account, good is by definition mixed with evil. In actual fact, human beings are faced with choices between good and evil. They do not dwell with Sheer Being, so they cannot say that nothing exists but good. Since they have been placed within the cosmos in a context of other existing things, they are forced to choose among alternatives, and these—in respect of certain criteria found in the cosmos and described by Ibn al-ʿArabī—will offer choices among the good, the better, the bad, and the worse. Though goods and evils all manifest God as Sheer Good, in relationship to the criteria set up by the nature of things and willed by God they cannot be considered equivalent in respect to human beings. Hence we cannot escape the reality of good and evil in our actual situation.

> In reality that which is named "evil" and that which is named "good" go back to one of four things: (1) The convention (*waḍʿ*) according to which have come the tongues of the revealed Laws (*sharāʾiʿ*). (2) Agreeableness with the constitution, so that the thing will be good in respect to someone; or disagreeableness with his constitution, so that it will be evil in respect to him. (3) A perfection which is established by proofs, so the thing will be good; or it will not attain to this degree of perfection and be evil. (4) Attaining to one's individual desire (*gharaḍ*), which will appear good to the person; or not attaining to it, which will appear evil.
>
> When the observer ceases looking at all these things, there remains nothing but the entities of existent things, qualified by neither good nor evil. When one is fair and verifies the situation, it comes down to this.
>
> However, what God has done is only that which has become actualized in existence, and this comprises all the perfection and imperfection, agreeableness and disagreeableness, revealed Laws with their conventions through which things are considered beautiful or ugly, and individual desires which souls sometimes attain and sometimes do not. Existence is not empty of these levels, and the speech of the Speaker [through the Laws] concerns only that which is actualized in existence, not the other point of view which is attributed to God's side.
>
> The root of all this lies both on the side of the existence of the Necessary Being through Himself, who is Sheer Good in whom there is no evil, and on the side of nondelimited nothingness, which stands opposite Nondelimited Being and which is sheer evil in which there is no good. Every evil that becomes manifest in the cosmos derives from this root [sheer evil], since the evil is the nonexistence of perfection, the nonexistence of agreeableness, and the nonexistence of reaching one's individual desire, which are all relationships. At the same time the agent of every good that becomes manifest is Nondelimited Being. (II 576.2)

As delimited creatures faced with perfection and imperfection, likes and dislikes, ambitions and desires, and the demands of the Law, human beings are forced to discern between good and evil at every stage of their existence in this world. If they could say that God is Incomparable and they, like Him, are infinitely beyond this world, they could ignore the secondary causes. But that would be absurd. In fact they must also acknowledge that God is Similar and that He manifests Himself to them wherever they turn in accordance with an indefinite variety of faces. Hence the secondary causes assume the properties of His names, and the cosmos is full of life-giving and slaying, forgiveness and vengeance, exalting and abasing, guidance and misguidance on all sorts of levels. In each case where human interests are involved, man has to see the secondary causes as good or evil. Even if he could, by some miracle, be totally indifferent to life and death, pleasure and pain, love and hate, still, he would be commanded by the Law to put each thing in its proper place. And to ignore the Law is to ignore felicity and embrace wretchedness. Hence human beings must always separate "God's point of view"—which is a corollary of His incomparability—from their own point of view, which is a corollary of His similarity and the fact that all things assume the divine names as their traits.

Ibn al-ʿArabī sometimes distinguishes these two points of view by speaking of two divine commands. In respect of the first command, God says "Be!" and the whole cosmos comes into existence. In respect of the second, He says to human beings, "Do this and avoid that, or you will fall into wretchedness." The first command is known as the "engendering command" (*al-amr al-takwīnī*) or the command without "intermediary" (*wāsiṭa*), that is, without the intermediary of a prophet, while the second is known as the "prescriptive command" (*al-amr al-taklīfī*) or the command "by intermediary." All created things obey the engendering command, so in this respect there is no evil in existence. But when the prescriptive command—the revealed Law—is taken into account, then some obey and some disobey. People bring both good and evil down upon themselves in respect of the prescriptive command.

The prescriptive command or the Scale of the Law is referred to in the many Koranic verses which tell human beings that they must have faith in God, perform the prayer, fast, pay the alms-tax, and so on. The engendering command is God's "desire" (*irāda*) for creation; "His command, when He desires a thing, is to say to it 'Be!', and it is" (36:82). Nothing can disobey God's desire, but man and jinn are free to disobey the command whereby He prescribes the Law for them.

> All acts performed by the servant are divided into two kinds: an act in which lies the servant's felicity, that is, the act to which he is called by God; and an act not connected to his felicity. The second kind does not derive from His call (*nidā'*), but it does derive from His desire (*irāda*) and His creation—but not from His call or the command of His Law. (II 593.10)

In general Ibn al-ʿArabī would rather apply the term "command" to the engendering command, which cannot be disobeyed, than to the prescriptive command, which can be disobeyed. If the Creator really commands something, how can the created thing disobey the command? To bring this home he sometimes points out that the prescriptive command is not really a command at all. To call it a command is to speak in grammatical terms, that is, to indicate that it takes the "imperative mood" (*ṣīghat al-amr*). But when God's desire—His engendering command—differs from this imperative mood, the engendering command will be carried out, not the prescriptive command. The engendering command always coincides with the divine desire. Whenever God desires a thing and says "Be," the object of the command comes into existence.

> The Divine Command never contradicts the Divine Desire, since the Desire enters into the Command's definition and reality. What happens is that confusion occurs because people confer the name "command" upon the imperative mood, though without doubt it is not a command, nor is the mood a desire. When God's "commands" come on the tongue of those who deliver His messages, these are imperative moods, not commands. Hence they can be disobeyed. Moreover, the Commander may command something [through the imperative mood] that He does not desire to be obeyed. Hence no one whatsoever disobeys God's command. (IV 430.28)

Since man follows the engendering command in any case, it is the prescriptive command which brings into existence the possibility of opposing God. Were there no revelation, there would be no opposition (*mukhālafa*), only conformity (*muwāfaqa*).

> All acts in respect of being acts belong to God, while they become acts of disobedience only in respect of God's decree making them so. But in respect of being acts, all God's acts are beautiful. (II 342.11)
>
> Nothing determines opposition except the prescription of the Law. When the prescription is lifted, wherever it may be lifted, so also is lifted the property of opposition. Then nothing remains but constant conformity and the continual obedience of the possible thing to the Necessary Being. In actual fact, at the time of opposition, this is the situation, since the disobeyer is obedient to the Divine Will (*mashī'a*). He opposes only the command by intermediary. (III 510.21)

The "lifting of prescription" takes place in the next world, when works are no longer relevant to human becoming, since disobedience is impossible.

> Every created thing other than mankind and jinn magnify and glorify God innately, and so also do all the bodily parts of mankind and jinn. However, this does not take place to bring about nearness to God or out of desire for the greatest station. On the contrary, for them glorification is like the breaths of a breather, because it derives from the demand of their own essences. So also will be the glorification of jinn and mankind in the Garden and the Fire—it will not be for the sake of nearness, nor will it bring about nearness for them. On the contrary, each of them will be in a "known station."[3] Hence worship will become natural, required by their realities. Prescription will have been lifted, and no opposition to the command of God that reaches them is conceivable, nor will there be any prohibitions, that is, after His words to the People of the Fire, "Slink you into it, and do not speak to Me!" (Koran 23:108). For we are talking about the situation after people have taken up their stations in each abode and the doors have been locked. (II 688.27)

The Perfection of Imperfection

If the engendering command alone is considered, there is no imperfection in the cosmos, since all creatures follow what God desires for them. In this respect, what is normally called "imperfection" is in fact perfection, since it allows for the actualization of the various levels of existence and knowledge. In other words, were there no imperfections—in the sense of diminishment, decrease, and lack—there would no creation. Were there no creation, the Hidden Treasure would remain hidden. Hence Being would be unseen in every respect. There would be no self-disclosure of the Divine Reality, Light would not shine, God would be the Nonmanifest but not the Manifest. But all this is absurd, since it demands the imperfection of Being Itself, which by definition is nondelimited perfection (*al-kamāl al-muṭlaq*). Being's perfection requires the manifestation of Its properties. The effects of the names and attributes must be displayed for God to be God.

In short, the nondelimited perfection of the Divine Reality is made possible only by the existence of imperfection, which is to say that this "imperfection" is demanded by existence itself. To be "other than God" is to be imperfect. It is to lack the divine attributes, beginning with Being. But it is precisely the "otherness" (*ghayriyya*) which allows the cosmos and all the creatures within it to exist. If the things were perfect in every respect, they would be identical with God Himself, and there would be nothing "other than God." But then we could not even speak about the cosmos, since there would be no cosmos and no speakers. Hence it is imperfection which separates the creatures from their Creator and makes possible the existence of the cosmos. Imperfection is itself a kind of perfection.

> God said, "He gave everything its creation" (20:50) and this is identical with the perfection of that thing, so it lacks (*naqṣ*) nothing. The reason for this is that we are created on the model of Him who possesses nondelimited perfection. . . . Nothing issues from the Perfect without being in accordance with the appropriate perfection. So there is no imperfect thing in the cosmos whatsoever. Were it not for the accidents which give birth to maladies, man would enjoy himself within the form of the cosmos, just as the cosmos enjoys itself, and he would delight in it, for it is the garden of the Real (*bustān al-ḥaqq*). . . . So perfection is an intrinsic attribute of the things, while imperfection is an accidental affair whose essence is perfection. (I 679.31)

Without imperfection, existence's perfection could not be actualized. All things are "imperfect" and thereby perfectly adapted to the roles they play in creation. In their roles as human beings, those who have not attained to the station of human perfection are no less perfect than other creatures. However, because of the peculiar human situation, people are born with the possibility of actualizing a second kind of perfection. Unlike other creatures, they are not fixed in a specific ontological situation, but can change their situation through the gifts they have been given—such as knowledge, desire, and speech—by following the prescriptive command, the Scale of the Law. The moment an animal is born, it is clearly this or that—a horse, an elephant, a mole, a mouse—and will never be anything else. But when a human being is born, only God knows what that person will be. He has the potentiality to become any one of a tremendous variety of human types, summarized by Ibn al-ʿArabī as unbeliever, believer, friend of God, prophet, and messenger (though the last two types are not possibilities in the present age). Whatever man becomes is a "perfection" in one sense at least. But he will not be perfect in both senses unless he becomes a "perfect man" (*insān kāmil*).

Both mankind and jinn—called, in Koranic terms, the two "weighty ones" (*al-thaqalān*)[4]—are born into an ambiguous situation which, from their own point of view, remains ambiguous until death, though God knows their destiny for all eternity. Their freedom allows them to make choices which effect their becoming. Whatever they do, they follow the engendering command (called below the "command of the Desire," *al-amr al-irādī*), but the extent to which they follow the prescriptive command determines whether they will join the felicitous in the Garden or the wretched in the Fire. In contrast, says Ibn al-ʿArabī, all other creatures are like the angels in that they are born into a "known station" which does not change.

> The angels say, "None of us there is, but has a known station" (Koran 37:164). So also is every existent thing except the two weighty ones. Though the two weighty ones are also created in their stations, these stations are designated and ordained within God's knowledge and unseen by them. Each individual among them reaches his station at the end of his breaths. So his last breath is his "known station" upon which he dies. That is why they have been called to travel (*sulūk*). Hence they travel, either upwardly by answering the summons of the Shariʿa, or downwardly by answering the command of the Desire from whence they know not, until after the object of the Desire has been attained.
>
> Hence each individual among the two weighty ones reaches in his traveling the known station for which he was created. "Among them are wretched and felicitous" (Koran 11:105). Every existent thing other than they—whether angel, animal, plant, or mineral—is created in its station, so it does not descend from its station, nor is it commanded to travel toward it, since it dwells within it. Hence it is felicitous with God. There is no wretchedness for it to reach. (I 258.35)

According to a hadith, "Saʿd is jealous, I am more jealous than Saʿd, and God is more jealous than I."[5] As a divine attribute "jealousy" (*ghayra*) is closely connected to the existence of the "other" (*ghayr*), through which the perfection of existence is made possible. In discussing this attribute and the fact that it demands the existence of the cosmos, Ibn al-ʿArabī alludes to the fact that all the divine names and realities mentioned in the Koran and the Hadith demand loci of manifestation in the cosmos. Some of these names are in fact "names of imperfection," in that they demand what we normally look upon as lacks and deficiencies. But since God is named by them—in the manner that is appropriate to His majesty and grandeur—man to be perfect must also be named by them. Otherwise he would not possess the Divine Form.

> Jealousy is a divine attribute that demands the "other," which is why it is called *ghayra*. Were the other not taken

into account, jealousy would not have been so named, nor would it have come into existence. The God (*al-ilāh*) who is the Powerful (*al-qādir*) demands the divine thrall (*ma'lūh*) which is the object of power (*maqdūr*), and this is the "other." The other must exist since the God demands it. Hence, He brought the cosmos into existence according to the most perfect mode that existence could take. The cosmos has to be perfect because of the impossibility of attributing imperfection to Him who is Perfect in power. That is why God said, "He gave everything its creation" (20:50), which is perfection. Had He not brought imperfection into existence in the cosmos, the cosmos would not be perfect. Hence part of the cosmos's perfection is the existence of relative imperfection within it. That is why we said that it came into existence in the most perfect form, since nothing remains in possibility (*imkān*) more perfect than it, since it is upon the Divine Form.[6]

According to the hadith, "God created Adam upon His form." Because of the Form, man possessed the potentiality to forget his servanthood. That is why God described man by forgetfulness (*nisyān*), since He said concerning Adam, "He forgot" (Koran 20:115). Forgetfulness is a divine attribute, and Adam only forgot since he was upon the Form. Hence [by forgetting] we do not deviate from what we are. God said, "They forgot God, so He forgot them" (9:67) in the manner that is appropriate to His majesty. (II 244.21)

Ibn al-ʿArabī summarizes the role of imperfection in existence and the type of perfection that is open to human beings as follows:

Part of the perfection of existence is the existence of imperfection within it, since, were there no imperfection, the perfection of existence would be imperfect. God said concerning everything other than God, "He gave everything its creation." So He made nothing of it imperfect, not even imperfection, for to it also "He gave its creation." So this is the perfection of the cosmos, which is everything other than God, but not that of God or man.

God possesses a perfection appropriate to Him, and man has a perfection which he receives. When someone lacks (*naqṣ*) this perfection, it is because of the imperfection which is in the cosmos, since man is a part of the cosmos, and not every human being receives perfection. But everything other than man is perfect in its level, not lacking in anything, according to the Koranic verse [just quoted].

Concerning human beings the Prophet said, "Many have become perfect among men, but among women only Mary and Āsiya; and the excellence of ʿĀ'isha over women is like the excellence of *tharīd* over other foods."[7] No imperfection has become manifest within the cosmos except in man. That is because he brings together all the realities of the cosmos. He is the concise epitome (*al-mukhtaṣar al-wajīz*), while the cosmos is the exhaustive elaboration. . . .

All existent things [other than God and man] receive their perfection. God is perfect, and man is divided into two kinds: One kind does not receive perfection. He is part of the cosmos, except that he brings together the cosmos in the way that an epitome brings together everything in something large.

A second kind of man receives perfection. Within him becomes manifest the preparedness for the Divine Presence in Its perfection and for all Its names. God appointed this kind a vicegerent and clothed him in the robe of bewilderment (*ḥayra*) toward Him.[8]. . . So man's perfection is through the preparedness for this specific self-disclosure. (II 307.11, 29,35)

Ibn al-ʿArabī sometimes points to the distinction between "completion" (*tamām*) and "perfection" (*kamāl*) in a manner relevant to the present context. Completion is the situation of something whose creation lacks nothing, while perfection is the situation of something which is not only complete, but also lives fully the "level" pertaining to its creation by actualizing the total range of possibilities inherent within it. Thus animal man is complete in creation, but imperfect in respect to the full possibilities of the human situation. In one passage Ibn al-ʿArabī offers other than his usual interpretation of the verse, "He gave everything its creation," by making it refer to completion, while the remainder of the verse, "and then guided" refers to perfection. "Guidance," it should be remembered, is the role of revelation; it can only be actualized through following the prophets.

> Perfection is what is sought, not completion, for completion lies in creation, but perfection lies in that which the complete acquires and the benefits it bestows. . . . "God gives to each thing its creation," and thereby it is complete, "then He guides" to the acquisition of perfection. He who is guided reaches perfection, but he who stops with his completion has been deprived. (III 405.3)

God's Conclusive Argument

The fact that some people follow the divine guidance by obeying the prescriptive command, while others refuse to follow it, goes back to the engendering command, since everything is rooted in God as designated by the name Allah. On the one hand, the prescriptive command is itself created by the engendering command, and on the other, it is Allah who says "Be!" to the faith and practice within us. No one can choose to enter into God's presence without having first been chosen to do so. From the point of view of "Allah," all things are predetermined and measured out.

But this does not mean that God compels the servant to choose the wrong path and then punishes him for it. As God's own form, man participates in God's freedom, so he makes his own choices and is held responsible for them. God compels (*jabr*) no one, though one might say that each person compels himself, since his destiny stems from his own nonexistent immutable entity, his own reality. God does not force anyone to do anything. He merely knows the entities for all eternity, and then He brings them into existence as they are in themselves. He does not "make" (*jaʿl*) them the way they are, since they are what they are in themselves. God does not make a pear tree into a pear tree; a pear tree is what it is. God merely brings it into existence, and it yields pears. God does not make a person into His friend or His enemy, since the person has been immutably fixed as His friend or enemy for all eternity. God merely shows mercy to the individual's entity through the Breath of the All-merciful. Once in existence, the friend is a friend and the enemy an enemy, without anyone having made them so. This, in Ibn al-ʿArabī's view, is one of the meanings of the Koranic verse, "To God belongs the conclusive argument" (6:149).

God creates all things on the basis of His knowledge of the things, and His knowledge of the things is identical with His knowledge of Himself. Hence the things become manifest upon the form of God, though only the cosmos in its entirety and man—the macrocosm and the microcosm—are forms of the name Allah as such.

> The cosmos is a divine transcription (*nuskha*) upon a form of the Real. Hence we say: God's knowledge of the things is His knowledge of Himself. (II 390.35)
>
> The Real knows Himself, He knows the cosmos from Himself, and He brought the cosmos into existence upon His own form. Hence it is a mirror within which He sees His own form. (II 326.26)
>
> God knows the things through His knowledge of Himself. Hence the cosmos emerges upon His form and no property whatsoever eludes Him, for He is the Lord and Master of each thing. (II 508.6)
>
> "Each day He is upon some task" (55:29), and each task derives from a divine attentiveness. The Real has given us the knowledge that He undergoes transmutation in forms. At each task He creates a divine form. Hence the cosmos became manifest upon the form of the Real. That is why we say: The Real knows

Himself, and hence He knows the cosmos. (II 385.8)

He created all things without any need for them and without anything which would make their creation necessary for Him. However, He knew beforehand that He would create what He created. For "He is the First and the Last, the Manifest and the Nonmanifest" (57:3). "He is powerful over all things" (11:4). "He encompasses everything in knowledge" (65:12). "He has enumerated everything in numbers" (72:28). "He knows the secret and that which is more hidden" (20:7). "He knows the treachery of the eyes and what the breasts conceal" (40:19). How should He not know that which He creates? "Shall He not know, He who created, while He is the All-subtle, the All-aware?" (67:14)

He knew the things in themselves before their existence. Then He brought them into existence according to the measure of His knowledge. He never ceases knowing the things, and no new knowledge accrues to Him when He newly brings the things forth. On the basis of His knowledge He makes the things properly and well. Through it He gives control over them to whomsoever He will and He exercises control. He knows the universals absolutely, and, according to the consensus and agreement of the people of sound consideration, He also knows the particulars. For He is the "knower of the unseen and the visible" (36:73). "God is high exalted above what they associate!" (7:189). (I 36.29)

The "possible thing" is called by this name because it stands equidistant between existence and nonexistence and needs a Preponderator to come into existence. If God wills, it comes into existence. But once the possible thing has come into existence, then we know that God's knowledge demanded its existence. Hence, in fact, it is a necessary existent, but "through the Other," not through itself.

Look at the mystery of God's words, "He gave each thing its creation" (20:50). Then you will know that things do not transgress what is worthy of them and that no level stands higher than knowledge. God says, "The Word is not changed with Me" (50:29), since that would contradict the object of His knowledge; hence it is impossible for it to occur. Though an affair appears to be a possible thing in respect of itself, this is not so in respect of the fact that God knows that one of the two possibilities will occur and in respect of the fact that His will is one. When God's will is connected to a thing's coming to be, then it must come to be and it cannot not occur. In respect of this reality it is not qualified by "possibility." That is why certain people who considered this situation ceased calling it the "possible thing" and named it "the necessary existent through the Other." (II 334.24)

When God creates something, He does so on the basis of His knowledge of that thing, and He knows it through knowing Himself. His knowledge has no effect upon what He knows. Rather, the object of knowledge determines the knowledge. In Ibn al-ʿArabī's way of speaking, "Knowledge follows its object" (*al-ʿilm tābiʿ li'l-maʿlūm*). God does not "make" the thing the way it is, He merely knows the way it is. This is one of the important themes of the *Fuṣūṣ al-ḥikam*.

Through this unveiling you will see that the Real Himself is the proof of Himself and of His Divinity, while the cosmos is nothing but His self-disclosure within the forms of the immutable entities, which cannot possibly exist without that self-disclosure. The self-disclosure becomes variegated and assumes diverse forms in accordance with the realities and states of the entities. We gain this knowledge after knowing that He is our God.

Then comes another unveiling through which our forms in Him will become manifest to you. Some of us become manifest to others in God; some of us know others; some of us are distinguished from others. Among us there are those who know that this knowledge of us through us takes place in God. Among us are those who are ignorant of the presence within which this knowledge of us occurs—I seek refuge in God lest I be one of the ignorant!

Through the two unveilings together [we come to know] that He does not determine our properties except through us. Or rather, we determine our own properties through ourselves, though within Him. Hence He says, "To God belongs the conclusive argument" (6:149), that is, against those who are veiled, those who [on the Day of Resurrection] will say to the Real, "Why didst Thou do to us such and such, which does not conform to our desires?" Then "The shank," which is that which was unveiled to the gnostics here, "shall be uncovered" (68:42).[9] They will see that the Real did not do to them what they claimed He did, since everything derived from themselves. He knew them only in keeping with their actual situation. Hence their argument is nullified and the conclusive argument remains with God.

You may object: "What then is the profit in His words [in the rest of verse 6:149], 'If He had willed, He would have guided you all'." We reply: Grammatically, the word "if" (*law*) indicates the impossibility of a thing which is impossible,[10] for He only wills in accordance with the actual situation. However, according to the proof of reason, the entity of the possible thing is receptive toward the one existence as well as its contrary. Whichever of the two intelligible properties occurs is what the possible thing possessed in the state of its immutability. . . .

The Divine Will becomes connected only to a single thing. Will is a relationship which follows knowledge, while knowledge is a relationship that follows the object of knowledge. The object of knowledge is you and your states. Knowledge displays no effect within the object of knowledge. On the contrary, the object of knowledge displays its effects in knowledge. The object gives to knowledge what it actually is in itself. . . .

"None of us there is but has a known station" (37:164). This "known station" is what you are in your immutability. Through it you become manifest in your existence, that is, if it is affirmed that you have existence. If it is affirmed that existence belongs to the Real and not to you, then without doubt you determine the properties within the Being of the Real. If it is affirmed that you are an existent thing, then again without doubt the property belongs to you. Even though the Real determines the property, He only effuses existence upon you, and you determine your own property. Hence you should praise none but yourself and blame none but yourself. For the Real only praise remains for effusing existence, since that belongs to Him, not to you. (*Fuṣūṣ* 81)

Recompense (*jazā'*) is a self-disclosure within the mirror of the Being of the Real. Hence nothing comes back to the possible things from the Real except that which is given by their own essences in their states, for they have a form in each state, and their forms become diverse in accordance with the diversity of their states. Then the self-disclosure becomes diverse according to the diversity of the state. Hence the effect that occurs within the servant accords with what he himself is. None gives him good except himself, and none gives him the opposite of good except himself. Indeed, he gives bliss to his own essence and he chastises it. So let him blame none but himself and let him praise none but himself. "To God belongs the conclusive argument" (6:149) through His knowledge of the creatures, for knowledge follows the object of knowledge. (*Fuṣūṣ* 96)

When God sent Himself down to the waystation of His servants, their properties exercised their influence over Him. Hence He only determines their properties through them. This is part of His "conclusive argument" against them. It is indicated in His words, "a suitable recompense" (78:26), a recompense for "what you were doing" (5:105), a recompense for "what you were earning" (7:39).[11] Their own works chastise them and their own works give them bliss. Nothing determines their properties but themselves. Hence they do not blame any but themselves, just as God has related to us concerning Satan's words:

"And Satan says, when the issue is decided, 'God surely promised you a true promise; and I promised you, then I failed you, for I had no authority over you'," that is, no strength, no argument, and no demonstration, "'but that I called you, and you answered me.'" But you are not required to answer everyone who calls you. That is why miracles give witness to the truthfulness of the calling of the messengers when they say that it is the call of God. But Satan set up no demonstration for them when he called them, as is indicated in his words, "I had no authority over you." How strange that people reject and disbelieve in the call of God, in spite of the demonstration which becomes manifest, while they answer the call of Satan, which is free of any demonstration. Then Satan says to them, "So do not blame me, but blame yourselves" (14:22). (III 112.13)

Even the gnostics do not know if God's engendering command will allow them to follow the Straight Path (*al-ṣirāṭ al-mustaqīm*) laid down by the prescriptive command, or if they will swerve from this path because their own realities demand deviation. In the sura of Hūd in the Koran, God says to the Prophet, "Go thou straight, as thou hast been commanded!" (11:112). The Prophet said, "Hūd and its sisters have whitened my hair."[12]

The gnostics experience nothing more difficult than the command of God to go straight, that is, His words, "Go thou straight as thou hast been commanded, and whoso repents with thee; and be thou not insolent" (11:112). In other words, do not leave aside His command because you find in yourselves that He has created you upon the divine form. Do not say, "The likes of us are not the objects of this command." For the knowers of God do not know if God's command will conform to His will in them. Will they obey His command, or will they oppose it? Hence God's command is difficult for them and they become distressed. This is indicated by the Prophet's words, "Hūd has whitened my hair," since Hūd is the sura within which "Go thou straight as thou hast been commanded" was sent down; "and its sisters," which have the same verse or something in the same meaning. (II 218.35)

The Messenger of God said, "Hūd and its sisters have whitened my hair," that is Hūd and all the verses which mention going straight. For he and the faithful are commanded by these verses. But the determining property belongs to the divine knowledge, not to the command. "God is never unjust toward His servants" (3:182), since He only knows what the objects of knowledge give to Him, since knowledge follows the object of knowledge. Nothing becomes manifest in existence except the actual situation of the object of knowledge. Hence "To God belongs the conclusive argument" (6:149). He who does not recognize that the situation is as we have described it has no news of the true situation.

But man is ignorant of what will come into existence from him before it comes to be. When something happens from him, it only happens on the basis of God's knowledge of him. And God knows nothing except what the object of knowledge is in itself. Hence His words, "He approves not misbelief in His servants" (39:7), are true. "Approval" (*riḍā*) is a desire (*irāda*). There is no contradiction between the command and the desire. The contradiction occurs between the command and that which is given by knowledge, which follows its object. God "accomplishes what He desires" (85:16), but He does not desire anything other than the actual situation as it is known. And we possess nothing of the divine command but the imperative mood, which is a created thing in the mouth of him who calls to God. It is desired, known, and existent in the mouth of the caller to God. So pay attention and take heed! "And say, 'My Lord, increase me in knowledge!'" (20:114). (IV 182.11)

The fact that the servants are ignorant of God's knowledge concerning them is of particular importance, for the feeling of freedom to which this gives rise allows them to assume responsibility for their own choices. Moreover, they do in fact share in the reality of freedom, since they are made upon God's form.

God does not prescribe through the Law that which cannot be borne, since it is impossible that One who is All-knowing and All-wise prescribe in the Law something which cannot be borne.

You might argue that He has prescribed faith for those—like Abū Jahl and his likes—whom He knew beforehand would not have faith. We reply: . . . I do not mean by "prescribing that which cannot be borne" anything other than what is customarily (*'āda*) meant by such a statement. In other words, the person for whom it is prescribed cannot accomplish it. For example: "Climb up to heaven" without any means, or "Bring together two opposites," such as "Stand while you are not standing." God only prescribed in the Law that which custom declares can be borne, such as having belief through faith, or pronouncing the formula of faith. Every human being finds in himself the ability for this, whether through performance (*kasb*) or creation; say whichever you like. That is why God's argument against the servant will be established on the Day of Resurrection. Hence He says, "Say: 'To God belongs the conclusive argument'" (6:149).

If He had prescribed for the servant something which he could not bear, these words would not be correct. On the contrary, He would have to say, "It is God's to do as He wills," just as He has said, "He shall not be questioned as to what He does" (21:23). The meaning of this is that no one will say to the Real, "Why didst Thou prescribe for us, prohibit us, and command us when Thou knewest that Thou hadst ordained for us opposition to Thee?" This is the place of "He shall not be questioned as to what He does." For He will say to them, "Did I command you to do that which you could not bear or that which you considered unbearable?" They will have to speak in accordance with what is customary: "We were able to bear it," since He prescribed that which they could in fact bear. Hence it is established that "To God belongs the conclusive argument," since they were ignorant of God's knowledge of them when the Law was prescribed for them. (II 336.12)

The Straight Path

In his daily prayers every Muslim recites the Fātiḥa, which mentions three different paths in the verses, "Guide us on (1) the straight path, the path of those whom Thou hast blessed, not (2) [the path] of those against whom Thou art wrathful, nor (3) of those who are astray" (1:5–7). One of these paths is straight and two are crooked. Yet, from a certain point of view, all paths are "straight," since each has been laid down by the engendering command. All paths come from God, and all lead back to Him. All paths are "good," since there is no evil in existence.

God gave news in His Book that His Prophet and Messenger said, "Surely my Lord is on a straight path" (11:56). Thereby He described Himself as being on a straight path. But He only said this after saying in the same verse, "There is no crawling creature but He takes it by the forelock." Hence in reality there is no one that is not "straight" upon the path of the Lord, since there is no one whom the Real has not taken by the forelock; none can extract his forelock from his Master's hand. . . .

The straightness demanded by the wisdom of "Allah" permeates every engendered thing. God said, in confirmation of Moses, "He gave each thing its creation" (20:50). Hence each thing has an actual straightness. The straightness of a plant is to move downwards, while the straightness of an animal is to move horizontally. Were this not so, no one would be able to profit from them: If a plant did not move downwards to drink water with its roots, it would give no benefit. . . .

All movements are straight. There is nothing but straightness and no way to opposition. . . . The "straightness" of a bow is its crookedness, because of what is desired from it. Hence there is nothing in engendered existence but straightness, since He who brought it into existence, God, is upon a straight path in respect of being a Lord. Though some of the paths enter into others and some become confused, they never cease being straight—the straightness of confusion and the straightness for which they came into existence. Hence the paths are in an absolute straightness which exercises its ruling property over every engendered thing. This is indicated by God's words, "To Him all affairs shall be returned," and He is upon a straight path; "so worship Him" (11:123), that is, make yourself lowly be-

> fore Him in any path within which He places you and do not make yourself lowly before any "other," since the other is nonexistence, and he who aims for nonexistence will attain to nothing. . . . Hence straightness pervades all entities, whether substances, accidents, states, or words. (II 217.1,26)
>
> It may be that in reality crookedness is straightness, like the crookedness of a bow: The straightness which is desired from it is its crookedness. So there is nothing in the cosmos except the straight, since He who "takes it by the forelock" walks with it, and He is "upon a straight path." Hence, every movement and rest in existence is divine, since it is in the hand of the Real and emerges from a Real who is described as being on a straight path. (II 563.23)

The straight paths which all things follow take them to Allah. But Allah is the all-comprehensive name (*al-ism al-jāmiʿ*), that is, "the name which brings together the properties of all the names" (II 236.5). The things of the cosmos manifest the traces and properties of the diverse divine names, but no matter which name they manifest, they also manifest the name Allah. "There is no thing," says God, "whose treasuries are not with Us" (15:21). In explaining the nature of this divine "withness" (*ʿindiyya*), Ibn al-ʿArabī reminds us of some of the specific properties of the name Allah.

> The "withness" of Allah is unknown, since, inasmuch as Allah is Allah, none of the divine names become designated to the exclusion of any other, since He is precisely that which brings together all the names. That which makes Him specific is only the states of the creatures. When someone says, "O Allah," his state specifies which of the names he desires from among those comprised in this name Allah. . . . For Allah is the name that receives all names, just as universal hyle receives all forms. (III 195.23)
>
> The name Allah comprehends all the names. So be mindful when you witness it, since you will never witness it non-delimited. When He whispers to you through this name, which is all-comprehensive, consider why He is whispering to you and consider the station which requires this whispering or this witnessing. Consider which divine name gazes upon this station. It is that name which is addressing you or which you are witnessing. This is what is called "self-transmutation in forms." Take the drowning man, for example. When he says, "O Allah," he means, "O Helper" or "O Deliverer" or "O Rescuer." When the person suffering pain says, "O Allah," he means, "O Healer" or "O Health-giver" or something of this sort. (*Rāzī* 5)

Since the straight path takes to Allah, and Allah as such is absolutely nondelimited, we have to inquire about the mode in which the straight path takes to Allah. In other words, does the path end up with the All-merciful and the All-compassionate? Or does it end up with the Vengeful and the Terrible in Punishment? As we have seen on more than one occasion, these names cannot be considered equivalent in respect of the properties which they exercise upon the creatures. Hence, concludes Ibn al-ʿArabī, the "straight path of Allah" is a fact of existence, but it cannot guarantee our felicity.

> There is no path which is not straight, since there is no path which does not take to Allah. But God said to His Prophet, "Go straight *as thou hast been commanded*" (11:112). He did not address him in terms of unqualified straightness. It has been established that "Unto Allah all things come home" (42:53) and that He is the end of every path. However, the important thing is which divine name you will reach and to which you will come home. For that name's effect—whether felicity and bliss or wretchedness and chastisement—will exercise its influence upon the one who reaches it. (II 218.13)
>
> The "path of Allah" is the all-inclusive path upon which all things walk, and it takes them to Allah. It embraces every divine Law and construction of the rational faculty, and then it takes to Allah, since it includes both wretched and felicitous. . . .
>
> This path is that concerning which the

Folk of Allah have said, "The paths to God are as numerous as the breaths of the creatures,"[13] since the breath emerges from the heart in accordance with the belief of the heart concerning Allah. The general belief is His existence. He who makes Him Time (*al-dahr*) will reach Allah in respect of His name Time, since Allah brings together all the contrary and non-contrary names. And we have already explained that He has named Himself by every name toward which there is poverty and need, for He said in His Book, "O people, you are the poor toward Allah, and Allah—He is the Independent, the Praiseworthy" (35:15). Though this may be denied, it is not denied by Allah, nor by the actual situation.

When someone believes that Allah is Nature, Allah will disclose Himself to him as Nature. When someone believes that Allah is such and such—whatever that might be—He will disclose Himself to him in the form of his belief. (III 410.24, 411.22)

The Koran alludes to several paths to Allah, but each one of them yields different results for those who follow them. In one chapter Ibn al-ʿArabī discusses five of these paths, including the path of Allah, the path of the Inaccessible (*al-ʿazīz*), the path of the Lord (*al-rabb*), the path of Muḥammad, and the path of the Blessing-giver (*al-munʿim*). In the present context, the last two of these paths are particularly relevant.

The path of the Blessing-giver is "the path of those whom" God "has blessed" (1:6). It is mentioned in His words, "He has laid down for you as Law what He charged Noah with, and what We have revealed to thee [O Muḥammad], and what We charged Abraham with, and Moses, and Jesus" (42:13). He mentions the prophets and the messengers, then says, "Those are they whom God has guided, so follow their guidance" (6:90). This is the path that brings together every prophet and messenger. It is the performance of religion, scattering not concerning it, and coming together in it.[14] It is that concerning which Bukhārī wrote a chapter entitled, "The chapter on what has come concerning the fact that the religion of the prophets is one." He brought the article which makes the word "religion" definite because all religion comes from God, even if some of the rulings are diverse. Everyone is commanded to perform the religion and to come together in it, that is, in the way upon which all agree. As for the rulings which are diverse, that is because of the Law which God assigned to each one of the messengers. He said, "To every one [of the prophets] We have appointed a Law and a way; and if God had willed, He would have made you one nation" (5:48). If He had done that, your revealed Laws would not be diverse, just as they are not diverse in the fact that you have been commanded to come together and to perform them. . . .

The specific path which pertains to the Prophet is that for which he was singled out to the exclusion of everyone else. It is the Koran, God's firm cord and all-comprehensive Law. This is indicated in His words, "This is My straight path, so follow it, and follow not diverse paths, lest they scatter you from its road" (6:153). (III 413.12, 24)

Hence the straight path which Muslims pray to be guided upon is the path of Muḥammad and the Koran, which alone leads them to felicity. When the faithful say, "Guide us on the straight path," they do not mean the nondelimited "path of Allah" but the delimited path of the Prophet.

Hence the meaning of "straightness" is motion and rest upon the path laid down by the Law. The "straight path" is the divine Law. Faith in God is the beginning of this path, and the "branches of faith" are its waystations. (II 218.16)

God says, "This is My straight path, so follow it, and follow not diverse roads, lest they scatter you from its road" (6:153), that is, the road wherein lies your felicity. Certainly, all roads lead to Allah, since He is the end of every road: "To Him all affairs shall be returned" (11:123). But not everyone who returns to Him gains felicity. The road of felicity is that set down by the Law (*al-mashrūʿa*), nothing else. (II 148.10)

Nobility of Character

Just as there is nothing but good in existence and all paths lead to Allah, so also all character traits are noble and none is base. But all character traits are noble only in relationship to their ontological roots. As soon as the four levels of good and evil are taken into account, some are noble and some base. In order to tell the difference between noble and base in what concerns ultimate felicity, human beings have need of the Law, or, what comes down to the same thing, the light of faith. In a chapter on perspicacity (*firāsa*), Ibn al-ʿArabī recalls the saying of the Prophet, "Be wary of the perspicacity of the man of faith, for he sees with the light of Allah."[15] Then he explains the nature of this "perspicacity through faith" (*al-firāsat al-īmāniyya*):[16]

> Perspicacity through faith is a divine light which God gives to the person of faith in the eye of his insight, just like the light which belongs to the eye of sight. When a person has this perspicacity, its mark is like the light of the sun through which sensory objects appear to sight. When the light of the sun is unveiled, sight differentiates among the sensory objects. It discerns the large from the small, the beautiful from the ugly, the white from the black, red, and yellow, the moving from the still, the far from the near, and the high from the low. In the same way, the light of perspicacity through faith discerns the praiseworthy from the blameworthy.
>
> The reason that the light of perspicacity is attributed to the name Allah, which is the name which brings together the properties of all the names, is that this light unveils both the praiseworthy and the blameworthy, both the movements of felicity pertaining to the next abode and the movements of wretchedness.
>
> Some of the possessors of perspicacity have reached a point where, upon seeing a person's footprint in the ground—though the person himself is not present—they are able to say that he is a felicitous person or a wretched person. This is similar to what is done by a tracker who follows footprints. The man of perspicacity says, for example, "The owner of this footprint was white and blind in one eye." Then he describes his character as if he sees him, including various accidental matters connected to his character. He sees all this without seeing the person himself. He judges concerning his lineage. He joins a child to its father when a disagreement arises because of the lack of the outward similarity which is usual between fathers and sons.
>
> This is why the light of perspicacity is attributed to Allah. If it were attributed to the name Praiseworthy, for example, the possessor of this light would see only the praiseworthy and felicitous. In the same way, if it were attributed to any divine name, the perspicacity would accord with what is given by the reality of that name. But since the light is attributed to Allah, its possessor perceives the good things and the evil which occur in matters of this world and the next, the blameworthy qualities and the praiseworthy, the noble character traits and the base, and what is given by Nature and by the spiritual domain. (II 235.35)

Man gains the light of perspicacity through assuming the noble character traits in perfect harmony, balance, and "equilibrium" (*iʿtidāl*). Just as physical illness is caused by a "disequilibrium" (*inḥirāf*) of the constitution, so also moral illness is caused by a disequilibrium of the character traits. In order to bring the traits into balance, man has need of the divine physician (*al-ṭabīb al-ilāhī*). It is his task to show the seeker how to employ his innate character traits, since nothing can be added to man's creation. The "assumption of traits" which a person should undergo, as we saw in the last chapter, can not mean that he comes to possess traits which did not already belong to him. On the contrary, the traits which he possesses innately are redirected such that they will always be pleasing to God.

> The divine physician treats the character traits and disciplines the individual de-

sires of the soul through reminder, admonition, and calling attention to the highest affairs and that which will come to belong to him who listens—the felicity as well as the praise of God, the people, and the high spirits. . . .

When the divine physician comes—and he is the prophet, or the inheritor of the prophet, or the sage—he examines what is required by the soul's configuration (*nash'a*). The soul submits itself to him and places its reins in his hands so that he will train it and take steps to achieve its felicity. If the soul is in disequilibrium, the physician returns it to the opposite of what its configuration requires by explaining to it how to put that disequilibrium to use in a manner which will be praised by God and within which the soul will find its felicity. For the physician cannot configure the soul in a new configuration, since "Thy Lord has finished with creation and character".[17] There remains nothing in our hands but clarifying the soul's proper occupations (*maṣraf*).

When the configuration of a person's soul is in equilibrium and he is ignorant of those affairs which lead to felicity with God and which require someone—that is, the Messenger of God—to acquaint him with them, he asks the learned masters about those affairs which will bring about felicity with God. But he has no need for anyone to acquaint him with the noble character traits, since his configuration's constitution and equilibrium will give him only noble character traits. Or rather, for some affairs he will need the person to acquaint him with the proper usage of disequilibrium. This is prescribed for him by the Law, since in that disequilibrium lie his best interests, whether in this world, the next, or both.

The person in disequilibrium will display blameworthy and base character traits. He will seek his own individual desires and will not care what outcome he may reach by attaining them. The disciplining physician leads him on step by step, state after state, by explaining to him the proper occupations, as mentioned. He comes to him with the perspicacity of faith and has knowledge of the best interest of this person. When he sees him perform an action which leads to something blameworthy, or that action itself brings about something blameworthy, he guides him to the extent he can until he submits his soul to him so that he may dominate over it.

If the person is in disequilibrium, his wayfaring will consist of struggle (*mujāhada*) and ascetic discipline (*riyāḍa*). If he is in equilibrium, he will be cheerful and joyous in his wayfaring, full of gaiety and happy. Affairs which are difficult for others will be easy for him, and he will not have to force himself in any of the noble character traits.

When the soul becomes limpid and wholesome, joins up with the world of purity, looks with the divine eye, hears through Him, and acts through His strength, then it knows the origins of things and their destinations, where they rise up and whence they return. This is called "perspicacity through faith." It is a gift from God which is attained by those who are sound in nature and those who are not.

Equilibrium and disequilibrium in the cosmos and that which causes the domination of some of the roots which determine the properties of compound things over others go back to the effects of the divine knowledge. On the basis of His knowledge God has mercy upon whom He will, He forgives and chastises, He dislikes, He approves, and He becomes wrathful. What does wrath have in common with satisfaction? What does pardon have in common with vengeance? What does approval have in common with disapproval? God has given reports of all these attributes in the revealed scriptures, while the people of unveiling know them through the witnessing of the eye. (II 236.31, 237.6)

The function of the prophets and the friends of God is to help bring out the noble character traits which are intrinsic to human nature. They must also provide proper guidance for the base character traits, since all character traits, noble and base, go back to man's essence. In the last analysis, a character trait is called base not because of its ontological root, but because of the way in which it is put to use. Everything that comes from God is good and follows the engendering command. Good and evil, as we saw above, need to be defined in terms of various relative factors: the Law, agreeableness to the constitution, perfection, and individual desire. The defining factor in questions of morality and character go back primarily to the Law, though the other factors may also be taken into account in certain cases and in various respects. The Law directs all character traits into proper channels so that people will employ their own innate attributes in the mode which corresponds to God's approval and satisfaction. Then these attributes are called "noble character traits." If employed wrongly, these same attributes become "base character traits." Right and wrong to back to the four factors just mentioned.

The Prophet said, "I was sent to complete (*itmām*) the noble character traits."[18] According to Ibn al-ʿArabī's interpretation, the noble character traits were incomplete because the earlier prophets did not deal with all of them. Muḥammad "completed" them by adding to the noble character traits all the base character traits, since his revealed law transforms the blameworthy traits into praiseworthy ones. The means of this transformation is to change the manner in which the so-called base character traits are applied or employed (*maṣraf*).

> "Completing the noble character traits" is to strip them of the baseness which has been attributed to them. Base character traits are an accidental thing, while noble character traits are an essential thing. The reason for this is that baseness has no divine support. It is an accidental relationship founded upon the individual desires of the soul. But noble character traits have a divine support, that is, the divine character traits. Hence the Prophet's completion of the noble character traits became manifest in his pointing out how they should be applied. He specified proper applications for them through which they become noble character traits and are stripped of the clothing of base character traits. (II 562.10)

> The Prophet said, "I was sent to complete the noble character traits." The meaning is as follows: Character traits have been divided into noble and base. The noble character traits have become manifest through the revealed religions to the prophets and messengers, all of whom distinguished the base traits from the noble.
>
> However, rational proofs, unveiling, and gnosis all show us that there is nothing in the cosmos except the character traits of God. Hence there are no base character traits.
>
> The Messenger of God was sent with the all-comprehensive Word to all mankind. He was given "the all-comprehensive words,"[19] while every prophet who preceded him possessed a specific Law. Hence he reported that he had been sent to complete the noble character traits, since they are the character traits of God. He joined what had been called base character traits to the noble character traits, and all became noble. He who understands what is meant by the revealed law sees that the Prophet did not leave a single base character trait in the cosmos.
>
> The Prophet explained for us how to apply what are called "base character traits," such as eager desire (*ḥirṣ*), envy (*ḥasad*), covetousness (*sharah*), miserliness (*bukhl*), timidity (*fazaʿ*), and every blameworthy attribute. He explained for us proper occupations for these attributes such that, if we employ them in these occupations, they will turn into noble character traits, the name of blame will disappear from them, and they will become praiseworthy. In this manner God completed the noble character traits through him. The noble character traits have no opposite, just as God has no opposite. All things in the cosmos are His character traits, so all are noble, though this is not recognized.
>
> God commanded us to avoid what we are commanded to avoid only because of our belief that they are base character traits. He revealed to His Prophet that he should explain to us how they can be properly employed, so that people would take notice. Among us there are those who know and others who do not. This then is the meaning of his words, "I was sent to complete the noble character traits." Through this he became the seal of the prophets. (II 363.23)

The attributes found in man's innate

disposition do not change, since they are essential to this world's configuration and man's specific constitution. These include cowardice (*jubn*), avarice (*shuḥḥ*), envy (*ḥasad*), eager desire (*ḥirṣ*), talebearing (*namīma*), arrogance (*takabbur*), harshness (*ghilẓa*), seeking subjugation (*ṭalab al-qahr*), and the like.

Since no one can set out to change them, God explained various proper applications for them toward which they can be directed by the rulings of the Law. If the soul directs the properties of these attributes toward these applications, it will attain to felicity and high degrees.

These proper applications are as follows: The soul should be cowardly toward committing forbidden things because of the loss it can expect. It should have avarice in respect to its religion. It should envy him who spends his possessions [in the way of religion] and him who seeks knowledge. It should be eagerly desirous toward good and try to spread it among the people. It should tell the tale of good, just as the garden tells the tale of the sweet smelling flowers within it. It should be arrogant in God toward him who is arrogant toward God's command. It should be harsh in its words and acts in the places where it knows that God approves of that. It should seek the subjugation of him who is hostile toward God and resists Him.

Such a soul does not leave its own attributes, but it directs them toward applications for which its Lord, His angels, and His messengers have praised it. Hence the Law has brought only that which aids nature (*ṭabʿ*). I do not know how it is that people suffer hardship, since they are not forbidden those attributes which their natures require. On the contrary, the Law explains their proper applications. Hence, people perish only when they are controlled by individual desires. It is that which allows them to suffer pain and to dislike things.

If man would direct his desire toward that which his Creator wants for him, he would be at rest. It was said to Abū Yazīd, "What do you desire?" He replied, "I desire not to desire." In other words, "Make me desire everything that Thou desirest," so that there may be nothing but what God desires. God "desires" for His servants only "ease, and He desires not hardship" (2:185) for them. He desires good for them, and evil does not return to Him, just as has been mentioned in the sound hadith: "The good, all of it, is in Thy hands, and evil does not go back to Thee," even if everything comes from God in respect to the root. Since it is impossible for man to cease desiring, the first thing this detracts from is his acts of obedience (*ṭāʿa*) in that he performs them without an intention (*niyya*) set down in the Law, and hence they are not acts of obedience. That is why Abū Yazīd sought deliverance from those individual desires of the soul which do not conform with the approval of God. (II 687.12)

Chapter 117 of the *Futūḥāt* is entitled, "On the station of covetousness (*sharah*) and eager desire (*ḥirṣ*)." These practically synonymous qualities are normally considered blameworthy, and *ḥirṣ* is commonly translated as "greed." But Ibn al-ʿArabī demonstrates that *ḥirṣ* is in fact a permanent attribute of every human being, and by following the Law man is able to apply it correctly. He refers to a hadith according to which someone arrived late for the communal prayer, and as he entered the mosque, people were just bowing, so he also bowed before joining up with the ranks of the worshipers. When told about this, the Prophet said to him, "May God increase you in eager desire [to obey Him], but do not repeat [your bowing outside of the ranks]."[20]

These two attributes belong to the innate disposition of human beings as human beings. This attribute is possessed as the innate disposition of every human. Hence it is impossible for it to disappear. Hence this is a station, not a state, since it is fixed.

If this station is blamed, that is because the object is blameworthy according to reason and the Law. God says, "You will find them the people most eagerly desirous of life" (2:96). The Prophet said, "May God increase you in eager desire, but do not repeat."

The Koranic verse could be interpreted either in terms of praise or blame, if it were not for the pronoun "them," which goes back to blameworthy people. The context shows that eager desire is meant in a blameworthy sense, in order to show that those people are liars in their claiming that "the last Abode is theirs exclusively, and not for other people" (2:94). But he who sees that here the eager desire is proof of their lying will see it as praiseworthy in them, since it is a divine proof of their lying. From God's side it is His argument against them, and "To God belongs the conclusive argument" (6:149). The blameworthy is completely blameworthy in respect to the fact that these people are in it, but not in respect to the fact that it is God's proof against them. . . .

As for the hadith which we mentioned, there eager desire is praiseworthy, since it is an eager desire to perform the obligatory worship.

With all this, these two attributes are two of the attributes of the perfected knower who is inheritor of the prophets, the guide of his community. For he looks at that wherein lies their best interest. Thus, God said concerning His Prophet, "[Grievous to him is your suffering,] eagerly desirous is he over you" (9:128). Hence God praised him for his eager desire to help his community. (II 198.28)

Ibn al-ʿArabī summarizes the relationship between noble and base character traits in the following passage:

The Prophet said, "I was sent to complete the noble character traits." "Noble character traits" in works and states are relative (*iḍāfī*). The reason for this is that people, who are the locus of noble character traits, have two states: free (*ḥurr*) and servant (*ʿabd*).

Character traits are either praiseworthy, and these are named noble character traits, or blameworthy, and these are named base character traits. Those in relation to whom noble and base character traits are employed are two and one. The one is God, and the two are your soul—when you place it in the station of a stranger—and the other, which is everything other than God.

Everything other than God is of two kinds, and you are included. One kind is elemental (*ʿunṣurī*) and the other kind is not elemental. Character traits are employed in relation to the elemental on the sensory level (*ḥissī*), while they are employed with the non-elemental on the supra-sensory level (*maʿnawī*).

The works which are called character traits are of two kinds, righteous (*ṣāliḥ*), which are the noble, and non-righteous, which are the base. Concerning the one kind God says, "Whoso works righteousness . . ." (2:62, etc.), while concerning the other kind He says, "[And Noah called upon his Lord, and said, 'O my Lord, my son is of my family . . . Said He, 'Noah, he is not of thy family;] it is a work not righteous.[21] Do not ask Me that whereof thou hast no knowledge. I admonish thee, lest thou shouldst be among the ignorant" (11:46). Thereby God taught Noah courtesy and the fact that one part of courtesy is to ask the unknown on the basis of knowledge. If he knows, and if he is one whose intercession and asking is accepted, then he should ask; but if he does not know, then he should not ask. However, a father's mercy and natural, elemental sympathy overcame him, so he employed them in other than their proper place. Hence God let him know that this was an attribute of the ignorant. There cannot be any good with ignorance, just as there cannot be any evil with knowledge.

When the Prophet said, "I was sent to complete the noble character traits," he meant that he knew what they were, how they should be employed, and where they should be employed.

Now, as I said, those addressed by the noble character traits are of two kinds, free and servant. The free man drinks of these traits as does the servant.

When you ascribe the character trait to God, everything other than God is God's servant. God says, "None is there in the heavens and the earth that comes not to the All-merciful as a servant" (19:93).

As for the share of the servant in the character traits, it is as follows: The absolute Master has declared (1) obligatory and (2) unlawful, so He has commanded and prohibited; He has also (3) declared indifferent, so He has bestowed free choice. He has preferred, so He has (4) recommended and (5) declared reprehensible. There is no sixth kind.[22]

A work may be obligatory because of the command of the Master, who is God, or recommended. If it is obligatory, its performance derives from the noble character traits in relation to God and yourself. If it is recommended, it derives from the noble character traits in relation to yourself. If the work includes a benefit for the other, it derives from the noble character traits in relation to the other. To refrain from a work having this property derives from the base character traits.

When an act has been declared unlawful or reprehensible, the division concerning it is like that in the obligatory and the recommended. Hence to refrain from that which is qualified by unlawfulness or reprehensibility derives from noble character traits, whereas to perform it derives from base character traits. To refrain from an act is a spiritual (*rūḥānī*) work, not a corporeal (*jismānī*) work, since "refraining" has no existence among the entities.

As for the work in which there is free choice—that is, the indifferent—to perform it derives from the noble character traits in relation to yourself in this world, but not the next world. However, if you do it because it is indifferent according to the Law, it derives from the noble character traits in relation to God and yourself in this world and the next. The wisdom in refraining from the indifferent follows exactly the same lines.

All the kinds pertain to the servant. The indifferent kind pertains to the free man. The reprehensible and recommended pertain to the free, though there is a breath of servanthood within them, but not its reality. . . .

If a person should be one of those whom no prophet has called, then in his case the noble character traits are those which are established by reason in respect to the existence of individual desire, perfection, and agreeableness to the constitution. For example, thanking one's benefactor is one of the noble character traits according to both reason and the Law, and showing ingratitude is one of the base character traits according to both. "God charges a soul only to its capacity" (2:286), whether or not a prophet's call has reached the soul. For in the actual situation, the Law judges the soul's works and it pardons him for his base character traits when no call from a prophet has reached him. Pardoning him is one of the noble character traits of God, and God is more worthy of noble attributes than the servant. Or rather, they belong to Him in reality and to the servant only by His solicitude in bestowing them. (II 616.34)

18. SAFETY IN SERVANTHOOD

Through following the Law the servant employs his innate character traits in the positive and praiseworthy manner that conforms to God's approval. As he continues in this path, more and more of the noble character traits will be attributed to him. But if he sees these traits as belonging to himself, he faces the grave danger of setting himself up as a rival to God, in practice if not in theory. Satan is always lying in wait, ready to ambush the man of piety by stirring up self-satisfaction and pride. The servant's only protection is to cling to his own nothingness, the fact that in the last analysis, he remains forever nonexistent. Nothing belongs to him except those attributes which manifest nonexistence, evil, and ignorance. Everything that manifests Being belongs to God. The servant must flee from every ontological attribute, since these are the properties of God's Lordship. He must dwell in his own non-ontological attributes, proper to servanthood.

The more perfect the actualization of servanthood, the more perfect is man. Paradoxically, the more perfect man's nothingness, the more perfectly he manifests God's attributes. The greatest "servant" of God is also His greatest locus of disclosure. Hence the first sobriquet of the Prophet Muḥammad is "His servant" (*ʿabduhu*)—only then is he "His messenger" (*rasūluhu*). Thus, in the general Islamic view, a human being can aspire to nothing higher than being a servant. Prophecy has come to an end, so no one can imitate Muḥammad in his role as messenger. Adhering to the Prophet's Sunna is to imitate him as servant.

The Servant's Worship of his Lord

The divine name Lord (*rabb*) denotes the relationship between the Divine Essence and all creatures. Though the Essence is Independent of the worlds, the creatures have need of It for everything they are. The name Lord alludes to the divine root of the existent things, since God is the "Lord" of all, and all things are His "vassals" (*marbūb*). The Koran employs this name about 900 times, but as Ibn al-ʿArabī often points out, it never employs it without ascribing it to something or someone. Thus God is "your Lord," "the Lord of your fathers," "the Lord of the heavens and the earth," "the Lord of the east and the west" and so on, but never just "the Lord." This is because the very meaning of the term Lord demands a vassal to which the Lord is ascribed. "The name 'Lord' is never employed without ascription, since it demands the vassal by its very existence" (II 437.8).[1]

The Lord of any vassal is the face of God turned toward it. In other words, the thing's Lord is God as He discloses Himself to it, and this is determined by the preparedness of its own immutable entity. "Things are ascribed to this name [Lord] because the cosmos has need of it more than any other name, since it names everything which governs the cosmos's interests (*maṣāliḥ*)" (II 442.20).

The opposite of Lord is "servant," or more literally, "slave" (*ʿabd*). This term is applied to everything other than God and more specifically to human beings. In many contexts Ibn al-ʿArabī uses the term interchangeably with "creature" (*khalq*). Thus he can say, "I mean by 'servant' the whole cosmos and man" (II 243.5). The Koran provides precedents for this usage in such verses as, "None is there in the heavens and earth that comes not to the All-merciful as a servant" (19:93). In this sense the term *ʿabd* corresponds to the philosophical expression "possible thing" (*mumkin*) and points to the poverty, need, and abasement of all creation before the Necessary Being. Hence, to be a servant is fundamentally an ontological situation. It indicates that the existence and attributes of the creature have been loaned to it by God. Man must come to a full understanding and realization of the radical poverty of all things, especially himself.

Human beings are servants of God in two manners. In one sense, God brings man into existence by the engendering command, and he follows it in all his states, whether he wants to or not. In another sense, man is addressed by the prescriptive command, and he may or may not follow it. In the first sense, man's acts are the acts of God, so they are ascribed directly to God. In the second case man is a locus of God's self-manifestation and possesses a certain degree of free choice. In the first case we speak of God's acts, in the second man's acts. In both cases man is a servant. To distinguish the two kinds of servanthood, Ibn al-ʿArabī calls the first *ʿubūda* and the second *ʿubūdiyya*, which can be translated as "servitude" and "servanthood," though it should be kept in mind that in the Shaykh's actual usage of the two terms, there is often no apparent difference between them.[2] The term "servitude" may suggest that free will is not envisaged, whereas "servanthood" is voluntary.

> "Servitude" is the servant's ascription to his Lord. Then, after that, there is "servanthood," which is his ascription to the divine locus of manifestation. Through

servitude he follows the command without any opposition. When He says to him, "Be!", he comes into existence without hesitation, for there is nothing there but the immutable entity receptive by its very essence to being engendered. Then, when the locus of manifestation is actualized, God says to it, "Do this and avoid that!" If he opposes the command, that is in respect of his being a locus of manifestation, but if he obeys it without delay, that is in respect of his entity. "Our only speech to a thing, when we desire it, is to say to it 'Be!', and it is" (16:40). . . .

In the house of this world the gnostics through God worship their Lord in respect to servitude, since they have no relationship except to Him. But everyone else is ascribed to servanthood, and it is said concerning them, "They have stood before Him in the station of servanthood." (II 88.26)

The word servant is closely connected to the term "worship" (*ʿibāda*), which translators often render as "service," i.e., of God. In the Koranic verse, "I created jinn and men only to worship Me" (51:56), "to worship Me" might also be translated "to serve Me" or "to be My servants." One way of distinguishing between servanthood and worship is to say that man is God's servant by the very fact of his existence, while he worships Him only inasmuch as he performs specifically devotional acts. Though this distinction may play a certain role in Ibn al-ʿArabī's writings, his analysis of the two terms has many more nuances than can be brought out by such a simple statement. Moreover, the Shaykh's primary interest is to bring out the ontological significance of the two terms, which is nearly identical. Hence, for example, he writes,

Know that existence is divided between worshiper (*ʿābid*) and worshiped (*maʿbūd*). The worshiper is everything other than God, that is, the cosmos, which is called and named "servant." The worshiped is that which is named God. (III 78.9)

Analyzed in terms of the existence of the creature, both worship and servanthood can be divided into essential and accidental kinds. Every creature is the servant of its Creator by its very essence: "None is there in the heavens and earth that comes not to the All-merciful as a servant" (19:93). So also everything worships Him, since "Everything in the heavens and the earth glorifies God" (57:1 etc.). On the level of the secondary and accidental qualities of the existent things, some of the jinn and men refuse to be God's servants or to worship Him, while others freely accept to do so. The distinction between essential and accidental worship parallels that between the engendering and prescriptive commands.

Worship is a real name of the servant, since it is his essence, his abode, his state, his entity, his self, his reality, and his face. (II 153.33)

Know that in everything other than God worship is of two kinds: (1) inherent (*dhātī*) worship, which is the worship which belongs by right to the Essence of the Real. This is a worship that derives from a divine self-disclosure. And (2) conventional (*waḍʿī*), commanded (*amrī*) worship, which derives from prophecy. (II 256.3)

When man becomes aware of the true knowledge of himself and occupies himself with the knowledge of his own realities in respect of the fact that he is human, he sees a difference between himself and the cosmos. He sees that the cosmos—that is, everything other than the jinn and mankind—has prostrated itself before God. It is obedient and has occupied itself with that worship of its Creator and Configurer which has been specified for it. Hence man seeks the reality which will bring him together with the cosmos, and he finds nothing but his possibility, poverty, lowliness, subjection, need, and misery. Then he considers the Real's description of the whole cosmos. He sees that He has described it as prostrating itself to Him, even its shadow. He sees that He has not described all of mankind—in contrast to the other kinds of the cosmos—as prostrating, only "many" (22:18).[3] He fears that he may be one of the "many" who merit chastisement.

Then he sees that the cosmos has been

given the innate character of worshiping God in its own essence. Hence this man finds in himself poverty and need toward someone who can guide him aright and show him the path which will take him to his felicity with God. When he hears God saying, "I created jinn and mankind only to worship Me" (51:56), he worships Him through poverty and need, just as the rest of the cosmos worships Him. But then he sees that God has set down bounds and designated various commands, while prohibiting him to step beyond them, and He has commanded things which he is able to perform. Hence knowledge of what God has set down for him in the Law becomes incumbent upon him, in order that he may perform the secondary (*far'ī*) worship, just as he has performed the primary (*aṣlī*) worship.

"Primary worship" is that which is demanded by the essences of the possible things inasmuch as they are possible. "Secondary worships" are all the acts for which the servant has need of a divine report in respect to what belongs to his Master by right and what is required by his servanthood.

When the servant knows that his Lord has commanded him and prohibited him, then he fulfills the right of his Master and the right of his servitude, for he has known himself. And everyone "who knows himself, knows his Lord." He who knows his Lord worships Him by His command.

No one combines the two forms of worship—the worship by command and the worship by prohibition—except mankind and the jinn. The angelic spirits have no prohibitions, which is why God said concerning them, "They disobey not God in what He commands them" (66:6), but He mentioned no prohibition for them. Concerning their inherent worship God said, "They glorify Him by night and day, and grow not weary" (41:38); "They glorify Him by night and day, and never fail" (21:20). The reality of their configuration bestows this, for this is the inherent worship, and it is a worship that permeates everything other than God.

Since, as we said, man brings together in himself all the realities of the cosmos, when he knows himself in respect of these realities, it becomes incumbent upon him to perform alone—in respect of himself —the worship of the whole cosmos. If he does not do this, he has not known himself in respect of his realities, for this is an inherent worship.

The form of his knowledge of this is as follows: He witnesses through unveiling all the realities without exception in their worship as they are in themselves, whether or not that has been unveiled for them. This is what I mean by knowledge of the realities, that is, through unveiling.

When man witnesses the realities, he cannot oppose the commands of his Master to worship, that is, the commands whose bounds and prescripts he observes both within and outside of himself. When he says, "Glory be to God" with his whole self as we have designated, then, in respect to that act of glorification, everything said by the whole cosmos is imprinted within the substance of his soul. . . . He is rewarded with the reward of the whole cosmos. (II 308.22)

The Perils of Lordship

As a general principle, Ibn al-'Arabī maintains that things never overstep the bounds of their own realities. Hence the servant and the Lord do not mix.

> It is impossible for realities to change, so the servant is servant and the Lord Lord; the Real is the Real and the creature creature. (II 371.5)

From this point of view, the servant cannot assume the character traits of God, since that would mean that he had come out of his own attributes. It would involve a sharing (*ishtirāk*) of attributes and a partnership (*mushāraka*) between Lord and servant. This would be an "association" (*shirk*) of other gods with God, which conflicts with Islam's fundamental axiom, *tawḥīd*, the declaration of God's Unity.

> God requires from those who declare His Unity that they not compete (*muzāḥama*) with Him, so that the Lord may re-

main Lord and the servant servant. The Lord does not compete with the servant in his servanthood, and the servant does not compete with the Lord in His Lordship, even while both servant and Lord exist. Hence he who declares God's Unity does not assume the traits of the divine names.

You may object: "It therefore becomes necessary that we do not accept what has been revealed by God concerning His becoming qualified by the attributes of the temporally originated things, such as withness, descent, sitting, and laughter, since these are all attributes of the servants. You just said that there is no competition, yet here we have Lordship competing with servanthood."

We answer: The situation is not as you suppose. The attributes you mentioned do not belong to servanthood. They are the attributes of Lordship in respect of Its manifestation within the loci of manifestation, not in respect of Its He-ness. Hence the servant is a servant according to its root, the Lordship is a Lordship according to Its root, and the He-ness is a He-ness according to Its root.

You may say: "But Lordship is not identical with the He-ness."

We reply: "Lordship" is the relationship of the He-ness to an entity, while the He-ness in itself does not require relationships. That which demands relationships from the He-ness is only the immutability of the entities. This is what is called "Lordship." (II 94.10)

Though Ibn al-ʿArabī claims in this passage that there is no assumption of traits, in many other passages, as we have already seen, he speaks of the reality of that assumption. Here he is looking at the actual ontological implications of the term, as he did in the last passage quoted in Chapter 16. From that point of view, all character traits are inherent in human nature, so none can be assumed. But in a looser sense, he frequently employs the term assumption of traits.

Through the assumption of traits, man gains the attributes normally associated with Lordship, including, for example, domination over the created things and the ability to "break habits" miraculously. Manifesting this power is a mark of spiritual immaturity, but the existence of the power is allowed by the "states" connected to the achievement of the spiritual stations. Ibn al-ʿArabī alludes to these "lordly attributes" (*al-ṣifāt al-rabbāniyya*) while contrasting a certain mode of self-disclosure connected to the Essence with another that takes place through the veil (*ḥijāb*).

[The first] is the form of the knowledge of declaring God's incomparability. . ., while [the second] is the form of the knowledge of declaring His similarity, that is, it is the servant's assumption of the traits of the divine names and his becoming manifest in His kingdom through the lordly attributes. In this station the created thing is a creator (*khāliq*) and manifests the properties of all the divine names. This is the level of the vicegerency (*khilāfa*) and the deputyship (*niyāba*) of the Real in the kingdom. Through it the servant can exercise governing control (*taḥakkum*) among the existent things by acting through his Resolve, by touching (*mubāshara*), or by speech (*qawl*).

As for Resolve, the servant desires something and that which he desires becomes imaginalized before him as he desires without increase or decrease. As for speech, he says to what he desires, "Be!", and it comes to be. Or he himself touches it, if it is a work, just as Jesus touched the clay in creating the bird and giving it form as a bird.[4] [The divine root of this touching is found in] God's words, "Him whom I created with My own two hands" (38:75). He who understands will recognize that man has a share in every divine presence. (II 667.22)

Man was not given governing control in the cosmos inasmuch as he is a man. On the contrary, he was given that through a divine, lordly power, since only an attribute of the Real can exercise governing control in the cosmos. In man this attribute is a trial (*ibtilāʾ*), not a bestowal of honor (*tashrīf*). (II 308.16)

The negative side to assuming the traits of the divine names can be seen in the case of such names as Overbearing, Magnificent, Inaccessible, Majestic,

Slayer, Avenger, and Terrible in Punishment. Though these are among God's "Most Beautiful Names," a human being who manifests them as his own character traits will face great danger. To the extent that he does assume them—and he cannot avoid this in some manner, since they are part of his innate disposition—he must take care to display them in the manner set down in the Law, or he runs the risk of turning into a Pharaoh. Ibn al-ʿArabī frequently points to the dangers of such names. In the passage below, taken from the longer version of his *Iṣṭilāḥāt*, he cites a Koranic verse in which two of God's names are attributed to the servant, but in a context which shows that the attributes are negative character traits. He is defining "adornment" (*al-taḥallī*):

> "Adornment" is to become qualified by the divine character traits. In the path it is called "assumption of the traits of the names." In our view adornment is the manifestation of the attributes of servitude continually, in spite of the existence of the assumption of the traits of the names. If the servant should cease being adorned in this manner, then the assumption of the names will go against him. God says, "In such a manner does God set a seal on every heart which is 'magnificent, overbearing'" (40:35).
>
> When the servant becomes adorned by the attributes of servitude, this itself derives from the assumption of the divine character traits, but most people cannot understand this with their rational faculties. Were they to know the meaning of those attributes by which the Real has described Himself in the Koran and the Sunna and which reason only accepts by interpreting in the sense of incomparability, they would not flee from such attributes when they hear them from people like myself.
>
> If servitude is conceived as an ontological quality, then it is identical with Him, since existence belongs only to Him. But since the entities of the possible things are the loci of manifestation for the Real, rational faculties find it distressing to ascribe to God what He ascribes to Himself. When this station beyond the stage of reason becomes manifest through prophecy, and then the Tribe act in accordance with it through faith, unveiling gives to them what reason considers impossible in respect to its reflection. (II 128.20)

In the preceding passage Ibn al-ʿArabī alludes to the fact that in the last analysis, servitude, to the extent that it can be considered an attribute of an existent thing, is itself taken from God, since existence belongs only to Him. This is what he means in a passage quoted earlier: "Even the name 'servant' does not belong to him; rather, he has assumed it as a trait, like all the Most Beautiful Names" (II 350.28).

Ibn al-ʿArabī discusses the dangers of assuming the traits of certain divine names while describing the station of the People of Blame (*al-malāmiyya*), who are the perfect gnostics.

> The divine root by which the People of Blame are supported is what we have mentioned: the fact that the majesty of the Real demands the acknowledgement of the tremendousness and magnificence due to the Divinity. At the same time, look at what is required by the abode of this world in respect to the Real: The servants make claims to lordship and they contend with the Real in His magnificence and tremendousness. Pharaoh said, "I am your lord the most high" (79:24), so he claimed magnificence and displayed overbearingness.
>
> The reason for all this is that this abode requires that the creatures be veiled from God. Were He to let them witness Himself in this world, then the property of decree (*qaḍāʾ*) and destiny (*qadar*)—that is, God's knowledge of what will take place from and in His creatures—would be nullified.[5] Hence His veil is a mercy toward them and it assures their subsistence, since by its essence His self-disclosure bestows overwhelming power (*qahr*) and allows no claims to remain along with it.[6]
>
> The Divinity yields to the property of the abodes (*mawṭin*), and this divine root is witnessed by the People of Blame, since they are sages and knowers. They say, "We are the branches of this root," since

everything in the cosmos has a divine root.

But if the servant should become qualified by a divine root, that is not necessarily praiseworthy. For example, without doubt magnificence (*kibriyā'*) is a divine root. But if the servant becomes qualified by it, makes himself a branch of this root, and employs it internally, then everyone agrees that this is blameworthy in every respect. However, if he should use it outwardly in a specific situation which occurs for him and in which it is permissible for him to employ it as an outward form without its spirit, then it is praiseworthy for the sake of the form. That is why the Tribe has held that it is obligatory for the friends to conceal miraculous breaking of habits, just as it is mandatory for the prophets to manifest it, since they are Lawgivers. (III 36.19)

In discussing the nature of a group of the friends of God known as "those who bow" (*al-rāki'ūn*), the Shaykh writes as follows:

Among the friends of God are "those who bow," whether men or women. God described them in His Book by this attribute (cf. 9:112). Bowing carries the sense of subjection and humility before God in respect of His He-ness and because of His inaccessibility and magnificence which become manifest in the cosmos.

The gnostic does not consider the cosmos in respect of its entity, but only in respect of the fact that it is a locus of manifestation for the attributes of the Real. God says, "In such a manner does God set a seal on every heart which is 'magnificent, overbearing'" (40:35). He says, "[Take him, and thrust him into the midst of Hell . . .] 'Taste! Surely thou art the "inaccessible, the generous"!'" (44:49). He says, "Magnificence is My cloak and tremendousness My shawl; if anyone contends with Me in either one, I will smash him."[7] Hence the entity is destroyed, while the attribute subsists. Those who bow do so before the attribute, not the entity. . . .

If the attributes of magnificence, overbearingness, inaccessibility, and tremendousness which are claimed by those servants who are magnificent, overbearing, inaccessible, and tremendous belonged to them in reality, He would not have blamed them. Nor would He have "seized them with a tightening grip" (69:10), any more than He seizes them for being lowly, submissive, mean, and abased—since meanness, lowliness, and smallness are their attributes. When someone manifests his own attributes, God does not take him to task for that—how could He take him to task for manifesting what is his by right? But, when they do not possess such attributes as overbearingness, yet they manifest them, God destroys them.

Hence the gnostics have verified the fact that these are the attributes of the Real. These attributes become manifest in those whom God desires to make wretched. Hence within the cosmos the gnostics humble themselves before the overbearing tyrants and those who are proudly magnificent, because of the attribute, not because of their entities, for the gnostics witness the Real in all things. This is even the case with bowing the head while extending their greetings when they meet someone. It may happen that the gnostics will bow their heads to one of their brothers when they greet him. Then this person becomes happy, but he is happy only because he is ignorant of himself, since he imagines that the person who bowed his head and bent himself over in front of him did so because of a high standing which belongs to him. When the rabble bow to each other, ignorance stands before ignorance out of custom and common usage, but they are not aware. But when the gnostics bow, they do so witnessing the overbearing power of God which demands that they bow themselves before it, for they see nothing but God. As Labīd said, "Is not everything other than God unreal?"[8] The unreal is nonexistence, without doubt, but existence is all the Real. Hence he who bows bows only before the ontological Real. (II 33.20)

God says to His Prophet, "Be thyself patient with those who call upon their Lord at morning and evening, desiring His face, and let not thine eye turn away from them, desiring the ornaments of the present life; and obey not him whose heart We have made neglectful of Our remembrance, so that he follows his own caprice and his affair has become all excess. Say: 'The Truth is from your Lord; so let whosoever will have faith, and let whosoever will disbelieve'" (18:28–29), that is, let no one's blaming you concerning God have any effect upon you.

The secondary cause of this verse was that the leaders of the disbelievers and the idolaters, such as al-Aqraʿ ibn Ḥābis, said, "Nothing prevents us from sitting with Muḥammad except the fact that these slaves sit with him," meaning by that Bilāl, Khubbāb ibn al-Aratt, and others. They were too proud to sit together with slaves at the same gathering. The Messenger of God was eagerly desirous that such as these would have faith. Hence he commanded the slaves that, when they saw him with these leaders, they should not approach until he finished with their business. Or, if the leaders approached while the slaves were with him, they should leave the gathering. Then God sent down this verse, out of jealousy toward the station of servanthood and poverty, lest the station be wronged by the attribute of exaltation and deiformity (*ta'alluh*) which became manifest outside of its proper place.

After this, whenever these slaves or their likes sat with the Messenger of God, he would not stand up from his place until they stood up and left, even if the session became prolonged. He used to say, "God has commanded me to restrain my soul with them." Hence, when the session became prolonged, some of the Companions, like Abū Bakr, would signal to them to stand up, so that the Messenger of God would be free to take care of various tasks. This derives from God's jealousy toward His poor and broken servant. It is one of the greatest proofs of the eminence of servitude and of dwelling within it.

This is the station to which we invite the people. For all souls see possessors of position and wealth as great, since exaltation and independence belong to God. Wherever this attribute discloses itself, people humble themselves and display their need for it. They do not differentiate between an intrinsic exaltation and independence and that which is accidental. They only witness this attribute. This is why people venerate those who display no need for them and renounce what the people possess. You see kings, in spite of their exaltation and authority, like slaves before the pious renouncers (*zuhhād*), because the latter are independent through God and have no need of the exaltation of the kings or the impermanent goods of this world which they possess. . . .

Wherever the attribute of the Real becomes manifest, it is loved and sought by the people, those who do not differentiate between its manifestation in him who deserves it and in him who does not deserve it. If these ignorant people only knew that the person most in need of possessions is he who has the most possessions! This is because the person who lives in abject poverty necessarily needs that which will remedy his lack, since this is intrinsic poverty. But the rich man—he who has so many possessions that, were they to be divided up for his lifetime and that of his children and grandchildren, it would be sufficient for all of them—leaves his wife and children and travels with his possessions. He risks the dangers of oceans and enemies, he crosses deserts to far cities in east and west, all in search of another dirham in addition to what he has. This he does because of the intensity of his poverty and need for it, even though he may well be destroyed in his search for additional wealth, or his possessions may suffer shipwreck or be confiscated. He may be taken prisoner in his travels or be slain. But in spite of all these difficulties, he does not refrain from traveling in search of additional wealth. Were it not for his ignorance and the intensity of his poverty and need, he would not risk the more precious for the more vile.

The poor man who renounces sees that this man of wealth is far poorer than he, and he is blameworthy in his poverty. Were this renouncer not rich through his Lord and free of these impermanent goods, he would be more intense in his eager desire in seeking them than the merchants and the kings. . . .

The people of our path have remained heedless of this route. They have held that independence through God is one of the greatest of levels, and this has veiled them from realizing the station of calling attention to poverty toward God, which is their real attribute. They have placed their real attribute in independence through

God by being included in His property, because of their love for independence, which is to come out of their own attribute.

But he alone is the Man who knows his own measure, achieves the realization of his own attribute, and does not emerge from his own abode. He keeps upon himself the robe, title, and name by which his Lord has titled and named him, for He said, "You are the poor toward God, and God—He is the Independent, the Praiseworthy" (35:15). (III 18.20)

In commenting on the inward significance of the Islamic rites of purity, Ibn al-ʿArabī points out that dust may be used in place of water in times of necessity because it reminds man of the lowliness of his origin and encourages him to claim nothing but what belongs to him by right.

Dust and the earth are the root of man's configuration, and this verifies his servanthood and lowliness. Then he was overcome by the accident of making claims, since the Messenger said concerning him that he was created upon the Form. In our view, this is because of the preparedness according to which God created him, that is, the fact that he is a receptacle for the assumption of the traits of the divine names in accordance with what his reality gives him. . . . Because of this relationship, man felt exalted and high and claimed magnificence. Hence he was commanded to purify himself from this prideful magnificence through the earth and dust, which is the reality of his servanthood. He becomes purified by considering the root of his own creation, that from which he was created. That is why God says to someone who has this attribute in order to provide medicine against the thought which gives rise to prideful magnificence, "Let man," that is, the children of Adam, "consider of what he was created; he was created of gushing water" (86:5), which is "mean water" (32:8 etc.). For one of the things he claims is power and bestowal, but his innate disposition is incapacity and greed. . . .

Hence it is said to him when he makes this claim and sees himself having the power, the munificence, the generosity, and the bestowal which become manifest from him: "Purify your soul from these attributes by considering the weakness and greed in accordance with which you are innately disposed." God says, "Whoso is guarded against the avarice of his own soul [—those, they are the prosperers]" (59:9), and He says, "[Surely man was created fretful . . .], when good visits him, grudging" (70:21). When man looks at this root, his soul becomes wholesome and he is purified of making claims. (I 373.33)

The Exaltation of Lowliness

Man can only stay safe from making claims by clinging to his own root, which is lowliness and servanthood. In effect, the divine names whose traits he assumes become a heavy burden upon him. Ibn al-ʿArabī points this out while explaining one of the senses of the Koranic verse, "God commands you to deliver trusts back to their owners" (4:58).

Do you not see that when someone deposits a possession with a person, he finds that it weighs him down? Guarding and preserving it are a burden for him. But if its owner says to him, "I give this to you and it no longer belongs to me," the carrying of that possession becomes easy for him, and he becomes tremendously happy, honoring the person who gave it to him. In the same way the attributes of the Real are a trust with the servant.

Because the divine attributes are a trust with the gnostic, he never ceases being weighed down by examining them. How should he employ them? Where should he put them to use? He fears to employ them in the way that their Owner might employ them. When he is weighed down in this way, he returns them to their Owner and remains happy and burden-free in servanthood, which is his own possession, or rather, his reality, since anything in addition to that may disappear from him. God praises him for delivering the trust back safely. So he who does not transgress his own measure will prosper, just as is said in the proverb: "No one who knows his own worth will come to ruin." (II 631.4)

The highest of waystations with God is for God to preserve His servant in the constant witnessing of his own servanthood, whether or not He has bestowed upon him any of the lordly robes. This is the most eminent of waystations given to a servant. It is indicated in His words to Moses, "I have made thee well for Myself" (20:41), and His words [concerning the *miʿrāj* of Muḥammad], "Glory be to Him who carried His servant by night" (17:1). Note how He links "His servant" with the declaration of incomparability [through the term "glorification"].[9] (III 32.9)

No one is a servant but he who is uniform in his servitude. If the servant deviates from this attribute through the slightest lordly description—even if that description is praiseworthy, like an attribute of mercy—he has left the level for which he was created and is deprived of perfection and knowledge of God to the extent that he is qualified by the attributes of the Real. (II 616.7)

The travelers on the spiritual path are constantly faced with the danger of leaving servanthood and ascribing God's attributes to themselves. No one can consider himself immune from the divine deception. If a person did so, that in itself would prove that he had been deceived. In one passage Ibn al-ʿArabī describes the various difficult ascents (*ʿaqaba*) which the spiritual traveler must pass in order to achieve the station of true servanthood.

This is the station which Niffarī in his *Mawāqif* called "equality" (*sawāʾ*),[10] since the servant becomes manifest in the form of the Real. If God does not favor this servant through preservation (*ʿiṣma*) and guarding and does not fix his feet in this difficult ascent by keeping his vision fixed upon his servanthood while he manifests the Form, then his feet will slip and the Form of the Real which he possesses in himself will come between him and his vision of his servanthood. Then he will see the Real in the form of his own servanthood, and the actual situation will be reversed in his eyes. This is a difficult locus of witnessing, for God descends from His station of independence from the worlds to that of seeking a loan from His servant.[11] It was in respect to this that it was said, "God is the poor," while in fact He is the Independent, "and we are the independent" (3:181), while in fact they are the poor. Thus the situation was reversed for them. This derives from the divine deception, of which man is not aware. He who desires the path to protection from the divine deception must cling to his servanthood and its concomitants in every state. That is the mark of his being protected from the deception of God. Nevertheless, he will not remain secure in respect to the future, since he has no security that he will keep this state. (III 147.5)

Were it not for the perfection of the Form in man, no one would have claimed lordship. Happy is he who is upon a form which requires such an elevated station and which has no effect upon him and does not bring him out of his servanthood! That is the preservation of which God has bestowed upon us an ample share at this time. May God assure our subsistence within it during the rest of our life until we are taken to Him—I and all our brothers and devotees, by His kindness! There is no Lord but He. (II 642.26)

All these warnings against the dangers of assuming God's attributes serve to remind us of our constant human situation. Every human being possesses himself and all his positive attributes as God's trust, so everyone must strive to handle the trust properly. The perfect servant combines servanthood with the assumption of the divine traits, just as he combines the declaration of God's incomparability (which demands that he be nothing) with the declaration of God's similarity (which means that he is God's self-disclosure).

Man can gain nothing better in his life than knowledge of God, the assumption of the traits of His names, halting with that which is demanded by his servant-

> hood, and fulfilling the obedience to his Master's commands appropriate for His level. (II 640.32)

Perfect man manifests the divine form while being firmly fixed in servanthood. Through the affirmation of his radical ontological deprivation, his absolute nothingness in face of the Necessary Being, he remains fixed in the distance (*buʿd*) from his Lord that his possibility and contingency demand. Yet, paradoxically, through his knowledge of his true situation, he is brought into God's nearness (*qurb*). Ibn al-ʿArabī points to the happy combination of distance and nearness, servanthood and manifesting the names of God, by quoting two apparently contradictory sayings of Abū Yazīd.

> When two things are conceived which never come together and which are different in each and every respect, that is the ultimate limit of "distance." Hence, nothing is farther from God than the cosmos, since nothing can bring the two together in respect of its own essence. This is found in God's words, "God is Independent of the worlds" (3:97) and in the hadith, "God is, and nothing is with Him."
>
> Then we descend to the next degree in distance and we say that the servant will not be the master (*sayyid*) of him in respect of whom he is a servant, so nothing is farther from the servant than his master. Hence servanthood is not a state of nearness. That which brings the servant near to his Master is his knowledge that he is His servant, and this knowledge is not identical with the servanthood. Servanthood demands distance from the Master, but the servant's knowledge of servanthood requires nearness to Him. When Abū Yazīd became bewildered about nearness and did not know how he should gain nearness to his Lord, the Real said to him in his inmost consciousness, "O Abū Yazīd! Come near to Me through that which I do not possess: lowliness and poverty." Hence He negated from Himself these two attributes, lowliness and poverty. That which He negates from Himself is an attribute of distance from Him. Hence, when those attributes which demand distance arise in someone, they determine his situation, and they demand distance.
>
> At another time Abū Yazīd said to his Lord, "Through what shall I gain nearness to Thee?" The Real said to him, "Leave aside your self and come!" Once he abandons himself, he will have abandoned the property of servanthood, since servanthood is identical with distance from Masterhood and the servant is far from the Master.
>
> Hence in lowliness and poverty Abū Yazīd sought nearness through servanthood, while in abandoning self he sought nearness through assuming the character traits of God. It is through this that there is a coming together. (II 561.11)

In order to understand the reality of his own servanthood, man needs to weigh it in the proper scale.

> Man's scale from the Divine Presence is found in the Prophet's words, "God created Adam upon His own Form." The divine generosity has placed man in this scale. Through his form he is weighed against the presence of Him who brought him into existence, in essence, attribute, and act. The fact of weighing does not necessitate a sharing (*ishtirāk*) of reality between the two things being weighed. That against which gold coin is weighed is the iron weight, which does not resemble the gold in its essence, attribute, or quantity. Hence it is known that what is being weighed through the human form is everything that the form demands through the divine names which turned their attentiveness toward bringing it into existence and which manifest their effects within it. So, just as the iron weight is not weighed against the gold in definition (*ḥadd*), reality, or the form of its entity, in the same way the servant does not come together with God in definition or reality—even though He created him upon His own form—since His Essence has no definition, while man is defined by a definition pertaining to his essence (*dhātī*), not merely designative (*rasmī*) or verbal (*lafẓī*), and every created thing is the same. But man is the most perfect and most comprehensive of created things in respect of his configuration and his level.

When you become aware of the reality of this Scale, you will cease imagining what you used to imagine about the "form"—that is, that He is an Essence and you are an essence and that you are qualified by the Alive, the Knowing, and the rest of the attributes, just as He is. Through this Scale you will come to know that this is not what is meant by the "form." That is why God brought together in a single sura "He created man" (55:3) and "He set up the Scale" (55:7). Then He commanded you to employ the Scale without exceeding or falling short (55:8–9). There is no way to employ it except as I have mentioned to you, since He is God, the Creator, and you are the servant, the created thing. How can the artifact know its artisan? What the artifact demands from the artisan is only the form of the artisan's knowledge of it, not the form of his essence. You are the artifact of your Creator. So your form corresponds to the form of His knowledge of you; and such is the case with every created thing.

Were this not the case, were the situation such that the two of you were brought together by a single definition and reality, as Zayd and ʿAmr are brought together [by their humanity], then you would be a god, or he would be a divine thrall (*ma'lūh*), and then a single definition would bring you together. But the situation is contrary to that!

So know by which scale you should weigh yourself against your Lord, and be not pleased with yourself! Know that you are the iron weight through which is weighed a unique ruby which has no sister. If you come together with it in quantity, you do not come together with it in measure, nor in essence, nor in specific character—God be high exalted! So cling to your servanthood and know your own measure. . . . Do not bring Him into your scale. For you are you, and He is He. "There is no god but He, the Inaccessible, the Wise!" (3:6). "Nothing is like Him, and He is Hearing, Seeing" (42:11). (III 8.23)

The outstanding gnostics always preserve courtesy toward God and are never overcome by heedlessness (*ghafla*). Lesser gnostics may at times succumb to the influence of a state, which explains why they sometimes utter such well-known sayings as the "I am the Real" of al-Ḥallāj or the two similar formulas of Abū Yazīd cited below.

> Do you not see that when the spirit is heedless of itself, it intrudes upon and is audacious toward the Divine Station? Then it claims lordship, like Pharaoh. When this state overcomes it, it says, "I am Allah" or "Glory be to me!", as one of the gnostics has said. This is because he was overcome by a state. That is why words like this have never issued from a messenger, or a prophet, or a friend who is perfect in his knowledge, his presence (*ḥuḍūr*), his clinging to the door of the station which belongs to him, his courtesy, and his observance of the material (*mādda*) within which he dwells and through which he becomes manifest.[12] (I 276.2)

When the great gnostics recognize the attributes of Lordship within themselves, it may be that they will preserve courtesy by seeing these as the attributes of the angelic hierarchy, not as God's attributes.

> Among the friends of God are those known as the "noble" (*al-kuramā'*), both men and women. God has befriended them through nobility of soul. He says concerning them, "When they pass by idle talk, they pass by with nobility" (25:72). In other words, they do not look at that which God has condemned looking upon. Hence they are not defiled by any of it, since they pass by with nobility, paying no attention to it, and it has no effect upon them. For idle talk is a station which souls find sweet, because of the opposition which God has kneaded into their innate disposition. But these are souls which refuse all vile qualities, since they are the souls of the noble among God's servants.
>
> In this attribute they join up with the Higher Plenum. Concerning the latter, God said that His scriptures have come "by the hands of noble and pious emissaries" (80:15), thereby describing them as noble. Every description which joins you to the Higher Plenum gives eminence to you.

When the gnostics among God's servants assume the traits of God's names, they place between themselves and the attributes of the Real the quality by which God has described the Higher Plenum. Hence they take the attribute in respect of its belonging to one of God's pure servants, not in respect of its being an attribute of the Real. For their eminence lies in that they never leave the station of servanthood. But among the gnostics, this tasting is rare, since most of the gnostics assume the traits of the Most Beautiful Names in respect of the fact that they are names of God, not in respect of what we just mentioned—that the Higher Plenum has been qualified by them as is proper. Hence the gnostic assumes their traits only after they have acquired the fragrances of servitude from the Higher Plenum. Gnostics such as these, in assuming the traits of the names, do not find any flavor of the Lordship appropriate to these names. He who knows what we have mentioned and puts it into practice will taste a knowledge of self-disclosure never tasted by anyone who finds the flavor of Lordship in his assumption of traits. (II 38.33)

The Perfect Servant

By definition, human beings are servants of God in two respects. On the one hand they are servants by their very essences, unable even to consider disobeying their Lord. On the other hand they can disobey God's prescriptive command. The "faithful" are those who, to a large degree, succeed in obeying the prescriptive command, though imperfections remain in their worship. But the worship and servanthood of a perfect man are without fault. His servanthood is so perfect that no distinction whatsoever can be drawn between the engendering and prescriptive commands. In other words, to perfect man God only says "Be!" But to animal men, He says, "Be! And now that you are, do this, and avoid doing that!"

Ibn al-ʿArabī refers to these points while explaining the nature of the "subsistence" (*baqāʾ*) of the servant after his "annihilation" (*fanāʾ*) in God, two terms frequently discussed in Sufi texts.

Subsistence is a relationship that does not disappear or change. Its property is immutably fixed in both the Real and the creature. It is a divine attribute. But annihilation is a relationship that disappears. It is an attribute of engendered existence and does not touch upon the Presence of the Real. Every attribute which is ascribed to both sides is more complete and higher than the attribute which is specific to the engendered side, except servitude. For its ascription to engendered existence is more complete and higher than the ascription of lordship and masterhood to it.

You may say: "Well then, 'annihilation' goes back to servitude and clings to it." We reply: Annihilation cannot be like servitude, since servitude is an immutably fixed attribute which is never lifted from engendered existence. But "annihilation" may annihilate the servant from his servitude and himself. Hence its property differs from the property of servitude.

If any affair causes a thing to leave its root and veils it from its own reality, that is not an eminence in the view of the Tribe, since it gives you the situation in contradiction to the way it is, thereby making you one of the ignorant. But subsistence is the immutable state of the servant which never disappears, since it is impossible for his immutable entity to cease to exist, just as it is impossible for his entity to be described as being identical with existence, since existence is its description after it was not. . . . The servant's entity subsists in immutability, while his existence is immutable in its servitude, his property everlasting in that. "None is there in the heavens and earth that comes not to the All-merciful as a servant" (19:93). (II 515.33)

In the last analysis, the gnostic is a servant and not a lord because only God truly exists. The attribute of the Lord is Being, while the attribute of the servant is nonexistence. The gnostic returns to the original state of his immutable entity.

In himself he is but a set of nonexistent properties, while the manifest is Being.

> The servant returns to his own specific characteristic, which is the servitude which does not compete with Lordship. He becomes adorned (*taḥallī*) by it and sits in the house of the thingness of his immutability, not the thingness of his existence, and he looks upon the way in which God turns him this way and that. In all of this he secludes himself from governing his own affair. (II 153.26)
>
> The exile (*ghurba*) of the gnostics from their homelands is their departure from their possibility. The homeland (*waṭan*) of the possible thing is possibility. Then it is unveiled for it that it is the Real. But the homeland of the Real is not possibility. So the possible thing departs from its homeland because of this witnessing. When the possible thing was in its homeland, that is, nonexistence—though its entity was immutably fixed—it heard the speech of the Real to it, "Be!", so it hurried into existence. It came to be in order to see Him who brought it into existence. Hence it went into exile from its homeland out of desire to see Him who said to it "Be!" When it opened its eye, the Real made it witness its own likenesses among the temporally originated things. It did not witness the Real, for whose sake it had hurried into existence. . . .
>
> But the perfected gnostics have no exile whatsoever. They are entities immutably fixed in their places; they never leave their homeland. Since the Real is their mirror, their forms become manifest within Him, exactly as forms become manifest within a mirror. So these forms are not their entities, since the forms become manifest in accordance with the shape of the mirror. Nor are those forms identical with the mirror, since in its own essence the mirror does not possess the differentiation of that which becomes manifest from them or of them themselves. So they do not go into exile. They are the people of witnessing (*shuhūd*) in existence (*wujūd*). I only ascribe existence to them because of the temporal origination of the properties, which do not become manifest except within an existent thing (*mawjūd*). Hence the level of exile is not one of the waystations of the Men. It is a lower waystation, within which alight those in the midst of the path (*al-mutawassiṭūn*) and the disciples (*al-murīdūn*). As for the great ones (*al-akābir*), they never see anything exiled from its homeland. On the contrary, the Necessary Being is Necessary, the possible thing is possible, and the impossible thing is impossible, so the homeland of each thing which has a homeland is determined. Were exile to occur within them, the realities would be overturned and the Necessary would become possible, the possible Necessary, and the impossible possible. But such is not the situation. (II 528.17, 529.19)

God's servant par excellence, the Prophet, said, "I will be master of mankind on the Day of Resurrection, without boasting." Yet, as Ibn al-ʿArabī explains, this is true not because he is a lord but because he is the perfect servant who has actualized his own nothingness. He has realized his own immutable entity, so he dwells in the domain of nonexistence.

> The Prophet means: I do not mean to boast over everyone else in the cosmos. Though I am the highest of the human loci of manifestation, I am also the most intense of all creatures in the realization of my own entity. The Man is not he who realizes his Lord. The Man is he who realizes his own entity. (II 74.6)

Not that boasting is necessarily negative, as Ibn al-ʿArabī seems to be indicating when he writes,

> On the night that I wrote this chapter I had a dream which filled me with joy. I awoke and composed a verse that I had previously worked on in my mind. It is a verse of boasting:
>
> Every age has one person through whom
> it soars—
> For the rest of this age, I am that one!
>
> This is because, to my knowledge, there is no one today who has realized the station of servanthood more than I, though there may be my equal. For I have reached the utmost limit of servanthood. I

am the pure and utter servant who knows nothing of the flavor of lordship. (III 41.23)

The gnostic enters into God's presence in his nothingness, but he returns illuminated.

There are those who undergo unveiling and then flee back to the visible world because they see that which terrifies them in their unveiling. One such was our companion Aḥmad al-ʿAṣṣād al-Ḥarīrī.[13] When he was taken, he would quickly return to his senses shaking and trembling. I used to scold him and tell him not to do that, but he would say, "I am frightened and terrified lest I lose myself through what I see." . . .

He who enters God's presence while having something of lordship in himself fears losing it there, so he flees back to the existence within which his lordliness becomes manifest. Hence there is little profit in his entering. But he who is firmly fixed enters as a receptive servant with a resolve inflamed for his root, so that God may give him those of His gentle favors which will habituate him. Then he comes out as a light from whom illumination is sought.

He who enters into that Exalted Side with his lordship is like him who enters in with a burning lamp, while he who enters in with his servanthood is like him who enters with a wick without flame, or with a handful of smoldering twigs. When the two of them enter like this, a breath from the All-merciful blows against them. The lamp is extinguished by that wind, while the twigs flame up. The possessor of the light comes out in darkness, while the possessor of the twigs comes out with a light from which illumination can be sought. So look at what his preparedness has given to him!

Thus everyone who flees from there fears that his lamp will be extinguished. He is afraid that his lordship will disappear, so he flees to the place where it is manifest. But he only comes out after his lamp has been extinguished. If he came out and it was still lit, such that the blowing of the wind had no effect upon it, then he would be right to claim lordship. But that still would have been through God's preserving him.

He who enters in as a servant has no fear. When his wick becomes ignited there, he knows who lit it and he sees His kindness in that. Then he comes out as an illuminated servant. Thus God said, "Glory be to Him who carried His servant by night" (17:1), that is, as a servant.[14] But when he came back out to his community, he came "calling unto God by His leave, and as a light-giving lamp" (33:46), just as he had entered in as a lowly servant, knowing that into which he was entering and to whom he was entering. (I 276.19)

Through seeking refuge in his own servanthood, the perfect servant manifests God's attributes almost in spite of himself. He seeks refuge in his own nothingness, but others perceive the attributes of God reflected within him.

At root the servant was created only to belong to God and to be a servant perpetually. He was not created to be a lord. So when God clothes him in the robe of mastership and commands him to appear in it, he appears as a servant in himself and a master in the view of the observer. This is the ornament of his Lord, the robe He has placed upon him.

Someone objected to Abū Yazīd that the people touched him with their hands and sought blessing from him. He replied, "They are not touching me, they are only touching an adornment with which my Lord has adorned me. Should I forbid them from that, when it does not belong to me?"

Someone remarked to Abū Madyan that the people were touching him with their hands with the intention of gaining blessing and he let them do that. "Do you not find in yourself the effect of that?"

He replied, "Does the Black Stone [of the Kaʿba] find in itself an effect which would remove it from being a stone, since it is kissed by the messengers, the prophets, and the friends, and since it is the right hand of God?"

The person replied that it did not.

Abū Madyan said, "I am that Stone."

Concerning this station God says to His

Prophet, "Those who swear allegiance to thee swear allegiance in truth to God" (48:10). Hence He negated after having affirmed, just as He did with the throwing—He both affirmed it and negated it: "You did not throw when you threw, but God threw" (8:17). (III 136.8)

Man should know that nothing brings servitude and Lordship together in any respect. Of all things, these two are the most intense in contrariety to each other. . . . Though black and white are contraries, they are brought together by color. Though motion and rest are contraries, they are brought together by an engendered thing. . . . Every set of two opposite or different things in the cosmos must have something which brings the two together, in spite of their contrariety, except servant and Lord, since the two do not come together in any affair whatsoever. The servant is he who has no face in Lordship, and the Lord is he who has no face in servanthood. Hence the Lord and the servant never come together.

The ultimate illusion is for a person to bring together Lord and servant through *wujūd* [Being/existence], for that does not bring them together. For I do not mean by "that which brings together" the ascription of words. I only mean the attribution of a meaning to one of the two in exactly the same sense as it is attributed to the other. But this is not found in the *wujūd* which is attributed to the Lord and the *wujūd* attributed to the servant. For the *wujūd* of the Lord is His own Entity, while the *wujūd* of the servant is a property which the servant is judged to possess. In respect of his entity, the servant may exist or may not exist, but the definition of his entity is the same in the two cases.

Since the *wujūd* of the servant is not his own entity, and since the *wujūd* of the Lord is identical with Himself, the servant should stand in a station within which no whiffs of lordship are smelt from him. For to have lordship would be falsehood and ignorance itself, so its possessor would not gain the station of servitude, though in fact he is a servant. To my words, "No whiff of lordship is smelt from him," I only add, "On his part, in himself," since he is never heedless of witnessing his servitude.

However, others might ascribe lordship to this servant, because of the effects of it which they see becoming manifest from him. But this belongs to God, not to him. And in himself he is different from that which he makes manifest to the cosmos.

It is impossible for the effect of lordship not to become manifest from him. When the disciple (*tilmīdh*) knows that the shaykh is of this sort, God opens up to the disciple that in which is his felicity. For he becomes disengaged from everything for God's side just as the shaykh is disengaged. He trusts in God, not in the shaykh. Then he remains looking upon the shaykh to see what state God will cause to pass over him in respect of the disciple, such as speaking with a command or a prohibition or uttering knowledge which will benefit him. Then the disciple takes that from God on the tongue of the shaykh. The disciple knows in himself about the shaykh what the shaykh knows about himself: that he is the locus for the flow of the properties of lordship.

Even if the shaykh should pass away, this disciple would not feel his loss as such, since he knows the state of his shaykh. Such was Abū Bakr al-Ṣiddīq with the Messenger of God, when the Messenger died. There was no one who was not terribly upset and did not say things which should not have been heard. Thereby each bore witness against himself for his own inadequacy and his lack of knowledge of the Messenger whom he followed. This was the case with everyone but Abū Bakr, since for him the situation had not changed. He knew what there was and the actual situation. Hence he climbed the pulpit and recited, "Muḥammad is naught but a messenger; messengers have passed away before him. Why, if he should die or is slain, will you turn about on your heels?" (3:144). So he whose illusions had overcome him came back to his senses, and then the people knew the excellence of Abū Bakr over everyone else. Hence he was worthy of the imamate and being given precedence. No one swore allegiance to him aimlessly. And no one failed to swear allegiance to him except those who were ignorant of the same thing in him of which they were ignorant in the Messenger of God. (III 371.27)

Worship Through Free Will Offerings

Islamic Law divides acts of worship into two basic kinds: *farḍ* (obligatory) and *nafl* (supererogatory). The literal significance of *nafl* is booty, bounty, gift; something in excess of what is expected. Each category of obligatory worship—e.g., praying, fasting, making the pilgrimage to Mecca—has its own supererogatory acts. In his chapter on these acts, Ibn al-ʿArabī discusses the divine roots of the various categories. The root of all supererogation is the fact that the servant is God's "supererogatory work" (*nāfila*), that is, something in excess of what is obligatory on God. He created us as His own free will offering to us.

> The supererogatory acts are ranked according to the excellence of the obligatory acts from which they derive, since they consist of each practice which has a root in the obligatory acts and which is born from that root and becomes manifest in its form. In the same way, we become manifest in the form of God. So we are His supererogatory work, and He is our root. That is why we say concerning Him that He is the Necessary Being through Himself, while we are necessary through Him, not through ourselves. (II 167.2)
>
> "Obligatory works" (*farāʾiḍ*) are acts to be performed or avoided which God has made incumbent (*wājib*) and unequivocally necessary for His servants. He who does not perform them has sinned. (II 168.13)

The difference between these two types of practices has been much discussed by the jurists and the Sufis. For many of the latter, the most significant knowledge which we have about them is what God says in the famous *ḥadīth qudsī*: "My servant draws near to Me through nothing I love more than that which I have made obligatory for him. My servant never ceases drawing near to Me through supererogatory works until I love him. Then, when I love him, I am his hearing through which he hears, his sight through which he sees, his hand through which he grasps, and his foot through which he walks."[15] From this hadith are derived the technical terms "the nearness of supererogatory works" (*qurb al-nawāfil*) and "the nearness of obligatory works" (*qurb al-farāʾiḍ*). (Often "nearness" is replaced by the term "worship" or "love" [*ḥubb*]). Ibn al-ʿArabī and his followers place these two nearnesses at the highest levels of human perfection. The Shaykh describes the nearness of supererogatory works, which is most often depicted as the lower of the two, in many different contexts.

> That which brings together all the supererogatory acts is the fact that the Real loves the servant, since these acts result in God's love for him. But this is not just any love. It is a love through which the Real is your hearing through which you hear, your sight through which you see, your hand through which you grasp, and your leg through which you run. (II 168.2)
>
> The Real is far too exalted to dwell (*ḥulūl*) within corporeal bodies. As for man, he sees through the sight which subsists through an organ, the eye in his head. He hears through the hearing which subsists through an organ, his ear. He speaks through the speech which exists in the movement and stillness of his tongue, his lips, and the places of articulation, from his chest to his lips. Then this same person practices acts of obedience to God in excess of what is obligatory for him, that is, the supererogatory good works (*nawāfil al-khayrāt*). This practice results in the negation of his hearing, his sight, his speech, and all his meanings, such as seizing and running, the properties of which had necessarily belonged to him. Because of the properties of these meanings, names such as hearing, seeing, and speaking had been applied to him. Now he hears through God, after he had been hearing through his own hearing. He sees through God, after he had been seeing through his own sight. Nevertheless, we know that God is far too exalted for the things to be His dwelling place (*maḥall*) or for Him to be their dwelling place. Hence the servant has heard through Him who does not subsist (*qiyām*) within him. He

has seen through that which does not subsist within him. And he has spoken through that which does not subsist within him, since the Real is his hearing, his sight, and his hand. (II 614.4)

God said concerning him whom He loves through the love of supererogatory works, "I am his hearing, and his sight, and his tongue through which he speaks." God gave witness that Muḥammad possesses supererogatory works through His words, "As for the night, keep vigil a part of it, as a supererogatory work for thee" (17:79). Hence his hearing must be the Real, his sight the Real, and his speech the Real. But He gave witness to this for no other creature specifically.

The mark of those whose obligatory works do not completely absorb their supererogatory works and who have an excess of supererogatory works is that God loves them through this specific love. He made its mark that the Real is their hearing, their sight, their hand, and all their faculties. Hence the Messenger of God used to pray that all of himself would be light,[16] since "God is the light of the heavens and the earth" (24:35).

This is why the philosophers allude to the fact that the servant's desired goal is becoming similar (*tashabbuh*) to the God, while the Sufis say concerning the same thing "assuming the traits of the names." The expressions are different, but the meaning is one. We beseech and implore God that He not veil us from our servitude when we assume the traits of the divine names! (II 126.3)

The Prophet said concerning Jesus, "Had his certainty increased, he would have walked upon the air,"[17] thereby alluding to his own *miʿrāj* (*isrāʾ*). It is obvious that Jesus's certainty is greater than ours, though not greater than the Prophet's. But we walk upon the air—through the property of following him whose community we are, not because we are greater in our certainty than Jesus. In the same way the community of Jesus may walk upon water, just as Jesus walked upon water. At the same time we know —even if in this situation we have this only through following—that the whole community does not walk upon air as Muḥammad walked upon air, since some members of his community do not follow him in everything they were commanded to follow him in. But he who fulfills the duty of following comes to possess his property, just as God said, "Say: 'I call to God upon insight, I and whoever follows after me'" (12:108).

But how can the eminence of him who walks upon air be compared with that of him for whom the Real is his hearing and sight? This belongs to him through perseverance in the supererogatory good works which result in God's love for him—or, it is the perseverance which results in this. This love results in the Real's being his hearing and his sight. (III 162.10)

In reality, it is the Real who "governs" (*mudabbir*) the cosmos [just as the spirit "governs" the body]. He Himself says, "He governs the affair, He differentiates the signs" (13:2). The "signs" are the proofs of the profession of His Unity: Each created thing gives a proof specific to itself of the Unity of Him who brought it into existence. . . . These are the "signs" which He "differentiates," thereby dividing them among His creatures according to the innate character which God has given to them.

So He is the spirit of the cosmos, its hearing, its sight, and its hand. Through Him the cosmos hears, through Him it sees, through Him it speaks, through Him it grasps, through Him it runs, since "There is no power and no strength save in God, the All-high, the Tremendous."[18]

This is known only by those who draw near to God through supererogatory good works, just as has been mentioned in the *Ṣaḥīḥ* in the divine prophetic reports: When the servant draws near to Him through supererogatory works, He loves him, and when He loves him He says, "I am his hearing, his sight, and his hand." Another version has, "For him I am hearing, sight, hand, and confirmer."

God's words "I am" show that this was already the situation, but the servant was not aware. Hence the generous gift which this nearness gives to him is the unveiling and the knowledge that God is his hearing and his sight. He had been imagining that he hears through his own hearing, but he was hearing through his Lord. In the same way, during his life, man supposes that he hears through his spirit, because of his ignorance, but in actual fact he hears only through his Lord. (III 67.29)

God is identical with Being/existence.

He is described as possessing attributes because the existent things have attributes. Then He reported that in respect of His own Entity, He is identical with the attributes and members of the servant, for He said, "I am his hearing." Thereby He attributed hearing to the entity of the existent thing which hears, while He ascribed it to Himself. But there is no Existent Being save He. So it is He who hears, and He is the hearing. So also is the case with the other faculties and perceptions: They are nothing but He. (II 563.29)

The servant draws near to God through the acts which are attributed to him. Then he reaches the nearness concerning which the Real reported that He is all his faculties and members through His He-ness. The servant cannot go nearer than this, since He establishes the entity of the servant by the fact that the pronoun in His words, "his hearing, his sight, his tongue, his hand, and his foot," goes back to him. He also establishes that he is not he, since he is only he through his faculties, because they belong to his essential definition. In the same way He said, "You did not throw when you threw, but God threw" (8:17). Both form and meaning belong to Him, so He owns the whole, since He is identical with the whole. Hence there is nothing in engendered existence but He, within the waystations of His Most Beautiful Names. There is none in relation to whom He can be glorified and declared Incomparable except Himself. (IV 272.22)

We have in our hands only revealed reports concerning God's descent, withness, two hands, hand, eye, eyes, foot, laughter, and so forth, all of which the Real attributes to Himself. This is the "form of Adam," and in all these reports, He gives us its differentiated details. Then He brings it all together in the Prophet's words, "God created Adam upon His own Form." Hence perfect man looks with the eye of God. This is indicated by His words, "I am his sight through which he sees" and so on. In the same way, he receives joyfully with God's joyful receiving, he laughs with God's laughter, he rejoices through God's rejoicing, he becomes wrathful through God's wrath, and he forgets through God's forgetting. God says, "They forgot God, so He forgot them" (9:67). (II 124.17)

God has explained to us that the He-ness of the Real is the hearing, the sight, and all the faculties of the servant. The servant only exists through his faculties, so he only exists through the Real. His outward dimension (*ẓāhir*) is a limited, creaturely form, while his inward dimension (*bāṭin*) is the He-ness of the Real, not limited by the form. In respect of his form, the servant is one of those who "glorify Him in praise," but in respect of his inward dimension, he is as we have mentioned. So the Real glorifies Himself.

The combined totality (*majmūʿ*) yields a subtle, abstruse meaning which neither of the two sides yields singly. Various things are ascribed to the form, such as conformity and opposition, obedience and disobedience. Because of the combined totality it is said that the Law makes prescriptions. Because of it the ritual prayer can correctly be divided between the servant and God. The servant says such and such, and God says such and such.[19]

There can be no servant without the combined totality. So look at the attributes which the Real acquires by describing Himself as being the faculties of the servant. Without Him, he would not be a servant, just as the Real would not be his faculties without him, for the name "servant" is only applied to the combined totality. . . .

God seeks from us [in the verse "They are commanded only to worship God, delivering the religion over to Him" (98:5)] to deliver our worship over to Him, since we are servants through worship, and we are only servants through His He-ness. Hence we deliver servanthood over to Him, as follows: We say to Him, "Thou art He through Thy I-ness, and Thou art He through my I-ness. Hence there is nothing but Thou. Hence Thou art named 'Lord' and 'servant'."

If the situation is not like this, we have not delivered worship over to Him. For He only seeks us to deliver worship in respect to the combined totality. Worship can have no existence or relationship without the combined totality, since on His own, He is "Independent of the worlds," but through the combined totality He says, "Lend to God a good loan" (73:20), so He delimited the loan by good-doing (*al-iḥsān*). Then He explained to us the meaning of good-doing, and He only did so in terms of the witnessing of the delimited, set up in the kibla.[20]

So the knowledge of God in the tongue of the Lawgiver who is God's spokesman is different from knowledge of Him through rational consideration. Hence there are two ways to knowledge of God, or if you like, you can say three. One way is our knowledge of Him in respect of our reflective consideration, a second in respect of His addressing us through the Law, and a third our knowledge of Him through the combined totality. And we know that we will not know Him as He knows Himself. (IV 140.25, 141.9)

Among human beings are those who seek Him through Him, but no angel seeks Him in this manner. This is because the perfect human being is upon the divine form in which God created him, but the angel does not have that. He who has this attribute is able to seek God through Him. And he who seeks Him through Him reaches Him, for no one else reaches Him. The perfect human being has supererogatory works in addition to his obligatory works. When the servant draws near to Him through them, He loves him. And when He loves him, He is his hearing and his sight.

When the Real is the sight of a servant in this manner, he sees Him and perceives Him through His sight, since his sight is the Real. Hence he only perceives Him through Him, not through himself. But no angel draws near to God through supererogatory works; on the contrary, they are all busy with obligatory works. Their obligatory works have absorbed all their breaths, so they have no supererogatory works. Hence they have no station which would result in the Real being their sight so that they could perceive Him through Him.

Hence the angels are servants by compulsion (*iḍṭirār*), while we are servants by compulsion through our obligatory works and by free choice (*ikhtiyār*) through our supererogatory works. In the same way, He is an essential Lord through our existence and a Lord of will through His property within us. The essential Lordship is compulsory (*ḍarūrī*), since it cannot be removed, but the Lordship of will is determined by the possibility of the possible things. He gives preponderance to whatever He wills. He who has no will cannot give preponderance, just as he who has no supererogatory works cannot have the Real as his sight. (IV 30.11)

Through being joined (*ittiṣāl*) to the Real, man is annihilated (*fanā'*) from himself. Then the Real becomes manifest so that He is his hearing and his sight. This is what is called a knowledge of "tasting." The Real is nothing of these organs until they are burned up by His Being, so that He is there, not they.

I have tasted that and felt the burning at the sensory level during my invocation of Allah through Allah. There He was, and I was not. I felt my tongue burning up. I suffered the pain of that burning with a sensory, animate suffering in the organ. In that state I continued invoking Allah through Allah for six hours or nearly so. Then God made my tongue grow back and I invoked Him through presence (*ḥuḍūr*) with Him, but not through Him.

The same is true of all the faculties: The Real will be nothing of them until His Being burns away that faculty, and He is there, whichever faculty it may be. This is indicated by His words, "I am his hearing, his sight, his tongue, and his hand." He who does not witness and feel the burning in his faculties has no tasting; it is only his illusion (*tawahhum*). This is the meaning of God's words concerning the divine veils, "Were they to be removed, the glories of His Face would burn away [everything perceived by the sight of the creatures]." Whenever the Real desires to burn away a faculty of His servant in order for him to acquire knowledge by way of tasting through lifting the veil that stands between man and the Real in respect to that faculty, He burns it away through the light of His face and fills up the fissure left by that faculty. If it is his hearing, the Real is his hearing at this time; if it is his sight or his tongue, the same is the case. In this meaning I composed the following poem:

Truly the invocation of Allah through
Allah burns—
My judgment in this is a verified
judgment.
For I—by the Lord of inspirations—
savored it,
so my judgment of its truth has been
confirmed.

That is why the Real says in the sound hadith, "I am his hearing and his sight." He identified His own attribute of being (*kaynūna*) with the hearing of the servant, described by a specific description. This is the greatest joining (*ittiṣāl*) that takes place between God and the servant, inasmuch as He causes one of the servant's faculties to disappear and stands through His own attribute of being within the servant in the station of what disappeared, as is proper to His majesty, and without any declaration of similarity, explanation of how (*takyīf*), constriction, encompassing, indwelling (*ḥulūl*), or substitution. "We have only witnessed what we know; we were no guardians of the Unseen. Enquire from the town," that is, the group, "wherein we were" (12:81), that is, the Folk of Allah, those of God's servants who are ascribed to this path, those who performed the supererogatory good works, persisted within them, and turned toward God through them. (III 298.17)

Obligations and Supererogations

In the nearness of supererogatory works, God is the hearing and sight of the servant. In the nearness of obligatory works, the servant is God's hearing and sight. It is through this station that perfect man is the "eye of God" and the protector of the cosmos. Though Ibn al-ʿArabī declares that the nearness of supererogatory works is possessed by the gnostics, the perfect men, and the Prophet himself, he states that the nearness of obligatory works is higher. There is no contradiction here, since perfect man may possess both nearnesses at once. In respect to one nearness he is nearer to God than in respect to the other.

In the first passage below, Ibn al-ʿArabī suggests that the nearness of supererogatory works is a state (as his own description of the burning of his tongue would indicate), while that of obligatory works is a station. In other passages he points out certain parallels which tie in topics already discussed, such as the fact that servanthood has two levels, servanthood through free choice (*ikhtiyār*) or supererogatory works, and servanthood through compulsion (*iḍṭirār*) or obligatory works. In the last analysis, the latter is higher and corresponds to "servitude" (*ʿubūda*).

Through supererogatory works, God is the servant's hearing and his seeing. Through obligatory works, the servant is the hearing and seeing of the Real, and by this the cosmos is established. For God looks at the cosmos only through the sight of this servant, and the cosmos does not disappear, since there is an affinity. But if He were to look at the cosmos with His own sight, the cosmos would be burnt away by the glories of His Face. Hence the Real looks at the cosmos only through the sight of the perfect servant who is created upon the Form. That servant is precisely the veil between the cosmos and the burning glories.[21] (II 354.19)

When the servant performs his obligations completely, he has fulfilled the servitude which is the rightful claim of Lordship upon him. The obligatory works result in an affair higher than that the Real should be his hearing. For when the Real is the hearing of the servant, this is a state of the servant, but the property of obligatory works comes between him and this state, for their property is that he becomes the hearing of the Real. Then the Real hears through the servant. This is pointed to by His words, "I was hungry, but you did not feed Me."[22] The fact that the obligatory works come between the servant and the Real's being his hearing is a verified and established station, as it is in the actual situation. In this station [in which the servant is God's hearing] the servant knows that the Real is he/not he. But the possessor of the "state" [in which God is his hearing] says "I." (II 168.20)

The servant draws near through performing obligatory works. When someone acquires the fruit of this, he is the hearing and sight of the Real. Hence the Real desires through his desire, though he does not know that his object of desire is what God desires should happen. If he knows that, he is not the possessor of this station. This is the scale with which is weighed the performance of obligatory works, and the servant draws near to God "through nothing that God loves more."

As for the nearness of supererogatory works, God also loves the servant through it. God's love gives him the Real as his hearing and his sight. This is the scale by which it is weighed. (II 559.25)

God chose obligatory works as the best of works, because they result in the servant being the attribute of the Real—His hearing and His sight—while the love of supererogatory works yields the Real as the hearing and sight of the servant. The supererogatory stands in a lower degree than the obligatory, since the obligatory possesses primacy.

The Real Himself does not descend to be "the hearing of the servant," as He said, because His majesty does not allow this. Hence, He must descend through His attribute, which means that the servant is the attribute of the Real, because of the form upon which he was created, since it is "cut out" from the Divine Form, just as "The womb (*raḥim*) is a branch of the All-merciful (*al-raḥmān*)."[23] [The root meaning of] "obligatory" is "to cut."

When the servant performs obligatory works, the fact that he is an attribute of the Real becomes manifest to him in them, but when he performs supererogatory works, the attribute of the Real belongs to him. Thereby the obligatory is differentiated from the supererogatory, and the higher degree belongs to the obligatory. Were it not for the fact that the obligatory yields that, it would not be established that He has said, "I was hungry, and you did not feed Me," and "I am more intense in my yearning to meet My servant than he is in desiring Me."[24] For He is "nearer" to us "than the jugular vein" (50:16), and He says, "I never waver in what I am doing [the way I waver . . .],"[25] and so on. (II 173.8)

The Prophet's station in the sciences is to encompass the knowledge of every knower of God, whether those who went before or those who came after. . . . He was singled out for six qualities never given to any prophet before him. . . . The second of these qualities is that he was given "the all-comprehensive words." "Words" is the plural of "word," and "The words of God are not exhausted."[26] Hence he was given the knowledge of that which is infinite. He knows that which is finite through its being restricted by existence, and he knows what has not entered into existence, which is infinite. He encompasses in knowledge the realities of the known things, and they are a divine attribute which belongs to no one but God. God's "Word" is words, just like the divine command, which is "but one" word, "like the twinkling of an eye" (54:50). There is nothing more similar to it in the sensory domain or more appropriate as a simile than the twinkling of an eye.

Since the Prophet knew the all-comprehensive words, he was given "inimitability" (*iʿjāz*) through the Koran, which is God's Word, and through it he acts as God's spokesman (*mutarjim*). Hence there is inimitability in his speaking on His behalf. One cannot conceive of "inimitability" in meanings disengaged from substrata, since inimitability is the connection of these meanings to the forms of the words which subsist through letters.

So the Prophet is the tongue of the Real, His hearing, and His sight. This is the highest of divine levels. One degree lower is the level of him whose hearing, sight, and tongue are the Real. Then He acts as His servant's spokesman, just as He acts as the spokesman through the Koran for the states of those who came before us and for what they said. This second degree does not have the same eminence, for here He acts as spokesman for His Folk and for the words of those brought near to Him, like the angels. He also acts as spokesman for Iblīs, in spite of his despair (*iblās*), satanity, and distance from what He said. But none acts as spokesman for God save him who has received an election (*ikhtiṣāṣ*) beyond which there is no election. (III 142.27, 143.6)

The Messenger of God said that God says, "My servant draws near to Me through nothing that I love more than what I have made obligatory for him," since this is a servanthood of compulsion. "And My servant never ceases drawing near to Me through supererogatory works," which is a servanthood of free choice, "until I love him," since He made them "supererogatory works," so they require distance from God. Then, when the servant fastens himself to the servanthood of free choice in the way he is fastened to the servanthood of compulsion, He loves him. This is the meaning of His words, "Until I love him." Then he says, "When I love him, I am his hearing through which he hears, his sight through which he sees," and so on.

When the Real is the sight of the servant through this state, how should there be concealed from him what is not concealed [from God]? Supererogatory works and clinging fast to them give the servant the properties of the attributes of the Real, while obligatory works give him the fact of being nothing but light. Then he looks through His Essence, not through His attributes, for His Essence is identical to His hearing and His seeing. That is the Real's Being, not the servant's existence. (II 65.21)

Most of the intelligent among the Folk of Allah are able to pave the way to the objects of their desire simply through their Resolve. Some of them achieve that in this world, and for others it is stored away until the Day of Resurrection. The great Men know that for which they were created, so if they were to halt at bringing things to be (*takwīn*), He would confront them with that. But they leave it to the Real to turn His creatures this way and that, as He does in actual fact. They refuse to be a locus for the manifestation of turning things this way and that. If something of that sort becomes manifest from them, this is not because of any intention of theirs. On the contrary, God has caused it to occur for them and made it manifest through them for the sake of a wisdom that He knows, while they are far removed from that. But that they should intend to do this—that cannot be imagined from them, unless they be commanded, such as the messengers. But this belongs to God, "And they disobey not God in what He commands them" (66:6), since they are preserved (*maʿṣūm*) from the attribution of acts to themselves. When acts become manifest from them, they say, "They belong to those names of His which are manifest in His loci of manifestation. What do we have to do with making claims? We are nothing (*lā shay'*) in the state of being loci of manifestation for Him and in every state."

This station is called "everlasting ease" (*rāḥat al-abad*). The person who stands in it is called "at ease" (*mustarīḥ*). He is the person who has fulfilled the right of Lordship, since the property belongs to the level, not to the entity. Do you not see that the sovereign's decrees are observed in his kingdom? So he is not disobeyed; he is feared, and people have hopes in him. This is not because he is a human being, for his humanness is his entity. This is only because he is a sovereign. Hence the intelligent person sees that what rules in the sovereign's kingdom is his level, not his entity. The sovereign does not rule because he is a human being, since there is no difference between him and every other human being. Such is the case with all loci of manifestation.

The Men of Allah consider themselves in respect of their entities, not in respect of their being loci of manifestation. So the level is the ruler, not themselves. This is the fruit of the Real which they pick when they rule through Him and reach servitude and servanthood—the worship of obligatory works and the worship of supererogatory works. (II 96.25)

7

Consummation

19. TRANSCENDING THE GODS OF BELIEF

"Faith" (*īmān*) was defined as belief, verbal expression of the belief, and putting the belief into practice. But the belief contained in faith is not just any belief, since the object of belief is implicit in the term. When the Koran commands human beings to have faith, as it often does, it means faith in "God, the angels, the prophets, the scriptures, and the Last Day," a formula occurring with slight variation in three verses (2:177, 2:285, 4:136). More specifically, this means faith in the Koran and the Prophet Muḥammad, and the putting of their teachings into practice.

The term "belief" (*iʿtiqād, ʿaqīda*) does not occur in the Koran, though other terms from the same root are employed. The basic meaning is to tie a knot, or to tie firmly. Belief is a knot tied in the heart, a conviction that something is true. In Ibn al-ʿArabī's way of looking at things, everyone has beliefs, since everyone is a delimited and defined existent thing with a delimited and defined consciousness, a knotting of the heart. An individual's belief goes back to the preparedness of his immutable entity, or its capacity to act as a receptacle for Being. However, his belief is never fixed at any moment of existence, since he constantly undergoes transformations as the possibilities inherent in his own entity make themselves manifest. Preparedness constantly changes.

Though preparedness goes back to the immutable entities, human beings are not puppets in this show. They are actors, which is to say that they possess the capacity, albeit limited, to direct the flow of their own unfolding. It is true that God has precedent knowledge of their choices, but they have no such knowledge. Whatever choice they make has a real effect upon their becoming. For example, if a person sincerely asks God for "increase in knowledge," he opens himself up to greater knowledge, since God answers prayers. Knowledge is light, and light is existence; greater knowledge means a greater capacity to manifest existence.

The process of transformation, whether by way of increase or decrease, continues ad infinitum. But where will a person's unfolding take him? From the human point of view, this depends upon the goal he sets for himself, which in turn is defined by his belief. The least one can say is that, in order for human development to end up in felicity in the next world, belief must be a part of "faith" as defined. In other words, the objects of belief must be those set down in revelation, and the concomitants of belief must be verbal attestation to faith and the following of the Law, the putting of belief into practice. As a matter of course every belief, every delimitation of the heart, will have certain effects upon activity. But that does not make belief equivalent to faith, unless the contents of the belief and the accompanying practice are both set down by a revealed Law.

Even in faith, however, every person's belief is not the same. Faith may be enough for felicity, but felicity has as many degrees as there are felicitous souls. Existence is by nature a "ranking according to excellence" (*tafāḍul*), whether in this world or the next. Just as no two people have exactly the same knowledge and awareness in the present plane of existence, so also no two people will have exactly the same degree of proximity to God in the next world. The degree a person achieves, within the context of his faith, goes back to his belief.

To the extent that a person ties his belief into a tighter knot, he will be further from the Divine Reality, which is Nondelimited by definition. To the extent he loosens all knots, he will be nearer to God. But that "tightening" and "loosening" cannot be defined by our own ego-centric vision of things. It must be delineated by God Himself, and this He does through the Law in all its degrees. What appears as tightening, constraint, limitation, and restriction of freedom from the human point of view may in fact, from the divine point of view, be loosening, opening, nondelimitation, and deliverance.

The Roots of Belief

No two people have exactly the same belief, because no two people are exactly the same. People are different because God's self-disclosure never repeats itself, so each existent thing, as a self-disclosure of God, differs from every other. The divine root of the diversity of God's self-disclosures is the diversity of the divine names, or the fact that God constantly undergoes "self-transmutation" (*taḥawwul*), or the infinite diversity of the immutable entities.

Ibn al-ʿArabī sometimes refers to God's self-transmutation as the "divine self-disclosure in the forms of beliefs" (e.g., II 311.25). According to the hadith already partly quoted in Chapter 6, God discloses Himself to the people at the Day of Resurrection, but they deny Him. Then, while still unrecognized by them, He says, "Is there a sign (*āya*) by which you will recognize God?" They reply that there is, and He shows it to them, so they acknowledge Him as their Lord. Ibn al-ʿArabī commonly refers to this "sign" as the "mark" (*ʿalāma*) that each group will recognize, and he identifies it as "the form of their belief concerning Him" (I 266.18).

> Every group have believed something about God. If He discloses Himself in other than that something, they will deny Him. But when He discloses Himself in the mark which this group have established with God in themselves, then they will acknowledge Him. Thus, for example, when He discloses Himself to an Ashʿarite in the form of the belief of his opponent, whose "knotting" (*ʿaqd*) concerning God is opposed to his, or He manifests Himself to his opponent in the form of the belief of the Ashʿarite, each of the two groups will deny Him. And so it is with all groups. (I 266.15)
>
> God says, "He gave each thing its creation" (20:50). Hence every existent thing has the stature (*taqwīm*) given to it by its creation. God says concerning man, "We indeed created man in the most beautiful stature" (95:4). In other words, the stature in which He created man is more excellent than any other stature. Man possesses the attribute of being more excellent than others only because God created him upon His own form.
>
> If you object that the changes which

man undergoes belong to himself, and the form of the Real does not accept change, we reply: God says in this station, "We shall finish with you, O mankind and jinn!" (55:31). The Prophet said, "Thy Lord has finished."[1] He also said that God will disclose Himself in the nearest form. Then, when they deny Him, He will transmute Himself into the form in which they will recognize Him by means of the mark which they recognize. Hence God has attributed this station to Himself.

He transcends the station of change and alteration in His Essence. However, this station [of change] bestows its name upon the self-disclosures in the divine loci of manifestation in the measure of the beliefs which are occasioned within the creatures instant by instant. Hence what we said is sound and this illusory objection is removed. High indeed is God exalted! (II 683.19)

God is with every object of belief. His existence in the conception (*taṣawwur*) of him who conceives of Him does not disappear when that person's conception changes into another conception. No, He has an existence in this second conception. In the same way, on the Day of Resurrection He will transmute Himself in self-disclosure from form to form. But that form from which He transmutes Himself does not disappear from Him, since the one who believed that concerning Him will see it. Hence He does nothing but remove the veil from the eye of the one who is perceiving the form, so that the person is then "upon insight." If they should blame Him, for their sake He transmutes Himself into the new form which possesses their mark. (IV 142.30)

God's *wujūd* is One in Him, but appears as the manifold existent things through self-disclosure. In other words, "Being" is attributed to God in respect of His incomparability and "existence" is attributed to Him in respect of His similarity. In the first case, God's Essence is unknowable and inaccessible; it is the Necessary Being through Itself. In the second case God manifests Himself within "formal existence" (*al-wujūd al-ṣūrī*), that is, the Breath of the All-merciful, which assumes the form of all the existent things of the cosmos.

If anyone wants entrance to God, let him abandon his reason and place before himself God's Law, for God does not accept delimitation (*taqyīd*), and reason is a delimitation. To Him belongs disclosing Himself in each form, just as to Him belongs "composing you in whatever form He desired" (82:8). So praise belongs to God, who has composed us within the form which neither delimits nor confines Him within a determinate form! On the contrary, I assign to Him what belongs to Him according to His own giving of knowledge, and that is His self-transmutation within forms. No one has "measured God with His true measure" (6:91) except God. He who halts with God in that by which He has described Himself will not place Him under the property of his own reason in respect of His Self—high indeed is God exalted above that! . . .

The Real has two relationships to *wujūd*: His relationship to the Necessary Being of Self, and His relationship to formal existence. He discloses Himself to His creatures in the second, since it is impossible for Him to disclose Himself in His Necessary Being of Self, since we have no eye by which to perceive that. Whether in the state of our existence or our nonexistence, we remain entities to whom the preponderance [of the one or the other] has been given. The property of possibility (*imkān*) never leaves us, so we never see Him except through ourselves, that is, in respect of what our realities give. Hence His self-disclosure must take place within formal existence, which is that which accepts self-transmutation and continual change. (III 515.33, 516.14)

In Himself God is One, while self-disclosures take the form of the many. This plurality of manifestation goes back to the divine names, which are one and many at the same time. Ibn al-ʿArabī refers to this while commenting on the sura of Unity (Koran 112). The first verse, "He is God, One" refers to the Unity of the One (*aḥadiyyat al-aḥad*), while the second verse, "God, the Everlasting Refuge" refers to the fact that all manyness returns to the names and finds refuge in them.

In respect of His Self, God possesses the Unity of the One, but in respect of

His names He possesses the Unity of the Many.

God is only one God. My proof?
  "Say: He is God, One."
When you wander in His names,
  this wandering derives from number.
But all return to Him. The reciter reads:
  "God, the Everlasting Refuge.
"He gives not birth" in truth, "nor was He born,
  nor is anyone equal" to God.
Reason is bewildered in Him, while
  imagination dominates it, helping. . . .
Through us properties are given to Him—
  when we disappear, He stands alone.

This is the cause which brings about His self-disclosure within the diverse forms and His self-transmutation within them: The diversity of beliefs in the cosmos demands this manyness. The root of the diversity of beliefs in the cosmos is this manyness in the One Entity. It explains why the people at the resurrection deny Him when He manifests Himself and says to them, "I am your Lord." Were He to disclose Himself to them in the form in which He made the Covenant with them, no one would deny Him. After they deny Him, He transmutes Himself into the form in which He had made the Covenant with them, so they acknowledge Him. . . .

Since God is the root of every diversity (*khilāf*) in beliefs within the cosmos, and since He also has brought about the existence of everything in the cosmos in a constitution not possessed by anything else, everyone will end up (*ma'āl*) with mercy. For it is He who created them and brought them into existence within the Cloud, which is the Breath of the All-merciful. So they are like the letters in the breath of the speaker at the places of articulation, which are diverse. In the same way, the cosmos is diverse in its constitution and its belief, even though it possesses unity through the fact that it is a temporally originated cosmos. (III 465.3,25)

The Breath of the All-merciful is Nondelimited Imagination. One reason it is called "imagination" is that the perception of forms within it depends upon the receptivity of the perceiving subjects. The divine self-disclosure is one, but those who "receive" (*qabūl*) it, or act as its "receptacles" (*qābil*), are many. Each receptacle perceives the self-disclosure according to its own preparedness. To say that a receptacle "perceives" the self-disclosure means that it "finds" it through its own existence. "Perception" and "existence" are one. Subjectivity and objectivity are two faces of the same reality.

The Real never ceases disclosing Himself constantly to hearts in this world. Hence man's incoming thoughts undergo variation because of the divine self-disclosure in a manner of which no one is aware except the Folk of Allah. In the same way, they know that the diversity of forms manifest in this world and the next in all existent things is nothing other than His variation, since He is the Manifest, for He is identical to each thing.

In the next world, the inward dimension (*bāṭin*) of man will be fixed, since it is identical with his outward dimension (*ẓāhir*) in this world, which undergoes continual change in a manner that is hidden, for this is its new creation at each moment, about which "They are in confusion" (50:15). But in the next world man's outward dimension will be like his inward dimension in this world: The divine self-disclosure will come to it constantly in actuality. Hence his outward dimension will undergo variation in the next world, just as his inward undergoes variation in this world within the forms taken by the divine self-disclosure, such that his inward dimension becomes colored by those forms.[2]

This is the imaginal conformity with God (*al-taḍāhī al-ilāhī al-khayālī*). However, in the next world this conformity will be manifest, while in this world it is nonmanifest. Hence the property of imagination accompanies man in the next world, and also the Real, in whose case it is called a "task": "Each day He is upon some task" (55:29). Hence He has always been so and always will be so. This is called "imagination," since we know that it goes back to the observer (*nāẓir*), not to the thing in itself. The thing in itself is fixed in its reality. It does not change, since realities do not change. But it becomes manifest to the observer within a variety of forms. This variation is also a reality; it never changes from its variation, so it does not accept fixity in a single form. On the contrary, its reality is to be fixed in variation. (III 470.16)

Man can never escape the property of imagination, since "everything other than God" is governed by it. Though from one point of view, the rational faculty is able to pierce the veils of imagination and perceive the Unity of God, from another point of view, even rational perception is governed by imagination.

> Everyone who perceives through one of the internal or external faculties in man imagines. . . . All beliefs are governed by this property. The sound hadith says, "Worship God *as if* you see Him"—such are beliefs. The locus of beliefs is the imagination. Though a rational proof is established that the object of belief is neither inside nor outside, nor is it similar to anything, yet man never stays safe from imagination, if he apprehends anything, since his configuration demands this. . . . So look how hidden and strong imagination is when it permeates man! He can never be safe from imagination and fantasy. How can he be safe? The rational faculty cannot escape his humanity. (IV 420.28)

In the *Fuṣūṣ* Ibn al-ʿArabī discusses a distinction between two levels of God's self-disclosure: He discloses Himself to Himself within His own knowledge as the entities and to the cosmos within the cosmos as formal existence colored and defined by the entities. We met these two levels in Chapter 17 in the discussion of God's creation of the cosmos according to His own knowledge of the cosmos. Having known all things at the level where He discloses Himself to Himself in Himself, He then bestows existence upon the things by disclosing Himself to them. One of these two self-disclosures pertains to the "unseen" world (*ghayb*) and the other to the "visible" world (*shahāda*), while both are perceived by the heart, the "locus" (*maḥall*) of self-disclosure to consciousness. Like other similar pairs of terms, "unseen" and "visible" are correlative and their meaning needs to be seen in context. Most often they refer to the spiritual and corporeal worlds. But here by "unseen" is meant God Himself—the Essence or He-ness—as contrasted with "everything other than God" or the cosmos, which is "visible" in relation to God. The unseen self-disclosure is God's own knowledge of the entities in their state of immutable nonexistence, while the visible self-disclosure is God's making Himself known and manifest to the entities by bringing them into existence.

> God has two self-disclosures: an "unseen" self-disclosure and a "visible" self-disclosure. Through the unseen self-disclosure He gives the heart its preparedness. This is the self-disclosure of the Essence, whose reality is the [Absolute] Unseen.[3] It is the "He-ness" (*huwiyya*) which is proper to Him and in accordance with which He calls Himself "He" in the Koran. This "He" belongs to Him perpetually and forever.
>
> When the heart gains this preparedness, He discloses Himself to it in the self-disclosure of witnessing in the visible world. Hence it sees Him and becomes manifest in the form of Him who disclosed Himself to it, as we have mentioned.
>
> He gives the heart the preparedness, as indicated in His words, "He gave each thing its creation" (20:50). Then He lifts the veil between Himself and His servant. The servant sees Him in the form of his own belief, so He is identical to the object of his belief. Hence neither the heart nor the eye ever witnesses anything but the form of the servant's belief concerning the Real. It is this Real within belief whose form is "embraced by" the heart [according to the hadith]. It is He who discloses Himself to the servant, and he recognizes Him. Hence the eye sees only the Real of belief.
>
> The great variety of beliefs is hidden from no one. He who delimits Him denies Him in other than his own delimitation, while acknowledging Him only when He discloses Himself in that

> whereby he has delimited Him. But He who frees Him from every delimitation never denies Him. On the contrary, he acknowledges Him in every form within which He undergoes self-transmutation and he gives to Him from himself the proper measure of the form in which He discloses Himself ad infinitum—since the forms of self-disclosure have no end at which they might stop. In the same way, the gnostic has no end to knowledge of God at which he might stop. At every instant the gnostic seeks increase of his knowledge of Him: "My Lord, increase me in knowledge!" "My Lord, increase me in knowledge!" "My Lord, increase me in knowledge!" Hence the situation has no end from either side, that is, when you say that there is Real and creature. (*Fuṣūṣ* 120)

A belief is a knotting, a tying, and a binding. God in Himself is unknowable to any "others," since He is absolutely nondelimited and undefined. No finite thing can perceive the Infinite. When God makes Himself known to others through His self-disclosure, He limits and restricts Himself, or else they could not know Him. His making Himself known to them corresponds to His bestowal of existence upon them. The self-disclosure through knowledge is the same as the self-disclosure through existence. Through His constricting Himself, He "ties Himself in a knot" and fits Himself into the beliefs of the creatures. God's "self-transmutation" takes place within "beliefs," since beliefs are another name for the individual delimitations which constitute the creatures. "Belief" is the creature's cognitive perception of the self-disclosure. Each person's belief is unique, since it defines his unique selfhood. Ibn al-ʿArabī makes many of these points in explaining the divine root of the state known as "contraction" (*qabḍ*), which means literally to grasp with the hand, to grip, or to be gripped and compressed.

> The "being gripped" on God's part from which emerges gripping within engendered existence is the attributes of the created things by which God becomes qualified, especially as indicated in His words, "The heart of My servant embraces Me." Then His "being gripped" is His self-disclosure in the form of the belief of everyone who has a belief concerning Him. The Real becomes, as it were, constricted and contracted by the beliefs. These are the "mark" which stands between Him and the common people among His servants. Were He not like this, He would not be a god; yet He is the God of the cosmos, without doubt. Hence He must be described as being embraced in this manner.
>
> The cosmos is dissimilar in its preparedness, and it must have a support. No part of the cosmos ever ceases worshiping God in respect of its own preparedness, so the Real necessarily discloses Himself to it in keeping with its preparedness to receive. For there is "nothing that does not glorify Him in praise," for He has gripped it with both of His hands in accordance with what it believes, "but you do not understand their glorification" (17:44). If their glorification went back to a single affair, no one would fail to understand the glorification of anyone else. But God has said that the glorification of the things is not understood, so this indicates that everyone glorifies his God in keeping with that of Him which he has in himself and others do not have.
>
> Since reason maintains that God cannot be restricted, while the actual situation demands the existence of restriction, He describes Himself at the end of the verse as "Clement." Hence He will not take to task—though He has power to do so—him who supposes that the Real is exclusively such and such and does not have some other description. At the end of the verse, He describes Himself as "Concealing" (*ghafūr*), since He curtains their hearts from knowledge of Him—except those of His servants He wills. . . . Every group other than the Folk of Allah have declared Him incomparable with such and such. That is why He reports about these groups by saying, "There is nothing that does not glorify Him," that is, declare Him incomparable, "in praise," that is, through laudation of Him. And declaring incomparable is distance. God does not report that He commanded them

to glorify Him, He merely reports that they glorify Him in praise. Hence, turn your attention in your recitation of the Koran to that which your Lord says about Himself, not to that which the cosmos says about Him. Have discernment, and have need concerning Him only for what He says about Himself, not what He narrates from the speech of the cosmos. Then you will be one of the Folk of the Koran, those who are God's Folk and Elect. (II 509.31)

Worshiping God and Self

People imagine that they believe in God. In fact, they believe in God's self-disclosure to themselves, and this always takes the shape of the receptacle. As Junayd said, "The water takes on the color of its cup." But what is God's self-disclosure to the individual if not the individual himself? In other words, no one worships God as He is in Himself; everyone worships God as he perceives Him in himself. More briefly: No one worships anyone but himself.

When a person sees something of the Real, he never sees anything but himself. (II 667.14)

The creatures are bound to worship only what they believe about the Real, so they worship nothing but a created thing. (IV 386.17)

Every man of reason who has a doctrine concerning the Essence of God worships that to which his reason has given birth. If he has faith, this discredits his faith. If he does not have faith, no more needs to be said—especially after Muḥammad has been sent to all mankind. (III 311.2)

Once we see that God "sent no messenger save with the tongue of his people" (14:4), we come to know that He never makes Himself known to us—when He desires that we know Him—except in accordance with our situation, not in accordance with what His Essence requires. Though His making Himself known to us accords with what His Essence requires, the requirement of His Essence becomes diversified between that which distinguishes Him from us and that through which He makes Himself known to us. (III 409.14)

You will know nothing of God except that which comes from Him and which He brings into existence within you, either as inspiration or the unveiling of a self-disclosure which has been occasioned. All of this is a temporally originated object of knowledge. Hence nothing knows anything except a temporally originated possible thing like itself. The possible things are infinite, since they do not enter into existence all at once. On the contrary, they are given existence instant by instant. Hence "None knows God but God," and the temporally originated engendered thing knows nothing but a temporally originated thing like itself, which the Real engenders within it. God says, "There comes not to them a remembrance from their Lord temporally originated, [but they listen to it yet playing, diverted their hearts]" (21:2). This "Remembrance" is His Speech, which had a temporal origination within them and became an object of their knowledge. Hence their knowledge only became attached to a temporally originated thing, [not to God's eternal speech]. (II 552.22)

Junayd was asked about knowledge (*maʿrifa*) and the knower (*ʿārif*). He replied, "The water takes on the color of its cup." In other words, the container displays its effects in what it contains. Junayd said this to let you know that you will never judge your object of knowledge except by yourself, since you will never know anything but yourself. Whatever may be the color of the cup, water becomes manifest in that color. The person without knowledge judges that the water is like that, since sight gives that to him. Water discloses itself in the forms of all the cups in respect to their colors, but it does not become delimited in its essence. You only see it that way. In the same manner, the shapes of the containers in which water appears display their effects in it, but in all of them it is still water. If the container is square, the water becomes manifest as square. . . .

He who sees the water only in the cup judges it by the property of the cup. But he who sees it simple and noncompound knows that the shapes and colors in which it becomes manifest are the effect of the containers. Water remains in its own definition and reality, whether in the cup or outside it. Hence it never loses the name "water." (III 161.24)

Having been asked about knowledge and the knower, Junayd said, "The water takes on the color of its cup." So also are the self-disclosures within the divine loci of manifestation, wherever these might be. The gnostic perceives them constantly. Self-disclosure belongs to him constantly, and he differentiates it constantly: The gnostic knows who is disclosing Himself and why He is disclosing Himself. But only the Real knows how (*kayf*) He discloses Himself. No one in the cosmos, no one other than God, knows that, neither angel nor prophet. For that is one of the specific characteristics of the Real, since the Essence is unknown at root. Hence the knowledge of how He discloses Himself in the loci of manifestation cannot be acquired or perceived by any of God's creatures. . . .

Since there are as many cups as drinkers at the Pool which will be found in the abode of the hereafter, and since the water in the cup takes the form of the cup in both shape and color, we know for certain that knowledge of God takes on the measure of your view, your preparedness, and what you are in yourself. No two people will ever come together in a single knowledge of God in all respects, since a single constitution is never found in two different people, nor can there be such a thing. When there are two, there must be that through which the distinction is made, since the entity of each is immutably established. Were this not so, they could not be two. Hence no one ever knows anything of the Real except his own self. (II 597.4,35)

Lights (*al-anwār*) are visible (*shahāda*), and the Real is a light, so He is witnessed and seen. Mysteries (*al-asrār*) are unseen (*ghayb*), so they possess the He (*al-huwa*), since the He never becomes manifest. In respect of the He, the Real is not witnessed, for the He is the Reality of the Real. In respect of His self-disclosure in forms, the Real is witnessed and seen, but He is seen only at the level of the viewer. That is what is bestowed by the viewer's preparedness. And his preparedness is of two kinds: an essential preparedness, through which there is an all-inclusive vision; and an accidental preparedness, which is the knowledge of God which he earns and by which his soul becomes adorned in respect of his rational consideration. Self-disclosure follows this specific preparedness, and within it there occurs ranking in degrees. (IV 443.33)

By knowing self, the servant comes to know God inasmuch as He has disclosed Himself to the soul. He knows God in His similarity, but can never know Him in His incomparability. It follows that by worshiping God, the servant is worshiping himself. He worships God as He discloses Himself to the soul, and that is determined and defined by the soul itself. It also follows that one cannot worship anything other than God, since whatever one worships is God's self-disclosure to the soul. Ibn al-ʿArabī sees one of the Koranic proofs of this last statement in the verse, "Thy Lord has decreed that you worship none but Him" (17:23). He explains that this verse is usually read as a commandment, similar to the commands "Perform the prayer" and "Pay the alms." But in fact, he says, it is a statement of the actual situation: Reality itself makes it impossible to worship anything but God.

When the vision of the Real takes place, it only takes place in a mutual waystation (*munāzala*) between an ascent and a descent. The ascent belongs to us and the descent to Him. To us belongs "drawing close" (*tadānī*) and to Him belongs "coming down" (*tadallī*), since "coming down" must stem from the high.[4] It is ours to climb (*taraqqī*) and His to receive (*talaqqī*) those who come to Him. All of this gives us knowledge of the form in which He discloses Himself to His servants and the fact that it possesses bounds and measure, in order that He might enter along with His servants under the property announced in His words, "We send it not down but in a known measure" (15:21).

"Surely We have created" or made "everything in measure" (54:49).

Vision is a created thing, so it occurs in measure. The variation of self-disclosure is the manifestation of a temporally originated thing to the recipient of self-disclosure, so it occurs in measure. Do you not see that, out of divine jealousy, He discloses Himself through His property in the entities which are taken as gods, since He has ordained and decreed that no one else be worshiped? He has reported this, for He says, "And thy Lord has decreed that you worship none but Him" (17:23).

The exoteric scholars take the word "decreed" to mean "commanded," but on the basis of unveiling we take it to be an ordainment, and this is correct. For those who associate others with God admit that they only worship these things "to bring" them "nigh in nearness to God" (39:3). Hence they give them the status of deputies manifest in the form of Him who has deputized them, and He has no form other than Divinity, which they attribute to those things. (III 117.3)

No one is loved but God, but the name of the created thing acts as a veil. In the same way, he who worships a created thing here worships none but God, though he does not know. He names his object of worship Manāt, al-ʿUzzā, or al-Lāt.[5] Then when he dies and the covering is removed, he knows that he only worshiped God, for God says, "And thy Lord has decreed," that is, ordained, "that you worship none but Him" (17:23). (IV 260.28)

In reality, he who associates others with God worships none but God, since, if he did not believe that there was divinity in the associate, he would not have worshiped it. "And thy Lord has decreed that you worship none but Him" (17:23). For this reason the Real shows jealousy for this description. He punishes them in this world if they do not show reverence to that which they suppose to be their god, and He provides for them and listens to their prayers when they ask from their god. For He knows that they have had recourse to this Level [of Divinity]. (I 328.14)

The Real is with the belief of everyone who has a belief. . . . In the same way, He is "with the opinion" which His servant has of Him.[6] However, the levels become ranked according to excellence, while God is wider, greater, and more tremendous than that He should be confined by any attribute which would restrain Him, such that He would be with one of His servants and not be with another. The "Divine Vastness" refuses that. For God says, "He is with you wherever you are" (57:4); "Whithersoever you turn, there is the face of God" (2:115), and the "face" of a thing is its reality and essence.

Were He to be with one person and not with another, the one with whom He was not would be worshiping his own illusion (*wahm*), not his Lord. But God has said, "And thy Lord has decreed," that is, ordained, "that you worship none but Him" (17:23). Because of Him the gods are worshiped, but the intention of every worshiper in his worship is only God. So nothing is worshiped in itself except God. He who associates others with God is only mistaken because he has set up for himself a special road of worship which was not established for him by a revealed Law from the Real. That is why he becomes one of the wretched. (I 405.27)

In the very last passage of the *Fuṣūṣ al-ḥikam*, Ibn al-ʿArabī summarizes his views concerning the God created by the servant's belief while discussing the ritual prayer (*ṣalāt*). Man must pray to God, but God also prays over man, as indicated in the verse, "It is He who prays over you" (33:43). In his usual fashion, Ibn al-ʿArabī searches for hidden significance by examining the root meaning of the word being discussed. In this case one of the meanings of *ṣalāt*'s root is "back" and "behind" (*ṣalā*), while the word *muṣallī*, which means "he who performs the prayer," also signifies "the horse which comes in behind the winner in a race." When man performs the prayer, he "lags behind" and follows God, and so also when God "performs the prayer," He lags behind man by following his belief.

The prayer is performed (2) by us or (1) by Him.

(1) When He performs the prayer, He prays through His name the Last, so He lags behind the existence of the servant. He is then identical with the Real which the servant creates in his own heart through his reflective consideration or through following authority. This is the God of belief, who assumes great variety in accordance with the preparedness of the locus. Thus, when Junayd was asked about knowledge of God and the knower, he replied, "The water takes on the color of the cup." This reply is precisely correct, giving news of the actual situation. This is the God who prays over us.

(2) When we ourselves pray, we possess the name "last." In this station we have the aforementioned state of Him who possesses this name. Hence we are with Him in accordance with our own state. He does not look upon us except in the form in which we come to Him, for the *muṣallī* is the horse which lags behind the leader on the racetrack. God says, "Each knows its own prayer," that is, its own level in lagging behind through worshiping its Lord, "and its own glorification" (24:41), that is, the glorification given to it by its own preparedness through which it declares God's incomparability. "There is nothing that does not glorify in praise" its Lord, the Clement, the Concealing (17:44). But we do not know the glorifications of the cosmos in differentiated detail, one by one.

The verse can also be read with the pronoun referring to the servant who glorifies: "There is nothing that does not glorify itself in praise." This is as we have said concerning the believer: He only praises the God who is in his belief and to whom he has tied himself. His practice all goes back to himself, so he praises only himself. For without doubt, he who praises the artifact praises its maker, since its beauty or lack of beauty goes back to its maker. The God of the believer is made by him who observes Him, so this God is his artifact. Hence his praise of what he has made is his praise of himself. That is why he blames the belief of others. If he were fair, he would not do so. But, of course, the possessor of this specific object of worship is ignorant of that, since he objects to others in what they believe concerning God. If he knew what Junayd said—that the water takes on the color of the cup—he would let every believer have his own belief and he would recognize God in the form of every object of belief. But the believer has an "opinion," not knowledge. That is why God said, "I am with My servant's opinion of Me," that is, "I do not become manifest to him except in the form of his belief." If he likes, he declares Him nondelimited, and if he likes, he delimits.

The God of beliefs assumes limitations. He is the God who is "embraced" by the heart of His servant. But nothing embraces the Nondelimited God, since He is identical with the things and identical with Himself. It cannot be said that a thing embraces itself, nor that it does not embrace it. So understand! "God speaks the truth, and He guides on the way" (Koran 33:4). (*Fuṣūṣ* 225)

Knowing Self

According to a famous hadith which we have already encountered several times, the Prophet said, "He who knows himself"—or "He who knows his own soul"—"knows His Lord." Ibn al-ʿArabī comments on this saying from various points of view. Often he cites it to encourage the seeker to come to know himself so that he may come to know God. But in the present context, he gives it a new shade of meaning: When the servant comes to know himself, thereby knowing God, he does not know God in Himself. Rather, he knows Him as his own Lord. This is the God who discloses Himself to the soul, and the self-disclosure is different from that experienced by any other soul. The God that I come to know through knowing myself is the God of my own belief, the water which has assumed the color of my cup.

We are many, deriving from One Entity—inaccessible and exalted is He! That Entity is related to us by bringing us into existence, and we are related to Him through existence. So "He who knows himself" as a creature and an existent thing "knows" the Real as a Creator and the one who brings into existence. (II 500.16)

"He who knows himself has known his Lord," for that creature who is the most knowing in respect of creation is the most knowing in respect of God. (III 404.28)

The Lawgiver said, "He who knows himself knows his Lord." This knowledge of God acquired after knowledge of self may be a knowledge of one's incapacity to attain to knowledge of God. One comes to know that there is Someone who cannot be known. The lack of a mark is a mark, for He is distinguished from His creatures though negation of attributes (*salb*), not affirmation (*ithbāt*).

The knowledge of Him may be knowledge of the fact that He is a god, so the servants come to know what is worthy of His Level. They make this an attribute of Him who stands in that Level and becomes manifest within it. Hence their knowledge of what the Level requires is their knowledge of the Possessor of the Level, since He is described by everything by which it is proper to describe it. But in reality it is known that this is knowledge of His Level, not of Him. (II 472.35)

"He who knows himself," the fact that his entity remains forever in its possibility, "knows His Lord," the fact that He is the Existent in Being. "He who knows" that the changes manifest within existence are the properties of the preparedness of the possible things "knows his Lord" by the fact that He alone makes them manifest. (III 101.18)

When the servant praises God, he does so either by names of incomparability or by names of acts. Our view in respect of unveiling is that first we begin with the names of incomparability. But in respect of rational consideration, we begin with the names of acts, since we cannot avoid witnessing the objects of the acts (*maf'ūlāt*). The first object of the acts that I witness is the nearest to me, and that is myself. Hence I praise Him through the names of His acts through me and in me. As often as I wish to pass beyond myself to other than myself, I become aware of another temporally originated thing which I occasion within myself through seeking, and that new thing demands that I praise God for it. I remain like this always, forever and ever, in this world and the next. And it cannot be otherwise. So consider how many are the waystations of praising God which remain for me by witnessing creatures other than myself! This station demands the Prophet's words, "I count not Thy praises before Thee—Thou art as Thou hast praised Thyself!" In the same way Abū Bakr said, "Incapacity to attain comprehension is itself comprehension."[7]

After finishing with myself and the created things, then I will begin praising Him with His names of incomparability. But finishing with myself is impossible, so attaining to the witnessing of the engendered things and finishing with the engendered things is impossible. Hence attaining to the names of incomparability is impossible.

Hence, whenever I see one of the common people or one of those who claim to have knowledge of God praising God by the names of incomparability by way of witnessing, or by the names of the acts in respect of the fact that they are connected to other than himself, I know that he has not known himself, nor has he witnessed it, nor has he sensed the effects of the Real within it. And whosoever is blind toward himself—which is nearest to him—is blind in relation to others and even further astray from the way. God says, "And whosoever is blind in this world (*dunyā*)," naming it *dunyā* ["closer"] since it is nearer to us than the next world . . . , "shall be blind in the world to come and even further astray from the way" (17:72). (II 641.6)

The root of the existence of knowledge of God is knowledge of self. So knowledge of God has the property of knowledge of self, which is the root. In the view of those who know the self, the self is an ocean without shore, so knowledge of it has no end. Such is the property of knowledge of the self. Hence, knowledge of God, which is a branch of this root, joins with it in property, so there is no end to knowledge of God. That is why in every state the knower says, "My Lord, increase me in knowledge!" (20:114). Then God increases him in knowledge of himself that he may increase in knowledge of his Lord. This is given by divine unveiling.

Some of the reflective thinkers maintain

> that knowledge of God is the root of knowledge of the self. But this can never be correct in the creature's knowledge of God. This is true exclusively in the Real's knowledge. This is a priority and a root through the level, not through existence, since through existence His knowledge of Himself is identical with His knowledge of the cosmos. Even if His knowledge is the root through the level, it is not so through existence. (III 121.25)

To say that "He who knows himself knows his Lord" means that he who knows himself knows his own specific Lord, who is God as He discloses Himself to his soul, not anyone else's Lord. One of Ibn al-ʿArabī's more succinct explanations of this point is found in the *Fuṣūṣ al-ḥikam*:

> Know that what is named "God" is One in Essence but All (*al-kull*) through the names. No existent thing has anything from God except its own specific Lord. It cannot possibly have the All. . . . That which becomes designated for it from the All is only that which corresponds to it, and that is its own Lord. No one takes from Him in respect of His Unity. That is why the Folk of Allah declare self-disclosure in Unity to be impossible. (*Fuṣūṣ* 90,91)

Paths of Belief

The tremendous variety of human beliefs can be classified in terms of whether people declare God's incomparability or recognize His similarity. Perfect knowledge, which puts every point of view in its place, combines these two basic beliefs.

The Essence in Its incomparability is nondelimited by any attribute or quality. We can only negate properties from It. There can be no question of saying that God is Creator, Preserver, Merciful, Vengeful, Guide, or Misguider, since these are all affirmative attributes that would declare His similarity with creation. But He in His Unknowability is far beyond them. We can only affirm that there is an Essence and that It cannot not be. Our own existence is somehow the shadow of Its existence. All created things are equal in their existence, so all things manifest the Essence inasmuch as they exist. This is the root of the engendering command, the divine word "Be!" In respect of this command, everything is as it should be, and everything follows a straight path. All beliefs are equal, since each of them exists, and existence is the sole attribute of any significance in respect to the Essence. There is no evil, since the Necessary Being through Himself is Sheer Good, and nothing arises from the Good but good. Everyone's specific Lord is embraced by the name Allah, which is the "Lord of Lords."

God in His similarity discloses Himself in all the forms of the cosmos. The All-merciful Breath articulates itself through every existential word. In this respect we say that inasmuch as God has disclosed Himself in the forms of the cosmos, the source of the self-disclosure is "Creator" and the locus of the self-disclosure is "creature." He who is able to disclose Himself is "Powerful," and that which manifests this self-disclosure is the "object of power." Thus become established all the relationships known as "names" or "attributes." In respect of this divine similarity, each name has specific properties, and the properties are diverse. The Life-giver is not equivalent to the Slayer, nor is the Guide equivalent to the Misguider. Each creature has its own specific Lord which is different from every other Lord, its own immutable entity which bestows upon it specific properties. The properties manifest in the cosmos cannot be ignored, since they are the "secondary causes" established by the Creator for a good purpose and according to wisdom. Each must be given its due (*ḥaqq*), which is to say that man must observe "courtesy" in all affairs. We attain to knowledge of courtesy through the Scale of the revealed Law, the prescriptive command.

The declaration of incomparability envisages the Divine Essence named Allah, the Lord of Lords, whose Path is followed by all things, whether existent or nonexistent. There are as many paths of Allah as there are "breaths of the creatures," and each leads to Him. The declaration of similarity allows us to perceive that each of these many paths leads to a different Lord, a different divine name, and that the properties of the names are diverse.

Each "belief" ties a knot in the heart of the believer and fixes him upon a path, the object of his belief being the end of the path. All beliefs are equivalent in that God is their ultimate object. But each belief is different in that it leads to a different name of God. Some of the names yield felicity, while others are connected to wretchedness. "Faith" comprises a belief along with a practice that will lead to felicity, while "misbelief" (*kufr*) is a belief and practice that will lead to wretchedness. The path of faith is wide, since it is that of the Blessing-giver and has been given to all the prophets, but the path of misbelief is even wider, since "my name is legion."

Like everything else in existence, the paths of belief are ranked in degrees. Some people see God only in negative terms through declaring His incomparability. Some see Him as possessing the Most Beautiful Names in the direction of incomparability, thus affirming that He possesses attributes but that these are totally different from those possessed by the creatures. Still others see God only in terms of His similarity, not being able to conceive of anything but what they can picture concretely in their imaginations. The highest of the paths combines all three ways and is followed by the gnostics, the Folk of Allah. Ibn al-ʿArabī discusses these four paths while pointing out that as soon as we consider the cosmos in its own state of possibility, then there is no "straightness" in the cosmos, since in itself the cosmos is He/not He; it is a mixture of light and darkness, good and evil.

When a person considers the cosmos's possibility (*imkān*), he sees that possibility is a cause of disease (*maraḍ*). Disease is a deviation (*mayl*), and deviation is the opposite of straightness. The cosmos's possibility is one of its essential attributes, so the disappearance of possibility cannot be imagined, whether in the state of the cosmos's nonexistence or in the state of its existence. Disease belongs to it essentially, so deviation belongs to it essentially. Hence there is no straightness. The disease of the cosmos is chronic. There is no hope for its cure.

However, the engendered universe is a locus for the existence of different sides attempting to throw each other into error. This is required by [the divine] wisdom and also by the sound rational faculty, which knows what will bring engendered existence out of its corruption, since the Law has set down prescriptions.

But it is impossible for the individuals of the cosmos to have a single constitution. Since constitutions are diverse, there is in the cosmos the knower and he who knows more, the excellent and he who is more excellent. Among them is he who knows God as nondelimited, without any delimitation. Among them is he who is not able to acquire any knowledge of God without delimiting Him by attributes which negate the suggestion of temporal origination and require the perfection of Him who is described. And among them is he who is not able to acquire knowledge of God without delimiting Him by the attributes of temporal origination; hence he brings Him under the property of being modified by time, place, bounds, and measure.

Since at the root of the creation of the cosmos, the situation of its knowledge of God accorded with this natural constitution, God sent down the revealed Laws according to these levels, so that the divine bounty would include all creatures.

God sent down, "Nothing is like Him" (42:11) for the sake of the person who knows God as nondelimited without any delimitation.

He sent down His words, "He encompasses everything in knowledge" (65:12), "He is powerful over everything" (5:120), "He performs whatsoever He desires" (11:107), "He is the Hearing, the Seeing" (42:11), "Allah, there is no god but He, the Alive, the Self-subsistent" (2:156), "Grant him protection till he hears the Speech of God" (9:6), "He knows everything" (2:29). All of this is for the sake of him who delimits Him by attributes of perfection.

God also sent down as part of the revealed Laws His words, "The All-merciful sat upon the Throne" (20:5), "He is with you wherever you are" (57:4), "He is God in the heavens and the earth" (6:3), "Running before Our eyes" (54:14), "Had We desired to take an amusement, We would have taken it to Us from Ourselves" (21:17).

In this way the revealed Laws include everything demanded by the constitutions of the cosmos. The object of belief is one of these kinds. But he who has a perfect constitution embraces all these beliefs. He knows where they come from and where they go, and nothing of them is absent from him. (II 219.23)

One of the many "stations" of the Sufi path is "examination" (*murāqaba*), through which the servant carefully guards over himself and observes God as He becomes manifest in the cosmos and in himself. Ibn al-ʿArabī sees its divine root in the name, "the Examiner" (*al-raqīb*). He points out that the term is applied to three different kinds of activity.

There are three types of examination by the servant, one of which cannot take place, while the other two can take place. The examination which cannot take place is the servant's examination of his Lord. He does not know His Essence, nor His relationship to the cosmos, so the existence of this kind of examination cannot be conceived, since it depends upon knowledge of the essence of the one who is examined. Another group says that this type of examination can take place, since the Law has defined Him as is proper to His majesty. So "He is with us wherever we are;"[8] "He sat upon the Throne" (20:5); He is "God in the earth; He knows" our "secrets and what" we "publish"; and He is also "God in the heavens" (6:3) and descends to us. He is the Manifest in the entity of every locus of manifestation among the possible things. Hence we know Him in this measure and examine Him to this extent. Hence our examination of the things is identical with our examination of Him, since He manifests Himself from everything. Among the people some have said, "I have never seen anything without seeing God before it," that is, without examining Him; another said, "after it," another said "with it," and another said, "in it."[9] Such people maintain that this kind of examination is correct.

The second kind is the examination of shame (*ḥayāʾ*), based upon the words of God, "Does he not know that God sees?" (96:14). The servant examines His seeing while He is seeing him. Hence he examines the Real's examination of himself. This is called the "examination of examination," and is established by the Law.

The third examination is that the servant examines his heart and his inward and outward self to see the signs of his Lord within it. Then he acts in accordance with the signs of his Lord which he sees. (II 208.34)

If God can be examined, this is the God who discloses Himself through the creatures. But God in Himself is beyond all examination. According to a *ḥadīth qudsī* already quoted, "My heavens and My earth embrace Me not, but the heart of My believing servant does embrace Me." This God embraced by the heart cannot be the God of incomparability, but rather the God of self-disclosure and similarity. The spiritual traveler reaches a point where he abandons all attempt to examine God in Himself, since he knows that the Essence remains forever unknown. Hence the Shaykh dedicates the chapter following the one on examination to "abandoning examination" (*tark al-murāqaba*).

Examination is an imaginal descent (*tanazzul mithālī*) which brings about nearness. But the level of the knowers of God demands that "Nothing is like Him" (42:11), so there are no likenesses and images. The actual situation of the Divinity does not become delimited or restricted and remains unknown. It is clear that He is not known when we believe that we know Him. No knowledge of Him provides us with any positive quality. On the contrary, there is a verified negation and an intelligible relationship allowing for the effects that exist within the entities. Hence there is no quality, location, time, position, correlation, accident, substance, or quantity. There is nothing of the ten categories, except for a verified passivity (*infiʿāl*) and a definite activity; or an act manifest from an unknown Agent whose effect is seen. His report is not recognized and His Entity is not known, though He is known to exist. So whom should we examine? For there is no one upon whom the eye falls or who is restricted by imagination, bounded by time, made plural by attributes and properties, qualified by states, distinguished by positions, made manifest by correlation. How can we examine Him who does not accept attributes? Knowledge is supposed to remove imagination. Hence He is the Examiner, not the examined. He is the Preserver, not the preserved.

That which man preserves in his heart is only his belief. That is what He embraces of his Lord. So if you examine, know whom it is that you examine. You will never leave yourself and you will never know any but your own essence, since the temporally originated thing never becomes connected to anything but that which corresponds to it (*al-munāsib*), and that is what you have of Him. What you have is temporally originated, so you will never depart from your own kind.

In reality, you worship nothing but what you have set up in yourself. That is why the doctrines concerning God are diverse and the states change. One group says, "He is like this." Another group says, "He is not like that, He is like this." A third group says concerning knowledge, "The water takes on the color of its cup." The third position holds that the cup affects the proof, thus affecting Him in the view of the eye.

So consider the bewilderment that pervades every believer. The perfect human being is he whose bewilderment has intensified and his regret is continuous—he does not reach his goal because of that which is his Object of worship, for he strives to achieve that which cannot possibly be achieved and he threads the path of Him whose path is not known.

He who is more perfect than the perfect is he who believes every belief concerning Him. He recognizes Him in faith, in proofs, and in heresy (*ilḥād*), since *ilḥād* is to deviate from one belief to another specific belief.

So if you want your eye to hit the mark, witness Him with every eye, for He pervades all things through self-disclosure. In every form He has a face and in every knower a state. So examine if you will, or do not examine. (II 211.29)

Belief and the Law

Although people worship God in whatever form they worship, they are commanded to worship Him as Allah, not inasmuch as He reveals Himself through various other names. All things worship their own Lords by their very existence, being subjected to them and following their commands, so "worship" is inherent to creation, that is, the worship brought about by the engendering command. But the specific worship that profits the servant and takes him to felicity is not inherent in creation, since it is determined and defined by the revealed Law, the prescriptive command.

God says, "They were commanded to worship but One God; there is no god but He; glory be to Him above what they associate!" (Koran 9:31). This is the *tawḥīd* of commanding to worship, and it is one of the most marvelous of affairs. How can there be a command in that which is inherent (*dhātī*) to him who is commanded? For worship is inherent to created things. So in what respect has worship been commanded?

As for the faithful, He commanded them to worship Him in respect of the Unity of the Entity (*aḥadiyyat al-ʿayn*), since He said concerning a group of them, "Call upon Allah or call upon the All-merciful; whichever you call upon, to Him belong the most beautiful names" (17:110). So this group which was commanded was not worshiping One God.

> He says: Do not consider the divine names in the respect that they denote diverse meanings. Otherwise, the names would make them slaves of their meanings and their worship would become defective. They would see that each reality within themselves is connected to a divine reality, and that they are poor and needy toward that divine reality; but these divine realities are numerous, since the reality of seeking provision worships the All-provider and the reality of seeking well-being worships the Healer. So God says to them, "Worship only One God!" For, although each divine name denotes a meaning that differs from the others, it also denotes a Single Entity demanded by all these diverse relationships. (II 409.4)

The mistake of him who associates others with God is that he devises for himself an original form of worship which God did not set down for him in a Law, so he worships something he has created. In order for the object of worship to have objective validity and pull man out of his subjective limitations, it must be defined by the One God Himself.

> When a person rationally considers God, he creates what he believes in himself through his consideration. Hence he worships only a god which he has created through his consideration. He has said to it "Be!", and it has come into existence. That is why God commanded us to worship the God brought by the Messenger and spoken of in the Book. For if you worship this God, you will be worshiping that which you have not created. On the contrary, you will be worshiping your Creator, and you will have fully given worship its due (*ḥaqq*). For knowledge of God derives only from following authority. It cannot possibly derive from proofs. That is why we have been prohibited from reflecting upon the Essence of God. But we have not been prohibited from ascribing the Level solely to Him—on the contrary, we have been commanded to do so—since there is no god but He. (IV 143.2)

Ibn al-ʿArabī summarizes the causes of divergent beliefs and the means of achieving felicity in spite of them while discussing the different types of human beings which God brings into existence. Each human being, in respect of the preparedness of his or her immutable entity, is a "locus" (*maḥall*) in which the Being of God discloses Itself. Each is a cup that colors the invisible water.

> Incapacity, timidity, and miserliness of character are inherent and necessary in man's innate disposition. The root of his creation is, "Surely man was created fretful, when evil visits him, impatient, when good visits him, grudging" (70:19–20). When man attacks and is valiant, he takes help from rank, earning, and assuming the character traits of God, since in his essence he has a spirit from Him. But the site displays effects, just as the site of water displays effects in the water—that is, the saltiness or bitterness or other tastes that are found therein. But in respect of its own ipseity (*huwiyya*), water has a single attribute in pleasantness (*ṭīb*) and flavor. So look how the site displays effects within it!
>
> In the same way, the spirits breathed into the bodies come from a pure and holy Root. If the locus has a pleasant constitution, it promotes the spirit in pleasantness, but if it is not pleasant, it makes it loathsome (*khabīth*) and brings it under the property of its own constitution.
>
> God's messengers, those who are His vicegerents, are the purest of human beings in locus. They are the sinless who increase the pleasant only in pleasantness. There are also vicegerents who become joined to the messengers; these are their inheritors in state, act, and word. There are those who are deficient in certain respects; these are the disobedient. Others are even more deficient; these are the hypocrites. Others dispute and war; they are the misbelievers and those who associate others with Him.
>
> God sends messengers to them so that they will excuse Him on their part when He punishes them for their rebelling against Him and attributing themselves to other than Him. . . . But they came to do this because of a correct principle. They saw the diversity of doctrines concerning God, though everyone came together concerning His Unity and that He is One,

there being no god but He. Then people disagreed as to what this God is. Each possessor of consideration said something to which he was led by his consideration. It became established for him that God is he who has such a property. What he did not know is that this is identical with his own making (*jaʿl*). Hence he worshiped only a god which he created and believed within himself, calling it a belief. Here the people diverged widely, even though the Single Thing is not diverse in Itself. Hence It has to accord with one of these doctrines or stand outside all of them.

Since this was the situation, it displayed its effects upon them. They found it easy to take stones, trees, stars, animals, and other such created things as their gods, each group in accordance with that which dominated over it. They did exactly the same thing as those who possess doctrines concerning God. They received aid in this from this principle, without being aware.

Hence you will see no one who worships an unmade god, since man creates in himself that which he worships and judges. But God is the Judge; He is not restricted by reason, nor does it rule over Him. On the contrary, to Him "belongs the command" in His creation, "before and after" (30:4). There is no god but He, the God and Master of everything.

All this belongs to the name, "He who sends forth" (*al-bāʿith*). It is He who sends forth to their inward selves (*bāṭin*) messengers—the reflective thoughts in accordance with which they speak and believe in God. In the same way He sends to their outward selves the messengers known as prophets, prophecy, and messengerhood. The intelligent person is he who abandons what he has in himself concerning God for what the messengers have brought from God concerning God. If what God's messengers have brought conforms to what the messengers of reflective powers have brought to their inward selves, so be it—and they should thank God for the agreement. But if disagreement appears, it is incumbent upon you to follow the messenger of the outward dimension. Beware of the calamity of the messengers of the inward dimension! Then you will attain to felicity, God willing. This is a piece of advice from me to every receptive person who possesses a sound rational faculty. "And say: 'My Lord, increase me in knowledge!'" (20:114). (IV 278.33)

After discussing the exalted station of perfect man, who worships God through direct witnessing, not as an unseen reality, Ibn al-ʿArabī turns to counselling his reader. He makes reference to the human constitution (*mizāj*), which reflects the preparedness of the immutable entity on the corporeal level. The more balanced the body's constitution, the more it is able to act as a perfect mirror for the spirit which God breathes into it.[10]

If you do not dwell in this waystation and have no entrance into this highest of all degrees, I will point to that through which you can attain to it:

You should know that God did not create the creatures with a single constitution. On the contrary, He made them disparate in constitution. This is obvious and self-evident to anyone who looks, because of the disparity among people in rational consideration and faith. God has told you that man is his brother's mirror.[11] Hence man sees in his brother something of himself that he would not see without him. For man is veiled by and enamored of his own caprice. But when he sees that attribute in the other, while it is his own attribute, he sees his own defect in the other. Then he comes to know its ugliness, if the attribute is ugly, or its beauty, if it should be beautiful.

Know that mirrors are diverse in shape and that they modify the object seen by the observer according to their own shapes, whether they be tall, wide, curved, bent, round, small, large, numerous, and so on—whatever may be given by the shape of the mirror. It is known that the messengers are the most balanced (*aʿdal*) of all people in constitution, since they receive the messages of their Lord. Each of them receives the message to the measure of the composition God has given him in his constitution. There is no prophet who was not sent specifically to a designated people, since he possessed a specific and curtailed constitution. But God sent Muḥammad with an all-inclusive message for all people without exception.[12] He was able to receive such a message because he possessed an all-inclusive constitution which comprises the constitution of every prophet and messenger, since he has the most balanced and most perfect of constitutions and the straightest of configurations.

Once you come to know this, and once you desire to see the Real in the most perfect manner in which He can become manifest in this human plane, then you need to know that this does not belong to you. You do not have a constitution like that possessed by Muḥammad. Whenever the Real discloses Himself to you within the mirror of your heart, your mirror will make Him manifest to you in the measure of its constitution and in the form of its shape. You know how far you stand below Muḥammad's degree in knowledge of his Lord through his plane. So cling to faith and follow him! Place him before you as the mirror within which you gaze upon your own form and the form of others. When you do this, you will come to know that God must disclose Himself to Muḥammad within his mirror. I have already told you that the mirror displays an effect in that which is seen from the point of view of the observer who sees. So the manifestation of the Real within the mirror of Muḥammad is the most perfect, most balanced, and most beautiful manifestation, because of the mirror's actuality. When you perceive Him in the mirror of Muḥammad, you will have perceived from Him a perfection which you could not perceive in respect of considering your own mirror. (III 251.3)

The Belief of the Gnostic

God in Himself is absolutely nondelimited. As we have seen, this means that He is not delimited by nondelimitation. Though in Himself He is free of all constriction and confinement, by this very fact He is able to assume, through His self-disclosure, every constriction and confinement. God created the human being upon His own form. Those who truly realize this form follow God in His nondelimitation. "God possesses the all-inclusiveness of *wujūd*, while they [i.e., the gnostics who realize the divine form] possess the all-inclusiveness of *shuhūd*" (III 161.16). On the level of belief, this means that the gnostic accepts every belief as true on its own level, while not restricting himself to any single belief, rather embracing them all. "Belief" is a knotting, so through his belief the gnostic ties all knots. But the heart accepts only one knot at a time.

> There is nothing wider than the reality of man, and nothing narrower. As for its wideness, that is because it is not too narrow for anything at all, except one thing. As for its narrowness, that is because it cannot embrace two incoming thoughts (*khāṭir*) at once, since it is one in essence, so it does not accept manyness. (II 515.9)

In order to tie a new knot in the heart, the gnostic must untie the first. In order to tie his heart in every knot, he must untie all knots. Like God, he assumes all delimitations without becoming delimited by them. He accepts the truth of every belief by assuming it as his own, yet he does not become constricted by it.

> The creatures have knotted their beliefs
>   concerning God
> and I bear witness to everything
>   they believe.
> When He appears to them in forms
>   through self-transmutation,
> they state what they witness,
>   not disclaiming Him. . . .
>
> The perfect gnostic recognizes Him in every form in which He discloses Himself and in every form in which He descends. Other than the gnostic recognizes Him only in the form of his own belief and denies Him when He discloses Himself to him in another form. He never ceases tying himself to his own belief and denying the belief of others.
>
> This is one of the most confusing affairs in the knowledge of God: To what does the diversity of forms go back? Does it go back to Him in Himself? This indeed

is what the divine news-giving has reported and what the proof of reason, provided by the reflective faculty, declares impossible. If the situation is as it is reported in the divine news-giving, then no one has seen anything but God. It is He Himself who is seen within the diverse forms, and He is identical to each form.

If the diversity of the forms goes back to the diversity of beliefs, and the forms are like the objects of belief, not the desired Object Itself, then no one has ever seen anything except his belief, whether he recognizes Him in every form—since he believes concerning Him that He accepts self-disclosure and manifestation to the object of self-disclosure in every form—or he recognizes Him only in a delimited form and in no other. (III 132.15,24)

The gnostic believes in every belief, yet he cannot express the fundamental root of his own belief concerning God, since it goes back to tasting, and tasting cannot be expressed through the technical terminology (*iṣṭilāḥ*) that becomes established in the sciences.

The science of tastings is the science of qualities (*kayfiyyāt*). Tastings cannot be told about except by those who experience them when they come together on a designated technical term. However, when they have not come together on a term, the tasters cannot communicate their tastings. This concerns knowledge of those things other than God which can be perceived only through tasting, such as sensory objects and taking pleasure in them and the pleasure which is found through knowledge acquired from reflective consideration. It is possible to establish technical terminology in all of this in an approximate manner.

As for the tasting which occurs during the witnessing of the Real, in that there can be no technical terminology. That is the tasting of the mysteries (*al-asrār*) and lies outside considerative and sensory tasting. The reason for this is as follows:

The things—I mean everything other than God—have likes and similars. Hence it is possible to establish technical terminology concerning them in order to make oneself understood to everyone who tastes the flavor of tasting within them, whatever kind of perception it may be. But as for the Author—"Nothing is like Him" (42:11). Hence it is impossible for a technical term to tie Him down, since that of Him which one individual witnesses is not the same as what another individual witnesses in any respect. This is the manner in which He is known by the gnostics. Hence no gnostic is able to convey to another gnostic what he witnesses of his Lord, for each of the two gnostics witnesses Him who has no likeness, and conveying knowledge can only take place through likenesses. If they shared a form in common, they would establish a technical term as they willed. If one of them accepted that, then everyone could accept it.

He does not disclose Himself in a single form to two individual gnostics. However, God may raise some of His servants through degrees which He does not give to other servants who are not worthy of them. These are the common people among the people of vision. He discloses Himself to them in the forms of similars. That is why the religious community (*al-umma*) can come together on a single knotting (*ʿaqd*) concerning God. Each member of the designated group believes concerning God what the others believe. Thus, for example, the Ashʿarites, the Muʿtazilites, the Ḥanbalīs, and the ancients may all agree on a single matter. All of them may agree on a single matter and not disagree, so it is permissible for them to establish technical terminology in that upon which they agree.

But the gnostics among the Folk of Allah know that "God never discloses Himself in a single form to two individuals, nor in a single form twice."[13] Hence for them the situation does not become tied down, since each individual has a self-disclosure specific to himself, and man sees Him through himself. When He discloses Himself to someone in a form, then discloses Himself to him in another form such that he comes to know about the Real from the second self-disclosure what he did not know through the first self-disclosure—and this happens constantly—then he knows that the actual situation is such in itself for himself and for others. Hence he cannot designate a technical term concerning this through which any positive knowledge would accrue to those who discuss it.

So the gnostics know, but what they know cannot be communicated. It is not in the power of the possessors of this most delightful station, higher than which there is no station among the possible things, to coin a word which would denote what they know. There is only what He has sent down—His words, "Nothing is like Him" (42:11). Hence He negated all likeness. Hence no form in which He discloses Himself to someone resembles any other form. . . .

Through our own delimitation we judge that He is nondelimited. But the actual situation in itself is described neither by delimitation nor nondelimitation. Rather, it is all-inclusive Being (*wujūd ʿāmm*). Hence He is identical with the things, but the things are not identical with Him. Nothing becomes manifest without His He-ness being identical with that thing. How should He whose Being is such accept nondelimitation or delimitation? In such manner have the gnostics known Him. He who declares Him nondelimited has not known Him, and he who declares Him delimited is ignorant of Him. (III 384.18)

Beatific Vision

No created thing can display God as He is in Himself, only as He discloses Himself. His self-disclosures are infinitely diverse in keeping with the infinite diversity of the entities. Among all the created things, human beings possess the particular characteristic of being able to participate actively in manifesting their own realities. The choices they make have a real effect upon the divine self-disclosure. God in His mercy revealed the Laws in order that people would be able to make the choices which lead directly to their felicity in the next stage of their existence. The touchstone of belief is death, since through death a person comes to witness the object of his belief. Man will see God in accordance with his own beliefs not only at the Greater Resurrection, when He transmutes Himself in forms, but already at the lesser resurrection known as physical death, when he enters into the *barzakh*, which is one of the realms of discontiguous imagination. Ibn al-ʿArabī explains this in Chapter 176 of the *Futūḥāt*, entitled "On the true knowledge of the states of the Tribe at death."

The Prophet said, "Man dies in accordance with the way he lived and he is mustered in accordance with the way he died."[14] God says [to the soul at death], "We have now unveiled from you your covering and your sight today is piercing" (50:22). In other words, at death man sees the actual situation, that which had been possessed solely by the Folk of Allah. . . .

When death is made present for the Tribe, they necessarily witness twelve forms. They may witness all of them or some of them, without any escape from this. The forms the person witnesses include the form of his practice, the form of his knowledge, the form of his station, the form of his state, the form of his messenger, the form of the angel, the form of one of the names of the acts, the form of one of the names of the attributes, the form of one of the names of the descriptions, the form of one of the names of incomparability, and the form of one of the names of the Essence. . . .

All of these are waystations of meanings (*maʿānī*), but when meanings are embodied and become manifest in shapes and measures, they assume forms, since witnessing takes place through sight. The imaginal, *barzakhī* presence determines this property. Death and sleep share in that into which meanings pass. . . .

Among the Tribe is the man who has a belief without knowledge, but the knotting of his belief conforms to knowledge of the actual situation. He believes concerning God what is believed by the learned master, but he believes it by following the authority of his teacher, one of the knowers of God. What he believes must necessarily become imaginalized, since he does not have the power to disengage it from imagination. This takes place when death is made present, since this is a state which gazes upon the presence of sound imagination into which no doubt enters. This is not the imagination which is a human faculty located in the front of the brain. On the contrary, this is imagination from the outside, like Gabriel in the form of Diḥya.[15] It is an independent and sound ontological presence which possesses embodied forms worn by meanings and spirits. This person will have a degree here that accords with what he believed. (II 295.21, 296.15)

Whenever Ibn al-ʿArabī discusses belief, he has in view the final outcome of belief, at the Resurrection and beyond. Belief determines human becoming in the next world, so all our effort needs to be directed toward putting it in correct order so that it will yield felicity. But more specifically, Ibn al-ʿArabī wants to clarify the position of the great gnostics and the nature of their unique knowledge of the Divine Reality, a knowledge which conforms to God's actual situation. They alone know God as He is, as combining incomparability and similarity, nondelimitation and delimitation.

No individual can escape having a belief concerning his Lord. Through it he resorts to Him and seeks Him. When the Real discloses Himself to him in his belief, he recognizes and acknowledges Him. But if He discloses Himself to him in other than his belief, he denies Him and seeks refuge from Him, thus displaying discourtesy toward Him in the actual situation, though he himself supposes that he has shown courtesy.

No believer believes in any God other than what he has made in himself, for the God of beliefs is made. The believers see nothing but themselves and what they have made within themselves. So consider: The levels of mankind in knowledge of God correspond exactly to their levels in vision of Him on the Day of Resurrection. I have told you the cause which brings this about.

Beware of becoming delimited by a specific knotting and disbelieving in everything else, lest great good escape you. Or rather, knowledge of the situation as it actually is in itself will escape you. Be in yourself a hyle for the forms of all beliefs, for God is wider and more tremendous than that He should be constricted by one knotting rather than another. For He says, "Whithersoever you turn, there is the Face of God" (2:115). He did not mention one place rather than another; and He said that the "face" of God is there, and the face of a thing is its reality. Through that He alerted the hearts of the gnostics, lest they busy themselves with the accidental affairs of the life of this world instead of keeping the like of this in mind. For the servant does not know in which breath he will be taken. He may be taken in the time of heedlessness, and he would not be equal to him who is taken in the time of presence. (*Fuṣūṣ* 113)

The Men are those who concur with the belief of every believer in respect of that which has conveyed it to him, taught it, and established it. On the Day of Visitation[16] the Men will see their Lord with the eye of every belief.

He who counsels his own soul should investigate, during his life in this world, all doctrines (*maqāla*) concerning God. He should learn from whence each possessor of a doctrine affirms the validity of his doctrine. Once its validity has been affirmed for him in the specific mode in which it is correct for him who holds it, then he should support it in the case of him who believes in it. He should not deny it or reject it, for he will gather its fruit on the Day of Visitation, whatever that belief might be. This is the all-embracing knowledge of God.

The root which shows the soundness of what we have said is the fact that every observer (*nāẓir*) of God is under the controlling property of one of the names of God. That name discloses itself to him and gives to him a specific belief through its self-disclosure, such that he is unaware. The divine names all possess a sound ascription to God. Hence his vision of God in each belief with all the diversity is sound; there is nothing of error within it. This is given to him by the most complete unveiling. . . .

So turn your attention to what we have mentioned and put it into practice! Then you will give the Divinity its due and you will be one of those who are fair toward their Lord in knowledge of Him. For God is exalted high above entering under delimitation. He cannot be tied down by one form rather than another. From here you will come to know the all-inclusiveness of felicity for God's creatures, and the all-embracingness of the mercy which embraces everything. (II 85.10,20)

20. SEEING WITH TWO EYES

God is One, which is to say that everything other than God is two or more. Absolute and nondelimited Oneness belongs to the Essence alone. But as soon as we speak of God in terms of His attributes, then we have in view God as Divinity—as Creator, Provider, Sustainer. We have to draw a real distinction between the Essence and the Divinity, between the Divinity and the cosmos, and among the many divine names. We are faced with plurality wherever we look, though not necessarily an ontological plurality, since there is only One Being. Hence Ibn al-ʿArabī, known as the great expositor of "Unity," devotes most of his attention to affirming the reality of multiplicity and explaining its relationship to the Oneness of God. But this, in fact, is the meaning of *tawḥīd*. As long as anything other than the Essence is envisaged, the term *tawḥīd* requires an affirmation of Oneness, and affirmation in turn demands duality: one who affirms and something affirmed.

Duality goes back to the Essence and the "other" (*al-ghayr*). God in His Essence is absolutely one from every point of view. But as soon as this is said, someone has said it, so in effect the reality of the other has also been affirmed. When we admit that there is a cosmos, we have to speak in terms of God and the cosmos, and here we dwell on the level of multiplicity. "There is no god but God" means that the Essence alone is one in every respect; if man is envisaged in the relationship, duality is affirmed. As Ibn al-ʿArabī remarks,

The Higher Plenum dispute only in respect to the Natural locus of manifestation within which they become manifest, as, for example, Gabriel, who became manifest in the form of Diḥya. Dispute takes place when they become manifest within the luminous, material frames (*al-hayākil al-nūriyyat al-māddiyya*), and these are the lights which the senses perceive, since the senses can only perceive the angels in elemental substrata of Nature.[1] However, when they become disengaged from these frames, there is no dispute and no quarrel, since there is no composition.

Whenever you say "two," dispute takes place. "Were there gods in heaven and earth other than Allah, the heaven and the earth would surely be corrupted" (21:22). Oneness in every respect is the perfection which accepts neither decrease or increase. You have to consider it in respect of itself, not in respect of him who declares it one (*muwaḥḥid*). If oneness is identical to him who declares it one, then it is itself. But if it is not identical to him who declares it one, then it is compound. A compound oneness is not what we mean, nor is it sought by the Men. (II 93.14)

In discussing Being, Ibn al-ʿArabī affirms the Unity of God while accepting that "others" possess a certain reality, though they remain forever nonexistent. But even here, Ibn al-ʿArabī admits that the things are not absolutely nonexistent, since they are known by God. Moreover, as soon as we speak of God's knowledge, we have entered into a multiplicity of relationships. Though these relationships have no independent existence, they are real in some respect, so we can no longer speak of Absolute Unity.

The "Oneness of Being" remains always inaccessible to us, since it corresponds to knowledge of the Essence Itself. The best we can do is approximate it on various levels, and this process is known in the common language of Islam as *tawḥīd*. It should thus not appear paradoxical that a book devoted to Ibn al-ʿArabī, famous as the great spokesman for the Oneness of Being, should end not with Oneness, but with duality, which can never be escaped in our relationship with the One.

As Ibn al-ʿArabī remarks with a tinge of exasperation in a slightly different context,

> The actual situation is nothing but knower and known, lord and vassal. Existence consists of this. So let the speaker speak about what is actually provided by existence and witnessing. Let him abandon the illusions of that which he calls "rationally conceivable"! (IV 102.31)

From a certain point of view the most fundamental of all dualities is that between Nondelimited Being and absolute nothingness, though the latter cannot possibly exist except in a tenuous fashion through imagination, by "supposing the impossible" (*farḍ al-muḥāl*). To the extent imagination is able to conceive of nothingness, its image becomes a *barzakh* between Being and nothingness. It is the existent image of nothingness.

But there is a second kind of nothingness, which we have been calling "nonexistence." Though it does not exist in itself, its existence can be imagined under certain circumstances; it may possibly exist. When God conceives of nonexistence, that conception affirms the reality of the conceiving subject and the conceived object, the knower and the known, the lord and the vassal. This is the level of the divine knowledge, and the divine knowledge knows everything that can possibly exist for all eternity. Hence God's very conception of nonexistence affirms the reality of the Supreme Barzakh, Nondelimited Imagination, Infinite Knowledge, the Breath of the All-merciful, the Divine Names.

It might be said that the most fundamental of all dualities is that between the Essence and the Divinity, though these two are a single Being. The Essence is Being as such, while the Divinity is that Level in respect to which it can be said that Being imagines or knows the cosmos. Hence the Divinity is the Supreme Barzakh, standing between the Essence and the cosmos, which arises out of the imaginalization of nonexistence.

When we as rational and created beings consider the actual situation of everything that exists and does not exist, we see God in Himself, God as related to the cosmos, the cosmos, and absolute nothingness. Strictly speaking, the last does not exist on any level, not even conceptualization, since we cannot conceive of it, except as an impossibility of conception. Hence we are left with the Essence, the Divinity, and the cosmos; or Being, the Barzakh, and existence. The cosmos or existence may also be called nonexistence, since it has no existence of its own. It is nonexistent inasmuch as it remains nonmanifest in God's knowledge and existent inasmuch as it becomes manifest when God discloses Himself.

When we consider God, we look at the Essence Itself or at the Divinity. In the first case we declare that He is absolutely incomparable and unknowable, and in the second we say that He is somehow similar to the cosmos. For Ibn al-ʿArabī, this duality in our conceptualization is merely the flip side of the duality of the "combined totality" (*al-majmūʿ*): The Real (*ḥaqq*) and creation (*khalq*), that is, God in Himself and God in His self-disclosure.

The relationships which become established because of the fundamental duality that grows up out of Unity are beyond count. Each divine name indicates a point of view in respect of which the Essence can be considered in relation to the cosmos. If the Shaykh often contradicts himself in explaining the reality of multiplicity, this has to do with the fact that he considers it from a wide variety of perspectives. When these shift, so also do the conclusions he draws. But it would be a terrible distortion of his teachings to try to eliminate the various perspectives and summarize what he has to say through a single doctrine, thereby eliminating all inconsistencies: "Ibn al-ʿArabī's position on *wujūd* is x or y." Yes, and no, we have to answer. Yes, because he accepts all positions which have an ontological grounding. No, because the acceptance of one position does not mean that he rejects other positions.

The men of reason—who are generally known today as "critical thinkers" of whatever shade or school—insist upon tying and binding. They want to know exactly what the situation is, and apply all the tools of their science to discover it. Ibn al-ʿArabī replies that the situation cannot be known, since, in the last analysis, God is the situation, and God's Essence is unknowable. What we can know depends upon our perspective. There are more perspectives than there are human minds. Each perspective throws a certain light upon the situation, but none of them can be final or definitive.

In short, if we want to say that Ibn al-ʿArabī affirms x, that may be true, but that is not all he has to say about the issue. Other perspectives are admissible and valid on their own levels. We cannot pin the Shaykh down as to what his position is on important intellectual problems, such as the nature of existence, God, the things, the human soul, and so on. The closest we can come to providing a succinct expression of his teachings is "Yes and no," "He/not He," "utter bewilderment."

When all this has been said, it is still vitally important—if the Shaykh's message to his fellow human beings is to be considered—to remember that bewilderment relates to the level of theory. When you ask about the ultimate reality of things, you cannot possibly be given a straightforward answer which will be valid in all situations. On another level, Ibn al-ʿArabī deals with the human situation, the existential plight which arises in face of the supreme unknowability of God. Where do we turn? What do we do? Here the Shaykh rejects all ambiguity, since in practical terms the human task is clear. We know that the universe is infused with mercy, and we also know that mercy by its very nature seeks our felicity. It has clearly set down the roads which lead to felicity, and our only choice—if we have any aspiration to rise beyond the level of "animal man"—is to follow the road which God has revealed to us.

In the last analysis, if Ibn al-ʿArabī continually affirms the utter incapacity (*ʿajz*) of the independent human reason, this is because he wants to direct human beings toward guidance and mercy. He tells us to give up trying to understand the nature of things with our rational faculties alone, since this is impossible. Reason in any case is congenitally deformed, since it ties and binds. Return to the heart, which unties all knots and loosens all deadening constrictions. But the heart can only be found in the direction of God, and we can only go toward God through the path that He has set down before us.

Duality and the Signs of Unity

Though duality displays its properties and effects throughout existence, each property and each effect is a sign (*āya*) of God's Oneness.

> Nothing makes one thing two other than itself, whether in the sensory or intelligible realms. As for the sensory realm, Adam was made two by that

which was opened up out of his short left rib, that is, the form of Eve. He was one in his entity, then he became a pair through her, though she was none other than himself. When she was in him, it was said that he was one.

As for the intelligible realm, the Divinity is nothing other than God's Essence, but what is intelligible from "Divinity" is different from what is intelligible from the fact that He is an "Essence." So the Essence of God made the Divinity two, though each is identical with the other.

In the sensory domain Adam was made two by Eve, who derived from his essence. Then God "scattered abroad from the pair of them many men and women" (Koran 4:1) in the form of the pair. In the same way God scattered abroad, from the Essence of God and the fact that He is the God of the cosmos, [many things] upon the form of these two intelligible things [the Essence and the Divinity]. Hence the cosmos emerged upon the form of That which brings about effects and That in which effects are displayed, for the sake of propagation (*tawālud*), that is, the propagation of the parts of the cosmos.

The Divinity is a property of the Essence. Through the Divinity the Essence has the property of bringing the cosmos into existence. Since the Essence prefers the property of bringing the cosmos into existence, the cosmos becomes manifest upon the form of that which brings it into existence. Hence it is divided into that which exercises effects and that within which effects are displayed, as in fact happens within the sensory domain. God did not create from Adam and Eve an earth, a heaven, a mountain, or anything other than their own kind. He created from them only their likes in form and property. . . .

Since the root is One and nothing made Him two except Himself, and since manyness only became manifest from His Entity, everything in the cosmos possesses a sign denoting the fact that He is One.

The whole of the cosmos is body and spirit, and through the two of these, existence is configured. The cosmos is to the Real as the body is to the spirit. Just as the spirit is not known except through the body [so also the Real is not known except through the cosmos]: When we look at the body and we see that its form subsists, but properties that we had been witnessing—that is, the perception of sensory things and meanings—disappear from the body and its form, then we know that beyond the manifest body there is another meaning which bestows the properties of the perceptions within it. We name that meaning the "spirit" of this body.

In the same way, we know that there is something that moves us or keeps us still, exercising its ruling properties within us as it wills, only when we look at our own souls. Then, when we know our souls, we know our Lord, like two exactly similar things. That is why the Prophet reported in the revelation through his words, "He who knows his soul knows his Lord," and why God sent down the report, "We shall show them Our signs upon the horizons and in themselves, until it is clear to them that He is the Real" (41:53), for the cosmos became manifest from God only in the form of the actual situation. (III 314.22)

Cosmologically speaking, duality begins with the First Intellect, the active pole of spiritual and intelligible existence, which is paired with the Universal Soul, the receptive pole. On a lower level, God sits upon the "Throne" and lets down His two feet, which rest upon the "Footstool." Though this topic deserves a thorough and detailed explication in another context, it is not inappropriate to recall here that these cosmic dualities all go back to the Essence and the Divinity, or to the declaration of incomparability and the affirmation of similarity.

Since the Footstool is the place of the two feet, it allows for only two abodes in the next world, the Fire and the Garden. Through the two feet, God produces two celestial spheres, the sphere of the constellations (*falak al-burūj*) and the sphere of the moon's mansions (*falak al-manāzil*), the latter of which is the earth of the Garden. These two will remain in the next world, while the order of everything below the sphere of the mansions will be destroyed. Its form will be changed and the light of the stars will disappear, just as God has said, "Upon the day the earth shall be changed into other than the earth, and the heavens" (14:48). He also says, "When the stars shall be extinguished" (77:8). But He means by "heavens" only that which is well-known as the heavens: the seven heavens specifically. As for the concave interior surface of the sphere of the mansions, that is the roof of the Fire.

Through the act of these two feet within this celestial sphere, there became manifest within the cosmos two of every kind, by the ordainment of the Inaccessible. This goes back to the existence of Nature's two active principles,[2] the two faculties of the Soul, the two faces of the Intellect, the two letters of the divine word "Be!" [*kun*, written *k.n.* in Arabic], and the two divine attributes in "Nothing is like Him"—which is one attribute—"and He is the Hearing, the Seeing" (42:11), which is the other attribute.

He who declares His incomparability does so on the basis of "Nothing is like Him," while he who declares His similarity does so on the basis of "He is the Hearing, the Seeing." Here there is an Unseen (*ghayb*) and a visible (*shahāda*). The unseen is incomparability, and the visible is similarity. So understand, if you can understand!

From here you will know the reality which exercised its governing property over the dualists—who are the Manichaeans—until they associated others with God. Though they went to great lengths and exerted themselves to the utmost in their rational consideration, they were not able to come out of this duality to the One Entity, which is nothing but God. "And he who calls upon another god with God has no proof for that" (23:117), so he will not be excused. (II 439.17)

God's two feet are the cosmic manifestation of the divine attributes of majesty (*jalāl*) and beauty (*jamāl*), which in turn go back to incomparability and similarity. Inasmuch as God is totally other, He produces in us feelings of awe (*hayba*) through His majesty, transcendence, power, inaccessibility, tremendousness, magnificence, overbearingness, and so on. But inasmuch as He is similar to us, He makes us feel intimate (*uns*) with Him through His beauty, gentleness, mercy, forgiveness, kindness, etc.

God—who is the All-merciful, none other—made the Throne the locus for the Unity of the Word (*aḥadiyyat al-kalima*). He created the Footstool, and the Word became divided into two commands, that He might create two of each kind. Then one of the two will be qualified by highness and the other by lowness, one by activity (*fiʿl*) and the other by receptivity (*infiʿāl*). Hence the concept of even numbers (*shafʿiyya*) became manifest from the Footstool in actuality, while it existed potentially within the One Word. Thereby it is known that the First Existent Being, though It is One in Entity in respect to Its Essence, also possesses the property of relationship with the cosmos that becomes manifest from It. Hence It is an Ontological Essence and a relationship. This is the root of all evenness in the cosmos.

There must also be an interconnecting factor (*rābiṭ*) which is conceived of between the Essence and the relationship, so that the Essence can accept this relationship. Hence oddness (*fardiyya*) becomes manifest through the concept of the interconnecting factor, since "three" is the first of the odd numbers[3] . . . , and these go on to infinity. And evenness, which is called "two," is the first of the pairs (*zawj*) among the numbers, and these also go on to infinity.

There is no even number which is not made odd by "one," and thus is found the oddness of that even number. And there is no odd number which is not made even by "one," and thus is found the evenness of that odd number. The factor which makes the odd even and the even odd is the Independent, which determines properties, but which is not determined by any properties. It has no need or poverty, and everything is poor toward It and in need of It.

The two feet were placed in the Footstool, and each foot rested in a place different from the place of the other. . . . The one place is named "Gehenna" and the other is named "Garden." There is no place after these two where the feet come to rest. These feet take replenishment only from the Root which they manifest, and that is the All-merciful. Hence they give nothing but mercy, for the property of the final end goes back to the root. . . .

[The Prophet said, "The Fire will continue to say, 'Are there any more'] until the Overbearing places His foot within it."[4] This is one of the two feet which are in the Footstool. The other foot, whose resting place is the Garden, is mentioned in His words, "Give thou good tidings to the faithful, that they have a foot of firmness with their Lord" (10:2). Hence the name "Lord" is with these, while the "Overbearing" is with the others, since the Fire is an abode of inaccessibility, overbearingness, and awe, while the Garden is an abode of beauty, intimacy, and the gentle divine descent. . . .

Through the two feet God gives wealth and poverty, through them "He makes to die and makes to live" (53:44), through them He fills with inhabitants or depopulates, through them "He creates the two kinds, male and female" (53:45), through them He abases and exalts, gives and withholds, harms and benefits. Were it not for these two, nothing would happen in the cosmos.

Were it not for the two feet, no one in the cosmos would associate others with God (*shirk*). For the two feet share properties in the cosmos. Each of them has both an abode in which it exercises governing control and certain people over whom it exercises governing control as God wills. . . .

The two feet consist of the contrariety of the divine names, such as the First and the Last, the Manifest and the Nonmanifest. Then the like of this becomes manifest from them in the cosmos: the world of the unseen and the world of the visible, majesty and beauty, nearness and distance, awe and intimacy, gathering and dispersion, curtaining and disclosure, absence and presence, contraction and expansion, this world and the next world, the Garden and the Fire.

In the same way, through "one," every object of knowledge possesses a unity through which it is distinguished from everything else. Likewise, oddness, which is the number "three," brings about the manifestation of the property of the two sides and the middle, which is the *barzakh*, the thing between the two, like the hot, the cold, and the lukewarm.

From oddness the odd numbers become manifest and from "two" the even numbers. Each number must be either even or odd, and so on ad infinitum. Through the power of the one the properties of the numbers become manifest, and the property belongs to "God, the One, the All-subjugating" (12:39, etc.). Were He not named by contrary names, He would not have been named "All-subjugating"—since it is impossible for any created thing to stand up to Him. Hence He is only "All-subjugating" in respect of the fact that He is named by contrary names. None stands up to Him but He, for He is the Exalter and the Abaser, and there occurs between the two names the properties of subjugator and subjugated, since only one of the two properties becomes manifest in the locus. (III 462.11, 463.12,27)

The Possessor of Two Eyes

Wherever the gnostic looks, he sees the One God, but, dwelling as he does in manyness, he sees Him from two points of view. On the one hand, he witnesses God as incomparable. Everything he sees is but a sign saying, "God is not this." On the other hand, he witnesses Him as similar. Everything he sees says, "God is like this; God is disclosing Himself in this; God is not other than this; God is this."

As the insight of the spiritual traveler is gradually illuminated by the light of faith and unveiling, he comes to see God from various perspectives, all of which go back to incomparability or similarity. On every level, he sees God as one or the other; rarely does he see Him as both. Only the perfect gnostics transcend the limitations of vision and see God with every eye and in every object of vision. When the gnostic attains this highest station, he deserves to be called the "Possessor of the Two Eyes" (*dhu'l-ʿaynayn*).

Every human being possesses two eyes to some degree, since everyone sees God as present and absent, whether he knows it or not. And everyone is included in the "man" to which the pronoun goes back in the Koranic verse, "Have We not appointed for him two eyes . . ., and guided him on the two highways?" (90:8–10). Ontologically speaking, one eye sees Being and the other perceives nothingness. Through the two eyes working together, man perceives that he himself and the cosmos are He/not He.

> The Real is sheer Light, while the impossible (*al-muḥāl*) is sheer darkness (*ẓulma*). Darkness never turns into light, nor does light turn into darkness. Creation is the Barzakh between Light and darkness. In its essence it is qualified neither by darkness nor by light, since it is the Barzakh and the Middle (*al-wasaṭ*) which has a property from each of its two sides. That is why He appointed for man two eyes and guided him on the two highways, since he exists between the two paths. Through one eye and one path he accepts light and looks upon it in the measure of his preparedness. Through the other eye and the other path he looks upon darkness and turns toward it.
>
> In himself, man is neither light nor darkness, since he is neither existent nor nonexistent. He is the firm impediment which prevents sheer light from dispelling darkness, and he prevents sheer darkness from taking away sheer light. He receives the two sides through his own essence, and he acquires, through this reception, that light whereby he is described as "existent" and that darkness whereby he is described as "nonexistent." So he shares in both sides and protects both sides. (III 274.28)
>
> Everything manifest in the cosmos is an imaginal, engendered form that conforms to a divine form. For He discloses Himself to the cosmos only in accordance with that which corresponds (*munāsaba*) to the cosmos—in the entity of an immutable substance, just as man is immutable in respect of his substance. Thus you see the immutable through the immutable, and that is "unseen" in respect to you and Him. You see the manifest through the manifest, and that is the "witnessed, the witnesser, and the witnessing" in respect to you and Him.
>
> Just as you perceive Him, you perceive your own essence. However, in every form you are known to be you, not other than you. Exactly in the same way, you know that Zayd is Zayd and no one else, even though he undergoes variation in his qualities, such as shame and fear, illness and health, satisfaction and wrath, and every state through which he fluctuates. Hence we say that so-and-so has changed from state to state and from form to form. Were it not for the fact that this is the situation, we would not know him once his state changed and we would say that he no longer exists.
>
> Hence we come to know that there are two eyes, as God said: "Have We not appointed for him two eyes?" (90:8). One eye is that through which he who undergoes transmutation is perceived, while the other eye is that through which the transmutation itself is perceived. These are two different paths which God has made clear to the Possessor of Two Eyes, as He said, "And guided him on the two highways" (90:10), that is, made clear for him the two paths. . . .
>
> Each eye has a path. So know whom you see and what you see. For this reason it is correct that, "You did not throw when you threw, but God threw" (8:17). The eye through which you perceive that the throwing belongs to God is different from the eye through which you perceive that the throwing belongs to Muḥammad. So know that you have two eyes, if you possess knowledge. Then you will know for certain that the thrower is God in the corporeal form of Muḥammad. Imaginalization and assuming imaginal forms is nothing but this. . . .
>
> This is the station of "God created Adam upon His own form." When someone makes something upon his own form, that thing is identical to the form, so it is it/not it. Hence it is correct to say, "You did not throw when you threw, but God threw," for the root of everything which became manifest from that form derives from Him upon whose form it is. (III 470.26, 471.12)

The eye which looks in the direction of the nonmanifest declares God's incomparability and places all emphasis upon His Unity, since it does not perceive the multiplicity of forms. The eye which looks in the direction of the manifest acknowledges the reality of manyness and declares His similarity, since it sees all things as God's self-disclosures. The Koran's fundamental teaching about God is that He is both incomparable and similar, so the very names of the Holy Book allude to this fact. Thus, as we have already seen, it is called both *qur'ān* or "that which brings together" and *furqān* or "that which differentiates." Ibn al-ʿArabī frequently alludes to the visions of the two eyes by these names. In the following, he mentions both, then describes his own experience of the unveiling of real differentiation in the cosmos. He points to the danger of seeing in one way but not the other, since those who see only *furqān* without *qur'ān* associate other gods with God. Though he does not mention them here, those who see *qur'ān* without *furqān* deny the reality of multiplicity and the ranking of the cosmos in degrees of excellence (*tafāḍul*). They are those deviated "esotericists" (*al-bāṭiniyya*) who declare that only the inward reality is true, thereby negating the necessity of the discernment between good and evil and the universal applicability of the revealed Law.

At the beginning of the passage, Ibn al-ʿArabī mentions the hadith, "There is no verse of the Koran which does not have an outward sense (*ẓahr*), an inward sense (*baṭn*), a limit (*ḥadd*), and a place to which one may ascend (*muṭṭalaʿ*)."[5] The "place to which one may ascend" is the face of God present in every existent thing. "When a person ascends, his eye does not fall upon the things, but only upon the face of God" (II 177.4).

> He who stops with the Koran inasmuch as it is a *qur'ān* has but a single eye which unifies all things. But when a person stops with it inasmuch as it is a totality of things brought together, then for him it is a *furqān*. It is he who witnesses the outward sense, the inward sense, the limit, and the place of ascent. For the Prophet said, "There is no verse of the Koran which does not have an outward sense, an inward sense, a limit, and a place to which one may ascend." But the first person does not say this, since his tasting is different.
>
> When we tasted this latter situation, we saw the Koranic descent as a *furqān*. Then we said: This is lawful (*ḥalāl*), that is unlawful (*ḥarām*), and this is indifferent (*mubāḥ*). The drinking places have become variegated and the religions diverse. The levels have been distinguished, the divine names and the engendered effects have become manifest, and the names and the gods have become many in the cosmos. People worship angels, stars, Nature, the elements, animals, plants, minerals, human beings, and jinn. So much is this the case that when the One presented them with His Oneness, they said, "What, has he made the gods One God? This is indeed a marvelous thing" (38:5). But in reality, one should not marvel at him who declares His Oneness, but at him who declares His manyness without proof or demonstration. That is why God said, "And he who calls upon another god with God has no proof for that" (23:117). . . .
>
> We have said that there is no effect in the cosmos which is not supported by a divine reality. So from whence do the gods become many? From the divine realities. Hence you should know that this derives from the names. For God was expansive with the names: He said, "Worship Allah" (4:36), "Fear Allah, your Lord" (65:1), "Prostrate yourselves to the All-merciful" (25:6). And He said, "Call upon Allah or call upon the All-merciful; whichever," that is Allah or the All-merciful, "you call upon, to Him belong the most beautiful names" (17:110). This made the situation more ambiguous for the people, since He did not say, "Call upon Allah or call upon the All-merciful; whichever you call upon, the Entity is One, and these two names belong to It." That would be the text which would remove the difficulty. God only left this difficulty as a mercy for those who associate others with Him, the people of rational consideration—those who associate others with

Him on the basis of obfuscation. (III 94.16)

Being With God Wherever You Are

Man has no access to the domain of Absolute Unity, that station in which God is One in every respect and no "other" can be conceived or imagined. The Essence remains inaccessible and unknowable to every created thing always and forever. God in His incomparability is absolutely incomparable. But in any case, that is not the practical concern of the traveler, since his goal is to annihilate all claims to independence and to become the perfect servant. The traveler strives to "return" to his own root, which is nonexistence, the station of "God is, and nothing is with Him." This "nothing" (*lā shay'*) as Ibn al-ʿArabī often points out, is precisely the immutable entity within the knowledge of God. Here the servant is one with God, since there can be no claims to any ontological two-ness; there is but One Being. Yet, from a certain point of view, the "reality" of the servant—that is, his entity—must still be affirmed, so this is the station of the Unity of Manyness (*aḥadiyyat al-kathra*), not the Unity of the One (*aḥadiyyat al-aḥad*), which belongs only to the Essence.

Having retired to the house of his own nothingness, the servant is totally at the bidding of his Lord, since he has nothing of his own. Here there is no servant, only the self-disclosure of God colored and shaped by the properties of the servant's entity. We see a servant like ourselves, but he has no self of his own and he witnesses nothing but God, inwardly and outwardly. God is his hearing and sight, his foot and his hand, and God alone appears to him in the guise of the others.

In order to achieve the perfection of servanthood, man must be "with" God, just as God is with him. It is true that God is with all things, but the things are not with God. This is the difficulty to which the traveler has addressed himself.

That about which it is said, "God is, and nothing is with Him," is the Divinity, not the Essence. In speaking of knowledge of God every property which is affirmed as belonging to the Essence belongs to the Divinity, which is relationships, attributions, and negations. Manyness belongs to these relationships, not to the Entity. (I 41.27)

The cosmos is never with God, whether it is qualified by existence or nonexistence. But it is correctly said that God, the Necessary Being, is with the cosmos, whether it is nonexistent or existent. (II 56.28)

The word "is" (*kān*) [in the saying, "God is, and nothing is with Him"] derives from "existence" (*kawn*), which is identical with *wujūd*. So the Prophet may as well have said, "God is Existent, and nothing is with Him in His Being." (II 692.25)

No one is with the Real in the respect that the Real belongs to Himself. A person is only with the Real in respect of that in which the Real has placed him. (II 507.12)

God said, "He is with you wherever you are" (57:4). He did not say, "And you are with Him," since the manner in which He accompanies us is unknown. He knows how He accompanies us, but we do not know how He accompanies us. So withness is affirmed for Him in relation to us, but it is negated from us in relation to Him. (II 582.10)

God says, "No indeed, but on that day they will be veiled from their Lord!" (Koran 83:15). The Prophet said, "God has seventy veils of light and darkness; were He to remove them, the glories of His Face would burn away everything perceived by the sight of His creatures." Look how subtle these veils are, and how hidden, for God says, "We are nearer to him than the jugular vein" (50:16), while these veils exist, preventing us from seeing Him in this mighty nearness. . . .

After examination, classification, and what has been given by the Eternal Speech, we see only that Thou art Thyself the veils. That is why the veils are also veiled and we do not see them, though they are light and darkness. They are what Thou hast named Thyself, the "Manifest" and the "Nonmanifest." . . . So Thou art the veil. We are veiled from Thee only through Thee, and Thou art veiled from us only through Thy manifestation. However, we do not recognize Thee, since we seek Thee from Thy name, just as we look for a king by his name and his attribute, even if he should be with us, but not manifest in that name and that attribute.

God has a manifestation through His Essence, so He talks to us and we talk to Him. He witnesses us and we witness Him. He recognizes us, but we do not recognize Him. This is the strongest proof that His attributes are negative, not positive. If they were positive, He would make them manifest when He became manifest in His Essence. But we do not recognize that He is He until He gives us knowledge, so we follow His authority in knowledge. Were His attributes positive, they would be identical with His Essence, and we would recognize Him through the very thing that we witness. But such is not the case. (II 159.11,27)

God accompanies us in every state in which we are, but we do not accompany Him except through halting at His bounds. So in reality, we accompany only His rulings (*aḥkām*), not Him, since He is with us, but we are not with Him. For He knows us, but we do not know Him. (II 287.7)

I saw in an Incident a spring of fresh milk. I had never seen milk so white and pleasant. I entered into it until it reached my breasts, while it was gushing forth, and I marveled at that. I heard a strange divine speech saying, "He who prostrates himself to other than God by God's command seeking nearness to God and obeying God will be felicitous and attain deliverance, but he who prostrates himself to other than God without God's command seeking nearness will be wretched. God says, 'The places of prostration belong to God; so call not upon anyone with God' (72:18)."

God is with the creatures, but the creatures are not with God. For He knows them, and "He is with" them "wherever" they "are" (57:4), within the confines of their places, their times, and their states. But the creatures are not with Him—majestic indeed is His majesty! For no creature knows Him that it should be with Him. Hence, he who calls upon God with the creatures is not like him who calls upon the creatures with God. "So call not upon anyone with God" (72:18).

In reality, there can be no prostration to other than God, except in respect to the fact that God is with the creatures wherever they are. Hence we neither know Him nor find Him except along with the creatures. In reality prostration is to God described by withness with the creatures. That is why the Law set down the kibla, as the Prophet said, "God is in the kibla of him who performs the prayer." The kibla is not God, but God is in it. He commanded us to prostrate ourselves to it because God is in it and with it.

He who sees the creature with his sight has seen the Real with his insight, without qualifications. But he should not prostrate himself when he sees that, unless he is commanded to do so. Then his prostration will be to God, though in the sensory domain it can never take place except to other than God, since one cannot prostrate himself to God. For God "encompasses everything" (41:54), so the relationship of all the directions to the Real, and of the Real to them, is the same. (III 376.22)

The Real is perpetually in a state of "union" (*waṣl*) with engendered existence. Through this He is a god. This is indicated by His words, "He is with you wherever you are" (57:4), that is, in whatever state you have in nonexistence, existence, and all qualities. Such is the actual situation.

What takes place for the people of solicitude, the Folk of Allah, is that God gives them vision and unveils their insights until they witness this withness. This—that is, the gnostic's witnessing—is what is called "union." So the gnostic has become joined (*ittiṣāl*) to witnessing the actual situation. Then this union cannot turn into separation (*faṣl*), just as knowledge cannot turn into ignorance. (II 480.12)

God says, "We are nearer to him than the jugular vein" (50:16), thereby describing Himself as being near to His servants. But what is desired from "nearness" (*qurb*) is that it be the attribute of the servant. The servant should be qualified as being near to the Real exactly as the Real is qualified as being near to him. He says, "He is with you wherever you are" (57:4). The Men seek to be with the Real forever in whatever form He discloses Himself. He never ceases disclosing Himself in the forms of His servants continuously, so the servant is with Him wherever He discloses Himself continuously. In the same way, the servant always has a "whereness" (*ayniyya*), and God is with him "wherever" he is continuously. Hence the whereness of the Real is the form of that in which He discloses Himself. The gnostics never cease witnessing nearness continuously, since they never cease witnessing forms within themselves and outside of themselves, and that is nothing but the self-disclosure of the Real. (II 558.27).

Two Perfections

Perfect man possesses two kinds of perfection, one related to his essential reality as a form of God, and the other to the various attributes and qualities which he manifests in his specific functions in this world and the next. In respect of the first, "essential" (*dhātī*) perfection, all perfect men are identical and one with God, and one might speak of "the Perfect Man" as a single reality. In respect to the second, "accidental" (*ʿaraḍī*) perfection, each perfect man has a specific function to play in the cosmic hierarchy, and hence there are many "perfect men" (*kummal*). In the first respect the inward reality of the perfect men is God as the Nonmanifest. In the second respect the perfect men are God as the Manifest, the Divine Form disclosed within the cosmos. From the second point of view, each perfect man is unique, since "Self-disclosure never repeats itself." In the next world, the perfect men dwell with God in respect of the essential perfection, while at the same time they populate various abodes of paradise in respect of the accidental perfection. Ibn al-ʿArabī sometimes calls the essential perfection that of servanthood (*ʿubūdiyya*) and the accidental perfection that of manliness (*rajūliyya*). The first manifests incomparability, the second similarity.

The essential perfection, which is different from the perfection of manliness, is that no lordliness (*rabbāniyya*) whatsoever should contaminate the fact that perfect man is a servant. Hence he is an existence while nonexistent, an affirmation while negated. It was for this that the Real brought him into existence.

The perfection of manliness is accidental, while the perfection of servanthood is essential. Between the two stations lies what lies between the two perfections. The degrees of the waystations of these two perfections are known to us wherever they might be.

The degree of the essential perfection is in the Self of the Real, while the degrees of accidental perfection are in the Gardens. The perfect men possess light, and they possess wages. God says, "[They are the just men and the witnesses in their Lord's sight;[they have their wage," that is, in respect of their accidental perfection and every accidental affair that requires a wage, "and they have their light" (57:19), in respect of their essential perfection. "God is the light of the heavens and the earth" (24:35), while the messengers—who are the perfect, without any dispute—all say, "My wage falls only on God" (10:72 etc.), for their station gives a wage, and necessarily so.

Ranking according to excellence (*tafāḍul*) takes place in accidental perfection, but not in essential perfection. God says, "Those messengers—some We have ranked in excellence above others" (2: 253). He also says, "They are degrees with God" (3:163). He does not say, "They have degrees with God." So He made them identical with the degrees, since they are identical with essential perfection, while through accidental perfection they possess degrees in the Garden. So know this!

May God place us among those who bring together the two perfections! And if He should deprive us of bringing them together, may He place us among the people of essential perfection through His kindness and generosity! (II 588.7)

Perfect man's essential perfection has to do with the fact that he manifests God Himself without taking any specific property or name into account. His accidental perfection appears when he manifests one or more of the divine names that are embraced by the all-comprehensive name Allah. Then he appears in the guise of God's generosity or knowledge or vengeance or some other attribute. The second situation distinguishes the perfect men from each other, since each manifests a unique commingling of the properties of the divine names. One perfect man may display greater knowledge, but less strength. Another may manifest more intense vengeance and weaker forgiveness. These accidental qualities depend upon the situation of the cosmos into which perfect man is placed. His activity is always appropriate to the cosmic context and historical circumstances—he is, after all, the perfect representative of God, His chosen vicegerent—but the nature of this activity will vary in accordance with the spatiotemporal situation. Ibn al-ʿArabī makes these points in continuing his discussion of the accidental perfection known as "manliness." Note that he distinguishes here between the perfection of the Essence, which pertains to God's incomparability, and the perfection of the Divinity, which pertains to His similarity through the names. He also brings in the distinction between the engendering command and the prescriptive command.

> The divine opening that is connected to engendered existence—e.g., help against enemies and vanquishing them, mercy and tenderness toward friends—is the result of manliness, nothing else. Once this station is achieved and its plane is perfected, God calls the servant in his inmost consciousness, a call from His own perfection to the servant's essential perfection. Then the servant declares the Essence of Him who brought him into existence incomparable with accidental perfection, which is the divine perfection. For in actuality, the divine perfection is found in the penetration of power into the objects of power, desire into the objects of desire, and the manifestation of the properties of the divine names. The essential perfection possessed by the Essence is absolute independence from all this.
>
> In this station the servant does not witness the Essence of Him who brought him into existence in the respect that He is qualified by Divinity. His locus of witnessing is His independence from the engendered effects (*al-āthār al-kawniyya*) which belong rightfully to the Divinity. The servant is poor toward the Essence with an essential poverty. In his worship he possesses an essential worship without any command (*amr*) joined to it, since a command is connected to accidental things, not the essential. It is not said to the servant, "Be a servant!", since he is a servant in his every essence. It is only said to him, "Do such and such a work, O servant!" This work is an accidental command, and the servant is commanded for the sake of the work. He may do the work or he may not. . . .
>
> In this station the servant declares the incomparability of the Essence of Him who brought him into existence with a praise which is appropriate to essential perfection. Then, because he also possesses accidental perfection—the perfection of manliness—he praises Him with a praise worthy of God, accident for accident, but not by way of declaring incomparability, since the way of declaring incomparability belongs only to the Essence. God says, "Nothing is like Him" because of the perfection of the Essence, and "He is the Hearing, the Seeing" (42:11) because of the perfection of the Divinity, which demands both the heard and the seen. Every demander calls for something demanded, and that which calls for something lacks the states of the servant [for which it calls]. But "God is Independent, Praiseworthy" (64:1), so the tongue of courtesy requires that it be said that He demands you for you, not for Himself. (II 588.27)

In his dual perfection, perfect man perceives God with two eyes. Through one he sees Him as incomparable, through the other as similar. This is the perfection of knowledge.

Man possesses an eminence (*sharaf*) over everything in the heaven and earth. He is God's sought-after goal among the existent things, since it is he whom God has taken as a locus of self-disclosure. I mean by "man" perfect man, since he is perfect only through God's form. In the same way a mirror, though complete in creation, is only perfect through the disclosure within it of the form of the looker. That is the "level" of the mirror, and the level is the goal. In the same way the Divinity is complete through the names which it demands from the divine thralls. So It lacks nothing. But Its perfection—I mean the level of which It is worthy—is independence from the worlds. Hence It possesses nondelimited perfection through independence from the worlds.

God willed to give His perfection its due (*ḥaqq*) and He wills this always. He created the cosmos to glorify Him in praise, not for anything else. The glorification is God's, while the glorifier does not possess the state of witnessing, since it is annihilated (*fanā'*) from the witnessing. But the cosmos does not lag in glorification for the blink of an eye, since its glorification is inherent (*dhātī*), like the breathing of a breather. This shows that the cosmos never ceases being veiled and it seeks witnessing through that glorification.

[Since God willed to give perfection its due,] He created perfect man upon His own form and gave news to the angels about his level. He told them that he is the vicegerent in the cosmos and that his home is the earth. He appointed the earth his abode, since He created him from it. He made the Higher Plenum busy with him in heaven and earth, since "He subjected" to him "what is in the heavens and what is in the earth, all together, for him" (Koran 45:12), that is, for his sake. Then God veiled Himself, for the deputy (*nā'ib*) has no property when He who has made him vicegerent is manifest. So "He is veiled from insights, just as He is veiled from sight": The Messenger of God, addressing people who resembled man in sensory form but who stood below the level of perfection, said, "God is veiled from insights just as He is veiled from sight; the Higher Plenum seeks Him just as you yourselves seek Him."[6] "Sight perceives Him not" (Koran 6:103), and in the same way, insights perceive Him not. "Insights" are rational faculties, which perceive Him not with their reflections, so they are incapable of reaching and winning the object they seek.

"And He taught Adam the names, all of them" (2:31). He commanded him to teach the Higher Plenum. He commanded everything[7] in the heavens and the earth to look after that which was appropriate for this deputy, since He subjected to him everything in the heavens and the earth, even that which is called "man" in respect of his completeness, not in respect of his perfection. As long as this kind which shares the name "man" with perfect man does not attain to perfection, he is one of those subjected to perfect man, who joins Him who is Independent of the worlds through his perfection. He alone—I mean perfect man—worships his Lord who is Independent of him. Perfect man's perfection is that his Lord is not without need for him, since there is no one who worships Him outside the mode of glorification but perfect man, since he receives self-disclosure constantly, and the property of witnessing never leaves him. Hence he is the most perfect of existent things in knowledge of God and the most constant of them in witnessing.

Perfect man has two visions (*naẓar*) of the Real, which is why He appointed for him two eyes. With one eye he looks upon Him in respect to the fact that He is Independent of the worlds. So he sees Him neither in any thing nor in himself. Through the other eye he looks upon Him in respect of His name All-merciful, which seeks the cosmos and is sought by the cosmos. He sees His Being permeating all things. Through the vision of this eye he is poor toward everything in respect to the fact that the things are the names of God, not in respect of their own entities. Hence, none is poorer toward the cosmos than perfect man, since he witnesses it subjected to himself. He knows that if he did not need the cosmos, those things that are subjected to him would not have been subjected to him. He knows in himself that he is more in need of the cosmos than the cosmos is in need of him. His all-inclusive poverty stands in the station of the all-inclusive divine Independence. In respect of poverty, he takes up a position in the cosmos like the position of the Real in respect to the divine names, which demand the displaying of effects in the cosmos. He only becomes manifest in his poverty by the manifestation of the names of the Real.

Perfect man is the Real in his independence from the cosmos, since the cosmos has been subjected for his sake by the divine names that display their effects within it. Nothing is subjected to him except that which possesses the display of effects, without respect to the entity of the cosmos. So he is poor only toward God.

Perfect man is also the Real in his poverty toward the cosmos. He knows that God subjected the cosmos to man only to distract the things, through the subjection imposed upon them, from seeking knowledge in respect to witnessing, for that does not belong to them, since they stand below the level of perfection. Therefore perfect man manifests need for that in which the cosmos has been subjected. Thereby subjection in the cosmos grows stronger, that they may not neglect that of it which the Real commanded them to perform; for "They disobey not God in what He commands them" (66:6). By making manifest this poverty, perfect man conforms to the Real in keeping the cosmos distracted.

Hence perfect man is the Real in his poverty, like the names, and the Real in his independence, since he does not see that which is subjected to him, only that which possesses effects. In other words, he sees the divine names, not the entities of the cosmos. Hence he is poor only toward God within the entities of the cosmos, while the cosmos knows nothing of that. (III 151.10)

Serving the Divine Names

In respect of God's Essence, or Being as such, perfect man manifests the all-comprehensive name Allah, but in respect of His self-disclosure and the perfection of manliness, he manifests the individual names of God. Each name of God has a servanthood specific to it, and the specific characteristics of the perfect men are determined by the specific names they serve. Viewed from the point of view of the spiritual journey, "assuming the traits of the divine names" is the process of becoming the servant of each name. In Ibn al-ʿArabī's view, this is the meaning of the hadith, "God has ninety-nine names, one hundred less one. He who counts (*iḥṣā'*) them will enter the Garden."[8] One of al-Tirmidhī's questions is, "How many are the shares of servanthood?" Ibn al-ʿArabī replies:

> There are ninety-nine shares, in keeping with the number of the divine names. If the servant counts those names, he enters the Garden. Each divine name has a servanthood specific to itself, through which it is worshiped by whichever of the created things worships it. Hence no one knows these divine names except a friend fixed in his friendship. For it has not been established for us that the Messenger of God has designated them. A number of people have counted them [in their books], but it is not known if they are the same ones concerning which the text has come. . . .
>
> Among the Men of Allah there are those whom God has given knowledge of these names in respect of the servanthood demanded by each of the names from the servant. So this gnostic friend serves God in accordance with the name which determines his property in his present moment (*waqt*).
>
> He who counts these divine names will enter the supra-sensory (*maʿnawī*) and sensory (*ḥissī*) Gardens. He will enter the supra-sensory Garden because of the knowledge of servanthood which these names demand as is appropriate to them. He will enter the sensory Garden because of the works which these names demand from the servants. (II 92.26)

The friends of God can be divided into a large variety of categories, as Ibn al-ʿArabī shows in a thirty-five page section of the *Futūḥāt* (II 6–39). Each type of friend displays various perfections of knowledge and character, the divine roots of which go back to certain specific names.[9] Thus Ibn al-ʿArabī describes the characteristics of the "Substitutes" (*abdāl*) as follows:

> The Substitutes are seven. They never increase and never decrease. Through them God preserves the seven climes. Each Substitute possesses a clime within which he is the governor and friend. . . . They know the affairs and mysteries that God has placed in the seven planets. . . . The names that pertain to them are names of attributes. Among them are ʿAbd al-Ḥayy ("Servant of the Alive"), ʿAbd al-ʿAlīm ("Servant of the Knowing"), ʿAbd al-Wadūd ("Servant of the Loving"), and ʿAbd al-Qādir ("Servant of the Powerful"). . . . Among them are ʿAbd al-Shakūr ("Servant of the Grateful"), ʿAbd al-Samīʿ ("Servant of the Hearing"), and ʿAbd al-Baṣīr ("Servant of the Seeing"). Each of these divine attributes has a Man from among these Substitutes. By means of the name God gazes upon them. The name is the attribute which dominates over them. In fact, there is none of the Men who does not have a relationship with a divine name, through which he receives the means to the good which he possesses. Each of them corresponds to the inclusiveness and compass that is given by the divine name. It determines the measure of the Man's knowledge. (II 7.9)

Ibn al-ʿArabī alludes to an experiential side of this special relationship between God's friend and the divine names while discussing the "opening of sweetness" (*futūḥ al-ḥalāwa*).

> When the Real named me a servant of His names and opened me up to this sweetness, I found no more intense effect than from the name Inaccessible. The meaning of this is that He makes man stand in the station of being a servant of each divine name so that he will acquire discrimination among the realities and actualize the divine sciences. (II 506.30)

Though many of God's friends are dominated by the properties of specific divine names, the perfect man displays all the names without any name dominating over the others, just as the divine Essence possesses all the names without being delimited and defined by any of them. Perfection, then, is an equilibrium (*iʿtidāl*) in which everything stays in balance. All names play their proper role without predominance. In contrasting the "lovers" (*muḥibb*) of God with the gnostics or perfect men, the Shaykh writes that the lovers become enraptured by His Beauty, but the gnostics remain in cold sobriety in face of the greatest of God's self-disclosures, since no name dominates over any other.

> The gnostics remain sober (*ṣaḥw*) and do not become enraptured in God in the way that the lovers become enraptured in Him, since He discloses Himself to the lovers in nondelimited beauty, but He discloses Himself to those who know Him in nondelimited perfection. What does perfection have in common with beauty?[10]
>
> In perfect man the names impede one another (*tamānuʿ*), and this mutual impeding leads to their not displaying effects in him who has this attribute. Hence he remains incomparable (*munazzah*) with the display of effects along with the Nondelimited Essence, concerning which no name or attribute gives any knowledge. So perfect man is in extreme sobriety, like the messengers, who are the most perfect of human types. For perfect man is in extreme nearness, and through it he becomes manifest in the perfection of his servanthood while witnessing the perfection of the Essence of Him who brought him into existence.
>
> Once you verify what we have said, you will understand that your tasting has nothing in common with the tasting of the Men, the perfect. It is they whom God has purified for Himself, selected for Himself, and made incomparable through Himself. Hence, they and He are like He and they. He named the perfect one from among them "al-ʿAṣr,"[11] since He "pressed" one thing together with another in order to extract what He sought. He pressed the essence of a servant, nondelimited in his servanthood such that he is untainted by any lordship whatsoever, together with the Essence of the Real, to-

> tally Nondelimited by any servanthood toward a divine name which would demand engendered existence. Once the two essences stood opposite each other in such a standing, that which was pressed out (*muʿtaṣar*) was identical to the perfection of the Real and the servant. This was the sought after goal for the sake of which the ʿAṣr came into existence. So if you have understand that to which we have alluded, you have attained to felicity and I have placed before you the ladder of perfection. Therefore climb! . . .
>
> Perfect man is more perfect than the cosmos in its totality, since he is a transcript of the cosmos letter for letter, and he adds to it the fact that his reality does not accept shrinking (*taḍāʾul*), though the highest of the angelic spirits, Seraphiel, accepts shrinking, since he shrinks seventy times a day.[12] . . . "Shrinking" only takes place in relation to a precedent elevation, but the universal servant (*al-ʿabd al-kullī*) has no elevation in his servanthood, since he is stripped of attributes (*maslūb al-awṣāf*). If Seraphiel brought forth the state of this universal servant in his servanthood, he would not again shrink. So understand my allusions! I have apprised you through this report that this angel is among those creatures who know the most about God. He shrinks time after time because God's self-disclosures continue time after time, since the Real never discloses Himself in a single form twice. In each self-disclosure Seraphiel sees what leads to shrinking. This is the sound doctrine, given by true knowledge of God. (II 615.22,34)

The "universal servant" is perfect man in respect of the fact that he is the servant of every (*kull*) divine name, not just this name or that. He cannot be called ʿAbd al-Karīm ("Servant of the Generous") or ʿAbd al-Majīd ("Servant of the Glorious") to the exclusion of any other epithet. On the contrary, he must be called the servant of every name, or, the "servant of Allah," the all-comprehensive name. Hence, though there are many kinds of "poles" (*quṭb*)—those friends of God around whom various realities of the universe turn—Ibn al-ʿArabī calls the absolute Pole (*al-quṭb*), around whom turns the whole of the cosmos, ʿAbd Allāh and ʿAbd al-Jāmiʿ ("Servant of the All-comprehensive").[13] These two names refer respectively to the Pole's essential and accidental perfections, which are as near as possible to being identical, since the "All-comprehensive" is both a name of God and the name of the name Allah, so it and Allah are practically synonymous. In any case, every pole is named by two names, Servant of Allah and servant of some other name.[14]

> When the poles and the righteous (*al-ṣāliḥūn*) are named by known names, they are named the servant only of that name which has taken charge of them. God says, "When the servant of Allah (i.e., the Prophet Muḥammad) stood calling on Him" (72:19). Hence God named him "ʿAbd Allāh," even if his father had named him "Muḥammad" and "Aḥmad." The Pole is forever specified by this all-comprehensive name, so he is ʿAbd Allāh in this world.
>
> Then the poles are ranked in excellence among themselves, even though they all come together in this name which is demanded by their station. Each of them is also specified by another divine name. He is attributed to it and called by it outside of the station of Polehood (*quṭbiyya*). Hence Moses' name is ʿAbd al-Shakūr ("Servant of the Grateful"), David's specific name is ʿAbd al-Malik ("Servant of the King"), and Muḥammad's name is ʿAbd al-Jāmiʿ. There is no pole who does not possess a name specific to him in addition to the all-inclusive name which he possesses, that is, ʿAbd Allāh. It makes no difference if the pole is a prophet in the time of prophecy which has now come to an end, or a friend of God in the time of the Shariʿa of Muḥammad. (II 571.18)

Perfect man serves God in the guise of the name Allah, not any other name. Just as Allah is Nondelimited Being, so perfect man is the nondelimited thrall of Allah (*al-maʾlūh al-muṭlaq*). He accompanies Allah in every self-disclosure. In other words, the perfect servant, through his nothingness and effacement, manifests all the divine names. He assumes the traits and fully realizes the properties of every name, without being delimited by any one name or group of names. Lesser friends of God, though they realize the name Allah to some degree by being human, manifest in practice only some of the names. Ordinary mortals assume various traits of the names in disequilibrium and imbalance, leading to deviation from the human norm and preventing them from passing beyond the level of "animal man."

> There can be no sheer servanthood, uncontaminated by any lordship whatsoever, except in perfect man alone. And there can be no sheer lordship, uncontaminated by any servanthood whatsoever, except in God. So man is upon the form of the Real through incomparability and being far removed from contamination in his reality, for he is the nondelimited divine thrall, and the Real is the Nondelimited God. And by all of this I mean perfect man.
>
> Perfect man is separated from him who is not perfect by a single intangible reality (*raqīqa*), which is that his servanthood is uncontaminated by any lordship whatsoever. Since perfect man has this high position, he alone is the goal sought after through the cosmos.
>
> This perfection became manifest in Adam in His words, "He taught Adam the names, all of them" (2:31). He added emphasis with "all," since it is a word that requires all-encompassingness. Thereby the Real gave witness to his perfection. In the same way it became manifest in Muḥammad, in his words, "I came to know the knowledge of the ancients and the later folk." So Adam's knowledge was included in his knowledge, since Adam is among the ancients. (II 603.14)

The People of Blame

By manifesting all the divine names without a trace of Lordship and thereby displaying perfect servanthood, perfect man becomes, one might say, totally ordinary. In him, nothing stands out, since he flows with all created things in perfect harmony and equilibrium. He is like a tree or a bird in his ordinariness, following the divine will wherever it takes him, with no friction, no protest, complete serenity, no waves. He is so much at ease with the continual flux of secondary causes that he remains unnoticed by his contemporaries. There may be outstanding spiritual masters who attract disciples through their teachings and miraculous gifts, but the most perfect of the masters are never even noticed except by those whom God chooses and guides. In respect of this characteristic, Ibn al-ʿArabī calls the most perfect of the gnostics the "People of Blame" (*malāmiyya*). Though the name "People of Blame" has historical precedents in Sufism, Ibn al-ʿArabī defines the term and describes those who deserve it in terms specific to his own teachings.[15]

> The People of Blame are those who know and are not known. (II 145.1)
>
> The People of Blame are the unknown, those whose stations are unknown. No divine affair dominates over them such that it might be known that God has a special solicitude towards them. Their states conceal their stations because of the wisdom of the abode: They never become manifest in the locus of contention, since sometimes people contend with their Master—who is God—in this house in respect of His Divinity. But this tribe have realized their Master, so this realization has prevented them from becoming manifest within the abode within which their Master is concealed. Hence they flow with the common people (*al-ʿāmma*) in respect of the outward acts of obedience which the common people perform. . . . No act becomes manifest from them which would distinguish them from the common people. This contrasts with the miraculous breaking of habits through states displayed by some of the friends. (II 501.25)
>
> The People of Blame are the masters and leaders of the folk of God's path. Among them is the master of the cosmos, that is, Muḥammad, the Messenger of God—God bless him and give him peace!

They are the sages, those who put things in their proper places. They do things well and put the secondary causes in their correct locations, while negating them in the places from which they should be negated. They violate nothing of what God has arranged in His creation, leaving it just as He has arranged it. Whatever is required for this world, they leave for this world, and whatever is required for the next world, they leave for the next world. They look at things with the same eye with which God looks at things. They never confuse realities.

A person who abolishes a secondary cause in the place where its Establisher—the Real—has established it has called its Establisher stupid and remained ignorant of His measure. A person who depends upon the secondary cause has associated others with God and becomes a heretic, so he will remain forever in the earth of Nature. Hence the People of Blame place secondary causes in their places, but they do not depend upon them. The disciples (*tilmīdh*) of the People of Blame, who are the Truthful (*al-ṣādiqūn*), undergo constant fluctuation within the stages of Manliness. But the disciples of others undergo constant fluctuation within the frivolities of the ego (*al-ruʿūnāt al-nafsiyya*).[16] The measures of the People of Blame are unknown. None knows them but their Master, who was partial toward them and singled them out for this station. (II 16.15)

In the following passage Ibn al-ʿArabī contrasts the "People of Blame" with two other types among the Men of Allah, the "worshipers" (*al-ʿubbād*) and the "Sufis." It is especially noteworthy that in this passage, as is frequently the case in his writings, the Shaykh employs the term "Sufi" not as a generic term for the seekers and finders of God, but as a designation for a particular type of spirituality which entails a certain amount of outward show and self-satisfaction, and thus denotes certain friends of God who are less than perfect.

The Men of Allah are three. There is no fourth:

Men who are dominated by renunciation (*zuhd*), constant devotion (*tabattul*), and pure acts, all of them praiseworthy. They purify their inward dimensions from every blameworthy attribute which has been blamed by the Lawgiver. However, they do not see anything beyond the works they perform. They have no knowledge of the states and the stations, nor do they possess the God-given sciences from Him, nor the mysteries, nor unveilings, nor anything of what is found by others. These are called the "worshipers" (*al-ʿubbād*). If anyone should come to ask them for a prayer, one of them may well chide him or say, "What thing am I that I should pray for you? What position have I?" He is wary lest he be stricken by self-satisfaction. He fears the calamities of the ego (*nafs*) and that making a show (*riyā'*) should enter into that. If one of them should busy himself with reading, his book will be the *Riʿāya* of al-Muḥāsibī or something of the same genre.[17]

The second kind are above the first. They see all acts as belonging to God and they understand that they possess no act whatsoever. Hence making a show disappears from them completely. If someone should ask them about something about which the people of the path are wary, they say, "Do you call upon any other than God, if you speak truly?" (6:40), and they say, "Say: 'Allah', then leave them alone" (6:91). They are like the worshipers in earnestness, striving, abstinence, renunciation, trust, and so on. However, while they possess all that, they see something beyond the situation of the worshipers, that is, states, stations, sciences, mysteries, unveilings, and charismatic gifts (*karāmāt*). So they attach their aspirations to acquiring those things. Once they reach something of that, they make it manifest among the common people as charismatic gifts, since they see no one but God. They are the people of good character (*khuluq*) and chivalry (*futuwwa*). This group is named the Sufis. In the view of the third group, they are the people of frivolity (*ruʿūna*) and the possessors of egos. Their students are like themselves: They make claims and pass by all God's creatures with a self-conceited gait, manifesting leadership over all the Men of Allah.

The third group add nothing to the five daily prayers and the supererogatory exercises (*rawātib*). They do not distinguish themselves from the faithful who perform God's obligations by any extra state whereby they might be known. They walk in the markets, they speak to the people, and none of God's creatures sees any of them distinguishing himself from the common people by a single thing; they add nothing to the obligatory works or the Sunna customary among the common folk. They are alone with God, firmly rooted, not wavering from their servanthood for the blink of an eye. They find no flavor in leadership, since Lordship has overcome their hearts and they are lowly before it. God has given them knowledge of the places of things and of appropriate works and states. They are veiled from the creatures and stay concealed from them by the covering of the common people. For they are sincere and purely devoted servants of their Master. They witness Him constantly in their eating and drinking, their waking and sleeping, and their speaking with Him among the people.

They put all secondary causes in their places and know the wisdom in them. You see them as if they were the ones who had created everything, since they affirm and emphasize the secondary causes. They are poor toward all things, since everything in their view is named "Allah." But no one has any need of them in anything, since in them has become manifest nothing of independence or exaltation through God, or any of the characteristics of the Divine Presence which would require things to have need for them. They see that the things have no poverty toward them. But they have poverty toward the things, in keeping with God's words to the people, "You are the poor toward God, and God—He is the Independent, the Praiseworthy" (35:15). Though they have gained independence through God, they never make manifest any attribute which would make it possible to ascribe to them the name by which God has described Himself, that is, the "Independent." They maintain for themselves outwardly and inwardly the name by which God has named them, that is, the "poor." From here they know that poverty is only toward God, the Independent. But they see that the people are poor toward all the secondary causes which have been put in their places. For the most part the people have been veiled from God. But in reality and in actual fact, the people are poor only toward Him in whose hand is the accomplishment of their needs, and that is God. So [the People of Blame] say: "Here God has named Himself by everything toward which there is poverty in reality. God is not poor toward anything, but everything is poor toward Him." These then are the People of Blame, the highest of the Men. Their students are the greatest of the Men, undergoing fluctuation in all the stages of Manliness.[18]

There is no one who has achieved the station of chivalry and good character with God, but not with anyone else, except they. They have achieved all the stations and have seen that God veils Himself from the creation in this world, while they are His elect. So they veil themselves from the creatures through the veil of their Master. From behind the veil they witness no one in the creatures other than their Master. When they reach the hereafter and the Real discloses Himself, they will also become manifest through the manifestation of their Master. But their rank in this world is unknown in entity.

For the common people, the worshipers are distinct by their mortification, their keeping away from people and people's states, and their avoidance of mixing with them in body. So they have their reward. The Sufis are distinct in the eyes of the common people by their claims and their miraculous breaking of habits, such as reading people's thoughts, and having their prayers answered. . . . They do not refrain from manifesting anything that will lead people to know about their nearness to God since, they suppose, they witness nothing but God. But a great knowledge escapes them. Moreover, this state of theirs is not safe from deception and being led on stage by stage.

The People of Blame do not distinguish themselves from any of God's creatures by anything, so they are unknown. Their state is the state of the common people.

They are called "People of Blame" for two reasons. One is that the term is ascribed to their students because they never cease blaming themselves next to God. They never perform a work with which they are happy, as part of their training. For no one can be happy with works until after they have been accepted, and this is unseen by their students. As for the great ones among them, the name is ascribed to them because they conceal their states and their rank with God when they see that people criticize their acts and blame what they do because the people do not see the acts as coming from God. They only see them as coming from him upon whose hand they become manifest. So they blame and criticize the acts. But were the covering to be removed and were they to see that the acts belong to God, no blame would attach to him upon whose hands they appeared. In this state all those acts would be noble and good. So also is it with this tribe themselves: Were their rank with God to become manifest to the people, the people would take them as gods. But since they have habitually been veiled from the common people, the blame which is ascribed to the common people when something worthy of it appears from them is also ascribed to them. It is as if their rank itself blames them because it is not manifest. (III 34.28)

The Station of No Station

Perfection is an equilibrium in which all divine names play their proper role without the predominance of one name or some names over others. Perfect man acts as God's deputy and vicegerent in every situation, since the perfect balance of the names within him means that God acts through him in respect of Allah, the all-comprehensive name, not in respect of one of the specific names that are embraced by the name Allah. Hence perfect man is not delimited by any specific attributes, since he encompasses all attributes. He assumes the attribute appropriate to the occasion, just as God always discloses Himself in keeping with the receptacle. It is in this sense that Ibn al-ʿArabī defines "perfection" in his *Iṣṭilāḥāt* as "being removed from attributes and effects."[19]

Because the perfect gnostic is not defined by any specific attribute, he is able to manifest conflicting and contradictory attributes, just as he is able to believe in every belief. The all-comprehensive name, Allah, brings together contrary attributes. The perfect gnostic, who is the locus of self-disclosure for this name, brings together all opposites. Ibn al-ʿArabī explains this while discussing the station of "expansion" (*basṭ*), whose opposite is "contraction" (*qabḍ*).

> The final end and ultimate return of the gnostics—though their entities remain immutably fixed—is that the Real is identical with them, while they do not exist. This station is possessed only by the gnostics. Hence they are contracted in the state of their expansion. A gnostic can never be contracted without expansion or expanded without contraction. But when anyone other than the gnostic is in the state of contraction, he does not have the state of expansion, and when he is in the state of expansion, he does not have the state of contraction. Hence the gnostic is known only through the fact that he brings opposites together, for all of him is the Real. Thus Abū Saʿīd al-Kharrāz was asked, "Through what have you known Allah?" He replied, "Through the fact that He brings opposites together," for he witnessed their coming together in himself, and he knew that he was upon His form. He had heard Him say, "He is the First and the Last, the Manifest and the Nonmanifest" (57:3); and it was this verse he brought in proof of his statement. (II 512.9)

In traversing the spiritual path, the gnostic passes from station to station, never losing a positive attribute after having gained it. One by one, in perfect harmony, he assumes the traits of the divine names. Having reached the highest station, he owns all stations. Having assumed the traits of all divine names, he now manifests the name Allah itself. Just as Allah designates nothing specific, but rather everything—Being and all its attributes—so also perfect man is nothing specific, since he is all things. Each station of the path represents a specific perfection of knowledge and character. Hence, Ibn al-ʿArabī calls the highest station which represents no specific perfection "no station" (*lā maqām*). He sees an allusion to it in the Koranic verse, "O people of Yathrib, you have no station (*lā muqām*)" (33:13). Everyone who resides below this station is delimited and defined by certain divine attributes rather than others. But the gnostic possesses all divine attributes and is delimited by none. He appears in each and every situation as wisdom requires and the secondary causes demand. He alone among created things is able to "put everything in its proper place" and "to give to each thing its due," since he alone manifests the name Allah in its perfection.

> The people of perfection have realized all stations and states and passed beyond these to the station above both majesty and beauty, so they have no attribute and no description. It was said to Abū Yazīd, "How are you this morning?" He replied, "I have no morning and no evening; morning and evening belong to him who becomes delimited by attributes, and I have no attributes." (II 133.19)
>
> The root of this knowledge of Allah is the station reached ultimately by the gnostics, that is, "no station," to which God alludes in the verse, "O people of Yathrib, you have no station" (33:13). This station becomes delimited by no attribute whatsoever. Abū Yazīd called attention to it with his words when it was said to him, "How are you this morning?" . . .
>
> "Morning" belongs to the eastern sun and evening to the western sun. The eastern sun pertains to manifestation, the world of the kingdom (*mulk*), and the visible, while the western sun pertains to curtaining, the world of the unseen, and the dominion (*malakūt*). In this station the gnostic is the "olive tree that is neither of the east nor of the west" (24:35), since no description determines the properties of this station, nor does he become delimited by it. This is his share of "Nothing is like Him" (42:11) and of "Glory be to thy Lord, the Lord of inaccessibility, above what they describe!" (37:180). (II 646.27)

The possessors of no station are called by several other names in various contexts. Perhaps the closest synonym, however, is the "Muhammadan" (Muḥammadī). The Muhammadan friend of God inherits his knowledge, stations, and states directly from the Prophet Muḥammad, without the intermediary of Jesus, Abraham, Moses, or any of the 124,000 other prophets. As Ibn al-ʿArabī points out, the term also has another meaning, but it plays a less important role in his teachings:

> The highest of all human beings are those who have no station. The reason for this is that the stations determine the properties of those who stand within them, but without doubt, the highest of all groups themselves determine the properties. They are not determined by properties. They are the divine ones (*al-ilāhiyyūn*), since the Real is identical with them, and He is "the strongest of those who determine properties" (95:8).
>
> This belongs to no human being except only the Muhammadans, as a divine solicitude already given to them. God has said concerning their likes, "But as for those unto whom the most beautiful reward has already gone forth from Us, they shall be kept far from it" (21:101), that is, from the Fire, since the Fire is one of these stations. So in reality, they are kept far from the stations. Hence the possessors of stations are those whose aspirations (*himma*) have become limited to certain goals and ends. When they reach those goals, they find in their hearts other, new goals, and these goals which they have reached become the beginning stages for other goals. Hence the goals determine their properties, since they seek them, and such is their situation forever.
>
> But the Muhammadan has no such property and witnesses no goal. His vastness is the vastness of the Real, and the Real has no goal in Himself which His Being might ultimately reach. The Real is witnessed by the Muhammadan, so he has no ultimate goal in his witnessing. But other than the Muhammadan wit-

nesses his own possibility. Hence he stands in a state or station which, in his eyes, may come to an end, or change, or cease to exist. He sees this as the ultimate goal of knowledge of God, since he has given the property its full due in respect to himself and his Lord.

Jesus is a Muhammadan. That is why he will descend at the end of time. Through him God will seal the Greater Friendship.[20] He is God's spirit and His word, and the words of the Real are never exhausted. So the Muhammadan has no ultimate goal in his mind which he might reach. (III 506.30)

In this Path no one is called a "Muhammadan" except two individuals: Either a person who has been singled out for inheriting knowledge of a ruling that did not exist in any Law before Muḥammad, or a person who brings together all the stations, then emerges from them, entering "no station," like Abū Yazīd and his equals. This person is also called a "Muhammadan," but everyone other than these two is ascribed to one of the prophets. That is why it has been reported that the Prophet said, "The learned masters (*ʿulamāʾ*) are the inheritors of the prophets."[21] He did not say that they were the inheritors of one prophet in particular. . . . Likewise he said, "The learned masters of this community are the prophets of the other communities," or in another version "like the prophets of the Children of Israel."[22] (I 223.2)

The Muhammadan Poles are those who inherit from Muḥammad in the revealed laws and the states which he possessed exclusively and which were not found in any Law or messenger that preceded him. If it was present in a Law that preceded his Law or a messenger who preceded him and was also present in him, the man inherits from that specific messenger, but by means of Muḥammad. Hence he is ascribed to that messenger. If he is a member of this community, he is called a Mūsawī if he inherited from Moses, or an ʿĪsawī [if he inherited from Jesus] or an Ibrāhīmī [if he inherited from Abraham], or whichever messenger or prophet it might be. No one is ascribed to Muḥammad except him who is like what we have said concerning that which belongs exclusively to him.

The most all-inclusive specification is that a person not be delimited by a station whereby he is distinguished. So the Muhammadan is only distinguished by the fact that he has no station specifically. His station is that of no station. The meaning of this is as follows:

A man may be dominated by his state so that he knows only by means of it, is attributed to it, and is designated by it. But the relationship of the stations to the Muhammadan is the same as the relationship of the names to God. He does not become designated by a station which is attributed to him. On the contrary, in every breath, in every moment, and in every state he takes the form which is required by that breath, moment, and state. Hence his delimitation does not last. For the divine properties are diverse at every moment, and he is diverse in accordance with their diversity. God is "each day upon some task" (55:29), and so also is the Muhammadan. This is indicated by God's words, "Surely in that there is a reminder for him who has a heart" (50:37). He did not say "rational faculty," which would delimit the person. The "heart" only has this name because of its fluctuation in states and affairs continuously and with each breath.

Among God's servants is he who knows how he undergoes constant fluctuation at each instant, and among them is he who is unaware of that. Both the Muhammadan Pole and the Solitary (*al-mufrad*)[23] undergo fluctuation in knowledge with each breath, just as every creature of God undergoes fluctuation in state with each breath. Hence this person is superior only through the knowledge of that within which and upon which he undergoes fluctuation, not through the fluctuation itself, since the latter permeates the entire cosmos. However, most people do not know this in a differentiated mode and specifically, though they do know it in an undifferentiated way. So their stations are measured by the extent of their awareness of that within and upon which they undergo fluctuation. (IV 76.27)

The perfect friend calls upon God in every station and tongue, but the messengers—who are many—stop with that which was revealed to them. What has been revealed to one of them may not have been revealed to another. But the Muhammadan gathers together through

> his level every call that has been dispersed among the messengers. Hence he is nondelimited because he calls with every tongue. For he is commanded to have faith in the messengers and in that which was sent down to them. So the Muhammadan friend does not stop with a specific revelation, except in respect to the rulings of lawful (*ḥalāl*) and unlawful (*ḥarām*). As for his calling, those things about which nothing was said, and those things concerning which nothing was sent down in Muḥammad's Law indicating that it should be avoided, he does not avoid it if it was brought by any revelation to any of the prophets, messenger or non-messenger. (III 167.3)

All creatures are poor (*faqīr*) toward God by definition, but the Muhammadan friend is destitute (*muflis*) of everything other than God. In explaining this point, Ibn al-ʿArabī turns to a hadith which divides the people of paradise into the poor and the rich. The Prophet said, "I stood at the gate of the Garden. Most of the people who entered it were from among the poor (*miskīn*), while the people of riches were imprisoned."[24]

> The Prophet said, "One dirham outstrips a thousand,"[25] since the possessor of the dirham has nothing else, so he spends it for God and returns to God, since he has no other support to which he might return. But the possessor of the thousand dirhams gives some of what is with him, and he leaves some, to which he returns, so he does not return to God. Hence the possessor of the single dirham has outstripped him in going to God. If the possessor of the thousand had spent everything he had, like the possessor of the single dirham, the two would be equal in station. Here the Lawgiver does not take into account the amount of the gift, he only considers that to which the giver goes back after giving. He is judged by that to which he returns.
>
> The returners to God are "destitute" of everything other than God. A rich man who sees the Real in every form will not reach the level of him who sees Him in no-thing (*lā shay'*), for the latter sees Him freed of all relationships, nondelimited, and without any delimitation.
>
> When the Real delimits Himself within a form to the recipient of self-disclosure, without doubt the form delimits the viewer. He is with each viewer in a form that is not seen by any other viewer. Hence, no one sees Him nondelimited by existence except him who is destitute, him from whose witnessing all forms have disappeared. Thus He says about the thirsty man, "[He supposes the mirage to be water,] until, when he comes to it, he finds it is no-thing," so He negates that it should be the thing sought, "and there he finds God" (24:39), that is, with no-thing. For "Nothing is like Him" (42:11), and He is "Independent of the worlds" (3:97). Hence no one perceives Him except him whom God has made destitute of the worlds. And he who is destitute of the worlds stands in extreme independence from the worlds. When secondary causes upset him, the Real brings him back to Himself. He knows to whom he returns and why he returns. He returns destitute in respect to Him who is Independent from him. He knows the Real as He should be known, so he follows Him. The right of his own entity is nonexistence and witnessing, while the right of his Lord is Being and witnessing.
>
> The Prophet, the possessor of perfect unveiling, said, "The possessors of riches are imprisoned," and he who is imprisoned is delimited. But he who is destitute has no riches to delimit or imprison him, so he is not delimited by this delimitation of the possessors of riches. Hence he is nearer to the divine form through nondelimitation than are the possessors of riches, since they are delimited.
>
> Hence the possessor of riches stands in the level of him who sees the Real in things and delimits Him by them, and necessarily so, since his station exercises its ruling property over him. But he who is destitute is a Muhammadan. He has no station. For it was said to the Prophet, "Nothing of the command belongs to thee" (3:128); so God made him destitute. "Riches" belong only to him who possesses the command, for everyone who possesses the command is the possessor of riches, since the "command" is that of engendering (*takwīn*), so that what the person desires comes to be. Hence he is not destitute. He who leaves his own reality has slipped in his path[26]. . . . Hence, re-

maining in one's own root is preferable, and this is what is indicated by His words to the noblest of mankind, the most complete of them in witnessing, and the highest of them in existence: "Nothing of the command belongs to thee." So He made him destitute.

"O People of Yathrib, you have no station, so return!" (33:13), for "God will give you a new configuration in that which you know not; you have known the first configuration," in other words, you knew that you were configured within that which you know not, "so why will you not remember?" (Koran 56:62). The Folk of Allah never leave the home of destitution, for in every breath they are "upon a clear sign" without any confusion, a new knowledge which they had not known. God gives them new configurations constantly in that which they know not. They do not possess consideration, circumspection, and deliberation, since no one considers anything but existent substrata, that is, the boundaries which imprison them, preventing them from knowing God, so that "They are in confusion as to a new creation" (50:15): They are in it, but they are unaware of it. When they enter the Garden on the Day of Resurrection, they step out of it only into "What no eye has seen, what no ear has heard, and what has never passed into the heart of any mortal."[27] Since it has not passed into the heart, which possesses constant fluctuation in its faces, then what do you think about reason, which has no fluctuation? May God place us among these destitute ones and separate us from the station of the people of riches, the prisoners! (III 105.8)

Ibn al-ʿArabī summarizes the perfection of perfect man and the meaning of the station of no station in discussing the true knowledge of "place" (*makān*).

God says, "O people of Yathrib, you have no station" (33:13). Concerning Idrīs He said, "We raised him up to a high place" (19:57). "Place" is a divine description in an all-inclusive and specific sense. The all-inclusive sense is indicated in His words, "The All-merciful sat upon the Throne" (20:5), and the specific sense in His words, "The heart of My faithful servant embraces Me." The most inclusive sense is that He is as you are, as indicated in His words, "He is with you wherever you are" (57:4), for here He mentions "whereness." "Place" among existent essences (*dhawāt*) corresponds to "rank" (*makāna*) among levels.

In the view of the Tribe, "place" is a waystation on God's carpet and belongs to the People of Perfection, who have passed beyond stations and states, majesty and beauty. They have no attributes, no descriptions, and no station, like Abū Yazīd.

Know that crossing over the stations and the states is one of the specific characteristics of the Muhammadans. It belongs only to the People of Courtesy, those who sit with the Real on the carpet of awe with intimacy. They are perpetually in equilibrium, fixity, and rest. However, they possess swift movements in their inward dimension with every breath. "You will see the mountains, that you supposed to be fixed, passing by like clouds" (27:88).

If the Real discloses Himself to them in a limited form, they bow their heads. In that state they see Him causing their states to fluctuate, not in accordance with the form within which He disclosed Himself to them. This causes them to bow their heads. So they stand between nondelimitation and delimitation. No station determines their properties, for there is none. They are the possessors of place upon the carpet of their configuration and the possessors of rank in their lack of lodging. In respect of their rank they undergo constant variation, and in respect of their place they are fixed. Through their own essences they are in their place, but through the divine names they are in their rank. In respect of the names they possess the "praiseworthy station"[28] and the near rank on the Day to be Witnessed, the Visitation,[29] and the Arrival.

Through their own essence they possess the limited place, the intended meaning, fixity in witnessing, the state of finding, vision of Him in every existent in rest and stillness. They witness Him in the Cloud with the eye through which they witness Him in the Sitting, with the eye through which they witness Him in the heaven of this world, with the eye through which they witness Him in the earth, with the eye through which they witness Him in the withness, with the eye through which they witness Him in "Nothing is like Him" (42:11). All of these are attributes of place.

As for their witnessing in respect to rank, their eyes are diverse in relationship. The eye with which they witness Him in such and such is not the same as the eye with which they witness Him in something else. The witnessed is in one eye, the witnesser views from one eye, and the vision differs in respect to that which is viewed. Some of us see the diversity of vision (*naẓar*) as deriving from the diversity of the Object of vision (*al-manẓūr*), while others see the diversity of the Object as deriving from the diversity of the vision. . . .

The real situation belongs to rank, since there can be no fixity in any single affair in existence. Hence place is fixed within rank. In the same way, we say that "stability" is "stability in variegation," not that variegation is opposed to stability. (II 386.19)

The true servant of God manifests the properties of the name Allah in the most perfect manner, giving everything its due just as God gives everything its creation. Ibn al-ʿArabī tells us that the all-comprehensive name yields all properties in the servant, yet three properties stand out from the rest: the declaration of incomparability, worship, and bewilderment (*ḥayra*).[30]

God says, "What is there after the Real but error?" (10:32), and it is nothing but creation. "Error" is bewilderment, and through the creatures the property of error became manifest.

The very Being of the Real
  is a verified Light,
The very existence of creation
  is a shadow following after. . . .

You look at creation in one respect and you say, "It is the Real." You look at it in another respect and you say, "It is creation." But in itself it is neither the Real, nor other than the Real. . . . The Real alone has only the name "Real," since it possesses Necessary Being through Itself. . . .

Hence the creatures have gone astray in creation, since it is a night from which daytime has been stripped away. They are in darkness, bewildered, astray. They have no light by which to find guidance, such as the stars which God has appointed for him who would be guided by them "in the darknesses of the land and the sea" (Koran 6:97). This is the view of the common people.

But the elect are "in darknesses, they do not see. Deaf, dumb, blind" (2:17), they do not understand. Sometimes they say, "We are we and He is He," sometimes they say, "He is we and we are He," and sometimes they say, "We are not purely we and He is not purely He." Then God declared that these elect ones speak the truth concerning their bewilderment, for He said to the most elect of His creatures in knowledge and gnosis, "You did not throw when you threw, but God threw" (8:17). Hence He negated the same thing that He affirmed, so He neither negated nor affirmed. Where are the common people in relation to this address? So knowledge of God is bewilderment, and knowledge of creation is bewilderment. (IV 279.26)

The gnostic is not bewildered because he is lost, but because he has found. He is nothing, yet he is everything. He has been freed from every delimitation, yet he assumes them all. He smells no whiff of Lordship, yet he rules the cosmos. He is known and unknown, affirmed and denied, existent and nonexistent, He/not He. Dwelling in no station, he determines the properties of every station. He even surpasses God's lover, if the lover is not also a gnostic.

Knowledge is more excellent than love, which is why God commanded His Prophet to seek increase in it from Him. It is identical to the divine friendship whereby God takes charge of His servants and ennobles them. Through knowledge they come to know that He cannot be known.

But if the lover is not a gnostic, he creates in himself a form by which he becomes enraptured and of which he is enamored. Hence he only worships and yearns for that which is under his own sway. Nothing can remove him from this station but knowledge.

The bewilderment of the gnostic in the Divine Side is the greatest of bewilderments, since he stands outside of restriction and delimitation. . . . He possesses all forms, yet no form delimits him. That is why the Messenger of God used to say, "O God, increase my bewilderment in Thee!" For this is the highest station, the clearest vision, the nearest rank, the most brilliant locus of manifestation, and the most exemplary path. . . .

No curtain and no veil remains, for this most elevated locus of witnessing rends and tears them all. The curtain delimits the curtained and the veil limits the veiled, but He has no limit upon His Essence and no delimitation to His majesty. How can anything veil Him? "Running before Our eyes—a recompense for him who denied" (54:14).

He who says, "Nothing is like Him" (42:11), has spoken the truth, since the only existent from which no eye is absent and which no "where" restricts is God, for all sensory and supra-sensory forms are His loci of manifestation. He speaks from every form, but not in every form. He is seen by every eye, He is heard by every hearing, but it is He from whom no speech is heard. He is conceived by the rational faculty, but no sight looks upon Him. He is defined, but He has no locus of manifestation within which to become delimited. The "He" is inseparable from Him. "There is no god but He, the Inaccessible, the Wise" (3:6). "He obliterates," but He is identical with what is obliterated, "and He establishes" (13:39), and He is identical with what is established. So "Nothing is like Him" (42:11) in this property, and through Him sound knowledge bestowed by Him bears witness to Him.

The knowledge of proofs negates this vision, since it has nothing of Him in its hands and since this vision has no connection to negation and the declaration of incomparability. But the knowledge of unveiling affirms it and preserves it. No locus of manifestation appears to it without its seeing Him within it. And both knowledges are correct.

He belongs to each faculty of perception in accordance with the faculty in order to teach it that it will never leave its own office and will not grasp with its hand anything of the knowledge of God except that which it is in itself. So it knows its own essence and describes itself. It emerges from delimitations and bounds by His manifestation within it, so that He may be the object of worship. For "He has decreed that" none be "worshiped but Him" (17:23). Hence the misbelievers suppose that the idols and statues are His loci of manifestation, so they apply the name "God" to them and worship only God, which is what is denoted by that locus of manifestation. Hence God takes care of their needs and gives them to drink, and He punishes them if they do not honor the Divine Side in this inanimate form, so they enter among the wretched. . . . So look at Being's permeation of these loci of manifestation. Look how one group reaches felicity, and others become wretched!

One of the Sufis said, "Whatever you imagine within yourself or give form to in your imagination—God is different from that." He is both right and wrong. He makes manifest and he veils.

Another one said, "God is not proven by any proof, nor conceived of by any rational faculties. Rational faculties reach Him not with their reflective powers, and gnostic sciences fail to call Him down with their invocations." For when He is invoked, He is invoked through Him. And through Him He is reflected upon and conceived of. He is the rational faculty of the rational thinkers, the reflection of the reflectors, the invocation of the invokers, the proof of the provers. Were He to come out of a thing, it would cease to be. And were He to be within a thing, it would cease to be. (II 661.10)

NOTES

Introduction

1. M. Joy, "Images and Imagination," *Encyclopedia of Religion* (New York: Macmillan, 1987), VII, p. 104; cf. G. Durand, "The Imaginal," ibid., pp. 109–14.

2. Translated by R. Manheim (Princeton: Princeton University Press, 1969).

3. Critics of Ibn al-ʿArabī have been many, as Osman Yahia has documented in *Histoire et classification de l'oeuvre d'Ibn ʿArabī* (Damascus: Institut Français de Damas, 1964), pp. 114–32; cf. his Arabic introduction to Sayyid Ḥaydar Āmulī, *Kitāb Naṣṣ al-nuṣūṣ fī sharḥ fuṣūṣ al-ḥikam*, ed. H. Corbin and O. Yahia (Tehran: Bibliothèque Iranienne, 1975), pp. 36–42. The present study takes for granted the positive nature of Ibn al-ʿArabī's contribution to Islamic intellectuality and therefore will not concern itself with the polemical issues that have arisen over the centuries. For a general classification of the different evaluations that have been made of Ibn al-ʿArabī's famous doctrine of the "Oneness of Being," cf. Chittick, "Rumi and *Waḥdat al-Wujūd*," in A. Banani and G. Sabagh (eds.), *The Heritage of Rumi* (Cambridge: Cambridge University Press, forthcoming).

4. Her thesis was presented at the University of Paris (Sorbonne): *Essai de Biographie du Shaykh al-Akbar Muhyi l-Din Ibn ʿArabi*, October, 1987.

5. Translated by R.W.J. Austin (London: George Allen & Unwin, 1971). See also S.H. Nasr, *Three Muslim Sages* (Cambridge: Harvard University Press, 1964). Corbin's introduction to *Creative Imagination* (pp. 38–77) provides many details of Ibn al-ʿArabī's life, though these are interwoven with interpretations with which not everyone would agree.

6. References to the *Futūḥāt al-makkiyya* (Būlāq, 1329/1911) will be made in the text in this form. The Roman numerals refer to the volume number, the Arabic numerals to the page and line numbers. In the notes, references will also be made to Osman Yahia's critical edition (Cairo: al-Hay'at al-Miṣriyyat al-ʿĀmma li'l-Kitāb, 1972–) in the form of Y 1,100.1 (Yahia, vol. 1, page 100, line 1).

7. He begins doing this systematically in Chapter 293, in response to the request of a disciple (II 669.11).

8. The "divine" entering thought is also called "merciful" (*raḥmānī*) and "lordly" (*rabbānī*). On *khawāṭir*, cf. I 281–84 (Y 4, 262–78); II 77.30, 132.29, 467.17, 563–66. The discussion was important in Kalām as well as Sufism. Cf. Wolfson, *The Philosophy of the Kalam* (Cambridge: Harvard University Press, 1976), pp. 624ff.

9. Even in the case of divine inrushes, there is no guarantee that the disciple will preserve his mental balance or sanity. Cf. Chapter 15, the section on "Spiritual States."

10. Reading *al-ibdār* for *al-abkār*. The second term, so far as I know, has no techni-

cal significance in Ibn al-ʿArabī's vocabulary, whereas he frequently employs the first and devotes chapter 256 of the *Futūḥāt* to it. He defines it in one of its senses as follows: "God set up the 'shining of the full moon' as an image in the cosmos for His disclosure of Himself within the cosmos through His ruling property. The shining of the full moon is the divine vicegerent (*al-khalīfat al-ilāhī*) who becomes manifest within the cosmos displaying the names of God and His properties, such as mercy, severity, vengeance, and pardon. In the same way, the sun becomes manifest in the moon itself, illuminating the whole of it, and is then called the 'full moon.' Hence the sun sees itself in the mirror of the full moon" (II 556.5). Cf. II 449.21, 554.29, 657.11; III 56.19, 115.35.

11. Ibn Sawdākīn, *Wasāʾil al-sāʾil*, p. 21 (edited in M. Profitlich, *Die Terminologie Ibn ʿArabīs im "Kitāb wasāʾil as-sāʾil" des Ibn Saudakīn* [Freiburg im Breisgau: Klaus Schwarz Verlag, 1973]). The *Fuṣūṣ* commentator Muʾayyid al-Dīn al-Jandī also tells us about Ibn al-ʿArabī's initial opening, though he differs concerning the number of months during which the Shaykh remained in retreat: "According to what has been related to us concerning the Shaykh, his first opening was opened up to him in the month of Muḥarram. He entered the retreat for the first time in the city of Seville in Andalus and for nine months he did not break his daily fast. He entered the retreat at the beginning of Muḥarram, and he was commanded to leave it on the day of the Feast of Fastbreaking [the first day of Shawwāl]. He was given the good news that he was the seal of Muhammadan sanctity and the Prophet's most perfect inheritor in knowledge, states, and station." (*Sharḥ fuṣūṣ al-ḥikam*, ed. S.J. Āshtiyānī [Mashhad: Dānishgāh, 1361/1982], p. 109, with corrections from a manuscript copy.) A somewhat longer version of this account is given in some manuscripts, but not in the printed version, of Jandī's Persian *Nafḥat al-rūḥ* [e.g., Istanbul, Hacı Mahmud 2447, folio 23b]). On Ibn al-ʿArabī's role as the "Seal of the Muhammadan Saints," that is, the last of those "friends of God" who inherit fully from the Prophet Muḥammad, cf. M. Chodkiewicz, *Le sceau des saints* (Paris: Gallimard, 1986).

12. Austin (*Sufis of Andalusia*, p. 23) and Chodkiewicz (*Le sceau*, p. 16) suggest that Ibn al-ʿArabī entered Sufism at the age of twenty, since he mentions "my entrance into this path (*ṭarīqa*) in the year 580 [1184]" (II 425.13). However, the context of this statement leaves some doubt as to what Ibn al-ʿArabī means by "this path." He may mean the Sufi way as such, but he also may mean the "path of God's solicitude," which makes possible quick and easy passage through the stations (mentioned a few lines earlier, II 425.4). He may also mean the particular path of ascension into the "Presence of Marriage and the Presence of Doubts" which he is discussing, or he may mean something else. Ibn al-ʿArabī could not have been twenty years old at his meeting with Ibn Rushd, since he says he had not yet sprouted a beard and a mustache. The present account suggests that he could have been as young as twelve or thirteen. This would not have been too unusual, from his point of view. He tells of the famous Sufi Sahl al-Tustarī reaching a high stage of realization at the age of six (II 20.19, translated in Chapter 15, note 18). In *Sufis of Andalusia* he tells of a master of ten or eleven years of age whom he met as a youth, and concludes the description with the words, "Some of the masters are young, some old" (p. 126). Chodkiewicz-Addas, on the basis of a good deal of evidence suggests that Ibn al-ʿArabī's "entrance into the path" refers to his discipleship at the hands of his first master, Abu'l-ʿAbbās al-ʿUryabī. In other words, at twenty he began his "wayfaring" (*sulūk*) in the technical Sufi sense, while in his early teens he had undergone his first opening as the result of a divine "attraction" (*jadhba*), through the intervention of the prophets Jesus, Moses, and Muhammad (*Essai*, pp. 75–82). However, it seems unlikely that a person would enter into a "retreat" (*khalwa*)—as Ibn al-ʿArabī mentions in his account of his meeting with Ibn Rushd—without the guidance of a master. The long retreat mentioned by Ibn Sawdakīn and al-Jandī must certainly have been directed by a shaykh, though it is not certain that this retreat is the same as the retreat mentioned by Ibn al-ʿArabī as preceding his meeting with Ibn Rushd. It is worth noting that the passage in which Ibn al-ʿArabī says he entered the path in the year 580 is highly mysterious, since he is discussing his visionary experiences and employs technical terminology whose significance is not clear. He writes: "The extremity of the cosmos which we have witnessed . . . through unveiling is 1000 worlds, no more. Those worlds which we have witnessed through tasting, which we

have passed through step by step, with which we have vied, and which we outstripped in two presences—the Presence of Marriage and the Presence of Doubts [?] (*shukūk*)—are sixteen worlds of eighty presences. We witnessed the rest of the worlds through unveiling and a giving of knowledge, not through tasting. We entered into everything we mentioned of these divine replenishments through tasting, with the common people among the Folk of Allah. But we added to them through a divine name, the 'Last.' Through it we acquired leadership (*riyāsa*) and the repose of God attained by those brought near Him, as mentioned in His words, 'Then, if he is one of those brought near, there shall be repose and ease, and a Garden of Delight' (56:89). I attained to these stations at my entrance into this path in the year 580 in a short period of time within the Presence of Marriage, with the People of Purity, and within the Presence of Doubts, with the People of Severity and Overcoming. . . . These are strange sciences and rare tastings. We met some men who possessed them in the Maghrib, some in Alexandria, two or three in Damascus, and one in Sīwās. The last was missing a little something from this station, so he presented it to us, and we completed it for him until he realized it in a short space of time. He was a stranger, not from that country, but from Akhlāṭ." (II 425.8)

13. Ibn al-ʿArabī had little respect for most of the learned masters of such rational sciences as Kalām and philosophy, but great respect for Ibn Rushd. He saw him primarily as a master of the Shariʿa, not as the heir to Aristotle as he has been perceived in the West. This is made clear in another passage, where Ibn al-ʿArabī describes Ibn Rushd as follows, again alluding to their meeting: "We have met very few truly intelligent men. They are those who have the greatest knowledge of the measure of God's messengers, follow most carefully the Sunna of the Messenger, and are most intensely concerned with its preservation. They know the veneration due to God's majesty, and they are aware of the knowledge about Himself that God gives only to His servants—the prophets and those who follow them—through a special divine effusion that is outside ordinary learning and cannot be acquired through study and effort or reached by reason through its own reflective powers. I met one of the great ones among them. He had seen what God had opened up to me without rational consideration or reading, but through a retreat in which I was alone with God, even though I had not been seeking such knowledge. He said, 'Praise belongs to God, that I should have lived in a time in which I saw "one whom God has given mercy from Him, and taught him knowledge from Him" (Koran 18:65)'" (I 325.16).

14. Abū Muḥammad ʿAbdallāh Badr ibn ʿAbdallāh the Ethiopian was Ibn al-ʿArabī's servant (*khādim*), disciple, and constant companion for twenty-three years until his death, which, Ibn al-ʿArabī tells us, occurred in Malatya (*Sufis of Andalusia*, p. 158), in about 618/1221.

15. In the introduction to a bibliography of some of his own works, he writes something similar: "I have not aimed in anything I have written for the goal of authors. Rather, inrushes have entered in upon me from God and nearly burned me alive. In order to distract myself from them, I have written down what can be written. Hence I left the path of authorship, though not because I intended to do that. I have also written books as the result of a divine command given to me by God in a dream or an unveiling." *Fihrist al-muʾallafāt*, ed. A. E. Affifi, "The Works of Ibn ʿArabī," *Revue de la faculté de lettres de l'Université d'Alexandrie* 8 (1954): 194.

16. A recent study by Masataka Takeshita throws light on the historical precedents of some of Ibn al-ʿArabī's ideas: *Ibn ʿArabī's Theory of the Perfect Man and its Place in the History of Islamic Thought* (Tokyo: Institute for the Study of Languages and Cultures of Asia and Africa, 1987).

17. Los Angeles: University of California Press, 1983. The work was originally published with the title *A Comparative Study of the Key Philosophical Concepts in Taoism and Sufism* (Tokyo: Keio University, 1966). Though the new edition has certain revisions, mainly stylistic, the old edition has the advantage of an index of Arabic terminology.

18. *Sharḥ fuṣūṣ al-ḥikam*, p. 5.

19. Qūnawī's commentary, *al-Fukūk*, deals only with the chapter headings of the *Fuṣūṣ*, but it was a major source of inspiration for later commentators. Cf. Chittick, "The Chapter Headings of the *Fuṣūṣ*," *Journal of the Muhyiddin Ibn ʿArabī Society* 2 (1984): 41–94.

20. Cf. Chittick, "The Last Will and Testament of Ibn ʿArabī's Foremost Disciple and Some Notes on its Author," *Sophia Perennis* 4/1 (1978): 43–58.

21. Cf. S.J. Āshtiyānī, *Sharḥ-i Muqaddima-yi Qayṣarī bar Fuṣūṣ al-ḥikam* (Mashhad: Bāstān, 1385/1965–66).

22. Cf. Chittick, "Mysticism versus Philosophy in Earlier Islamic History: The al-Ṭūsī, al-Qūnawī Correspondence," *Religious Studies* 17 (1981): 87–104.

23. Cf. Izutsu, *The Concept and Reality of Existence* (Tokyo: The Keio Institute of Cultural and Linguistic Studies, 1971); M. Mohaghegh and Izutsu (trans.), *The Metaphysics of Sabzavārī* (Delmar, N.Y.: Caravan Books, 1977).

24. Cf. the chapter, "An Analysis of *Waḥdat al-Wujūd*: Toward a Metaphilosophy of Oriental Philosophies," in Izutsu, *Concept and Reality*.

25. Ibn ʿArabī, *Al-Futūḥāt al-Makkiyya: Textes choisis/Selected Texts*, by Michel Chodkiewicz, with the collaboration of W.C. Chittick, Cyrille Chodkiewicz, Denis Gril, and James W. Morris (Paris: Sindbad, 1989). Especially welcome is Chodkiewicz's, "introduction à la lecture de *Futūḥāt al-Makkiyya*."

26. *Ibn Alʿ Arabī: The Bezels of Wisdom*, New York: Paulist Press, 1980.

27. A basic outline of Ibn al-ʿArabī's cosmology, with diagrams, is provided in Chittick, "Ibn al-ʿArabī and his School," in *Islamic Spirituality: Manifestations*, ed. S.H. Nasr (vol. 20 of *World Spirituality: An Encyclopedic History of the Religious Quest*; New York: Crossroad, forthcoming).

Chapter 1. The Divine Presence

1. *Le sceau des saints*, p. 26.

2. As in the sometimes abused phrase often heard in Persian Sufi poetry, *hama ūst*. Cf. A. Schimmel, *Mystical Dimensions of Islam* (Chapel Hill: University of North Carolina Press, 1975), pp. 147, 274, 283, 362, 376.

3. For a detailed explanation of several versions of this scheme, cf. Chittick, "The Five Divine Presences: From al-Qūnawī to al-Qayṣarī," *Muslim World* 72 (1982): 107–128.

4. The use of the first person plural to refer to God is common in the Koran, as is the use of the first person singular. Ibn al-ʿArabī says that the singular pronoun refers to the Divine Essence Itself, i.e., the name Allah, whereas "We" refers to more than one divine name (IV 319.3).

5. The most well-known example of a discussion of the states and stations as ascending levels is Anṣārī's *Manāzil al-sāʾirīn*, ed. and transl. S. de Laugier de Beaurecueil, *Les Étapes des itinérants vers Dieu* (Cairo: Imprimerie de l'Institut Français d'Archéologie Orientale, 1962).

6. The term *al-musammā* is commonly used by Ibn al-ʿArabī as a synonym for Essence. The rationale for this is eminently clear as soon as we remember that the original meaning of *dhāt* ("Essence") in Arabic is "possessor of," that is, possessor of attributes. Since attributes and names are in this context synonymous, Essence has practically the same literal meaning as the "Named": that which is signified by the names or attributes.

7. I say "explaining through language" since Ibn al-ʿArabī discerns the divine root through tasting and unveiling. If God gives the taste, one knows immediately and without intermediary; but explaining the "taste" is something quite different.

8. Repeating what was said earlier, nothingness has no existence whatsoever, except inasmuch as we conceive of it in our minds as the opposite of Being, or a "direction" toward which existence gushes forth. Ibn al-ʿArabī calls the Void (*al-khalaʾ*)—which is the "place" where the cosmos takes shape—a "supposed extension" (*imtidād mutawahham*), since it has no existence other than as a device we employ to explain the situation of existing things. On the Void, cf. *Cosmology*.

9. See especially his *Spiritual Body and Celestial Earth* (Princeton: Princeton University Press, 1977).

10. The Arabic *insān*, a key term in Ibn al-ʿArabī's vocabulary, will be translated either as "human being" or, on occasion, in deference to the traditions and music of the English language, as "man," the non-gendered sense of the term being meant. In Arabic *insān* has no gender connotations, though it is grammatically masculine. Men and women are equally *insān*.

11. Cf. II 677.13: "The first thing God brought into existence [after the sphere of the mansions of the moon] was the earth, which is the limit of the Void, the utmost limit of the dense things and the darknesses. The earth has kept on descending (*nāzil*) constantly until now, while the Void has no end, since it is a supposed extension not in a body. So the whole cosmos, all together, is descending forever in search of the center. This search is the search for knowledge, while the 'center' is that wherein it can find rest, after

which there will be no search. But this will never happen. Hence its descent in its search is continual and without end. This is called 'the search for the Real', since the Real is the object of the search."

12. See the chapter on jinn in *Cosmology*.

13. All these hadiths and many more like them are found in the standard sources such as Bukhārī, Muslim, and Tirmidhī. See Wensinck, *Concordance* II 74–75.

14. The divine attribute is *ʿilm*, "knowledge," while the word *ʿaql*, "intelligence" or "reason" or "intellect" is not attributed to God Himself. Intelligence is the means of knowing, and He who already knows all things has no need for a means, since there is nothing else He could possibly learn. On the human level, the word "intelligence" perhaps suggests more clearly the implications of the divine attribute, since it is not primarily a question of "what is known," i.e., "knowledge" as "information," but the consciousness, awareness, discernment, and wisdom of the knowing subject.

15. This is one way of approaching the subject implicit in many of Ibn al-ʿArabī's formulations. But more central to his own teachings is the idea that every attribute—positive or negative—manifests a divine perfection of some sort, though it may be viewed as a lack from the point of view of other attributes. The Shariʿa then functions to redirect even seemingly negative attributes into positive channels, on the basis of those attributes' ontological content. Cf. Chapters 16–18.

16. Translated by G.M. Wickens as *The Nasirean Ethics* (London: George Allen and Unwin, 1964). See especially the discussion of "justice" (*ʿadl*), which derives from the same root as the word "equilibrium" (*iʿtidāl*); on the relationship between justice and wisdom, see p. 81.

17. In Arabic several significant words applied to God are grammatically feminine, so it is not unusual to speak of God as "She" (e.g., *dhāt Allāh hiya . . .*).

18. This is a generalization. As always Ibn al-ʿArabī's teachings do not fit into neat categories. Not all the figures he deals with would necessarily be considered prophets (e.g., Luqmān and Khālid), nor do all the attributes that he ascribes to them fit into the category of the Most Beautiful Names, though they are certainly divine attributes.

Chapter 2. The Names of God

1. M. Asin Palacios writes that the "whole of the *Futūḥāt*" is based upon "belief in the esoteric virtue of the divine names" (*The Mystical Philosophy of Ibn Masarra and His Followers* [Leiden: Brill, 1978], pp. 174–75). Corbin calls the doctrine of the divine names "One of the most characteristic themes of Ibn ʿArabī's thinking" (*Creative Imagination*, p. 114). S.H. Nasr is careful to remind us that the Shaykh's emphasis upon the names follows naturally upon the whole tradition: "It is through [the names] that Ibn ʿArabī, like other Ṣūfīs, envisages the process of creation as well as that of spiritual realization so that the Names and Qualities play a fundamental role in every aspect of his world view and provide the 'language,' based on the terminology of the Quran, with which he expounds the doctrines of Sufism" (*Three Muslim Sages* [Cambridge: Harvard University Press, 1964], p. 109).

2. Cf. IV 294.11, translated in Chapter 3.

3. On the Void, cf. Chapter 1, notes 8 and 11.

4. A similar passage (II 360.10) repeats these names and adds the names of God in Greek, "Iēsos" [?] (*īshā*), Armenian, "Astuac" (*aṣfāj*), and Turkish, "Tangri" (*tankarī*). Wāq means God in several Cushitic languages, including Somali and Oromo. Ibn al-ʿArabī may have known the word through his disciple Badr the Ethiopian.

5. Both realities and levels are important technical terms and will be discussed in what follows.

6. Ibn Qasī is best known for his involvement in the political disturbances which led to the overthrow of the Almoravid dynasty and the landing of Almohad troops in Spain. He was assassinated in 546/1151 by followers dismayed at his decision to ally himself with the Portuguese of Coimbra against the Almohads. Cf. *Encyclopedia of Islam* (new edition), III 817–18. Ibn al-ʿArabī wrote a commentary on his *Khalʿ al-naʿlayn* (cf. Yahia, *Histoire et classification*, no. 681). The Shaykh refers to Ibn Qasī's view on this question of the names in II 686.25; *Dhakhāʾir* 207. He refers to some of his other views in II 52.7, 60.34, 160.22, 257.11, 693.23; III 24.28, 165.7. In an especially interesting passage, the Shaykh severely criticizes Ibn Qasī—though without mentioning him by name—for his view of the "scale of justice" (*mīzān al-ʿadl*).

He attributes his mistakes to the fact that he did not have a master thoroughly versed in the Sharīʿa (III 176.7; cf. I 749.20; III 7.13). In his commentary on *Khalʿ al-naʿlayn*, Ibn al-ʿArabī calls Ibn Qasī "ignorant" and an "imposter" (Chodkiewicz-Addas, *Essai*, p. 88).

7. Cf. Izutsu, *Sufism*, p. 100. Cf. the following: "Though each name bestows a specific reality, each divine name has in its power to bestow what is bestowed by all the divine names. God says, 'Call upon Allah or call upon the All-merciful; whichever you call upon, to it belong the most beautiful names' (Koran 17:110). In the same way, had He mentioned any other of His names, He would have said about it, 'To it belong the most beautiful names'. This is because of the Unity of the Named (*aḥadiyyat al-musammā*). So know that!" (I 214.27; Y 3, 318).

8. Ibn al-ʿArabī probably quotes Abū Yazīd more frequently than any other Sufi, while considering him one of the "People of Blame," the highest ranking friends of God (III 34.11; cf. II 40.16). For another explanation of this saying, see III 212.34.

9. Muslim, Īmān 302. Ibn al-ʿArabī quotes most of the hadith in III 44.29 and a good deal of it in II 309.26. He devotes Chapter 311 of the *Futūḥāt* largely to the power of some of God's friends to undergo imaginalization. The chapter is translated into English in Chodkiewicz et al., *Al-Futūḥāt*.

10. Here the term *aḥkām* is used as a synonym for relationships and attributes instead of effects. This is not usual, but it is typical of the manner in which Ibn al-ʿArabī employs his terminology—sometimes emphasizing one side of a thing's reality (e.g., that pertaining to the cosmos and manifestation) and sometimes the other (that pertaining to God and nonmanifestation).

11. For a few of Ibn al-ʿArabī's explanations of this saying, cf. II 16.31, 214.9, 263.18, 487.8, 561.15; III 405.12; IV 231.3.

12. In no way does this imply that God is "compelled" to create the universe. See Chapter 4.

13. On the important concept of "independence," see Chapter 4.

14. That is, possibility in the philosophical sense, as opposed to the necessity of the Necessary Being. The relationship of a possible thing to existence and nonexistence is the same. It may or may not come to exist within the cosmos, but there is nothing in its own reality that would demand its existence. According to the Peripatetic philosophers (in a position which Ibn al-ʿArabī accepts as one valid mode of expressing the situation), in order for the possible thing to exist, the Necessary Being must "give preponderance" (*tarjīḥ*) to the side of its existence over its nonexistence. Therefore, in the Shaykh's terms, the possible thing constantly "asks" God—with the "tongue of its state" (*lisān al-ḥāl*) to bestow existence upon it. The Most Beautiful Names demand the cosmos because it alone is able to display their properties and effects. See Chapter 5.

15. According to the Prophet, "Heralding visions are the dreams of the Muslim, and they are one of the parts of prophecy" (Tirmidhī, Ru'yā 2). Another hadith found in all the standard sources tells us, "Nothing remains of prophecy but heralding visions," (*Concordance* I 181); most versions add that the Prophet defined heralding visions as "sound dreams" (*al-ru'yā al-ṣāliḥa*). Cf. Chapter 13, notes 18 and 24.

16. Ibn al-ʿArabī enumerates the "mothers" of the names differently according to the context: Seven: Alive, Knowing, Desiring, Powerful, Speaking, Generous, and Just (I 100.15 [Y 2,126.11]). Four: Knowing, Desiring, Powerful, Speaking (II 66.23) or Alive, Knowing, Desiring, Powerful (I 469.24 [Y 7,122.3]). Three: Allah, All-merciful, Lord (I 427.4 [Y 6,304.3]; II 437.5, 442.21). On the "Presences of the Names," cf. the longest chapter in the *Futūḥāt*, Chapter 558 (IV 196–326), which is divided into ninety-nine sections, each dealing with the "presence" of one of the names.

17. Ibn al-ʿArabī employs the term "common people" (*al-ʿumūm*; also *al-ʿāmma*) in at least three different senses, which must be understood from the context. The expression is contrasted with the "elect" (*al-khuṣūṣ, al-khāṣṣa*), and the "elect of the elect" (*khuṣūṣ al-khuṣūṣ, khāṣṣat al-khāṣṣa*), terms which also vary according to the context. In the present instance, he seems to have in mind the first of the following possibilities: 1. The common people are jurists (*fuqahā'*), theologians (*aṣḥāb ʿilm al-kalām*), and the Muslim philosophers (*ḥukamā' al-islām*), the elect are the Sufis, and the elect of the elect the highest degree of the friends of God, the "Verifiers" or "People of Blame." 2. The common people are the general run of the faithful, and the elect the jurists, theologians, and philosophers (cf. II 591.34). The elect of the elect would then be

the Sufis. 3. The "common people" are the majority of the Sufis, the "elect" are the accomplished Sufi masters, and the "elect of the elect" are the Verifiers.

18. In his *Iṣṭilāḥāt*, Ibn al-ʿArabī identifies "adornment" with "assumption of the traits of the names." Cf. II 128.20, translated in Chapter 18.

19. For explanations of these terms, see Chapter 5.

20. "Folk of Allah" (*ahl Allāh*), synonymous with "Folk of the Koran," is one of the many epithets by which Ibn al-ʿArabī refers to the greatest friends of God. The two terms derive from the hadith, "God has folk [i.e., family] among the people: the Folk of the Koran, who are the Folk of Allah and His Elect (*khāṣṣa*)" (Aḥmad III 128, 242). The Shaykh often quotes or paraphrases this hadith (e.g., II 299.18, 352.27, 372.14, 510.10; III 103.34, 121.35).

21. In other words, the Most Beautiful Names belong to God alone, but the servant comes to be described by them when he gains proximity to Him. The lover imagined that in the same way, when God "descends" to the creaturely level in order to speak to the creatures, He borrows the names of created things in order to be understood.

22. Literally, the "knowledge of the traces" or "of the outward descriptions," that is, such sciences as jurisprudence and Kalām (cf. II 330.23, 523.10). Ibn al-ʿArabī frequently employs the term *ʿulamāʾ al-rusūm*, "the exoteric scholars" or "scholars of the outward appearances." Often he employs the term pejoratively, but not always (cf. III 167.8), since these sciences are valid on their own levels.

23. I.e., the word of God through which He brings the engendered things into existence. Of the several Koranic passages in which it is mentioned, Ibn al-ʿArabī quotes most commonly the verse, "Our only speech to a thing, when We desire it, is to say to it 'Be!', and it is" (16:40).

24. For a detailed discussion of the two kinds of worship, see Chapter 18.

25. God's "jealousy" (*ghayra*) removes the properties of the "other" (*ghayr*), since it demands that the "other" cannot have true existence. "The Divine Jealousy requires that none be qualified by existence but God" (II 226.29). At the same time, jealousy is one of the divine roots of the "other." "Jealousy requires affirming the other, but in reality there are no others, except the entities of the possible things in respect of their immutability, not in respect of their existence. Jealousy becomes manifest through the immutability of the possible things. . . . God is jealous lest the possible things accept existence" (II 10.12). Cf. II 244–46, 500–502.

26. Allusion to several Koranic verses, such as, "Have you not seen how God has subjected to you everything in the heavens and the earth?" (31:20).

27. "God's qualifying Himself through jealousy" most likely refers to a hadith concerning the Prophet's companion Saʿd: "He is jealous, I am more jealous than he, and God is more jealous than I; because of His jealousy He has forbidden indecencies (*al-fawāḥish*)" (Bukhārī, Tawḥīd 20; Muslim, Liʿān 17). Here the "property of jealousy" is that no "other" can have true existence (cf. above, note 25).

Chapter 3. The Divine Roots of Hierarchy and Conflict

1. "Existence" here quite obviously does not imply any sort of separate or independent existence, since the names—as Ibn al-ʿArabī never tires of stressing—are only relationships, not entities.

2. As we saw in the previous chapter, in one respect all names denote the Essence, but in another respect each has its own specific meaning. Here Ibn al-ʿArabī looks at the name Allah in terms of its specificity, so it does not denote the Essence. Elsewhere he maintains that it denotes the Essence better than any other name. "[The name Allah] denotes the Essence Itself" (*Azal* 14). Cf. IV 197.1, translated in the next chapter, and II 174.26.

3. Cf. III 397.4: "It is no surprise when an existent thing displays effects (*taʾthīr*)—what is surprising is when a nonexistent thing displays effects. All relationships are nonexistent things, yet they possess effects and properties. In reality, everything that is nonexistent in entity but manifest in property and effect is called 'unseen' (*ghayb*), for the thing whose entity is absent is 'unseen'."

4. Allusion to the Koranic verse which Ibn al-ʿArabī constantly quotes, "Nothing is like Him" (42:11).

5. The hadith is provided with minor variations in Muslim, Musāfirīn 172. Cf. Aḥmad

II 433, III 34; for versions in most of the standard sources, see *Concordance* II 152.

6. The hadith is not mentioned in the *Concordance*, but Ibn al-ʿArabī cites it frequently, e.g., I 225.24 (Y 3,372), 306.8 (Y 4,417), 385.16 (Y 5,502); IV 321.17.

7. On this "Principle of Plenitude" in Western thought, see A.O. Lovejoy, *The Great Chain of Being* (Cambridge: Harvard University Press, 1936).

8. The statement goes back to the use of the word "desire" in such Koranic contexts as, "Our only word to a thing, when We desire it, is to say to it 'Be!', and it is" (16:40). As Ibn al-ʿArabī points out, once the object of desire (*murād*) is achieved, the property of desire leaves the thing (II 522.8). The Shaykh frequently makes this point concerning love (*maḥabba*), which is a specific kind of desire. "Love never becomes connected to anything but the nonexistent thing—that which has no existence when the connection becomes established. Love desires the existence or occurrence of its object. . . . What the lover loves is the desire of union with the specific person, whoever it might be. If it is someone who can be embraced, he loves embracing his beloved. If it is someone with whom intercourse can be had, he loves the intercourse. If it is someone to be sat with, he loves the sitting. Hence his love only becomes attached to that of the person which is nonexistent at the moment, but he imagines that he loves the person." (II 327.2; cf. II 113.9, 232.14, 264.1, 332.9, 334.3, 337.18, 522.4). "Desire" (*irāda*) differs from "will" (*mashīʾa*) primarily in the nature of the object, and this has important theological consequences. For example, the Shaykh writes, "Desire has no free choice (*ikhtiyār*). Nothing in the Koran or Sunna has spoken of any such thing, nor does the rational faculty point to it. Free choice belongs only to will, for if He wills, the thing comes to be, and if He wills, it does not come to be. . . . Desire is the connection of the will to the object of desire, as indicated in His words, 'Our only speech to a thing, when We desire it . . .' (16:40)" (III 48.12).

9. Once a possible thing comes into existence, it is clear that God has known that it would come into existence for all eternity, so its existence is necessary, not through itself, but through the "other"—the Being of God.

10. The expression *ʿayn al-shayʾ huwa ʿayn al-shayʾ* is normally translated as "one thing is identical with another thing." This is clearly one meaning of "the entity of one thing is the entity of another thing." But in the present context, Ibn al-ʿArabī has in mind the identity of all the names and attributes with the Divine Essence, and the normal translation would not convey this point as clearly.

11. In general the Shaykh al-Akbar applies the term "Verifiers" (*al-muḥaqqiqūn*) to the highest category of the friends of God. They follow no one's authority (*taqlīd*), since in themselves they have "verified" (*taḥqīq*) and "realized" (*taḥaqquq*)—through unveiling and finding—the truth (*ḥaqq*) and reality (*ḥaqīqa*) of all things, i.e., the Real Himself (*al-ḥaqq*). Cf. Chapter 165 (II 267–68), 388.13; IV 31.8. They are the same as the People of Blame (*Mawāqiʿ* 29).

12. As was done recently by one of his detractors in Egypt in an episode which once again has confirmed the living relevance of his teachings. See Th. E. Homerin, "Ibn Arabi in the People's Assembly: Religion, Press, and Politics in Sadat's Egypt," *The Middle East Journal* 40 (1986): 462–77, especially p. 471.

13. *Muḥāḍarat al-asmāʾ al-ilāhiyya wa muḥāwaratuhā wa mujārātuhā fī ḥilbat al-munāẓara* (I 210.3 [Y 3, 297]). In this passage from the *Futūḥāt* he refers to his depiction of the Conference of the Names in *ʿAnqā mughrib* (pp. 33ff.) and *Inshāʾ al-dawāʾir* (pp. 36–38), but he seems to be unaware that later on in the same volume of the *Futūḥāt* he will provide its fullest description. He also refers to his description of the Conference in *Dhakhāʾir* 201.

14. This term usually refers to God as revealer of the Koran, though it may often refer to the Prophet inasmuch as he established elements of the Law through his Hadith and Sunna.

15. The entity or specific characteristic of the name cannot become manifest within God, since He is One in every respect and the manifestation of the entities of all the names depends upon multiplicity. Hence the entities of the names can only become apparent in the cosmos through their effects and properties.

16. Ibn al-ʿArabī adds this clarification because the term "creation" (*khalq*) has two basic meanings: *ījād* or "to bring into existence" and *taqdīr* or "to ordain," that is, to establish and define the states of the things before they come into existence in this world. The Shaykh writes that in the hadith, "God created the creatures in darkness," "created" means "ordained." "Hence, the first divine effect in creatures was ordainment, before they

came to exist. . . . The divine ordainment in their case is like the architect who pictures in his mind what he wants to build" (II 62.3). Cf. II 95.28, 430.4, IV 210.18; *Muʿjam* 426–27.

17. Cf. II 57.6: "The first of the divine names is the One/Unique (*al-wāḥid al-aḥad*), which is a single, compound name, just as Baʿlbak, Rāmhurmuz, and *al-raḥmān al-raḥīm* (The All-merciful/All-compassionate) are compound. By it we do not mean two names. The One/Unique is the first of the names because . . . it denotes the Essence Itself, without any relationship by which It is described, just like concrete names for things. There is nothing more exact as a proper name, since it is a name of the Essence. . . . You may object that it is fitting that the name 'Allah' be the first divine name rather than the One/Unique, since Allah is called the One/Unique, but the One/Unique is not called Allah. I will reply: What is denoted by the name Allah demands the cosmos and everything within it. Hence it belongs to Him like the name 'king' or 'sultan': It is a name of the Level, not of the Essence. But 'Unique' is a name of the Essence. . . . Nothing is understood from 'One' but the Entity."

18. Here Ibn al-ʿArabī alludes to "the Most Beautiful Names."

19. These two are discussed in detail in Chapter 18.

20. *Mala' aʿlā aw adnā*, i.e., the spiritual and corporeal worlds. The "higher plenum" —discussed in the next chapter—is a Koranic term often taken to refer to the highest angels or archangels, but Ibn al-ʿArabī employs the term to refer to the angelic or spiritual world in general.

21. The term *faṣl* in a philosophical context is normally translated as specific difference or *differentia* and is contrasted with *jins* or genus. Ibn al-ʿArabī certainly has this meaning in mind, but he is attempting to tie the term into a much broader discussion. This is indicated by the fact that this chapter—devoted to *faṣl*—is preceded by a chapter devoted to *waṣl* or "joining." Hence I have used a non-philosophical term to translate the word.

Chapter 4. The Essence and the Divinity

1. Inasmuch as the Divinity is a "level" and therefore nonexistent as such, it can never be witnessed; that is, it cannot be seen through unveiling (on "witnessing," cf. Chapter 13). Hence, when a person "witnesses" God, he witnesses an "entity" which is the Essence, since God has no other entity. However, this Entity can never be known in Itself, only in respect of the relationship It establishes with the one who witnesses it, i.e., His self-disclosure to the witnesser.

2. Since attributes can only be negated from the Essence, no "positive attributes of Self" can be attributed to It. All positive attributes which can be attributed to God are attributed to Him only in respect of the Divinity, and these attributes are shared with the creatures. "The Real did not name Himself by any name or describe Himself by any positive attribute unless the creatures are also qualified by it. The attribute is ascribed to each described object in accordance with what the reality of the object demands. In the Real it is prior because the Real is prior in existence, and in the creatures it is posterior because they are posterior in existence. It is said concerning the Real that He is an Essence who is described as Alive, Knowing, Powerful, Desiring, Speaking, Hearing, and Seeing. It is said concerning man the creature that he is alive, knowing, powerful, desiring, speaking, hearing, and seeing—no one disagrees on this" (II 432.35).

3. Al-Suyūṭī provides five variations on this hadith in *al-Jāmiʿ al-ṣaghīr* (*Fayḍ al-qadīr fī sharḥ al-jāmiʿ al-ṣaghīr* [Beirut: Dār al-Maʿrifa, 1972]), III, pp. 262–63.

4. Here "names of majesty" are synonymous with "names of incomparability" (cf. the last section of the previous chapter).

5. A well-known Sufi who died in 286/899. Ibn al-ʿArabī accords him the highest respect by calling him one of the People of Blame (III 34.1).

6. The Arabic term is *shubha*, which means something similar, a likeness, a resemblance. As a technical term in the sciences it refers to doubt and wavering over the exact status of something, e.g., whether it is lawful or unlawful, true or false. Ibn al-ʿArabī uses the term to refer to an argument which throws a person into doubt after he has established a position through rational proofs (*dalīl*).

7. Allusion to several Koranic verses, such as, "What, is he who is upon a clear sign from his Lord like one unto whom evil deeds have been decked out fair?" (47:14).

8. The references are probably to the famous Ashʿarites Abu'l-Maʿālī ʿAbd al-Malik al-Juwaynī (d. 487/1085), al-Qāḍī Abū Bakr

Muḥammad al-Bāqillānī (d. 403/1013), al-Ustādh Abū Isḥāq Ibrāhīm al-Isfarāyinī (d. 418/1027), and al-Shaykh Abu'l-Ḥasan al-Ash'arī (d. 324/935), founder of the school.

9. Abū Yazīd was asked, "How are you this morning?" He replied, "I have no morning and no evening; morning and evening belong to him who becomes delimited by attributes, but I have no attributes." On the significance of this saying, see II 133.21 and 646.29, translated in Chapter 20. Cf. II 187.11; III 106.16.

10. *Al-Ṣifātiyyūn*, i.e., the proponents of Kalām, since, as mentioned in Chapter 2, it is they who employ this term among the three mentioned here. For another instance of this title, cf. II 60.1 (reading *ṣifātiyyīn* for *ṣifātīn*).

11. Allusion to the station of *khilāfa*, "vicegerency" or "successorship" of God in the earth, granted—in the Shaykh's interpretation—to the perfect men in virtue of their full actualization of the divine form. "No one is called the 'vicegerent' except through the perfection of the Divine Form within him" (III 156.35). Cf. *Cosmology*.

12. The fact that God knew this is stated clearly in the text of the Koran: "O you who have faith, void not your freewill offerings by making people feel obliged and by injury, as one who shows off to men and has no faith in God and the Last Day" (2:264). If God has forbidden it for the faithful—who are attempting to assume His character traits—then certainly He has also forbidden it for Himself.

13. Reference to the following saying, which Ibn al-'Arabī cites as coming from the Torah: "O son of Adam! I created the things for you and I created you for Myself" (I 295.32 [Y 4,358.10]).

14. This saying, attributed in Sufi texts to the Prophet, is better known in the form, "I was a Hidden Treasure, so I loved to be known. Hence I created the creatures that I might be known." The scholars of Hadith consider it a forgery, as the Shaykh is well aware. However, in his view its authenticity has been proven by unveiling (*kashf*), or vision of the Prophet in the imaginal world. Hence he writes that this hadith "is sound on the basis of unveiling, but not established by way of transmission (*naql*)" (II 399.28). On establishing the soundness of hadiths through unveiling, see the last section of Chapter 14.

15. Cf. II 300.29, 301.3, 619.21.

16. Reading *bi 'aynihi* in place of *ya'ummuhu*.

17. Reference to the hadith of the Hidden Treasure quoted above, where God says, "I loved to be known."

18. Reference to a hadith which has come in several versions, such as, "God surely rejoices more through the repentance of one of His servants than any of you rejoice when you find your stray camel in the desert." Muslim, Tawba 1–9; Bukhārī, Da'awāt 4; etc. (*Concordance* I, p. 284).

19. Cf. II 40.35, 379.8, 476.29, 500.11, 512.12, 605.9, 660.14; III 316.16; IV 282.31, 325.5; *Dhakhā'ir* 112.

20. On the importance of divine courtesy, cf. Chapter 11.

21. The Fundamental Scale (*al-mīzān al-aṣlī*), of which the Scale of the Law is the branch, is that through which the works of the servants are weighed on the Day of Resurrection. On scales, see Chapter 11.

22. Cf. I 114.15 (Y 2,199.6); III 157.34, 361.27, 441.26.

23. Several versions of the hadith are related in standard sources, including Dārimī, Ru'yā 12; and Aḥmad I 378, IV 66, V 243, 378. The Shaykh provides a detailed commentary on the hadith in Chapter 306 of the *Futūḥāt* (III 26–28).

24. These are the four "natures" (*ṭabā'i'*), i.e., the four constituent qualities of Nature. Cf. the following footnote.

25. "Nature" (*ṭabī'a*) is the forever invisible materia which allows everything below the world of the spirits (*'ālam al-arwāḥ*) to become manifest, that is, everything within the worlds of imagination and corporeal bodies. In this sense it makes up the "body" as opposed to the spirit of a thing; or, it is the thing's "darkness" as opposed to its "light." Nature is composed of four basic tendencies, known as the "natures" (*ṭabā'i'*): heat, cold, wetness, and dryness. In a second sense, Nature is synonymous with the Breath of the All-merciful. See Chapter 8.

26. On the hierarchy of the cosmos in Ibn al-'Arabī's teachings, cf. *Cosmology*.

27. *The Philosophy of the Kalam*, pp. 8ff.

28. A slightly more sophisticated classification would make these into three kinds of names: Those that (1.) designate the Essence in Itself and (2.) those that designate the Divinity in respect of (a.) names of incomparability and (b.) attributes of acts (I 563.19 [Y 7,81]). As mentioned earlier, the Shaykh provides several ways of classifying the names, not all of them completely consistent with what we are discussing here.

29. Allusion to Koran 41:44. "To the faithful [the Koran] is a guidance and a healing;

but as for those who have no faith, in their ears is a heaviness, and to them it is a blindness; those—they are called from a far place."

30. The "delimitation" of the Essence is discussed in the last section of Chapter 6.

31. Koran translators generally render the term *ʿizza* as might or glory, but Ibn al-ʿArabī states that the term in this verse means that no laudation on the part of the creatures can attain to Him (III 148.23). He defines the divine name Inaccessible (*al-ʿazīz*) as "He who is wanted but cannot be attained" (III 153.18). In explaining the Koranic verse, he writes "The Inaccessible is the unapproachable (*al-manīʿ*) and the unreachable (*al-ḥimā*). If something can be attained in any respect—through an attribute, a description, knowledge, or gnosis—it is not unapproachable and unreachable" (II 542.2).

32. On the fact that none knows any but himself, see Chapter 19.

33. Ibn al-ʿArabī frequently cites these attributes on the basis of various hadiths: 1. Receiving joyfully (*tabashbush*): "No Muslim takes up an abode in the mosques for the sake of prayer and invocation without God receiving him joyfully, just as the family of an absent man receives him joyfully when he returns" (Ibn Māja, Masājid 19; Aḥmad II 307, 328, 340, 453). 2. Rejoicing. Cf. the hadith cited in note 18. 3. Wonder (*taʿajjub*). "Surely God wonders at a youth who has no sensual desire" (Aḥmad IV 151). 4. "Being our deputies" is explained in the hadith of hunger, thirst, and illness partly cited here. The Shaykh often refers to this hadith, which parallels Matthew 25:41–45, by mentioning its three central clauses together: "I was hungry, but you did not feed Me; I was thirsty, but you did not give Me to drink; I was ill, but you did not visit Me" (I 297.27 [Y 4,369.11], 407.16 [Y 6,173.11], 481.22 [Y 7,203.2], 570.13 [Y 8,360.11]). In Muslim (Birr 43) the wording is slightly different, but the meaning is the same. The first part of the hadith reads as follows: "On the Day of Resurrection God will say, 'O son of Adam, I was ill and you did not visit Me.' He will reply, 'How should I visit Thee, when Thou art Lord of the worlds?' He will reply, 'Did you not know that my servant so-and-so was ill, but you did not visit him? Did you not know that had you visited him, you would have found Me with him (*ʿindahu*)?'" Cf. W. Graham, *Divine Word and Prophetic Word in Early Islam* (The Hague: Mouton, 1977), pp. 179–80.

34. By "companions" (*aṣḥāb*) Ibn al-ʿArabī on occasion means his own disciples, but more commonly he means those Sufis who have written about the subject under discussion; in the present context, he means his spiritual peers, whether or not he has met them. Thus he uses the expression to refer to great Sufis such as Abū Yazīd (II 657.34) or al-Ghazālī (III 316.11). He writes, "I mean by 'our companions' the possessors of hearts, witnessings, and unveilings, not the worshipers (*al-ʿubbād*), nor the pious renouncers (*al-zuhhād*), nor the 'Sufis' without restriction—only those among them who are the people of realities and verification (*taḥqīq*)" (I 261.10). Cf. III 34.28, translated in Chapter 20, which explains the three basic degrees of God's friends—worshipers, Sufis, and the People of Blame (the Verifiers).

35. For the sources of some of these terms, see note 33 above. The others are found in the Koran or various hadiths: 1. Laughter (*ḍiḥk*). This attribute is ascribed to God in several hadiths found in the standard sources (cf. *Concordance* III, pp. 483–85). Ibn al-ʿArabī most often cites the hadith related through Abū Zarīn: "The Messenger of God said, 'Our Lord laughs at the despondency of His servants and the nearness of their change of state.' I asked him, 'O Messenger of God. Does the Lord laugh?' He replied, 'Yes.' I said, 'We will not lack any good from a Lord who laughs'" (Ibn Māja, Muqaddima 13; cf. III 452.28; *Dhakhāʾir* 143). 2. Descent (*nuzūl*). Reference to the hadith quoted in the previous chapter, "Our Lord descends . . . " (cf. note 5). 3. Withness (*maʿiyya*). Allusion to Koran 57:4, "God is with you wherever you are." 4. Love (*maḥabba*). Attributed to God in many Koranic verses. 5. Yearning (*shawq*). Reference to a hadith not mentioned in the *Concordance*. In one passage the Shaykh refers to it as follows: "It has been mentioned in a report (*khabar*), concerning whose soundness (*ṣiḥḥa*) I have no knowledge, that God mentioned those who yearn for Him. Then He said concerning Himself that He is 'more intense in yearning for them,' in a manner appropriate for His majesty" (II 364.19). Having explained the meaning of the hadith, the Shaykh goes on to say, "This is so if the report is sound. But I have no knowledge concerning it, neither by way of unveiling nor by way of a sound transmission (*riwāya ṣaḥīḥa*). However, it is mentioned and well-known" (II 364.22). He provides a more complete text for the hadith in II 173.13, translated in Chapter 18.

36. Tasting (*dhawq*) may be defined as the direct knowledge of something through

opening or unveiling. It is the first stage of the experience of God's self-disclosure, while "drinking" (*shurb*) is the next stage, and "quenching" (*rī*) is the third stage (cf. II 133.2 and 548.4, translated in Chapter 13). In some passages Ibn al-ʿArabī adds "intoxication" (*sukr*) as a fourth stage (*Dhakhāʾir* 67).

37. Cf. the passage in which Ibn al-ʿArabī recounts his conversation with the king al-Malik al-Ẓāhir, the son of Saladin (III 69.33, translated in Chapter 12).

38. Elsewhere the Shaykh points out that no verse or hadith can be interpreted exclusively as indicating the declaration of similarity, since in each case the Arabs will understand a number of senses, including the declaration of incomparability (I 95.18 [Y 2,104.3]). In the process of mentioning a number of examples, he cites *istīlāʾ* as a valid explanation of *istiwāʾ* (I 98.7 [Y 2,116.7]).

39. Allusion to the hadith, "God created Adam upon His own Form." Cf. Chapter 10, note 4.

40. Reference to the Prophet's words mentioned in many hadiths in most of the standard sources (cf. *Concordance* I, p. 216, col. 1, line 17–22).

41. In other words, the theologians have denied the truth of the revelation by interpreting God's hand, for example, as signifying "power" or some other abstract concept.

42. On *tashabbuh*, which Ibn al-ʿArabī sometimes considers synonymous with "assuming the traits of the divine names" (*al-takhalluq bi'l-asmāʾ al-ilāhiyya*), cf. Chapter 16.

43. God's forgetting, deception, trickery, and guile are all mentioned in the Koran: "They forgot God, so He forgot them" (9:67). "They deceived, and God deceived, and God is the best of deceivers" (3:54). "They are devising guile, and I am devising guile" (86:16). "The hypocrites seek to trick God, but He is tricking them" (4:142).

44. This statement refers both to the hadith of the Hidden Treasure and to the Koranic verse, "I created jinn and mankind only to worship Me" (51:56). The Prophet's companion Ibn ʿAbbās interpreted "to worship Me" as meaning "to know Me" (II 214.16).

Chapter 5. Existence and Nonexistence

1. For an introduction to the history of the usage of the term *waḥdat al-wujūd* among Ibn al-ʿArabī's followers, see Chittick, "Rumi and *Waḥdat al-Wujūd*."

2. Allusion to the hadith of the Hidden Treasure. Cf. Chapter 4, note 14.

3. As opposed to "the necessary through the other" (*al-wājib bi'l-ghayr*), i.e., the possible thing which has come into existence. Cf. Chapter 3, note 9.

4. See II 232.11 and III 47.30, both translated in Chapter 12.

5. Cf. Chittick and P.L. Wilson, *Fakhruddin ʿIraqi: Divine Flashes* (New York: Paulist Press, 1982), introduction; and Chittick, "Ṣadr al-Dīn Qūnawī on the Oneness of Being," *International Philosophical Quarterly* 21 (1981): 171–84.

6. The distinction between entified and mental existence is especially important in discussions of "impossible things," which cannot exist in the cosmos but can be conceived of in the mind. To mental existence Ibn al-ʿArabī adds two more categories of existence: verbal (*lafẓī*), and written (*kitābī* or *khaṭṭī* or *raqamī*). Concerning verbal existence he writes, "Every object of knowledge enters into this existence, even the impossible thing and nonexistence. For the impossible thing is found in words but never receives entified existence. As for nonexistence, if it is the nonexistence by which the possible thing is described, it receives entified existence, whereas if it is the nonexistence which is the impossible, it does not receive entified existence" (II 309.29). Cf. I 45.34 (Y 1,208.5).

7. The term "elemental" is applied to things compounded of the four elements—earth, air, fire, and water. Cf. *Cosmology*.

8. These are the faculties of the vegetal, animal, and rational souls. Cf. *Cosmology*.

9. Cf. Chittick, "Ibn al-ʿArabī's Myth of the Names," *Theories of Knowledge: Ancient and Medieval*, ed. P. Morewedge, forthcoming.

10. Muslim, Birr 55. For a translation of the whole text, cf. Graham, *Divine Word*, pp. 205–206.

11. The other two types of marriage pertain to the spiritual world (*rūḥānī*) and the realm of Nature (*ṭabīʿī*). Cf. III 516.29; also I 170–171 (Y 3,100–109); *Muʿjam* 1069–71.

12. III 295.18; cf. *Fuṣūṣ al-ḥikam* 187 and ʿAfīfī's commentary thereon.

13. This hadith is often translated as "God was, and nothing was with Him," but as the Shaykh points out, the verb *kān* here is a word which denotes existence (*ḥarf wujūdī*), without temporal implication (II 56.6, translated below, and II 692.24). As for the saying

"And He is now as He was" (*wa huwa'l-ān kamā kān*) sometimes mentioned as part of the hadith, Ibn al-ʿArabī tells us that it adds nothing to the meaning and indicates ignorance on the part of the person who said it (I 41.25 [Y 1,189.14]; II 56.7, 458.31, 692.24). According to the *Fuṣūṣ* commentator Qayṣarī, that person was Junayd (cf. *al-Tawḥīd wa'l-nubuwwa wa'l-walāya*, ed. S.J. Āshtiyānī in *Rasā'il-i Qayṣarī* [Mashhad: Dānishgāh, 1357/1978], p. 13; Jāmī, *Naqd al-nuṣūṣ fī sharḥ naqsh al-fuṣūṣ*, ed. W. Chittick [Tehran: Imperial Iranian Academy of Philosophy, 1977], p. 67).

14. The hadith is found in four of the standard sources (*Concordance* VI 260.26).

15. The term He-ness is basically synonymous with Essence. "*Huwiyya* signifies the Unseen Reality" (II 130.10) or "the Reality in the world of the Unseen" (*Iṣṭilāḥāt* 14). It is God inasmuch as He is designated by the name "He" (*huwa*), which is a pronoun designating absence and therefore nonmanifestation. The term *huwa* is mentioned in many Koranic verses, such as that which is being discussed in the present passage—"He is the First and the Last, the Manifest and the Nonmanifest." Often the term can be translated more accurately as "it-ness," since the word *huwa* can designate anything absent or anything to which allusion can be made and is thus more general than the gender-specific "he" might suggest. "The word '*huwa*' is more inclusive than the word 'Allah,' since it designates Allah, every absent thing, and everything which possesses an it-ness. And there is nothing that does not possess an itness. It makes no difference if the known or mentioned thing is existent or nonexistent" (III 514.22). Cf. IV 443.33 (translated in Chapter 19) and II 579–81.

16. Here the Shaykh employs the terminology of logic, but he considers this a universal law, not limited to the mental domain. Three things are needed for any result (*natīja*) to be produced, whether we envisage reproduction in the animal world (male, female, and union), conclusions in the logical domain (the major, minor, and middle terms of a syllogism), or the creation of the cosmos (God's Essence, His Desire, and His creative Word "Be"). Cf. II 412.26, 440.25; III 106.27, 126.4. See also *Muʿjam* 247–50; *Fuṣūṣ* 116 (BW 142); Jāmī, *Naqd al-nuṣūṣ*, 194–97 (partly translated in Chittick, "Ibn 'Arabī's own Summary of the Fuṣūṣ," *Sophia Perennis* 2/1 (1976): 67–68; also *Journal of the Muhyiddin Ibn ʿArabi Society* 1 (1982): 63–64).

17. E.g., Farghānī, *Mashāriq al-darārī*, ed. S.J. Āshtiyānī, (Tehran: Anjuman-i Islāmī-yi Ḥikmat wa Falsafa-yi Īrān), 1358/1979, p. 30 (quoted in Jāmī, *Naqd al-nuṣūṣ*, p. 118).

18. The terminology of some of Ibn al-ʿArabī's followers suggests that the divine names as such are the "universal divine names" (*al-asmā' al-ilāhiyyat al-kulliyya*), while the existent things are the "particular divine names" (*al-asmā' al-ilāhiyyat al-juz'iyya*). Cf. Farghānī, *Mashāriq al-darārī*, pp. 58–59. Since the terms "universal" and "particular" are relative, the two terms may also be used simply to distinguish those names which have a wider scope from those which have a narrower scope. Cf. Farghānī, *Muntaha'l-madārik* (Cairo: Maktab al-Ṣanā'iʿ, 1293/1876), I, p. 87.

19. As explained in the introduction, "opening" (*fatḥ* or *futūḥ*) is more or less synonymous with "unveiling" (*kashf*) and "tasting" (*dhawq*). Hence it signifies direct, experiential knowledge of the realities of things, a knowledge that God gives to the servant through "self-disclosure" (*tajallī*). Cf. Chapter 13.

20. This verse is one of the scriptural sources for Ibn al-ʿArabī's "Real Through Whom Creation Takes Place" (*al-ḥaqq al-makhlūq bihi*) discussed in Chapter 8.

Chapter 6. The New Creation

1. Cf. Izutsu, *Sufism and Taoism*, pp. 205–15; also Izutsu, "The Concept of Perpetual Creation in Islamic Mysticism and Zen Buddhism," in S.H. Nasr (ed.), *Mélanges offerts à Henry Corbin* (Tehran: McGill University, Institute of Islamic Studies, 1977), especially pp. 142–46.

2. Cf. his *Ayyām al-sha'n* in *Rasā'il*; also I 121.23 (Y 2,234.15), 291.35 (Y 4,236.5); II 441.32; III 45.28, 201–203; *Muʿjam* 1253–54.

3. "Individual moment" would be a more literal translation. But Ibn al-ʿArabī himself glosses *fard* as "that which does not receive division" (*alladhī lā yaqbal al-qisma*, II 384.31).

4. Ibn al-ʿArabī's analogy may seem farfetched, but it is characteristic of his methodology to employ to the extent possible Koranic imagery or principles established by the Koran. Here one should recall the verse, "God is not ashamed to strike a similitude even of a gnat, or aught above it" (2:26); nor is the Shaykh.

5. In view of the fact that the obvious meaning of the verse is that "next" should be read "next world," it may seem that Ibn al-ʿArabī is forcing an unintended meaning upon the text. But he has no need to force things, since there are other verses that could serve to make his point as well. What he is in fact doing is bringing out the richness of the original text, while at the same time illustrating a fundamental principle of his own hermeneutics: Any meaning that can be understood from the text without doing violence to the language is meant by God, who revealed it with full knowledge of all interpretations. Cf. Chapter 14.

6. Muslim, Īmān 302.

7. God is called "Time" according to the hadith, "Say not, 'Oh, the disappointment of time!' [or, in another version, "Curse not time"], for God is time." Muslim, Alfāẓ 4, 5; cf. Bukhārī, Adab 101; *Muwaṭṭa'*, Kalām 3; Aḥmad II 259, 272, 275, 318, 934. The Shaykh writes (III 202.4) that in respect of being "Time," God is a single beginningless and endless "Day," without nighttime or daytime; but the properties of God's names and attributes divide this single Day into many days, and these are the "Days of God" mentioned in the Koranic verse, "We sent Moses with Our signs: 'Bring forth thy people from the shadows to the light and remind them of the Days of God!'" (14:5). The Shaykh clarifies the connection between Time and the constant fluctuation of states in the following passage: "Having let us know that He is Time, God mentioned to us that He possesses days. These are the 'Days of God.' They became entified by the properties of God's names within the cosmos. Each name possesses days, which are the time (*zamān*) of the ruling property of that name. But all are God's Days, and all are the differentiations of the property of Time in the cosmos. These Days commingle (*tawāluj*), interpenetrate, and cover each other. This is the diversity of properties that is seen in the cosmos at a single time. It derives from the interpenetration, covering, transformation, and repetition of the Days. Each of these Divine Days has a night and a daytime. Their night is the unseen, i.e., that of them which is unseen by us. . . . Their daytime is the visible, and it is identical with their property within the corporeal bodies, down to the last elemental body, i.e., everything below Nature" (III 201.12).

8. The reference is to the divine names which are also human attributes (e.g., generosity, justice, patience, etc.) and the human attributes by which God describes Himself in the Koran and the hadith (e.g., hand, foot, laughter, rejoicing, etc.). Cf. Chapter 3, last section.

9. This saying is found embedded in a number of different hadiths in the standard sources; e.g., Bukhārī, Īmān 32; Tahajjud 18, Ṣawm 52, Libās 43; Muslim, Musāfirīn 215, 221, Ṣiyām 177.

10. These words are attributed in sequence to Adam, Noah, Abraham, Moses, and Jesus in a long hadith about the Prophet's intercession on the Day of Resurrection. (Muslim, Īmān 327; cf. Bukhārī, Anbiyā' 3, Tafsīr Sūra 17, 5; Tirmidhī, Qiyāma 10; Aḥmad II, 435, 436).

11. These words belong to Abū Bakr (II 514.28).

12. For another commentary on the first sentence of the *Futūḥāt*, cf. II 310.34.

13. I 266.9 (Y 4,190.11). In the same passage he mentions that others have also said the same thing, and elsewhere he quotes it from "a group of the Folk of Tasting" (III 127.32) and mentions that it is the position of the "Verifiers" (II 657.14); cf. II 77.27.

14. The text is found with the addition of the words "among His creatures" after "thing" in Ibn Māja, Iqāma 152. Another version has *badā* in place of *tajallā* (Nasā'ī, Kusūf 16). On the verification of hadith through "unveiling," see the last section of Chapter 14.

15. Abū Dāwūd, Adab 91; Tirmidhī, Adab 2, 3, Daʿawāt 128.

16. *Al-Rijāl* (sing. *rajul*), i.e., the great friends of God. This term is more or less synonymous with *al-akābir*, "the great ones." The term "man" is not gender specific, as Ibn al-ʿArabī often points out, e.g., "At this point the person is called a *rajul*. . . . So the perfection of manliness (*rajūliyya*) lies in what we have mentioned, whether the person is male or female" (II 588.6). Cf. *Cosmology*, where several such passages are quoted.

17. Reference to two hadiths: 1. "I came to know the knowledge of the ancients and the later folk" is mentioned in one version of the hadith of the dispute of the higher plenum (quoted in Chapter 4; cf. note 23). This version is not indexed in the *Concordance*, but Ibn al-ʿArabī cites it in I 137.15 (Y 2,302.12); II 603.20, 608.20. Other versions of the hadith have, "I came to know everything in the heavens and the earth" (Tirmidhī, Tafsīr Sūra

38, 2; Aḥmad I 368); "I came to know everything between the east and the west" (Tirmidhī, ibid.). 2. "I was sent with the all-comprehensive words" (Bukhārī, Jihād 122, Taʿbīr 22, Iʿtiṣām 1; Nasāʾī, Jihād 1, Taṭbīq 100).

18. Muslim, Qadar 17; cf. Tirmidhī, Qadar 7, Daʿawāt 89; Ibn Māja, Muqaddima 13; Aḥmad II 168, 173; VI 182, 251, 302, 315.

19. Cf. *Concordance* V 459.

20. This hadith is frequently cited in Sufi texts, as well as by al-Ghazālī in *Iḥyāʾ ʿulūm al-dīn* (III.1.5; III, p. 12), but it is not acknowledged as authentic by most of the exoteric scholars. Cf. *Muʿjam* 1265–66.

21. Cf. above, note 7.

22. This famous saying, usually quoted as a hadith, is not accepted by the specialists (cf. *Muʿjam* 1261). Ibn al-ʿArabī frequently comments on it; cf. Chapter 19.

23. As mentioned in the introduction, associating others with God (*shirk*) is the opposite of *tawḥīd*, or professing God's Unity.

24. The reference is to the situation of the people in hell according to a short section of the long hadith of *taḥawwul*: "The angels intercede, the prophets intercede, the faithful intercede, and none remains but the Most Merciful of the merciful. He takes a handful of the Fire and removes from it a people who have never done any good at all after they have become coals. He throws them into a river in the Garden, called the 'River of Life'. They sprout up like seeds sprout up in the wake of a flood" (Muslim, Imān 302, 304).

25. Al-Ḥakīm al-Tirmidhī (fl. 3rd/9th century) drew up a list of 157 questions which could only be answered, so he said, by the elect among the friends of God. Ibn al-ʿArabī was the first and only person to take up the challenge, writing a treatise called *al-Jawāb al-mustaqīm*. Later he incorporated a vastly expanded version of this treatise into Chapter 73 of the *Futūḥāt* (II 39–139). Cf. al-Tirmidhī, *Kitāb khatm al-awliyāʾ*, ed. O. Yahia (Beirut: Imprimerie Catholique, 1965); Chodkiewicz, *Le sceau*, passim.

26. This is a *ḥadīth qudsī* recorded in most of the standard sources. Cf. Graham, *Divine Word*, pp. 127ff.

27. I.e., in answering the previous question of Tirmidhī, II 111–113.

28. Cf. Chapter 3, note 5.

29. This saying is found in many versions in the standard sources. Cf. Graham, *Divine Word*, pp. 129, 175–76.

30. Allusion to the hadith cited above, "My heavens and My earth embrace Me not, but the heart of My believing servant does embrace Me."

31. *al-ʿAjz ʿan dark al-idrāk idrāk*. Ibn al-ʿArabī frequently cites this saying, attributing it to Abū Bakr, as a description of the highest level of human knowledge. Cf. II 619.35 (translated in Chapter 9); III 132.35; *Dhakhāʾir* 202.

Chapter 7. Cosmic Imagination

1. These seven divine attributes are sometimes called the "Seven Leaders" or "Seven Mothers," since all the remaining divine and cosmic attributes can be traced back to them. Cf. I 100.6ff. (Y 2,126–27); II 134.33, 460.11, 493.20; *Inshāʾ* 33. Cf. Chapter 2, note 16.

2. Tirmidhī, Tafsīr Sūra 113, 3.

3. The more complete form of this hadith, which is narrated from ʿIkrima and whose authenticity is disputed by the specialists, is as follows: "I saw my Lord in the form of a beardless youth, wearing a cloak of gold, upon his head a crown of gold, and upon his feet sandals of gold" (*Dhakhāʾir* 71). Naturally Ibn al-ʿArabī is aware that it is not considered sound (I 97.27 [Y 2,114.6]).

4. Diḥya Kalbī was known as the most beautiful contemporary of the Prophet, and a hadith tells us that Gabriel used to come to the Prophet in his form (Aḥmad II 107). Cf. II 492.3, 495.12, 612.33; III 42.10; *Dhakhāʾir* 170.

5. Bukhārī, ʿIlm 38, Adab 109, Taʿbīr 10; Muslim, Ruʾyā 10, 11, etc. Cf. *Concordance* VI 169–70.

6. Bukhārī, ʿIlm 22, Faḍāʾil al-Ṣaḥāba 6; Taʿbīr 15, 16, 34; Muslim, Faḍāʾil al-Ṣaḥāba 16; Dārimī, Ruʾyā 13.

7. Though frequently cited by the Shaykh and other Sufis as a hadith, it is not found in the standard collections. Abū Ibrāhīm Mustamlī Bukhārī (d. 434/1042–43) attributes it to ʿAlī ibn Abī Ṭālib (*Sharḥ-i Taʿarruf* [Lucknow, 1328], III, p. 98).

8. Allusion to Koran 78:9–11: "And We appointed your sleep for a rest; and We appointed night for a garment; and We appointed daytime for livelihood" (cf. 25:47).

9. See above, note 3.

10. Abū Dāwūd, Adab 88. He also used to say, "If any of you has seen a dream, let him tell it to me, and I will interpret it for him" (Dārimī, Ruʾyā 13; Aḥmad II 146).

11. Allusion to the hadith, "The veridical [or good, or sound] dream [or, the dream of the person of faith] is one-forty-sixth part of prophecy." The text is found in most of the standard sources (*Concordance* I 343, s.v. *juz'*).

12. This hadith is not indexed in the *Concordance*, though a number of hadiths speak of the Trumpet as a "horn" (*qarn*).

13. The first hadith is part of the famous hadith of Gabriel, in which Gabriel comes to the Prophet in the form of a man and asks the Prophet about *al-islām* ("submission"), *al-īmān* ("faith"), and *al-iḥsān* ("virtue" or "good-doing" or "perfection"). The Prophet then explains to his Companions that the man had been Gabriel, and he had come to teach them their religion (Bukhārī, Tafsīr Sūra 31, 2; Īmān 37; Muslim, Īmān 1; etc.). On the second hadith, cf. Chapter 3, note 6.

14. Most, if not all of these examples, are drawn from hadiths. 1. Knowledge as milk: cited above. 2. Islam as a pillar (Bukhārī, Taʿbīr 23, Manāqib al-Anṣār 19; Muslim, Faḍā'il al-Ṣaḥāba 148, 150). 3. Koran: butter and honey (Bukhārī, Taʿbīr 47; Muslim, Ru'yā 17; Abū Dāwūd, Sunna 8; Ibn Māja, Ru'yā 10; Dārimī, Ru'yā 13; Aḥmad I 236). 4. Religion as a cord (*qayd*): Probably a reference to the hadith, "I love a cord (in dreams), for it is constancy (*thabāt*) in religion" (Bukhārī, Taʿbīr 26; Muslim, Ru'yā 6; etc.). 5. God. a. As a human being: the hadith of ʿIkrima, mentioned above. b. As a light. Probably a reference to the Prophet's answer to Abū Dharr, who asked him if he had seen his Lord: "I saw a light" (Muslim, Īmān 292); "I saw Him as a light—how should I see Him?" (Aḥmad V 147).

15. Allusion to various Koranic verses (e.g., Koran 7:8–9, 21:47, 23:102–3, 101:6–8) as well as hadiths concerning the Scales set up on the Day of Resurrection. For example, "Two sentences are loved by the All-merciful, light on the tongue, and heavy in the Scale: 'Glory be to God, and praise' and 'Glory be to God the Mighty'" (Bukhārī, Tawḥīd 58; Muslim, Dhikr 30; etc.).

16. Reference to the following hadith: "Death will be brought (on the Day of Resurrection) as a salt-colored ram, and a caller will call, 'O people of the Garden!' They will crane their necks and look. He will say, 'Do you recognize this?" They will say, 'Yes, this is death,' for each of them has seen it. Then he will call, 'O people of the Fire!' They will crane their necks and look. He will say, 'Do you recognize this?' They will say, 'Yes, this is death,' for each of them has seen it. Then it will be sacrificed. Then he will say, 'O people of the Garden! Everlastingness, and no death! O people of the Fire! Everlastingness, and no death!'" (Bukhārī, Tafsīr Sūra 19, 1; Aḥmad III 9; other versions are found in Tirmidhī, Janna 20, Tafsīr Sūra 19, 2; Aḥmad II 377).

Chapter 8. The Supreme Barzakh

1. Tirmidhī, Tafsīr Sūra 11, 1; Ibn Māja, Muqaddima 13; Aḥmad IV 11, 12.

2. The hadith is found in Bukhārī, Daʿawāt 14, and other standard sources.

3. The three types of creation are referred to in the Koran and the hadith: 1. Several Koranic verses refer to God's creation of the things through "Be!", which, as we have seen, Ibn al-ʿArabī calls the "Word of the Presence" (*kalimat al-ḥaḍra*). 2. A hadith which Ibn al-ʿArabī often quotes tells us that "He created the Garden of Eden with His hand, He wrote the Torah with His hand, and He planted the tree of Ṭūbā [in Paradise] with His hand." This is not found in the *Concordance*, but Suyūṭī gives us the text, "God created the Garden of Eden and planted its trees with His hand" (*al-Jāmiʿ al-ṣaghīr* III, 444). 3. Adam was created through both of God's hands, as mentioned in God's words to Iblis: "What prevented thee from prostrating thyself before him whom I created with My two hands?" (Koran 38:75). Cf. I 122.14 (Y 2,237.16).

4. On the different kinds of corporeal bodies and their relationship to Nature, cf. *Cosmology*.

5. Reference to a hadith, cited in Chapter 7, note 14.

6. On Diḥya, see Chapter 7, note 4. According to the accounts of the Battle of Badr referred to in the preceding chapter, at the point when the Prophet threw a handful of sand toward the enemy, the angels joined the battle and turned it in favor of the Muslims. This event is mentioned in Koran 8:12: "When thy Lord revealed to the angels, 'I am with you, so confirm the faithful. I shall cast terror into the unbelievers' hearts, so strike off their heads and smite their every finger.'"

7. Labīd ibn Rābiʿa (d. ca. 41/661) was one of the foremost Arab poets and a contemporary of the Prophet. He is said to have entered Islam in the year 9/630–31, when he accom-

panied a delegation from his tribe to Medina (cf. *Encyclopedia of Islam* V 583–84). The hadith is found in Bukhārī, Manāqib al-Anṣār 26, Adab 90; Muslim, Shiʿr 3–7, etc.

8. I 97.21 (Y 2, 113.3). Lane cites the first hadith in the *Lexicon* (s.v. *nafas*), but the versions of these two hadiths given in the standard collections do not mention the All-merciful. A typical version of the first runs, "The wind comes from the Spirit of God. It brings mercy and it brings chastisement. So when you see it, curse it not, but ask God for its good and seek refuge in Him from its evil" (Ibn Māja, Adab 29; Aḥmad II 268, 409, 518; V 123; cf. Tirmidhī, Fitan 65; Abū Dāwūd, Adab 104; Aḥmad II 437). The second hadith is given in the form, "I find the breath of your Lord coming from the direction of Yemen" (Aḥmad II 541).

9. Lane gives *nafas* as a synonym for *tanfīs*, citing these hadiths as examples (*Arabic-English Lexicon*, s.v. *nafas*).

10. II 394–95. Cf. the diagram provided in T. Burckhardt, *Mystical Astrology according to Ibn ʿArabi*, translated by B. Rauf (Gloucestershire: Beshara Publications, 1977).

11. On the two kinds of mercy cf. Chittick, "The Chapter Headings of the *Fuṣūṣ*," *Journal of the Muhyiddin Ibn ʿArabi Society* 2 (1984): 72–74.

12. Allusion to the hadith of the Hidden Treasure (Chapter 4, note 14).

13. On the significance of this remark for Ibn al-ʿArabī's approach to the study of Hadith, see Chapter 14, last section.

14. Cf. Chapter 3, note 8.

15. Ibn Barrajān (d. 536/1141) was called by some the al-Ghazālī of al-Andalus. He was a leader of the resistance movement against the Almoravids, and was summoned to the capital at Marrākush by the Almoravid prince and thrown into prison, where he soon died (cf. *Encyclopedia of Islam* III 732). The Shaykh mentions that he took this term from Ibn Barrajān in II 60.12, 104.6; III 77.25.

16. Ibn al-ʿArabī mentions these two verses specifically as Ibn Barrajān's source of inspiration (II 60.12), but there are several similar verses employing the term *al-ḥaqq* (6:73, 10:5, 14:19, 16:3, 29:44, 39:5, 45:22, 46:3, 64:3).

17. By quoting this partial Koranic verse, the Shaykh shows that he is commenting on the meaning of the whole verse from which it derives, "He is the First and the Last, the Manifest and the Nonmanifest, and He has knowledge of everything."

18. This fact has important ramifications in cosmology. See *Cosmology*; also Chittick, "Death and the World of Imagination."

19. "The Reality of Realities is that which includes both creature and the Real. None of the considerative thinkers have mentioned it, only the Folk of Allah. However, the Muʿtazilites gave news of something near to it. They said that God is Speaker through a quality of being a Speaker (*qāʾiliyya*), Knower through a quality of being a Knower, Powerful through a quality of being Powerful, because they fled from affirming any superadded attribute to the Essence of the Real in order to declare His incomparability. They strove in this direction and came near" (II 433.14).

20. *Li-kull ḥaqq ḥaqīqa*. The hadith is not indexed in the *Concordance*.

21. *Inshāʾ al-dawāʾir*, pp. 15ff. Cf. Izutsu, *Sufism*, pp. 161–63; also the study of M. Takeshita, "An Analysis of Ibn ʿArabī's *Inshāʾ al-Dawāʾir* with Particular Reference to the Doctrine of the 'Third Thing'," *Journal of Near Eastern Studies* 41 (1982): 243–60.

22. Thus it is the father which impregnates the Hyle to give birth to the Universal Body.

23. See *Cosmology*.

24. The heavens and celestial spheres are translucent corporeal bodies.

25. See *Cosmology*.

Chapter 9. Knowledge and the Knower

1. Ibn Māja, Muqaddima 17.

2. Reference to a Koranic verse, repeatedly cited by the Shaykh, which alludes to the special knowledge inherited by the friends of God from the Prophet: "Say [O Muḥammad!]: 'This is my way. I call to God upon insight, I and whoever follows after me'" (12:108). Cf. Chapter 15.

3. Life is often said to have a certain priority over knowledge, since that which is not alive cannot know, but the compass of knowledge is absolute in a manner that does not apply to life.

4. Concerning his use of the term *aṣḥāb* in this sense, cf. Chapter 4, note 34.

5. On Sahl, cf. Chapter 15, note 18; on Abū Madyan, cf. Chapter 13, note 19. Ibn al-ʿArīf (d. 536/1141) was an important Andalusian Sufi. He headed a group in Almeria which was a focal point for opposition to the

Almoravid jurists. He was summoned along with Ibn Barrajān (Chapter 8, note 15) to Marrākush, but well treated by the prince. Fragments of his correspondence with Ibn Barrajān have been published (P. Nwyia, "Notes sur quelques fragments inédits de la correspondence d'Ibn al-ʿArīf avec Ibn Barrajān," *Hespéris* 43 (1956): 217–21). His *Maḥāsin al-majālis*, sometimes quoted by Ibn al-ʿArabī, was edited and translated into French by M. Asin Palacios (Paris: Librairie Orientaliste Paul Geuthner, 1933). Cf. the introduction to this work, and *Encyclopedia of Islam* III 712–13. Others whom Ibn al-ʿArabī considers Verifiers include Farqad al-Sabakhī of Basra (d. 131/748–49), Junayd, and al-Ḥasan al-Baṣrī (*Isfār* 7).

6. Cf. *Mawāqiʿ al-nujūm* (Cairo: Maktaba Muḥammad ʿAlī Ṣabīḥ, 1965), esp. pp. 29–32.

7. Muslim, Dhikr 73; Tirmidhī, Daʿawāt 68, etc.

8. Ibn al-ʿArabī uses the term *al-ʿilm al-ilāhī*, which translates literally as "the divine science" or "theology," but either of these terms would be misleading. He uses this expression more or less synonymously with *al-ilāhiyyāt*, which translates literally as "the divine things." For a few other examples of usage of the term *al-ʿilm al-ilāhī* in this sense, cf. II 451.33, 459.12, 33, 646.27, 660.20; III 97.20, 132.26; for *al-ilāhiyyāt*, cf. II 404.15, 521.12, 523.16, 526.33, 537.13, 536.18, 541.10, 551.34, 560.24, 609.7, 644.23, 658.10, 668.7; III 127.31.

9. Cf. II 214.15: "Ibn al-ʿAbbās said that the meaning [of 'to worship Me'] is 'to know Me'."

10. For the source of this hadith, cf. Chapter 6, note 17.

11. These words derive from the Koranic account of how the angels were commanded to prostrate themselves to Adam. After teaching Adam the names, God tells the angels to name the things, and they reply, "Glory be to Thee! We have no knowledge save what Thou hast taught us." Then God has Adam tell them the names, and only then does He command the angels to prostrate themselves.

12. Allusion to Koran 16:49: "Their shadows incline to the right and to the left, prostrating themselves to God."

13. On the "prostration of the heart," cf. Chapter 15, note 18. On its fluctuation, cf. Chapter 6.

14. Hadiths to this effect, though not in the exact same wording, are found in Bukhārī, Tawḥīd 36; Muslim, Īmān 326, 327; Aḥmad II 436; III 248.

15. Allusion to Koran 18:109 and 31:27.

16. Allusion to the famous prophetic saying, "He who knows himself knows his Lord." Cf. Chapter 19.

17. When the famous Sufi Dhu'l-Nūn (d. 246/861) was asked about the verse "Am I not your Lord?," he said, "It is as if it is still ringing in my ears" (II 108.31, 566.1).

18. Aḥmad I 391, 452.

19. The hadith is found in most sources, including Muslim, Ṣalāt 222; Dārimī, Ṣalāt 148 (*Concordance* I 304).

20. I.e., the Breath of the All-merciful, the Barzakh. The Breath is articulated speech, so it cannot subsist without words.

21. Allusion to Koran 41:53: "We shall show them Our signs upon the Horizons and in themselves, until it is clear to them that He is the Real."

Chapter 10. Acquiring Knowledge

1. See *Cosmology*.

2. The philosophers employed the terms *shahwa* and *ghaḍab* or "anger" in a neutral sense to indicate the two basic powers of the animal soul, through which the soul finds what is necessary for its survival and repels danger. In the philosophical or psychological context the two terms have often been translated as "concupiscence" (or "appetite") and "irascibility."

3. Their outward forms possess innate knowledge since they are inanimate, compounded of the four elements. But their spirits—that is, their rational souls—need to gain knowledge of God.

4. The text of the hadith is found in a number of contexts, not all of which would suggest that the pronoun in "his form" returns to God (Bukhārī, Isti'dhān 1; Muslim, Birr 115, Janna 28; Aḥmad II 244, 251, 315, 323, 434, 463, 519). Though Ibn al-ʿArabī almost always reads the pronoun as referring back to God, he recognizes that it may also be read as referring to Adam, as in the following passage: "If an Islamic philosopher (*faylasūf islāmī*) [had asked me the meaning of this hadith], I would have answered that the pronoun goes back to Adam. The meaning is that Adam did not pass through stages (*aṭwār*) of creation, as the sperm passes from being

water to a human being, one creation after another. On the contrary, God created him as he became manifest, and he did not pass by stages, e.g., from infancy to youth to manhood to old age, nor did he pass from smallness of body to largeness, as does a child among Adam's progeny. This is the way in which such a questioner should be answered, since every questioner has an answer appropriate to him" (II 124.23). Ibn al-ʿArabī points to another version of the hadith which reads, "upon the Form of the All-merciful," thus removing the ambiguity. Though this version is not accepted by the authorities in the transmission of hadith (*aṣḥāb al-naql*), "it has been shown to be sound (*ṣaḥīḥ*) by unveiling (*kashf*)" (II 490.7).

5. The Universal Soul stands below the First Intellect and represents the receptive dimension of the spiritual world. See *Cosmology*.

6. Bukhārī, Riqāq 38. Cf. Graham, *Divine Word*, pp. 173–75.

7. This last phrase, *wa qalīl mā hum*, is normally read, "And they are few" or "How few they are," with *mā* understood as extraneous or emphatic. Ibn al-ʿArabī's reading seems a bit forced, but not completely unallowable. He is certainly being consistent with his own principles of Koran commentary; cf. Chapter 14.

8. Literally, the "spirituals" (*al-rūḥāniyyūn*).

9. Reference to the famous "hadith of supererogatory works," according to which God loves the servant who seeks nearness to Him through supererogatory works and becomes all his faculties (Bukhārī, Riqāq 38). This station of knowledge, achieved only by the greatest friends of God, is discussed in detail in Chapter 18.

10. The technical sense of this allusion to Koran 12:108 is explained below in Chapter 13.

11. Allusion to the hadith, "Verily the Trusted Spirit [Gabriel] blew into my heart that no soul will die until it completes its term" (Suyūṭī, *al-Jāmiʿ al-ṣaghīr* II, 450). Cf. Ibn al-ʿArabī's words, "By God, I neither speak nor judge except through a blowing into my heart from a divine, holy spirit" (III 101.6; cf. II 637.8).

Chapter 11. The Scale of the Law

1. Cf. W. Chittick, "A Sufi Approach to Religious Diversity: Ibn al-ʿArabī on the Metaphysics of Revelation."

2. Presumably this refers to Bukhārī's *Ṣaḥīḥ*, but I was not able to find the chapter. Ibn al-ʿArabī defines the Sunna of the Prophet in a manner which ties it into this universal message of all the prophets: It is "coming together in religion, performing it, and not scattering in it" (II 168.26).

3. *Ahl al-ḥaqq*, a term Ibn al-ʿArabī employs synonymously with *ahl Allāh* (cf. III 385.26).

4. Several of these passages are quoted in *Cosmology*.

5. Every messenger is also a prophet, but not every prophet is a messenger. See *Cosmology*.

6. Cf. III 6.22.

7. Allusion to Koran 56:27–55.

8. On the four natures, cf. Chapter 8.

9. This sentence is taken from a hadith found in Muslim (Īmān 293, 295), Ibn Māja (Muqaddima 13), and Aḥmad (IV 395, 401, 405).

10. *Taklīf*, or "being addressed by the Law" and being required to follow its injunctions, ceases only at death. Cf. below.

11. II 269.33, III 36.17. On the People of Blame, cf. Chapter 20.

12. The hadith is found in several variants and in practically all the standard sources. A typical version runs, "Surely your soul has a right against you, your Lord has a right against you, your guest has a right against you, and your wife has a right against you; so give to each one who [or which] possesses a right his [her, its] right." Cf. *Concordance* I 486.

13. Allusion to the well-known hadith, "One of the beauties of a man's Islam is that he refrains from that which is not his concern" (Tirmidhī, Zuhd 11; Ibn Māja, Fitan 12; *Muwaṭṭa'*, Ḥusn al-Khuluq 3, Kalām 17).

14. Suyūṭī, *al-Jāmiʿ al-ṣaghīr* I 224.

15. *al-Ṭā'ifat al-ʿāliya*, i.e., the great Sufis.

16. This is an abbreviated form of the "hadith of supererogatory works" (Bukhārī, Riqāq 38). See Chapter 18.

17. Allusion to several Koranic verses which allude to the "sealing of the heart," e.g., "God has set a seal on their hearts, so they know not" (9:93).

18. On the divine jealousy, cf. Chapter 2, note 27.

19. Allusion to the "hadith of the veils": "God has seventy"—or "seventy thousand"—"veils of light and darkness; were they to be removed, the Glories of His Face would burn away everything perceived by the sight of His creatures." Ibn al-ʿArabī frequently quotes it in this form (e.g., II 80.34, 110.31, 460.7, 488.10, 542.3, 554.9). The *Concordance* gives a text which states "His veil is light" in place of "God has . . . darkness" (Muslim, Īmān 293; Ibn Māja, Muqaddima 13).

20. The hadith is found in Muslim (Īmān 164) and other standard sources.

21. Allusion to Koran 6:97: "He appointed for you the stars, that by them you might be guided in the darknesses of land and sea." Cf. 27:63.

22. Ibn al-ʿArabī adds the phrase "in this station" since, from the point of view of another "station" (*maqām*), there is a certain similarity between God and man.

23. Part of the long version of the hadith of the Hidden Treasure, quoted in Chapter 8.

24. Here Ibn al-ʿArabī alludes to the famous definition of *al-iḥsān*: "Worship God *as if* you see Him." Cf. Chapter 7, note 13.

25. Reference to several hadiths (cf. Chapter 4, notes 33 and 35) and the Koranic verse, "He is with you wherever you are" (57:4).

26. Another reference to the hadith mentioned above; cf. footnote 16.

27. Here the term one entity refers to the Barzakh, the "entity of the cosmos," whereas a few lines down it refers to Being, as is more normally the case.

28. For this analogy, cf. II 519.17; III 127.26.

29. I employ the term "corporeous" to distinguish the term *jasadī* from the term *jismī* (or *jismānī*), "corporeal." Ibn al-ʿArabī often uses the first to refer to imaginal objects witnessed in the World of Imagination and the second to refer to corporeal things of the world of everyday experience. Cf. *Cosmology*.

Chapter 12. Faith and Rational Interpretation

1. As pointed out earlier, this sentence, cited by some authors as a hadith, is frequently given as a definition of knowledge.

2. In a slightly different form the hadith is found in Tirmidhī (Īmān 12), Nasāʾī (Īmān 8), Ibn Māja (Fitan 2), etc.

3. Tirmidhī, Qiyāma 60. The hadith is found in several sources in the form, "A person has no faith if his neighbor does not feel secure from his calamity" (Bukhārī, Adab 29; Muslim, Īmān 73; etc.).

4. Bukhārī, Janāʾiz 80, 92, Tafsīr 30:1; Muslim, Qadar 22–24, etc.

5. The hadith is well-known in the form, "You are more knowledgeable in the affair (*amr*) of this world of yours" (Muslim, Faḍāʾil 143; Ibn Māja, Ruhūn 15; Aḥmad V 5, 16, 298; VI 128).

6. On the hadith, cf. Chapter 6, note 24.

7. Muslim, Īmān 43.

8. Allusion to the hadith, "If a person sets down in Islam a good custom (*sunna ḥasana*) which is put into practice, he will have written for him the wage of those who put it into practice, while nothing will be diminished from their wages; and if a person sets down in Islam a bad custom which is put into practice, he will have written for him the load of those who put it into practice, while nothing will be diminished from their loads" (Muslim, ʿIlm 15, Zakāt 69; Nasāʾī, Zakāt 64; etc.).

9. Nature, in the more limited sense of the term (cf. Chapter 8), is the domain of both imagination and sense perception, that is, everything below the spiritual world. The "natural" includes everything which takes bodily form, whether in the corporeal or the imaginal worlds. The corporeal world, in addition to being natural, is also "elemental" (*ʿunsurī*), that is, composed of the four elements; but the imaginal domains are natural without being elemental. Cf. *Cosmology*; also Chittick, "Death and the World of Imagination," pp. 73–77.

10. Though Ibn al-ʿArabī frequently cites the saying, it is not found in the standard sources. Al-Ghazālī among others considers it a hadith. Cf. *Muʿjam* 1263.

11. Corbin has been so successful in getting across the idea that *taʾwīl* is central to Ibn al-ʿArabī that an Arab scholar has written a book on him called the "philosophy of *taʾwīl*" (N. H. Abū Zayd, *Falsafat al-taʾwīl* [Beirut: Dār al-Tanwīr, 1983]). Cf. Chodkiewicz's review (*Studia Islamica* 60 [1984]: 177–80), which points out that Ibn al-ʿArabī rarely uses the term in a favorable sense.

12. *Creative Imagination*, p. 50.

13. Corbin goes on to say that any mention of *ta'wīl* during Ibn al-ʿArabī's era "sufficed to alarm the authorities, jealous of the legalitarian religion and the literal truth." By now the reader will have realized that few of the authorities could have been more jealous "of the legalitarian religion and the literal truth" than Ibn al-ʿArabī himself, though this did not prevent him from seeing inward meanings in addition to outward forms. On the question of "Shiʿite leanings" in Ibn al-ʿArabī, cf. Chodkiewicz's remarks in *Sceau*, pp. 15, 34, 67–68, 174. The present author agrees with Chodkiewicz that there is no basis in Ibn al-ʿArabī's works for suggesting a kinship with Shiʿism on the formal level. Whenever Ibn al-ʿArabī mentions Shiʿism, he does so with a certain amount of hostility (cf., e.g., I 282.4 [Y 4,280.8]; II 8.19; III 36.15, 138.9). The fact that the Shaykh expresses a view of certain things similar to what is found among some Shiʿites merely proves that neither he nor they were prevented by literal-mindedness from seeing God manifesting Himself in the cosmos, the Unseen entering into the visible, the spiritual present in the corporeal, or mercy preceding wrath.

14. Allusion to a number of Koranic verses, including 6:57: "Say: 'I stand upon a clear sign from my Lord'."

15. The third son of Saladin, he ruled over Aleppo from 582/1186 to 615/1218.

16. Reference to Koran 13:15: "To God prostrate themselves all who are in the heavens and the earth, willingly or unwillingly, as do their shadows in the mornings and the evenings."

17. In employing the more normal sense of the word *tawḥīd*, Ibn al-ʿArabī claims that none of the groups is able to escape from a certain "association" or sharing (*ishtirāk*) in the question of the acts (III 211–12).

18. In the present context this term seems to refer to the spiritual realities which govern the corporeal world, or to the Breath of the All-merciful itself (cf. *Dhakhā'ir* 141, 143, 208). Elsewhere Ibn al-ʿArabī identifies the world of the breaths with the world which is unveiled during God's self-disclosure (*Dhakhā'ir* 149, 166, 194) and he defines breaths as the "assaults (*saṭawāt*) of the awe of self-disclosure" (ibid., 68). He also defines "breaths" as the "fragrances of nearness to God" and adds, "When the gnostics smell the perfume of these breaths . . . , they come to know a divine person who has the mystery which they are seeking and the knowledge which they want to acquire. God sets up within themselves a pole around which their spheres begin to turn" (I 152.14). Ibn al-ʿArabī often identifies the "world of the breaths" with the Men of Allah (*rijāl Allāh*), that is, the great friends of God (II 6.21; cf. II 11.9, 425.23).

19. On the determining property of God's knowledge and its relationship to this Koranic verse, see Chapter 17, section on "God's Conclusive Argument."

20. As pointed out earlier, *taklīf*, or the prescription of the Law, comes to an end at death. *Al-Ṣirāṭ* is usually interpreted to mean the bridge over hell leading to paradise on the Day of Resurrection. On the "inherent worship" of all things, cf. Chapter 18, first section.

21. Cf. M. Schwartz, "'Acquisition' (*kasb*) in Early Islam," in S.M. Stern and A. Hourani, *Islamic Philosophy and the Classical Tradition* (Columbia, S.C.: University of South Carolina Press, 1972), pp. 355–87; R.M. Frank, "Moral Obligation in Classical Muslim Theology," *Journal of Religious Ethics* 11 (1983): 204–23, esp. 218–19; *Encyclopedia of Islam* IV 692–94; Wolfson, *Philosophy*, pp. 663–719.

22. In this verse Ibn al-ʿArabī reads *maghfira* in its primary, literal sense. The term is usually translated as "forgiveness."

23. Allusion to the hadith of "self-transmutation" (*taḥawwul*) at the resurrection.

24. One of Ibn al-ʿArabī's foremost disciples (cf. the mention of him in the introduction).

25. Cf. Bukhārī, Tafsīr 6,7; 7,1; Nikāḥ 107; Tawḥīd 15, 20; Muslim, Liʿān 17; Tawba 32–35.

26. Here, of course, Ibn al-ʿArabī's analogy is weakened by the picture of the cosmos drawn by modern astronomy.

Chapter 13. Knowing God's Self-Disclosure

1. The definitions of *wajd* given in *Iṣṭilāḥāt* 5 and *Futūḥāt* II 133.13 lack the last phrase and have copyist errors; in place of *mufniya* the first reads *mughayyiba* and the second *mughniya*.

2. The term *ṣuḥuf* (plural of *ṣaḥīfa*) is employed generically for scriptures. Here Ibn al-

ʿArabī probably has the scriptures of Abraham in mind, since the Koran attributes the term specifically only to Moses and Abraham (87:19), and he has already mentioned the Torah.

3. Farghānī translates *wujūd* as *yāft wa yābandagī* (*Mashāriq al-darārī*, p. 18).

4. This is the sign by which each group will recognize its Lord on the Day of Resurrection. Cf. Chapter 19.

5. For details on this cosmology, see *Cosmology*.

6. In respect of their bodies, which are inanimate, these creatures glorify God like other inanimate things, as is pointed out at the end of the paragraph. The "bodies" of angels and jinn are imaginal or "corporeous," not corporeal. Cf. *Cosmology*.

7. See also II 485–89 (fifteen kinds), 550 (four kinds), 666–69 (four kinds), and III 56.19 (two kinds).

8. Muslim, Īmān 291; Tirmidhī, Tafsīr Sūra 53,7.

9. Cf. Chapter 11, note 19.

10. The hadith is found in many versions. The closest to that mentioned here is Muslim, Īmān 302, Zuhd 16; Bukhārī, Tafsīr Sūra 4, 8; Ibn Māja, Muqaddima 13. Cf. Muslim, Īmān 299; Bukhārī, Mawāqīt al-Ṣalāt 16, 26; Tafsīr Sūra 50, 2; Bukhārī, Adhān 129; Riqāq 52; etc.

11. Allusion to Koran 7:40: "Nor shall they enter the Garden until the camel passes through the eye of the needle."

12. Cf. *Iṣṭilāḥāt* 6, and the detailed discussion of these three stages in *Futūḥāt*, Chapters 248–50 (II 547–52).

13. The verses are from *Futūḥāt* I 10.26 (Y 1,73.10).

14. Abu'l-ʿAbbās ʿAlī ibn ʿĪsā (d. 386/996), a well-known grammarian and Muʿtazilite rhetorician.

15. The hadith is not indexed in the *Concordance*, though Ibn al-ʿArabī often cites it (e.g., I 95.15 [Y 2,102.18]; III 151.1).

16. The term "rust" is derived from Koran 83:14: "No indeed, but what they were earning has rusted upon their hearts."

17. Allusion to the words, "We lay coverings upon their hearts lest they understand" (Koran 6:25, 17:46, 18:57).

18. The "revelation" (*waḥy*) mentioned here is one kind of unveiling. It is not identical with the revelation given to prophets in the form of scriptures. Following Koranic usage, Ibn al-ʿArabī divides revelation into a number of kinds. "Revelation may be given to every kind of creature, including angel, jinn, man, animal, plant, and inanimate object (*jamād*). Among animals God mentioned the bee (Koran 16:68), and among inanimate objects He mentioned the heaven (41:12) and the earth (99:5)—even if, in our view, everything is alive, for here we follow customary usage according to ordinary sense perception" (II 631.35). In the most specific sense, revelation is the descent of the angel upon the hearing and heart of the messenger or prophet, and it no longer takes place, since there is no prophet after Muḥammad (II 253.3). "In this respect, that which pertains specifically to the prophet and not to the friend is 'Law-giving revelation'" (II 376.6; cf. *Cosmology*). In a more general sense, revelation is "that which God casts into the hearts of His servants without intermediary. He makes them hear a speech (*ḥadīth*) in their hearts, but hearing does not grasp how it takes place, limits do not define it, and imagination does not give it form. Nevertheless, he understands it, but he does not know how it has come, from whence it has come, nor what is its cause" (II 375.19). In this last sense, revelation is experienced by the friends of God, and it is identified with unveiling or "heralding visions" (*mubashshira*), a term derived from the hadith literature (Chapter 2, note 15). "The revelation of heralding visions is the most inclusive kind of revelation. It reaches the servant from the Real without intermediary, though it may also come through an intermediary. One of the characteristics of prophecy is that it comes through an intermediary, since there must be an angel involved. But heralding visions are not like that. Hence the gnostic servant does not care about the prophecy which has escaped him, since heralding visions remain for him" (III 86.14). But Ibn al-ʿArabī warns his reader to be wary of private "revelations": "O friend, if you suppose that God has given you revelation, look into yourself for wavering or opposition [to the Law]. If you find any trace of that—through governing (*tadbīr*), differentiation (*tafṣīl*), or reflection (*tafakkur*)—you are not a possessor of revelation. If He exercises governing control over you, makes you blind and deaf, and comes between you and your reflection and governing, while putting His command into effect through you, then that is revelation, and at that point you are the possessor of revelation. Then you will know that He has raised you and elevated your position so that you have reached those animals, plants, and inanimate objects about

whom you say, 'They are below me.' For everything other than mankind and the jinn—in respect of their totality—has an inborn knowledge of God. Mankind and jinn have an inborn knowledge of God only in respect of the differentiation of their parts, like everything other than they—angels, plants, animals, and inanimate objects. There is nothing in man—whether hair, skin, flesh, veins, blood, spirit, soul, nails, and teeth—which does not have an inborn knowledge of God through revelation, through which God discloses Himself to it. But, in respect of man's totality and the properties of the coming together of all his parts, he is ignorant of God. . . . If God were to allow him to hear the speech of his skin, his hand, his tongue, or his foot, he would hear it speaking through knowledge of its Lord, glorifying His majesty and calling Him holy. 'On the day when their tongues, their hands, and their feet shall testify against them for what they were doing' (Koran 24:24). 'They will say to their skins, "Why did you testify against us?"' (41:21). So in respect of his differentiated parts, man is a knower of God, but in respect of his totality, he is ignorant of God, until he learns—that is, he comes to know what lies in his differentiated parts. So he is the knower while ignorant. 'No soul knows what comfort is laid up for them secretly' (32:17). Hence man, in respect of his differentiation, is the possessor of revelation. But in respect of his totality, he does not possess revelation all the time" (II 78.20).

19. Allusion to Koran 35:12: "Not equal are the two seas; this is sweet . . . and that is salt . . . , yet of both you eat fresh flesh." Abū Madyan (d. 594/1197) was born near Seville and went to Fez and then to the East in search of knowledge. He returned to al-Andalus and settled in Bijāya (Bugia), becoming famous for his piety and exemplary life. Summoned to the court at Marrākush because of his fame, he died en route and was buried in Tlemcen. Ibn al-ʿArabī frequently cites his words or tells anecdotes about him heard from his disciples, though he himself does not appear to have met him. Nevertheless, he often refers to him as "our shaykh," which would indicate a spiritual if not personal contact (I 251.14; II 11.31, 22.24, 261.16, 505.19, 520.7, 551.29; III 117.19; IV 141.25; other references to him include II 201.21, 222.6, 648.24, 683.3; III 94.2, 130.12, 136.11). Cf. *Sufis of Andalusia*, index; *Encyclopedia of Islam* I 137–38.

20. *Ajʿalnī nūran*. The Prophet's supplication from which this phrase is taken is found in several versions, usually without this particular phrase. In Muslim, Musāfirīn 187, the text reads as follows: "He used to say in his prayer or in the prostration, 'O God, place in my heart a light, in my hearing a light, in my sight a light, on my right hand a light, on my left hand a light, before me a light, behind me a light, above me a light, below me a light, and appoint for me a light' or 'make me into a light'." This last phrase is found as an integral part of the text of the supplication in Aḥmad I 284.

21. Cf. Chittick, "Rumi and *Waḥdat al-Wujūd*," which provides a history of the early usage of the term *waḥdat al-wujūd* and explains the different meanings which have been given to it.

22. On the hadith of God's self-transmutation, see Chapter 2, note 9.

23. A disciple of Abū Madyan, he was one of Ibn al-ʿArabī's important spiritual teachers. Cf. *Sufis of Andalusia*, pp. 69–73 et passim; II 682.33; III 45:16.

24. An "incident" (*wāqiʿa*) is a true dream or vision. The name is taken from that of sura 56 of the Koran, which begins, "When the Incident falls—and none denies its falling—abasing, exalting." In the Koranic context the verse refers to the Last Day, when God comes, and all doubt disappears, since things are seen in their proper places. Ibn al-ʿArabī says that "Incidents come from inside, since they derive from the essence of man. Some people see them in the state of sleep, some in the state of annihilation (*fanāʾ*), and others in the state of wakefulness. They do not veil man from the objects of his sense perception at the time" (II 491.6). He identifies Incidents with "heralding visions" (*mubashshirāt*) and the "beginnings of divine revelation." The first of these terms is found in hadiths mentioned in Chapter 2, note 15, while the second derives from a hadith related from ʿĀʾisha: "The first thing through which revelation began for the Messenger of God was veridical [or sound] dreams (*al-ruʾyā al-ṣādiqa* or *al-ṣāliḥa*) during sleep. He never saw a dream without it coming [true] like the breaking of dawn" (Bukhārī, Taʿbīr 1, Tafsīr Sūra 96, 1–3; Muslim, Īmān 252). Cf. II 58.7.

25. Desiring an object but not attaining to it means that one perceives the object as distant and inaccessible, cold and unkind. Being oneself the object of desire means that one perceives the desirer as loving and warm.

26. A saying of Abū Ṭālib Makkī (cf. Chapter 6, note 13).
27. On this saying, cf. Chapter 7, note 7.

Chapter 14. Understanding the Koran

1. Passages in which Ibn al-ʿArabī refers to al-Ghazālī in a positive light include II 289.6, 290.30, 496.29; IV 12.18. Passages which may be read as criticisms of one sort or another include II 19.16, 262.10, 622.19; *Dhakhā'ir* 181.
2. The hadith is found in Aḥmad III 128, 242. Ibn al-ʿArabī quotes or alludes to it frequently. Cf. II 299.18, 352.27, 372.14, 510.10; III 103.34, 121.35.
3. Tirmidhī, Manāqib 1; Ibn Māja, Zuhd 37; Dārimī, Muqaddima 8; Aḥmad I 281, 295; III 144.
4. The station is mentioned in the Koran: "It may be that thy Lord will raise thee up to a praiseworthy station" (17:79). The Prophet says that he will indeed be given this station in Aḥmad I 398, III 456 (cf. Dārimī, Riqāq 80: "I will stand at the right hand of God in a station for which the ancients and the later folk will envy me").
5. Cf. Chapter 6, note 17.
6. Bukhārī, Anbiyā' 3; Muslim, Īmān 327, 328; etc. Some versions add, "without boasting" (Tirmidhī, Tafsīr Sūra 17, 18; Aḥmad I 281, 295, etc.).
7. Cf. Chapter 6, note 17.
8. Ibn al-ʿArabī and others frequently cite the hadith in this form, but the *Concordance* lists only the following: The Prophet was asked, "When did prophecy become your obligation [or: When did you become a prophet]?" He replied, "When Adam was between spirit and body" (Tirmidhī, Manāqib 1; Aḥmad IV 66, V 59, 379).
9. Ibn al-ʿArabī summarizes the excellencies and superiorities of the Prophet primarily on the basis of Hadith in Chapter 337, "On the True Knowledge of the Station of Muḥammad" (III 140–146).
10. Allusion to Koran 18:109, 31:27.
11. The hadith is not indexed in the *Concordance*. Ibn al-ʿArabī cites it again in III 141.7.
12. Reference to the hadith, often quoted by Ibn al-ʿArabī, "The learned masters of this community are the prophets of the Children of Israel." It is not found in the *Concordance*.
13. Muslim, Musāfirīn 139.
14. Allusion to al-Kharrāz's previously quoted saying concerning God's bringing opposites together.
15. Allusion to the Koranic principle, "God charges a soul only to its capacity" (2:286).
16. In al-Tirmidhī, the book on Tafsīr begins with a chapter entitled, "Concerning that which has come about the one who comments on the Koran according to his own opinion." Of the three hadiths, the closest to what is mentioned here reads, "He who speaks (*qawl*) about the Koran according to his own opinion has taken up his place in the Fire."
17. The verse is normally translated, "Let him not associate anyone with . . .".
18. The primary sense of the term *ghafūr* is "He who covers and conceals," though in the religious vocabulary it has the technical sense of "Forgiving."
19. Allusion to Koran 90:10. The "possessors of two eyes" are discussed in detail in Chapter 20.
20. Ibn al-ʿArabī was well acquainted with the work of al-Qushayrī (d. 465/1072–73) and often refers to his famous *Risāla* (cf. II 117.8, 143.20, 245.17, 537.27, 569.15, 649.30, 679.1; III 213.20, 372.22).
21. The reference is to a position taken by the Peripatetic philosophers; they are "without faith," since they "interpret" instead of accepting the Koran on face value.
22. The term came to be employed in the Islamic sciences to mean "jurist," that is, specialist in the Shariʿa, but in the Koranic sense it means "one who understands."
23. The term is employed in the "principles of jurisprudence" to indicate how the jurist reaches "certainty" (*yaqīn*) concerning the rulings of the Shariʿa.
24. For more references to this saying, cf. II 253.34; III 140.35, 413.35.
25. For the hadith, cf. Chapter 2, note 15.
26. Reference to the sound hadith, "When someone comes to Me running, I come to him rushing" (cf. Chapter 6, note 29).
27. A slight modification of the verse, "He is with you wherever you are" (57:4).
28. Muslim, Istiqsā' 13; Abū Dāwūd, Adab 105.
29. The hadith is found in Bukhārī (Shurūṭ 15) and Aḥmad (IV 330).
30. In this sense "locus of manifestation" (*maẓhar*) refers to the appearance of a corporeous body (*jasad*) in the World of Imagination.

31. On this hadith, cf. Chapter 7, note 13.

32. Pp. 21ff.

33. For a similar passage on the friend's knowledge of Hadith, cf. II 376.11.

34. Allusion to the hadith, "Satan does not become imaginalized in my form." Cf. Chapter 7, note 5.

Chapter 15. Weighing Self-Disclosure

1. See *Cosmology*.

2. For Koranic mentions of God's deception and guile, cf. Chapter 4, note 43. Leading on step by step is mentioned in 7:182: "And those who cry lies to Our signs—We will lead them on step by step from whence they know not."

3. For other references to this saying, cf. II 162.16 and III 8.13 (quoted below).

4. The source of this sound hadith is given in Chapter 12, note 8.

5. Allusion to the hadith, "In the days of your time, your Lord has fragrant blasts of mercy. Address yourselves to them, so that you may be struck by one of them, never afterwards to be wretched" (Sūyūṭī, *al-Jāmiʿ al-ṣaghīr* II 505).

6. *Raqāʾiq*, sing. *raqīqa*. Literally, the term designates something thin, delicate, or flimsy. Ibn al-ʿArabī employs it to describe subtle forms or relationships which tie together different levels of existence. He often employs it with verbs from the root *m.d.d.*, meaning to extend or to stretch. "God created rank (*makāna*) before He created place (*makān*). Then He stretched tenuities from rank to specific places within the seven heavens and the earth. Then He brought into existence the spatially confined things in their places to the measure of their rank" (II 582.26). "There are tenuities which extend from the Universal Soul to the Throne. . . . These are like ladders for the angels, while the meanings which descend in these tenuities are like angels" (III 28.32). "Know that there is no form in the lower world without a likeness (*mithl*) in the higher world. The forms of the higher world preserve the existence of their likenesses in the lower world. . . . Between the two worlds there are tenuities which extend from each form to its likeness, such that they are connected and not disconnected. Ascent and descent take place upon those tenuities, so they are ascending and descending ladders. Sometimes they are called 'affinities' (*munāsaba*)" (III 260.6). Cf. II 80.24, 81.15, 446.12, 680.2; III 14.31, 61.27; *Dhakhāʾir* 194).

7. These are four of the five *ḥukms* or "rulings" of the Shariʿa. The first two categories mentioned are synonymous.

8. Tirmidhī, Ruʾyā 2; Aḥmad III 267.

9. Allusion to the already cited hadith, "The veridical dream is one-forty-sixth part of prophecy" (Chapter 7, note 11).

10. On the four natures—heat, cold, wetness, and dryness—cf. Chapter 8.

11. On the hadith from which the term "inblowing" or "blowing" is derived, cf. Chapter 10, note 11.

12. These two prophets have not died but still live among us. "After the Messenger of God, God has left three messengers alive in their bodies within the abode of this world: Idrīs, who was left alive in his body and whom God made to dwell in the fourth heaven—for the seven heavens belong to this world and they remain as long as it subsists, while their form disappears when it disappears, so they are a part of the abode of this world. . . . God also left upon the earth Elias and Jesus, both of whom are messengers. They practice the primordial religion brought by Muḥammad. Everyone agrees that these three are messengers. As for Khaḍir—who is the fourth—there is disagreement concerning him among others, but not in our view. All of them subsist in their bodies in the abode of this world" (II 5.25). Cf. Chodkiewicz, *Le Sceau*, pp. 118–19.

13. Ibn Māja, Zuhd 3. Later on in the same passage, Ibn al-ʿArabī adds a sentence to the hadith which he seems to consider part of it: "They have been ground down by afflictions and encompassed by misfortunes, but they do not waver and they resort to none but God" (II 385.22).

14. Cf. II 566–67.

15. Ibn al-ʿArabī explains: "By 'rational madmen', the Sufis mean to say that their madness is not caused by a corruption of their constitution through some engendered affair, such as food, or hunger, or something else. Their madness derives only from a divine self-disclosure to their hearts. The Real comes to them suddenly and takes away their rational faculties. Their rational faculties remain imprisoned with Him, enjoying the bliss of witnessing Him, completely occupied by His Presence, purified by His beauty. They are possessors of rational faculties without ratio-

nal faculties. But they are known outwardly as 'madmen,' i.e., [according to the literal sense of the term], as 'curtained' (*mastūr*) from the governance of their rational faculties" (I 248.12). Cf. II 522.23ff.

16. For other references to Abū 'Iqāl, cf. I 167.8, 251.33; II 188.4, 239.30, 384.18.

17. The darkness of "Nature" (*ṭabī 'a*), it should be remembered, is contrasted with the light of the spirit, to which the rational faculty is intimately connected.

18. Sahl ibn 'Abdallāh al-Tustarī (d. 283/896) was one of the greatest of the Sufis, and Ibn al-'Arabī cites him frequently. The Shaykh tells the circumstances of the "prostration of the heart" mentioned here as follows: "Sahl ibn 'Abdallāh had seen that his heart prostrated itself. He mentioned this to a number of the shaykhs of his time, but they did not know what he was saying, since they had not tasted that. Hence he set out seeking someone who would recognize it. When he reached 'Abbādān, he went to see a shaykh and said to him, 'O master, does the heart prostrate itself?' The shaykh replied, 'Until eternity without end.' In other words, the heart never lifts up its head from its prostration. Through his question Sahl recognized that God had given the shaykh knowledge of the prostration of his heart. Hence his heart clung to that attribute, and it did not lift up its head from its prostration in this world—nor will it lift it up in the next world. After that he never supplicated God to lift up something which had come down, nor to push down something which had risen up" (III 86.22). "Sahl ibn 'Abdallāh attained to this station when he was a boy of six years. That is why his beginning in this path was the prostration of the heart. How many a friend of God there has been, great in consequence, long in life, who died without achieving the prostration of heart and without even knowing that the heart prostrates itself—even though he realized the station of friendship and his feet became firmly grounded within it. When the prostration of the heart is actualized, the heart never lifts up its head again. From his fixity in this one step, many steps branch out, while he remains fixed in it. Most of the friends see the fluctuation of the heart from state to state—which is why it is called a 'heart.' But, although the states of the possessor of this station undergo fluctuation, they derive from a single entity upon which he is fixed. This is called 'prostration of the heart'" (II 20.19). See also I 76.28, II 102.12. Qushayrī relates that Sahl's uncle taught him the invocation of God's name in the heart at a very young age. Then at six or seven Sahl went to school to learn the Koran, fasting every day. At thirteen he was faced with a problem which no one could solve, so he received permission from his family to travel from Tustar to Baṣra to find a teacher. Then he went to the island of 'Abbādān, where Shaykh Abū Ḥabīb Ḥamza ibn 'Abdallāh al-'Abbādānī (unknown except in this account) provided the answer. He remained with him for a while, profiting from his words and learning the rules of courtesy (*ādāb*), then returned to Tustar (*Risālat al-Qushayrī*, ed. 'Abd al-Ḥalīm Maḥmūd and Maḥmūd ibn al-Sharīf, vol. I [Cairo: Dār al-Kutub al-Ḥadītha, 1972], pp. 104–107). Cf. G. Boewering, *The Mystical Vision of Existence in Classical Islam: The Qur'ānic Hermeneutics of the Ṣūfī Sahl at-Tustarī (d. 283/896)*, (New York: de Gruyter, 1980), p. 40. For references to Sahl in the *Futūḥāt*, cf. II 12.1, 40.17, 45.12, 60.11, 93.27, 104.7, 171.21, 318.31, 355.14, 479.27, 543.4, 551.5, 662.11; III 41.8, 77.26, 150.7; cf. *Dhakhā'ir* 150; *Mawāqi'* 26.

19. This may be an allusion to his master Abu'l-'Abbās al-'Uryabī, who towards the end of his life was an 'Īsawī, that is, a friend of God inheriting the sciences of Jesus (I 223.21 [Y 3,361.10]; III 208.27). Cf. Austin, *Sufis of Andalusia*, pp. 63–69; Chodkiewicz, *Le sceau*, p. 98.

20. Allusion to the hadith, "Faith has seventy or sixty and some branches, the best of which is the words, 'There is no god but God,' and the least of which is the removal of harm from the path" (Muslim, Īmān 58 etc.).

Chapter 16. Names and Stations

1. On this famous *ḥadīth qudsī*, cf. Chapter 6, note 20.

2. On these two hadiths, cf. Chapter 7, note 13.

3. "Descends" and "alight" are both translations of the word *nuzūl*. The word *manzil* or "waystation" means "place of *nuzūl*," while *munāzala* means "mutual *nuzūl*." By changing the pronouns, Ibn al-'Arabī gives different shades of meanings to the word *nuzūl* as indicated in the translation.

4. Cf. II 154.4, where he specifically refers to this section as dealing with the stations.

5. Cf. II 386.5 for a similar passage.

6. Normally this name would be translated as "All-forgiving," but Ibn al-ʿArabī takes it back to its root meaning.

7. One of the clearest discussions of this division within the context of Ibn al-ʿArabī's school is found in Farghānī's *Muntaha'l-madārik* (I 93, II 81–84). Cf. the briefer Persian original of the same work, *Mashāriq al-darārī*, pp. 467–69.

8. Many Sufis, especially those of the later periods, place the world of invincibility beyond the world of dominion, but Ibn al-ʿArabī makes clear that he means by the term the intermediary world of imagination. Cf. *Iṣṭilāḥāt* 16(II 129.17); also II 203.3; IV 208.27.

9. For an earlier discussion of the term, cf. al-Ghazālī, *al-Maqṣad al-asnā*, ed. F.A. Shehadi (Beirut: Dar el-Machreq, 1971), pp. 42ff.; translated in R.J. McCarthy, *Freedom and Fulfillment: An Annotated Translation of al-Ghazālī's al-Munqidh min al-Dalāl and other Relevant Works of al-Ghazālī* (Boston: Twayne, 1980), pp. 340–43.

10. At the same time, the Shaykh has reservations about this term. He writes, "As for those who say that 'gaining similarity to the Divine Presence to the extent of capacity'—that is, assuming the traits of the divine names—is the goal and perfection, that is true in regards to wayfaring (*sulūk*), but not in the actual acquisition. For there is no gaining similarity through the acquisition itself, since that is God Himself, and a thing cannot gain similarity to itself" (II 93.30). Cf. II 483.27, translated in Chapter 4.

11. This should be the same as Abū Bakr ibn al-Maʿāfirī, according to Massignon the author of *Kitāb al-jawāmid wa'l-ʿawāṣim* attributed to Ibn al-ʿArabī (Yahia, *Histoire et classification*, # 193, p. 274).

12. The hadith is not indexed in the *Concordance*; Ibn al-ʿArabī also quotes it in I 285.8 and I 742.33. In II 241.27 he calls it a "sound" (*ṣaḥīḥ*) hadith.

13. Al-Ghazālī makes clear that he wrote his *al-Maqṣad al-asnā* (above, note 9) to assist the servant in assuming the traits of God's names.

14. In *Inshā'* (28) Ibn al-ʿArabī provides a table in which he classifies ninety-seven names in keeping with these seven basic names, though the printed edition of *Inshā'* does not allow for a clear understanding of how the division works. Later on in the same treatise, he writes that "The 'Leaders of the Names' (*a'immat al-asmā'*) are seven in all, according to both reason and the Law, while the remaining names are their followers" (33). He then lists seven names, replacing "Hearing" and "Seeing," found in the table, with "Generous" (*al-jawād*) and "Just" (*al-muqsit*). Ibn al-ʿArabī based the table on a classification provided by the theologian Abū Isḥāq al-Isfarāyinī in *al-Jalī wa'l-khafī*, with one minor change (cf. II 134.33, 460.12). For a similar classification of 108 names on the basis of the same seven names (employing *al-jawād* and *al-muqsit*), with a detailed explanation of the rationale behind the classification, cf. Farghānī, *Muntaha'l-madārik* I 27–42.

15. Nasā'ī, Imāma 28; Abū Dāwūd, Ṣalāt 93, 98; Aḥmad III 154, 260, 283; V 263.

16. Allusion to Koran 3:26: "Say: 'O God, Master of the Kingdom. Thou givest the kingdom to whom Thou wilt, and seizest the kingdom from whom Thou wilt.'"

17. Muslim, Īmān 25,26; Tirmidhī, Birr 66; Aḥmad III 23. Al-Ashajj al-ʿAṣarī and his fellow members of the ʿAṣar family are said to have come before the Prophet to accept Islam in the year 8 or 10 of the hijra.

18. Abū Dāwūd, Adab 149.

Chapter 17. Pitfalls of the Path

1. Fazlur Rahman, *Islam*, 2nd. ed. (Chicago: University of Chicago Press, 1979), p. 146. This particular criticism rests upon the words, "a thoroughly monistic system," and it should be obvious that neither "monism" nor "system" can easily be applied to Ibn al-ʿArabī's teachings.

2. Muslim, Musāfirīn 201; Nasā'ī, Iftitāḥ 17.

3. Allusion to the words of the angel in the Koran, "None of us there is but has a known station" (37:164).

4. Ibn al-ʿArabī explains the sobriquet as having to do with the fact that the jinn and men are latecomers in existence. "God named us 'the weighty ones' because of the heaviness in us, which is identical with our being late (*ta'akhkhur*) in existence and which made us slow. For heavy things habitually move slowly, just as light things habitually move quickly. So we and the jinn are among the

heavy things, while we are heavier than the jinn, because of the element which dominates over us, i.e., earth" (III 315.25).

5. Cf. Chapter 2, note 27.

6. By mentioning "possibility," Ibn al-ʿArabī is alluding to the famous saying of al-Ghazālī, "There is nothing in possibility more wondrous than what is." On the debate which this saying set off, cf. E.L. Ormsby, *Theodicy in Islamic Thought: The Dispute over Al-Ghazālī's "Best of All Possible Worlds"* (Princeton: Princeton University Press, 1984). Ibn al-ʿArabī refers to and explains the saying in many contexts. Cf. I 4.33 (Y 1,53), 259.35 (Y 4, 154), 441.11 (Y 6,392), 463.6 (Y 7,82), 552.14 (Y 8,221); II 96.13, 103.34, 321.19, 345.22, 395.25; III 11.15, 110.4, 166.19, 360.21, 398.18, 449.9,; IV 101.11, 260.10; *Inshāʾ* 18; *Masāʾil* (*Rasāʾil*, no. 22) 27; *Dhakhāʾir* 208–209.

7. Bukhārī, Anbiyāʾ 32, 46; Faḍāʾil Aṣḥāb al-Nabī 30; Aṭʿima 25; Muslim, Faḍāʾil al-Ṣaḥāba 70; Tirmidhī, Aṭʿima 31; Ibn Māja, Aṭʿima 14. Āṣiya was the wife of Pharoah. The exact nature of the *tharīd* meant by the Prophet is not completely clear; it seems to be a kind of meat stew in which bread is dipped.

8. On the high station of bewilderment, cf. Chapter 20.

9. This is the literal significance of the Koranic verse. "To uncover the shank" means something like "To gird the loins." It is to prepare oneself for a difficult task and for the terror which it occasions. The verse is in reference to the Day of Judgment and is usually interpreted to mean, "On the day when man will face calamity and terror."

10. The word *law* is employed in this sort of context to indicate that something which is supposed could not have happened. In *A Grammar of the Arabic Language* (3rd. ed., Cambridge: Cambridge University Press, 1971), Wright states that the particle "implies that what is supposed either does not take place or is not likely to do so" (II 347), whereas Ibn al-ʿArabī holds strictly that the supposed thing does not occur. He frequently refers to the manner in which *law* is employed in the Koran to explain the nature of the divine will and its relationship to knowledge and power. Cf. II 116.2, 194.7, 252.1, 334.29, 580.15, 665.30; IV 30.27, 45–46.

11. There are other Koranic allusions here as well, including "a recompense for what they were earning" (9:82) and "a recompense for what they were doing" (46:14).

12. Ibn al-ʿArabī gives the hadith in this form. In Tirmidhī (Tafsīr Sūra 56, 6), it is found as follows: "Hūd, the Terror (56), the Envoys (77), the Tiding (78), and the Darkening (81) have whitened my hair."

13. This saying is frequently cited in Sufi texts as a hadith, but Ibn al-ʿArabī does not consider it so. Cf. II 317.14

14. Allusion to Koran 42:13; cf. II 414.13, translated in Chapter 11.

15. Suyūṭī, *al-Jāmiʿ al-ṣaghīr* I 142.

16. The word *firāsa* is also applied to the science of physiognomy, and the chapter includes a discussion of bodily signs, markings, shapes, and colors whereby experienced physicians (*al-ḥukamāʾ min ahl al-tajriba min al-ʿulamāʾ biʾl-ṭabīʿa*, II 239.19) are able to read people's constitutions and characters (II 237.35–239.23), as well as a discussion of the spiritual roots of these signs.

17. This hadith is found in al-Munāwī, *Kunūz al-ḥaqāʾiq fī ḥadīth khayr al-khalāʾiq* (on the margin of Suyūṭī, *al-Jāmiʿ al-ṣaghīr*, Cairo, 1358/1939) II 24. Two other versions of the text are found in *al-Jāmiʿ al-ṣaghīr* (1972) IV 428–29.

18. Though Ibn al-ʿArabī frequently cites the hadith in this form, the collections indexed in the *Concordance* have "I was sent to complete the good (*ḥusn*) character traits" (*Muwaṭṭaʾ* 8) or "the righteous (*ṣāliḥ*) character traits" (Aḥmad II 381). There is also the hadith, "I saw him [the Prophet] commanding noble character traits" (Bukhārī, Manāqib al-Anṣār 33, Adab 39; Muslim, Faḍāʾil al-Ṣaḥāba 133).

19. Allusion to the hadith cited in Chapter 6, note 17.

20. Bukhārī, Adhān 114; Abū Dāwūd, Ṣalāt 100; Nasāʾī, Imāma 63; Aḥmad V 39, 43, 45, 46, 50.

21. Ibn al-ʿArabī reads the "it" here as referring to Noah's asking. Most translators and commentators have read the verse as "He"—i.e., Noah's son—"is (possessor of) a work not righteous." Arberry translates as "it," conforming to the natural flow of the Arabic, but without explaining what "it" refers to. By interpreting "it" to refer to Noah's asking, Ibn al-ʿArabī reads the text in a way that conforms exactly to the structure of the sentence. No doubt the commentators have avoided this reading in order not to attribute an unrighteous deed to a prophet.

22. These, of course, are the five "rulings" by which the Shariʿa includes all human activity.

Chapter 18. Safety in Servanthood

1. Cf. *Futūḥāt* II 442.20; III 129.10, 199.32.

2. The minor orthographical distinction between *ʿubūda* and *ʿubūdiyya* (much less apparent in Arabic than in English) may sometimes have been ignored by scribes or printers, a fact which further complicates the task of trying to maintain a clear distinction between the two terms.

3. Cf. Ibn al-ʿArabī's commentary on this verse in II 305.12, translated in Chapter 10.

4. This miracle of Jesus is mentioned in Koran 3:49 and 5:110. Ibn al-ʿArabī often refers to it, e.g., II 143.3, 274.23; III 149.25.

5. Cf. the discussion of the "Conclusive Argument" in the previous chapter, especially the fact that "man is ignorant of what will come into existence from him before it comes to be." There is also an allusion to the hadith of the seventy veils, the removal of which would burn away the creatures.

6. Allusion to the properties of the name the "Overwhelming" (*al-qahhār*) as mentioned in a verse concerning the Day of Resurrection: "The day they sally forth, and naught of theirs is hidden from God. 'Whose is the kingdom today?' 'God's, the One, the Overwhelming'" (40:16). Cf. 14:48.

7. In the sources indexed in the *Concordance*, the last clause is given as, "I shall throw him into the Fire" or "into Gehenna" (Ibn Māja, Zuhd 16; Abū Dāwūd, Libās 25; Aḥmad II 244, 376, 414, 427, 442; cf. Graham, *Divine Word*, pp. 162–63).

8. On Labīd and this verse, cf. Chapter 8, note 7.

9. On the identity of *tasbīḥ* or glorification and *tanzīh* or the declaration of God's incomparability, see Chapter 4.

10. Neither the text as published by Arberry nor the additions made by Nwyia have this particular *Mawqif.*

11. Allusion to several Koranic verses, such as 57:11: "Who is he that will lend to God a good loan, and He will multiply it for him, and his shall be a generous wage?"

12. Elsewhere Ibn al-ʿArabī employs this same saying of Abū Yazīd to illustrate a station of perfection, that of the nearness of supererogatory works discussed below. He writes, "No creature of God says 'I am Allah,' only Allah. . . . And the perfect servant also says it, he whose tongue, hearing, sight, faculties, and organs are God, like Abū Yazīd and his equals. But other than these two, none says 'I am Allah'" (IV 11.16).

13. In *Sufis of Andalusia* (pp. 91–95), he is called Abu'l-ʿAbbās Aḥmad al-Jarrār (though "al-Ḥarrār" is correct). Cf. Chodkiewicz-Addas, *Essai*, index, s.v. Abu'l-ʿAbbās.

14. The verse refers to God's taking the Prophet on the *miʿrāj*, the ascent or "night journey" into His Presence.

15. The hadith is found in this form in Bukhārī, Riqāq 38; cf. Graham, *Divine Word*, pp. 173–74.

16. Reference to the hadith cited in Chapter 13, note 20.

17. The hadith is not indexed in the *Concordance*. Al-Ghazālī cites it in *Iḥyāʾ ʿulūm al-dīn* I.2.14 (IV, p. 71); cf. Bukhārī, *Sharḥ-i taʿarruf* II 173; III 37.

18. This oft-repeated formula occurs in many hadiths in all sources (cf. *Concordance* I 532).

19. Allusion to a *ḥadīth qudsī* which Ibn al-ʿArabī often discusses: "I have divided the ritual prayer into two halves between Me and My servant . . . " (Graham, *Divine Word*, pp. 182–84). Cf. I 229.35 (Y 3,394); II 100.30, 167.27, 517.19; *Fuṣūṣ* 222 (BW 280).

20. Reference to the hadith of Gabriel, in which the Prophet says, "Good-doing [or, virtue] is that you worship God as if you see Him [in your kibla], for if you do not see Him, He sees you." Cf. Chapter 7, note 13.

21. According to the Shaykh's teachings, perfect man is the axis of the cosmos without whom it could not subsist. Cf. *Cosmology*; also Chittick, "Ibn ʿArabī's own Summary," Chap. 1.

22. On this hadith, see Chapter 4, note 33.

23. This hadith is found in Bukhārī, Adab 13; Tirmidhī, Birr 16; Aḥmad I 321; II 295, 383, 406, 455.

24. On the first hadith, see Chapter 4, note 33; on the second, Chapter 4, note 35.

25. Cf. Chapter 10, note 6.

26. This is a near quotation of Koran 31:27.

Chapter 19. Transcending the Gods of Belief

1. The verb "to finish with" (*farāgh*) is attributed to God in several hadiths, such as, "Your Lord has finished with the servants:

a group in the Garden and a group in the Burning" (Tirmidhī, Qadar 8). Here Ibn al-ʿArabī has in mind the hadith cited in Chapter 17, note 17.

2. This reversal of relationships between this world and the next is the key to Ibn al-ʿArabī's eschatology. Cf. Chittick, "Death and the World of Imagination."

3. Like many other pairs of terms, "unseen" and "visible" are relative. As a result, the world of imagination is "unseen" in relation to the world of corporeal bodies, but "visible" in relation to the spiritual world. The Divine Essence, however, is the Absolute Unseen (*al-ghayb al-muṭlaq*; cf. II 648.9), which is to say that "None knows God but God." "The 'He' (*al-huwa*) descends to the waystation of the visible thing while It remains in Itself Incomparable. But the He never descends except in forms perceived by sense perception, whether in the sensory or the imaginal realm. It is called 'the He' at the time of the manifestation of the form, in order that it might be known that the He is the spirit of that form and the object of its denotation. Then it is known that none knows the meaning of that form except God. Thus God said, 'With Him are the keys to the Unseen; none knows them but He' (6:59). He who is 'with' the He is the same as the He, and the He is unseen, so He who is with the unseen is unseen. Since He is unseen with the unseen, the visible does not know Him; only the unseen knows Him. Hence none knows what is in the unseen except He who is unseen" (II 638.31).

4. These two terms derive from Koran 53:8, which describes the Prophet's *miʿrāj*. Most commentators read both verbs with Gabriel as subject, as indicated, for example, in Pickthall's translation: "Then he drew nigh and came down." But the verses are obscure, and Ibn al-ʿArabī's interpretation makes perfect sense in the context of the *miʿrāj*: "Then he [the Prophet] drew close and He [God] came down."

5. Three pre-Islamic idols mentioned in Koran 53:19–20.

6. Allusion to the sound *ḥadīth qudsī* found in Bukhārī, Muslim, and other sources: "I am with My servant's opinion of Me" (cf. Graham, *Divine Word*, p. 130).

7. Cf. II 619ff. (translated in Chapter 9).

8. Almost a direct quote of Koran 57:4.

9. The first of these sayings is by Abū Bakr, as we have seen in several passages. The four sayings together have sometimes been attributed to the first four caliphs, representing four different degrees of *tawḥīd* (cf. Schimmel, *Mystical Dimensions of Islam*, p. 147). The last saying, "I have never seen anything without seeing God in it" is attributed to the Sufi Muḥammad ibn Wāsiʿ (d. 123/741; Kalābādhī, *The Doctrine of the Sufis*, trans. A.J. Arberry [Lahore: Ashraf, 1966], p. 53; Hujwīrī, *Kashf al-mahjūb*, trans. R.A. Nicholson [London: Luzac, 1911], pp. 91, 330); in a slightly different form it is attributed to ʿAlī ibn Abī Ṭālib (ʿAyn al-Quḍāt Hamadānī, *Tamhīdāt*, ed. ʿA. ʿUsayrān [Tehran: Dānishgāh, 1341/1962], pp. 279–80).

10. This principle is explained in detail in *Cosmology*.

11. Allusion to the hadith, "The man of faith is the mirror of the man of faith" (Abū Dāwūd, Adab 49; Tirmidhī, Birr 18).

12. Reference to 34:28: "We have sent thee not, except to all people without exception, good tidings to bear and warning."

13. Ibn al-ʿArabī attributes the saying, as noted in Chapter 6, to Abū Ṭālib al-Makkī.

14. The hadith is not found in the *Concordance*.

15. Cf. Chapter 7, note 4.

16. This is the day in the paradisial week when the faithful go to visit their Lord and gaze upon Him. The term is derived from a hadith, the relevant portion of which reads, "Then they are given permission to the measure of Friday among the days of this world, and they visit their Lord." Tirmidhī, Janna 15; Ibn Māja, Zuhd 39.

Chapter 20. Seeing with Two Eyes

1. Perception of the angels with the senses must take place within the domains within which sense perception functions, i.e., the domains of the elements and of "Nature," or the corporeal and imaginal worlds.

2. Heat and cold are active (*fāʿil*), while wetness and dryness are passive (*munfaʿil*). Cf. Chapter 8.

3. According to a position taken by Muslim mathematicians, "One is the principle and origin of the numbers. . . . And . . . two is . . . the first number" (The Brethren of Purity, quoted in S.H. Nasr, *Science and Civili-*

zation in Islam [Cambridge: Harvard University Press, 1968], p. 154). In Ibn al-ʿArabī's own words, "One is not a number, though all the numbers originate from it" (I 253.31). Two is the first of the even numbers, and three the first of the odd numbers, a position Ibn al-ʿArabī found confirmed through a visionary conversation with the Prophet (II 215.13). "The source of number (*al-ʿadad*) is the one which accepts a second, not the One in Being (*al-wāḥid al-wujūd*). Then one accepts multiplication and composition in the levels and expands with a tremendous expansion ad infinitum. . . . So 'one' is the narrowest of things. In respect of its essence, it is not a number in itself, only through being two, three, or four" (I 307.2). "The entities of two, three, four, ad infinitum become manifest through the manifestation of one" (II 519.17). Cf. II 581.13; III 127.26.

4. The words, "Are there any more?" are attributed to Gehenna in Koran 50:30. Several versions of the hadith are provided in the standard sources, but in place of the name Overbearing (*al-jabbār*) are found names such as the Lord of Inaccessibility, our Lord, and the All-merciful (Bukhārī, Tawḥīd 7, 25; Muslim, Janna 35, 37, 38; Tirmidhī, Janna 20; Tafsīr Sūra 50; Aḥmad II 369, 507, III 13).

5. The Sufis often cite this hadith, and Lane records it (*Arabic-English Lexicon*, s.v. *muṭṭalaʿ*), but Ibn al-ʿArabī recognizes that it is not found in the usual sources, since he writes concerning it, "Our companions, the people of unveiling, all agree concerning the soundness of this report from the Prophet" (I 187.14).

6. Cf. Chapter 13, note 15.

7. Literally "everyone" (*man*). But Ibn al-ʿArabī quite consciously employs this term to refer to all things, since all things are alive. He writes, "Certain grammarians believe that the word *man* can be employed only for that which understands (*ʿaql*). But everything glorifies God in praise, and no one 'glorifies' who does not understand the worthiness of him whom he is glorifying and praising. Hence the word *man* applies to all things, since all things understand from God that for which they glorify Him" (III 258.32).

8. Bukhārī, Tawḥīd 12, Shurūṭ 18; Tirmidhī, Daʿawāt 82; Aḥmad II 258, 267, 314, 427, 499, 503, 516.

9. Particularly in his chapters on the individual divine names, Ibn al-ʿArabī often discusses those friends of God who have a special relationship with specific names. Certain of his followers paid a great deal of attention to this teaching. For example, ʿAbd al-Razzāq Kāshānī devotes a long section of his *Iṣṭilāḥāt al-ṣūfiyya* to describing the servant of each of the ninety-nine most beautiful names of God. Cf. *The Most Beautiful Names* by Sheikh Tosun Bayrak al-Jerrahi al-Halveti (Putney Vermont: Threshold Books, 1985), where these descriptions have been translated or paraphrased at the end of each section.

10. Beauty (*jamāl*), it should be remembered, is the opposite of majesty (*jalāl*), while perfection embraces all opposition.

11. Al-ʿAṣr, "the Afternoon" or "Time" or "the Age" is the name of sura 103. In this passage Ibn al-ʿArabī is explaining the various allusions contained in the word and its usage in Islamic terminology, for example, as the name of the afternoon prayer. The root meaning of the term is to press, compress, squeeze, extract.

12. Seraphiel (Isrāfīl) is the greatest of the archangels and blows the Trumpet on the Day of Resurrection. The "shrinking" mentioned here refers to the accounts of the Prophet's vision of Gabriel. According to one version, the Prophet told Gabriel, who had appeared to him, that he would like to see him in the form in which God had originally created him. Gabriel replied that the Prophet would not be able to bear the vision. The Prophet insisted, so Gabriel revealed himself and filled the horizons, and the Prophet fainted. When he regained consciousness, Gabriel had returned to the first form. The Prophet said, "I did not imagine that any creature of God could be like that." Gabriel replied, "What if you had seen Seraphiel? The Throne is upon his shoulders, while his two feet have passed beyond the limits of the lowest earth. Yet he shrinks because of God's tremendousness until he becomes like a tiny sparrow" (al-Qazwīnī, *ʿAjāʾib al-makhlūqāt*, on the margin of al-Damīrī, *Ḥayāt al-ḥayawān* [n.p.: al-Maktabat al-Islāmiyya, n.d.], I, p. 97).

13. "The Pole is the 'servant of Allah' and the 'servant of the All-comprehensive', so he is described by all the names through having assumed their traits and realized them. He is the mirror of God, the locus of disclosure for the holy descriptions and for the divine loci of self-manifestation. He is the Possessor of the Present Moment, the Eye of Time, and the Mystery of Destiny" (II 573.19).

14. It is this fact to which the *Fuṣūṣ al-ḥikam* alludes in its very structure: The first

chapter refers to "The Wisdom of the name Allah as embodied in the prophetic word, Adam," and, as Ibn al-ʿArabī informs us, he means by "Adam" the human being, made upon the form of Allah. Then each of the remaining chapters of the book is devoted to the manner in which a specific prophet manifests a specific divine attribute; but each prophet, by also being "Adam," manifests the name Allah.

15. Cf. Chodkiewicz, *Le Sceau*, esp. pp. 136–38; see also *Muʿjam* 1003–06.

16. The next passage translated below makes clear that these "disciples of others" are the "Sufis."

17. *al-Riʿāya li ḥuqūq Allāh*, by al-Ḥārith al-Muḥāsibī (d. 243/857), on whom, cf. Schimmel, *Mystical Dimensions*, pp. 54 et passim. Books "of the same genre" include *Qūt al-qulūb* of Abū Ṭālib al-Makkī (d. 386/996) and al-Ghazālī's *Iḥyāʾ ʿulūm al-dīn*. These deal largely with the psychological and spiritual attitudes which must accompany the outward observance of the Law.

18. "Manliness," as pointed out above, is the "accidental" as opposed to the essential perfection of the perfect men, the means whereby they manifest the names and attributes of God in their multiplicity.

19. I read *tanazzuh* as in the *Futūḥāt* (II 129.19) rather than *tanzīh* as in the Hyderabad edition of *Iṣṭilāḥāt* (16).

20. On Jesus as the universal "seal of friendship" or "sanctity," see Chodkiewicz, *Le Sceau*, especially chap. VIII.

21. Bukhārī, ʿIlm 10; Abū Dāwūd, ʿIlm 1; Ibn Māja, Muqaddima 17; Dārimī, Muqaddima 32; Aḥmad V 196.

22. Neither version is found in the *Concordance*, though both are frequently cited in Sufi texts.

23. The "Solitary" (more commonly *fard* [pl. *afrād*] than *mufrad*) stands at a rank equal to that of the Pole, but the Pole is given a specific function not given to the Solitary. The Pole rules the cosmos, but the Solitary does not come under his rule. Hence Ibn al-ʿArabī compares the Solitaries to the "Enraptured Angels" (*al-malāʾikat al-muhayyamūn*), who stand at an equal rank with the First Intellect (*al-ʿaql al-awwal*). But the attention of the Intellect is turned toward bringing the cosmos into existence, while the Enraptured Angels are turned solely toward the contemplation of God (cf. I 93.5 [Y 2,91.9], 199–202 [Y 3,245–58]; II 19.9, 53.14,20, 488.33, 675.6; III 137.12; *Muʿjam* 876–78). For use of the term *mufrad*, cf. III 86.28; IV 77.19. Cf. Chodkiewicz, *Le sceau*, esp. chaps. VII and VIII.

24. Bukhārī, Riqāq 51, Nikāḥ 87; Muslim, Dhikr 93.

25. The text as found in one of the standard sources reads, "One dirham outstrips 100,000 dirhams." When the Prophet was asked to explain, he replied: "One man has two dirhams, and he gives one of them in alms. Another man goes to the midst of his wealth, takes from it 100,000 dirhams, and gives them in alms" (Nasāʾī, Zakāt 49).

26. Here again Ibn al-ʿArabī alludes to those imperfect gnostics who employ their powers and in particular their Resolve (*himma*) to create what they desire.

27. This *ḥadīth qudsī* begins with the words, "I have prepared for My righteous servants what. . . ." The text is found in Bukhārī, Muslim, and other standard sources (Graham, *Divine Word*, pp. 117–19).

28. Allusion to the station of the Prophet at the Resurrection (cf. Chapter 14, note 4).

29. The "Day to be Witnessed" is mentioned in Koran 11:103: "That is a Day mankind will be gathered to, a day to be witnessed." On the "Visitation," cf. Chapter 19, note 16.

30. Cf. IV 197.17, translated in Chodkiewicz et al., *Al-Futūḥāt*.

BIBLIOGRAPHY

I. Works by Ibn al-ʿArabī

A. Arabic

ʿAnqā mughrib fī khatm al-awliyāʾ wa shams al-maghrib. Cairo: Maktaba Muḥammad ʿAlī Ṣabīḥ, 1954.

Ayyām al-shaʾn. In *Rasāʾil*.

Azal. In *Rasāʾil*.

Dhakhāʾir al-aʿlāq: Sharḥ tarjumān al-ashwāq. Ed. M. ʿAbd al-Raḥmān al-Kurdī. Cairo, 1968.

Fihrist al-muʾallafāt. Ed. A. E. Affifi. "The Works of Ibn ʿArabī." *Revue de la faculté de lettres de l'Université d'Alexandrie* 8 (1954): 109–117, 193–207.

Fuṣūṣ al-ḥikam. Ed. A. ʿAfīfī. Beirut: Dār al-Kutub al-ʿArabī, 1946.

Futūḥāt al-makkiyya, al-. Cairo, 1911; repr. Beirut: Dār Ṣādir, n.d. Ed. O. Yahia, Cairo: Al-Hayʾat al-Miṣriyyat al-ʿĀmma li'l-Kitāb, 1972–.

Ijāza li'l Malik al-Muẓaffar. Ed. A. Badawi. "Autobibliografía de Ibn ʿArabī." *Al-Andalus* 20 (1955): 107–28.

Inshāʾ al-dawāʾir. Ed. H.S. Nyberg. In *Kleinere Schriften des Ibn al-ʿArabī*. Leiden: E.J. Brill, 1919.

Isfār ʿan natījat al-asfār, al-. In *Rasāʾil*.

Iṣṭilāḥāt al-ṣūfiyya. In *Rasāʾ*il. Longer version in *Futūḥāt* II 128–134.

Masāʾil. In *Rasāʾil*.

Mawāqiʿ al-nujūm. Cairo: Maktaba Muḥammad ʿAlī Ṣabīḥ, 1965.

Rasāʾil Ibn al-ʿArabī. Hyderabad-Deccan: The Dāiratu'l-Maʿārifi'l-Osmania, 1948.

Rāzī, Risālat al-Shaykh ila'l-imām al-. In *Rasāʾil*.

Tarjumān al-ashwāq. In *Dhakhāʾir al-aʿlāq*. Also ed. and trans. R.A. Nicholson. London: Oriental Translation Fund, 1911; repr. London: Theosophical Publishing House, 1978.

B. Translations

al-Anwār. Trans. R. Harris as *Journey to the Lord of Power*. New York: Inner Traditions, 1981.

al-Durrat al-fākhira. Partly trans. in Austin. *Sufis of Andalusia*.

al-Fanāʾ fi'l-mushāhada. Trans. Michel Vâlsan. *Le Livre de l'extinction dans la contemplation*. Paris: Les Editions de l'Oeuvre, 1984.

Fuṣūṣ al-ḥikam. Trans. R.W.J. Austin. *Ibn alʿArabī: The Bezels of Wisdom*. Ramsey, N.J.: Paulist Press, 1981. Trans. A.A. at-Tarjumana. *The Seals of Wisdom—Muhyiddin Ibn al-ʿArabī*. Norwich: Diwan Press, 1980. Partial French trans. by T. Burckhardt, rendered into English by A. Culme-Seymour. *The Wisdom of the Prophets*. Gloucestershire: Beshara Publications, 1975.

al-Futūḥāt al-Makkiyya: Textes choisis/Selected

Texts. Trans. M. Chodkiewicz, W.C. Chittick, Ch. Chodkiewicz, D. Gril, and J. Morris. Paris: Sindbad, 1989.

al-Ittiḥād al-kawnī. Trans. D. Gril. *Le Livre de l'Arbre et des Quatre Oiseaux*. Paris: Les Deux Océans, 1984.

Kunh mā lā budda minhu'l-murīd. Trans. A. Jeffrey. "Instructions to a Postulant." In *A Reader on Islam*. The Hague: Mouton, 1962, pp. 640–55.

Mishkāt al-anwār. Trans. Muhammad Vâlsan. *La Niche des Lumières*. Paris: Les Editions de l'Oeuvre, 1983.

Naqsh al-fuṣūṣ. Trans. W. C. Chittick. "Ibn 'Arabi's own Summary of the *Fuṣūṣ*: 'The Imprint of the Bezels of Wisdom'." *Sophia Perennis* 1/2 (1975): 88–128; 2/1 (1976): 67–106; reprinted in the *Journal of the Muhyiddin Ibn 'Arabi Society* (1982): 30–93.

Rūḥ al-quds. Partly trans. in Austin. *Sufis of Andalusia*.

Shajarat al-kawn. Trans. A. Jeffrey. "Ibn al-'Arabī's Shajarat al-Kawn." *Studia Islamica* 10 (1959): 43–77; 11 (1960): 113–60.

Tarjumān al-ashwāq. Ed. and trans. R.A. Nicholson. London: Oriental Translation Fund, 1911; repr. London: Theosophical Publishing House, 1978.

II. Other Works

Abū Dāwūd. *al-Sunan*. Ed. A. S. 'Alī, Cairo: Muṣṭafā al-Bābī al-Ḥalabī, 1952.

Abū Zayd, N. H. *Falsafat al-ta'wīl*. Beirut: Dār al-Tanwīr, 1983.

Affifi, A. *The Mystical Philosophy of Muhyīd-Dīn Ibn al-'Arabī*. Cambridge: Cambridge University Press, 1939.

Aḥmad ibn Ḥanbal. *al-Musnad*. Beirut: Dār Ṣādir, n.d.

Āmulī, Sayyid Ḥaydar. *Kitāb naṣṣ al-nuṣūṣ fī sharḥ fuṣūṣ al-ḥikam*. Ed. H. Corbin and O. Yahia. Tehran: Bibliothèque Iranienne, 1975.

Anṣārī, 'Abdallāh. *Manāzil al-sā'irīn*. Ed. and trans. S. de Laugier de Beaurecueil. *Les Étapes des itinérants vers Dieu*. Cairo: Imprimerie de l'Institut Français d'Archéologie Orientale, 1962.

Āshtiyānī. S.J. *Sharḥ-i muqaddima-yi Qayṣarī bar Fuṣūṣ al-ḥikam*. Mashhad: Bāstān, 1385/1965–66.

Asin Palacios, M. *El Islam cristianizado*. Madrid, 1931. French trans. as *L'Islam christianisé: Etude sur le Soufisme d'Ibn 'Arabī de Murcie*. Paris: Guy Trédaniel, 1982.

———. *The Mystical Philosophy of Ibn Masarra and His Followers*. Leiden: Brill, 1978.

Ateş, A. "Ibn al-'Arabī." *Encyclopedia of Islam* (new edition). London and Leiden: Luzac and Brill, 1960 on, vol. 3, pp. 707–11.

Austin, R.W.J. *Sufis of Andalusia*. London: George Allen & Unwin, 1971.

Balyānī, Awḥad al-Dīn. *Épître sur l'Unicité Absolue*. Trans. M. Chodkiewicz. Paris: Les Deux Océans, 1982.

Bayrak al-Jerrahi al-Halveti, Sheikh Tosun. *The Most Beautiful Names*. Putney Vermont: Threshold Books, 1985.

Boewering, G. *The Mystical Vision of Existence in Classical Islam: The Qur'ānic Hermeneutics of the Ṣūfī Sahl at-Tustarī (d. 283/896)*. New York: de Gruyter, 1980.

Bukhārī, al-. *al-Ṣaḥīḥ*. N.p.: Maṭābi' al-Shu'ab, 1378/1958–59.

Bukhārī, Abū Ibrāhīm Mustamlī. *Sharḥ-i Ta'arruf*. Lucknow, 1328/1910.

Burckhardt, T. *Mystical Astrology According to Ibn 'Arabī*. Gloucestershire: Beshara Publications, 1977.

BW. See *Ibn al'Arabī: The Bezels of Wisdom* (above, IB), under *Fuṣūṣ al-ḥikam*.

Chittick, W.C. "Belief and Transformation: The Sufi Teachings of Ibn al-'Arabī." *The American Theosophist* 74/5 (1986): 181–192.

———. "The Chapter Headings of the *Fuṣūṣ*." *Journal of the Muhyiddin Ibn 'Arabi Society* 2 (1984): 41–94.

———. "Death and the World of Imagination: Ibn al-'Arabī's Eschatology." *The Muslim World* 78 (1988): 51–82.

———. "The Five Divine Presences: From al-Qūnawī to al-Qayṣarī." *The Muslim World* 72 (1982): 107–128.

———. "From the *Meccan Openings*: The Myth of the Origin of Religion and the Law." *The World and I* 3/1 (1988): 655–65.

———. "Ibn al-'Arabī and his School." *Islamic Spirituality: Manifestations*. Ed. S.H. Nasr (vol. 20 of *World Spirituality: An Encyclopedic History of the Religious Quest*). New York: Crossroad, forthcoming.

———. "Ibn al-'Arabī's Myth of the Names." *Theories of Knowledge: Ancient and Medieval*. Ed. P. Morewedge, forthcoming.

———. "The Last Will and Testament of Ibn 'Arabī's Foremost Disciple and Some Notes on its Author." *Sophia Perennis* 4/1 (1978): 43–58.

———. "Mysticism vs. Philosophy in

Earlier Islamic History: The al-Ṭūsī, al-Qūnawī Correspondence." *Religious Studies* 17 (1981): 87–104.

———. "Rūmī and *Waḥdat al-wujūd*." *The Heritage of Rumi*. Ed. A. Banani and G. Sabagh. Cambridge: Cambridge University Press, forthcoming.

———. "Ṣadr al-Dīn Qūnawī on the Oneness of Being." *International Philosophical Quarterly* 21 (1981): 171–184.

———. "A Sufi Approach to Religious Diversity: Ibn al-ʿArabī on the Metaphysics of Revelation." Forthcoming.

———. "The World of Imagination and Poetic Imagery: Thoughts on the *Tarjumān al-Ashwāq*." *Temenos*, forthcoming.

Chodkiewicz, M. *Le Sceau des saints, prophétie et sainteté dans la doctrine d'Ibn Arabī*. Paris: Gallimard, 1986.

———. "Ibn ʿArabī, la lettre et la loi." *Actes du colloque: Mystique, culture et société*. Éd. M. Meslin. Paris: Université de Paris–Sorbonne, 1983, pp. 27–40.

Chodkiewicz-Addas, C. *Essai de Biographie du Shaykh al-Akbar Muhyi l-Din Ibn ʿArabi*. Thèse de Doctorat nouveau régime, Université de Paris I, UER de Philosophie. October, 1987.

Concordance. See Wensinck.

Corbin, H. *Creative Imagination in the Ṣūfism of Ibn ʿArabī*. Princeton: Princeton University Press.

———. *Spiritual Body and Celestial Earth*. Princeton: Princeton University Press, 1977.

Dārimī, al-. *al-Sunan*. N.p.: Dār Iḥyā' al-Sunnat al-Nabawiyya, n.d.

Farghānī, Saʿīd al-Dīn. *Mashāriq al-darāri*. Ed. S.J. Āshtiyānī. Tehran: Anjuman-i Islāmī-i Ḥikmat wa Falsafa-yi Īrān, 1358/1979.

———. *Muntaha'l-madārik*. Cairo: Maktab al-Ṣanā'iʿ, 1293/1876.

Frank, R.M. "Moral Obligation in Classical Muslim Theology." *Journal of Religious Ethics* 11 (1983): 204–23.

Friedmann, Y. *Shaykh Aḥmad Sirhindī: An Outline of His Thought and a Study of His Image in the Eyes of Posterity*. Montreal and London: McGill-Queen's University Press, 1971.

Ghazālī, Abū Ḥāmid al-. *Iḥyā' ʿulūm al-dīn*. Cairo: Maṭbaʿat al-ʿAmirat al-Sharafiyya, 1326–27/1908–09.

———. *al-Maqṣad al-asnā*. Ed. F.A. Shehadi. Beirut: Dar el-Machreq, 1971.

Graham, W. *Divine Word and Prophetic Word in Early Islam*. The Hague: Mouton, 1977.

Ḥakīm, Suʿād al-. *al-Muʿjam al-ṣūfī*. Beirut: Dandara, 1981.

Hamadānī, ʿAyn al-Quḍāt. *Tamhīdāt*. Ed. ʿA. ʿUsayrān. Tehran: Dānishgāh, 1341/1962.

Homerin, Th. E. "Ibn Arabi in the People's Assembly: Religion, Press, and Politics in Sadat's Egypt." *The Middle East Journal* 40 (1986): 462–77.

Hujwīrī. *Kashf al-maḥjūb*. Trans. R.A. Nicholson. London: Luzac, 1911.

Ibn al-ʿArīf. *Maḥāsin al-majālis*. Ed. and trans. M. Asin Palacios. Paris: Librairie Orientalist Paul Geuthner, 1933.

Ibn Māja. *al-Sunan*. Ed. M.F. ʿAbd al-Bāqī. Cairo: Dār Iḥyā' al-Kutub al-ʿArabiyya, 1952.

Ibn Taymiyya. *Majmūʿat al-rasā'il wa'l-masā'il*. Ed. Muḥammad Rashīd Riḍā. N.p., n.d.

ʿIrāqī, Fakhr al-Dīn. *Fakhruddin ʿIraqi: Divine Flashes*. Trans. W.C. Chittick and P.L. Wilson. New York: Paulist Press (Classics of Western Spirituality), 1982.

Izutsu, T. *The Concept and Reality of Existence*. Tokyo: The Keio Institute of Cultural and Linguistic Studies, 1971.

———. "The Concept of Perpetual Creation in Islamic Mysticism and Zen Buddhism." In S.H. Nasr (ed.). *Mélanges offerts à Henry Corbin*. Tehran: McGill University, Institute of Islamic Studies, 1977, pp. 115–48.

———. *Sufism and Taoism*. Los Angeles: University of California Press, 1983. First edition as *A Comparative Study of the Key Philosophical Concepts in Taoism and Sufism*. Tokyo: Keio University, 1966.

Jahāngīrī, M. *Muḥyī al-Dīn ibn al-ʿArabī*. Tehran: Dānishgāh, 1361/1982.

Jāmī, ʿAbd al-Raḥmān. *Naqd al-nuṣūṣ fī sharḥ naqsh al-fuṣūṣ*. Ed. W. C. Chittick. Tehran: Imperial Iranian Academy of Philosophy, 1977.

Jandī, Muʿayyid al-Dīn. *Nafḥat al-rūḥ wa tuḥfat al-futūḥ*. Ed. N. Māyil Harawī. Tehran: Mawlā, 1362/1983. Also ms. Istanbul, Hacı Mahmud 2447.

———. *Sharḥ fuṣūṣ al-ḥikam*. Ed. S.J. Āshtiyānī. Mashhad: Dānishgāh, 1361/1982.

Kalābādhī. *The Doctrine of the Sufis*. Trans. A.J. Arberry, Lahore: Ashraf, 1966.

Kāshānī, ʿAbd al-Razzāq. *Sharḥ fuṣūṣ al-ḥikam*. Cairo: Muṣṭafā al-Bābī al-Ḥalabī, 1966.

Lane, E.W. *An Arabic-English Lexicon*. Repr. Cambridge: Islamic Texts Society, 1984.

McCarthy, R.J. *Freedom and Fulfillment: An Annotated Translation of al-Ghazālī's al-*

Munqidh min al-Ḍalāl and other Relevant Works of al-Ghazālī. Boston: Twayne, 1980.
Madkūr, I. (ed.). *al-Kitāb al-Tidhkārī: Muḥyī al-Dīn Ibn al-ʿArabi.* Cairo: al-Hay'at al-Miṣriyyat al-ʿĀmma li'l-Ta'līf wa'l-Nashr, 1969.
Makkī, Abū Ṭālib. *Qūt al-qulūb.* Cairo: Muṣṭafā al-Bābī al-Ḥalabī, 1961.
Mālik ibn Anas. *al-Muwaṭṭa'.* As cited in Wensinck, *Concordance.*
Mohaghegh, M. and Izutsu, T. *The Metaphysics of Sabzavārī.* Delmar, N.Y.: Caravan Books, 1977.
Morris, J. "Ibn ʿArabī and his Interpreters." *Journal of the American Oriental Society* 106 (1986): 539–51, 733–56; 107 (1987): 101–19.
Muḥāsibī, al-Ḥārith al-. *al-Riʿāya li ḥuqūq Allāh.* Ed. ʿA. Maḥmūd and ʿA. Aḥmad ʿAṭā'. Cairo: Dār al-Kutub al-Ḥadītha, 1970.
Muʿjam. See Ḥakīm.
Munāwī, al-. *Kunūz al-ḥaqā'iq fī ḥadīth khayr al-khalā'iq.* On the margin of al-Suyūṭī. *al-Jāmiʿ al-ṣaghīr.* Cairo, 1939.
Muslim. *al-Ṣaḥīḥ.* Cairo: Maṭbaʿa Muḥammad ʿAlī Ṣabīḥ, 1334/1915–16.
Muwaṭṭa'. See Mālik.
Nasā'ī, al-. *al-Sunan.* Beirut: Dār Iḥyā' al-Turāth al-ʿArabī, 1348/1929–30.
Nasr, S.H. *Science and Civilization in Islam.* Cambridge: Harvard University Press, 1968.
———. *Three Muslim Sages.* Cambridge: Harvard University Press, 1964.
Niffarī, Muḥammad al-. *The Mawāqif and Mukhāṭabāt.* Ed. and trans. by A.J. Arberry. London: Luzac, 1935.
———. "Textes inédits." In Paul Nwyia. *Trois oeuvres inédits de Mystiques Musulmans.* Beirut: Dar el-Machreq, 1973.
Nwyia, P. "Notes sur quelques fragments inédits de la correspondence d'Ibn al-ʿArīf avec Ibn Barrajān." *Hespéris* 43 (1956): 217–21.
Ormsby, E.L. *Theodicy in Islamic Thought: The Dispute over Al-Ghazālī's "Best of All Possible Worlds".* Princeton: Princeton University Press, 1984.
Profitlich, M. *Die Terminologie Ibn ʿArabīs im "Kitāb wasā'il as-sā'il" des Ibn Saudakīn.* Freiburg im Breisgau: Klaus Schwarz Verlag, 1973.
Qayṣarī, Sharaf al-Dīn Dāwūd. *Sharḥ fuṣūṣ al-ḥikam.* Tehran: Dār al-Funūn, 1299/1881–82.
———. *Rasā'il-i Qayṣarī.* Ed. S.J. Āshtiyānī. Mashhad: Dānishgāh, 1357/1978.
Qazwīnī, al-. *ʿAjā'ib al-makhlūqāt.* On the margin of al-Damīrī. *Ḥayāt al-ḥayawān.* N.p.: al-Maktabat al-Islāmiyya, n.d.
Qūnawī, Ṣadr al-Dīn. *al-Fukūk.* On the margin of ʿAbd al-Razzāq Kāshānī. *Sharḥ manāzil al-sā'irīn.* Tehran: Ibrāhīm Lārījānī, 1315/1897–98, pp. 183–300.
Rahman, Fazlur. *Islam.* Second ed., Chicago: University of Chicago Press, 1979.
Schimmel, A. *Mystical Dimensions of Islam.* Chapel Hill: University of North Carolina Press, 1975.
Schuon, F. *Sufism: Veil and Quintessence.* Bloomington: World Wisdom Books, 1981.
Schwartz, M. "'Acquisition' (*kasb*) in Early Islam." In S.M. Stern and A. Hourani. *Islamic Philosophy and the Classical Tradition.* Columbia, S.C.: University of South Carolina Press, 1972, pp. 355–87.
Suyūṭī, al-. *al-Jāmiʿ al-ṣaghīr.* In al-Munāwī, *harḥ al-jāmiʿ al-ṣaghīr.* Beirut: Dār al-Maʿrifa, 1972.
Takeshita, Masataka. "An Analysis of Ibn ʿArabī's *Inshā' al-Dawā'ir* with Particular Reference to the Doctrine of the 'Third Thing'." *Journal of Near Eastern Studies* 41 (1982): 243–60.
———. *Ibn ʿArabī's Theory of the Perfect Man and its Place in the History of Islamic Thought.* Tokyo: Institute for the Study of Languages and Cultures of Asia and Africa, 1987.
Tirmidhī, al-. *al-Jāmiʿ al-ṣaḥīḥ, wa huwa sunan al-Tirmidhī.* Ed. A.M. Shākir. Cairo: al-Maktabat al-Islāmiyya, 1938.
Tirmidhī, al-Ḥakīm al-. *Kitāb khatm al-awliyā'.* Ed. O. Yahia. Beirut: Imprimerie Catholique, 1965.
Ṭūsī, Naṣīr al-Dīn. *The Nasirean Ethics.* Trans. G.M. Wickens. London: George Allen and Unwin, 1964.
Wensinck, A.J., Mensing, J.P., and Brugman, J. *Concordance et indices de la tradition musulmane.* Leiden: E.J. Brill, 1936–1969.
Wolfson, H. *The Philosophy of the Kalam.* Cambridge: Harvard University Press, 1976.
Wright, W. *A Grammar of the Arabic Language.* Third ed., Cambridge: Cambridge University Press, 1971.
Yahia, O. *Histoire et classification de l'oeuvre d'Ibn ʿArabī.* Damascus: Institut Français de Damas, 1964.

INDEX OF SOURCES

INDEX OF KORANIC VERSES

INDEX OF HADITHS AND SAYINGS

INDEX OF NAMES AND TERMS

Khudāy, 35
khuluq, 21, 241, 283, 373; *akhlāq*, 21, 283; *khuluq ʿaẓīm*, 21, 241; *ḥusn al-akhlāq*, 22; *makārim al-akhlāq*, 22, 175, 241, 286; *safsāf al-akhlāq*, 286; *takhalluq*, 21, 43, 60, 65, 71, 73, 95, 114, 208, 283, 286; *al-takhulluq bi akhlāq Allāh*, 22, 283; *al-takhalluq bi'l-asmā'*, 265; *al-takhulluq bi asmā' Allāh*, 22; *al-takhulluq bi'l-asmā' al-ilāhiyya*, 275, 393n42
khurūj, 157, 219; *makhraj*, 128
khuṣūṣ, 268, 387n17; *khuṣūṣ al-khuṣūṣ*, 268, 387n17; *khāṣṣ*, 130; *khāṣṣa*, 387n17, 388n20; *khāṣṣat al-khāṣṣa*, 387n17; *takhaṣṣuṣ*, 85; *ikhtiṣāṣ*, 54, 330
kibla, 122, 180, 228, 277, 328, 365
kibriyā'. See *kabīr*.
king (sovereign) (*malik*), 64, 120, 196, 267, 316, 365, 390n17; level of, 48, 49, 50, 110, 152, 240, 331; support of jurists by, 72, 202; and subject, 48, 152, 247; kingdom (*mulk*), 87, 313; of God, 85, 88; world of, 282, 376
kitāb, 19; *umm al-kitāb*, 240; *al-wujūd al-kitābī*, 396n6; *kitāba*, 258
kiyānī. See *kawn*.
knowers, men of knowledge (*ʿulamā'*), 349; divine, 236; perfected, 308; of God, 73; through God, 202; most knowledgeable of, 155. *See* learned.
Knowing (*al-ʿālim, al-ʿalīm*), 37, 54, 174, 285, 389n19; great scope of, 48, 49, 51, 52
knowledge (possessed by man) (*ʿilm, maʿrifa*), (defined), 148–149, 220; all-embracing (of God), 355; all-encompassing, 170; all-inclusive, 236; bestowed (contrasted with earned), 200 (*see also* bestowal); certain, 166; destructive, 269; divine, 111; engendered (contrasted with divine), 153; God-given, 235, 236, 237, 249, 252, 373; innate (of God), 158, 162, 399n3, 404n18; Law-defined, 173; perfect, 320; positive, 354; rational, 173, 258; self-evident (*see* self-evident); sound, 170, 188, 201, 210, 381; transmitted, 232; unlettered, 235–237; useful, 149–150; useless, 150, 242; verified, 168, 243, 288; as the basis of nearness to God, 151; of certainty, 155; of divine things, 150, 235; of God, xxi, 150, 271, 318, 328, 353–354, 355, 368, 376–377; of God as the life of the soul, 234; of God as the purpose of creation, 76, 150, 216; of God by all things (except jinn and man), 157, 158, 163, 216–217, 404n18; of God determined by knower, 341–342, 349; of God through God, 166, 167; of God through cosmos (self-disclosure), 153, 156, 164; of God must come through Law or God's knowledge-giving, 163, 213, 233; of God must come through following authority, 350; of God must come through self, 71, 167, 176, 216, 341, 345–346; of God must come through things, 157, 225; of God's appropriate attributes (through reason), 233; of God's existence, 233, 234; of God's Level, 345; as the greatest blessing, 148, 156; of the infinite, 154; as the means to pass to the nonmanifest, 217; of other than God, 150; of other than temporally originated things as impossible, 154, 341, 349; as a perfection, 266; of the realities, 312; as recollection, 154; as the root of felicity (deliverance), 151, 153; of self, 229, 230, 311, 341; of self and Lord, 154, 177, 312, 344–346, 359; of self as the fruit of existence, 278; of self-disclosure, 94, 111, 169, 185, 216, 218, 219, 238, 262, 321; of self-disclosure cannot be communicated, 353–354; of servanthood as bringing about nearness, 319; as the source of all good, 148; of things as they are in themselves, 245; of things through God, 167; ascent in, 123; constant renewal of, 156, 157, 218, 262; decrease of, 218–220; highest kind of, 112, 218; increase of, 148, 151, 153, 156, 157, 158, 176, 218–220, 340, 345, 380; infinity of, 154, 156–158, 330; light of, 196, 197, 257; limitations on, 188; pain through, 156; passage from one to another, 280; perfection of, 367; root of, 150; search of the cosmos for, 385n11; seeker of, 153; three kinds of, 188; three ways to, 328, 347; two kinds of, 168–169, 173, 197, 200, 218; all present in man, 154; always better than ignorance, 175; always determined by the knower, 219; contrasted with entities, 218; contrasted with faith, 193–195, 196–197; contrasted with ignorance (*see* ignorance); contrasted with imaginal perception, 209; contrasted with practice (*see* practice); contrasted with reason, 255; contrasted with tasting, 222; derives from imagination, 121; derives from marks, 255; derives from mercy, 148; gained through godfearing (*see* godfearing); identical with existence, 4, 91, 188, 258; knowledge that God cannot be known, 112, 132, 143, 154, 155, 380; more excellent than love, 380; knowledge/not knowledge, 156; negates evil, 308; object(s) of knowledge (*maʿlūm*), 11, 37, 79, 123, 153, 214, 217, 298, 299, 341, 361; three, 204–205; four, 136; none but God, 214; known thing (*maʿlūm*), 119, 122; three levels of, 115. *See also* gnosis, science, tasting, unveiling, witnessing.
knowledge (possessed by God) (*ʿilm*), 19, 38, 121, 295, 298, 357, 386n14; eternal, 247; precedent, 157, 195, 238; as an attribute of all-encompassingness, 148, 398n3; of cosmos through Self, 38, 84, 131, 167, 297–298, 339, 346; of particulars, 248, 249; of universals, 298; effects of, 305; existence of things in, 88; (infinite) objects of, 11, 38, 153, 154; man's ignorance of, 180, 255, 300–301; presence of, 5; relation of to destiny, 314; Scale of, 178, 255; compared to man's rational faculty, 238; followed by existent forms, 320; follows the object of knowledge, 206, 298–300, 305; identical with Himself (His Essence), 38, 154, 167, 297–298; knowledge-giving, bestowal of knowledge (*taʿrīf*), divine, 76, 171, 180, 201, 217, 257, 259, 263, 277, 337
Konya, xviii
Koran (*qur'ān*), 35, 238–244; tremendous, 241; as the character of Muḥammad, 241; as containing all knowledge, 239; as light, 215; as the straight path of Muḥammad, 303; all-comprehensiveness of, 239, 240; all meanings of intended by God, 243–244, 245; carriers of, 241; context of, 242; diverse understandings of, 92; explanation of through allusions, 247, 249–250; Folk of, 239, 340; inimita-

nā'ib. See *niyāba*.
na'īm, 106, 227
najāt, 150
nakirāt, min ankar al-, 12, 88
Named (*al-musammā*), (defined), 385n6; (mentioned), 36–37, 39, 40, 53, 54, 57, 67, 86, 183, 281; identity of with name, 37, 39, 96; unity of, 387n7
names (*asmā'*), (defined), 5, 8–11, 34, 40, 41, 42, 53, 155; (discussed), 65, 139, 183, 386n1; all-comprehensive (*see* all-comprehensive); contrary (and non-contrary), 67, 68, 303, 361; creaturely, 43; engendered, 95; engendered (contrasted with divine), 124, 220; merciful (contrasted with wrathful), 151, 157; Most Beautiful, 8, 11, 22, 33, 37, 40, 41, 43, 53, 61, 62, 86, 95, 107, 276, 283, 284, 314, 327, 387n14; ninety-nine, 8, 44, 129, 135, 369; particular (contrasted with universal), 394n18; proper, 66, 155, 245, 390n7; seven, 284, 408n14; as abodes, 281; of acts (*see* acts); of attributes, 354; as a *barzakh*, 39, 68; as boughs of tree, 100; as causes of manifestation, 95; as darknesses (and lights), 58; of deputation, 210; as diverse places of homecoming, 302; of engendered existence, 41–44; of the Essence, 245, 276, 354, 390n17, 391n28; as the goal in ascent, 257; as God's character traits, 22, 283; as God's family, 41, 52, 56; of good, 157; as the human kingdom, 276; of imperfection, 43; of incomparability, 354, 390n4 (*see* acts); of majesty and beauty, 23, 150; of the names, 34–35, 36, 37; of perfection, 43, 112; of praise, 155; as relationships, 35–36, 52, 59, 60, 156; as the root of hierarchy, 51; of secondary causes, 46; as sources of the many gods, 363; of taking to task, 157; as waystations, 281; all things as, 42, 44, 94, 210, 368; assuming the traits of (*see* traits); attentiveness of, 48, 279, 280, 319; authority of, 53; classification of, 58, 210, 391n28, 408n14; conditionality of, 41, 42; conference of, 53–54; conflict of, 55–56, 67; diversity of, 35, 55; effects of (*see* effects); effusion of knowledge by, 257; equilibrium among, 27; gnostic as companion of, 281; God's knowledge of, 36; hierarchy (levels, ranking) of, 23, 39, 47–52, 68; infinity of, 42: influence of on the heart, 266; interaction with in a mutual waystation, 281; joy of, 53; leaders of, 408n14; manifestation of (as cosmos), 16, 40, 48–49, 52–53, 96, 114, 284, 331, 369; many faces of, 281; manyness (and oneness) of, 57; Mothers of, 42, 387n16; mutual impeding of, 370; negation of, 93; nonexistence of, 50; prescripton of Law by, 208; Presences of, 28, 42, 387n16; pronouns as, 210; proofs of, 187; properties of (*see* properties); relief of, 130; scopes of, 48; secondary causes as, 44; servanthood toward, 370; sharing of, 137, 183, 390n2; two denotations of, 35, 36–38, 47, 66, 350, 388n2; belong only to God, 43, 95; bestow only existence, 55; correspond to stations of the Muhammadan, 377; demand engendered existence, 41, 52, 64–65, 177, 369, 387n14; demanded by states of entities, 40, 183; determine belief, 355; determine the finding of the Real, 212; determine the friend's knowledge, 370; do not make the One many, 35–36, 52, 53, 56–57, 183, 278; exist only through creatures, 62; manifested fully only in man, 30, 276, 286; not ontological (contrasted with entities), 35, 50, 52; rule over creatures, 152; rule over the poles, 371; solidly joined together, 285
namīma, 307
naqīḍayn, 66, 112; *tanāquḍ*, 188
naql, 131, 161, 215, 250, 391n14; *aṣḥāb al-naql*, 400(a)n4
naqṣ, 43, 266, 294, 296; *ahl al-naqṣ*, 269
narration, possessor of (*muḥaddath*), 262
nash'a, 68, 129, 184, 305
naṣīb, 276
Nasirean Ethics, 22
naskh, 108, 171
Nasr, S.H., xxii, 382n5, 385n27, 386n1, 411n3
naṣṣ, 219
na't: *nu'ūt al-jalāl*, 50
natīja, 279, 394n16
nāṭiq. See *nuṭq*.
natural (*ṭabī'ī*), 142, 143; locus of manifestation, 356; bodies, 234; intoxication, 198; world, 223; worship, 294; contrasted with elemental, 401n9
Nature (*ṭabī'a*), (defined), 139–142, 391n25, 401n9; (mentioned), 68, 105, 120, 126, 303, 307, 395n7; disengaged, 142; First, 143, greatest, 140; primordial (*see* primordial); as darkness, 140, 142; as evil, 142; as mother, 140, 160; as place of forgetfulness, 195; earth of, 371; science of, 271; two active principles of, 141, 360; contrasted with light, 163, 407n17; contrasted with reason, 271; contrasted with spirit, 140, 142, 304; natures (*ṭabā'i'*), 142, 262; four, 141, 173
nawāfil. See *nāfila*.
nawm, 120
naẓar, 71, 110, 159, 165, 197, 217, 233, 368, 380; *al-naẓar al-fikrī*, 60, 149, 159; *naẓar ṣaḥīḥ*, 84; *ahl al-naẓar*, 52, 160; *ṣāḥib al-naẓar*, 165; *aṣḥāb al-naẓar*, 121; *naẓarī*, 63; *nāẓir*, 338, 355; *nuẓẓār*, 51, 160; *nāẓirūn*, 84; *manẓūr*, 380
nāzil. See *nuzūl*.
nāẓir. See *naẓar*.
nearness (*qurb, qurba*), 280, 348; to God, 151, 196, 201, 294, 365–366; of God to man, 154, 249, 365; of obligatory and supererogatory works, 325, 327 (*see also* supererogatory); contrasted with distance, 151, 223, 319, 361; depends upon God's giving knowledge, 171
necessary (*wājib*), 121, 122, 123; through the Other, 51, 90, 298, 325, 389n9, 393n3; contrasted with impossible, 94, 196; Necessary Being (*wājib al-wujūd*), (defined), 81–82; (mentioned), xxi, 51, 80, 81, 87, 90, 132, 204, 213, 287, 325, 337, 364, 380; as distinct from the one entity of the cosmos, 183; contrasted with possible thing(s), 69, 82, 90, 123, 124, 246, 291, 293, 310, 319, 322, 337, 387n14; "necessary finding," 212
necessity (*wujūb*), of Being, 50, 53; of immutability (contrasted with that of Being), 183; negated from creation, 298
negation (*salb*), of attributes from God, 9, 62, 163–

Printed in the United States
31017LVS00001B/195-206

9 780887 068850